Head First C#

Second Edition

> Wouldn't it be dreamy if there was a C# book that was more fun than endlessly debugging code? It's probably nothing but a fantasy....

Andrew Stellman
Jennifer Greene

O'REILLY®

Beijing • Cambridge • Köln • Sebastopol • Taipei • Tokyo

Head First C#

Second Edition

by Andrew Stellman and Jennifer Greene

Published by O'Reilly Media, Inc., 1005 Gravenstein Highway North, Sebastopol, CA 95472.

O'Reilly Media books may be purchased for educational, business, or sales promotional use. Online editions are also available for most titles (*http://my.safaribooksonline.com*). For more information, contact our corporate/institutional sales department: (800) 998-9938 or *corporate@oreilly.com*.

Series Creators:	Kathy Sierra, Bert Bates
Cover Designers:	Louise Barr, Karen Montgomery
Production Editor:	Rachel Monaghan
Proofreader:	Emily Quill
Indexer:	Lucie Haskins
Page Viewers:	Quentin the whippet and Tequila the pomeranian

Printing History:

November 2007: First Edition.
May 2010: Second Edition.

The O'Reilly logo is a registered trademark of O'Reilly Media, Inc. The *Head First* series designations, *Head First C#*, and related trade dress are trademarks of O'Reilly Media, Inc.

Microsoft, Windows, Visual Studio, MSDN, the .NET logo, Visual Basic and Visual C# are registered trademarks of Microsoft Corporation.

Many of the designations used by manufacturers and sellers to distinguish their products are claimed as trademarks. Where those designations appear in this book, and O'Reilly Media, Inc., was aware of a trademark claim, the designations have been printed in caps or initial caps.

While every precaution has been taken in the preparation of this book, the publisher and the authors assume no responsibility for errors or omissions, or for damages resulting from the use of the information contained herein.

No bees, space aliens, or comic book heroes were harmed in the making of this book.

ISBN: 978-1-449-38034-2

[SB]

"I've never read a computer book cover to cover, but this one held my interest from the first page to the last. If you want to learn C# in depth and have fun doing it, this is THE book for you."

> **— Andy Parker, fledgling C# programmer**

"It's hard to really learn a programming language without good engaging examples, and this book is full of them! *Head First C#* will guide beginners of all sorts to a long and productive relationship with C# and the .NET Framework."

> **—Chris Burrows, developer for Microsoft's C# Compiler team**

"With *Head First C#*, Andrew and Jenny have presented an excellent tutorial on learning C#. It is very approachable while covering a great amount of detail in a unique style. If you've been turned off by more conventional books on C#, you'll love this one."

> **—Jay Hilyard, software developer, co-author of *C# 3.0 Cookbook***

"I'd reccomend this book to anyone looking for a great introduction into the world of programming and C#. From the first page onwards, the authors walks the reader through some of the more challenging concepts of C# in a simple, easy-to-follow way. At the end of some of the larger projects/labs, the reader can look back at their programs and stand in awe of what they've accomplished."

> **—David Sterling, developer for Microsoft's Visual C# Compiler team**

"*Head First C#* is a highly enjoyable tutorial, full of memorable examples and entertaining exercises. Its lively style is sure to captivate readers—from the humorously annotated examples, to the Fireside Chats, where the abstract class and interface butt heads in a heated argument! For anyone new to programming, there's no better way to dive in."

> **—Joseph Albahari, C# Design Architect at Egton Medical Information Systems,
> the UK's largest primary healthcare software supplier,
> co-author of *C# 3.0 in a Nutshell***

"[*Head First C#*] was an easy book to read and understand. I will recommend this book to any developer wanting to jump into the C# waters. I will recommend it to the advanced developer that wants to understand better what is happening with their code. [I will recommend it to developers who] want to find a better way to explain how C# works to their less-seasoned developer friends."

> **—Giuseppe Turitto, C# and ASP.NET developer for Cornwall Consulting Group**

"Andrew and Jenny have crafted another stimulating Head First learning experience. Grab a pencil, a computer, and enjoy the ride as you engage your left brain, right brain, and funny bone."

> **—Bill Mietelski, software engineer**

"Going through this *Head First C#* book was a great experience. I have not come across a book series which actually teaches you so well….This is a book I would definitely recommend to people wanting to learn C#"

> **—Krishna Pala, MCP**

Praise for other *Head First books*

"Kathy and Bert's *Head First Java* transforms the printed page into the closest thing to a GUI you've ever seen. In a wry, hip manner, the authors make learning Java an engaging 'what're they gonna do next?' experience."

> —**Warren Keuffel,** *Software Development Magazine*

"Beyond the engaging style that drags you forward from know-nothing into exalted Java warrior status, *Head First Java* covers a huge amount of practical matters that other texts leave as the dreaded "exercise for the reader...." It's clever, wry, hip and practical—there aren't a lot of textbooks that can make that claim and live up to it while also teaching you about object serialization and network launch protocols. "

> —**Dr. Dan Russell, Director of User Sciences and Experience Research**
> **IBM Almaden Research Center (and teaches Artificial Intelligence at**
> **Stanford University)**

"It's fast, irreverent, fun, and engaging. Be careful—you might actually learn something!"

> —**Ken Arnold, former Senior Engineer at Sun Microsystems**
> **Co-author (with James Gosling, creator of Java),**
> ***The Java Programming Language***

"I feel like a thousand pounds of books have just been lifted off of my head."

> —**Ward Cunningham, inventor of the Wiki and founder of the Hillside Group**

"Just the right tone for the geeked-out, casual-cool guru coder in all of us. The right reference for practical development strategies—gets my brain going without having to slog through a bunch of tired stale professor-speak."

> —**Travis Kalanick, Founder of Scour and Red Swoosh**
> **Member of the MIT TR100**

"There are books you buy, books you keep, books you keep on your desk, and thanks to O'Reilly and the Head First crew, there is the penultimate category, Head First books. They're the ones that are dog-eared, mangled, and carried everywhere. *Head First SQL* is at the top of my stack. Heck, even the PDF I have for review is tattered and torn."

> — **Bill Sawyer, ATG Curriculum Manager, Oracle**

"This book's admirable clarity, humor and substantial doses of clever make it the sort of book that helps even non-programmers think well about problem-solving."

> — **Cory Doctorow, co-editor of Boing Boing**
> **Author, *Down and Out in the Magic Kingdom***
> **and *Someone Comes to Town, Someone Leaves Town***

Praise for other *Head First books*

"I received the book yesterday and started to read it…and I couldn't stop. This is definitely très 'cool.' It is fun, but they cover a lot of ground and they are right to the point. I'm really impressed."

— **Erich Gamma, IBM Distinguished Engineer, and co-author of** ***Design Patterns***

"One of the funniest and smartest books on software design I've ever read."

— **Aaron LaBerge, VP Technology, ESPN.com**

"What used to be a long trial and error learning process has now been reduced neatly into an engaging paperback."

— **Mike Davidson, CEO, Newsvine, Inc.**

"Elegant design is at the core of every chapter here, each concept conveyed with equal doses of pragmatism and wit."

— **Ken Goldstein, Executive Vice President, Disney Online**

"I ♥ Head First HTML with CSS & XHTML—it teaches you everything you need to learn in a 'fun coated' format."

— **Sally Applin, UI Designer and Artist**

"Usually when reading through a book or article on design patterns, I'd have to occasionally stick myself in the eye with something just to make sure I was paying attention. Not with this book. Odd as it may sound, this book makes learning about design patterns fun.

"While other books on design patterns are saying 'Bueller… Bueller… Bueller…' this book is on the float belting out 'Shake it up, baby!'"

— **Eric Wuehler**

"I literally love this book. In fact, I kissed this book in front of my wife."

— **Satish Kumar**

Other related books from O'Reilly

Programming C# 4.0

C# 4.0 in a Nutshell

C# Essentials

C# Language Pocket Reference

Other books in O'Reilly's *Head First* series

Head First Java

Head First Object-Oriented Analysis and Design (OOA&D)

Head Rush Ajax

Head First HTML with CSS and XHTML

Head First Design Patterns

Head First Servlets and JSP

Head First EJB

Head First PMP

Head First SQL

Head First Software Development

Head First JavaScript

Head First Ajax

Head First Statistics

Head First Physics

Head First Programming

Head First Ruby on Rails

Head First PHP & MySQL

Head First Algebra

Head First Data Analysis

Head First Excel

This book is dedicated to the loving memory of Sludgie the Whale,
who swam to Brooklyn on April 17, 2007.

You were only in our canal for a day,
but you'll be in our hearts forever.

the *authors*

Thanks for buying our book! We really love writing about this stuff, and we hope you get a kick out of reading it...

Andrew

...because we know you're going to have a great time learning C#.

Jenny

This photo (and the photo of the Gowanus Canal) by Nisha Sondhe

Andrew Stellman, despite being raised a New Yorker, has lived in Pittsburgh *twice*. The first time was when he graduated from Carnegie Mellon's School of Computer Science, and then again when he and Jenny were starting their consulting business and writing their first book for O'Reilly.

When he moved back to his hometown, his first job after college was as a programmer at EMI-Capitol Records—which actually made sense, since he went to LaGuardia High School of Music and Art and the Performing Arts to study cello and jazz bass guitar. He and Jenny first worked together at that same financial software company, where he was managing a team of programmers. He's had the privilege of working with some pretty amazing programmers over the years, and likes to think that he's learned a few things from them.

When he's not writing books, Andrew keeps himself busy writing useless (but fun) software, playing music (but video games even more), experimenting with circuits that make odd noises, studying taiji and aikido, having a girlfriend named Lisa, and owning a pomeranian.

Jennifer Greene studied philosophy in college but, like everyone else in the field, couldn't find a job doing it. Luckily, she's a great software engineer, so she started out working at an online service, and that's the first time she really got a good sense of what good software development looked like.

She moved to New York in 1998 to work on software quallity at a financial software company. She managed a team of testers at a really cool startup that did artificial intelligence and natural language processing.

Since then, she's traveled all over the world to work with different software teams and build all kinds of cool projects.

She loves traveling, watching Bollywood movies, reading the occasional comic book, playing PS3 games (especially LittleBigPlanet!), and owning a whippet.

Jenny and Andrew have been building software and writing about software engineering together since they first met in 1998. Their first book, *Applied Software Project Management*, was published by O'Reilly in 2005. They published their first book in the Head First series, *Head First PMP*, in 2007.

They founded Stellman & Greene Consulting in 2003 to build a really neat software project for scientists studying herbicide exposure in Vietnam vets. When they're not building software or writing books, they do a lot of speaking at conferences and meetings of software engineers, architects and project managers.

Check out their blog, *Building Better Software*: http://www.stellman-greene.com

viii

Table of Contents (Summary)

Table of Contents (the real thing)

Intro

Your brain on C#. You're sitting around trying to *learn* something, but your *brain* keeps telling you all that learning *isn't important*. Your brain's saying, "Better leave room for more important things, like which wild animals to avoid and whether nude archery is a bad idea." So how *do* you trick your brain into thinking that your life really depends on learning C#?

get productive with C#

1

Visual Applications, in 10 minutes or less

Want to build great programs really fast?

With C#, you've got a **powerful programming language** and a **valuable tool** at your fingertips. With the **Visual Studio IDE**, you'll never have to spend hours writing obscure code to get a button working again. Even better, you'll be able to **focus on getting your work done**, rather than remembering which method parameter was for the *name* of a button, and which one was for its *label*. Sound appealing? Turn the page, and let's get programming.

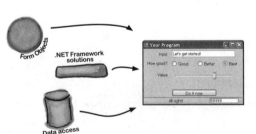

it's all just code

Under the hood

You're a programmer, not just an IDE user.

2

You can get a lot of work done using the IDE. But there's only so far it can take you. Sure, there are a lot of **repetitive tasks** that you do when you build an application. And the IDE is great at doing those things for you. But working with the IDE is *only the beginning*. You can get your programs to do so much more—and **writing C# code** is how you do it. Once you get the hang of coding, there's *nothing* your programs can't do.

Build this form ➞

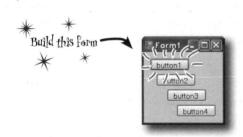

Every time you make a new program, you define a namespace for it so that its code is separate from the .NET Framework classes.

A class contains a **piece** of your program (although some very small programs can have just one class).

A class has one or more methods. Your methods always have to live **inside a class**. And methods are made up of statements — like the ones you've already seen.

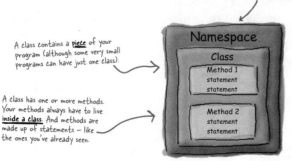

objects: get oriented!

Making Code Make Sense

Every program you write solves a problem.

3

When you're building a program, it's always a good idea to start by thinking about what *problem* your program's supposed to solve. That's why ***objects*** are really useful. They let you structure your code based on the problem it's solving, so that you can spend your time *thinking about the problem* you need to work on rather than getting bogged down in the mechanics of writing code. When you use objects right, you end up with code that's *intuitive* to write, and easy to read and change.

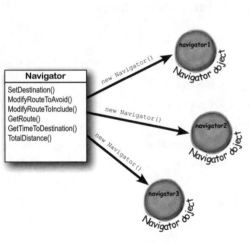

Navigator

SetDestination()
ModifyRouteToAvoid()
ModifyRouteToInclude()
GetRoute()
GetTimeToDestination()
TotalDistance()

new Navigator()

navigator1
Navigator object

new Navigator()

navigator2
Navigator object

new Navigator()

navigator3
Navigator object

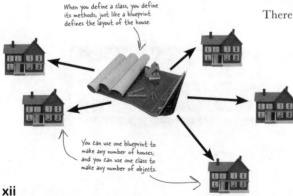

When you define a class, you define its methods, just like a blueprint defines the layout of the house.

You can use one blueprint to make any number of houses, and you can use one class to make any number of objects.

types and references

It's 10:00. Do you know where your data is?

4

**Data type, database, Lieutenant Commander Data…
it's all important stuff.** Without data, your programs are useless. You
need **information** from your users, and you use that to look up or produce new
information to give back to them. In fact, almost everything you do in programming
involves **working with data** in one way or another. In this chapter, you'll learn the
ins and outs of C#'s **data types**, see how to work with data in your program, and
even figure out a few dirty secrets about **objects** (*pssst…objects are data, too*).

```
Dog fido;
Dog lucky = new Dog();
```

```
fido = new Dog();
```

```
lucky = null;
```

C# Lab 1

A Day at the Races

Joe, Bob, and Al love going to the track, but they're tired of losing all their money. They need you to build a simulator for them so they can figure out winners before they lay their money down. And, if you do a good job, they'll cut you in on their profits.

encapsulation

Keep your privates... private

Ever wished for a little more privacy?

5

Sometimes your objects feel the same way. Just like you don't want anybody you don't trust reading your journal or paging through your bank statements, good objects don't let *other* objects go poking around their fields. In this chapter, you're going to learn about the power of **encapsulation**. You'll **make your object's data private**, and add methods to **protect how that data is accessed**.

ciaAgent

kgbAgent

mi5Agent

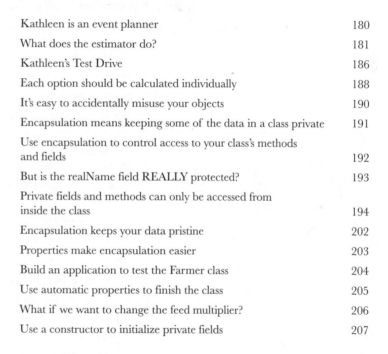

inheritance

Your object's family tree

6

Sometimes you *DO* want to be just like your parents.

Ever run across an object that *almost* does exactly what you want *your* object to do? Found yourself wishing that if you could just *change a few things*, that object would be perfect? Well, that's just one reason that **inheritance** is one of the most powerful concepts and techniques in the C# language. Before you're through with this chapter, you'll learn how to **subclass** an object to get its behavior, but keep the **flexibility** to make changes to that behavior. You'll **avoid duplicate code**, **model the real world** more closely, and end up with code that's **easier to maintain**.

7

interfaces and abstract classes
Making classes keep their promises

Actions speak louder than words.

Sometimes you need to group your objects together based on the **things they can do** rather than the classes they inherit from. That's where **interfaces** come in—they let you work with any class that can do the job. But with **great power comes great responsibility**, and any class that implements an interface must promise to **fulfill all of its obligations**…or the compiler will break their kneecaps, see?

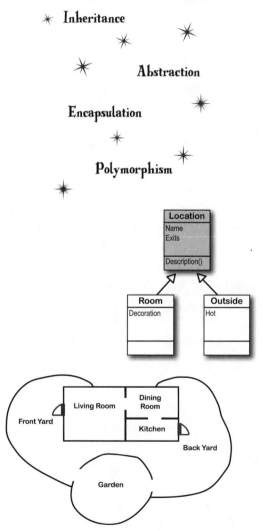

* Inheritance
* Abstraction
* Encapsulation
* Polymorphism

enums and collections

Storing lots of data

When it rains, it pours.

In the real world, you don't get to handle your data in tiny little bits and pieces. No, your data's going to come at you in **loads, piles, and bunches**. You'll need some pretty powerful tools to organize all of it, and that's where **collections** come in. They let you **store, sort, and manage** all the data that your programs need to pore through. That way, you can think about writing programs to work with your data, and let the collections worry about keeping track of it for you.

8

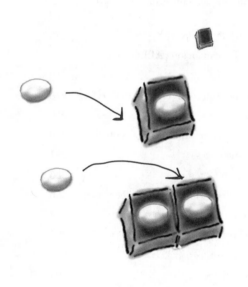

poof!

C# Lab 2

The Quest

Your job is to build an adventure game where a mighty adventurer is on a quest to defeat level after level of deadly enemies. You'll build a turn-based system, which means the player makes one move and then the enemies make one move. The player can move or attack, and then each enemy gets a chance to move and attack. The game keeps going until the player either defeats all the enemies on all seven levels or dies.

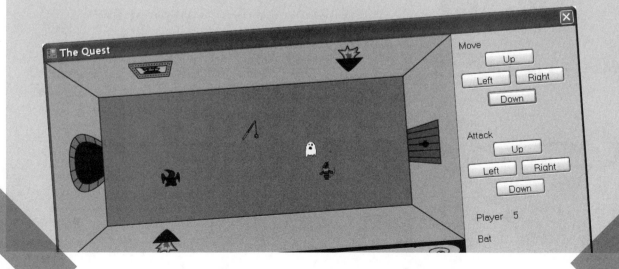

reading and writing files

Save the byte array, save the world

Sometimes it pays to be a little persistent.

So far, all of your programs have been pretty short-lived. They fire up, run for a while, and shut down. But that's not always enough, especially when you're dealing with important information. You need to be able to **save your work**. In this chapter, we'll look at how to **write data to a file**, and then how to **read that information back in** from a file. You'll learn about the .NET **stream classes**, and also take a look at the mysteries of **hexadecimal** and **binary**.

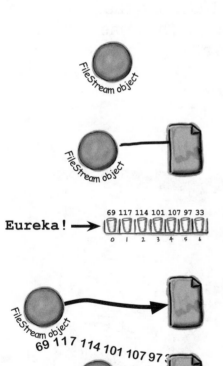

Eureka! ➔

69 117 114 101 107 97 33

exception handling
Putting out fires gets old

10

Programmers aren't meant to be firefighters.

You've worked your tail off, waded through technical manuals and a few engaging Head First books, and you've reached the pinnacle of your profession: **master programmer**. But you're still getting panicked phone calls in the middle of the night from work because **your program crashes**, or **doesn't behave like it's supposed to**. Nothing pulls you out of the programming groove like having to fix a strange bug… but with **exception handling**, you can write code to **deal with problems** that come up. Better yet, you can even react to those problems, and **keep things running**.

Work's boring today. I want to go scuba diving. Time to fire up the Excuse generator.

11

events and delegates

What your code does when you're not looking

Your objects are starting to think for themselves.

You can't always control what your objects are doing. Sometimes things…happen. And when they do, you want your objects to be smart enough to **respond to anything** that pops up. And that's what events are all about. One object *publishes* an event, other objects *subscribe*, and everyone works together to keep things moving. Which is great, until you want your object to take control over who can listen. That's when **callbacks** will come in handy.

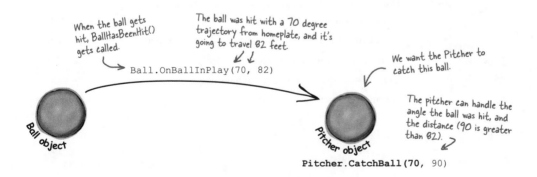

When the ball gets hit, BallHasBeenHit() gets called.

`Ball.OnBallInPlay(70, 82)`

The ball was hit with a 70 degree trajectory from homeplate, and it's going to travel 82 feet.

We want the Pitcher to catch this ball.

The pitcher can handle the angle the ball was hit, and the distance (90 is greater than 82).

Ball object

Pitcher object

`Pitcher.CatchBall(70, 90)`

review and preview
Knowledge, power, and building cool stuff

12

Learning's no good until you BUILD something.

Until you've actually written working code, it's hard to be sure if you really *get* some of the tougher concepts in C#. In this chapter, we're going to use what we've learned to do just that. We'll also get a preview of some of the new ideas coming up soon. And we'll do all that by building phase I of a **really complex application** to make sure you've got a good handle on what you've already learned from earlier chapters. So buckle up...it's time to **build some software**!

Life and death of a flower

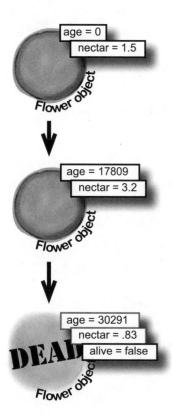

controls and graphics
Make it pretty

13

Sometimes you have to take graphics into your own hands.

We've spent a lot of time relying on controls to handle everything visual in our applications. But sometimes that's not enough—like when you want to **animate a picture**. And once you get into animation, you'll end up **creating your own controls** for your .NET programs, maybe adding a little **double buffering**, and even **drawing directly onto your forms**. It all begins with the **Graphics** object, **bitmap**s, and a determination to not accept the graphics status quo.

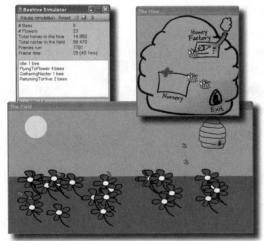

14 CAPTAIN AMAZING
THE DEATH OF THE OBJECT

15

LINQ

Get control of your data

It's a data-driven world…you better know how to live in it.

Gone are the days when you could program for days, even weeks, without dealing with **loads of data**. But today, *everything is about data*. In fact, you'll often have to work with data from **more than one place**…and in more than one format. Databases, XML, collections from other programs…it's all part of the job of a good C# programmer. And that's where **LINQ** comes in. LINQ not only lets you **query data** in a simple, intuitive way, but it lets you **group data**, and **merge data from different data sources**.

C# Lab 3

Invaders

In this lab you'll pay homage to one of the most popular, revered and replicated icons in video game history, a game that needs no further introduction. It's time to build Invaders.

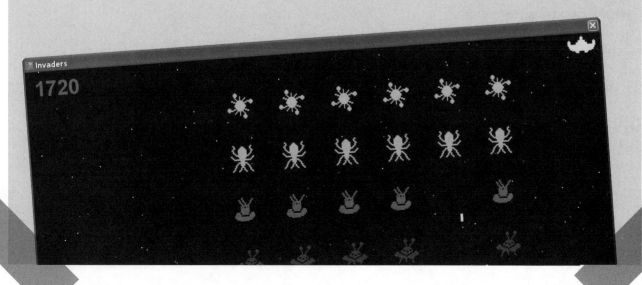

leftovers

The top 11 things we wanted to include in this book

The fun's just beginning!

We've shown you a lot of great tools to build some really **powerful software** with C#. But there's no way that we could include **every single tool, technology, or technique** in this book—there just aren't enough pages. We had to make some *really tough choices* about what to include and what to leave out. Here are some of the topics that didn't make the cut. But even though we couldn't get to them, we still think that they're **important and useful**, and we wanted to give you a small head start with them.

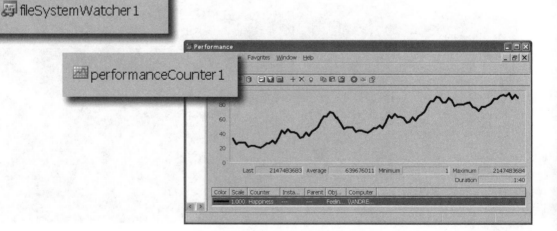

how to use this book

Intro

*I can't believe they put **that** in a C# programming book!*

In this section, we answer the burning question:
"So why DID they put that in a C# programming book?"

Who is this book for?

If you can answer "yes" to all of these:

(1) Do you want to **learn** C#?

(2) Do you like to tinker—do you learn by doing, rather than just reading?

(3) Do you prefer **stimulating dinner party conversation** to **dry, dull, academic lectures**?

this book is for you.

Who should probably back away from this book?

If you can answer "yes" to any of these:

(1) Does the idea of writing a lot of code make you bored and a little twitchy?

(2) Are you a kick-butt C++ or Java programmer looking for a reference book?

(3) Are you **afraid to try something different**? Would you rather have a root canal than mix stripes with plaid? Do you believe that a technical book can't be serious if C# concepts are anthropomorphized?

this book is not for you.

[Note from marketing: this book is for anyone with a credit card.]

We know what you're thinking.

"How can *this* be a serious C# programming book?"

"What's with all the graphics?"

"Can I actually *learn* it this way?"

And we know what your *brain* is thinking.

Your brain craves novelty. It's always searching, scanning, *waiting* for something unusual. It was built that way, and it helps you stay alive.

So what does your brain do with all the routine, ordinary, normal things you encounter? Everything it *can* to stop them from interfering with the brain's *real* job—recording things that *matter*. It doesn't bother saving the boring things; they never make it past the "this is obviously not important" filter.

How does your brain *know* what's important? Suppose you're out for a day hike and a tiger jumps in front of you, what happens inside your head and body?

Neurons fire. Emotions crank up. *Chemicals surge.*

And that's how your brain knows…

This must be important! Don't forget it!

But imagine you're at home, or in a library. It's a safe, warm, tiger-free zone. You're studying. Getting ready for an exam. Or trying to learn some tough technical topic your boss thinks will take a week, ten days at the most.

Just one problem. Your brain's trying to do you a big favor. It's trying to make sure that this *obviously* non-important content doesn't clutter up scarce resources. Resources that are better spent storing the really *big* things. Like tigers. Like the danger of fire. Like how you should never have posted those "party" photos on your Facebook page.

And there's no simple way to tell your brain, "Hey brain, thank you very much, but no matter how dull this book is, and how little I'm registering on the emotional Richter scale right now, I really *do* want you to keep this stuff around."

Your brain thinks THIS is important.

Great. Only 700 more dull, dry, boring pages.

Your brain thinks THIS isn't worth saving.

We think of a "Head First" reader as a learner.

So what does it take to *learn* something? First, you have to *get* it, then make sure you don't *forget* it. It's not about pushing facts into your head. Based on the latest research in cognitive science, neurobiology, and educational psychology, *learning* takes a lot more than text on a page. We know what turns your brain on.

Some of the Head First learning principles:

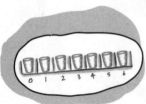

Make it visual. Images are far more memorable than words alone, and make learning much more effective (up to 89% improvement in recall and transfer studies). It also makes things more understandable. **Put the words within or near the graphics** they relate to, rather than on the bottom or on another page, and learners will be up to *twice* as likely to solve problems related to the content.

Use a conversational and personalized style. In recent studies, students performed up to 40% better on post-learning tests if the content spoke directly to the reader, using a first-person, conversational style rather than taking a formal tone. Tell stories instead of lecturing. Use casual language. Don't take yourself too seriously. Which would *you* pay more attention to: a stimulating dinner party companion, or a lecture?

Get the learner to think more deeply. In other words, unless you actively flex your neurons, nothing much happens in your head. A reader has to be motivated, engaged, curious, and inspired to solve problems, draw conclusions, and generate new knowledge. And for that, you need challenges, exercises, and thought-provoking questions, and activities that involve both sides of the brain and multiple senses.

Get—and keep—the reader's attention. We've all had the "I really want to learn this but I can't stay awake past page one" experience. Your brain pays attention to things that are out of the ordinary, interesting, strange, eye-catching, unexpected. Learning a new, tough, technical topic doesn't have to be boring. Your brain will learn much more quickly if it's not.

Touch their emotions. We now know that your ability to remember something is largely dependent on its emotional content. You remember what you care about. You remember when you *feel* something. No, we're not talking heart-wrenching stories about a boy and his dog. We're talking emotions like surprise, curiosity, fun, "what the…?", and the feeling of "I Rule!" that comes when you solve a puzzle, learn something everybody else thinks is hard, or realize you know something that "I'm more technical than thou" Bob from engineering *doesn't*.

Metacognition: thinking about thinking

If you really want to learn, and you want to learn more quickly and more deeply, pay attention to how you pay attention. Think about how you think. Learn how you learn.

Most of us did not take courses on metacognition or learning theory when we were growing up. We were *expected* to learn, but rarely *taught* to learn.

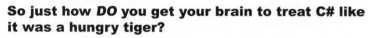

I wonder how I can trick my brain into remembering this stuff...

But we assume that if you're holding this book, you really want to learn how to build programs in C#. And you probably don't want to spend a lot of time. If you want to use what you read in this book, you need to *remember* what you read. And for that, you've got to *understand* it. To get the most from this book, or *any* book or learning experience, take responsibility for your brain. Your brain on *this* content.

The trick is to get your brain to see the new material you're learning as Really Important. Crucial to your well-being. As important as a tiger. Otherwise, you're in for a constant battle, with your brain doing its best to keep the new content from sticking.

So just how *DO* you get your brain to treat C# like it was a hungry tiger?

There's the slow, tedious way, or the faster, more effective way. The slow way is about sheer repetition. You obviously know that you *are* able to learn and remember even the dullest of topics if you keep pounding the same thing into your brain. With enough repetition, your brain says, "This doesn't *feel* important to him, but he keeps looking at the same thing *over* and *over* and *over*, so I suppose it must be."

The faster way is to do **anything that increases brain activity,** especially different *types* of brain activity. The things on the previous page are a big part of the solution, and they're all things that have been proven to help your brain work in your favor. For example, studies show that putting words *within* the pictures they describe (as opposed to somewhere else in the page, like a caption or in the body text) causes your brain to try to makes sense of how the words and picture relate, and this causes more neurons to fire. More neurons firing = more chances for your brain to *get* that this is something worth paying attention to, and possibly recording.

A conversational style helps because people tend to pay more attention when they perceive that they're in a conversation, since they're expected to follow along and hold up their end. The amazing thing is, your brain doesn't necessarily *care* that the "conversation" is between you and a book! On the other hand, if the writing style is formal and dry, your brain perceives it the same way you experience being lectured to while sitting in a roomful of passive attendees. No need to stay awake.

But pictures and conversational style are just the beginning.

Here's what WE did:

We used ***pictures***, because your brain is tuned for visuals, not text. As far as your brain's concerned, a picture really *is* worth a thousand words. And when text and pictures work together, we embedded the text *in* the pictures because your brain works more effectively when the text is *within* the thing the text refers to, as opposed to in a caption or buried in the text somewhere.

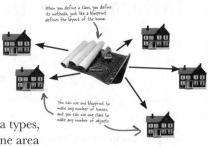

When you define a class, you define its methods, just like a blueprint defines the layout of the house.

You can use one blueprint to make any number of houses, and you can use one class to make any number of objects.

We used ***redundancy***, saying the same thing in *different* ways and with different media types, and *multiple senses*, to increase the chance that the content gets coded into more than one area of your brain.

We used concepts and pictures in ***unexpected*** ways because your brain is tuned for novelty, and we used pictures and ideas with at least *some* ***emotional*** *content*, because your brain is tuned to pay attention to the biochemistry of emotions. That which causes you to *feel* something is more likely to be remembered, even if that feeling is nothing more than a little ***humor***, ***surprise***, or ***interest***.

We used a personalized, ***conversational style***, because your brain is tuned to pay more attention when it believes you're in a conversation than if it thinks you're passively listening to a presentation. Your brain does this even when you're *reading*.

We included more than 80 ***activities***, because your brain is tuned to learn and remember more when you ***do*** things than when you *read* about things. And we made the exercises challenging-yet-do-able, because that's what most people prefer.

We used ***multiple learning styles***, because *you* might prefer step-by-step procedures, while someone else wants to understand the big picture first, and someone else just wants to see an example. But regardless of your own learning preference, *everyone* benefits from seeing the same content represented in multiple ways.

BULLET POINTS

We include content for ***both sides of your brain***, because the more of your brain you engage, the more likely you are to learn and remember, and the longer you can stay focused. Since working one side of the brain often means giving the other side a chance to rest, you can be more productive at learning for a longer period of time.

And we included ***stories*** and exercises that present ***more than one point of view,*** because your brain is tuned to learn more deeply when it's forced to make evaluations and judgments.

Fireside Chats

We included ***challenges***, with exercises, and by asking ***questions*** that don't always have a straight answer, because your brain is tuned to learn and remember when it has to *work* at something. Think about it—you can't get your *body* in shape just by *watching* people at the gym. But we did our best to make sure that when you're working hard, it's on the *right* things. That ***you're not spending one extra dendrite*** processing a hard-to-understand example, or parsing difficult, jargon-laden, or overly terse text.

We used ***people***. In stories, examples, pictures, etc., because, well, because *you're* a person. And your brain pays more attention to *people* than it does to *things*.

Here's what YOU can do to bend your brain into submission

So, we did our part. The rest is up to you. These tips are a starting point; listen to your brain and figure out what works for you and what doesn't. Try new things.

Cut this out and stick it on your refrigerator.

---

(1) Slow down. The more you understand, the less you have to memorize.

Don't just *read*. Stop and think. When the book asks you a question, don't just skip to the answer. Imagine that someone really *is* asking the question. The more deeply you force your brain to think, the better chance you have of learning and remembering.

(2) Do the exercises. Write your own notes.

We put them in, but if we did them for you, that would be like having someone else do your workouts for you. And don't just *look* at the exercises. **Use a pencil.** There's plenty of evidence that physical activity *while* learning can increase the learning.

(3) Read the "There are No Dumb Questions"

That means all of them. They're not optional sidebars—*they're part of the core content!* Don't skip them.

(4) Make this the last thing you read before bed. Or at least the last challenging thing.

Part of the learning (especially the transfer to long-term memory) happens *after* you put the book down. Your brain needs time on its own, to do more processing. If you put in something new during that processing time, some of what you just learned will be lost.

(5) Drink water. Lots of it.

Your brain works best in a nice bath of fluid. Dehydration (which can happen before you ever feel thirsty) decreases cognitive function.

(6) Talk about it. Out loud.

Speaking activates a different part of the brain. If you're trying to understand something, or increase your chance of remembering it later, say it out loud. Better still, try to explain it out loud to someone else. You'll learn more quickly, and you might uncover ideas you hadn't known were there when you were reading about it.

(7) Listen to your brain.

Pay attention to whether your brain is getting overloaded. If you find yourself starting to skim the surface or forget what you just read, it's time for a break. Once you go past a certain point, you won't learn faster by trying to shove more in, and you might even hurt the process.

(8) Feel something.

Your brain needs to know that this *matters*. Get involved with the stories. Make up your own captions for the photos. Groaning over a bad joke is *still* better than feeling nothing at all.

(9) Write a lot of software!

There's only one way to learn to program: **writing a lot of code**. And that's what you're going to do throughout this book. Coding is a skill, and the only way to get good at it is to practice. We're going to give you a lot of practice: every chapter has exercises that pose a problem for you to solve. Don't just skip over them—a lot of the learning happens when you solve the exercises. We included a solution to each exercise—don't be afraid to **peek at the solution** if you get stuck! (It's easy to get snagged on something small.) But try to solve the problem before you look at the solution. And definitely get it working before you move on to the next part of the book.

What you need for this book:

We wrote this book using Visual C# 2010 Express Edition, which uses C# 4.0 and .NET Framework 4.0. All of the screenshots that you see throughout the book were taken from that edition, so we recommend that you use it. If you're using Visual Studio 2010 Professional, Premium, Ultimate or Test Professional editions, you'll see some small differences, which we've pointed out wherever possible. You can download the Express Edition for free from Microsoft's website—it installs cleanly alongside other editions, as well as previous versions of Visual Studio.

SETTING UP VISUAL STUDIO 2010 EXPRESS EDITION

- It's easy enough to download and install Visual C# 2010 Express Edition. Here's the link to the Visual Studio 2010 Express Edition download page:

  ```
  http://www.microsoft.com/express/downloads/
  ```

  You don't need to check any of the options in the installer to get the code in this book to run, but feel free to if you want.

  If you absolutely must use an older version of Visual Studio, C# or the .NET Framework, then please keep in mind that you'll come across topics in this book that won't be compatible with your version. The C# team at Microsoft has added some pretty cool features to the language. Keep in mind that if you're not using the latest version, there will be some code in this book that won't work.

- Download the installation package for Visual C# 2010 Express Edition. Make sure you do a complete installation. That should install everything that you need: the IDE (which you'll learn about),.NET Framework 4.0, and other tools.

- Once you've got it installed, you'll have a new Start menu option: ***Microsoft Visual C# 2010 Express Edition***. Click on it to bring up the IDE, and you're all set.

Read me

This is a learning experience, not a reference book. We deliberately stripped out everything that might get in the way of learning whatever it is we're working on at that point in the book. And the first time through, you need to begin at the beginning, because the book makes assumptions about what you've already seen and learned.

We use a lot of diagrams to make tough concepts easier to understand.

The activities are NOT optional.

The exercises and activities are not add-ons; they're part of the core content of the book. Some of them are to help with memory, some for understanding, and some to help you apply what you've learned. ***Don't skip the written problems.*** The pool puzzles are the only things you don't *have* to do, but they're good for giving your brain a chance to think about twisty little logic puzzles.

The redundancy is intentional and important.

One distinct difference in a Head First book is that we want you to *really* get it. And we want you to finish the book remembering what you've learned. Most reference books don't have retention and recall as a goal, but this book is about *learning*, so you'll see some of the same concepts come up more than once.

You should do ALL of the "Sharpen your pencil" activities

Sharpen your pencil

Do all the exercises!

The one big assumption that we made when we wrote this book is that you want to learn how to program in C#. So we know you want to get your hands dirty right away, and dig right into the code. We gave you a lot of opportunities to sharpen your skills by putting exercises in every chapter. We've labeled some of them "Do this!"—when you see that, it means that we'll walk you through all of the steps to solve a particular problem. But when you see the Exercise logo with the running shoes, then we've left a big portion of the problem up to you to solve, and we gave you the solution that we came up with. Don't be afraid to peek at the solution—**it's not cheating**! But you'll learn the most if you try to solve the problem first.

Activities marked with the Exercise (running shoe) logo are really important! Don't skip them if you're serious about learning C#.

Exercise

We've also placed all the exercise solutions' source code on the web so you can download it. You'll find it at http://www.headfirstlabs.com/books/hfcsharp/

The "Brain Power" exercises don't have answers.

For some of them, there is no right answer, and for others, part of the learning experience of the Brain Power activities is for you to decide if and when your answers are right. In some of the Brain Power exercises you will find hints to point you in the right direction.

If you see the Pool Puzzle logo, the activity is optional, and if you don't like twisty logic, you won't like these either.

The technical review team

Lisa Kellner

Chris Burrows

We're especially grateful for Chris's insight and almost ridiculously helpful feedback.

Not pictured (but just as awesome are the reviewers from the first edition): Joe Albahari, Jay Hilyard, Aayam Singh, Theodore, Peter Ritchie, Bill Meitelski Andy Parker, Wayne Bradney, Dave Murdoch, Bridgette Julie Landers. And special thanks to Jon Skeet for his thorough review and suggestions for the first edition!

Nick Paladino

David Sterling

David really helped us out, especially with some very neat IDE tricks.

Technical Reviewers:

When we wrote this book, it had a bunch of mistakes, issues, problems, typos, and terrible arithmetic errors. OK, it wasn't quite that bad. But we're still really grateful for the work that our technical reviewers did for the book. We would have gone to press with errors (including one or two big ones) had it not been for the most kick-ass review team EVER....

First of all, we really want to thank **Chris Burrows** and **David Sterling** for their enormous amount of technical guidance. We also want to thank **Lisa Kellner**—this is our sixth book that she's reviewed for us, and she made a huge difference in the readability of the final product. Thanks, Lisa! And special thanks to **Nick Paladino.** Thanks!

Chris Burrows is a developer at Microsoft on the C# Compiler team who focused on design and implementation of language features in C# 4.0, most notably dynamic.

David Sterling has worked on the Visual C# Compiler team for nearly 3 years.

Nicholas Paldino has been a Microsoft MVP for .NET/C# since the discipline's inception in the MVP program and has over 13 years of experience in the programming industry, specifically targeting Microsoft technologies.

Acknowledgments

Our editor:

We want to thank our editors, **Brett McLaughlin and Courtney Nash**, for editing this book. Brett helped with a lot of the narrative, and the comic idea in Chapter 14 was completely his, and we think it turned out really well. Thanks!

Brett McLaughlin

Courtney Nash

The O'Reilly team:

Lou Barr

Lou Barr is an amazing graphic designer who went above and beyond on this one, putting in unbelievable hours and coming up with some pretty amazing visuals. If you see anything in this book that looks fantastic, you can thank her (and her mad InDesign skillz) for it. She did all of the monster and alien graphics for the labs, and the entire comic book. Thanks so much, Lou! You are our hero, and you're awesome to work with.

Sanders Kleinfeld

There are so many people at O'Reilly we want to thank that we hope we don't forget anyone. Special thanks to production editor **Rachel Monaghan**, indexer **Lucie Haskins**, **Emily Quill** for her sharp proofread, **Ron Bilodeau** for volunteering his time and preflighting expertise, and **Sanders Kleinfeld** for offering one last sanity check—all of whom helped get this book from production to press in record time. And as always, we love **Mary Treseler**, and can't wait to work with her again! And a big shout out to our other friends and editors, **Andy Oram** and **Mike Hendrickson**. And if you're reading this book right now, then you can thank the greatest publicity team in the industry: **Marsee Henon**, **Sara Peyton**, **Mary Rotman**, **Jessica Boyd**, **Kathryn Barrett**, and the rest of the folks at Sebastopol.

Safari® Books Online

 Safari Books Online is an on-demand digital library that lets you easily search over 7,500 technology and creative reference books and videos to find the answers you need quickly.

With a subscription, you can read any page and watch any video from our library online. Read books on your cell phone and mobile devices. Access new titles before they are available for print, and get exclusive access to manuscripts in development and post feedback for the authors. Copy and paste code samples, organize your favorites, download chapters, bookmark key sections, create notes, print out pages, and benefit from tons of other time-saving features.

O'Reilly Media has uploaded this book to the Safari Books Online service. To have full digital access to this book and others on similar topics from O'Reilly and other publishers, sign up for free at *http://my.safaribooksonline.com/?portal=oreilly.*

Visual Applications, in 10 minutes or less

> Don't worry, Mother. With Visual Studio and *C#*, you'll be able to program so fast that you'll never burn the pot roast again.

Want to build great programs really fast?

With C#, you've got a **powerful programming language** and a **valuable tool** at your fingertips. With the **Visual Studio IDE**, you'll never have to spend hours writing obscure code to get a button working again. Even better, you'll be able to **focus on getting your work done**, rather than remembering which method parameter was for the *name* of a button, and which one was for its *label*. Sound appealing? Turn the page, and let's get programming.

Why you should learn C#

C# and the Visual Studio IDE make it easy for you to get to the business of writing code, and writing it fast. When you're working with C#, the IDE is your best friend and constant companion.

> The IDE—or Visual Studio Integrated Development Environment—is an important part of working in C#. It's a program that helps you edit your code, manage your files, and publish your projects.

Here's what the IDE automates for you...

Every time you want to get started writing a program, or just putting a button on a form, your program needs a whole bunch of repetitive code.

```
using System;
using System.Collections.Generic;
using System.Windows.Forms;
namespace A_New_Program
{
    static class Program
    {
        /// <summary>
        /// The main entry point for the application.
        /// </summary>
        [STAThread]
        static void Main()
        {
            Application.EnableVisualStyles();
            Application.SetCompatibleTextRenderingDefault(false);
            Application.Run(new Form1());
        }
    }
}
```

```
private void InitializeComponent()
{
    this.button1 = new System.Windows.Forms.Button();
    this.SuspendLayout();
    //
    // button1
    //
    this.button1.Location = new System.Drawing.Point(105, 56);
    this.button1.Name = "button1";
    this.button1.Size = new System.Drawing.Size(75, 23);
    this.button1.TabIndex = 0;
    this.button1.Text = "button1";
    this.button1.UseVisualStyleBackColor = true;
    this.button1.Click += new System.EventHandler(this.button1_Click);
    //
    // Form1
    //
    this.AutoScaleDimensions = new System.Drawing.SizeF(8F, 16F);
    this.AutoScaleMode = System.Windows.Forms.AutoScaleMode.Font;
    this.ClientSize = new System.Drawing.Size(292, 267);
    this.Controls.Add(this.button1);
    this.Name = "Form1";
    this.Text = "Form1";
    this.ResumeLayout(false);
```

> It takes all this code just to draw a button on a form. Adding a few more visual elements to the form could take 10 times as much code.

What you get with Visual Studio and C#...

With a language like C#, tuned for Windows programming, and the Visual Studio IDE, you can focus on what your program is supposed to **do** immediately:

> The result is a better looking application that takes less time to write.

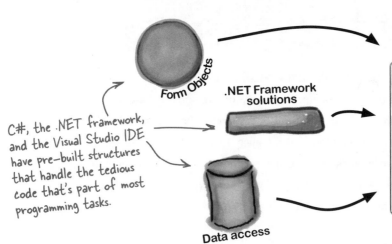

> C#, the .NET framework, and the Visual Studio IDE have pre-built structures that handle the tedious code that's part of most programming tasks.

Form Objects
.NET Framework solutions
Data access

C# and the Visual Studio IDE make lots of things easy

When you use C# and Visual Studio, you get all of these great features, without having to do any extra work. Together, they let you:

1 **Build an application, FAST.** Creating programs in C# is a snap. The language is powerful and easy to learn, and the Visual Studio IDE does a lot of work for you automatically. You can leave mundane coding tasks to the IDE and focus on what your code should accomplish.

2 **Design a great looking user interface.** The Form Designer in the Visual Studio IDE is one of the easiest design tools to use out there. It does so much for you that you'll find that making stunning user interfaces is one of the most satisfying parts of developing a C# application. You can build full-featured professional programs without having to spend hours writing a graphical user interface entirely from scratch.

3 **Create and interact with databases.** The IDE includes an easy-to-use interface for building databases, and integrates seamlessly with SQL Server Compact Edition and many other popular database systems.

4 **Focus on solving your REAL problems.** The IDE does a lot for you, but *you* are still in control of what you build with C#. The IDE just lets you focus on your program, your work (or fun!), and your customers. But the IDE handles all the grunt work, such as:

   ★ Keeping track of all your projects

   ★ Making it easy to edit your project's code

   ★ Keeping track of your project's graphics, audio, icons, and other resources

   ★ Managing and interacting with databases

All this means you'll have all the time you would've spent doing this routine programming to put into **building killer programs**.

You're going to see exactly what we mean next.

Help the CEO go paperless

The Objectville Paper Company just hired a new CEO. He loves hiking, coffee, and nature...and he's decided that to help save forests, he wants to become a paperless executive, starting with his contacts. He's heading to Aspen to go skiing for the weekend, and expects a new address book program by the time he gets back. Otherwise...well...it won't be just the old CEO who's looking for a job.

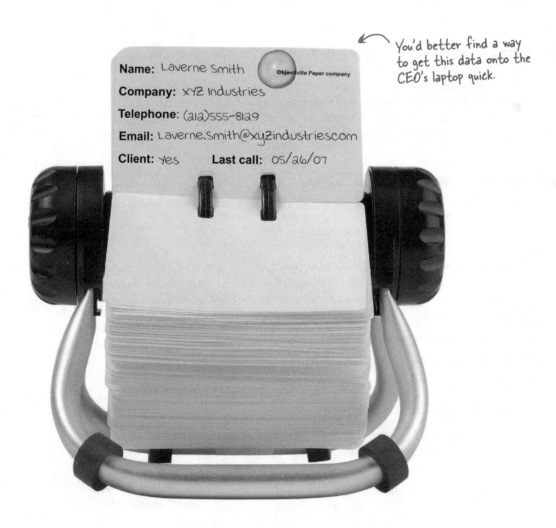

You'd better find a way to get this data onto the CEO's laptop quick.

Name: Laverne Smith

Company: XYZ Industries

Telephone: (212)555-8129

Email: Laverne.Smith@xyzindustries.com

Client: Yes   Last call: 05/26/07

Get to know your users' needs <u>before</u> you start building your program

Before we can start writing the address book application—or *any* application—we need to take a minute and think about **who's going to be using it**, and **what they need** from the application.

① The CEO needs to be able to run his address book program at work and on his laptop, too. He'll need an installer to make sure that all of the right files get onto each machine.

The CEO wants to be able to run his program on his desktop and laptop, so an installer is a must.

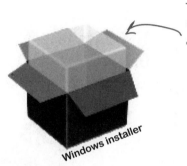

Windows installer

Think about your users and their <u>needs</u> before you start building the code, and they'll be happy with the final product once you're done!

② The Objectville Paper Company sales team wants to access his address book, too. They can use his data to build mailing lists and get client leads for more paper sales.

The CEO figures a database would be the best way for everyone in the company to see his data, and then he can just keep up with one copy of all his contacts.

We already know that Visual C# makes working with databases easy. Having contacts in a database lets the CEO and the sales team all access the information, even though there's only one copy of the data.

SQL Database

Here's what you're going to build

You're going to need an application with a graphical user interface, objects to talk to a database, the database itself, and an installer. It sounds like a lot of work, but you'll build all of this over the next few pages.

Here's the structure of the program we're going to create:

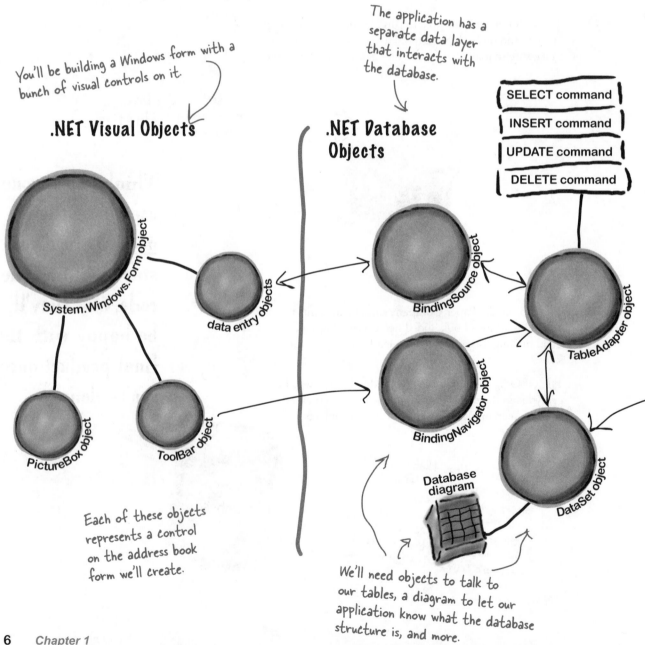

The application has a separate data layer that interacts with the database.

You'll be building a Windows form with a bunch of visual controls on it.

.NET Visual Objects

.NET Database Objects

SELECT command

INSERT command

UPDATE command

DELETE command

System.Windows.Form object

data entry objects

BindingSource object

TableAdapter object

BindingNavigator object

PictureBox object

ToolBar object

Database diagram

DataSet object

Each of these objects represents a control on the address book form we'll create.

We'll need objects to talk to our tables, a diagram to let our application know what the database structure is, and more.

The data is all stored in a table in a SQL Server Compact database.

Once the program's built, it'll be packaged up into a Windows installer.

Data Storage

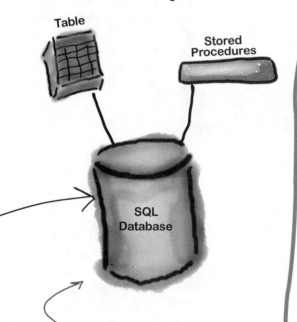

Table

Stored
Procedures

SQL
Database

Here's the database itself, which Visual Studio will help us create and maintain.

Deployment Package

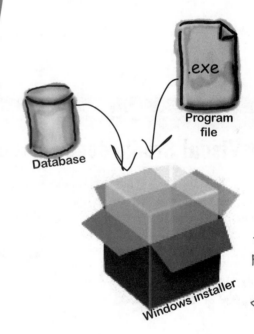

.exe

Program
file

Database

Windows installer

The sales department will just need to point and click to install and then use his program.

What you do in Visual Studio...

Go ahead and start up Visual Studio, if you haven't already. Skip over the start page and select New Project from the **File** menu. Name your project "Contacts" and click OK. There are several project types to choose from. Select **Windows Forms Application** and choose "Contacts" as the name for your new project.

Things may look a bit different in your IDE.

This is what the "New Project" window looks like in Visual Studio 2010 Express Edition. If you're using the Professional or Team Foundation edition, it might be a bit different. But don't worry, everything still works exactly the same.

What Visual Studio does for you...

As soon as you save the project, the IDE creates `Form1.cs`, `Form1.Designer.cs`, and `Program.cs` file, when you create a new project. It adds these to the Solution Explorer window, and by default, puts those files in `My Documents\Visual Studio 2010\Projects\Contacts\`.

Make sure that you save your project as soon as you create it by selecting "Save All" from the File menu—that'll save all of the project files out to the folder. If you select "Save", it just saves the one you're working on.

This file contains the C# code that defines the behavior of the form.

This has the code that starts up the program and displays the form.

The code that defines the form and its objects lives here.

Form1.cs

Program.cs

Form1.Designer.cs

Visual Studio creates all three of these files automatically.

Sharpen your pencil

Below is what your screen probably looks like right now. You should be able to figure out the purpose of most of these windows and files based on what you already know. Make sure you open the Toolbox and Error List windows by **choosing them from the View >> Other Windows menu**. Then in each of the blanks, try and fill in an annotation saying what that part of the IDE does. We've done one to get you started.

This toolbar has buttons that apply to what you're currently doing in the IDE.

If your IDE doesn't look exactly like this picture, you can select "Reset Window Layout" from the Window menu.

We've blown up this window below so you have more room.

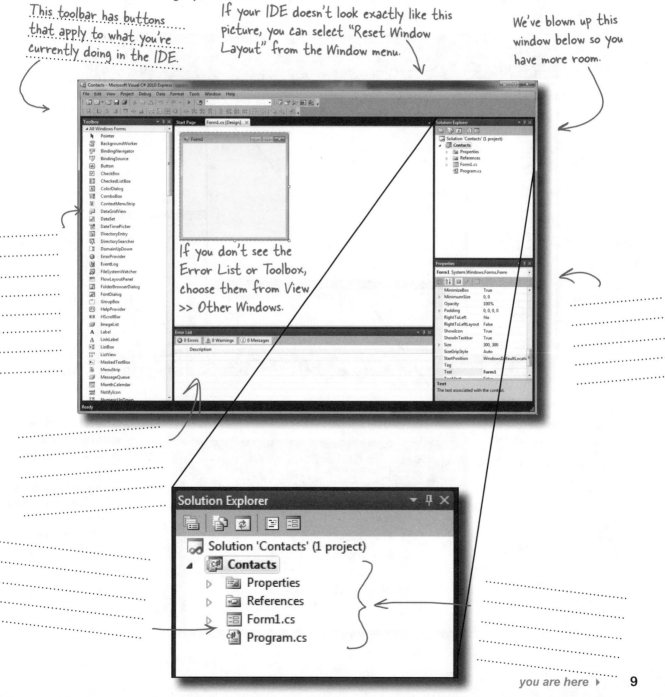

If you don't see the Error List or Toolbox, choose them from View >> Other Windows.

Sharpen your pencil
Solution

We've filled in the annotations about the different sections of the Visual Studio C# IDE. You may have some different things written down, but you should have been able to figure out the basics of what each window and section of the IDE is used for.

This toolbar has buttons that apply to what you're currently doing in the IDE.

This is the toolbox. It has a bunch of visual controls that you can drag onto your form.

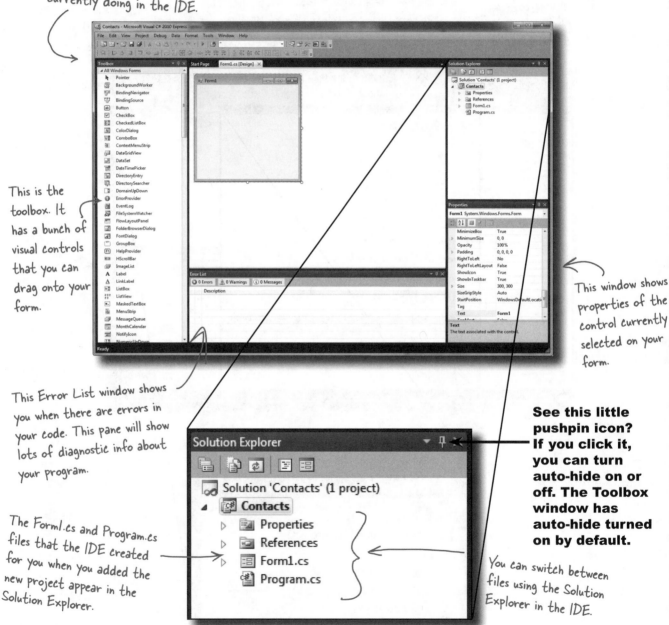

This window shows properties of the control currently selected on your form.

This Error List window shows you when there are errors in your code. This pane will show lots of diagnostic info about your program.

The Form1.cs and Program.cs files that the IDE created for you when you added the new project appear in the Solution Explorer.

See this little pushpin icon? If you click it, you can turn auto-hide on or off. The Toolbox window has auto-hide turned on by default.

You can switch between files using the Solution Explorer in the IDE.

Q: So if the IDE writes all this code for me, is learning C# just a matter of learning how to use the IDE?

A: No. The IDE is great at automatically generating some code for you, but it can only do so much. There are some things it's really good at, like setting up good starting points for you, and automatically changing properties of controls on your forms. But the hard part of programming—figuring out what your program needs to do and making it do it—is something that no IDE can do for you. Even though the Visual Studio IDE is one of the most advanced development environments out there, it can only go so far. It's *you*—not the IDE—who writes the code that actually does the work.

Q: I created a new project in Visual Studio, but when I went into the "Projects" folder under My Documents, I didn't see it there. What gives?

A: When you first create a new project in Visual Studio 2010 Express, the IDE creates the project in your `Local Settings\ Application Data\Temporary Projects` folder. When you save the project for the first time, it will prompt you for a new filename, and save it in the `My Documents\Visual Studio 2010\Projects` folder. If you try to open a new project or close the temporary one, you'll be prompted to either save or discard the temporary project. *(NOTE: The other, non-Express versions of Visual Studio do not use a temporary projects folder. They create the project directly in Projects!)*

Q: What if the IDE creates code I don't want in my project?

A: You can change it. The IDE is set up to create code based on the way the element you dragged or added is most commonly

used. But sometimes that's not exactly what you wanted. Everything the IDE does for you—every line of code it creates, every file it adds—can be changed, either manually by editing the files directly or through an easy-to-use interface in the IDE.

Q: Is it OK that I downloaded and installed Visual Studio Express? Or do I need to use one of the versions of Visual Studio that isn't free in order to do everything in this book?

A: There's nothing in this book that you can't do with the free version of Visual Studio (which you can download from Microsoft's website). The main differences between Express and the other editions (Professional and Team Foundation) aren't going to get in the way of writing C# and creating fully functional, complete applications.

Q: Can I change the names of the files the IDE generates for me?

A: Absolutely. When you create a new project, the IDE gives you a default form called `Form1` (which has files called `Form1.cs`, `Form1.Designer.cs`, and `Form1. resx`). But you can use the Solution Explorer to change the names of the files to whatever you want. By default, the names of the files are the same as the name of the form. If you change the names of the files, you'll be able to see in the Properties window that the form will still be called `Form1`. You can change the name of the form by changing the "(Name)" line in the Properties window. If you do, the filenames won't change.

C# doesn't care what names you choose for your files or your forms (or any other part of the program), although there are a few rules for this. But if you choose good names, it makes your programs easier to work with. For now, don't worry about names—we'll talk a lot more about how to choose good names for parts of your program later on.

Q: I'm looking at the IDE right now, but my screen doesn't look like yours! It's missing some of the windows, and others are in the wrong place. What gives?

A: If you click on the "Reset Window Layout" command under the "Window" menu, the IDE will restore the default window layout for you. Then you can use the "View >> Other Windows" menu to make your screen look just like the ones in this chapter.

Visual Studio will generate code you can use as a starting point for your applications.

Making sure the application does what it's supposed to do is entirely up to you.

Develop the user interface

Adding controls and polishing the user interface is as easy as
dragging and dropping with the Visual Studio IDE. Let's add a
logo to the form:

1 **Use the PictureBox control to add a picture.**
Click on the PictureBox control in the Toolbox, and drag it
onto your form. In the background, the IDE added code to
`Form1.Designer.cs` for a new picture control.

> If you don't see
> the toolbox, try
> hovering over the
> word "Toolbox"
> that shows up
> in the upper
> left-hand corner
> of the IDE. If it's
> not there, select
> "Toolbox" from
> the View menu to
> make it appear.

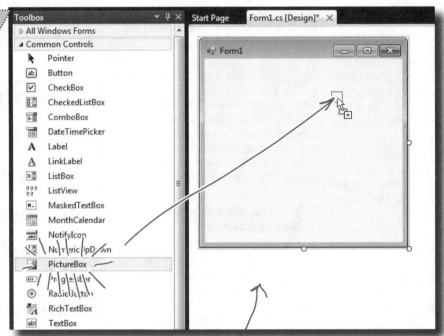

Every time you make a change to a control's properties on the form, the code in Form1.Designer.cs is getting changed by the IDE.

Form1.Designer.cs

Relax

It's OK if you're not a pro at user interface design.

We'll talk a lot more about designing
good user interfaces later on. For now,
just get the logo and other controls on your form, and
worry about **behavior**. We'll add some style later.

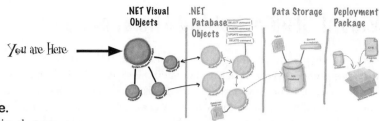

You are Here ➞

2 **Set the PictureBox to Zoom mode.**

Every control on your form has properties that you can set. Click the little black arrow for a control to access these properties. Change the PictureBox's Size property to "Zoom" to see how this works:

Click on this little black arrow to access a control's properties.

You can also use the "Properties" window in the IDE to set the Size property. The little black arrow is just there to make it easy to access the most common properties of any control.

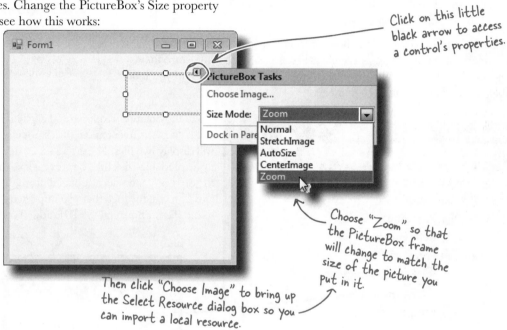

Choose "Zoom" so that the PictureBox frame will change to match the size of the picture you put in it.

Then click "Choose Image" to bring up the Select Resource dialog box so you can import a local resource.

3 **Download the Objectville Paper Company logo.**

Download the Objectville Paper Co. logo from Head First Labs (**http://www.headfirstlabs.com/books/hfcsharp**) and save it to your hard drive. Then click the PictureBox properties arrow, and select Choose Image. You'll see a Select Resources window pop up. Click the "Local Resource" radio button to enable the "Import…" button at the top of the form. Click that button, find your logo, and you're all set.

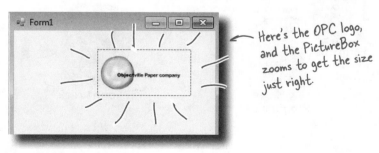

Here's the OPC logo, and the PictureBox zooms to get the size just right.

Visual Studio, behind the scenes

Every time you do something in the Visual Studio IDE, the IDE is *writing code for you*. When you created the logo and told Visual Studio to use the image you downloaded, Visual Studio created a resource and associated it with your application. A **resource** is any graphics file, audio file, icon, or other kind of data file that gets bundled with your application. The graphics file gets integrated into the program, so that when it's installed on another computer, the graphic is installed along with it and the PictureBox can use it.

When you dragged the PictureBox control onto your form, the IDE automatically created a resource file called `Form1.resx` to store that resource and keep it in the project. Double-click on this file, and you'll be able to see the newly imported image.

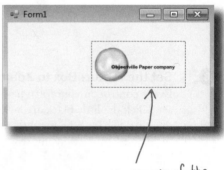

This image is now a resource of the Contact List application.

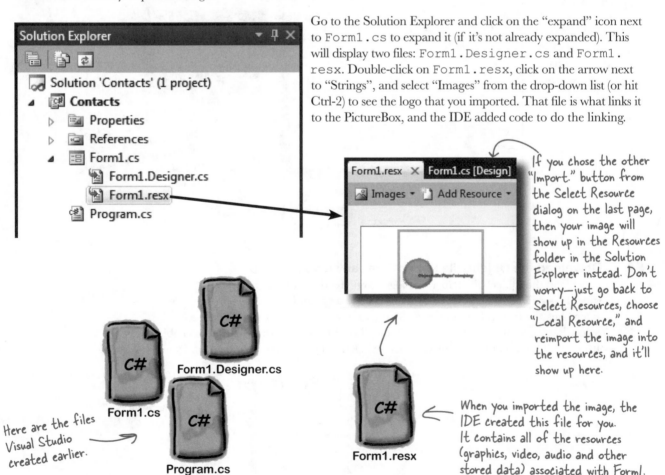

Go to the Solution Explorer and click on the "expand" icon next to `Form1.cs` to expand it (if it's not already expanded). This will display two files: `Form1.Designer.cs` and `Form1.resx`. Double-click on `Form1.resx`, click on the arrow next to "Strings", and select "Images" from the drop-down list (or hit Ctrl-2) to see the logo that you imported. That file is what links it to the PictureBox, and the IDE added code to do the linking.

If you chose the other "Import." button from the Select Resource dialog on the last page, then your image will show up in the Resources folder in the Solution Explorer instead. Don't worry—just go back to Select Resources, choose "Local Resource," and reimport the image into the resources, and it'll show up here.

Here are the files Visual Studio created earlier.

When you imported the image, the IDE created this file for you. It contains all of the resources (graphics, video, audio and other stored data) associated with Form1.

Add to the auto-generated code

The IDE creates lots of code for you, but you'll still want to get into this code and add to it. Let's set the logo up to show an About message when the users run the program and click on the logo.

When you're editing a form in the IDE, double-clicking on any of the toolbox controls causes the IDE to automatically add code to your project. Make sure you've got the form showing in the IDE, and then double-click on the PictureBox control. The IDE will add code to your project that gets run any time a user clicks on the PictureBox. You should see some code pop up that looks like this:

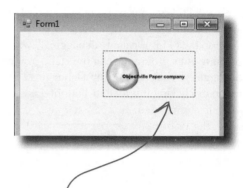

```
public partial class Form1 : Form
{

    public Form1()
    {

        InitializeComponent();

    }

    private void pictureBox1_Click(object sender, EventArgs e)

    {

        MessageBox.Show("Contact List 1.0.\nWritten by: Your Name", "About");

    }
}
```

When you double-clicked on the PictureBox control, the IDE created this method. It will run every time a user clicks on the logo in the running application.

This method name gives you a good idea about when it runs: when someone clicks on this PictureBox control.

When you double-click on the PictureBox, it will open this code up with a cursor blinking right here. Ignore any windows the IDE pops up as you type; it's trying to help you, but we don't need that right now.

Type in this line of code. It causes a message box to pop up with the text you provide. The box will be titled "About".

Once you've typed in the line of code, save it using the Save icon on the IDE toolbar or by selecting "Save" from the File menu. Get in the habit of doing "Save All" regularly!

---

there are no
Dumb Questions

Q: What's a method?

A: A **method** is just a *named block of code*. We'll talk a lot more about methods in Chapter 2.

Q: What does that \n thing do?

A: That's a line break. It tells C# to put "Contact List 1.0." on one line, and then start a new line for "Written by:".

You can <u>already</u> run your application

Press the F5 key on your keyboard, or click the green arrow button (▶) on the toolbar to check out what you've done so far. (This is called "debugging," which just means running your program using the IDE.) You can stop debugging by selecting "Stop Debugging" from the Debug menu or clicking this toolbar button: ■ .

All three of these buttons work—and you didn't have to write any code to make them work.

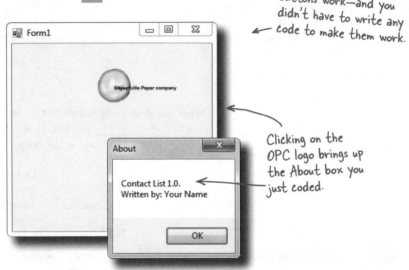

Clicking on the OPC logo brings up the About box you just coded.

Where are my files?

When you run your program, Visual Studio copies your files to My Documents\Visual Studio 2010\Projects\Contacts\Contacts\bin\debug. You can even hop over to that directory and run your program by double-clicking on the .exe file the IDE creates.

C# turns your program into a file that you can run, called an **executable**. You'll find it in here, in the debug folder.

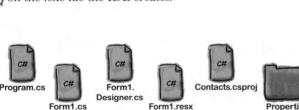

Program.cs · Form1.cs · Form1.Designer.cs · Form1.resx · Contacts.csproj · Properties · bin

This isn't a mistake; there are two levels of folders. The inner folder has the actual C# code files.

there are no Dumb Questions

Q: In my IDE, the green arrow is marked as "Debug." Is that a problem?

A: No. Debugging, at least for our purposes right now, just means running your application inside the IDE. We'll talk a lot more about debugging later, but for now, you can simply think about it as a way to run your program.

Q: I don't see the Stop Debugging button on my toolbar. What gives?

A: The Stop Debugging button shows up in a special toolbar that **only shows up** when your program is running. Try starting the application again, and see if it appears.

Here's what we've done so far

We've built a form and created a PictureBox object that pops up a message box when it's clicked on. Next, we need to add all the other fields from the card, like the contact's name and phone number.

Let's store that information in a database. Visual Studio can connect fields directly to that database for us, which means we don't have to mess with lots of database access code (which is good). But for that to work, we need to create our database so that the controls on the form can hook up to it. So we're going to jump from the .NET Visual Objects straight to the Data Storage section.

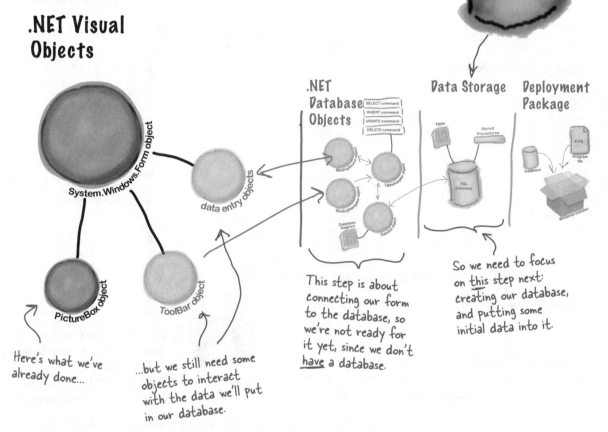

So we need to focus on this step next: creating our database, and putting some initial data into it.

This step is about connecting our form to the database, so we're not ready for it yet, since we don't <u>have</u> a database.

Here's what we've already done...

...but we still need some objects to interact with the data we'll put in our database.

Visual Studio can generate code to connect your form to a database, but you need to have the database in place BEFORE generating that code.

We need a database to store our information

Before we add the rest of the fields to the form, we need to create a database to hook the form up to. The IDE can create lots of the code for connecting our form to our data, but we need to define the database itself first.

Make sure you've stopped debugging before you continue.

❶ **Add a new SQL database to your project.**
In the Solution Explorer, **right-click the Contacts project**, select Add, and then choose New Item. Choose the SQL Database icon, and name it **ContactDB.sdf.**

This file is our new database.

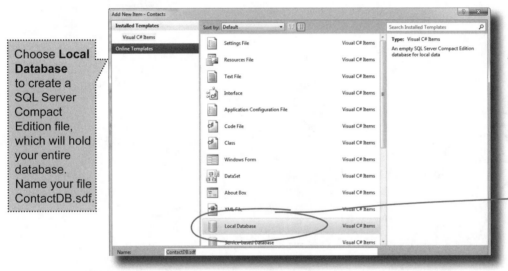

ContactDB.sdf

Choose **Local Database** to create a SQL Server Compact Edition file, which will hold your entire database. Name your file ContactDB.sdf.

A Local Database is actually a SQL Server Compact Edition database file, which typically has the extension SDF. It gives you an easy way to embed a database into your program.

❷ **Click on the Add button in the Add New Item window.**

❸ **Cancel the Data Source Configuration Wizard.**
For now, we want to skip configuring a data source, so click the Cancel button. We'll come back to this once we've set up our database structure.

❹ **View your database in the Solution Explorer.**
Go to the Solution Explorer, and you'll see that ContactDB has been added to the file list. Double-click ContactDB.sdf in the Solution Explorer and look at the left side of your screen. The Toolbox has changed to a Database Explorer.

Watch it!

If you're not using the Express edition, you'll see "Server Explorer" instead of "Database Explorer."

The Visual Studio 2010 Professional and Team Foundation editions don't have a Database Explorer window. Instead, they have a Server Explorer window, which does everything the Database Explorer does, but also lets you explore data on your network.

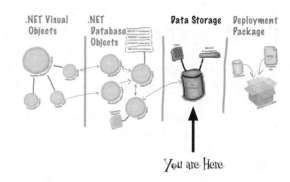

You are Here

The IDE created a database

When you told the IDE to add a new SQL database to your project, the IDE created a new database for you. A **SQL database** is a system that stores data for you in an organized, interrelated way. The IDE gives you all the tools you need to maintain your data and databases.

Data in a SQL database lives in tables. For now, you can think of a table like a spreadsheet. It organizes your information into columns and rows. The columns are the data categories, like a contact's name and phone number, and each row is the data for one contact card.

A SQL database stores your data, and has information about how it's structured and SQL code to help you access it.

Your data's stored in a table with columns and rows, like in a spreadsheet.

Tables

Stored Procedures

SQL Database

SQL is its own language

SQL stands for **Structured Query Language**. It's a programming language for accessing data in databases. It's got its own syntax, keywords, and structure. SQL code takes the form of **statements** and **queries**, which access and retrieve the data. A SQL database can hold **stored procedures**, which are a bunch of SQL statements and queries that are stored in the database and can be run at any time. The IDE generates SQL statements and stored procedures for you automatically to let your program access the data in the database.

ContactDB.sdf

The SQL database is in this file. We're just about to define tables and data for it, and all of that will be stored in here too.

[note from marketing: Can we get a plug for Head First SQL in here?]

Creating the table for the Contact List

We have a database, and now we need to store information in it. But our information actually has to go into a table, the data structure that databases use to hold individual bits of data. For our application, let's **create a table called "People"** to store all the contact information:

① **Add a table to the ContactDB database.**
Right-click on Tables in the Database Explorer, and select Create Table. This will open up a window where you can define the columns in the table you just created.

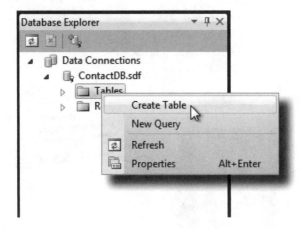

Now we need to add columns to our table. First, let's add a column called ContactID to our new People table, so that each Contact record has its own unique ID.

② **Add a ContactID column to the People table.**
Type "ContactID" in the Column Name field, and select Int from the Data Type drop-down box. Be sure to select "No" for Allow Nulls.

Finally, let's make this the primary key of our table. Highlight the ContactID column you just created, and click the Primary Key button. This tells the database that each entry will have a unique primary key entry.

Column Name	Data Type	Length	Allow Nulls	Unique	Primary Key
ContactID	int	4	No	Yes	Yes

Add a new column called "ContactID" with data type "int". Make sure to set "Allow Nulls" to No, "Unique" to Yes, and Primary Key to "Yes."

---

there are no Dumb Questions

Q: What's a column again?

A: A column is one field of a table. So in a People table, you might have a FirstName and LastName column. It will always have a data type, too, like String or Date or Bool.

Q: Why do we need this ContactID column?

A: It helps to have a unique ID for each record in most database tables. Since we're storing contact information for individual people, we decided to create a column for that, and call it ContactID.

Q: What's that Int from Data Type mean?

A: The data type tells the database what type of information to expect for a column. Int stands for integer, which is just a whole number. So the ContactID column will have whole numbers in it.

Q: This is a lot of stuff. Should I be getting all of this?

A: No, it's OK if you don't understand everything right now. Your goal right now should be to start to get familiar with the basics of using the Visual Studio IDE to lay out your form and run your program. (If you're dying to know more about databases, you can always pick up *Head First SQL*.)

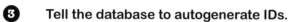

.NET Visual Objects   .NET Database Objects   **Data Storage**   Deployment Package

You are Here

③ Tell the database to autogenerate IDs.

Since ContactID is a number for the database, and not our users, we can tell our database to handle creating and assigning IDs for us automatically. That way, we don't have to worry about writing any code to do this.

In the properties below your table, set Identity to "True" to make ContactID an identity column for your table.

And make sure you specify the table name "People" in the Name box at the top of the window.

This window is what you use to define your table and the data it will store.

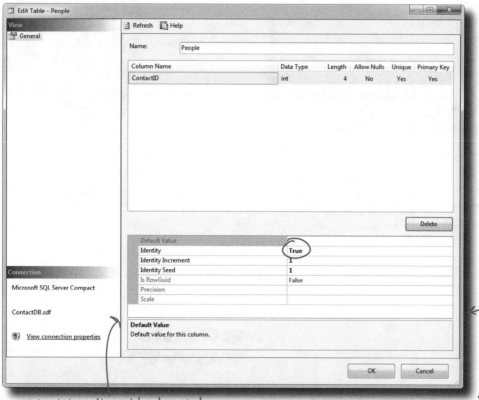

A primary key helps your database look up records quickly. Since the primary key is the main way your program will locate records, it always needs to have a value.

This will make it so that the ContactID field updates automatically whenever a new record is added.

You'll need to click on the right column and select "True" from the drop-down next to Identity to designate ContactID as your table's record Identifier.

The blanks on the contact card are columns in our People table

Now that you've created a primary key for the table, you need to define all of the fields you're going to track in the database. Each field on our written contact card should become a column in the People table.

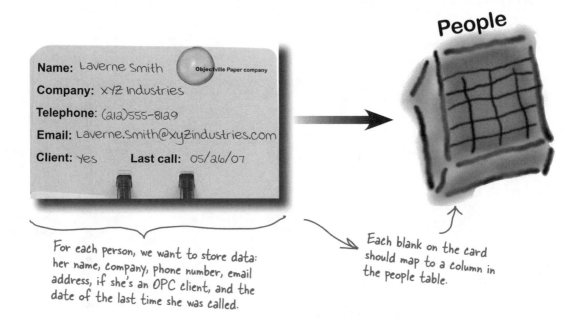

For each person, we want to store data: her name, company, phone number, email address, if she's an OPC client, and the date of the last time she was called.

Each blank on the card should map to a column in the People table.

BRAIN POWER

What kinds of problems could result from having multiple rows stored for the same person?

Now that you've created a People table and a primary key column, you need to add columns for all of the data fields. See if you can work out which data type goes with each of the columns in your table, and also match the data type to the right description.

Column Name	Data Type	Description
Last Call		This type stores a date and time
	int	
Name		A Boolean true/false type
	bit	
ContactID		A string of letters, numbers, and other characters with a maximum length of 100
	nvarchar(100)	
Client?		A whole number
	datetime	

WHO DOES WHAT?

Now that you've created a People table and a primary key column, you need to add columns for all of the data fields. See if you can work out which data type goes with each of the columns in your table, and also match the data type to the right description.

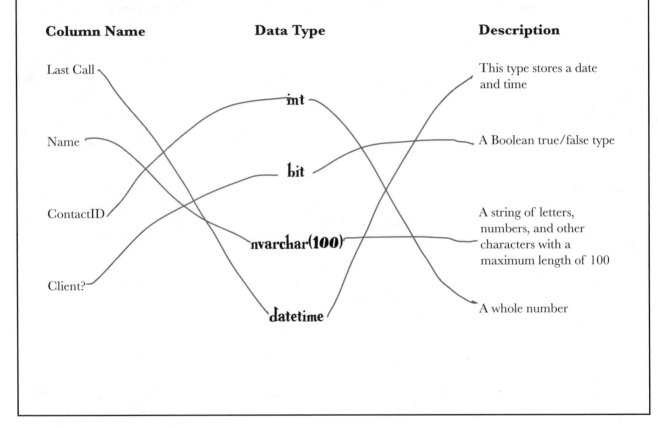

Column Name	Data Type	Description
Last Call	int	This type stores a date and time
Name	bit	A Boolean true/false type
ContactID	nvarchar(100)	A string of letters, numbers, and other characters with a maximum length of 100
Client?	datetime	A whole number

Finish building the table

Go back to where you entered the ContactID column and add the other five columns from the contact card. Here's what your database table should look like when you're done:

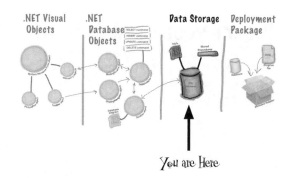

You are Here

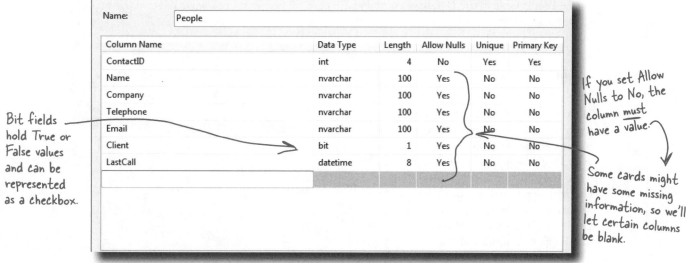

Name: People

Column Name	Data Type	Length	Allow Nulls	Unique	Primary Key
ContactID	int	4	No	Yes	Yes
Name	nvarchar	100	Yes	No	No
Company	nvarchar	100	Yes	No	No
Telephone	nvarchar	100	Yes	No	No
Email	nvarchar	100	Yes	No	No
Client	bit	1	Yes	No	No
LastCall	datetime	8	Yes	No	No

Bit fields hold True or False values and can be represented as a checkbox.

If you set Allow Nulls to No, the column *must* have a value.

Some cards might have some missing information, so we'll let certain columns be blank.

Click on the **OK** button to save your new table. This will add an empty table to your database.

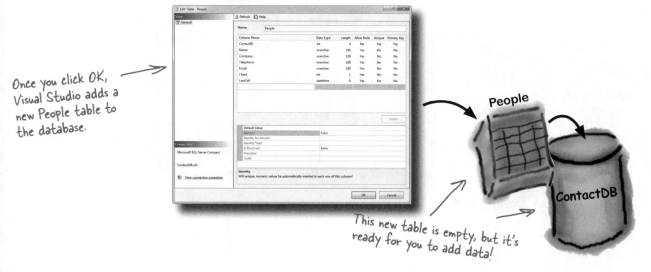

Once you click OK, Visual Studio adds a new People table to the database.

People

ContactDB

This new table is empty, but it's ready for you to add data!

Insert your card data into the database

Now you're ready to start entering cards into the database.
Here are some of the boss's contacts—we'll use those to
set up the database with a few records.

*Your job is to enter
the data from all six
of these cards into
the People table.*

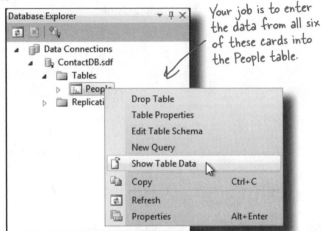

(1) Expand Tables and then right-click
on the People table in the Database
Explorer (or Server Explorer) and
select Show Table Data.

(2) Once you see the Table grid in the
main window, go ahead and add all
of the data below. (You'll see all null
values at first—just type over them
when you add your first row. And
ignore the exclamation points that
appear next to the data.) You don't
need to fill in the ContactID column;
that happens automatically.

*Type "True" or "False"
in the Client column.
That'll get translated
to the way SQL stores
yes or no info.*

Name: Liz Nelson   Objectville Paper company

Company: JTP

Telephone: (419)555-2578

Email: LizNelson@JTP.ORG

Client: Yes   **Last call:** 03/04/09

Name: Lloyd Jones   Objectville Paper company

Company: Black Box inc.

Telephone: (718)555-5638

Email: LJones@xblackboxinc.com

Client: Yes   **Last call:** 05/26/10

Name: Lucinda Ericson   Objectville Paper company

Company: Ericson Events

Telephone: (212)555-9523

Email: Lucy@ericsonevents.info

Client: No   **Last call:** 05/17/10

Name: matt Franks

Objectville Paper company

Company: XYZ Industries

Telephone: (212)555-8125

Email: matt.Franks@xyzindustries.com

Client: Yes   **Last call:** 05/26/10

Name: Sarah Kalter

Objectville Paper company

Company: Kalter, Riddle and Stoft

Telephone: (614)555-5641

Email: Sarah@KRS.org

Client: no   **Last call:** 12/10/08

Objectville Paper Company is in the United States, so the CEO writes dates so that 05/26/10 means May 26, 2010. If your machine is set to a different location, you may need to enter dates differently; you might need to use 26/05/10 instead.

Name: Laverne Smith

Objectville Paper company

Company: XYZ Industries

Telephone: (212)555-8129

Email: Laverne.Smith@xyzindustries.com

Client: Yes   **Last call:** 04/11/10

(3) Once you've entered all six records, select Save All from the File menu again. That should save the records to the database.

"Save All" tells the IDE to save everything in your application. That's different from "Save", which just saves the file you're working on.

there are no Dumb Questions

Q: So what happened to the data after I entered it? Where did it go?

A: The IDE automatically stored the data you entered into the People table in your database. The table, its columns, the data types, and all of the data inside it is all stored in the SQL Server Compact database file, ContactDB.sdf. That file is stored as part of your project, and the IDE updates it just like it updates your code files when you change them.

Q: OK, I entered these six records. Will they be part of my program forever?

A: Yes, they're as much a part of the program as the code that you write and the form that you're building. The difference is that instead of being compiled into an executable program, the ContactDB.sdf file is copied and stored along with the executable. When your application needs to access data, it reads and writes to ContactDB.sdf, in the program's output directory.

This file is actually a SQL database, and your program can use it with the code the IDE generated for you.

ContactDB.sdf

Connect your form to your database objects with a data source

We're finally ready to build the .NET database objects that our form will use to talk to your database. We need a **data source**, which is really just a collection of SQL statements your program will use to talk to the ContactDB database.

Once you're done entering data, close the data entry window to get back to your form.

1 **Go back to your application's form.**

Close out the People table and the ContactDB database diagram. You should now have the Form1.cs [Design] tab visible.

People: Query(C:\U...cts\ContactDB.sdf) ✕

	ContactID	Name	Company	Telephone	Email	Client	LastCall
	1	Lloyd Jones	Black Box Inc.	(718)555-5638	LJones@xblack...	True	5/26/2010 12:00...
	2	Lucinda Ericson	Ericson Events	(212)555-9523	lucy@ericsonev...	False	5/17/2010 12:00...
	3	Liz Nelson	JTP	(419)555-2578	liznelson@JTP....	True	3/4/2009 12:00:...
	4	Matt Franks	XYZ Industries	(212)555-8125	Matt.Franks@x...	True	5/26/2010 12:00...
	5	Sarah Kalter	Kalter, Riddle a...	(614)555-5641	sarah@krs.org	False	12/10/2008 12:0...
	6	Laverne Smith	XYZ Industries	(212)555-8129	Laverne.Smith...	True	4/11/2010 12:00...
▶*	*NULL*	*NULL*	*NULL*	*NULL*	*NULL*	*NULL*	*NULL*

2 **Add a new data source to your application.**

This should be easy by now. Click the Data menu, and then select Add New Data Source...from the drop-down.

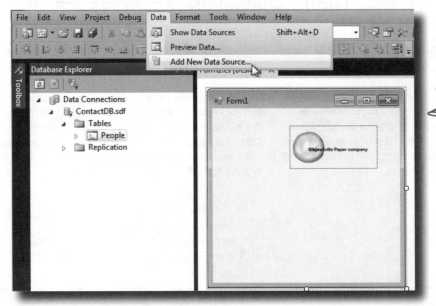

The data source you're creating will handle all the interactions between your form and your database.

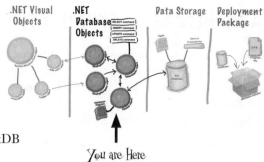

You are Here

③ Configure your new data source.

Now you need to set up your data source to use the ContactDB
database. Here's what to do:

★ Step 1: Choose a Data Source Type. Select **Database**
and click the Next button.

★ Step 2: Choose a Database Model. Select **Dataset** and
click the Next button.

★ Step 3: Choose Your Data Connection. You should see
your Contact database in the drop-down. Click Next.

★ Step 4: Choose Your Database Objects. Click the
Tables checkbox.

★ In the Dataset Name field, make sure it says
"ContactDBDataSet" and **click Finish**.

*These steps connect your
new data source with
the People table in the
ContactDB database.*

*In the non-Express editions, you may be
asked to save the connection in the app
config. Answer "Yes."*

*Now your form can use the data
source to interact with the
ContactDB database.*

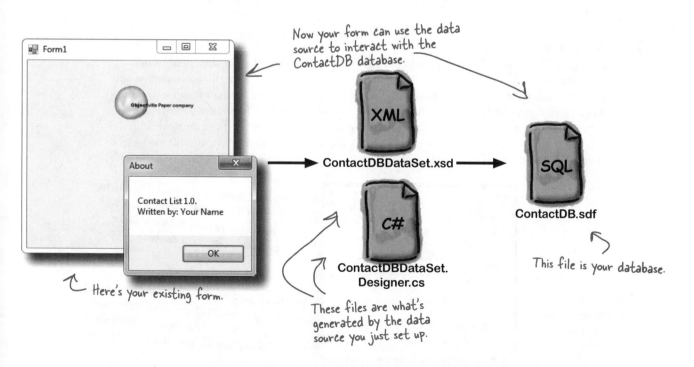

ContactDBDataSet.xsd

ContactDB.sdf

**ContactDBDataSet.
Designer.cs**

This file is your database.

Here's your existing form.

*These files are what's
generated by the data
source you just set up.*

bind it all together

Add database-driven controls to your form

Now we can go back to our form and add some more controls. But these aren't just any controls—they are controls that are *bound* to our database and the columns in the People table. That just means that a change to the data in one of the controls on the form automatically changes the data in the matching column in the database.

Here's how to create several database-driven controls:

← It took a little work, but now we're back to creating form objects that interact with our data storage.

1 **Select the data source you want to use.**
Select Show Data Sources from the Data pull-down menu. This will bring up the Data Sources window, showing the sources you have set up for your application.

If you don't see this tab, select Show Data Sources from the Data menu.

This window shows you all your data sources. We've only got one setup, but you could have more for different tables or databases.

You can also look for, and click on, the Data Sources tab along the bottom of your Database Explorer window.

2 **Select the People table.**
Under the ContactDBDataSet, you should see the People table and all of the columns in it. Click the "expand" icon next to the People table to expand it—you'll see the columns that you added to your table. When you click on the People table in the Data Sources window and drag it onto your form, the IDE automatically adds data controls to your form that the user can use to browse and enter data. By default it adds a DataGridView, which lets the user work with the data using one big spreadsheet-like control. Click the arrow next to the People table and select Details—that tells the IDE to add individual controls to your form for each column in the table.

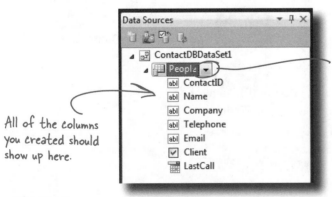

Click this arrow and choose Details to tell the IDE to add individual controls to your form rather than one large spreadsheet-like data control.

All of the columns you created should show up here.

You'll only see this drop-down if you've got a form designer window open in the IDE. It lets you **drag data controls** directly out of your data source and onto your form.

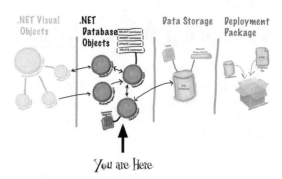

.NET Visual Objects

.NET Database Objects

Data Storage

Deployment Package

You are Here

3 **Create controls that bind to the People table.**

Drag and drop the People table onto your form in the form designer window. You should see controls appear for each column in your database. Don't worry too much about how they look right now; just make sure that they all appear on the form.

> If you accidentally click out of the form you're working on, you can always get back to it by clicking the "Form1.cs [Design]" tab, or opening `Form1.cs` from the Solution Explorer.

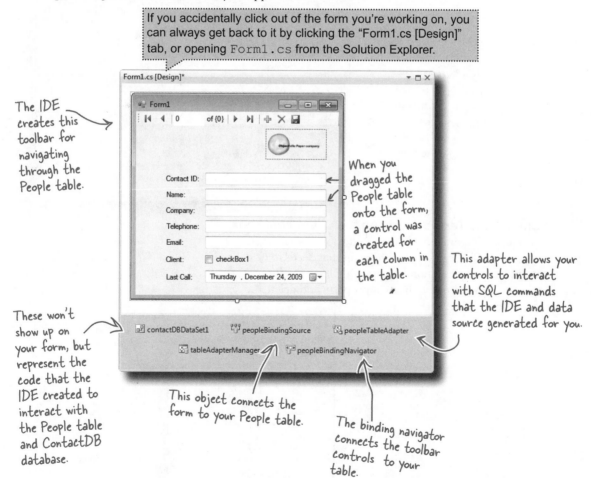

The IDE creates this toolbar for navigating through the People table.

When you dragged the People table onto the form, a control was created for each column in the table.

This adapter allows your controls to interact with SQL commands that the IDE and data source generated for you.

These won't show up on your form, but represent the code that the IDE created to interact with the People table and ContactDB database.

This object connects the form to your People table.

The binding navigator connects the toolbar controls to your table.

Good programs are <u>intuitive</u> to use

Right now, the form works. But it doesn't look that great. Your application has to do more than be functional. It should be easy to use. With just a few simple steps, you can make the form look a lot more like the paper cards we were using at the beginning of the chapter.

Our form would be more intuitive if it looked a lot like the contact card.

① **Line up your fields and labels.**
Line up your fields and labels along the left edge of the form. Your form will look like other applications, and make your users feel more comfortable using it.

Blue lines will show up on the form as you drag controls around. They're there to help you line the fields up.

② **Change the Text Property on the Client checkbox.**
When you first drag the fields onto the form, your Client checkbox will have a label to the right that needs to be deleted. Right below the Solution Explorer, you'll see the Properties window. Scroll down to the Text property and delete the "checkbox1" label.

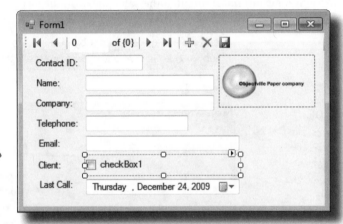

Delete this word to make the label go away.

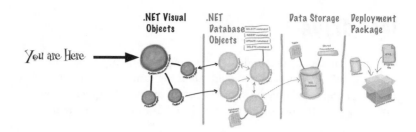

You are Here ➤

.NET Visual Objects   **.NET Database Objects**   **Data Storage**   **Deployment Package**

③ **Make the application look professional.**

You can change the name of the form by clicking on any empty space within the form, and finding the Text property in the Properties window of your IDE. Change the name of the form to *Objectville Paper Company Contact List.*

The reason you want to turn off the Maximize button is that maximizing your form won't change the positions of the controls, so it'll look weird.

You can also turn off the Maximize and Minimize buttons in this same window, by looking for the MaximizeBox and MinimizeBox properties. Set these both to False.

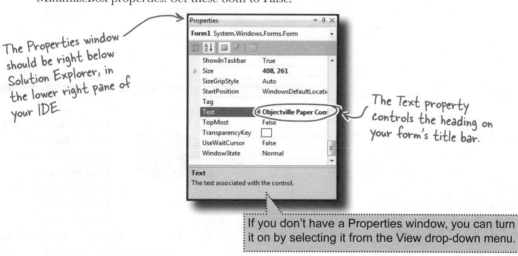

The Properties window should be right below Solution Explorer, in the lower right pane of your IDE.

The Text property controls the heading on your form's title bar.

If you don't have a Properties window, you can turn it on by selecting it from the View drop-down menu.

A good application not only works, but is easy to use. It's always a good idea to make sure it behaves as a typical user would expect it to.

Test drive

OK, just one more thing to do... run your program and make sure it works the way you think it should! Do it the same way you did before—press the F5 key on your keyboard, or click the green arrow button ▶ on the toolbar (or choose "Run" from the Debug menu).

Click the X box in the corner to stop the program so you can move on to the next step.

You can always run your programs at any time, even when they're not done—although if there's an error in the code, the IDE will tell you and stop you from executing it.

These controls let you page through the different records in the database.

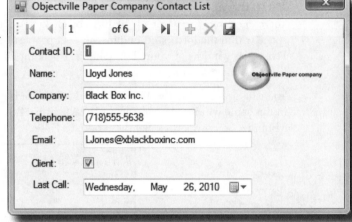

Building your program overwrites the data in your database.

We'll spend more time on this in the next chapter.

The IDE builds first, then runs

When you run your program in the IDE it actually does two things. First it **builds** your program, then it **executes** it. This involves a few distinct parts. It **compiles** the code, or turns it into an executable file. Then it places the compiled code, along with any resources and other files, into a subdirectory underneath the bin folder.

In this case, you'll find the executable and SQL database file in `bin/debug`. Since it copies the database out each time, any changes you make will be lost the next time you run inside the IDE. But if you run the executable from Windows, it'll save your data—until you build again, at which point the IDE will overwrite the SQL database with a new copy that contains the data you set up from inside the Database Explorer.

Watch it!

Every time you build your program, the IDE puts a fresh copy of the database in the bin folder. This will overwrite any data you added when you ran the program.

When you debug your program, the IDE rebuilds it if the code has changed—which means that your database will sometimes get overwritten when you run your program in the IDE. If you run the program directly from the `bin/debug` or `bin/release` folder, or if you use the installer to install it on your machine, then you won't see this problem.

How to turn YOUR application into EVERYONE'S application

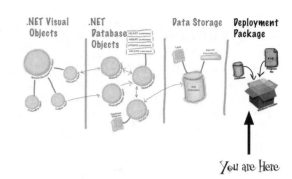

At this point, you've got a great program. But it only runs on your machine. That means that nobody else can use the app, pay you for it, see how great you are and hire you... and your boss and customers can't see the reports you're generating from the database.

C# makes it easy to take an application you've created, and **deploy** it. Deployment is taking an application and installing it onto other machines. And with the Visual C# IDE, you can set up a deployment with just two steps.

You are Here

1 Select *Publish Contacts* from the Project menu.

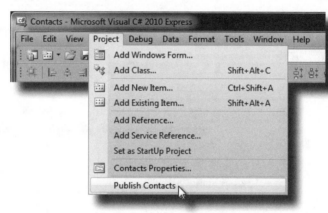

Building the solution just copies the files to your local machine. Publish creates a Setup executable and a configuration file so that any machine could install your program.

2 Just accept all of the defaults in the Publish Wizard by clicking Finish. You'll see it package up your application and then show you a folder that has your Setup. exe in it.

If you're using Visual Studio Express, you'll find "Publish" in the Project menu, but in other editions it may be in the Build menu.

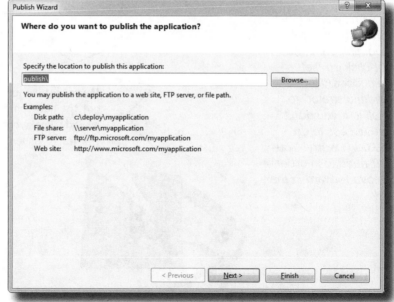

Give your users the application

Once you've created a deployment, you'll have a new folder
called `publish/`. That folder has several things in it, all
used for installation. The most important for your users is
`setup`, a program that will let them install your program on
their own computers.

This is where all of the supporting files for the installer are stored.

You may need to run the installer as administrator.

If SQL Server Compact isn't already installed on the machine, the installer will automatically download and install it. On some machines, this won't work unless you run the setup as administrator, so right-click on "setup" and choose "Run as administrator" to install it. If you don't have access to do that, don't worry! You don't need to in order to move forward in the book.

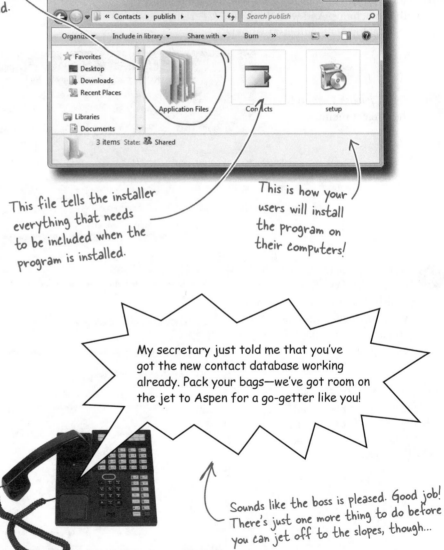

This file tells the installer everything that needs to be included when the program is installed.

This is how your users will install the program on their computers!

My secretary just told me that you've got the new contact database working already. Pack your bags—we've got room on the jet to Aspen for a go-getter like you!

Sounds like the boss is pleased. Good job! There's just one more thing to do before you can jet off to the slopes, though...

You're NOT done: test your installation

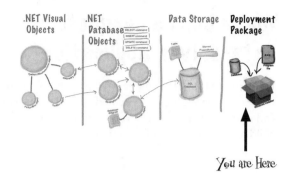

Before you pop the cork on any champagne bottles, you need to test your deployment and installation. You wouldn't give anyone your program without running it first, would you?

Close the Visual Studio IDE. Click the setup program, and select a location on your own computer to install the program. Now run it from there, and make sure it works like you expect. You can add and change records, too, and they'll be saved to the database.

You are Here

Now you can make changes to the data, and they'll get saved to the database.

You can use the arrows and the text field to switch between records.

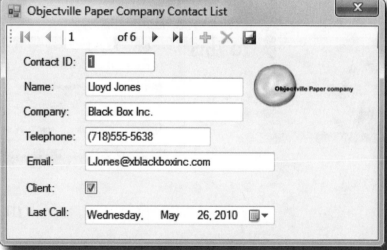

Go ahead...make some changes. You've deployed it so this time, they'll stick.

The contacts you entered are all there. They're part of the ContactDB. sdf database file, which gets installed along with your program.

TEST EVERYTHING!
Test your program, test your deployment, test the data in your application.

You've built a complete data-driven application

The Visual Studio IDE made it pretty easy to create a Windows application, create and design a database, and hook the two together. You even were able to build an installer with a few extra clicks.

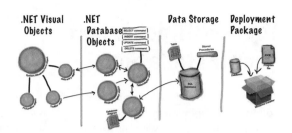

From this

to this

in no time flat.

The power of Visual C# is that you can quickly get up and running, and then focus on what your <u>program's supposed to do</u>...not lots of windows, buttons, and SQL access code.

ok

yes

CSharpcross

Take some time to sit back and exercise your C# vocabulary with this crossword; all of the solution words are from this chapter.

Across

3. The _____ explorer is where you edit the contents of your SQL tables and bind them to your program
5. An image, sound, icon, or file that's attached to your project in a way that your code can access easily
9. You build one of these so you can deploy your program to another computer
12. What the "I" in IDE stands for
14. When you double-clicked on a control, the IDE created this for you and you added code to it
15. Every row contains several of these, and all of them can have different data types
16. The _____ Explorer shows you all of the files in your project

Down

1. What's happening when code is turned into an executable
2. What you change to alter the appearance or behavior of controls on your form
3. What you're doing when you run your program from inside the IDE
4. The "About" box in the Objectville Paper Company Contact List program was one of these
6. You displayed the Objectville Paper Company logo with one of these
7. Before you start building a program, you should always think about users and their _____
8. A database can use many of these to store data
10. The data type in a SQL database that you use to store true/false values
11. Before you can run your program, the IDE does this to create the executable and move files to the output directory
13. You drag controls out of this and onto your form

 CSharpcross Solution

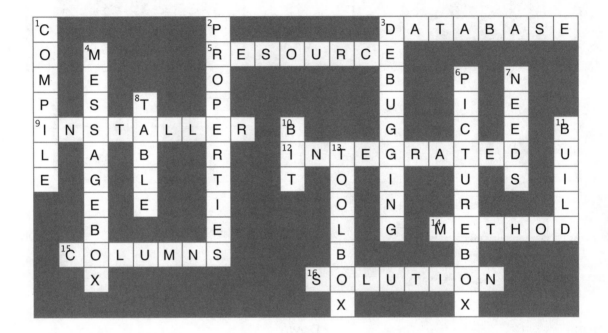

2 it's all just code

Under the hood

One of these days I'll figure out what's going on under there...

You're a programmer, not just an IDE user.

You can get a lot of work done using the IDE. But there's only so far it can take you. Sure, there are a lot of **repetitive tasks** that you do when you build an application. And the IDE is great at doing those things for you. But working with the IDE is *only the beginning*. You can get your programs to do so much more—and **writing C# code** is how you do it. Once you get the hang of coding, there's *nothing* your programs can't do.

When you're doing this...

The IDE is a powerful tool—but that's all it is, a *tool* for you to use. Every time you change your project or drag and drop something in the IDE, it creates code automatically. It's really good at writing **boilerplate** code, or code that can be reused easily without requiring much customization.

Let's look at what the IDE does in typical application development, when you're…

All of these tasks have to do with standard actions and boilerplate code. Those are the things the IDE is great for helping with.

①

Creating a Windows Forms Application project

There are several kinds of applications the IDE lets you build, but we'll be concentrating on Windows Forms applications for now. Those are programs that have visual elements, like forms and buttons.

Make sure you always create a Windows Forms Application project—that tells the IDE to create an empty form and add it to your new project.

②

Dragging a button out of the toolbox and onto your form, and then double-clicking it

Buttons are how you make things happen in your form. We'll use a lot of buttons to explore various parts of the C# language. They're also a part of almost every C# application you'll write.

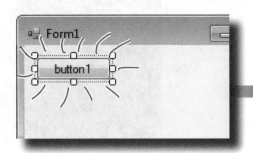

③

Setting a property on your form

The **Properties window** in the IDE is a really powerful tool that you can use to change attributes of just about everything in your program: all visual and functional properties for the controls on your form, attributes of your databases, and even options on your project itself.

The Properties window in the IDE is a really easy way to edit a specific chunk of code in Form1.Designer.cs automatically. It would take a lot longer to do it by hand. Use the F4 shortcut to open the Properties window if it's closed.

...the IDE does this

Every time you make a change in the IDE, it makes a
change to the code, which means it changes the files that
contain that code. Sometimes it just modifies a few lines,
but other times it adds entire files to your project.

These files are created from a predefined template that contains the basic code to create and display a form.

① **...the IDE creates the files and folders
for the project.**

WindowsApplication1   Form1.cs   Form1.Designer.cs   Program.cs   Properties
.csproj

② **...the IDE adds code to the Form1.Designer.cs file that adds
the button to the form, and then adds code to the Form1.cs
file to handle the button click.**

```
private void button1_Click(object sender, EventArgs e)
{

}
```

Form1.Designer.cs

*The IDE knows how to add an empty method
to handle a button click. But it doesn't know
what to put inside it—that's your job.*

This code gets added to Form1.cs.

Form1.cs

③ **...the IDE opens the Form1.Designer.cs file and
updates a line of code.**

The IDE went into this file...

```
partial class Form1
{
    ⋮
        this.Text = "Objectville Paper Company Contact List";
    ⋮
}
```

Form1.Designer.cs

...and updated this line of code.

Where programs come from

A C# program may start out as statements in a bunch of files, but it ends up as a program running in your computer. Here's how it gets there.

Every program starts out as source code files

You've already seen how to edit a program, and how the IDE saves your program to files in a folder. Those files **are** your program—you can copy them to a new folder and open them up, and everything will be there: forms, resources, code, and anything else you added to your project.

You can think of the IDE as a kind of fancy file editor. It automatically does the indenting for you, changes the colors of the keywords, matches up brackets for you, and even suggests what words might come next. But in the end, all the IDE does is edit the files that contain your program.

The IDE bundles all of the files for your program into a **solution** by creating a solution (`.sln`) file and a folder that contains all of the other files for the program. The solution file has a list of the project files (which end in `.csproj`) in the solution, and the project files contain lists of all the other files associated with the program. In this book, you'll be building solutions that only have one project in them, but you can easily add other projects to your solution using the IDE's Solution Explorer.

There's no reason you couldn't build your programs in Notepad, but it'd be a lot more time-consuming.

The .NET Framework gives you the right tools for the job

C# is just a language—by itself, it can't actually **do** anything. And that's where the **.NET Framework** comes in. Remember that Maximize button you turned off for the Contacts form? When you click the Maximize button on a window, there's code that tells the window how to maximize itself and take up the whole screen. That code is part of the .NET Framework. Buttons, checkboxes, lists… those are all pieces of the .NET Framework. So are the internal bits that hooked your form up to the database. It's got tools to draw graphics, read and write files, manage collections of things…all sorts of tools for a lot of jobs that programmers have to do every day.

The tools in the .NET Framework are divided up into **namespaces**. You've seen these namespaces before, at the top of your code in the "using" lines. One namespace is called `System.Windows.Forms`—it's where your buttons, checkboxes, and forms come from. Whenever you create a new Windows Forms Application project, the IDE will add the necessary files so that your project contains a form, and those files have the line "`using System.Windows.Forms;`" at the top.

Build the program to create an executable

When you select "Build Solution" from the Build menu, the IDE **compiles** your program. It does this by running the **compiler**, which is a tool that reads your program's source code and turns it into an **executable**. The executable is a file on your disk that ends in .exe— that's what you double-click on to run your program. When you build the program, it creates the executable inside the bin folder, which is inside the project folder. When you publish your solution, it copies the executable (and any other files necessary) into the folder you're publishing to.

When you select "Start Debugging" from the Debug menu, the IDE compiles your program and runs the executable. It's got some more advanced tools for **debugging** your program, which just means running it and being able to pause (or "break") it so you can figure out what's going on.

Your program runs inside the CLR

When you double-click on the executable, Windows runs your program. But there's an extra "layer" between Windows and your program called the **Common Language Runtime**, or CLR. Once upon a time, not so long ago (but before C# was around), writing programs was harder, because you had to deal with hardware and low-level machine stuff. You never knew exactly how someone was going to configure his computer. The CLR—often referred to as a **virtual machine**—takes care of all that for you by doing a sort of "translation" between your program and the computer running it.

You don't really have to worry about the CLR much right now. It's enough to know it's there, and takes care of running your program for you automatically. You'll learn more about it as you go.

You'll learn about all sorts of things the CLR does for you. For example, it tightly manages your computer's memory by figuring out when your program is finished with certain pieces of data and getting rid of them for you. That's something programmers used to have to do themselves, and it's something that you don't have to be bothered with. You won't know it at the time, but the CLR will make your job of learning C# a whole lot easier.

The IDE helps you code

You've already seen a few of the things that the IDE can do.
Let's take a closer look at some of the tools it gives you.

⭐ **The Solution Explorer shows you everything in your project**

You'll spend a lot of time going back and forth between classes, and the easiest way to do that is to use the Solution Explorer. Here's what the Solution Explorer looks like after creating the Objectville Paper Company Contact List program:

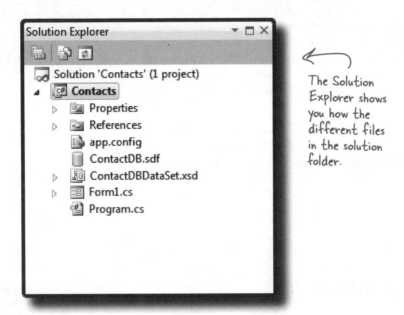

The Solution Explorer shows you how the different files in the solution folder.

⭐ **Use the tabs to switch between open files**

Since your program is split up into more than one file, you'll usually have several code files open at once. When you do, each one will be in its own tab in the code editor. The IDE displays an asterisk (*) next to a filename if it hasn't been saved yet.

Here's the form's resource file that you added the Objectville Paper Company logo to.

When you're working on a form, you'll often have two tabs for it at the same time—one for the form designer, and one to view the form's code. Use **control-tab** to switch between open windows quickly.

The IDE helps you write code

Did you notice little windows popping up as you typed code into the IDE? That's a feature called IntelliSense, and it's really useful. One thing it does is show you possible ways to complete your current line of code. If you type MessageBox and then a period, it knows that there are three valid ways to complete that line:

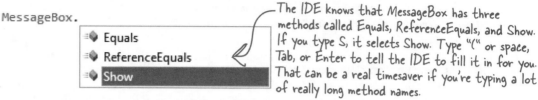

The IDE knows that MessageBox has three methods called Equals, ReferenceEquals, and Show. If you type S, it selects Show. Type "(" or space, Tab, or Enter to tell the IDE to fill it in for you. That can be a real timesaver if you're typing a lot of really long method names.

If you select Show and type **(**, the IDE's IntelliSense will show you information about how you can complete the line:

This means that there are 21 different ways that you can call the MessageBox's Show method (like ways to display different buttons or icons).

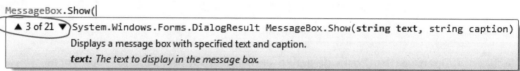

The IDE also has shortcuts called **snippets** that let you type an abbreviation to tell it to fill in the rest of the code. Here's a useful one: type mbox and press the Tab key twice, and the IDE will fill in the MessageBox.Show method for you:

```
MessageBox.Show("Test");
```

When you use Start Debugging to run your program inside the IDE, the first thing it does is build your program. If it compiles, then your program runs. If not, it won't run, and will show you errors in the Error List.

The Error List helps you troubleshoot compiler errors

If you haven't already discovered how easy it is to make typos in a C# program, you'll find out very soon! Luckily, the IDE gives you a great tool for troubleshooting them. When you build your solution, any problems that keep it from compiling will show up in the Error List window at the bottom of the IDE:

A missing semicolon at the end of a statement is one of the most common errors that keeps your program from building!

	Description	File	Line	Column	Project
⊗ 1	'System.Windows.Forms.MessageBox' does not contain a definition for 'XYZ'	Form1.cs	45	24	Contacts
⊗ 2	; expected	Form1.cs	45	33	Contacts

Error List — ● 2 Errors — ⚠ 0 Warnings — ⓘ 0 Messages

Double-click on an error, and the IDE will jump to the problem in the code:

```
private void pictureBox1_Click(object sender, EventArgs e)
{
    MessageBox.XYZ("hi")
}
```

The IDE will show a red underscore to show you that there's an error.

When you change things in the IDE, you're also changing your code

When you see a "Do this!", pop open the IDE and follow along. We'll tell you exactly what to do, and point out what to look for to get the most out of the example we show you.

The IDE is great at writing visual code for you. But don't take our word for it. Open up Visual Studio, **create a new Windows Forms Application project**, and see for yourself.

Do this!

① Open up the designer code

Open the `Form1.Designer.cs` file in the IDE. But this time, instead of opening it in the Form Designer, open up its code by right-clicking on it in the Solution Explorer and selecting "View Code." Look for the Form1 class declaration:

```
partial class Form1
```

Notice how it's a partial class? We'll talk about that in a minute.

② Open up the Form designer and add a PictureBox to your form

Get used to working with more than one tab. Go to the Solution Explorer and open up the Form designer by double-clicking on `Form1.cs`. **Drag a new PictureBox** onto a new form.

② Find and expand the designer-generated code for the PictureBox control

Then go back to the Form1.Designer.cs tab in the IDE. Scroll down and look for this line in the code:

Click on the plus sign

```
⊞   Windows Form Designer generated code
```

Click on the + on the left-hand side of the line to expand the code. Scroll down and find these lines:

```
//
// pictureBox1
//
this.pictureBox1.Location = new System.Drawing.Point(276, 28);

this.pictureBox1.Name = "pictureBox1";

this.pictureBox1.Size = new System.Drawing.Size(100, 50);

this.pictureBox1.TabIndex = 0;

this.pictureBox1.TabStop = false;
```

Don't worry if the numbers in your code for the Location and Size lines are a little different than these...

Wait, wait! What did that say?

Scroll back up for a minute. There it is, at the top of the Windows Form Designer–generated code section:

```
///  <summary>
///  Required method for Designer support - do not modify
///  the contents of this method with the code editor.
///  </summary>
```

Most comments only start with two slashes (//). But the IDE sometimes adds these three-slash comments.

These are XML comments, and you can use them to document your code. Flip to "Leftovers" section #1 in the Appendix of this book to learn more about them.

There's nothing more attractive to a kid than a big sign that says, "Don't touch this!" Come on, you know you're tempted... let's go modify the contents of that method with the code editor! **Add a button to your form, and then go ahead and do this:**

① **Change the code that sets the button1.Text property. What do you think it will do to the Properties window in the IDE?**
Give it a shot—see what happens! Now go back to the form designer and check the Text property. Did it change?

② **Stay in the designer, and use the Properties window to change the Name property to something else.**
See if you can find a way to get the IDE to change the Name property. It's in the Properties window at the very top, under "(Name)". What happened to the code? What about the comment in the code?

③ **Change the code that sets the Location property to (0,0) and the Size property to make the button really big.**
Did it work?

④ **Go back to the designer, and change the button's BackColor property to something else.**
Look closely at the Form1.Designer.cs code. Were any lines added?

You don't have to save the form or run the program to see the changes. Just make the change in the code editor, and then click on the tab labeled "Form1.cs [Design]" to flip over to the form designer—the changes should show up immediately.

It's always easier to use the IDE to change your form's Designer-generated code. But when you do, any change you make in the IDE ends up as a change to your project's code.

Anatomy of a program

Every C# program's code is structured in exactly the same way. All programs use **namespaces**, **classes**, and **methods** to make your code easier to manage.

Every time you make a new program, you define a namespace for it so that its code is separate from the .NET Framework classes.

A class contains a piece of your program (although some very small programs can have just one class).

A class has one or more methods. Your methods always have to live inside a class. And methods are made up of statements—like the ones you've already seen.

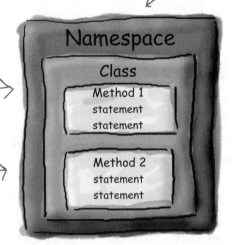

Let's take a closer look at your code

Open up the code from your Contacts project's `Form1.cs` so we can go through it piece by piece.

❶ The code file starts by using the .NET Framework tools

You'll find a set of `using` lines at the top of every program file. They tell C# which parts of the .NET Framework to use. If you use other classes that are in other namespaces, then you'll add `using` lines for them, too. Since forms often use a lot of different tools from the .NET Framework, the IDE automatically adds a bunch of `using` lines when it creates a form and adds it to your project.

```
using System;
using System.Collections.Generic;
using System.ComponentModel;
using System.Data;
using System.Drawing;
using System.Linq;
using System.Text;
using System.Windows.Forms;
```

These using lines are at the top of every code file. They tell C# to use all of those .NET Framework classes. Each one tells your program that the classes in this particular .cs file will use all of the classes in one specific .NET Framework namespace.

One thing to keep in mind: you don't actually *have* to use a `using` statement. You can always use the fully qualified name. So if you leave out `using System.Windows.Forms`, you can still show a message box by calling `System.Windows.Forms.MessageBox.Show()`, and the compiler will know what namespace you're talking about.

❷ C# programs are organized into classes

Every C# program is organized into **classes**. A class can do anything, but most classes do one specific thing. When you created the new program, the IDE added a class called `Form1` that displays a form.

When you called your program Contacts, the IDE created a namespace for it called Contacts by adding the namespace keyword at the top of your code file. Everything inside its pair of curly brackets is part of the Contacts namespace.

```
namespace Contacts
{
    public partial class Form1 : Form
    {
```

This is a class called Form1. It contains all of the code to draw the form and the Toolbox controls on it. The IDE created it when you told it to create a new Windows Forms Application project.

❸ Classes contain methods that perform actions

When a class needs to do something, it uses a **method**. A method takes an input, performs some action, and sometimes produces an output. The way you pass input into a method is by using **parameters**. Methods can behave differently depending on what input they're given. Some methods produce output. When they do, it's called a **return value**. If you see the keyword `void` in front of a method, that means it doesn't return anything.

Look for the matching pairs of brackets. Every { is eventually paired up with a }. Some pairs can be inside others.

```
public Form1()
{
    InitializeComponent();
}
```

This line calls a method named InitializeComponent(), which the IDE also created for you.

❹ A statement performs one single action

When you added the `MessageBox.Show()` line to your program, you were adding a **statement**. Every method is made up of statements. When your program calls a method, it executes the first statement in the method, then the next, then the next, etc. When the method runs out of statements or hits a `return` statement, it ends, and the program resumes after the statement that originally called the method.

This is a method called pictureBox1_Click() that gets called when the user clicks on the picture box.

This method has two parameters called sender and e.

```
private void pictureBox1_Click(object sender, EventArgs e)
{
    MessageBox.Show("Contact List 1.0", "About");
}
}
```

This is a statement. You already know what it does—it pops up a little message box window.

Your statement called the Show() method, which is part of the MessageBox class, which is inside the System.Windows.Forms namespace.

Your statement passed two parameters to the Show() method. The first one was a string of text to display in the message box, and the second one was a string to display in its title bar.

Your program knows where to start

When you created the new Windows Application solution, one of the files the IDE added was called **Program.cs**. Go to the Solution Explorer and double-click on it. It's got a class called `Program`, and inside that class is a method called `Main()`. That method is the **entry point**, which means that it's the very first thing that's run in your program.

Every C# program can only have one entry point method, and it's always called Main(). That's how it knows where to start when you run it.

Here's some code the IDE built for you automatically in the last chapter. You'll find it in Program.cs.

Your Code Up Close

❶
```csharp
using System;
using System.Linq;
using System.Collections.Generic;
using System.Windows.Forms;

❷
namespace Contacts
{
```
The namespace for all this code is Contacts. We'll talk about namespaces more in a few pages.

```csharp
    ❸
    static class Program
    {
```
Lines that begin with two or more slashes are comments, which you can add anywhere you want. The slashes tell C# to ignore them.

```csharp
        /// <summary>
        /// The main entry point for the application.
        /// </summary>

        [STAThread]

        static void Main()
        {   ❺

            Application.EnableVisualStyles();

        ❹Application.SetCompatibleTextRenderingDefault(false);

            Application.Run(new Form1());
        }

    }

}
```
Every time you run your program, it starts here, at the entry point.

This statement creates and displays the Contacts form, and ends the program when the form's closed.

I do declare!

The first part of every class or method is called a <u>declaration</u>.

Remember, this is just a starting point for you to dig into the code. But before you do, you'll need to know what you're looking at.

1 **C# and .NET have lots of built-in features.**

You'll find lines like this at the top of almost every C# class file. System.Windows.Forms is a **namespace**. The using System.Windows.Forms line makes everything ← in that namespace available to your program. In this case, that namespace has lots of visual elements in it like buttons and forms.

> Your programs will use more and more namespaces like this one as you learn about C# and .NET's other built-in features throughout the book.
>
> If you didn't specify the "using" line, you'd have to explicitly type out System.Windows.Forms every time you use anything in that namespace.

2 **The IDE chose a namespace for your code.**

Here's the namespace the IDE created for you—it chose Contacts based on your project's name. All of the code in your program lives in this namespace.

> Namespaces let you use the same name in different programs, as long as those programs aren't also in the same namespace.

3 **Your code is stored in a class.**

This particular class is called Program. The IDE created it and added the code that starts the program and brings up the Contacts form.

> You can have multiple classes in a single namespace.

4 **This code has one method, and it contains several statements.**

A namespace has classes in it, and classes have methods. Inside each method is a set of statements. In this program, the statements handle starting up the Contacts form. Methods are where the action happens—every method **does** something.

> Technically, a program can have more than one Main() method, and you can tell C# which one is the entry point... but you won't need to do that now.

5 **Each program has a special kind of method called the entry point.**

Every C# program **must** have exactly one method called Main. Even though your program has a lot of methods, only one can be the first one that gets executed, and that's your Main method. C# checks every class in your code for a method that reads static void Main(). Then, when the program is run, the first statement in this method gets executed, and everything else follows from that first statement.

Every C# program must have exactly one method called Main. That method is the entry point for your code.

When you run your code, the code in your Main() method is executed FIRST.

You can change your program's entry point

As long as your program has an entry point, it doesn't matter which class your entry point method is in, or what that method does. **Open up the program you wrote in Chapter 1**, remove the Main method in Program.cs, and create a new entry point.

Do this!

① Go back to Program.cs and change the name of the Main method to NotMain. Now **try to build and run** the program. What happens?

_____

_____

> Write down what happened when you changed the method name, and why you think that happened.

② Now let's create a new entry point. **Add a new class** called AnotherClass. cs. You add a class to your program by right-clicking on the project name in the Solution Explorer and selecting "Add>>Class…". Name your class file AnotherClass.cs. The IDE will add a class to your program called AnotherClass. Here's the file the IDE added:

> Right-click on the project in Properties and select "Add" and "Class..."

```csharp
using System;
using System.Linq;
using System.Collections.Generic;
using System.Text;

namespace Contacts
{
    class AnotherClass
    {
    }
}
```

> These four standard using lines were added to the file.

> This class is in the same Contacts namespace that the IDE added when you first created the Windows Application project.

> The IDE automatically named the class based on the filename.

③ Add a new using line to the top of the file: **using System.Windows.Forms;** Don't forget to end the line with a semicolon!

④ Add this method to the **AnotherClass** class by typing it in between the curly brackets:

> MessageBox is a class that lives in the System.Windows.Forms namespace, which is why you had to add the using line in step #3. Show() is a method that's part of the MessageBox class.

```csharp
class AnotherClass
{
    public static void Main()
    {
        MessageBox.Show("Pow!");
    }
}
```

Now run it!

Pow!

OK

So what happened?

Instead of popping up the Contacts application, your program now shows this message box. When you made the new Main() method, you gave your program a new entry point. Now the first thing the program does is run the statements in that method—which means running that MessageBox.Show() statement. There's nothing else in that method, so once you click the OK button, the program runs out of statements to execute and then it ends.

5 Figure out how to fix your program so it pops up Contacts again.

Hint: You only have to change two lines in two files to do it.

Sharpen your pencil

Fill in the annotations so they describe the lines in this C# file that they're pointing to. We've filled in the first one for you.

```
using System;
using System.Linq;
using System.Text;
using System.Windows.Forms;


namespace SomeNamespace

{

    class MyClass {

        public static void DoSomething() {

            MessageBox.Show("This is a message");

        }

    }

}
```

C# classes have these "using" lines to add methods from other namespaces

there are no Dumb Questions

Q: What's with all the curly brackets?

A: C# uses curly brackets (or "braces") to group statements together into **blocks**. Curly brackets always come in pairs. You'll only see a closing curly bracket after you see an opening one. The IDE helps you match up curly brackets—just click on one, and you'll see it and its match get shaded darker.

Q: I don't quite get what the entry point is. Can you explain it one more time?

A: Your program has a whole lot of statements in it, but they're not all run at once. The program starts with the first statement in the program, executes it, and then goes on to the next one, and the next one, etc. Those statements are usually organized into a bunch of classes. So when you run your program, how does it know which statement to start with?

That's where the entry point comes in. The compiler will not build your code unless there is **exactly one method called** `Main()`, which we call the entry point. The program starts running with the first statement in `Main()`.

Q: How come I get errors in the Error List window when I try to run my program? I thought that only happened when I did "Build Solution."

A: Because the first thing that happens when you choose "Start Debugging" from the menu or press the toolbar button to start your program running is that it saves all the files in your solution and then tries to compile them. And when you compile your code—whether it's when you run it, or when you build the solution—if there are errors, the IDE will display them in the Error List instead of running your program.

A lot of the errors that show up when you compile your code also show up in the Error List window and as red squiggles under your code.

Sharpen your pencil Solution

Fill in the annotations so they describe the lines in this C# file that they're pointing to. We've filled in the first one for you.

C# classes have these "using" lines to add methods from other namespaces.

```
using System;
using System.Linq;
using System.Text;
using System.Windows.Forms;

namespace SomeNamespace

{

    class MyClass {

        public static void DoSomething() {

            MessageBox.Show("This is a message");

        }

    }

}
```

All of the code lives in classes, so the program needs a class here.

This class has one method. Its name is "DoSomething," and when it's called it pops up a MessageBox..

This is a statement. When it's executed, it pops up a little window with a message inside of it.

WHAT'S MY PURPOSE?

Match each of these fragments of code generated by the IDE to what it does.
(Some of these are new—take a guess and see if you got it right!)

```
partial class Form1
{
  :
  this.BackColor = Color.DarkViolet;
  :
}
```

Set properties for a label

```
// This loop gets executed three times
```

Nothing—it's a comment that the programmer added to explain the code to anyone who's reading it

```
partial class Form1
{
  private void InitializeComponent()
  {
  :
  }
}
```

Disable the maximize icon (⬜) in the title bar of the Form1 window

```
number_of_pit_stopsLabel.Name
        = "number_of_pit_stopsLabel";
number_of_pit_stopsLabel.Size
        = new System.Drawing.Size(135, 17);
number_of_pit_stopsLabel.Text
        = "Number of pit stops:";
```

A special kind of comment that the IDE uses to explain what an entire block of code does

```
/// <summary>
/// Bring up the picture of Rover when
/// the button is clicked
/// </summary>
```

Change the background color of the Form1 window

```
partial class Form1
{
  :
  this.MaximizeBox = false;
  :
}
```

A block of code that executes whenever a program opens up a Form1 window

Match each of these fragments of code generated by the IDE to what it does.
(Some of these are new—take a guess and see if you got it right!)

```
partial class Form1
{
  :
  this.BackColor = Color.DarkViolet;
  :
}
```

Set properties for a label

```
// This loop gets executed three times
```

Nothing—it's a comment that the programmer added to explain the code to anyone who's reading it

```
partial class Form1
{
  private void InitializeComponent()
  {
    :
  }
}
```

Disable the maximize icon (⬜) in the title bar of the Form1 window

```
number_of_pit_stopsLabel.Name
        = "number_of_pit_stopsLabel";
number_of_pit_stopsLabel.Size
        = new System.Drawing.Size(135, 17);
number_of_pit_stopsLabel.Text
        = "Number of pit stops:";
```

A special kind of comment that the IDE uses to explain what an entire block of code does

```
/// <summary>
/// Bring up the picture of Rover when
/// the button is clicked
/// </summary>
```

Change the background color of the Form1 window

```
partial class Form1
{
  :
  this.MaximizeBox = false;
  :
}
```

A block of code that executes whenever a program opens up a Form1 window

Two classes can be in the same namespace

Take a look at these two class files from a program called `PetFiler2`. They've got three classes: a Dog class, a Cat class, and a Fish class. Since they're all in the same `PetFiler2` namespace, statements in the `Dog.Bark()` method can call `Cat.Meow()` and `Fish.Swim()`. It doesn't matter how the various namespaces and classes are divided up between files. They still act the same when they're run.

When a class is "public" it means every other class in the program can access its methods.

SomeClasses.cs

```
namespace PetFiler2 {

    class Dog {

        public void Bark() {
            // statements go here
        }

    }

    partial class Cat {

        public void Meow() {
            // more statements
        }

    }

}
```

MoreClasses.cs

```
namespace PetFiler2 {

    class Fish {

        public void Swim() {
            // statements
        }

    }

    partial class Cat {

        public void Purr() {
            // statements
        }

    }

}
```

Since these classes are in the same namespace, they can all "see" each other—even though they're in different files. A class can span multiple files too, but you need to use the partial keyword when you declare it.

You can only split a class up into different files if you use the partial keyword. You probably won't do that in any of the code you write in this book, but the IDE used it to split your form up into two files, Form1.cs and Form1.Designer.cs.

There's more to namespaces and class declarations, but you won't need them for the work you're doing right now. Flip to #2 in the "Leftovers" appendix to read more.

Your programs use <u>variables</u> to work with data

When you get right down to it, every program is basically a data cruncher. Sometimes the data is in the form of a document, or an image in a video game, or an instant message. But it's all just data. And that's where **variables** come in. A variable is what your program uses to store data.

Watch it!

Are you already familiar with another language?

If so, you might find a few things in this chapter seem really familiar. Still, it's worth taking the time to run through the exercises anyway, because there may be a few ways that C# is different from what you're used to.

Declare your variables

Whenever you **declare** a variable, you tell your program its *type* and its *name*. Once C# knows your variable's type, it'll keep your program from compiling if you make a mistake and try to do something that doesn't make sense, like subtract "Fido" from 48353.

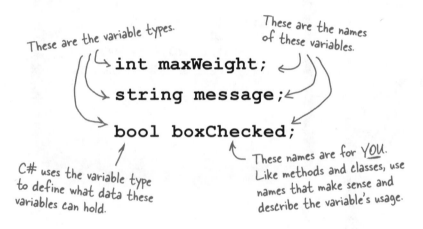

These are the variable types.

These are the names of these variables.

```
int maxWeight;
string message;
bool boxChecked;
```

C# uses the variable type to define what data these variables can hold.

These names are for YOU. Like methods and classes, use names that make sense and describe the variable's usage.

Variables vary

A variable is equal to different values at different times while your program runs. In other words, a variable's value *varies*. (Which is why "variable" is such a good name.) This is really important, because that idea is at the core of every program that you've written or will ever write. So if your program sets the variable `myHeight` equal to 63:

```
int myHeight = 63;
```

any time `myHeight` appears in the code, C# will replace it with its value, 63. Then, later on, if you change its value to 12:

```
myHeight = 12;
```

C# will replace `myHeight` with 12—but the variable is still called `myHeight`.

Whenever your program needs to work with numbers, text, true/false values, or any other kind of data, you'll use variables to keep track of them.

You have to assign values to variables before you use them

Try putting these statements into a C# program:

```
int z;
MessageBox.Show("The answer is " + z);
```

Go ahead, give it a shot. You'll get an error, and the IDE will refuse to compile your code. That's because the compiler checks each variable to make sure that you've assigned it a value before you use it. The easiest way to make sure you don't forget to assign your variables values is to combine the statement that declares a variable with a statement that assigns its value:

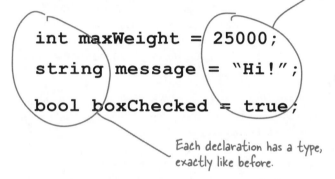

These values are assigned to the variables.

```
int maxWeight = 25000;
string message = "Hi!";
bool boxChecked = true;
```

Each declaration has a type, exactly like before.

If you write code that uses a variable that hasn't been assigned a value, your code won't compile. It's easy to avoid that error by combining your variable declaration and assignment into a single statement.

↑

Once you've assigned a value to your variable, that value can change. So there's no disadvantage to assigning a variable an initial value when you declare it.

A few useful types

Every variable has a type that tells C# what kind of data it can hold. We'll go into a lot of detail about the many different types in C# in Chapter 4. In the meantime, we'll concentrate on the three most popular types. `int` holds integers (or whole numbers), `string` holds text, and `bool` holds Boolean true/false values.

> var-i-a-ble, adjective.
> able to be changed or adapted.
> *The drill's **variable** speed bit let Bob change the drill speed from slow to fast based on the job he had to do.*

C# uses familiar math symbols

To programmers, the word "string" almost always means a string of text, and "int" is almost always short for integer.

Once you've got some data stored in a variable, what can you do with it? Well, if it's a number, you'll probably want to add, subtract, multiply, or divide it. And that's where **operators** come in. You already know the basic ones. Let's talk about a few more. Here's a block of code that uses operators to do some simple math:

We declared a new int variable called number and set it to 15. Then we added 10 to it. After the second statement, number is equal to 25.

```
int number = 15;
number = number + 10;
number = 36 * 15;
number = 12 - (42 / 7);
number += 10;
number *= 3;
number = 71 / 3;
```

The third statement changes the value of number, setting it equal to 36 times 15, which is 540. Then it resets it again, setting it equal to 12 - (42 / 7), which is 6.

This operator is a little different. += means take the value of number and add 10 to it. Since number is currently equal to 6, adding 10 to it sets its value to 16.

The *= operator is similar to +=, except it multiplies the current value of number by 3, so it ends up set to 48.

Normally, 71 divided by 3 is 23.666666.... But when you're dividing two ints, you'll always get an int result, so 23.666... gets truncated to 23.

```
int count = 0;
count ++;
count --;
```

You'll use int a lot for counting, and when you do, the ++ and -- operators come in handy. ++ increments count by adding one to the value, and -- decrements count by subtracting one from it, so it ends up equal to zero.

This MessageBox will pop up a box that says "hello again hello"

```
string result = "hello";
result += " again " + result;
MessageBox.Show(result);
result = "the value is: " + count;
result = "";
```

When you use the + operator with a string, it just puts two strings together. It'll automatically convert numbers to strings for you.

The "" is an empty string. It has no characters. (It's kind of like a zero for adding strings.)

A bool stores true or false. The ! operator means NOT. It flips true to false, and vice versa.

```
bool yesNo = false;
bool anotherBool = true;
yesNo = !anotherBool;
```

Don't worry about memorizing these operators now.

You'll get to know them because you'll see 'em over and over again.

Use the debugger to see your variables change

The debugger is a great tool for understanding how your programs work. You can use it to see the code on the previous page in action.

Debug this!

① Create a new Windows Forms Application project

Drag a button onto your form and double-click it. Enter all of the code on the previous page. Then take a look at the comments in the screenshot below:

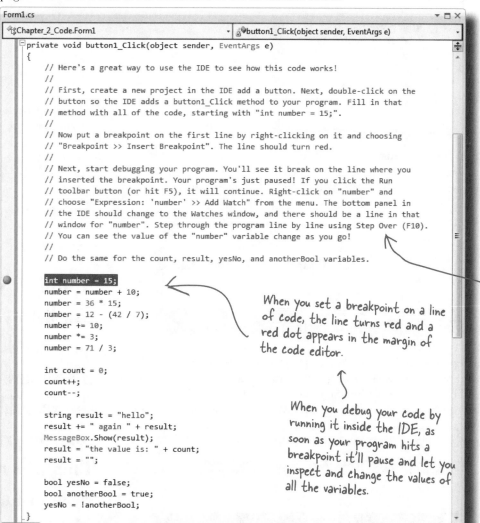

```
Form1.cs
Chapter_2_Code.Form1                                    button1_Click(object sender, EventArgs e)
private void button1_Click(object sender, EventArgs e)
{
    // Here's a great way to use the IDE to see how this code works!
    //
    // First, create a new project in the IDE add a button. Next, double-click on the
    // button so the IDE adds a button1_Click method to your program. Fill in that
    // method with all of the code, starting with "int number = 15;".
    //
    // Now put a breakpoint on the first line by right-clicking on it and choosing
    // "Breakpoint >> Insert Breakpoint". The line should turn red.
    //
    // Next, start debugging your program. You'll see it break on the line where you
    // inserted the breakpoint. Your program's just paused! If you click the Run
    // toolbar button (or hit F5), it will continue. Right-click on "number" and
    // choose "Expression: 'number' >> Add Watch" from the menu. The bottom panel in
    // the IDE should change to the Watches window, and there should be a line in that
    // window for "number". Step through the program line by line using Step Over (F10).
    // You can see the value of the "number" variable change as you go!
    //
    // Do the same for the count, result, yesNo, and anotherBool variables.

    int number = 15;
    number = number + 10;
    number = 36 * 15;
    number = 12 - (42 / 7);
    number += 10;
    number *= 3;
    number = 71 / 3;

    int count = 0;
    count++;
    count--;

    string result = "hello";
    result += " again " + result;
    MessageBox.Show(result);
    result = "the value is: " + count;
    result = "";

    bool yesNo = false;
    bool anotherBool = true;
    yesNo = !anotherBool;
}
```

When you set a breakpoint on a line of code, the line turns red and a red dot appears in the margin of the code editor.

When you debug your code by running it inside the IDE, as soon as your program hits a breakpoint it'll pause and let you inspect and change the values of all the variables.

Creating a new Windows Forms Application project will tell the IDE to create a new project with a blank form and an entry point. You might want to name it something like "Chapter 2 program 1"—you'll be building a whole lot of programs throughout the book.

Comments (which either start with two or more slashes or are surrounded by / and */ marks) show up in the IDE as green text. You don't have to worry about what you type in between those marks, because comments are always ignored by the compiler.*

② Insert a breakpoint on the first line of code

Right-click on the first line of code (int number = 15;) and choose "Insert Breakpoint" from the Breakpoint menu. (You can also click on it and choose Debug >> Toggle Breakpoint or press F9.)

→ *Flip the page and keep going!*

3 **Start debugging your program**

Run your program in the debugger by clicking the Start Debugging button (or by pressing F5, or by choosing Debug >> Start Debugging from the menu). Your program should start up as usual and pop up the form.

4 **Click on the button to trigger the breakpoint**

As soon as your program gets to the line of code that has the breakpoint, the IDE automatically brings up the code editor and highlights the current line of code in yellow.

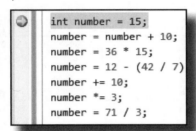

```
int number = 15;
number = number + 10;
number = 36 * 15;
number = 12 - (42 / 7)
number += 10;
number *= 3;
number = 71 / 3;
```

> You can also **hover** over a variable while you're debugging to see its value displayed in a tooltip...and you can pin it so it says open!

5 **Add a watch for the number variable**

Right-click on the number variable (any occurrence of it will do!) and choose **Expression: 'number' >> Add Watch** from the menu. The Watch window should appear in the panel at the bottom of the IDE:

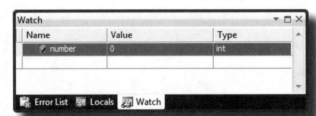

6 **Step through the code**

Press F10 to step through the code. (You can also choose Debug >> Step Over from the menu, or click the Step Over button in the Debug toolbar.) The current line of code will be executed, setting the value of number to 15. The next line of code will then be highlighted in yellow, and the Watch window will be updated:

As soon as the number variable gets a new value (15), its watch is updated.

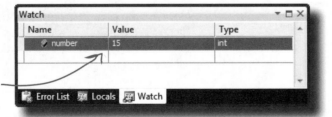

> **Adding a watch can help you keep track of the values of the variables in your program. This will really come in handy when your programs get more complex.**

7 **Continue running the program**

When you want to resume, just press F5 (or Debug >> Continue), and the program will resume running as usual.

Loops perform an action over and over

Here's a peculiar thing about most large programs: they almost always involve doing certain things over and over again. And that's what **loops** are for—they tell your program to keep executing a certain set of statements as long as some condition is true (or false!).

```
while (x > 5)
{
    x = x - 3;
}
```

That's a big part of why booleans are so important. A loop uses a test to figure out if it should keep looping.

In a while loop, all of the statements inside the curly brackets get executed as long as the condition in the parentheses is true.

IDE Tip: Brackets

If your brackets (or braces—either name will do) don't match up, your program won't build, which leads to frustrating bugs. Luckily, the IDE can help with this! Put your cursor on a bracket, and the IDE highlights its match:

```
bool test;
while (test == true)
{
    // Contents of the loop
}
```

Every for loop has three statements. The first sets up the loop. The statement will keep looping as long as the second one is true. And the third statement gets executed after each time through the loop.

```
for (int i = 0; i < 8; i = i + 2)
{
    MessageBox.Show("I'll pop up 4 times");
}
```

Use a code snippet to write simple for loops

You'll be typing for loops in just a minute, and the IDE can help speed up your coding a little. Type for followed by two tabs, and the IDE will automatically insert code for you. If you type a new variable, it'll automatically update the rest of the snippet. Press tab again, and the cursor will jump to the length.

Press tab to get the cursor to jump to the length. The number of times this loop runs is determined by whatever you set length to. You can change length to a number or a variable.

```
for (int i = 0; i < length; i++)
{
}
```

If you change the variable to something else, the snippet automatically changes the other two occurrences of it.

Time to start coding

The real work of any program is in its statements. But statements don't exist in a vacuum. So let's set the stage for digging in and getting some code written. **Create a new Windows Forms Application project**.

Build this form

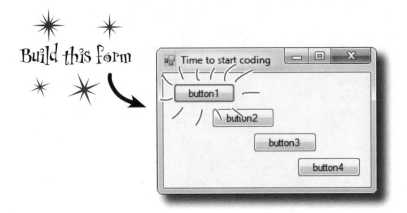

Add statements to show a message

Get started by double-clicking on the first button. Then add these statements to the `button1_Click()` method. Look closely at the code and the output it produces.

A few helpful tips

✦ Don't forget that all your statements need to end in a semicolon:

```
name = "Joe";
```

✦ You can add comments to your code by starting them with two slashes:

```
// this text is ignored
```

✦ Variables are declared with a **name** and a **type** (there are plenty of types that you'll learn about in Chapter 4):

```
int weight;
// weight is an integer
```

✦ The code for a class or a method goes between curly braces:

```
public void Go() {
    // your code here
}
```

✦ Most of the time, extra whitespace is fine:

```
int j        =        1234   ;
```

is the same as:

```
int j = 1234;
```

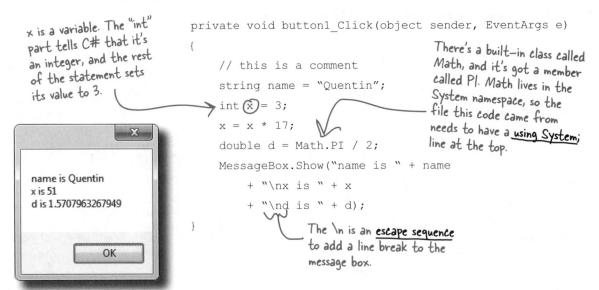

x is a variable. The "int" part tells C# that it's an integer, and the rest of the statement sets its value to 3.

```
private void button1_Click(object sender, EventArgs e)
{
    // this is a comment
    string name = "Quentin";
    int x = 3;
    x = x * 17;
    double d = Math.PI / 2;
    MessageBox.Show("name is " + name
        + "\nx is " + x
        + "\nd is " + d);
}
```

There's a built-in class called Math, and it's got a member called PI. Math lives in the System namespace, so the file this code came from needs to have a <u>using System;</u> line at the top.

name is Quentin
x is 51
d is 1.5707963267949

The \n is an **escape sequence** to add a line break to the message box.

if/else statements make decisions

Use **if/else statements** to tell your program to do certain
things only when the **conditions** you set up are (or aren't)
true. A lot of if/else statements check if two things are equal.
That's when you use the == operator. That's different from the
single equals sign (=) operator, which you use to set a value.

Every if statement
starts with a
conditional test.

```
if (someValue == 24)
{
    MessageBox.Show("The value was 24.");
}
```

The statement inside
the curly brackets is
executed only if the
test is true.

Always use two equals signs to check if
two things are equal to each other.

```
if (someValue == 24)
{
    // You can have as many statements
    // as you want inside the brackets

    MessageBox.Show("The value was 24.");
} else {
    MessageBox.Show("The value wasn't 24.");
}
```

if/else statements are
pretty straightforward.
If the conditional
test is true, the
program executes the
statements between the
first set of brackets.
Otherwise, it executes
the statements between
the second set.

Don't confuse the two equals sign operators!

*You use one equals sign (=) to set a variable's value, but two equals
signs (==) to compare two variables. You won't believe how many bugs in
programs—even ones made by experienced programmers!—are caused
by using = instead of ==. If you see the IDE complain that you "cannot implicitly
convert type 'int' to 'bool'", that's probably what happened.*

Watch it!

Set up conditions and see if they're true

Use **if/else statements** to tell your program to do certain things only when the **conditions** you set up are (or aren't) true.

Use logical operators to check conditions

You've just looked at the == operator, which you use to test whether two variables are equal. There are a few other operators, too. Don't worry about memorizing them right now—you'll get to know them over the next few chapters.

★ The != operator works a lot like ==, except it's true if the two things you're comparing are **not equal**.

★ You can use > and < to compare numbers and see if one is bigger or smaller than the other.

★ The ==, !=, >, and < operators are called **conditional operators**. When you use them to test two variables or values, it's called performing a **conditional test.**

★ You can combine individual conditional tests into one long test using the && operator for AND and the || operator for OR. So to check if i equals 3 or j is less than 5, do (i == 3) || (j < 5).

> **When you use a conditional operator to compare two numbers, it's called a conditional test.**

Set a variable and then check its value

Here's the code for the second button. It's an if/else statement that checks an integer **variable** called x to see if it's equal to 10.

Make sure you stop your program before you do this—the IDE won't let you edit the code while the program's running. You can stop it by closing the window, using the stop button on the toolbar, or selecting "Stop Debugging" from the Debug menu.

```
private void button2_Click(object sender, EventArgs e)
{
    int x = 5;
    if (x == 10)
    {
        MessageBox.Show("x must be 10");
    }
    else
    {
        MessageBox.Show("x isn't 10");
    }
}
```

First we set up a variable called x and make it equal to 5. Then we check if it's equal to 10.

Here's the output. See if you can tweak one line of code and get it to say "x must be 10" instead.

Add another conditional test

The third button makes this output. Now make a change to
two lines of code so that it pops up both message boxes.

This line checks someValue to
see if it's equal to 3, and then
it checks to make sure name
is "Joe".

```
private void button3_Click(object sender, EventArgs e)
{
    int someValue = 4;
    string name = "Bobbo Jr.";
    if ((someValue == 3) && (name == "Joe"))
    {
        MessageBox.Show("x is 3 and the name is Joe");
    }
    MessageBox.Show("this line runs no matter what");
}
```

Add loops to your program

Here's the code for the last button. It's got two loops. The first is a **while** loop,
which repeats the statements inside the brackets as long as the condition is true—do
something *while* this is true. The second one is a **for** loop. Take a look and see how it
works.

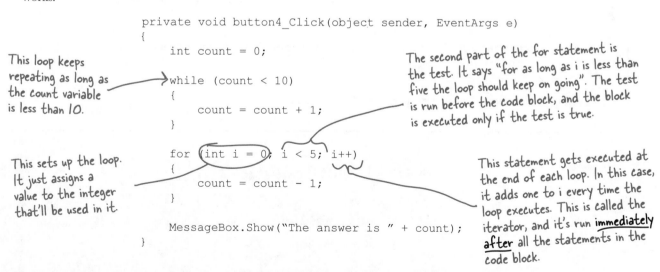

```
private void button4_Click(object sender, EventArgs e)
{
    int count = 0;

    while (count < 10)
    {
        count = count + 1;
    }

    for (int i = 0; i < 5; i++)
    {
        count = count - 1;
    }

    MessageBox.Show("The answer is " + count);
}
```

This loop keeps
repeating as long as
the count variable
is less than 10.

This sets up the loop.
It just assigns a
value to the integer
that'll be used in it.

The second part of the for statement is
the test. It says "for as long as i is less than
five the loop should keep on going". The test
is run before the code block, and the block
is executed only if the test is true.

This statement gets executed at
the end of each loop. In this case,
it adds one to i every time the
loop executes. This is called the
iterator, and it's run immediately
after all the statements in the
code block.

**Before you click on the button, read through the code and try to figure out what the
message box will show. Then click the button and see if you were right!**

over and over and over and...

Sharpen your pencil

Let's get a little more practice with conditional tests and loops. Take a look at the code below. Circle the conditional tests, and fill in the blanks so that the comments correctly describe the code that's being run.

```
int result = 0; // this variable will hold the final result
int x = 6; // declare a variable x and  set it to 6  ←—— We filled in the first one for you.
while (x > 3) {
   // execute these statements as long as ..........................................................

   result = result + x; // add x ....................................................................

   x = x - 1; // subtract ..........................................................................
}
for (int z = 1; z < 3; z = z + 1) {
   // start the loop by .............................................................................
   // keep looping as long as ......................................................................
   // after each loop, .............................................................................
   result = result + z; // ........................................................................
}
// The next statement will pop up a message box that says
// ...............................................................
MessageBox.Show("The result is " + result);
```

More about conditional tests

You can do simple conditional tests by checking the value of a variable using a comparison operator. Here's how you compare two ints, x and y:

```
x < y (less than)
x > y (greater than)
x == y (equals—and yes, with two equals signs)
```

These are the ones you'll use most often.

Wait up! There's a flaw in your logic. What happens to my loop if I write a conditional test that never becomes false?

Then your loop runs forever!

Every time your program runs a conditional test, the result is either **true** or **false**. If it's **true**, then your program goes through the loop one more time. Every loop should have code that, if it's run enough times, should cause the conditional test to eventually return **false**. But if it doesn't, then the loop will keep running until you kill the program or turn the computer off!

This is sometimes called an infinite loop, and there are actually times when you'll want to use one in your program.

Sharpen your pencil

Here are a few loops. Write down if each loop will repeat forever or eventually end. If it's going to end, how many times will it loop?

Loop #1
```
int count = 5;
while (count > 0) {
    count = count * 3;
    count = count * -1;
}
```
For Loop #3, how many times will this statement be executed?

Loop #2
```
int i = 0;
int count = 2;
while (i == 0) {
    count = count * 3;
    count = count * -1;
}
```

Loop #3
```
int j = 2;
for (int i = 1; i < 100;
     i = i * 2)
{
    j = j - i;
    while (j < 25)
    {
        j = j + 5;
    }
}
```

Loop #4
```
while (true) { int i = 1;}
```

For Loop #5, how many times will this statement be executed?

Loop #5
```
int p = 2;
for (int q = 2; q < 32;
     q = q * 2)
{
    while (p < q)
    {
        p = p * 2;
    }
    q = p - q;
}
```
*Hint: q starts out equal to 2. Think about when the iterator "q = q * 2" is executed.*

Remember, a for loop always runs the conditional test at the beginning of the block, and the iterator at the end of the block.

BRAIN POWER

Can you think of a reason that you'd want to write a loop that never stops running? (Hint: You'll use one in Chapter 13....)

Sharpen your pencil
Solution

Let's get a little more practice with conditional tests and loops. Take a look at the code below. Circle the conditional tests, and fill in the blanks so that the comments correctly describe the code that's being run.

```
int result = 0; // this variable will hold the final result
int x = 6; // declare a variable x and  set it to 6
while (x > 3) {
    // execute these statements as long as  x is greater than 3

    result = result + x; // add x  to the result variable

    x = x - 1; // subtract  1 from the value of x
}
for (int z = 1; (z < 3;) z = z + 1) {
    // start the loop by  declaring a variable z and setting it to 1
    // keep looping as long as  z is less than 3
    // after each loop,  add 1 to z
    result = result + z; //  add the value of z to result

}
// The next statement will pop up a message box that says
//  The result is 18

MessageBox.Show("The result is " + result);
```

This loop runs twice—first with z set to 1, and then a second time with z set to 2. Once it hits 3, it's no longer less than 3, so the loop stops.

Sharpen your pencil
Solution

Here are a few loops. Write down if each loop will repeat forever or eventually end. If it's going to end, how many times will it loop?

Loop #1
This loop executes once

Loop #2
This loop runs forever

Loop #3
This loop executes 7 times

Loop #4
Another infinite loop

Loop #5
This loop executes 8 times

Take the time to really figure this one out. Here's a perfect opportunity to try out the debugger on your own! Set a breakpoint on the statement q = p − q; Add watches for the variables p and q and step through the loop.

there are no
Dumb Questions

Q: Is every statement always in a class?

A: Yes. Any time a C# program does something, it's because statements were executed. Those statements are a part of classes, and those classes are a part of namespaces. Even when it looks like something is not a statement in a class—like when you use the designer to set a property on an object on your form—if you search through your code you'll find that the IDE added or changed statements inside a class somewhere.

Q: Are there any namespaces I'm not allowed to use? Are there any I *have* to use?

A: Yes, there are a few namespaces that are not recommended to use. Notice how all of the `using` lines at the top of your C# class files always said `System`? That's because there's a `System` namespace that's used by the .NET Framework. It's where you find all of your important tools to add power to your programs, like `System.Data`, which lets you work with tables and databases, and `System.IO`, which lets you work with files and data streams. But for the most part, you can choose any name you want for a namespace (as long as it only has letters, numbers, and underscores). When you create a new program, the IDE will automatically choose a namespace for you based on the program's name.

Q: I still don't get why I need this partial class stuff.

A: Partial classes are how you can spread the code for one class between more than one file. The IDE does that when it creates a form—it keeps the code you edit in one file (like `Form1.cs`), and the code it modifies automatically for you in another file (`Form1.Designer.cs`). You don't need to do that with a namespace, though. One namespace can span two, three, or a dozen or more files. Just put the namespace declaration at the top of the file, and everything within the curly brackets after the declaration is inside the same namespace. One more thing: you can have more than one class in a file. And you can have more than one namespace in a file. You'll learn a lot more about classes in the next few chapters.

Q: Let's say I drag something onto my form, so the IDE generates a bunch of code automatically. What happens to that code if I click "Undo"?

A: The best way to answer this question is to try it! Give it a shot— do something where the IDE generates some code for you.

Drag a button on a form, change properties. Then try to undo it. What happens? Well, for simple things you'll see that the IDE is smart enough to undo it itself. But for more complex things, like adding a new SQL database to your project, you'll be given a warning message. It still knows how to undo the action, but it may not be able to redo it.

Q: So exactly how careful do I have to be with the code that's automatically generated by the IDE?

A: You should generally be pretty careful. It's really useful to know what the IDE is doing to your code, and once in a while you'll need to know what's in there in order to solve a serious problem. But in almost all cases, you'll be able to do everything you need to do through the IDE.

BULLET POINTS

- You tell your program to perform actions using statements. Statements are always part of classes, and every class is in a namespace.

- Every statement ends with a semicolon (;).

- When you use the visual tools in the Visual Studio IDE, it automatically adds or changes code in your program.

- Code blocks are surrounded by curly braces { }. Classes, `while` loops, if/else statements, and lots of other kinds of statements use those blocks.

- A conditional test is either `true` or `false`. You use conditional tests to determine when a loop ends, and which block of code to execute in an if/else statement.

- Any time your program needs to store some data, you use a variable. Use = to assign a variable, and == to test if two variables are equal.

- A `while` loop runs everything within its block (defined by curly braces) as long as the *conditional test* is `true`.

- If the conditional test is `false`, the `while` loop code block won't run, and execution will move down to the code immediately after the loop block.

Code Magnets

Part of a C# program is all scrambled up on the fridge. Can you rearrange the code snippets to make a working C# program that produces the message box? Some of the curly braces fell on the floor and they were too small to pick up, so feel free to add as many of those as you need! (Hint: you'll definitely need to add a couple. Just write them in!)

The "" is an empty string—it means Result has no characters in it yet.

```
if (x == 1) {

Result = Result + "d";

x = x - 1;

}
```

```
if (x == 2) {

Result = Result + "b c";

}
```

```
if (x > 2) {

Result = Result + "a";

}
```

```
int x = 3;
```

```
x = x - 1;

Result = Result + "-";
```

```
while (x > 0) {
```

```
string Result = "";
```
This magnet didn't fall off the fridge...

```
MessageBox.Show(Result);
```

Output:

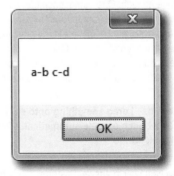

a-b c-d

OK

→ Answers on page 82.

We'll give you a lot of exercises like this throughout the book. We'll give you the answer in a couple of pages. If you get stuck, don't be afraid to peek at the answer—it's not cheating!

You'll be creating a lot of applications throughout this book, and you'll need to give each one a different name. We recommend naming this one "2 Fun with if—else statements" based on the chapter number and the text in the title bar of the form.

Exercise

Time to get some practice using if/else statements. Can you build this program?

Here's the form.

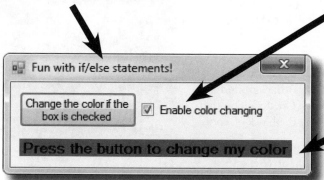

Add this checkbox.
Drag it out of the toolbox and onto your form. Use the **Text** property to change the text that's next to it. (You also use the **Text** property to change the button and label text.)

This is a label.
You can use the properties to change the font size and make it boldface. Use the **BackColor** property to set to red—choose "**Red**" from the selection of web colors.

Pop up this message if the user clicks the button but the box IS NOT checked.
If your checkbox is named **checkBox1** (you can change the **Name** property if you want), then here's the conditional test to see if it's checked:

```
checkBox1.Checked == true
```

If the user clicks the button and the box IS checked, change the background color of the label.
If the label background color is red, change it to blue when the button is clicked. If it's blue, change it back to red. Here's a statement that sets the background color of a label called **label1**:

```
label1.BackColor = Color.Red;
```

(Hint: The conditional test to check whether a label's background color is red looks a lot like that statement—but with one important difference!)

Let's build something **flashy**! Start by creating a new Windows Forms Application in the IDE.

Exercise

① **Here's the form to build** ————————➤

Hint: If you declare a variable inside a for loop—for (int c = 0; ...)—then that variable's only valid inside the loop's curly brackets. So if you have two for loops that both use the variable, you'll either declare it in each loop or have one declaration outside the loop. And if the variable c is already declared outside of the loops, you can't use it in either one.

② **Make the form background go all psychedelic!**
When the button's clicked, make the form's background color cycle through a whole lot of colors! Create a loop that has a variable **c** go from 0 to 253. Here's the block of code that goes inside the curly brackets:

```
this.BackColor = Color.FromArgb(c, 255 - c, c);

Application.DoEvents(); ⟵
```

This line tells the program to stop your loop momentarily and do the other things it needs to do, like refresh the form, check for mouse clicks, etc. Try taking out this line and seeing what happens. The form doesn't redraw itself, because it's waiting until the loop is done before it deals with those events. ↖

> For now, you'll use Application.DoEvents() to make sure your form stays responsive while it's in a loop, but it's kind of a hack. You shouldn't use this code outside of a toy program like this. Later on in the book, you'll learn about a much better way to let your programs do more than one thing at a time!

③ **Make it slower**
Slow down the flashing by adding this line after the `Application.DoEvents()` line:

```
System.Threading.Thread.Sleep(3);
```

Color me impressed!
.NET has a bunch of predefined colors like Blue and Red, but it also lets you make your own colors using the Color.FromArgb() method, by specifying three numbers: a red value, a green value, and a blue value.

This statement inserts a 3 millisecond delay in the loop. It's a part of the .NET library, and it's in the `System.Threading` namespace.

④ **Make it smoother**

Let's make the colors cycle back to where they started. Add another loop that has **c** go from 254 down to 0. Use the same block of code inside the curly brackets.

⑤ **Keep it going**

Surround your two loops with another loop that continuously executes and doesn't stop, so that when the button is pressed, the background starts changing colors and then keeps doing it. (Hint: The `while (true)` loop will run forever!)

When one loop is inside another one, we call it a "nested" loop.

Uh-oh! The program doesn't stop!

Run your program in the IDE. Start it looping. Now close the window. Wait a minute—the IDE didn't go back into edit mode! It's acting like the program is still running. You need to actually stop the program using the square stop button in the IDE (or select "Stop Debugging" from the Debug menu).

---

⑥ **Make it stop**

Make the loop you added in step #5 stop when the program is closed. Change your outer loop to this:

```
while (Visible)
```

Now run the program and click the X box in the corner. The window closes, and then the program stops! Except…there's a delay of a few seconds before the IDE goes back to edit mode.

When you're checking a Boolean value like Visible in an if statement or a loop, sometimes it's tempting to test for (Visible == true). You can leave off the "== true"—it's enough to include the Boolean.

When you're working with a form or control, Visible is true as long as the form or control is being displayed. If you set it to false, it makes the form or control disappear.

Hint: The && operator means "AND". It's how you string a bunch of conditional tests together into one big test that's true only if the first test is true AND the second is true AND the third, etc. And it'll come in handy to solve this problem.

Can you figure out what's causing that delay? Can you fix it so the program ends immediately when you close the window?

Time to get some practice using if/else statements. Can you build this program?

```
using System;
using System.Collections.Generic;
using System.ComponentModel;
using System.Data;
using System.Drawing;
using System.Linq;
using System.Text;
using System.Windows.Forms;

namespace Fun_with_If_Else
{
    public partial class Form1 : Form
    {
        public Form1()
        {
            InitializeComponent();
        }

        private void button1_Click(object sender, EventArgs e)
        {
            if (checkBox1.Checked == true)
            {
                if (label1.BackColor == Color.Red)
                {
                    label1.BackColor = Color.Blue;
                }
                else
                {
                    label1.BackColor = Color.Red;
                }
            }
            else
            {
                MessageBox.Show("The box is not checked");
            }
        }
    }
}
```

Here's the code for the form. We named our solution "Fun with If Else", so the IDE made the namespace Fun_with_If_Else. If you gave your solution a different name, it'll have a different namespace.

The IDE added the method called button1_Click() to your form when you double-clicked on the button. The method gets run every time the button's clicked.

The inner if statement checks the label's color. If the label is currently red, it executes a statement to turn it blue.

The outer if statement checks the checkbox to see if it's been checked. Check!

This statement's run if the label's background color is not red to make it set back to red.

This MessageBox pops up if the checkbox isn't checked.

You can download the code for all of the exercise solutions in this book from www.headfirstlabs.com/books/hfcsharp/

Exercise Solution

Let's build something **flashy!**

Sometimes we won't show you the entire code in the solution, just the bits that changed. All of the logic in the FlashyThing project is in this button1_Click() method that the IDE added when you double-clicked the button in the form designer.

When the IDE added this method, it added an extra return before the curly bracket. Sometimes we'll put the bracket on the same line like this to save space—but C# doesn't care about extra space, so this is perfectly valid.

Consistency is generally really important to make it easy for people to read code. But we're purposefully showing you different ways, because you'll need to get used to reading code from different people using different styles.

```csharp
private void button1_Click(object sender, EventArgs e) {
    while (Visible) {
        for (int c = 0; c < 254 && Visible; c++) {
            this.BackColor = Color.FromArgb(c, 255 - c, c);
            Application.DoEvents();
            System.Threading.Thread.Sleep(3);
        }
        for (int c = 254; c >= 0 && Visible; c--) {
            this.BackColor = Color.FromArgb(c, 255 - c, c);
            Application.DoEvents();
            System.Threading.Thread.Sleep(3);
        }
    }
}
```

The outer loop keeps running as long as the form is visible. As soon as it's closed, Visible is false, and the while will stop looping.

We used && Visible instead of && Visible == true. It's just like saying "if it's visible" instead of "if it's true that it's visible"—they mean the same thing.

The first for loop makes the colors cycle one way, and the second for loop reverses them so they look smooth.

We fixed the extra delay by using the && operator to make each of the for loops also check Visible. That way the loop ends as soon as Visible turns false.

Can you figure out what's causing that delay? Can you fix it so the program ends immediately when you close the window?

The delay happens because the for loops need to finish before the while loop can check if Visible is still true. You can fix it by adding **&& Visible** to the conditional test in each for loop.

Was your code a little different than ours? There's more than one way to solve any programming problem—like you could have used while loops instead of for loops. If your program works, then you got the exercise right!

Pool Puzzle

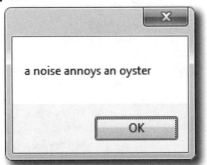

Your *job* is to take code snippets from the pool and place them into the blank lines in the code. You may **not** use the same snippet more than once, and you won't need to use all the snippets. Your *goal* is to make a class that will compile and run. Don't be fooled—this one's harder than it looks.

Output

a noise annoys an oyster

OK

We included these "Pool Puzzle" exercises throughout the book to give your brain an extra-tough workout. If you're the kind of person who loves twisty little logic puzzles, then you'll love this one. If you're not, give it a shot anyway—but don't be afraid to look at the answer to figure out what's going on. And if you're stumped by a pool puzzle, definitely move on.

```
int x = 0;
String Poem = "";

while ( _____ ) {

    _____

    if ( x < 1 ) {

    _____
    }

    _____

    if ( _____ ) {


    _____


    _____
    }
    if ( x == 1 ) {

    _____
    }
    if ( _____ ) {

    _____
    }

    _____

}

_____
```

Note: each snippet from the pool can only be used once!

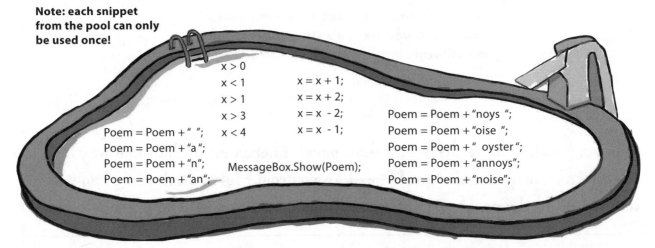

```
                x > 0
                x < 1        x = x + 1;
                x > 1        x = x + 2;
                x > 3        x = x - 2;
Poem = Poem + " ";    x < 4        x = x - 1;         Poem = Poem + "noys ";
Poem = Poem + "a ";                                   Poem = Poem + "oise ";
Poem = Poem + "n";                                    Poem = Poem + " oyster ";
Poem = Poem + "an";   MessageBox.Show(Poem);          Poem = Poem + "annoys";
                                                      Poem = Poem + "noise";
```

➞ Answers on page 83.

Csharpcross

How does a crossword help you learn C#? Well, all the words are C#-related and from this chapter. The clues also provide mental twists and turns that will help you burn alternative routes to C# right into your brain.

Across

3. You give information to a method using these _____

4. `button1.Text` and `checkBox3.Name` are examples of

8. Every statement ends with one of these

10. The name of every C# program's entry point

11. Contains methods

12. Your code statements live in one of these

14. A kind of variable that's either true or false

15. A special method that tells your program where to start

16. This kind of class spans multiple files

Down

1. The output of a method is its _____ value

2. `System.Windows.Forms` is an example of one of these

5. A tiny piece of a program that does something

6. A block of code is surrounded by _____

7. The kind of test that tells a loop when to end

9. You can call _____.`Show()` to pop up a simple Windows dialog box

13. The kind of variable that contains a whole number

Code Magnets Solution

Part of a C# program is all scrambled up on the fridge. Can you rearrange the code snippets to make a working C# program that produces the message box? Some of the curly braces fell on the floor and they were too small to pick up, so feel free to add as many of those as you need!

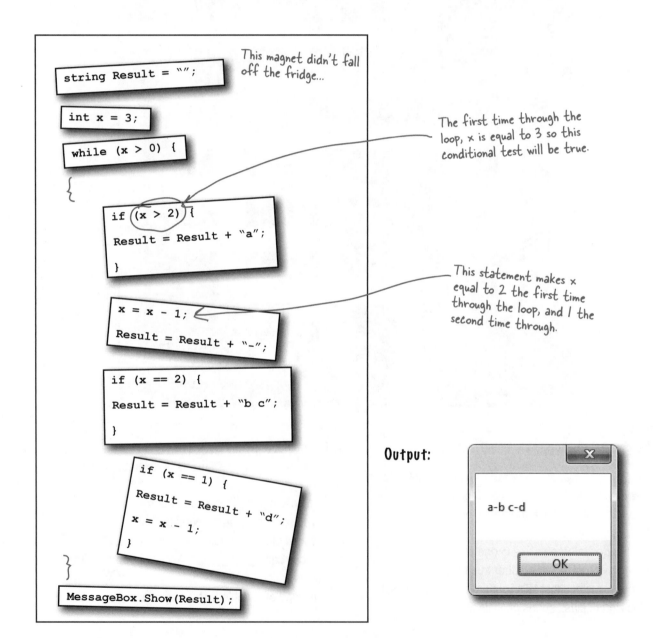

This magnet didn't fall off the fridge...

```
string Result = "";
```

```
int x = 3;
```

```
while (x > 0) {
```

{

The first time through the loop, x is equal to 3 so this conditional test will be true.

```
if (x > 2) {
Result = Result + "a";

}
```

```
x = x - 1;
Result = Result + "-";
```

This statement makes x equal to 2 the first time through the loop, and 1 the second time through.

```
if (x == 2) {
Result = Result + "b c";

}
```

```
if (x == 1) {
Result = Result + "d";
x = x - 1;
}
```

}

```
MessageBox.Show(Result);
```

Output:

a-b c-d

OK

Pool Puzzle Solution

Your *job* was to take code snippets from the pool and place them into the blank lines in the code. Your *goal* was to make a class that will compile and run.

```
int x = 0;
String Poem = "";

while ( x < 4 ) {

   Poem = Poem + "a";
   if ( x < 1 ) {
      Poem = Poem + " ";
   }
   Poem = Poem + "n";

   if ( x > 1 ) {

      Poem = Poem + " oyster";

      x = x + 2;
   }
   if ( x == 1 ) {

      Poem = Poem + "noys ";
   }
   if ( x < 1 ) {

      Poem = Poem + "oise ";
   }

   x = x + 1;
}
MessageBox.Show(Poem);
```

Output:

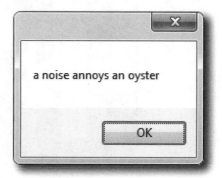

a noise annoys an oyster

Did you get a different solution? Type it into the IDE and see if it works! There's more than one correct solution to the pool puzzle.

If you want a real challenge, see if you can figure out what it is! Here's a hint: There's another solution that keeps the word fragments in order.

Csharpcross Solution

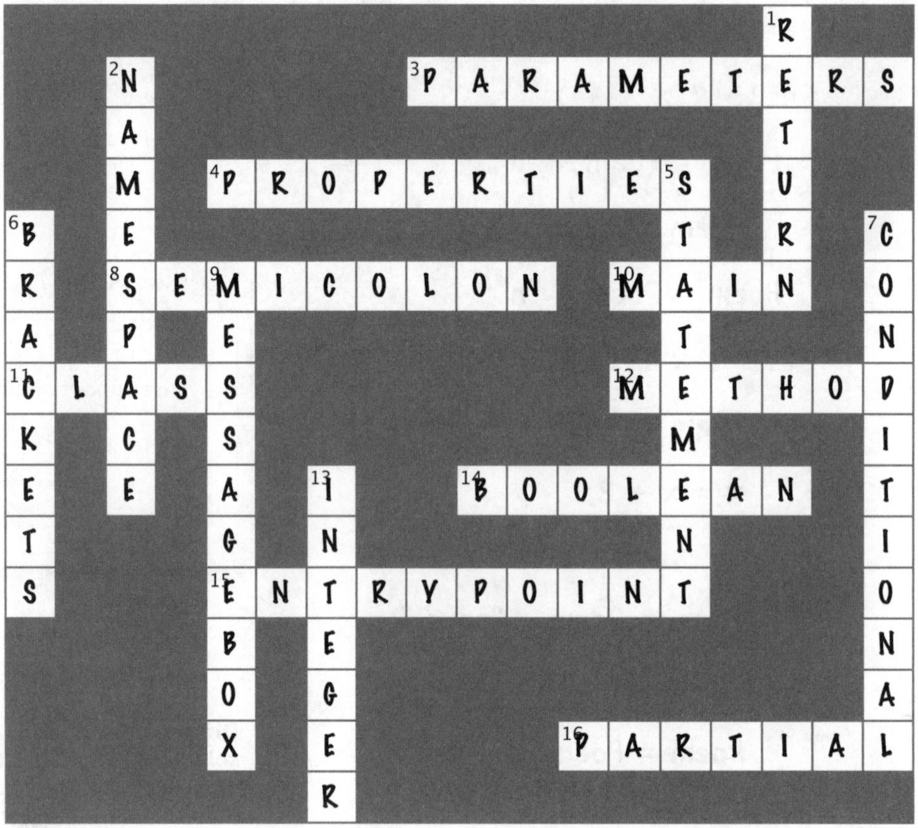
1 RETURN
2 NAMESPACE
3 PARAMETERS
4 PROPERTIES
5 STATEMENT
6 BRACKETS
7 CONDITIONAL
8 SEMICOLON
9 MESSAGEBOX
10 MAIN
11 CLASS
12 METHOD
13 INTEGER
14 BOOLEAN
15 ENTRYPOINT
16 PARTIAL

3 objects: get oriented!

Making code make sense

...and that's why my Husband class doesn't have a HelpOutAroundTheHouse() method or a PullHisOwnWeight() method.

Every program you write solves a problem.

When you're building a program, it's always a good idea to start by thinking about what *problem* your program's supposed to solve. That's why **objects** are really useful. They let you structure your code based on the problem it's solving, so that you can spend your time *thinking about the problem* you need to work on rather than getting bogged down in the mechanics of writing code. When you use objects right, you end up with code that's *intuitive* to write, and easy to read and change.

How Mike thinks about his problems

Mike's a programmer about to head out to a job interview. He can't wait to show off his C# skills, but first he has to get there—and he's running late!

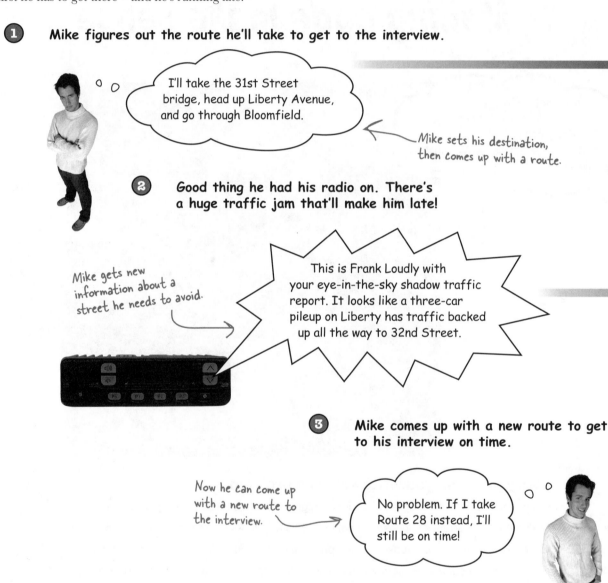

1 Mike figures out the route he'll take to get to the interview.

I'll take the 31st Street bridge, head up Liberty Avenue, and go through Bloomfield.

Mike sets his destination, then comes up with a route.

2 Good thing he had his radio on. There's a huge traffic jam that'll make him late!

Mike gets new information about a street he needs to avoid.

This is Frank Loudly with your eye-in-the-sky shadow traffic report. It looks like a three-car pileup on Liberty has traffic backed up all the way to 32nd Street.

3 Mike comes up with a new route to get to his interview on time.

Now he can come up with a new route to the interview.

No problem. If I take Route 28 instead, I'll still be on time!

How Mike's car navigation system thinks about his problems

Mike built his own GPS navigation system, which he uses to help him get around town.

Here's a diagram of a class in Mike's program. It shows the name on top, and the methods on the bottom.

Navigator
SetCurrentLocation()
SetDestination()
ModifyRouteToAvoid()
ModifyRouteToInclude()
GetRoute()
GetTimeToDestination()
TotalDistance()

```
SetDestination("Fifth Ave & Penn Ave");
string route;
route = GetRoute();
```

Here's the output from the GetRoute() method—it's a string that contains the directions Mike should follow.

The navigation system sets a destination and comes up with a route.

"Take 31st Street Bridge to Liberty Avenue to Bloomfield"

The navigation system gets new information about a street it needs to avoid.

```
ModifyRouteToAvoid("Liberty Ave");
```

Now it can come up with a new route to the destination.

```
string route;
route = GetRoute();
```

"Take Route 28 to the Highland Park Bridge to Washington Blvd"

GetRoute() gives a new route that doesn't include the street Mike wants to avoid.

Mike's navigation system solves the street navigation problem the same way he does.

Mike's Navigator class has methods to set and modify routes

Mike's `Navigator` class has methods, which are where the action happens. But unlike the `button_Click()` methods in the forms you've built, they're all focused around a single problem: navigating a route through a city. That's why Mike stuck them together into one class, and called that class `Navigator`.

Mike designed his `Navigator` class so that it's easy to create and modify routes. To get a route, Mike's program calls the `SetDestination()` method to set the destination, and then uses the `GetRoute()` method to put the route into a string. If he needs to change the route, his program calls the `ModifyRouteToAvoid()` method to change the route so that it avoids a certain street, and then calls the `GetRoute()` method to get the new directions.

> *Mike chose method names that would make sense to someone who was thinking about how to navigate a route through a city.*

```
class Navigator {

    public void SetCurrentLocation(string locationName) { ... }

    public void SetDestination(string destinationName) { ... };

    public void ModifyRouteToAvoid(string streetName) { ... };

    public string GetRoute() { ... };

}
```

> *This is the **return type** of the method. It means that the statement calling the GetRoute() method can use it to set a string variable that will contain the directions. When it's **void**, that means the method doesn't return anything.*

```
string route =
        GetRoute();
```

Some methods have a return value

Every method is made up of statements that do things. Some methods just execute their statements and then exit. But other methods have a **return value**, or a value that's calculated or generated inside the method, and sent back to the statement that called that method. The type of the return value (like `string` or `int`) is called the **return type**.

The **return** statement tells the method to immediately exit. If your method doesn't have a return value—which means it's declared with a return type of `void`—then the `return` statement just ends with a semicolon, and you don't always have to have one in your method. But if the method has a return type, then it must use the `return` statement.

> *Here's an example of a method that has a return type—it returns an int. The method uses the two **parameters** to calculate the result and uses the **return** statement to pass the value back to the statement that called it.*

```
public int MultiplyTwoNumbers(int firstNumber, int secondNumber) {
        int result = firstNumber * secondNumber;
        return result;
    }
```

Here's a statement that calls a method to multiply two numbers. It returns an `int`:

```
int myResult = MultiplyTwoNumbers(3, 5);
```

> *Methods can take values like 3 and 5. But you can also use variables to pass values to a method.*

BULLET POINTS

- Classes have methods that contain statements that perform actions. You can design a class that is easy to use by choosing methods that make sense.

- Some methods have a **return type**. You set a method's return type in its declaration. A method with a declaration that starts "`public int`" returns an int value. Here's an example of a statement that returns an int value: `return 37;`

- When a method has a return type, it **must** have a `return` statement that returns a value that matches a return type. So if you've got a method that's declared "`public string`" then you need a `return` statement that returns a string.

- As soon as a `return` statement in a method executes, your program jumps back to the statement that called the method.

- Not all methods have a return type. A method with a declaration that starts "`public void`" doesn't return anything at all. You can still use a `return` statement to exit a `void` method: `if (finishedEarly) { return; }`

Use what you've learned to build a program that uses a class

Let's hook up a form to a class, and make its button call a method inside that class.

Do this!

1 Create a new Windows Forms Application project in the IDE. Then add a class file to it called `Talker.cs` by right-clicking on the project in the Solution Explorer and selecting "Class…" from the Add menu. When you name your new class file "Talker.cs", the IDE will automatically name the class in the new file `Talker`. Then it'll pop up the new class in a new tab inside the IDE.

2 Add `using System.Windows.Forms;` to the top of the class file. Then add code to the class:

```
class Talker {
    public static int BlahBlahBlah(string thingToSay, int numberOfTimes)
    {
        string finalString = "";
        for (int count = 1; count <= numberOfTimes; count++)
        {
            finalString = finalString + thingToSay + "\n";
        }
        MessageBox.Show(finalString);
        return finalString.Length;
    }
}
```

This statement declares a finalString variable and sets it equal to an empty string.

This line of code adds the contents of thingToSay and a line break ("\n") onto the end of it to the finalString variable.

The BlahBlahBlah() method's return value is an integer that has the total length of the message it displayed. You can add ".Length" to any string to figure out how long it is.

*This is called a **property**. Every string has a property called Length. When it calculates the length of a string, a line break ("\n") counts as one character.*

→ **Flip the page to keep going!**

So what did you just build?

The new class has one method called `BlahBlahBlah()` that takes two parameters. The first parameter is a string that tells it something to say, and the second is the number of times to say it. When it's called, it pops up a message box with the message repeated a number of times. Its return value is the length of the string. The method needs a string for its `thingToSay` parameter and a number for its `numberOfTimes` parameter. It'll get those parameters from a form that lets the user enter text using a **TextBox** control and a number using **NumericUpDown** control.

Now add a form that uses your new class!

> Set the default text of the TextBox to "Hello!" using its Text property.

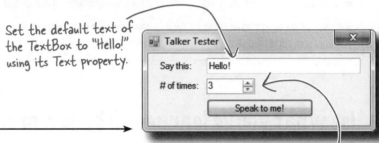

3 Make your project's form look like this. ──────────────→

Then double-click on the button and have it run this code that calls `BlahBlahBlah()` and assigns its return value to an integer called `len`:

> This is a NumericUpDown control. Set its Minimum property to 1, its Maximum property to 10, and its Value property to 3.

```
private void button1_Click(object sender, EventArgs e)
{
    int len = Talker.BlahBlahBlah(textBox1.Text, (int)numericUpDown1.Value);
    MessageBox.Show("The message length is " + len);
}
```

4 Now run your program! Click the button and watch it pop up two message boxes. The class pops up the first message box, and the form pops up the second one.

> The BlahBlahBlah() method pops up this message box based on what's in its parameters.

> When the method returns a value, the form pops it up in this message box.

You can add a class to your project and share its methods with the other classes in the project.

Mike gets an idea

The interview went great! But the traffic jam this morning got Mike thinking about how he could improve his navigator.

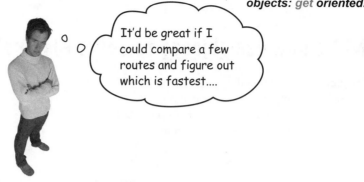

It'd be great if I could compare a few routes and figure out which is fastest....

He could create three different Navigator classes...

Mike *could* copy the `Navigator` class code and paste it into two more classes. Then his program could store three routes at once.

This box is a **class diagram**. It lists all of the methods in a class, and it's an easy way to see everything that it does at a glance.

Navigator
SetDestination()
ModifyRouteToAvoid()
ModifyRouteToInclude()
GetRoute()
GetTimeToDestination()
TotalDistance()

Navigator2
SetDestination()
ModifyRouteToAvoid()
ModifyRouteToInclude()
GetRoute()
GetTimeToDestination()
TotalDistance()

Navigator3
SetDestination()
ModifyRouteToAvoid()
ModifyRouteToInclude()
GetRoute()
GetTimeToDestination()
TotalDistance()

Whoa, that can't be right! What if I want to change a method? Then I need to go back and fix it in three places.

Right! Maintaining three copies of the same code is really messy. A lot of problems you need to solve need a way to represent one ***thing*** a bunch of different times. In this case, it's a bunch of routes. But it could be a bunch of turbines, or dogs, or music files, or anything. All of those programs have one thing in common: they always need to treat the same kind of thing in the same way, no matter how many of the thing they're dealing with.

Mike can use <u>objects</u> to solve his problem

Objects are C#'s tool that you use to work with
a bunch of similar things. Mike can use objects
to program his `Navigator` class just once, but
use it *as many times as he wants* in a program.

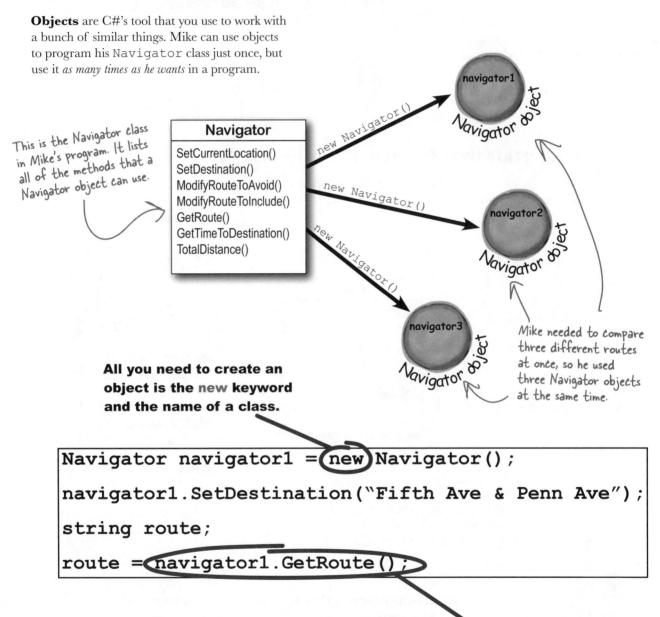

This is the Navigator class in Mike's program. It lists all of the methods that a Navigator object can use.

Navigator
SetCurrentLocation()
SetDestination()
ModifyRouteToAvoid()
ModifyRouteToInclude()
GetRoute()
GetTimeToDestination()
TotalDistance()

new Navigator()

navigator1
Navigator object

new Navigator()

navigator2
Navigator object

new Navigator()

navigator3
Navigator object

Mike needed to compare three different routes at once, so he used three Navigator objects at the same time.

**All you need to create an
object is the new keyword
and the name of a class.**

```
Navigator navigator1 = new Navigator();
navigator1.SetDestination("Fifth Ave & Penn Ave");
string route;
route = navigator1.GetRoute();
```

**Now you can use the object! When you
create an object from a class, that object
has all of the methods from that class.**

You use a <u>class</u> to build an <u>object</u>

A class is like a blueprint for an object. If you wanted to build five identical houses in a suburban housing development, you wouldn't ask an architect to draw up five identical sets of blueprints. You'd just use one blueprint to build five houses.

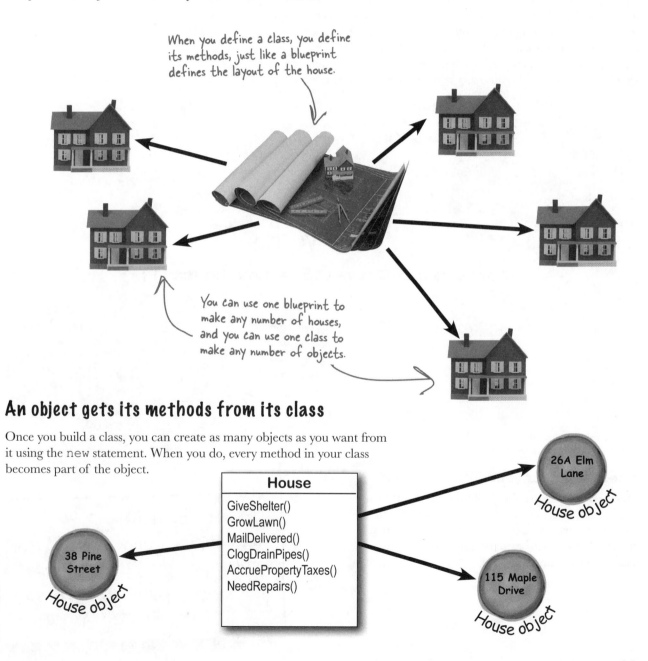

When you define a class, you define its methods, just like a blueprint defines the layout of the house.

You can use one blueprint to make any number of houses, and you can use one class to make any number of objects.

An object gets its methods from its class

Once you build a class, you can create as many objects as you want from it using the new statement. When you do, every method in your class becomes part of the object.

House

GiveShelter()
GrowLawn()
MailDelivered()
ClogDrainPipes()
AccruePropertyTaxes()
NeedRepairs()

26A Elm Lane
House object

38 Pine Street
House object

115 Maple Drive
House object

When you create a new object from a class, it's called an <u>instance</u> of that class

Guess what…you already know this stuff! Everything in the toolbox is a class: there's a `Button` class, a `TextBox` class, a `Label` class, etc. When you drag a button out of the toolbox, the IDE automatically creates an instance of the `Button` class and calls it `button1`. When you drag another button out of the toolbox, it creates another instance called `button2`. Each instance of `Button` has its own properties and methods. But every button acts exactly the same way, because they're all instances of the same class.

Before: Here's a picture of your computer's memory when your program starts.

Your program executes a new statement.

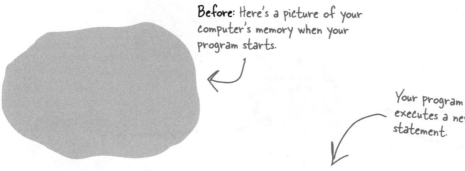

```
House mapleDrive115 = new House();
```

After: Now it's got an instance of the House class in memory.

115 Maple Drive

House object

Check it out for yourself!

Do this!

Open any project that uses a button called `button1`, and use the IDE to search the entire project for the text "**button1 = new**". You'll find the code that the IDE added to the form designer to create the instance of the `Button` class.

> **in-stance, noun.**
> an example or one occurrence of something. *The IDE search-and-replace feature finds every **instance** of a word and changes it to another.*

A better solution...brought to you by objects!

Mike came up with a new route comparison program that uses objects to find the shortest of three different routes to the same destination. Here's how he built his program.

GUI stands for Graphical User Interface, which is what you're building when you make a form in the form designer.

1 Mike set up a GUI with a text box—`textBox1` contains the **destination** for the three routes. Then he added `textBox2`, which has a street that one of the routes should **avoid**; and `textBox3`, which contains a different street that the third route has to **include**.

The navigator1 object is an instance of the Navigator class.

2 He created a `Navigator` object and set its destination.

Navigator
SetCurrentLocation()
SetDestination()
ModifyRouteToAvoid()
ModifyRouteToInclude()
GetRoute()
GetTimeToDestination()
TotalDistance()

navigator1
3.5 miles
Navigator object

```
string destination = textBox1.Text;
Navigator navigator1 = new Navigator();
navigator1.SetDestination(destination);
route = navigator1.GetRoute();
```

3 Then he added a second `Navigator` object called `navigator2`. He called its `SetDestination()` method to set the destination, and then he called its `ModifyRouteToAvoid()` method.

The SetDestination(), ModifyRouteToAvoid(), and ModifyRouteToInclude() methods all take a string as a parameter.

4 The third `Navigator` object is called `navigator3`. Mike set its destination, and then called its `ModifyRouteToInclude()` method.

navigator1
3.5 miles
Navigator object

navigator2
3.8 miles
Navigator object

navigator3
4.2 miles
Navigator object

Any time you create a new object from a class, it's called creating an instance of that class.

5 Now Mike can call each object's `TotalDistance()` method to figure out which route is the shortest. And he only had to write the code once, not three times!

Wait a minute! You didn't give me nearly enough information to build the navigator program.

That's right, we didn't. A geographic navigation program is a really complicated thing to build. But complicated programs follow the same patterns as simple ones. Mike's navigation program is an example of how someone would use objects in real life.

Theory and practice

Speaking of patterns, here's a pattern that you'll see over and over again throughout the book. We'll introduce a concept or idea (like objects) over the course of a few pages, using pictures and small code excerpts to demonstrate the idea. This is your opportunity to take a step back and try to understand what's going on without having to worry about getting a program to work.

House object

```
House mapleDrive115 = new House();
```

When we're introducing a new concept (like objects), keep your eyes open for pictures and code excerpts like this.

After we've introduced a concept, we'll give you a chance to get it into your brain. Sometimes we'll follow up the theory with a writing exercise—like the *Sharpen your pencil* exercise on the next page. Other times we'll jump straight into code. This combination of theory and practice is an effective way to get these concepts off of the page and stuck in your brain.

A little advice for the code exercises

If you keep a few simple things in mind, it'll make the code exercises go smoothly:

★ It's easy to get caught up in syntax problems, like missing parentheses or quotes. One missing bracket can cause many build errors.

★ It's *much better* to look at the solution than get frustrated with a problem. When you're frustrated, your brain doesn't like to learn.

★ All of the code in this book is tested and definitely works in Visual Studio 2010! But it's easy to accidentally type things wrong (like typing a one instead of a lowercase L).

★ If your solution just won't build, try downloading it from the Head First Labs website: **http://www.headfirstlabs.com/hfcsharp**

When you run into a problem with a coding exercise, don't be afraid to peek at the solution. You can also download the solution from the Head First Labs website.

Sharpen your pencil

Follow the same steps that Mike followed on the facing page to write the code to create `Navigator` objects and call their methods.

```
string destination = textBox1.Text;
string route2StreetToAvoid = textBox2.Text;
string route3StreetToInclude = textBox3.Text;
```

We gave you a head start. Here's the code Mike wrote to get the destination and street names from the textboxes.

```
Navigator navigator1 = new Navigator();
navigator1.SetDestination(destination);
int distance1 = navigator1.TotalDistance();
```

And here's the code to create the navigator object, set its destination, and get the distance.

1. Create the **navigator2** object, set its destination, call its **ModifyRouteToAvoid()** method, and use its **TotalDistance()** method to set an integer variable called **distance2**.

`Navigator navigator2 =` ....

`navigator2.` ....

`navigator2.` ....

`int distance2 =` ....

2. Create the **navigator3** object, set its destination, call its **ModifyRouteToInclude()** method, and use its **TotalDistance()** method to set an integer variable called **distance3**.

....

....

....

....

The Math.Min() method built into the .NET Framework compares two numbers and returns the smallest one. Mike used it to find the shortest distance to the destination.

```
int shortestDistance = Math.Min(distance1, Math.Min(distance2, distance3));
```

Sharpen your pencil
Solution

Follow the same steps that Mike followed on the facing page to write the code to create Navigator objects and call their methods.

```
string destination = textBox1.Text;
string route2StreetToAvoid = textBox2.Text;
string route3StreetToInclude = textBox3.Text;
```

We gave you a head start. Here's the code Mike wrote to get the destination and street names from the textboxes.

```
Navigator navigator1 = new Navigator();
navigator1.SetDestination(destination);
int distance1 = navigator1.TotalDistance();
```

And here's the code to create the navigator object, set its destination, and get the distance.

---

1. Create the **navigator2** object, set its destination, call its **ModifyRouteToAvoid()** method, and use its **TotalDistance()** method to set an integer variable called **distance2**.

```
Navigator navigator2 =    new Navigator()

navigator2.    SetDestination(destination);

navigator2.    ModifyRouteToAvoid(route2StreetToAvoid);

int distance2 =    navigator2.TotalDistance();
```

---

2. Create the **navigator3** object, set its destination, call its **ModifyRouteToInclude()** method, and use its **TotalDistance()** method to set an integer varable called **distance3**.

```
Navigator navigator3 = new Navigator()

navigator3.SetDestination(destination);

navigator3.ModifyRouteToInclude(route3StreetToInclude);

int distance3 = navigator3.TotalDistance();
```

The Math.Min() method built into the .NET Framework compares two numbers and returns the smallest one. Mike used it to find the shortest distance to the destination.

```
int shortestDistance = Math.Min(distance1, Math.Min(distance2, distance3));
```

> I've written a few classes now, but I haven't used "new" to create an instance yet! So does that mean I can call methods without creating objects?

Yes! That's why you used the `static` keyword in your methods.

Take another look at the declaration for the `Talker` class you built a few pages ago:

```
class Talker
{
    public static int BlahBlahBlah(string thingToSay, int numberOfTimes)
    {
        string finalString = "";
```

When you called the method you didn't create a `new` instance of `Talker`. You just did this:

```
Talker.BlahBlahBlah("Hello hello hello", 5);
```

That's how you call `static` methods, and you've been doing that all along. If you take away the `static` keyword from the `BlahBlahBlah()` method declaration, then you'll have to create an instance of `Talker` in order to call the method. Other than that distinction, static methods are just like object methods. You can pass parameters, they can return values, and they live in classes.

There's one more thing you can do with the `static` keyword. You can mark your **whole class** as static, and then all of its methods **must** be `static` too. If you try to add a non-static method to a static class, it won't compile.

there are no Dumb Questions

Q: When I think of something that's "static," I think of something that doesn't change. Does that mean non-static methods can change, but static methods don't? Do they behave differently?

A: No, both static and non-static methods act exactly the same. The only difference is that static methods don't require an instance, while non-static methods do. A lot of people have trouble remembering that, because the word "static" isn't really all that intuitive.

Q: So I can't use my class until I create an instance of an object?

A: You can use its static methods. But if you have methods that aren't static, then you need an instance before you can use them.

Q: Then why would I want a method that needs an instance? Why wouldn't I make all my methods static?

A: Because if you have an object that's keeping track of certain data—like Mike's instances of his `Navigator` class that each kept track of a different route—then you can use each instance's methods to work with that data. So when Mike called his `ModifyRouteToAvoid()` method in the `navigator2` instance, it only affected the route that was stored in that particular instance. It didn't affect the `navigator1` or `navigator3` objects. That's how he was able to work with three different routes at the same time—and his program could keep track of all of it.

Q: So how does an instance keep track of data?

A: Turn the page and find out!

An instance uses <u>fields</u> to keep track of things

You change the text on a button by setting its `Text` property in the
IDE. When you do, the IDE adds code like this to the designer:

```
button1.Text = "Text for the button";
```

Technically, it's setting a <u>property</u>. A property is very similar to a field—but we'll get into all that a little later on.

Now you know that `button1` is an instance of the `Button` class.
What that code does is modify a **field** for the `button1` instance.
You can add fields to a class diagram—just draw a horizontal line in
the middle of it. Fields go above the line, methods go underneath it.

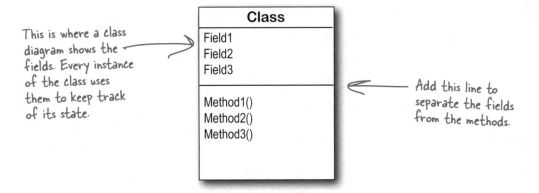

This is where a class diagram shows the fields. Every instance of the class uses them to keep track of its state.

Class

Field1
Field2
Field3

Method1()
Method2()
Method3()

Add this line to separate the fields from the methods.

Methods are what an object <u>does</u>. Fields are what the object <u>knows</u>.

When Mike created three instances of `Navigator` classes, his program created three objects.
Each of those objects was used to keep track of a different route. When the program created the
`navigator2` instance and called its `SetDestination()` method, it set the destination for that
one instance. But it didn't affect the `navigator1` instance or the `navigator3` instance.

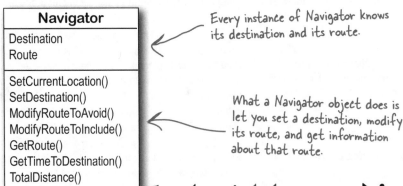

Navigator

Destination
Route

SetCurrentLocation()
SetDestination()
ModifyRouteToAvoid()
ModifyRouteToInclude()
GetRoute()
GetTimeToDestination()
TotalDistance()

Every instance of Navigator knows its destination and its route.

What a Navigator object does is let you set a destination, modify its route, and get information about that route.

An object's behavior is defined by its methods, and it uses fields to keep track of its state.

Let's create some instances!

It's easy to add fields to your class. Just declare variables outside of any methods. Now every instance gets its own copy of those variables.

> Remember, when you see "void" in front of a method, it means that it doesn't return any value.

```
class Clown {
    public string Name;
    public int Height;

    public void TalkAboutYourself() {
        MessageBox.Show("My name is "
            + Name + " and I'm "
            + Height + " inches tall.");
    }
}
```

Clown
Name
Height
TalkAboutYourself()

When you want to create instances of your class, **don't use** the static keyword in either the class declaration or the method declaration.

> Remember, the *= operator tells C# to take whatever's on the left of the operator and multiply it by whatever's on the right.

Sharpen your pencil

Write down the contents of each message box that will be displayed after the statement next to it is executed.

```
Clown oneClown = new Clown();
oneClown.Name = "Boffo";
oneClown.Height = 14;
```

oneClown.TalkAboutYourself();   "My name is _____ and I'm _____ inches tall."

```
Clown anotherClown = new Clown();
anotherClown.Name = "Biff";
anotherClown.Height = 16;
```

anotherClown.TalkAboutYourself();   "My name is _____ and I'm _____ inches tall."

```
Clown clown3 = new Clown();
clown3.Name = anotherClown.Name;
clown3.Height = oneClown.Height - 3;
```

clown3.TalkAboutYourself();   "My name is _____ and I'm _____ inches tall."

```
anotherClown.Height *= 2;
```

anotherClown.TalkAboutYourself();   "My name is _____ and I'm _____ inches tall."

Thanks for the memory

When your program creates an object, it lives in a part of the computer's memory called the **heap**. When your code creates an object with a new statement, C# immediately reserves space in the heap so it can store the data for that object.

Here's a picture of the heap before the project starts. Notice that it's empty.

Let's take a closer look at what happened here

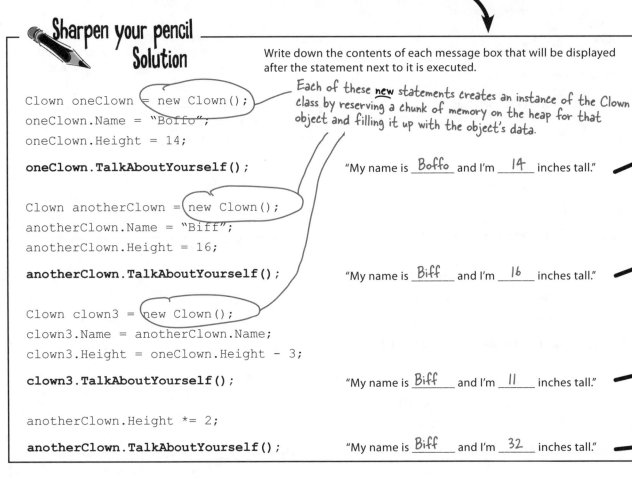

Sharpen your pencil
Solution

Write down the contents of each message box that will be displayed after the statement next to it is executed.

> *Each of these <u>new</u> statements creates an instance of the Clown class by reserving a chunk of memory on the heap for that object and filling it up with the object's data.*

```
Clown oneClown = new Clown();
oneClown.Name = "Boffo";
oneClown.Height = 14;

oneClown.TalkAboutYourself();
```
"My name is __Boffo__ and I'm __14__ inches tall."

```
Clown anotherClown = new Clown();
anotherClown.Name = "Biff";
anotherClown.Height = 16;

anotherClown.TalkAboutYourself();
```
"My name is __Biff__ and I'm __16__ inches tall."

```
Clown clown3 = new Clown();
clown3.Name = anotherClown.Name;
clown3.Height = oneClown.Height - 3;

clown3.TalkAboutYourself();
```
"My name is __Biff__ and I'm __11__ inches tall."

```
anotherClown.Height *= 2;
anotherClown.TalkAboutYourself();
```
"My name is __Biff__ and I'm __32__ inches tall."

When your program creates a new object, it gets added to the heap.

What's on your program's mind

This object is an instance of the Clown class.

Here's how your program creates a new instance of the Clown class:

```
Clown myInstance = new Clown();
```

That's actually two statements combined into one. The first statement declares a variable of type Clown (Clown myInstance;). The second statement creates a new object and assigns it to the variable that was just created (myInstance = new Clown();). Here's what the heap looks like after each of these statements:

1
```
Clown oneClown = new Clown();
oneClown.Name = "Boffo";
oneClown.Height = 14;
oneClown.TalkAboutYourself();
```
The first object is created, and its fields are set.

2
```
Clown anotherClown = new Clown();
anotherClown.Name = "Biff";
anotherClown.Height = 16;
anotherClown.TalkAboutYourself();
```
These statements create the second object and fill it with data.

3
```
Clown clown3 = new Clown();
clown3.Name = anotherClown.Name;
clown3.Height = oneClown.Height - 3;
clown3.TalkAboutYourself();
```
Then the third Clown object is created and populated.

4
```
anotherClown.Height *= 2;
anotherClown.TalkAboutYourself();
```

There's no new command, which means these statements don't create a new object. They're just modifying one that's already in memory.

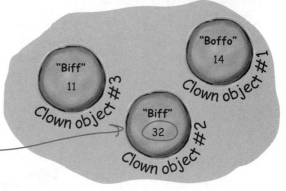

You can use class and method names to make your code intuitive

When you put code in a method, you're making a choice about how to structure your program. Do you use one method? Do you split it into more than one? Or do you even need a method at all? The choices you make about methods can make your code much more intuitive—or, if you're not careful, much more convoluted.

1 Here's a nice, compact chunk of code. It's from a control program that runs a machine that makes candy bars.

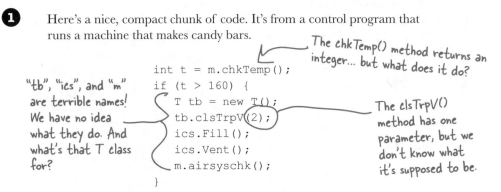

The chkTemp() method returns an integer... but what does it do?

```
int t = m.chkTemp();
if (t > 160) {
    T tb = new T();
    tb.clsTrpV(2);
    ics.Fill();
    ics.Vent();
    m.airsyschk();
}
```

"tb", "ics", and "m" are terrible names! We have no idea what they do. And what's that T class for?

The clsTrpV() method has one parameter, but we don't know what it's supposed to be.

Take a second and look at that code. Can you figure out what it does?

2 Those statements don't give you any hints about why the code's doing what it's doing. In this case, the programmer was happy with the results because she was able to get it all into one method. But making your code as compact as possible isn't really useful! Let's break it up into methods to make it easier to read, and make sure the classes are given names that make sense. But we'll start by figuring out what the code is supposed to do.

How do you figure out what your code is supposed to do? Well, all code is written for a reason. So it's up to you to figure out that reason! In this case, we can look up the page in the specification manual that the programmer followed.

> ### General Electronics Type 5 Candy Bar Maker Specification Manual
>
> The nougat temperature must be checked every 3 minutes by an automated system. If the temperature **exceeds 160°C**, the candy is too hot, and the system must **perform the candy isolation cooling system (CICS) vent procedure**.
>
> - Close the trip throttle valve on turbine #2
> - Fill the isolation cooling system with a solid stream of water
> - Vent the water
> - Verify that there is no evidence of air in the system

3 That page from the manual made it a lot easier to understand the code. It also gave us some great hints about how to make our code easier to understand. Now we know why the conditional test checks the variable **t** against 160—the manual says that any temperature above 160°C means the nougat is too hot. And it turns out that **m** was a class that controlled the candy maker, with static methods to check the nougat temperature and check the air system. So let's put the temperature check into a method, and choose names for the class and the methods that make the purpose obvious.

```
public boolean IsNougatTooHot() {
    int temp = Maker.CheckNougatTemperature();
    if (temp > 160) {
        return true;
    } else {
        return false;
    }
}
```

The IsNougatTooHot() method's return type

By naming the class "Maker" and the method "CheckNougatTemperature", the code is a lot easier to understand.

This method's return type is Boolean, which means it returns a true or false value.

4 What does the specification say to do if the nougat is too hot? It tells us to perform the candy isolation cooling system (or CICS) vent procedure. So let's make another method, and choose an obvious name for the T class (which turns out to control the turbine) and the `ics` class (which controls the isolation cooling system, and has two static methods to fill and vent the system):

```
public void DoCICSVentProcedure() {
    Turbine turbineController = new Turbine();
    turbineController.CloseTripValve(2);
    IsolationCoolingSystem.Fill();
    IsolationCoolingSystem.Vent();
    Maker.CheckAirSystem();
}
```

A void return type means the method doesn't return any value at all.

5 Now the code's a lot more intuitive! Even if you don't know that the CICS vent procedure needs to be run if the nougat is too hot, **it's a lot more obvious what this code is doing**:

```
if (IsNougatTooHot() == true) {
    DoCICSVentProcedure();
}
```

You can make your code easier to read and write by thinking about the problem your code was built to solve. If you choose names for your methods that make sense to someone who understands that problem, then your code will be a lot easier to decipher...and develop!

Give your classes a <u>natural</u> structure

Take a second and remind yourself why you want to make your methods intuitive: **because every program solves a problem or has a purpose.** It might not be a business problem—sometimes a program's purpose (like FlashyThing) is just to be cool or fun! But no matter what your program does, the more you can make your code resemble the problem you're trying to solve, the easier your program will be to write (and read, and repair, and maintain…).

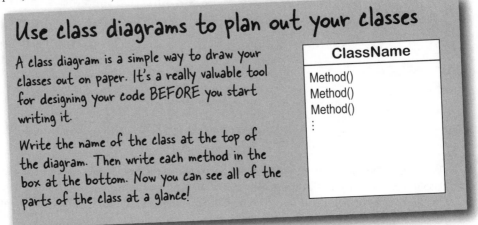

Use class diagrams to plan out your classes

A class diagram is a simple way to draw your classes out on paper. It's a really valuable tool for designing your code BEFORE you start writing it.

Write the name of the class at the top of the diagram. Then write each method in the box at the bottom. Now you can see all of the parts of the class at a glance!

ClassName
Method()
Method()
Method()
⋮

Let's build a class diagram

Take another look at the `if` statement in #5 on the previous page. You already know that statements always live inside methods, which always live inside classes, right? In this case, that `if` statement was in a method called `DoMaintenanceTests()`, which is part of the `CandyController` class. Now take a look at the code and the class diagram. See how they relate to each other?

```
class CandyController {

  public void DoMaintenanceTests() {

    ...
    if (IsNougatTooHot() == true) {
      DoCICSVentProcedure();
    }
    ...
  }

  public void DoCICSVentProcedure() ...

  public boolean IsNougatTooHot() ...

}
```

CandyController
DoMaintenanceTests()
DoCICSVentProcedure()
IsNougatTooHot()

Sharpen your pencil

The code for the candy control system we built on the previous page called three other classes. Flip back and look through the code, and fill in their class diagrams.

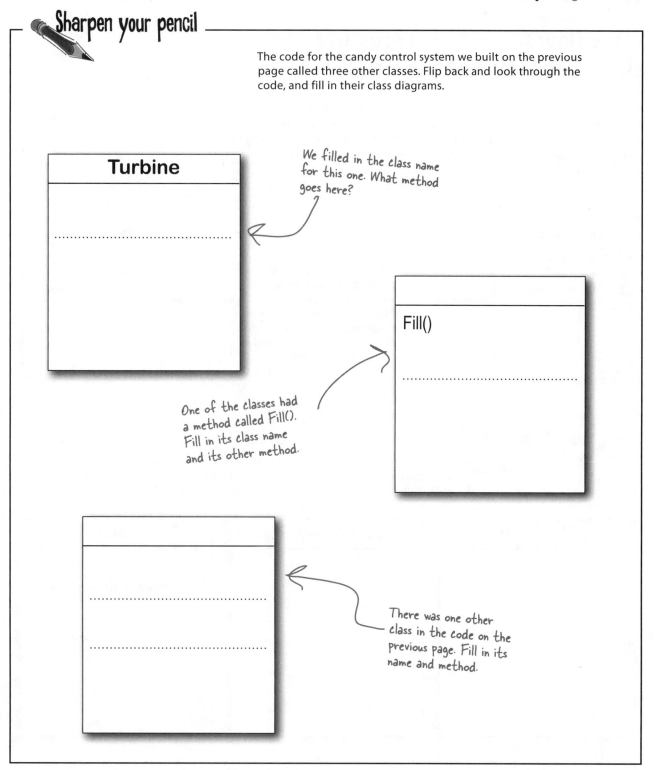

Turbine

....

We filled in the class name for this one. What method goes here?

Fill()

....

One of the classes had a method called Fill(). Fill in its class name and its other method.

....

....

There was one other class in the code on the previous page. Fill in its name and method.

Class diagrams help you organize your classes so they make sense

Writing out class diagrams makes it a lot easier to spot potential problems in your classes **before** you write code. Thinking about your classes from a high level before you get into the details can help you come up with a class structure that will make sure your code addresses the problems it solves. It lets you step back and make sure that you're not planning on writing unnecessary or poorly structured classes or methods, and that the ones you do write will be intuitive and easy to use.

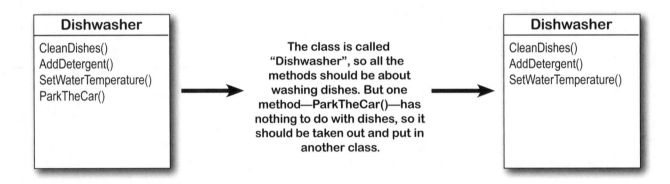

Dishwasher
CleanDishes()
AddDetergent()
SetWaterTemperature()
ParkTheCar()

The class is called "Dishwasher", so all the methods should be about washing dishes. But one method—ParkTheCar()—has nothing to do with dishes, so it should be taken out and put in another class.

Dishwasher
CleanDishes()
AddDetergent()
SetWaterTemperature()

Sharpen your pencil

Solution   The code for the candy control system we built on the previous page called three other classes. Flip back and look through the code, and fill in their class diagrams.

You could figure out that Maker is a class because it appears in front of a dot in Maker.CheckAirSystem().

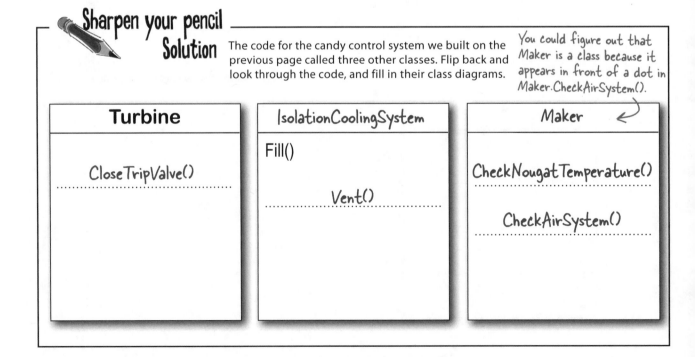

Turbine
CloseTripValve()

IsolationCoolingSystem
Fill()
Vent()

Maker
CheckNougatTemperature()
CheckAirSystem()

Sharpen your pencil

Each of these classes has a serious design flaw. Write down what you think is wrong with each class, and how you'd fix it.

Class23

CandyBarWeight()
PrintWrapper()
GenerateReport()
Go()

This class is part of the candy manufacturing system from earlier.

....

....

....

....

DeliveryGuy

AddAPizza()
PizzaDelivered()
TotalCash()
ReturnTime()

DeliveryGirl

AddAPizza()
PizzaDelivered()
TotalCash()
ReturnTime()

These two classes are part of a system that a pizza parlor uses to track the pizzas that are out for delivery.

....

....

....

....

CashRegister

MakeSale()
NoSale()
PumpGas()
Refund()
TotalCashInRegister()
GetTransactionList()
AddCash()
RemoveCash()

The CashRegister class is part of a program that's used by an automated convenience store checkout system.

....

....

....

....

Sharpen your pencil
Solution

Here's how we corrected the classes. We show just one possible way to fix the problems—but there are plenty of other ways you could design these classes depending on how they'll be used.

This class is part of the candy manufacturing system from earlier.

The class name doesn't describe what the class does. A programmer who sees a line of code that calls Class23.Go() will have no idea what that line does. We'd also rename the method to something that's more descriptive—we chose MakeTheCandy(), but it could be anything.

CandyMaker
CandyBarWeight()
PrintWrapper()
GenerateReport()
MakeTheCandy()

These two classes are part of a system that a pizza parlor uses to track the pizzas that are out for delivery.

It looks like the DeliveryGuy class and the DeliveryGirl class both do the same thing—they track a delivery person who's out delivering pizzas to customers. A better design would replace them with a single class that adds a field for gender.

DeliveryPerson
Gender
AddAPizza()
PizzaDelivered()
TotalCash()
ReturnTime()

We added the Gender field because we assumed there was a reason to track delivery guys and girls separately, and that's why there were two classes for them.

The CashRegister class is part of a program that's used by an automated convenience store checkout system.

All of the methods in the class do stuff that has to do with a cash register—making a sale, getting a list of transactions, adding cash... except for one: pumping gas. It's a good idea to pull that method out and stick it in another class.

CashRegister
MakeSale()
NoSale()
Refund()
TotalCashInRegister()
GetTransactionList()
AddCash()
RemoveCash()

```
public partial class Form1 : Form
{
  private void button1_Click(object sender, EventArgs e)
  {
    String result = "";
    Echo e1 = new Echo();

    _____

    int x = 0;
    while ( _____ ) {
      result = result + e1.Hello() + "\n";

      _____

      if ( _____ ) {
        e2.count = e2.count + 1;
      }
      if ( _____ ) {
        e2.count = e2.count + e1.count;
      }
      x = x + 1;
    }
    MessageBox.Show(result + "Count: " + e2.count);
  }

  class _____ {
    public int _____ = 0;
    public string _____ {
      return "helloooo...";
    }
  }
}
```

Póol Puzzle

Your *job* is to take code snippets from the pool and place them into the blank lines in the code. You **may** use the same snippet more than once, and you won't need to use all the snippets. Your *goal* is to make classes that will compile and run and produce the output listed.

Output

```
helloooo...
helloooo...
helloooo...
helloooo...
Count: 10
```
```
OK
```

Bonus Question!

If the last line of output was **24** instead of **10,** how would you complete the puzzle? You can do it by changing just one statement.

Note: Each snippet from the pool can be used more than once!

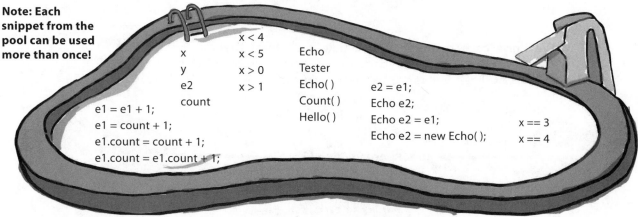

```
x < 4
x                  x < 5        Echo
y                  x > 0        Tester
e2                 x > 1        Echo()
count                           Count()      e2 = e1;
                                Hello()      Echo e2;
    e1 = e1 + 1;                             Echo e2 = e1;
    e1 = count + 1;                          Echo e2 = new Echo( );     x == 3
    e1.count = count + 1;                                               x == 4
    e1.count = e1.count + 1;
```

Answers on page 122.

working *class* *guys*

Build a class to work with some guys

Joe and Bob lend each other money all the time. Let's create a class to
keep track of them. We'll start with an overview of what we'll build.

Guy
Name
Cash
GiveCash()
ReceiveCash()

① **We'll create a Guy class and add two instances of it to a form**
The form will have two fields, one called `joe` (to keep track of the first object),
and the other called `bob` (to keep track of the second object).

The new statements
that create the two
instances live in the
code that gets run as
soon as the form is
created. Here's what
the heap looks like
after the form is
loaded.

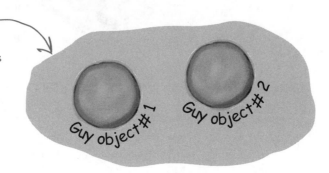

We chose names for the
methods that make sense.
You call a Guy object's
GiveCash() method to tell
him to give up some of his
cash, and his ReceiveCash()
method when you want him
to take some cash back.
We could have called them
GiveCashToSomeone() and
ReceiveCashFromSomeone(),
but that would have been
very long!

② **We'll set each Guy object's cash and name fields**
The two objects represent different guys, each with his own name and a
different amount of cash in his pocket.

Each guy has a Name
field that keeps track of
his name, and a Cash field
that has the number of
bucks in his pocket.

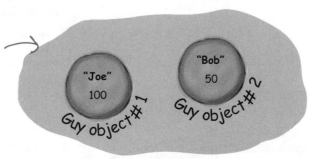

When you take an instance
of Guy and call its
ReceiveCash() method, you
pass the amount of cash
the guy will take as a
parameter. So calling joe.
ReceiveCash(25) tells Joe
to receive 25 bucks and
add them to his wallet.

③ **We'll give cash to the guys and take cash from them**
We'll use each guy's `ReceiveCash()` method to increase a guy's cash,
and we'll use his `GiveCash()` method to reduce it.

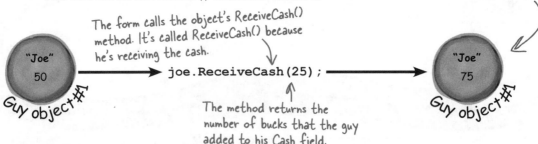

The form calls the object's ReceiveCash()
method. It's called ReceiveCash() because
he's receiving the cash.

`joe.ReceiveCash(25);`

The method returns the
number of bucks that the guy
added to his Cash field.

Create a project for your guys

Create a new Windows Forms Application project (because we'll be using a form). Then use the Solution Explorer to add a new class to it called Guy. Make sure to add "using System. Windows.Forms;" to the top of the Guy class file. Then fill in the Guy class. Here's the code for it:

Do this!

The Guy class has two fields. The Name field is a string, and it'll contain the guy's name ("Joe"). And the Cash field is an int, which will keep track of how many bucks are in his pocket.

```
class Guy {
    public string Name;
    public int Cash;

    public int GiveCash(int amount) {
        if (amount <= Cash && amount > 0) {
            Cash -= amount;
            return amount;
        } else {
            MessageBox.Show(
             "I don't have enough cash to give you " + amount,
             Name + " says...");
            return 0;
        }
    }
```

The GiveCash() method has one parameter called amount that you'll use to tell the guy how much cash to give you.

He uses an if statement to check whether he has enough cash—if he does, he takes it out of his pocket and returns it as the return value.

The Guy makes sure that you're asking him for a positive amount of cash, otherwise he'd add to his cash instead of taking away from it.

If the guy doesn't have enough cash, he'll tell you so with a message box, and then he'll make GiveCash() return 0.

```
    public int ReceiveCash(int amount) {
        if (amount > 0) {
            Cash += amount;
            return amount;
        } else {
            MessageBox.Show(amount + " isn't an amount I'll take",
                    Name + " says...");
            return 0;
        }
    }
}
```

The ReceiveCash() method works just like the GiveCash() method. It's passed an amount as a parameter, checks to make sure that amount is greater than zero, and then adds it to his cash.

If the amount was positive, then the ReceiveCash() method returns the amount added. If it was zero or negative, the guy shows a message box and then returns 0.

Be careful with your curly brackets. It's easy to have the wrong number—make sure that every opening bracket has a matching closing bracket. When they're all balanced, the IDE will **automatically indent** them for you when you type the last closing bracket.

Build a form to interact with the guys

The Guy class is great, but it's just a start. Now put together a form that uses two instances of the Guy class. It's got labels that show you their names and how much cash they have, and buttons to give and take cash from them.

Build this!

1 **Add two buttons and three labels to your form**

The top two labels show how much cash each guy has. We'll also add a field called bank to the form—the third label shows how much cash is in it. We're going to have you name some of the labels that you drag onto the forms. You can do that by **clicking on each label** that you want to name and **changing its "(Name)" row** in the Properties window. That'll make your code a lot easier to read, because you'll be able to use "joesCashLabel" and "bobsCashLabel" instead of "label1" and "label2".

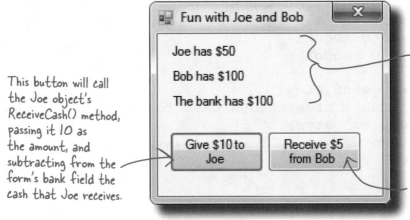

This button will call the Joe object's ReceiveCash() method, passing it 10 as the amount, and subtracting from the form's bank field the cash that Joe receives.

Name the top label joesCashLabel, the label underneath it bobsCashLabel, and the bottom label bankCashLabel. You can leave their Text properties alone; we'll add a method to the form to set them.

This button will call the Bob object's GiveCash() method, passing it 5 as the amount, and adding the cash that Bob gives to the form's bank field.

2 **Add fields to your form**

Your form will need to keep track of the two guys, so you'll need a field for each of them. Call them joe and bob. Then add a field to the form called bank to keep track of how much money the form has to give to and receive from the guys.

```
namespace Your_Project_Name {
    public partial class Form1 : Form {

        Guy joe;
        Guy bob;
        int bank = 100;

        public Form1() {
            InitializeComponent();
        }
}
```

Since we're using Guy objects to keep track of Joe and Bob, you declare their fields in the form using the Guy class.

The amount of cash in the form's bank field goes up and down depending on how much money the form gave to and received from the Guy objects.

③ Add a method to the form to update the labels

The labels on the right-hand side of the form show how much cash each guy has and how much is in the bank field. So add the UpdateForm() method to keep them up to date—**make sure the return type is void** to tell C# that the method doesn't return a value. Type this method into the form right underneath where you added the bank field:

```
public void UpdateForm() {
    joesCashLabel.Text = joe.Name + " has $" + joe.Cash;
    bobsCashLabel.Text = bob.Name + " has $" + bob.Cash;
    bankCashLabel.Text = "The bank has $" + bank;
}
```

Notice how the labels are updated using the Guy objects' Name and Cash fields.

This new method is simple. It just updates the three labels by setting their Text properties. You'll have each button call it to keep the labels up to date.

④ Double-click on each button and add the code to interact with the objects

Make sure the left-hand button is called button1, and the right-hand button is called button2. Then double-click each of the buttons—when you do, the IDE will add two methods called button1_Click() and button2_Click() to the form. Add this code to each of them:

```
private void button1_Click(object sender, EventArgs e) {
    if (bank >= 10) {
        bank -= joe.ReceiveCash(10);
        UpdateForm();
    } else {
        MessageBox.Show("The bank is out of money.");
    }
}
```

When the user clicks the "Give $10 to Joe" button, the form calls the Joe object's ReceiveCash() method—but only if the bank has enough money.

The bank needs at least $10 to give to Joe. If there's not enough, it'll pop up this message box.

```
private void button2_Click(object sender, EventArgs e) {
    bank += bob.GiveCash(5);
    UpdateForm();
}
```

The "Receive $5 from Bob" button doesn't need to check how much is in the bank, because it'll just add whatever Bob gives back.

If Bob's out of money, GiveCash() will return zero.

---

⑤ Start Joe out with $50 and start Bob out with $100

It's up to you to **figure out how to get Joe and Bob to start out with their Cash and Name fields set properly.** Put it right underneath InitializeComponent() in the form. That's part of that designer-generated method that gets run once, when the form is first initialized. Once you've done that, click both buttons a number of times—make sure that one button takes $10 from the bank and adds it to Joe, and the other takes $5 from Bob and adds it to the bank.

```
public Form1() {
    InitializeComponent();
    // Initialize joe and bob here!
}
```

Add the lines of code here to create the two objects and set their Name and Cash fields.

Exercise

Exercise Solution

It's up to you to **figure out how to get Joe and Bob to start out with their Cash and Name fields set properly.** Put it right underneath InitializeComponent() in the form.

```
public Form1() {
        InitializeComponent();
```

Here's where we set up the first instance of Guy. The first line creates the object, and the next two set its fields.

```
        bob = new Guy();
        bob.Name = "Bob";
        bob.Cash = 100;

        joe = new Guy();
        joe.Name = "Joe";
        joe.Cash = 50;
```

Then we do the same for the second instance of the Guy class.

Make sure you call UpdateForm() so the labels look right when the form first pops up.

```
        UpdateForm();
}
```

there are no Dumb Questions

Make sure you save the project now—we'll come back to it in a few pages.

Q: Why doesn't the solution start with "Guy bob = new Guy()"? Why did you leave off the first "Guy"?

A: Because you already declared the bob field at the top of the form. Remember how the statement "int i = 5;" is the same as the two statements "int i" and "i = 5;"? This is the same thing. You could try to declare the bob field in one line like this: "Guy bob = new Guy();". But you already have the first part of that statement ("Guy bob;") at the top of your form. So you only need the second half of the line, the part that sets the bob field to create a new instance of Guy().

Q: OK, so then why not get rid of the "Guy bob;" line at the top of the form?

A: Then a variable called bob will only exist inside that special "public Form1()" method. When you declare a variable inside a method, it's only valid inside the method—you can't access it from any other method. But when you declare it outside of your method but inside the form or a class that you added, then you've added a field accessible from *any other method* inside the form.

Q: What happens if I don't leave off that first "Guy"?

A: You'll run into problems—your form won't work, because it won't ever set the form's bob variable. Think about it for a minute, and you'll see why it works that way. If you have this code at the top of your form:

```
public partial class Form1 : Form {
    Guy bob;
```

and then you have this code later on, inside a method:

```
Guy bob = new Guy();
```

then you've declared *two* variables. It's a little confusing, because they both have the same name. But one of them is valid throughout the entire form, and the other one—the new one you added—is only valid inside the method. The next line (bob.Name = "Bob";) only updates that *local* variable, and doesn't touch the one in the form. So when you try to run your code, it'll give you a nasty error message ("NullReferenceException not handled"), which just means you tried to use an object before you created it with new.

There's an easier way to initialize objects

Almost every object that you create needs to be initialized in some way. And the Guy object is no exception—it's useless until you set its Name and Cash fields. It's so common to have to initialize fields that C# gives you a shortcut for doing it called an **object initializer**. And the IDE's IntelliSense will help you do it.

> **Object intializers save you time and make your code more compact and easier to read...and the IDE helps you write them.**

1 Here's the original code that you wrote to initialize Joe's Guy object.

```
joe = new Guy();
joe.Name = "Joe";
joe.Cash = 50;
```

2 Delete the second two lines and the semicolon after "Guy ()," and add a right curly bracket.

```
joe = new Guy() {
```

3 Press space. As soon as you do, the IDE pops up an IntelliSense window that shows you all of the fields that you're able to initialize.

```
joe = new Guy() {
```

4 Press tab to tell it to add the Cash field. Then set it equal to 50.

```
joe = new Guy() { Cash = 50
```

5 Type in a comma. As soon as you do, the other field shows up.

```
joe = new Guy() { Cash = 50,
```

5 Finish the object initializer. Now you've saved yourself two lines of code!

```
joe = new Guy() { Cash = 50, Name = "Joe" };
```

This new declaration does exactly the same thing as the three lines of code you wrote originally. It's just shorter and easier to read.

A few ideas for designing intuitive classes

* **You're building your program to solve a problem.**
  Spend some time thinking about that problem. Does it break down into pieces easily? How would you explain that problem to someone else? These are good things to think about when designing your classes.

  It'd be great if I could compare a few routes and figure out which is fastest....

* **What real-world things will your program use?**
  A program to help a zoo keeper track her animals' feeding schedules might have classes for different kinds of food and types of animals.

ROAD CLOSED
CHEMIN FERMÉ

* **Use descriptive names for classes and methods.**
  Someone should be able to figure out what your classes and methods do just by looking at their names.

  myInst
  obj Object

  bestRoute
  Navigator object

* **Look for similarities between classes.**
  Sometimes two classes can be combined into one if they're really similar. The candy manufacturing system might have three or four turbines, but there's only one method for closing the trip valve that takes the turbine number as a parameter.

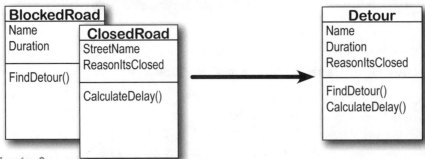

BlockedRoad
Name
Duration
FindDetour()

ClosedRoad
StreetName
ReasonItsClosed
CalculateDelay()

Detour
Name
Duration
ReasonItsClosed
FindDetour()
CalculateDelay()

Exercise

Add buttons to the "Fun with Joe and Bob" program to make the guys give each other cash.

1 Use an object initializer to initialize Bob's instance of Guy
You've already done it with Joe. Now make Bob's instance work with an object initializer too.

If you already clicked the button, just delete it, add it back to your form, and rename it. Then delete the old button3_Click() method that the IDE added before, and use the new method it adds now.

2 Add two more buttons to your form
The first button tells Joe to give 10 bucks to Bob, and the second tells Bob to give 5 bucks back to Joe. **Before you double-click on the button,** go to the Properties window and change each button's name using the "(Name)" row—it's **at the top** of the list of properties. Name the first button **joeGivesToBob**, and the second one **bobGivesToJoe**.

This button tells Joe to give 10 bucks to Bob, so you should use the "(Name)" row in the Properties window to name it joeGivesToBob.

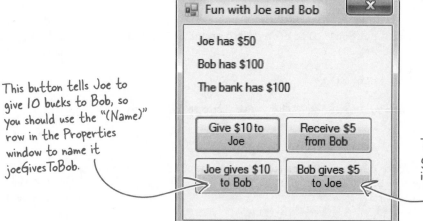

This button tells Bob to give 5 bucks to Joe. Name it bobGivesToJoe.

3 Make the buttons work
Double-click on the joeGivesToBob button in the designer. The IDE will add a method to the form called joeGivesToBob_Click() that gets run any time the button's clicked. Fill in that method to make Joe give 10 bucks to Bob. Then double-click on the other button and fill in the new bobGivesToJoe_Click() method that the IDE creates so that Bob gives 5 bucks to Joe. Make sure the form updates itself after the cash changes hands.

Exercise Solution

Add buttons to the "Fun with Joe and Bob" program to make the guys give each other cash.

```
public partial class Form1 : Form {
    Guy joe;
    Guy bob;
    int bank = 100;

    public Form1() {
        InitializeComponent();
        bob = new Guy() { Cash = 100, Name = "Bob" };
        joe = new Guy() { Cash = 50, Name = "Joe" };
        UpdateForm();
    }

    public void UpdateForm() {
        joesCashLabel.Text = joe.Name + " has $" + joe.Cash;
        bobsCashLabel.Text = bob.Name + " has $" + bob.Cash;
        bankCashLabel.Text = "The bank has $" + bank;
    }

    private void button1_Click(object sender, EventArgs e) {
        if (bank >= 10) {
            bank -= joe.ReceiveCash(10);
            UpdateForm();
        } else {
            MessageBox.Show("The bank is out of money.");
        }
    }

    private void button2_Click(object sender, EventArgs e) {
        bank += bob.GiveCash(5);
        UpdateForm();
    }

    private void joeGivesToBob_Click(object sender, EventArgs e) {
        bob.ReceiveCash(joe.GiveCash(10));
        UpdateForm();
    }

    private void bobGivesToJoe_Click(object sender, EventArgs e) {
        joe.ReceiveCash(bob.GiveCash(5));
        UpdateForm();
    }

}
```

Here are the object initializers for the two instances of the Guy class. Bob gets initialized with 100 bucks and his name.

To make Joe give cash to Bob, we call Joe's GiveCash() method and send its results into Bob's ReceiveCash() method.

Take a close look at how the Guy methods are being called. The results returned by GiveCash() are pumped right into ReceiveCash() as its parameter.

The trick here is thinking through who's giving the cash and who's receiving it.

Before you go on, take a minute and flip to #1 in the "Leftovers" appendix, because there's some basic syntax that we haven't covered yet. You won't *need* it to move forward, but it's a good idea to see what's there.

Objectcross

It's time to give your left brain a break, and put that right brain to work: all the words are object-related and from this chapter.

Across

2. If a method's return type is _____, it doesn't return anything

7. An object's fields define its _____

9. A good method _____ makes it clear what the method does

10. Where objects live

11. What you use to build an object

13. What you use to pass information into a method

14. The statement you use to create an object

15. Used to set an attribute on controls and other classes

Down

1. This form control lets the user choose a number from a range you set

3. It's a great idea to create a class _____ on paper before you start writing code

4. An object uses this to keep track of what it knows

5. These define what an object does

6. An object's methods define its _____

7. Don't use this keyword in your class declaration if you want to be able to create instances of it

8. An object is an _____ of a class

12. This statement tells a method to immediately exit, and can specify the value that should be passed back to the statement that called the method

Pool Puzzle Solution

Your *job* was to take code snippets from the pool and place them into the blank lines in the code. Your *goal* was to make classes that will compile and run and produce the output listed.

```
public partial class Form1 : Form
{
  private void button1_Click(object sender, EventArgs e)
  {
    String result = "";
    Echo e1 = new Echo();
    Echo e2 = new Echo();
    int x = 0;
    while (     x < 4     ) {
      result = result + e1.Hello() + "\n";
      e1.count = e1.count + 1;
      if (     x == 3     ) {
        e2.count = e2.count + 1;
      }
      if (     x > 0     ) {
        e2.count = e2.count + e1.count;
      }
      x = x + 1;
    }
    MessageBox.Show(result + "Count: " + e2.count);
  }

  class     Echo     {
    public int  count     = 0;
    public string  Hello()     {
      return "helloooo...";
    }
  }
}
```

> That's the correct answer.
> And here's the bonus answer!
> Echo e2 = e1;

Objectcross Solution

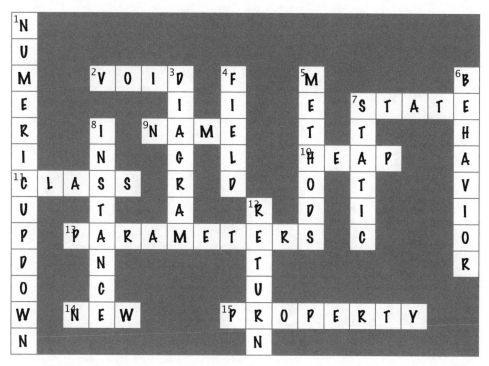

4 types and references

It's 10:00.
Do you know where your data is?

This data just got garbage collected.

Data type, database, Lieutenant Commander Data...
it's all important stuff. Without data, your programs are useless. You need **information** from your users, and you use that to look up or produce new information to give back to them. In fact, almost everything you do in programming involves **working with data** in one way or another. In this chapter, you'll learn the ins and outs of C#'s **data types**, see how to work with data in your program, and even figure out a few dirty secrets about **objects** (*pssst...objects are data, too*).

The variable's type determines what kind of data it can store

There are a bunch of **types** built into C#, and each one stores a different kind of data. You've already seen some of the most common ones, and you know how to use them. But there are a few that you haven't seen, and they can really come in handy, too.

Types you'll use all the time

It shouldn't come as a surprise that `int`, `string`, `bool`, and `double` are the most common types.

★ `int` can store any **whole** number from −2,147,483,648 to 2,147,483,647.

A whole number doesn't have a decimal point.

★ `string` can hold text of any length (including the empty string `""`).

★ `bool` is a Boolean value—it's either `true` or `false`.

★ `double` can store **real** numbers from $\pm 5.0 \times 10^{-324}$ to $\pm 1.7 \times 10^{308}$ with up to 16 significant figures. That range looks weird and complicated, but it's actually pretty simple. The "significant figures" part means the *precision* of the number: 35,048,410,000,000, 1,743,059, 14.43857, and 0.00004374155 all have seven significant figures. The 10^{308} thing means that you can store any number as large as 10^{308} (or 1 followed by 308 zeroes)—as long as it only has 16 or fewer significant figures. On the other end of the range, 10^{-324} means that you can store any number as small as 10^{-324} (or a decimal point followed by 324 zeroes followed by 1)… but, you guessed it, as long as it only has 16 or fewer significant figures.

"float" is short for "floating point"—as opposed to a "fixed point" number, which always has the same number of decimal places.

More types for whole numbers

Once upon a time, computer memory was really expensive, and processors were really slow. And, believe it or not, if you used the wrong type, it could seriously slow down your program. Luckily, times have changed, and most of the time if you need to store a whole number you can just use an `int`. But sometimes you really need something bigger… and once in a while, you need something smaller, too. That's why C# gives you more options:

A lot of times, if you're using these types it's because you're solving a problem where it really helps to have the "wrapping around" effect that you'll read about in a few minutes.

★ `byte` can store any **whole** number between 0 and 255.

★ `sbyte` can store any **whole** number from −128 to 127

★ `short` can store any **whole** number from −32,768 to 32,767.

★ `ushort` can store any **whole** number from 0 to 65,535.

The "u" stands for "unsigned"

★ `uint` can store any **whole** number from 0 to 4,294,967,295.

★ `long` can store any **whole** number between minus and plus 9 billion billion.

★ `ulong` can store any **whole** number between 0 and about 18 billion billion.

The "s" in sbyte stands for "signed" which means it can be negative (the "sign" is a minus sign).

Types for storing *really* **HUGE** and *really* tiny **numbers**

Sometimes 7 significant figures just isn't precise enough. And, believe it or not, sometimes 10^{38} isn't big enough and 10^{-45} isn't small enough. A lot of programs written for finance or scientific research run into these problems all the time, so C# gives us two more types:

When your program needs to deal with currency, you usually want to use a decimal to store the number.

★ float can store any number from $\pm1.5. \times 10^{-45}$ to $\pm3.4 \times 10^{38}$ with 7 significant digits.

★ decimal can store any number from $\pm1.0 \times 10^{-28}$ to $\pm7.9 \times 10^{28}$ with 28–29 significant digits.

A "literal" just means a number that you type into your code. So when you type "int i = 5;", the 5 is a literal.

When you used the Value property in your numericUpDown control, you were using a decimal.

Literals have types, too

When you type a number directly into your C# program, you're using a **literal**... and every literal is automatically assigned a type. You can see this for yourself—just enter this line of code that assigns the literal 14.7 to an int variable:

```
int myInt = 14.7;
```

Now try to build the program. You'll get this: ——————

	Description
⊗ 1	Cannot implicitly convert type 'double' to 'int'. An explicit conversion exists (are you missing a cast?)

That's the same error you'll get if you try to set an int equal to a double variable. What the IDE is telling you is that the literal 14.7 has a type—it's a double. You can change its type to a float by sticking an F on the end (14.7F). And 14.7M is a decimal.

The "M" stands for "money"—seriously!

If you try to assign a float literal to a double or a decimal literal to a float, the IDE will give you a helpful message reminding you to add the right suffix. Cool!

A few more useful built-in types

Sometimes you need to store a single character like Q or 7 or $, and when you do you'll use the char type. Literal values for char are always inside single quotes ('x', '3'). You can include **escape sequences** in the quotes, too ('\n' is a line **break**, '\t' is a tab). You write an escape sequence in your C# code using two characters, but your program stores each escape sequence as a single character in memory.

And finally, there's one more important type: **object**. You've already seen how you can create objects by creating instances of classes. Well, every one of those objects can be assigned to an object variable. You'll learn all about how objects and variables that refer to objects work later in this chapter.

You'll learn a lot more about how char and byte relate to each other in Chapter 9.

BRAIN POWER

Windows 7 has a really neat feature in Calculator called "Programmer" mode, where you can see binary and decimal at the same time!

You can use the Windows calculator to convert between decimal (normal, base-10) numbers and binary numbers (base-2 numbers written with only ones and zeroes)—put it in Scientific mode, enter a number, and click the **Bin** radio button to convert to binary. Then click **Dec** to convert it back. Now **enter some of the upper and lower limits for the whole number types** (like −32,768 and 255) and convert them to binary. Can you figure out *why* C# gives you those particular limits?

A variable is like a data to-go cup

All of your data takes up space in memory. (Remember the heap from last chapter?) So part of your job is to think about how *much* space you're going to need whenever you use a string or a number in your program. That's one of the reasons you use variables. They let you set aside enough space in memory to store your data.

Not all data ends up on the heap. Value types usually keep their data in another part of memory called the stack. You'll learn all about that in Chapter 14.

Think of a variable like a cup that you keep your data in. C# uses a bunch of different kinds of cups to hold different kinds of data. And just like the different sizes of cups at the coffee shop, there are different sizes of variables, too.

int is commonly used for whole numbers. It holds numbers up to 2,147,483,647.

A short will hold whole numbers up to 32,767.

You'll use long for whole numbers that are going to be really big.

byte holds numbers between zero and 255.

long	int	short	byte
64	32	16	8

These are the number of bits of memory set aside for the variable when you declare it.

Numbers that have decimal places are stored differently than whole numbers. You can handle most of your numbers that have decimal places using `float`, the smallest data type that stores decimals. If you need to be more precise, use a `double`. And if you're writing a financial application where you'll be storing currency values, you'll want to use the `decimal` type.

float	double	decimal
32	64	128

These types are for fractions. Larger variables store more decimal places.

It's not always about numbers, though. (You wouldn't expect to get hot coffee in a plastic cup or cold coffee in a paper one.) The C# compiler also can handle characters and non-numeric types. The `char` type holds one character, and `string` is used for lots of characters "strung" together. There's no set size for a `string` object, either. It expands to hold as much data as you need to store in it. The `bool` data type is used to store true or false values, like the ones you've used for your `if` statements.

bool	char	string
8	16	depends on the size of the string

10 pounds of data in a 5 pound bag

When you declare your variable as one type, that's how your compiler looks at it. Even if the value is nowhere near the upper boundary of the type you've declared, the compiler will see the cup it's in, not the number inside. So this won't work:

```
int leaguesUnderTheSea = 20000;

short smallerLeagues = leaguesUnderTheSea;
```

20,000 would fit into a `short`, no problem. But since `leaguesUnderTheSea` is declared as an `int`, the compiler sees it as `int`-sized and considers it too big to put in a `short` container. The compiler won't make those translations for you on the fly. You need to make sure that you're using the right type for the data you're working with.

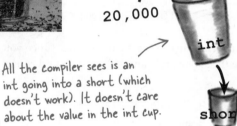

20,000

int

short

All the compiler sees is an int going into a short (which doesn't work). It doesn't care about the value in the int cup.

This makes sense. What if you later put a larger value in the int cup, one that wouldn't fit into the short cup? The compiler is trying to protect you.

Sharpen your pencil

Three of these statements won't compile, either because they're trying to cram too much data into a small variable or because they're putting the wrong type of data in. Circle them.

```
int hours = 24;                    string taunt = "your mother";

short y = 78000;                   byte days = 365;

bool isDone = yes;                 long radius = 3;

short RPM = 33;                    char initial = 'S';

int balance = 345667 - 567;        string months = "12";
```

Even when a number is the right size, you can't just assign it to any variable

Let's see what happens when you try to assign a decimal value to an int variable.

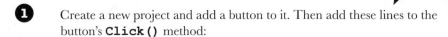
Do this

1 Create a new project and add a button to it. Then add these lines to the button's **Click()** method:

```
decimal myDecimalValue = 10;
int myIntValue = myDecimalValue;

MessageBox.Show("The myIntValue is " + myIntValue);
```

2 Try building your program. Uh oh—you got an error that looks like this:

Error List

⊗ 1 Error ⚠ 0 Warnings ⓘ 0 Messages

Description

⊗ 1 Cannot implicitly convert type 'decimal' to 'int'. An explicit conversion exists (are you missing a cast?)

Check out how the IDE figured out that you were probably missing a cast.

3 Make the error go away by **casting** the decimal to an int. Once you change the second line so it looks like this, your program will compile and run:

```
int myIntValue = (int) myDecimalValue;
```
Here's where you **cast** the decimal value to an int.

So what happened?

The compiler won't let you assign a value to a variable if it's the wrong type—even if that variable can hold the value just fine—because that's the underlying cause behind an enormous number of bugs. When you use casting, you're essentially making a promise to the compiler that you know the types are different, and that in this particular instance it's OK for C# to cram the data into the new variable.

Take a minute to flip back to the beginning of the last chapter and check out how you used casting when you passed the NumericUpDown.Value to the Talker Tester form.

Sharpen your pencil
Solution

Three of these statements won't compile, either because they're trying to cram too much data into a small variable or because they're putting the wrong type of data in. Circle them.

short y = 78000;

The short type holds numbers from −32,767 to 32,768. This number's too big!

byte days = 365;

A byte can only hold a value of up to 256. You'll need a short for this.

bool isDone = yes;

You can only assign a value of "true" or "false" to a bool.

When you cast a value that's too big, C# will adjust it automatically

You've already seen that a `decimal` can be cast to an `int`. It turns out that *any* number can be cast to *any other* number. But that doesn't mean the **value** stays intact through the casting. If you cast an `int` variable that's set to 365 to a `byte` variable, 365 is too big for the **byte**. But instead of giving you an error, the value will just **wrap around**: for example, 256 cast to a `byte` will have a value of 0. 257 would be converted to 1, 258 to 2, etc., up to 365, which will end up being **109**. And once you get back to 255 again, the conversion value "wraps" back to zero.

> Hey, I've been combining numbers and strings in my message boxes since I learned about loops in Chapter 2! Have I been converting types all along?

Yes! The + operator converts for you.

What you've been doing is using the + operator, which **does a lot of converting for you automatically**—but it's especially smart about it. When you use + to add a number or Boolean to a string, then it'll automatically convert that value to a string, too. If you use + (or *, /, or −) with two different types, it **automatically converts the smaller type to the bigger one**. Here's an example:

```
int myInt = 36;
double myFloat = 16.4D;
myFloat = myInt + myFloat;
```

Since an `int` can fit into a `float` but a `float` can't fit into an `int`, the + operator converts `myInt` to a `float` before adding it to `myFloat`.

When you're assigning a number value to a double, you need to add a D to the end of the number to tell the compiler that it's a float, and not a double.

Wrap it yourself!

There's no mystery to how casting "wraps" the numbers—you can do it yourself. Just pop up the Windows calculator, switch it to Scientific mode, and calculate 365 Mod 256 (using the "Mod" button, which does a modulo calculation). You'll get 109.

Sharpen your pencil

You can't always cast any type to any other type. Create a new project, drag a button onto a form, double-click on it, and type these statements in. Then build your program—it will give lots of errors. Cross out the ones that give errors. That'll help you figure out which types can be cast, and which can't!

```
int myInt = 10;
byte myByte = (byte)myInt;
double myDouble = (double)myByte;
bool myBool = (bool)myDouble;
string myString = "false";
myBool = (bool)myString;
myString = (string)myInt;
myString = myInt.ToString();
myBool = (bool)myByte;
myByte = (byte)myBool;
short myShort = (short)myInt;
char myChar = 'x';
myString = (string)myChar;
long myLong = (long)myInt;
decimal myDecimal = (decimal)myLong;
myString = myString + myInt + myByte
+ myDouble + myChar;
```

C# does some casting automatically

There are two important conversions that don't require you to do the casting. The first is done automatically any time you use arithmetic operators, like in this example:

```
long l = 139401930;

short s = 516;

double d = l - s;

d = d / 123.456;

MessageBox.Show("The answer is " + d);
```

The — operator subtracted the short from the long, and the = operator converted the result to a double.

When you use + it's smart enough to convert the decimal to a string.

The other way C# converts types for you automatically is when you use the + operator to **concatenate** strings (which just means sticking one string on the end of another, like you've been doing with message boxes). When you use + to concatenate a string with something that's another type, it automatically converts the numbers to strings for you. Here's an example. The first two lines are fine, but the third one won't compile.

```
long x = 139401930;

MessageBox.Show("The answer is " + x);

MessageBox.Show(x);
```

The C# compiler spits out an error that mentions something about invalid arguments (an argument is what C# calls the value that you're passing into a method's parameter). That's because the parameter for MessageBox.Show() is a string, and this code passed a long, which is the wrong type for the method. But you can convert it to a string really easily by calling its ToString() method. That method is a member of every value type and object. (All of the classes you build yourself have a ToString() method that returns the class name.) That's how you can convert x to something that MessageBox.Show() can use:

```
MessageBox.Show(x.ToString());
```

Sharpen your pencil Solution

You can't always cast any type to any other type. Create a new project, drag a button onto a form, and type these statements into its method. Then build your program—it will give lots of errors. Cross out the ones that give errors. That'll help you figure out which types can be cast, and which can't!

```
int myInt = 10;

byte myByte = (byte)myInt;

double myDouble = (double)myByte;

bool myBool = (bool)myDouble;

string myString = "false";

myBool = (bool)myString;

myString = (string)myInt;

myString = myInt.ToString();

myBool = (bool)myByte;

myByte = (byte)myBool;

short myShort = (short)myInt;

char myChar = 'x';

myString = (string)myChar;

long myLong = (long)myInt;

decimal myDecimal = (decimal)myLong;

myString = myString + myInt + myByte
+ myDouble + myChar;
```

When you call a method, the arguments must be compatible with the types of the parameters ←

A parameter is what you define in your method. An argument is what you pass to it. A method with an int parameter can take a byte argument.

Try calling `MessageBox.Show(123)`—passing `MessageBox.Show()` a literal (123) instead of a string. The IDE won't let you build your program. Instead, it'll show you an error in the IDE: "Argument '1': cannot convert from 'int' to 'string'." Sometimes C# can do the conversion automatically—like if your method expects an `int`, but you pass it a `short`—but it can't do that for `int`s and `string`s.

But `MessageBox.Show()` isn't the only method that will give you compiler errors if you try to pass it a variable whose type doesn't match the parameter. *All* methods will do that, even the ones you write yourself. Go ahead and try typing this completely valid method into a class:

```
public int MyMethod(bool yesNo) {

    if (yesNo) {
        return 45;
    } else {
        return 61;
    }

}
```

One reminder—the code that calls this parameter doesn't have to pass it a variable called yesNo. It just has to pass it a Boolean value or variable. The only place it's called yesNo is inside the method's code.

It works just fine if you pass it what it expects (a `bool`)—call `MyMethod(true)` or `MyMethod(false)`, and it compiles just fine.

But what happens if you pass it an integer or a string instead? The IDE gives you a similar error to the one that you got when you passed 123 to `MessageBox.Show()`. Now try passing it a Boolean, but assigning the return value to a string or passing it on to `MessageBox.Show()`. That won't work, either—the method returns an `int`, not a `long` or the `string` that `MessageBox.Show()` expects.

When the compiler gives you an "invalid arguments" error, it means that you tried to call a method with variables whose types didn't match the method's parameters.

You can assign anything to a variable, parameter, or field with the type object.

if statements always test to see if something's true

Did you notice how we wrote our if statement like this:

    if (yesNo) {

We didn't have to explicitly say "if (yesNo == true)". That's because an if statement always checks if something's true. You check if something's false using ! (an exclamation point, or the NOT operator). "if (!yesNo)" is the same thing as "if (yesNo == false)". In our code examples from now on, you'll usually just see us do "if (yesNo)" or "if (!yesNo)", and not explicitly check to see if a Boolean is true or false.

Exercise

Actually, C# does give you a way to use reserved keywords as variable names, by putting @ in front of the keyword. You can do that with non-reserved names too, if you want to.

There are about 77 **reserved words** in C#. These are words reserved by the C# compiler; you can't use them for variable names. You'll know a lot of them really well by the time you finish the book. Here are some you've already used. Write down what you think these words do in C#.

namespace

for

class

public

else

new

using

if

while

⟶ Answers on page 164.

Exercise

Create a reimbursement calculator for a business trip. It should allow the user to enter a starting and ending mileage reading from the car's odometer. From those two numbers, it will calculate how many miles she's traveled and figure out how much she should be reimbursed if her company pays her $.39 for every mile she puts on her car.

1 **Start with a new Windows project.**
Make the form look like this:

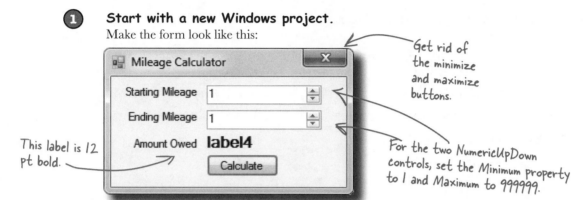

Get rid of the minimize and maximize buttons.

This label is 12 pt bold.

For the two NumericUpDown controls, set the Minimum property to 1 and Maximum to 999999.

When you're done with the form, double-click on the button to add some code to the project.

2 **Create the variables you'll need for the calculator.**
Put the variables in the class definition at the top of Form1. You need two whole number variables to track the starting odometer reading and the ending odometer reading. Call them startingMileage and endingMileage. You need three numbers that can hold decimal places. Make them doubles and call them milesTraveled, reimburseRate, and amountOwed. Set the value for reimburseRate to .39.

3 **Make your calculator work.**
Add code in the button1_Click() method to:

★ Make sure that the number in the Starting Mileage field is smaller than the number in the Ending Mileage field. If not, show a message box that says "The starting mileage must be less than the ending mileage". Make the title for the message box "Cannot Calculate".

★ Subtract the starting number from the ending number and then multiply it by the reimburse rate using these lines:

```
milesTraveled = endingMileage -= startingMileage;

amountOwed = milesTraveled *= reimburseRate;

label4.Text = "$" + amountOwed;
```

4 **Run it.**
Make sure it's giving the right numbers. Try changing the starting value to be higher than the ending value and make sure it's giving you the message box.

You were asked to create a reimbursement calculator for a business trip. Here's the code for the first part of the exercise.

```
public partial class Form1 : Form
{
    int startingMileage;
    int endingMileage;
    double milesTraveled;
    double reimburseRate = .39;
    double amountOwed;
    public Form1() {
        InitializeComponent();
    }
    private void button1_Click(object sender, EventArgs e){
        startingMileage = (int) numericUpDown1.Value;
        endingMileage = (int)numericUpDown2.Value;
        if (startingMileage <= endingMileage){
            milesTraveled = endingMileage -= startingMileage;
            amountOwed = milesTraveled *= reimburseRate;
            label4.Text = "$" + amountOwed;
        } else {
            MessageBox.Show(
        "The starting mileage must be less than the ending mileage",
                        "Cannot Calculate Mileage");
        }
    }
}
```

int works great for whole numbers. This number could go all the way up to 999,999. So a `short` or a `byte` won't cut it.

Did you remember that you have to change the `decimal` value from the numericUpDown control to an `int`?

This block is supposed to figure out how many miles were traveled and then multiply them by the reimbursement rate.

We used an alternate way of calling the MessageBox. Show() method here. We gave it two parameters: the first one is the message to display, and the second one goes in the title bar.

This button seems to work, but it has a pretty big problem. Can you spot it?

1 **Now add another button to the form.**

Let's track down that problem by adding a button to your form that shows the value of the milesTraveled field. (You could also use the debugger for this!)

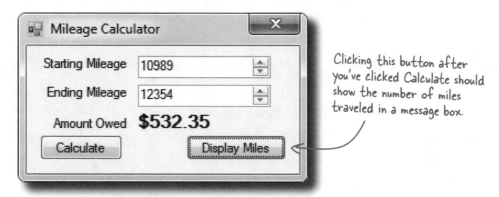

Clicking this button after you've clicked Calculate should show the number of miles traveled in a message box.

When you're done with the form, double-click on the Display Miles button to add some code to the project.

2 **One line should do it.**

All we need to do is get the form to display the milesTraveled variable, right? So this line should do that:

```
private void button2_Click(object sender, EventArgs e) {

        Messagebox.Show(milesTraveled + " miles", "Miles Traveled");

}
```

3 **Run it.**

Type in some values and see what happens. First enter a starting mileage and ending mileage, and click the Calculate button. Then click the Display Miles button to see what's stored in the milesTraveled field.

4 **Um, something's not right...**

No matter what numbers you use, the number of miles always matches the amount owed. Why?

Combining = with an operator

Take a good look at the operator we used to subtract ending mileage from starting mileage (-=). The problem is it doesn't just subtract, it also assigns a value to the variable on the left side of the subtraction sign. The same thing happens in the line where we multiply number of miles traveled by the reimbursement rate. We should replace the -= and the *= with just - and *:

```
private void button1_Click(object sender, EventArgs e)
{
    startingMileage = (int) numericUpDown1.Value;

    endingMileage = (int)numericUpDown2.Value;

    if (startingMileage <= endingMileage){

        milesTraveled = endingMileage -= startingMileage;

        amountOwed = milesTraveled *= reimburseRate;

        label4.Text = "$" + amountOwed;

    } else {

        MessageBox.Show("The starting mileage number must
                        be less than the ending mileage number",
                        "Cannot Calculate Mileage");

    }
```

These are called compound operators. This one subtracts startingMileage from endingMileage but also assigns the new value to endingMileage and milesTraveled at the same time.

This is better—now your code won't modify endingMileage and milesTraveled.

```
milesTraveled = endingMileage - startingMileage;

amountOwed = milesTraveled * reimburseRate;
```

So can good variable names help you out here? Definitely! Take a close look at what each variable is supposed to do. You already get a lot of clues from the name milesTraveled—you know that's the variable that the form is displaying incorrectly, and you've got a good idea of how that value ought to be calculated. So you can take advantage of that when you're looking through your code to try to track down the bug. It'd be a whole lot harder to find the problem if the incorrect lines looked like this instead:

```
mT = eM -= sM;
aO = mT *= rR;
```

Variables named like this are essentially useless in telling you what their purpose might be.

Objects use variables, too

So far, we've looked at objects separate from other types. But an object is just another data type. Your code treats objects exactly like it treats numbers, strings, and Booleans. It uses variables to work with them:

Using an int

① Write a statement to declare the integer.

```
int myInt;
```

② Assign a value to the new variable.

```
myInt = 3761;
```

③ Use the integer in your code.

```
while (i < myInt) {
```

Using an object

① Write a statement to declare the object.

```
Dog spot;
```

When you have a class like Dog, you use it as the type in a variable declaration statement.

② Assign a value to the object.

```
spot = new Dog();
```

③ Check one of the object's fields.

```
while (spot.IsHappy) {
```

> So it doesn't matter if I'm working with an object or a numeric value. If it's going into memory, and my program needs to use it, I use a variable.

Objects are just one more type of variable your program can use.

If your program needs to work with a whole number that's really big, use a long. If it needs a whole number that's small, use a short. If it needs a yes/no value, use a boolean. And if it needs something that barks and sits, use a Dog. No matter what type of data your program needs to work with, it'll use a variable.

Refer to your objects with reference variables

That's called instantiating the object.

When you create a new object, you use code like **new Guy()**. But that's not enough; even though that code creates a new **Guy** object on the heap, it doesn't give you a way to *access* that object. **You need a reference to the object.** So you create a **reference variable**: a variable of type **Guy** with a name, like **joe**. So **joe** is a reference to the new **Guy** object you created. Any time you want to use that particular guy, you can reference it with the reference variable called **joe**.

So when you have a variable that is an object type, it's a reference variable: a reference to a particular object. Take a look:

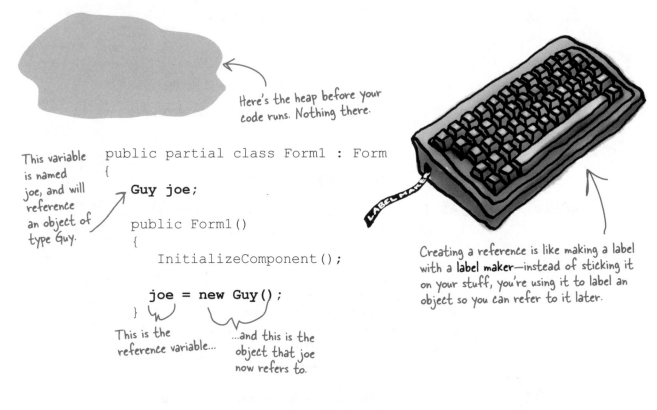

Here's the heap before your code runs. Nothing there.

This variable is named joe, and will reference an object of type Guy.

```
public partial class Form1 : Form
{
    Guy joe;

    public Form1()
    {
        InitializeComponent();

        joe = new Guy();
    }
```

This is the reference variable...

...and this is the object that joe now refers to.

Creating a reference is like making a label with a **label maker**—instead of sticking it on your stuff, you're using it to label an object so you can refer to it later.

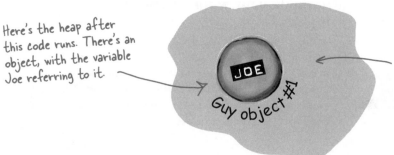

Here's the heap after this code runs. There's an object, with the variable Joe referring to it.

JOE

Guy object #1

The ONLY way to reference this Guy object is through the reference variable called joe.

References are like labels for your object

In your kitchen, you probably have a container of salt and sugar. If you switched their labels, it would make for a pretty disgusting meal—even though the labels changed, the contents of the containers stayed the same. **References are like labels.** You can move labels around and point them at different things, but it's the **object** that dictates what methods and data are available, not the reference itself.

This object is of type Guy. It's a SINGLE object with MULTIPLE references.

Form1's button1_Click method has a variable called "Joe" that references this object.

JOE PROGRAMMER
CUSTOMER
BROTHER
DAD HEYYOU
UNCLEJOE

An instance of the Guy class is keeping a reference to this object in a variable called "Dad".

Every one of these labels is a different reference variable, but they all point to the SAME Guy object.

When your code needs to work with an object in memory, it uses a reference, which is a variable whose type is a class of the object it's going to point to. A reference is like a label that your code uses to talk about a specific object.

There are lots of different references to this same Guy, because a lot of different methods use him for different things. Each reference has a different name that makes sense in its context.

You never refer to your object directly. For example, you can't write code like **Guy.GiveCash()** if **Guy** is your object type. The C# compiler doesn't know which **Guy** you're talking about, since you might have several instances of **Guy** on the heap. So you need a reference variable, like **joe**, that you assign to a specific instance, like **Guy joe = new Guy()**.

Now you can call methods, like **joe.GiveCash()**. **joe** refers to a specific instance of the **Guy** class, and your C# compiler knows exactly which instance to use. And, as you saw above, you might have *multiple labels pointing to the same instance*. So you could say **Guy dad = joe**, and then call **dad.GiveCash()**. That's OK, too—that's what Joe's kid does every day.

If there aren't any more references, your object gets garbage-collected

If all of the labels come off of an object, programs can no longer access that object. That means C# can mark the object for **garbage collection**. That's when C# gets rid of any unreferenced objects, and reclaims the memory those objects took up for your program's use.

For an object to stay in the heap, it has to be referenced. Some time after the last reference to the object disappears, so does the object.

① **Here's some code that creates an object.**

```
Guy joe = new Guy()
  { Name = "Joe", Cash = 50 };
```

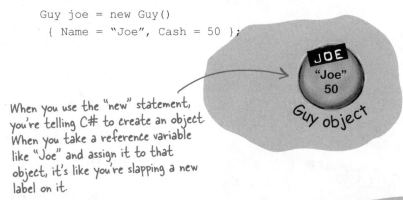

When you use the "new" statement, you're telling C# to create an object. When you take a reference variable like "Joe" and assign it to that object, it's like you're slapping a new label on it.

② **Now let's create a second object.**

```
Guy bob = new Guy()
  { Name = "Bob", Cash = 75 };
```

Now we have two Guy object instances, and two reference variables: one for each Guy.

③ **Let's take the reference to the first object, and change it to point at the second object.**

```
joe = bob;
```

Now joe is pointing to the same object as bob.

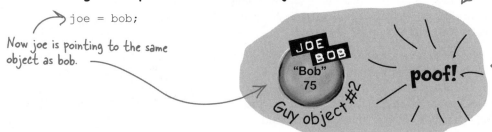

But there is no longer a reference to the first Guy object...

...so C# marks the object for garbage collection, and eventually trashes it. It's gone!

Typecross

Take a break, sit back, and give your right brain something to do. It's your standard crossword; all of the solution words are from this chapter.

When you're done, turn the page and take on the rest of the chapter.

Across

1. The second part of a variable declaration

4. "namespace", "for", "while", "using", and "new" are examples of _____ words

6. What (int) does in this line of code: x = (int) y;

8. When an object no longer has any references pointing to it, it's removed from the heap using _____ collection

10. What you're doing when you use the + operator to stick two strings together

14. The numeric type that holds the biggest numbers

15. The type that stores a single letter or number

16. \n and \r are _____ sequences

17. The four whole number types that only hold positive numbers

Down

2. You can combine the variable declaration and the _____ into one statement

3. A variable that points to an object

5. What your program uses to work with data that's in memory

7. If you want to store a currency value, use this type

9. += and -= are this kind of operator

11. A variable declaration always starts with this

12. Every object has this method that converts it to a string

13. When you've got a variable of this type, you can assign any value to it

→ Answers on page 165.

Multiple references and their side effects

You've got to be careful when you start moving around reference
variables. Lots of times, it might seem like you're simply pointing
a variable to a different object. But you could end up removing all
references to another object in the process. That's not a bad thing, but
it may not be what you intended. Take a look:

❶
```
Dog rover = new Dog();
rover.Breed = "Greyhound";
```

Objects: <u>1</u>

References: <u>1</u>

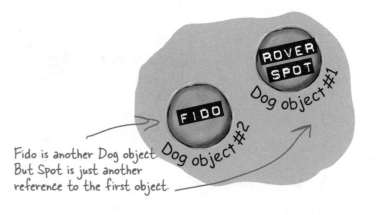

❷
```
Dog fido = new Dog();
fido.Breed = "Beagle";
Dog spot = rover;
```

Objects: <u>2</u>

References: <u>3</u>

Fido is another Dog object.
But Spot is just another
reference to the first object.

❸
```
Dog lucky = new Dog();
lucky.Breed = "Dachshund";
fido = rover;
```

Objects: <u>2</u>

References: <u>4</u>

poof!

Lucky is a third object.
But Fido is now pointing
to Object #1. So, Object
#2 has no references.
It's done as far as the
program is concerned.

Sharpen your pencil

Now it's your turn. Here's one long block of code. Figure out how many objects and references there are at each stage. On the right-hand side, draw a picture of the objects and labels in the heap.

1
```
Dog rover = new Dog();
rover.Breed = "Greyhound";
Dog rinTinTin = new Dog();
Dog fido = new Dog();
Dog quentin = fido;
```

Objects:_____

References:_____

2
```
Dog spot = new Dog();
spot.Breed = "Dachshund";
spot = rover;
```

Objects:_____

References:_____

3
```
Dog lucky = new Dog();
lucky.Breed = "Beagle";
Dog charlie = fido;
fido = rover;
```

Objects:_____

References:_____

4
```
rinTinTin = lucky;
Dog laverne = new Dog();
laverne.Breed = "pug";
```

Objects:_____

References:_____

5
```
charlie = laverne;
lucky = rinTinTin;
```

Objects:_____

References:_____

Sharpen your pencil Solution

Now it's your turn. Here's one long block of code. Figure out how many objects and references there are at each stage. On the right-hand side, draw a picture of the objects and labels in the heap.

①
```
Dog rover = new Dog();
rover.Breed = "Greyhound";
Dog rinTinTin = new Dog();
Dog fido = new Dog();
Dog quentin = fido;
```

Objects: 3

References: 4

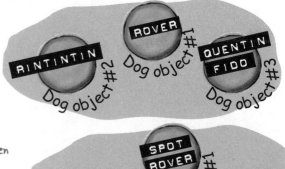

One new Dog object is created but Spot is the only reference to it. When Spot is set = to Rover, that object goes away.

②
```
Dog spot = new Dog();
spot.Breed = "Dachshund";
spot = rover;
```

Objects: 3

References: 5

Here a new Dog object is created, but when Fido is set to Rover, Fido's object from #1 goes away.

③
```
Dog lucky = new Dog();
lucky.Breed = "Beagle";
Dog charlie = fido;
fido = rover;
```

Charlie was set to Fido when Fido was still on object #3. Then, after that, Fido moved to object #1, leaving Charlie behind.

Objects: 4

References: 7

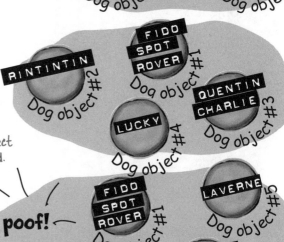

Dog #2 lost its last reference, and it went away.

poof!

④
```
rinTinTin = lucky;
Dog laverne = new Dog();
laverne.Breed = "pug";
```

Objects: 4

References: 8

When Rin Tin Tin moved to Lucky's object, the old Rin Tin Tin object disappeared.

⑤
```
charlie = laverne;
lucky = rinTinTin;
```

Objects: 4

References: 8

Here the references move around but no new objects are created. And setting Lucky to Rin Tin Tin did nothing because they already pointed to the same object.

Exercise

Create a program with an elephant class. Make two elephant instances and then swap the reference values that point to them, ***without*** getting any Elephant instances garbage-collected.

1 Start with a new Windows Application project.
Make the form look like this:

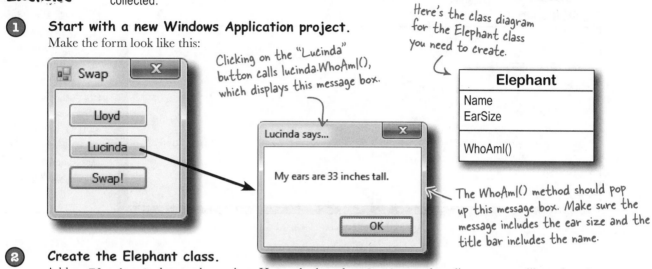

Clicking on the "Lucinda" button calls lucinda.WhoAmI(), which displays this message box.

Here's the class diagram for the Elephant class you need to create.

Elephant
Name
EarSize
WhoAmI()

The WhoAmI() method should pop up this message box. Make sure the message includes the ear size and the title bar includes the name.

2 Create the Elephant class.
Add an Elephant class to the project. Have a look at the Elephant class diagram—you'll need an int field called EarSize and a String field called Name. (Make sure both are public.) Then add a method called WhoAmI() that displays a message box that tells you the name and ear size of the elephant.

3 Create two Elephant instances and a reference.
Add two Elephant fields to the Form1 class (in the area right below the class declaration) named Lloyd and Lucinda. Initialize them so they have the right name and ear size. Here are the **Elephant** object initializers to add to your form:

```
lucinda = new Elephant() { Name = "Lucinda", EarSize = 33 };
lloyd = new Elephant() { Name = "Lloyd", EarSize = 40 };
```

4 Make the "Lloyd" and "Lucinda" buttons work.
Have the Lloyd button call lloyd.WhoAmI() and the Lucinda button call lucinda.WhoAmI().

5 Hook up the swap button.
Here's the hard part. Make the Swap button ***exchange*** the two references, so that when you click Swap, the Lloyd and Lucinda variables swap objects and a "Objects swapped" box is displayed. Test out your program by clicking the Swap button and then clicking the other two buttons. The first time you click Swap, the Lloyd button should pop up Lucinda's message box, and the Lucinda button should pop up Lloyd's message box. If you click the Swap button again, everything should go back.

C# garbage-collects any object with no references to it. So here's your hint: If you want to pour a glass of beer into another glass that's currently full of water, you'll need a third glass to pour the water into....

Exercise Solution

Create a program with an elephant class. Make two elephant instances and then swap the reference values that point to them, **without** getting any Elephant instances garbage-collected.

This is the Elephant class definition code in the Elephant.cs file we added to the project. Don't forget the "using System. Windows.Forms;" line at the top of the class. Without it, the MessageBox statement won't work.

```
using System.Windows.Forms;

class Elephant {

  public int EarSize;
  public string Name;

  public void WhoAmI() {
     MessageBox.Show("My ears are " + EarSize + " inches tall.",
        Name + " says...");
  }
}
```

Here's the Form1 class code from Form1.cs.

```
public partial class Form1 : Form {

    Elephant lucinda;
    Elephant lloyd;

    public Form1()
    {
        InitializeComponent();
        lucinda = new Elephant()
            { Name = "Lucinda", EarSize = 33 };
        lloyd = new Elephant()
            { Name = "Lloyd", EarSize = 40 };
    }

    private void button1_Click(object sender, EventArgs e) {
        lloyd.WhoAmI();
    }

    private void button2_Click(object sender, EventArgs e) {
        lucinda.WhoAmI();
    }

    private void button3_Click(object sender, EventArgs e) {
        Elephant holder;
        holder = lloyd;
        lloyd = lucinda;
        lucinda = holder;
        MessageBox.Show("Objects swapped");
    }
}
```

If you just point Lloyd to Lucinda, there won't be any more references pointing to Lloyd and his object will be lost. That's why you need to have the Holder reference hold onto the Lloyd object until Lucinda can get there.

There's no new statement for the reference because we don't want to create another instance of Elephant.

strings and arrays are different from all of the other data types you've seen, because they're the only ones without a set size (think about that for a bit).

BRAIN POWER

Why do you think we didn't add a Swap() method to the Elephant class?

Two references means TWO ways to change an object's data

Besides losing all the references to an object, when you have multiple references to an object, you can unintentionally change an object. In other words, one reference to an object may *change* that object, while another reference to that object has *no idea* that something has changed. Watch:

Do this

1   Add another button to your form.

2   Add this code for the button. Can you guess what's going to happen when you click it?

```
private void button4_Click(object sender, EventArgs e)
{
    lloyd = lucinda;
    lloyd.EarSize = 4321;
    lloyd.WhoAmI();
}
```

This statement says to set EarSize to 4321 on whatever object the lloyd reference happens to point to.

You're calling the WhoAmI() method from the **lloyd** object.

After this code runs, both the lloyd and lucinda variables reference the SAME Elephant object.

But lloyd points at the same thing that lucinda does.

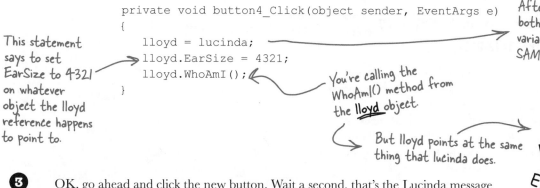

Elephant Object

3   OK, go ahead and click the new button. Wait a second, that's the Lucinda message box. Didn't we call the `WhoAmI()` method from Lloyd?

It's lucinda's message box...

Lucinda says...

My ears are 4321 inches tall.

OK

Elephant Object

But we set this EarSize using the lloyd reference! What gives?

Note that the data is NOT being overwritten—the only things changing are the references.

lloyd and lucinda are now interchangeable. Changes to one affect the object that BOTH are pointing at... there's no longer a real difference between lloyd and lucinda, since they point to the SAME object.

A special case: <u>arrays</u>

If you have to keep track of a lot of data of the same type, like a list of heights or a group of dogs, you can do it in an **array**. What makes an array special is that it's a **group of variables** that's treated as one object. An array gives you a way of storing and changing more than one piece of data without having to keep track of each variable individually. When you create an array, you declare it just like any other variable, with a name and a type:

> You could combine the declaration of the myArray variable with its initialization—just like any other variable. Then it'd look like this:
>
> bool[] myArray = new bool[15];

> You declare an array by specifying its type, followed by square brackets.

```
bool[] myArray;

myArray = new bool[15];

myArray[4] = true;
```

> This array has 15 elements within it.

> You use the new keyword to create an array because it's an object. So an array variable is a kind of reference variable.

> This line sets the value of the fifth element of myArray to true. It's the fifth one because the first is myArray[0], the second is myArray[1], etc.

Use each element in an array like it is a normal variable

When you use an array, first you need to **declare a reference variable** that points to the array. Then you need to **create the array object** using the new statement, specifying how big you want the array to be. Then you can **set the elements** in the array. Here's an example of code that declares and fills up an array—and what's happening on the heap when you do it. The first element in the array has an **index** of zero.

> In memory, the array is stored as one chunk of memory, even though there are multiple int variables within it.

> The type of each element in the array.

```
int[] heights;
heights = new int[7];
heights[0] = 68;
heights[1] = 70;
heights[2] = 63;
heights[3] = 60;
heights[4] = 58;
heights[5] = 72;
heights[6] = 74;
```

> name

> You reference these by index, but each one works essentially like a normal int variable.

> 7 int variables
>
> 0 1 2 3 4 5 6
> int int int int int int int

> HEIGHTS
> Array

> Notice that the array is an object, even though the 7 elements are just value types—like the ones on the first two pages of this chapter.

Arrays can contain a bunch of reference variables, too

You can create an array of object references just like you create an array of numbers or strings. Arrays don't care what type of variable they store; it's up to you. So you can have an array of `int`s, or an array of `Duck` objects, with no problem.

Here's code that creates an array of 7 Dog variables. The line that initializes the array only creates reference variables. Since there are only two `new Dog()` lines, only two actual instances of the Dog class are created.

When you set or retrieve an element from an array, the number inside the brackets is called the index. The first element in the array has an index of zero.

```
Dog[] dogs = new Dog[7];
dogs[5] = new Dog();
dogs[0] = new Dog();
```

This line declares a dogs variable to hold an array of references to Dog objects, and then creates a 7-element array.

These two lines create new instances of Dog() and put them at indexes 0 and 5.

The first line of code only created the array, not the instances. The array is a list of seven Dog reference variables.

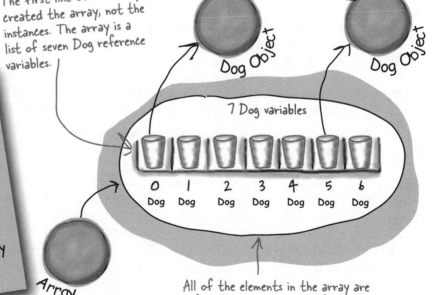

Dog Object

Dog Object

7 Dog variables

| 0 | 1 | 2 | 3 | 4 | 5 | 6 |
| Dog | Dog | Dog | Dog | Dog | Dog | Dog |

Array

All of the elements in the array are references. The array itself is an object.

An array's length

You can find out how many elements are in an array using its Length property. So if you've got an array called heights, then you can use heights.Length to find out how long it is. If there are 7 elements in the array, that'll give you 7—which means the array elements are numbered 0 to 6.

Welcome to Sloppy Joe's Budget House o' Discount Sandwiches!

Sloppy Joe has a pile of meat, a whole lotta bread, and more condiments than you can shake a stick at. But what he doesn't have is a menu! Can you build a program that makes a new *random* menu for him every day?

Do this

MenuMaker
Randomizer
Meats
Condiments
Breads
GetMenuItem()

1 **Start a new project and add a MenuMaker class**

If you need to build a menu, you need ingredients. And arrays would be perfect for those lists. We'll also need some way of choosing random ingredients to combine together into a sandwich. Luckily, the .NET Framework has a built-in class called `Random` that generates random numbers. So we'll have four fields in our class: a Randomizer field that holds a reference to a `Random` object, and three arrays of `strings` to hold the meats, condiments, and breads.

> The class has three fields to store three different arrays of strings. It'll use them to build the random menu items.

The field called Randomizer holds a reference to a Random object. Calling its Next() method will generate random numbers.

```
class MenuMaker {
    public Random Randomizer;

    string[] Meats = { "Roast beef", "Salami", "Turkey", "Ham", "Pastrami" };

    string[] Condiments = { "yellow mustard", "brown mustard",
            "honey mustard", "mayo", "relish", "french dressing" };

    string[] Breads = { "rye", "white", "wheat", "pumpernickel",
            "italian bread", "a roll" };
}
```

> Remember, use square brackets to access a member of an array. The value of Breads[2] is "wheat".

Notice how you're initializing these arrays? That's called a collection initializer, and you'll learn all about them in Chapter 8.

2 **Add a GetMenuItem() method to the class that generates a random sandwich**

The point of the class is to generate sandwiches, so let's add a method to do exactly that. It'll use the `Random` object's `Next()` method to choose a random meat, condiment, and bread from each array. When you pass an `int` parameter to `Next()`, the method returns a random that's less than that parameter. So if your `Random` object is called `Randomizer`, then calling `Randomizer.Next(7)` will return a random number between 0 and 6.

So how do you know what parameter to pass into the `Next()` method? Well, that's easy—just pass in each array's `Length`. That will return the index of a random item in the array.

```
public string GetMenuItem() {
    string randomMeat = Meats[Randomizer.Next(Meats.Length)];
    string randomCondiment = Condiments[Randomizer.Next(Condiments.Length)];
    string randomBread = Breads[Randomizer.Next(Breads.Length)];
    return randomMeat + " with " + randomCondiment + " on " + randomBread;
}
```

The GetMenuItem() method returns a string that contains a sandwich built from random elements in the three arrays.

> The method puts a random item from the Meats array into randomMeat by passing Meats.Length to the Random object's Next() method. Since there are 5 items in the Meats array, Meats.Length is 5, so Next(5) will return a random number between 0 and 4.

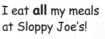

I eat **all** my meals at Sloppy Joe's!

How it works...

The randomizer.Next(7) method gets a random number that's less than 7. Meats.Length returns the number of elements in Meats. So `randomizer.Next(Meats.Length)` gives you a random number that's greater than or equal to zero, but less than the number of elements in the Meats array.

```
Meats[Randomizer.Next(Meats.Length)]
```

Meats is an array of strings. It's got five elements, numbered from zero to 4. So Meats[0] equals "Roast Beef", and Meats[3] equals "Ham".

3 Build your form

Add six labels to the form, `label1` through `label6`. Then add code to set each label's `Text` property using a `MenuMaker` object. You'll need to initialize the object using a new instance of the `Random` class. Here's the code:

Use an object initializer to set the MenuMaker object's Randomizer field to a new instance of the Random class.

```
public Form1() {
    InitializeComponent();

    MenuMaker menu = new MenuMaker() { Randomizer = new Random() };

    label1.Text = menu.GetMenuItem();
    label2.Text = menu.GetMenuItem();
    label3.Text = menu.GetMenuItem();
    label4.Text = menu.GetMenuItem();
    label5.Text = menu.GetMenuItem();
    label6.Text = menu.GetMenuItem();
}
```

Now you're all set to generate six different random sandwiches using the GetMenuItem() method.

Here's something to think about. What would happen if you forgot to initialize the MenuMaker object's Randomizer field? Can you think of a way to keep this from happening?

When you run the program, the six labels show six different random sandwiches.

Sloppy Joe's Menu

Salami with honey mustard on rye
Roast beef with french dressing on wheat
Turkey with yellow mustard on wheat
Turkey with mayo on white
Pastrami with relish on italian bread
Roast beef with french dressing on pumpernickel

Objects use references to talk to each other

Elephant
Name
EarSize
WhoAmI()
TellMe()
SpeakTo()

So far, you've seen forms talk to objects by using reference variables to call their methods and check their fields. Objects can call one another's methods using references, too. In fact, there's nothing that a form can do that your objects can't do, because **your form is just another object**. And when objects talk to each other, one useful keyword that they have is `this`. Any time an object uses the `this` keyword, it's referring to itself—it's a reference that points to the object that calls it.

 Here's a method to tell an elephant to speak

Let's add a method to the `Elephant` class. Its first parameter is a message from an `elephant`. Its second parameter is the `elephant` that said it:

```
public void TellMe(string message, Elephant whoSaidIt) {
    MessageBox.Show(whoSaidIt.Name + " says: " + message,);
}
```

Here's what it looks like when it's called. You can add to `button4_Click()`, but add it **before the statement that resets the references!** (`lloyd = lucinda;`)

```
lloyd.TellMe("Hi", lucinda);
```

We called Lloyd's `TellMe()` method, and passed it two parameters: "Hi" and a reference to Lucinda's object. The method uses its `whoSaidIt` parameter to access the `Name` parameter of whatever elephant was passed into `TellMe()` using its second parameter.

2 **Here's a method that calls another method**

Now let's add this `SpeakTo()` method to the `Elephant` class. It uses a special keyword: `this`. That's a reference that **lets an object talk about itself**.

```
public void SpeakTo(Elephant whoToTalkTo, string message) {
    whoToTalkTo.TellMe(message, this);
}
```
This method in the Elephant class calls another elephant's TalkTo() method. It lets one elephant communicate with another one.

Let's take a closer look at how this works.

```
lloyd.SpeakTo(lucinda, "Hello");
```

When Lloyd's `SpeakTo()` method is called, it uses its `talkTo` parameter (which has a reference to Lucinda) to call Lucinda's `TellMe()` method.

```
whoToTalkTo.TellMe(message, this);
```

Lloyd uses whoToTalkTo (which has a reference to Lucinda) to call TellMe ()

this is replaced with a reference to Lloyd's object

```
lucinda.TellMe(message, [a reference to Lloyd]);
```

So Lucinda acts as if she was called with ("`Hello`", `lloyd`), and shows this message:

Where no object has gone before

There's another important keyword that you'll use with objects. When you create a new reference and don't set it to anything, it has a value. It starts off set to null, which means it's not pointing to anything.

```
Dog fido;
```

Right now, there's only one object. The fido reference is set to null.

```
Dog lucky = new Dog();
```

Now that fido's pointing to an object, it's no longer equal to null.

```
fido = new Dog();
```

When we set lucky to null, it's no longer pointing at its object, so it gets garbage-collected.

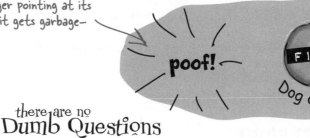

```
lucky = null;
```

poof!

there are no Dumb Questions

Q: One more time—my form is an object?

A: Yes! That's why your class code starts with a class declaration. Open up code for a form and see for yourself. Then open up Program.cs in any program you've written so far and look inside the Main() method—you'll find "new Form1()".

Q: Why would I ever use null?

A: There are a few ways you see null used in typical programs. The most common way is testing for it:

```
if (lloyd == null) {
```

That test will return true if the lloyd reference is set to null.

Another way you'll see the null keyword used is when you **want** your object to get garbage-collected. If you've got a reference to an object and you're finished with the object, setting the reference to null will immediately mark it for collection (unless there's another reference to it somewhere).

Q: You keep talking about garbage collecting, but what's actually doing the collecting?

A: Remember how we talked about the **Common Language Runtime (or CLR)** back at the beginning of the first chapter? That's the virtual machine that runs all .NET programs. A *virtual machine* is a way for it to isolate running programs from the rest of the operating system. One thing that virtual machines do is manage the memory that they use. That means that it keeps track of all of your objects, figures out when the last reference to the object disappears, and frees up the memory that it was using.

this and that

Dumb Questions

Q: I'm still not sure I get how references work.

A: References are the way you use all of the methods and fields in an object. If you create a reference to a Dog object, you can then use that reference to access any methods you've created for the Dog object. If you have a (non-static) method called Dog.Bark() or Dog.Beg(), you can create a reference called spot. Then you can use that to access spot.Bark() or spot.Beg(). You could also change information in the fields for the object using the reference. So you could change a Breed field using spot.Breed.

Q: Wait, then doesn't that mean that every time I change a value through a reference I'm changing it for all of the other references to that object, too?

A: Yes. If rover is a reference to the same object as spot, changing rover.Breed to "beagle" would make it so that spot.Breed was "beagle."

Q: I still don't get that stuff about different types holding different sized values. What's the deal with that?

A: OK. The thing about variables is they assign a size to your number no matter how big its value is. So if you name a variable and give it a long type even though the number is really small (like, say, 5), the CLR sets aside enough memory for it to get really big. When you think about it, that's really useful. After all, they're called variables because they change all the time.

The CLR assumes you know what you're doing and you're not going to give a variable a type that you don't need. So even though the number might not be big now, there's a chance that after some math happens, it'll change. The CLR gives it enough memory to handle whatever type of number you call it.

Q: Remind me again—what does "this" do?

A: this is a special variable that you can only use inside an object. When you're inside a class, you use this to refer to any field or method of that particular instance. It's especially useful when you're working with a class whose methods call other classes. One object can use it to send **a reference to itself** to another object. So if Spot calls one of Rover's methods passing this as a parameter, he's giving Rover a reference to the Spot object.

Any time you've got code in an object that's going to be instantiated, the instance can use the special this variable that has a reference to itself.

BULLET POINTS

There's actually a very specific case where you don't declare a type – you'll learn about it when you use the "var" keyword in Chapter 14.

- When you declare a variable you ALWAYS give a type. Sometimes you combine it with setting the value.

- There are **value types** for variables that hold different sizes of numbers. The biggest numbers should be of the type long and the smallest ones (up to 255) can be declared as bytes.

- Every value type has a size, and you can't put a value of a bigger type into a smaller variable, no matter what the actual size of the data is.

- When you're using literal values, use the F suffix to indicate a float (15.6F) and M for a decimal (36.12M).

- There are a few types (like short to int) that C# knows how to convert automatically. When the compiler won't let you set a variable equal to a value of a different type, that's when you need to cast it.

- There are some words that are reserved by the language and you can't name your variables with them. They're words like for, while, using, new, and others that do specific things in the language.

- References are like labels: you can have as many references to an object as you want, and they all refer to the same thing.

- If an object doesn't have any references to it, it eventually gets garbage-collected.

156 *Chapter 4*

Sharpen your pencil

Here's an array of `Elephant` objects and a loop that will go through it and find the one with the biggest ears. What's the value of the `biggestEars.Ears` **after** each iteration of the `for` loop?

```
private void button1_Click(object sender, EventArgs e)
{
    Elephant[] elephants = new Elephant[7];
    elephants[0] = new Elephant() { Name = "Lloyd", EarSize = 40 };
    elephants[1] = new Elephant() { Name = "Lucinda", EarSize = 33 };
    elephants[2] = new Elephant() { Name = "Larry", EarSize = 42 };
    elephants[3] = new Elephant() { Name = "Lucille", EarSize = 32 };
    elephants[4] = new Elephant() { Name = "Lars", EarSize = 44 };
    elephants[5] = new Elephant() { Name = "Linda", EarSize = 37 };
    elephants[6] = new Elephant() { Name = "Humphrey", EarSize = 45 };

    Elephant biggestEars = elephants[0];
    for (int i = 1; i < elephants.Length; i++)
    {
        if (elephants[i].EarSize > biggestEars.EarSize)
        {
            biggestEars = elephants[i];
        }
    }
    MessageBox.Show(biggestEars.EarSize.ToString());
}
```

We're creating an array of 7 Elephant() references.

Every array starts with index 0, so the first elephant in the array is Elephants[0].

This line makes the biggestEars reference point at whatever elephant elephants[i] points to.

Be careful—this loop starts with the second element of the array (at index 1) and iterates six times until i is equal to the length of the array.

Iteration #1 biggestEars.EarSize = _____

Iteration #2 biggestEars.EarSize = _____

Iteration #3 biggestEars.EarSize = _____

Iteration #4 biggestEars.EarSize = _____

Iteration #5 biggestEars.EarSize = _____

Iteration #6 biggestEars.EarSize = _____

➤ Answers on page 166.

Code Magnets

The code for a button is all scrambled up on the fridge. Can you reconstruct the code snippets to make a working method that produces the output listed below?

```
int y = 0;
```

```
refNum = index[y];
```

```
islands[0] = "Bermuda";
islands[1] = "Fiji";
islands[2] = "Azores";
islands[3] = "Cozumel";
```

```
int refNum;

while (y < 4) {
```

```
result += islands[refNum];
```

```
MessageBox.Show(result);
```

```
index[0] = 1;
index[1] = 3;
index[2] = 0;
index[3] = 2;
```

```
}
```

```
}
```

```
string[] islands = new string[4];
```

```
result += "\nisland = ";
```

```
int[] index = new int[4];
```

```
y = y + 1;
```

```
private void button1_Click (object sender, EventArgs e)
{
```

```
string result = "";
```

X

island = Fiji
island = Cozumel
island = Bermuda
island = Azores

OK

→ **Answers on page 167.**

Pōōl Puzzle

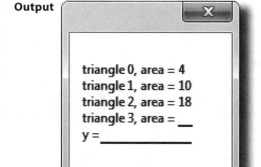

Your **job** is to take code snippets from the pool and place them into the blank lines in the code. You **may** use the same snippet more than once, and you won't need to use all the snippets. Your **goal** is to make a class that will compile and run and produce the output listed.

Output

```
triangle 0, area = 4
triangle 1, area = 10
triangle 2, area = 18
triangle 3, area = __
y = _____
```

OK

Bonus Question!

For extra bonus points, use snippets from the pool to fill in the two blanks missing from the output.

Note: Each snippet from the pool can be used more than once.

Here's the entry point for the application. Assume it's in a file with the right "using" lines at the top.

```
class Triangle
{
    double area;
    int height;
    int length;
    public static void Main(string[] args)
    {
        string results = "";

        _____

        _____

        while ( _____ )
        {

            _____
            _____.height = (x + 1) * 2;
            _____.length = x + 4;

            _____
            results += "triangle " + x + ", area";
            results += " = " + _____.area + "\n";

            _____

        }

        _____
        x = 27;
        Triangle t5 = ta[2];
        ta[2].area = 343;
        results += "y = " + y;
        MessageBox.Show(results +
            ", t5 area = " + t5.area);
    }
    void setArea()
    {

        _____ = (height * length) / 2;

    }
}
```

Hint: SetArea() is NOT a static method. Flip back to Chapter 3 for a refresher on what the static keyword means.

Pool:

area
ta.area
x   ta.x.area
y   ta[x].area

Triangle [ ] ta = new Triangle(4);
Triangle ta = new [ ] Triangle[4];
Triangle [ ] ta = new Triangle[4];

4, t5 area = 18
4, t5 area = 343
27, t5 area = 18
27, t5 area = 343

ta[x] = setArea();
ta.x = setArea();
ta[x].setArea();

int x;
int y;
int x = 0;
int x = 1;
int y = x;
28
30.0

x = x + 1;   ta.x
x = x + 2;   ta(x)
x = x - 1;   ta[x]
ta = new Triangle();
ta[x] = new Triangle();
ta.x = new Triangle();

x < 4
x < 5

➡️ **Answers on page 168.**

Build a typing game

You've reached a milestone...you know enough to build a game! Here's how your game will work. The form will display random letters. If the player types one of them, it disappears and the accuracy rate goes up. If the player types an incorrect letter, the accuracy rate goes down. As the player keeps typing letters, the game goes faster and faster, getting more difficult with each correct letter. If the form fills up with letters, the game is over!

Do this

 Build the form.
Here's what the form will look like in the form designer:

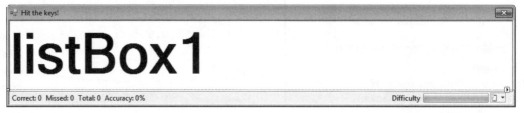

You'll need to:

★ Turn off the minimize box and maximize box. Then set the form's **FormBorderStyle** property to **Fixed3D**. That way, the player won't be able to accidentally drag and resize it. Then resize it so that it's much wider than it is tall (we set our form's size to 876, 174).

★ Drag a **ListBox** out of the Toolbox onto the form. Set its **Dock** property to Fill, and its **MultiColumn** property to True. Set its **Font** to 72 point bold.

★ In the Toolbox, expand the "All Windows Forms" group at the top. This will display many controls. Find the **Timer** control and double-click on it to add it to your form.

★ Find the **StatusStrip** in the "All Windows Forms" group in the Toolbox and double-click on it to add a status bar to your form. You should now see the **StatusStrip** and **Timer** icons in the gray area at the bottom of the form designer:

See how you can use a Timer to make your form do more than one thing at once? Take a minute and flip to #3 in the "Leftovers" appendix to learn about another way to do that.

❷ Set up the StatusStrip control.
Take a closer look at the status bar at the bottom of the screenshot. On one side, it's got a series of labels:

And on the other side, it's got a label and a progress bar:

Add a `StatusLabel` to your `StatusStrip` by clicking its drop-down and selecting `StatusLabel`:

★ Set the `StatusStrip`'s `SizingGrip` property to False.

★ Use the Properties window to set its (Name) to `correctLabel` and its Text to "Correct: 0". Add three more `StatusLabels`: `missedLabel`, `totalLabel`, and `accuracyLabel`.

★ Add one more `StatusLabel`. Set its `Spring` to True, `TextAlign` to `MiddleRight`, and Text to "Difficulty". Finally, add a `ProgressBar` and name it `difficultyProgressBar`.

❸ Set up the Timer control.
Did you notice how your Timer control didn't show up on your form? That's because the Timer is a *non-visual control*. It doesn't actually change the look and feel of the form. It does exactly one thing: it **calls a method over and over again**. Set the Timer control's **Interval** property to 800, so that it calls its method every 800 milliseconds. Then **double-click on the *timer1* icon** in the designer. The IDE will do what it always does when you double-click on a control: it will add a method to your form. This time, it'll add one called **timer1_Tick**. Here's the code for it:

```
private void timer1_Tick(object sender, EventArgs e)
{
    // Add a random key to the ListBox
    listBox1.Items.Add((Keys)random.Next(65, 90));
    if (listBox1.Items.Count > 7)
    {
        listBox1.Items.Clear();
        listBox1.Items.Add("Game over");
        timer1.Stop();
    }
}
```

You'll add a field called "random" in just a minute. Can you guess what its type will be?

4 **Add a class to keep track of the player stats.**

If the form is going to display the total number of keys the player pressed, the number that were missed and the number that were correct, and the player's accuracy, then we'll need a way to keep track of all that data. Sounds like a job for a new class! Add a class called `Stats` to your project. It'll have four `int` fields called `Total`, `Missed`, `Correct`, and `Accuracy`, and a method called `Update` with one `bool` parameter: `true` if the player typed a correct letter that was in the ListBox, or `false` if the player missed one.

Stats
Total Missed Correct Accuracy
Update()

```
class Stats
{
    public int Total = 0;
    public int Missed = 0;
    public int Correct = 0;
    public int Accuracy = 0;

    public void Update(bool correctKey)
    {
        Total++;

        if (!correctKey)
        {
            Missed++;
        }
        else
        {
            Correct++;
        }

        Accuracy = 100 * Correct / (Missed + Correct);
    }
}
```

Every time the Update() method is called, it recalculates the % correct and puts it in the Accuracy field.

5 **Add fields to your form to hold a Stats object and a Random object.**

You'll need an instance of your new **Stats** class to actually store the information, so add a field called **stats** to store it. And you already saw that you'll need a field called **random**—it'll contain a **Random** object.

Add the two fields to the top of your form:

```
public partial class Form1 : Form
{
    Random random = new Random();
    Stats stats = new Stats();
    ...
```

⑥ Handle the keystrokes.

There's one last thing your game needs to do: any time the player hits a key, it needs to check if that key is correct (and remove the letter from the ListBox if it is), and update the stats on the `StatusStrip`.

Go back to the form designer and select the form. Then go to the Properties window and click on the lightning bolt button. Scroll to the **KeyDown** row and **double-click on it**. This tells the IDE to add a method called `Form1_KeyDown()` that gets called every time the user presses a key. Here's the code for the method:

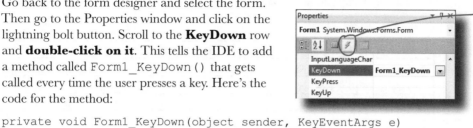

Click this button to change the Properties window's view. The button to the left of it switches the Properties window back to showing you properties.

```
private void Form1_KeyDown(object sender, KeyEventArgs e)
{
    // If the user pressed a key that's in the ListBox, remove it
    // and then make the game a little faster
    if (listBox1.Items.Contains(e.KeyCode))
    {
        listBox1.Items.Remove(e.KeyCode);
        listBox1.Refresh();
        if (timer1.Interval > 400)
            timer1.Interval -= 10;
        if (timer1.Interval > 250)
            timer1.Interval -= 7;
        if (timer1.Interval > 100)
            timer1.Interval -= 2;
        difficultyProgressBar.Value = 800 - timer1.Interval;

        // The user pressed a correct key, so update the Stats object
        // by calling its Update() method with the argument true
        stats.Update(true);
    }
    else
    {
        // The user pressed an incorrect key, so update the Stats object
        // by calling its Update() method with the argument false
        stats.Update(false);
    }

    // Update the labels on the StatusStrip
    correctLabel.Text = "Correct: " + stats.Correct;
    missedLabel.Text = "Missed: " + stats.Missed;
    totalLabel.Text = "Total: " + stats.Total;
    accuracyLabel.Text = "Accuracy: " + stats.Accuracy + "%";
}
```

This if statement checks the ListBox to see if it contains the key the player pressed. If it does, then the key gets removed from the ListBox and the game difficulty is increased.

These are called events, and you'll learn a lot more about them later on.

This is the part that increases the difficulty as the player gets more keys right. You can make the game easier by reducing the amounts that are subtracted from timer1.Interval, or make it harder by increasing them.

When the player presses a key, the Form1_KeyDown() method calls the stats object's Update() method to update the player stats, and then it displays them in the StatusStrip.

⑦ Run your game.

Your game's done! Give it a shot and see how well you do. You may need to adjust the font size of the ListBox to make sure it holds exactly 7 letters, and you can change the difficulty by adjusting the values that are subtracted from `timer1.Interval` in the `Form1_KeyDown()` method.

EXERCISE SOLUTION

There are about 77 **reserved words** in C#. These are words reserved by the C# compiler; you can't use them for variable names. You'll know a lot of them really well by the time you finish the book. Here are some you've already used. Write down what you think these words do in C#.

namespace
Namespaces make sure that the names you are using in your program don't collide with the ones in the .NET Framework or other external classes you've used in your program. All of the classes and methods in a program are inside a namespace.

for
This lets you do a loop that executes three statements. First it declares the variable it's going to use, then there's the statement that evaluates the variable against a condition. The third statement does something to the value.

class
A class is how you define an object. Classes have properties and methods. Properties are what they know and methods are what they do.

public
A public class can be used by every other class in the project. When a variable or method is declared as public, it can be used by classes and called by methods that are outside of the one it's being declared in.

else
Code that starts with else will get executed if the if statement preceding it fails.

new
You use this to create a new instance of an object.

using
This is a way of listing off all of the namespaces you are using in your program. using lets you use code from the .NET Framework and predefined classes from third parties as well as classes you can make yourself.

if
One way of setting up a conditional statement in a program. It says if one thing is true, do one thing and if not do something else.

while
while loops are loops that keep on going as long as the condition in them is true.

Typecross Solution

```
 ¹N ²A  M  E
³R     S           ⁴R  E  S  E  R ⁵V  E  D
 E     S                          A
 F     I                          R
 E     G              ⁶C  A  S  T  I  N  G
 R     N                          A        ⁷D
 E     M              ⁸G  A  R  B  A  G  E
 N     E                          L        C        ⁹C
¹⁰C  O  N  C  A ¹¹T  E  N  A ¹²T  E        I        O
 E     T           Y            O           M        M
          ¹³O      P            S           A        P
¹⁴D  O  U  B  L  E              T           L        O
          J           ¹⁵C  H  A  R           I        U
          E            R        I                    N
      ¹⁶E  S  C  A  P  E     ¹⁷U  N  S  I  G  N  E  D
          T                    G
```

Sharpen your pencil
Solution

Here's an array of `Elephant` objects and a loop that will go through it and find the one with the biggest ears. What's the value of the `biggestEars.Ears` **after** each iteration of the `for` loop?

```
private void button1_Click(object sender, EventArgs e)
{

    Elephant[] elephants = new Elephant[7];

    elephants[0] = new Elephant() { Name = "Lloyd", EarSize = 40 };

    elephants[1] = new Elephant() { Name = "Lucinda", EarSize = 33 };

    elephants[2] = new Elephant() { Name = "Larry", EarSize = 42 };

    elephants[3] = new Elephant() { Name = "Lucille", EarSize = 32 };

    elephants[4] = new Elephant() { Name = "Lars", EarSize = 44 };

    elephants[5] = new Elephant() { Name = "Linda", EarSize = 37 };

    elephants[6] = new Elephant() { Name = "Humphrey", EarSize = 45 };
```

Did you remember that the loop starts with the second element of the array? Why do you think that is?

Iteration #1 biggestEars.EarSize = __40__

```
    Elephant biggestEars = elephants[0];

    for (int i = 1; i < elephants.Length; i++)

    {
```

Iteration #2 biggestEars.EarSize = __42__

```
        if (elephants[i].EarSize > biggestEars.EarSize)
```

↑ The biggestEars reference is used to keep track of which element we've seen while going through the for loop has the biggest ears so far.

```
        {

            biggestEars = elephants[i];
```

} Use the debugger to check this! Put your breakpoint here and watch biggestEars.EarSize.

Iteration #3 biggestEars.EarSize = __42__

```
        }
    MessageBox.Show(biggestEars.EarSize.ToString());
```

Iteration #4 biggestEars.EarSize = __44__

```
}
```

The for loop starts with the second elephant and compares it to whatever elephant biggestEars points to. If its ears are bigger, it points biggestEars at that elephant instead. Then it moves to the next one, then the next one...by the end of the loop biggestEars points to the one with the biggest ears.

Iteration #5 biggestEars.EarSize = __44__

Iteration #6 biggestEars.EarSize = __45__

Code Magnets Solution

The code for a button is all scrambled up on the fridge. Can you reconstruct the code snippets to make a working method that produces the output listed below?

```
private void button1_Click (object sender, EventArgs e)
{
    string result = "";

    int[] index = new int[4];

    index[0] = 1;

    index[1] = 3;

    index[2] = 0;

    index[3] = 2;

    string[] islands = new string[4];

    islands[0] = "Bermuda";

    islands[1] = "Fiji";

    islands[2] = "Azores";

    islands[3] = "Cozumel";

    int y = 0;

    int refNum;

    while (y < 4) {

        refNum = index[y];
        result += "\nisland = ";
        result += islands[refNum];
        y = y + 1;

    }

    MessageBox.Show(result);
}
```

Here's where the index[] array gets initialized.

The islands[] array is initialized here.

The result string is built up using the += operator to concatenate lines onto it.

This while loop pulls a value from the index[] array and uses it for the index in the islands[] array.

```
island = Fiji
island = Cozumel
island = Bermuda
island = Azores
```

OK

Pool Puzzle Solution

Notice how this class contains the entry point, but it also creates an instance of itself? That's completely legal in C#.

```
class Triangle
{
    double area;
    int height;
    int length;
    public static void Main(string[] args)
    {
        string results = "";
        int x = 0;
        Triangle[] ta = new Triangle[4];
        while (  x < 4  )
        {
            ta[x] = new Triangle();
            ta[x] .height = (x + 1) * 2;
            ta[x] .length = x + 4;
            ta[x].setArea();
            results += "triangle " + x + ", area";
            results += " = " + ta[x] .area + "\n";
            x = x + 1;
        }
        int y = x;
        x = 27;
        Triangle t5 = ta[2];
        ta[2].area = 343;
        results += "y = " + y;
        MessageBox.Show(results +
            ", t5 area = " + t5.area);
    }
    void setArea()
    {
        area            = (height * length) / 2;
    }
}
```

After this line, we've got an array of four Triangle references—but there aren't any Triangle objects yet!

The while loop creates the four instances of Triangle by calling the new statement four times.

Bonus Answer

triangle 0, area = 4
triangle 1, area = 10
triangle 2, area = 18
triangle 3, area = 28
y = 4, t5 area = 343

OK

The setArea() method uses the height and length fields to set the area field. Since it's not a static method, it can only be called from inside an instance of Triangle.

C# Lab

A Day at the Races

This lab gives you a spec that describes a program for you to build, using the knowledge you've gained over the last few chapters.

This project is bigger than the ones you've seen so far. So read the whole thing before you get started, and give yourself a little time. And don't worry if you get stuck—there's nothing new in here, so you can move on in the book and come back to the lab later.

We've filled in a few design details for you, and we've made sure you've got all the pieces you need...and nothing else.

It's up to you to finish the job. You can download an executable for this lab from the website...but we won't give you the code for the answer.

The spec: build a racetrack simulator

Joe, Bob, and Al love going to the track, but they're tired of losing all their money. They need you to build a simulator for them so they can figure out winners *before* they lay their money down. And, if you do a good job, they'll cut you in on their profits.

Here's what you're going to build for them....

The Guys

Joe, Bob, and Al want to bet on a dog race. Joe starts with 50 bucks, Bob starts with 75 bucks, and Al starts with 45 bucks. Before each race, they'll each decide if they want to bet, and how much they want to put down. The guys can change their bets right up to the start of the race…but once the race starts, all bets are final.

The Betting Parlor

The betting parlor keeps track of how much cash each guy has, and what bet he's placed. There's a minimum bet of 5 bucks. The parlor only takes one bet per person for any one race.

The parlor checks to make sure that the guy who's betting has enough cash to cover his bet—so the guys can't place a bet if they don't have the cash to cover the bet.

Welcome to Curly's Betting Parlor
Minimum Bet: $5
One bet per person per race
Got enough cash?

Betting

Every bet is double-or-nothing—either the winner doubles his money, or he loses what he bet. There's a minimum bet of 5 bucks, and each guy can bet up to 15 bucks on a single dog. If the dog wins, the bettor ends up with twice the amount that he bet (after the race is complete). If he loses, that amount disappears from his pile.

> Say a guy places a $10 bet at the window. At the end of the race, if his dog wins, his cash goes up by $10 (because he keeps the original $10 he bet, plus he gets $10 more from winning). If he loses, his cash goes down by $10.

All bets: double-or-nothing
Minimum Bet: $5
Up to $15 per dog
Win: $$ added
Lose: $$ removed

The Race

There are four dogs that run on a straight track. The winner of the race is the first dog to cross the finish line. The race is totally random, there are no handicaps or odds, and a dog isn't more likely to win his next race based on his past performance.

> If you want to build a handicap system, by all means do it! It'll be really good practice writing some fun code.

Sound fun? We've got more details coming up... ⟶

You'll need three classes and a form

You'll build three main classes in the project, as well as a GUI for the simulator. You should have an array of three Guy objects to keep track of the three guys and their winnings, and an array of four Greyhound objects that actually run the race. Also, each instance of Guy should have its own Bet object that keeps track of his bet and pays out (or takes back) cash at the end of the race.

We've gotten you started with class descriptions and some snippets of code to work from. You've got to finish everything up.

> You'll need to add "using System.Windows.Forms" to the top of the Greyhound and Guy classes. And you'll need to add "using System. Drawing;" to Greyhound, because it uses Point.

We've given you the skeleton of the class you need to build. Your job is to fill in the methods.

```
class Greyhound {
    public int StartingPosition; // Where my PictureBox starts
    public int RacetrackLength; // How long the racetrack is
    public PictureBox MyPictureBox = null; // My PictureBox object
    public int Location = 0; // My Location on the racetrack
    public Random Randomizer; // An instance of Random

    public bool Run() {
        // Move forward either 1, 2, 3 or 4 spaces at random
        // Update the position of my PictureBox on the form
        // Return true if I won the race
    }
    public void TakeStartingPosition() {
        // Reset my location to the start line
    }
}
```

You only need one instance of Random—each Greyhound's Randomizer reference should point to the same Random object.

Greyhound

Greyhound
StartingPosition
RacetrackLength
MyPictureBox
Location
Randomizer
Run()
TakeStartingPosition()

See how the class diagram matches up with the code?

The Greyhound object initializer is pretty straightforward. Just make sure you pass a reference to the right PictureBox on the form to each Greyhound object.

We've added comments to give you an idea of what to do.

Don't overthink this... sometimes you just need to set a variable, and you're done.

Your object can control things on your form...

The Greyhound class keeps track of its position on the racetrack during the race. It also updates the location of the PictureBox representing the dog moving down the race track. Each instance of Greyhound uses a field called MyPictureBox to reference the PictureBox control on the form that shows the picture of the dog. Suppose the distance variable contains the distance to move the dog forward. Then this code will update the location of MyPictureBox by adding distance to its X value:

You'll have to make sure the form passes the right picture box into each Greyhound's object initializer.

```
Point p = MyPictureBox.Location;
p.X += distance;
MyPictureBox.Location = p;
```

You get the current location of the picture...

...add the value to move forward to its X coordinate...

...and then update the picture box location on the form.

Guy
Name
MyBet
Cash
MyRadioButton
MyLabel
UpdateLabels()
PlaceBet()
ClearBet()
Collect()

When you initialize the Guy object, make sure you set its MyBet field to null, and call its UpdateLabels() method as soon as it's initialized.

This is the object that Guy uses to represent bets in the application.

Bet
Amount
Dog
Bettor ←
GetDescription
PayOut

Hint: You'll instantiate Bet in the Guy code. Guy willl use the **this** keyword to pass a reference to himself to the Bet's initializer.

```
class Guy {
    public string Name; // The guy's name
    public Bet MyBet; // An instance of Bet() that has his bet
    public int Cash; // How much cash he has


    // The last two fields are the guy's GUI controls on the form
    public RadioButton MyRadioButton; // My RadioButton
    public Label MyLabel; // My Label

    public void UpdateLabels() {
        // Set my label to my bet's description, and the label on my
        // radio button to show my cash ("Joe has 43 bucks")
    }v

    public void ClearBet() { } // Reset my bet so it's zero

    public bool PlaceBet(int Amount, int Dog) {
        // Place a new bet and store it in my bet field
        // Return true if the guy had enough money to bet
    }

    public void Collect(int Winner) { } // Ask my bet to pay out
}
```

Once you set MyLabel to one of the labels on the form, you'll be able to change the label's text using MyLabel.Text. And the same goes for MyRadioButton!

Add your code here.

Remember that bets are represented by instances of Bet.

The key here is to use the Bet object...let it do the work.

The object initializer for Bet just sets the amount, dog, and bettor.

```
class Bet {
    public int Amount; // The amount of cash that was bet
    public int Dog; // The number of the dog the bet is on
    public Guy Bettor; // The guy who placed the bet

    public string GetDescription() {
        // Return a string that says who placed the bet, how much
        // cash was bet, and which dog he bet on ("Joe bets 8 on
        // dog #4"). If the amount is zero, no bet was placed
        // ("Joe hasn't placed a bet").
    }

    public int PayOut(int Winner) {
        // The parameter is the winner of the race. If the dog won,
        // return the amount bet. Otherwise, return the negative of
        // the amount bet.
    }
}
```

This is a common programming task: assembling a string or message from several individual bits of data.

Here's your application architecture

Spend some time looking closely at the architecture. It looks pretty complicated at first, but there's nothing here you don't know. Your job is to recreate this architecture yourself, starting with the Greyhound and Guy arrays in your main form.

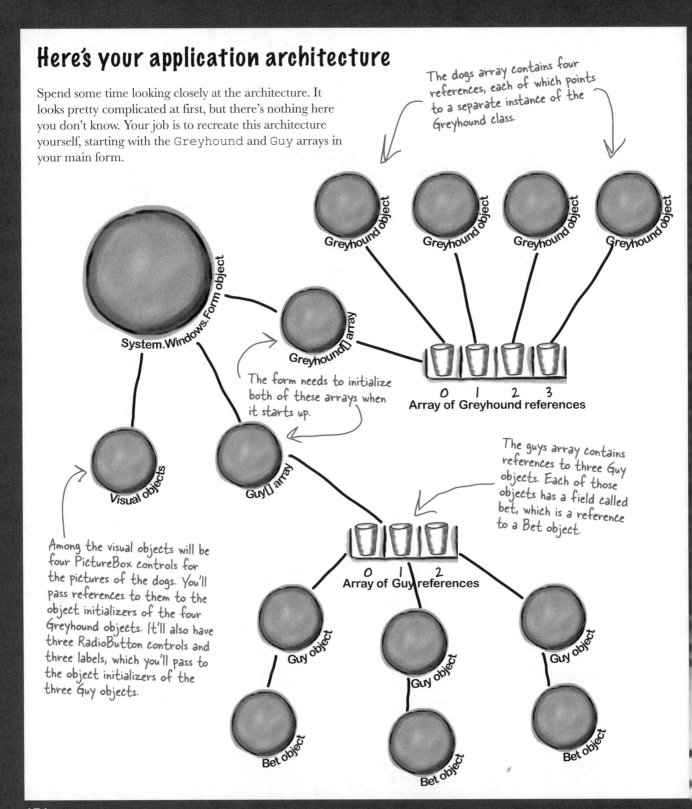

The dogs array contains four references, each of which points to a separate instance of the Greyhound class.

Greyhound object
Greyhound object
Greyhound object
Greyhound object

System.Windows.Form object

Greyhound[] array

The form needs to initialize both of these arrays when it starts up.

0   1   2   3
Array of Greyhound references

Visual objects

Guy[] array

The guys array contains references to three Guy objects. Each of those objects has a field called bet, which is a reference to a Bet object.

Among the visual objects will be four PictureBox controls for the pictures of the dogs. You'll pass references to them to the object initializers of the four Greyhound objects. It'll also have three RadioButton controls and three labels, which you'll pass to the object initializers of the three Guy objects.

0   1   2
Array of Guy references

Guy object
Guy object
Guy object

Bet object
Bet object
Bet object

A Day at the Races

When a Guy places a bet, he creates a new Bet object

First the form tells Guy #2 to place a bet for 7 bucks on dog #3...

Guy[1].PlaceBet(7, 3)

...so Guy #2 creates a new instance of Bet, using the this keyword to tell the Bet object that he's the bettor...

```
MyBet = new Bet()
{ Amount = 7, dog = 3, Bettor = this };
```

Form object   Guy object   Bet object

true

...and since the Guy had enough money to place the bet, PlaceBet() returns true.

The form tells the dogs to keep running until there's a winner

When the user tells the form to start the race, the form starts a loop to animate each dog running along the track.

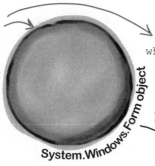

System.Windows.Form object

Each dog's Run() method checks to see if that dog won the race, so the loops should end immediately as soon as one of the dog wins.

```
while ( there's no winner ) {
   for ( loop through each dog, making
         sure there's still no winner ) {
      have the dog run one pace
   }
}
```

Greyhound[] array

The Bet object figures out if it should pay out

The betting parlor in the form tells each Guy which dog won so he can collect any winnings from his bet.

Guy[1].Collect(winningDog)   MyBet.PayOut(winningDog)

Form object   Guy object   Bet object

The Guy will add the result of Bet.PayOut() to his cash. So if the dog won, it should return Amount; otherwise, it'll return -Amount.

```
if ( my dog won ) {
   return Amount;
} else {
   return -Amount;
}
```

175

Here's what your GUI should look like

The graphical user interface for the "Day at the Races" application consists of a form that's divided into two sections. The top is the racetrack: a `PictureBox` control for the track, and four more for the dogs. The bottom half of the form shows the betting parlor, where three guys (Joe, Bob, and Al) can bet on the outcome of the race.

Each of the four dogs has its own PictureBox control. When you initialize each of the four Greyhound objects, each one's MyPicturebox field will have a reference to one of these objects. You'll pass the reference (along with the racetrack length and starting position) to the Greyhound's object initializer.

You'll use the Length property of the racetrack PictureBox control to set the racetrack length in the Greyhound object, which it'll use to figure out if it won the race.

Make sure you set each PictureBox's SizeMode property to Zoom.

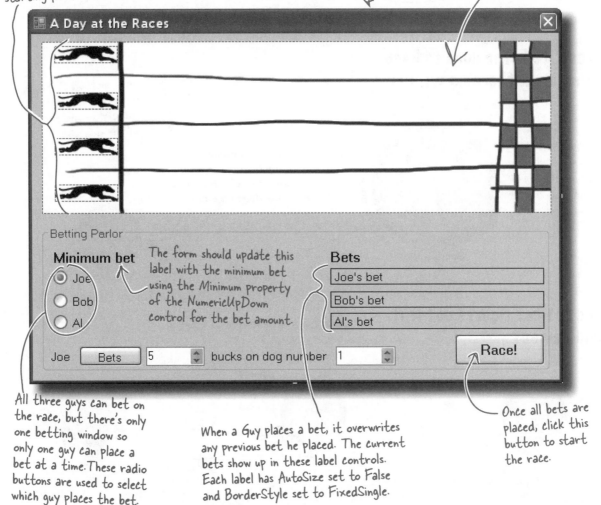

All three guys can bet on the race, but there's only one betting window so only one guy can place a bet at a time. These radio buttons are used to select which guy places the bet.

The form should update this label with the minimum bet using the Minimum property of the NumericUpDown control for the bet amount.

When a Guy places a bet, it overwrites any previous bet he placed. The current bets show up in these label controls. Each label has AutoSize set to False and BorderStyle set to FixedSingle.

Once all bets are placed, click this button to start the race.

You can download the graphics files from www.headfirstlabs.com/books/hfcsharp/

Placing bets

Use the controls in the Betting Parlor group box to place each guy's bet. There are three distinct stages here:

> When a guy places a bet, his Guy object updates this label using the MyLabel reference. He also updates the cash he has using his MyRadioButton reference.

(1) No bets have been placed yet

When the program first starts up, or if a race has just finished, no bets have been placed in the betting parlor. You'll see each guy's total cash next to his name on the left.

> Each guy's cash shows up here.

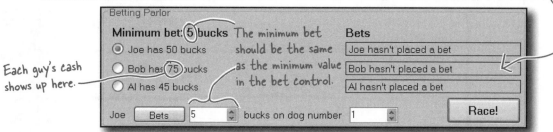

> The minimum bet should be the same as the minimum value in the bet control.

(2) Each guy places his bets

To place a bet, select the guy's radio button, select an amount and a dog, and click the Bets button. His PlaceBet() method will update the label and radio button.

> Once Bob places his bet, his Guy object updates this label and the radio button text.

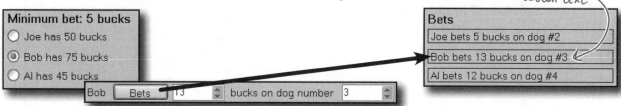

(3) After the race, each guy collects his winnings (or pays up!)

Once the race is complete and there's a winner, each Guy object calls his Collect() method and adds his winnings or losses to his cash.

> Since Al bet 12 bucks on the winning dog, his cash goes up by 12. The other two guys lose the money they bet.

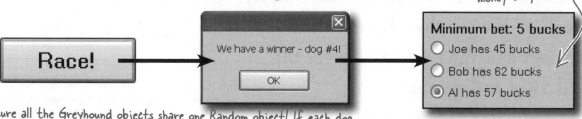

Make sure all the Greyhound objects share one Random object! If each dog creates its own new instance of Random, you might see a bug where all of the dogs generate the same sequence of random numbers.

The Finished Product

You'll know your "Day at the Races" application is
done when your guys can place their bets and watch
the dogs race.

During the race, the four dog
images run across the racetrack
until one of them wins the race.

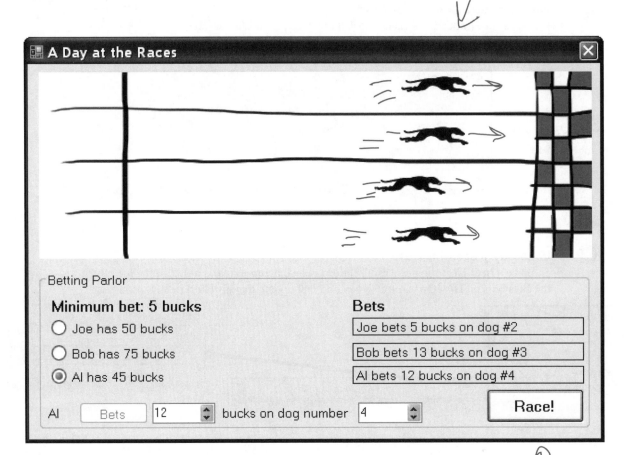

You can download a finished executable,
as well as the graphics files for the
four dogs and the racetrack, from the
Head First Labs website:
www.headfirstlabs.com/books/hfcsharp

During the race, no bets can be
placed...and make sure you can't
start a new race while the dogs
are running!

But you won't find the source code! In real life, you
don't get a solution to your programming problems.
Here's your chance to really test your C# knowledge
and see just how much you've learned!

5 encapsulation

Keep your privates...
private

No peeking!

Ever wished for a little more privacy?

Sometimes your objects feel the same way. Just like you don't want anybody you don't trust reading your journal or paging through your bank statements, good objects don't let *other* objects go poking around their fields. In this chapter, you're going to learn about the power of **encapsulation**. You'll **make your object's data private**, and add methods to **protect how that data is accessed**.

Kathleen is an event planner

She's been planning dinner parties for her clients and she's doing really well. But lately she's been having a hard time responding to clients fast enough with an estimate for her services.

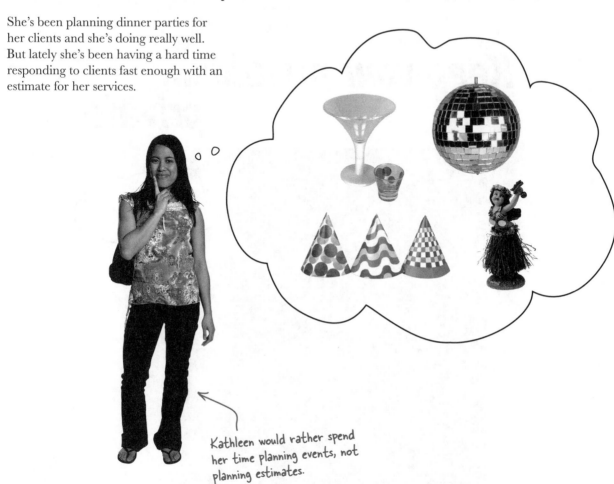

Kathleen would rather spend her time planning events, not planning estimates.

When a new client calls Kathleen to do a party, she needs to find out the number of guests, what kind of drinks to serve, and what decorations she should buy. Then she uses a pretty complicated calculation to figure out the total cost, based on a flow chart she's been using for years. The bad news is that it takes her a long time to work through her chart, and while she's estimating, her potential clients are checking out other event planners.

It's up to you to build her a C#-driven event estimator and save her business. Imagine the party she'll throw you when you succeed!

What does the estimator do?

Kathleen runs down some of the basics of her system for figuring out the costs of an event. Here's part of what she came up with:

Kathleen's Party Planning Program—Cost Estimate for a Dinner Party

- For each person on the guest list there's a $25 food charge.

- Clients have a choice when it comes to drinks. Most parties serve alcohol, which costs $20 per person. But they can also choose to have a party without alcohol. Kathleen calls that the "Healthy Option," and it only costs $5 per person to have soda and juice instead of alcohol. Choosing the Healthy Option is a lot easier for her, so she gives the client a 5% discount on the entire party, too.

- There are two options for the cost of decorations. If a client goes with the normal decorations, it's $7.50 per person with a $30 decorating fee. A client can also upgrade the party decorations to the "Fancy Option"—that costs $15 per person with a $50 one-time decorating fee.

Here's another look at this same set of costs, broken down into a little flow chart to help you see how it works:

Some of these choices involve a change to the final price of the event, as well as individual per-person costs.

While most choices affect the cost for each guest, there are also one-time fees to figure in.

Exercise

Build a program to solve Kathleen's party estimating problem.

1 Create a new Windows Application project and add a class file to it called `DinnerParty.cs`, and build the `DinnerParty` class using the class diagram to the left. It's got three methods: `CalculateCostOfDecorations()`, `SetHealthyOption()`, and `CalculateCost()`. For the fields, use `decimal` for the two costs, `int` for the number of people, and `bool` to keep track of whether or not the Healthy Option was selected. Make sure you **add an M after every literal** you assign to a decimal value (`10.0M`).

DinnerParty
NumberOfPeople
CostOfBeveragesPerPerson
CostOfDecorations
SetHealthyOption()
CalculateCostOfDecorations()
CalculateCost()

Here's the class diagram for the DinnerParty class you'll need to create.

2 Here's a useful C# tool. Since the cost of food won't be changed by the program, you can declare it as a **constant**, which is like a variable except that its value can never be changed. Here's the declaration to use:

```
public const int CostOfFoodPerPerson = 25;
```

3 Flip back to the previous page to be sure you've got all of the logic right for the methods. Only one of them returns a value (a `decimal`)—the other two are `void`. The `CalculateCostOfDecorations()` method figures out the cost of decorations for the number of people attending the party. Use the `CalculateCost()` method to figure out the total cost by adding the cost of the decorations to the cost of drinks and food per person. If the client wants the Healthy Option, you can apply the discount inside the `CalculateCost()` method after you've figured out the total cost.

4 Add this code to your form:

You'll declare the dinnerParty field in the form, and then add these four lines below InitializeComponent().

```
DinnerParty dinnerParty;
public Form1() {
    InitializeComponent();
    dinnerParty = new DinnerParty() { NumberOfPeople = 5 }
    dinnerParty.SetHealthyOption(false);
    dinnerParty.CalculateCostOfDecorations(true);
    DisplayDinnerPartyCost();
}
```

The SetHealthyOption() method uses a bool parameter (healthyOption) to update the CostOfBeveragesPerPerson field based on whether or not the client wants the Healthy Option.

5 Here's what the form should look like. Use the `NumericUpDown` control's properties to set the maximum number of people to 20, the minimum to 1, and the default to 5. Get rid of the maximize and minimize buttons, too.

You don't need to add "using System.Windows.Forms;" to your DinnerParty class, because it doesn't use MessageBox.Show() or anything else from that .NET Framework namespace.

Set the default value to 5. The minimum should be 1 and the maximum should be 20.

Set the Fancy Decorations checkbox's Checked property to True.

This is a label named labelCost. The Text Property is empty, the BorderStyle property set to Fixed3D, and the AutoSize property set to false.

6 Instead of using a button to calculate the costs, this form will update the cost label automatically as soon as you use a checkbox or the NumericUpDown control. The first thing you need to do is create a method in the form that displays the cost.

Add this method to Form1(). It'll get called when the NumericUpDown control is clicked:

This method will get called by all of the other methods you create on the form. It's how you update the cost label with the right value whenever anything changes.

Add this method to the form—it'll recalculate the cost of the party and put it in the Cost label.

```
private void DisplayDinnerPartyCost()
{
    decimal Cost = dinnerParty.CalculateCost(checkBox2.Checked);
    costLabel.Text = Cost.ToString("c");
}
```

Change the name of the label that displays the cost to costLabel.

Passing "c" to ToString() tells it to format the cost as a currency value. If you're in a country that uses dollars, it'll add a dollar sign.

This is true if the checkbox for the Healthy Option is checked.

7 Now hook up the NumericUpDown field to the NumberOfPeople variable you created in the DinnerParty class and display the cost in the form. Double-click on the NumericUpDown control—the IDE will add an ***event handler*** to your code. That's a method that gets run every time the control is changed. It'll reset the number of people in the party. Fill it in like this:

You've been using event handlers all along—when you double-click on a button, the IDE adds a Click event handler. Now you know what it's called.

```
private void numericUpDown1_ValueChanged(
                            object sender, EventArgs e)
{
    dinnerParty.NumberOfPeople = (int) numericUpDown1.Value;
    DisplayDinnerPartyCost();
}
```

You need to cast numericUpDown.Value to an int because it's a Decimal property.

Uh-oh—there's a problem with this code. Can you spot it? Don't worry if you don't see it just yet. We'll dig into it in just a couple of minutes!

The value you send from the form to the method will be fancyBox.Checked. That will be passed as a boolean parameter to the method in the class.

These are just two-line methods. The first line will call the method you created in the class to figure out the costs, and the second will display the total cost on the form.

8 Double-click on the Fancy Decorations checkbox on the form and make sure that it first calls CalculateCostOfDecorations() and then DisplayDinnerPartyCost(). Next, double-click the Healthy Option checkbox and make sure that it calls the SetHealthyOption() method in the DinnerParty class and then calls the DisplayDinnerPartyCost() method.

Exercise
Solution

Here's the code that goes into `DinnerParty.cs`.

> Using a constant for CostOfFoodPerPerson ensures the value can't be changed. It also makes the code easier to read—it's clear that this value never changes.

> When the form first creates the object, it uses the initializer to set NumberOfPeople. Then it calls SetHealthyOption() and CalculateCostOfDecorations() to set the other fields.

```
class DinnerParty {
    const int CostOfFoodPerPerson = 25;
    public int NumberOfPeople;
    public decimal CostOfBeveragesPerPerson;
    public decimal CostOfDecorations = 0;

    public void SetHealthyOption(bool healthyOption) {
        if (healthyOption) {
            CostOfBeveragesPerPerson = 5.00M;
        } else {
            CostOfBeveragesPerPerson = 20.00M;
        }
    }

    public void CalculateCostOfDecorations(bool fancy) {
        if (fancy)
        {
            CostOfDecorations = (NumberOfPeople * 15.00M) + 50M;
        } else {
            CostOfDecorations = (NumberOfPeople * 7.50M) + 30M;
        }
    }
    public decimal CalculateCost(bool healthyOption) {
        decimal totalCost = CostOfDecorations +
                ((CostOfBeveragesPerPerson + CostOfFoodPerPerson)
                    * NumberOfPeople);

        if (healthyOption) {
            return totalCost * .95M;
        } else {
            return totalCost;
        }
    }
}
```

> We used "if (Fancy)" instead of typing "if (Fancy == true)" because the if statement always checks if the condition is true.

> We used parentheses to make sure the math works out properly.

> This applies the 5% discount to the overall event cost if the non-alcoholic option was chosen.

We had you use a decimal for the prices because it's designed for monetary values. Just make sure you always put an "M" after every literal—so if you want to store $35.26, make sure you write 35.26M. You can remember this because the M stands for *Money*!

```csharp
public partial class Form1 : Form {
    DinnerParty dinnerParty;
    public Form1() {
        InitializeComponent();
        dinnerParty = new DinnerParty() { NumberOfPeople = 5 };
        dinnerParty.CalculateCostOfDecorations(fancyBox.Checked);
        dinnerParty.SetHealthyOption(healthyBox.Checked);
        DisplayDinnerPartyCost();
    }

    private void fancyBox_CheckedChanged(object sender, EventArgs e) {
        dinnerParty.CalculateCostOfDecorations(fancyBox.Checked);
        DisplayDinnerPartyCost();
    }

    private void healthyBox_CheckedChanged(object sender, EventArgs e) {
        dinnerParty.SetHealthyOption(healthyBox.Checked);
        DisplayDinnerPartyCost();
    }

    private void numericUpDown1_ValueChanged(object sender, EventArgs e) {
        dinnerParty.NumberOfPeople = (int)numericUpDown1.Value;
        DisplayDinnerPartyCost();
    }

    private void DisplayDinnerPartyCost() {
        decimal Cost = dinnerParty.CalculateCost(healthyBox.Checked);
        costLabel.Text = Cost.ToString("c");
    }
}
```

We call DisplayDinnerPartyCost to initialize the label that shows the cost as soon as the form's loaded.

Changes to the checkboxes on the form set the healthyOption and Fancy booleans to true or false in the SetHealthyOption() and CalculateCostOfDecorations() methods.

We named our checkboxes "healthyBox" and "fancyBox" so you could see what's going on in their event handler methods.

The new dinner party cost needs to be recalculated and displayed any time the number changes or the checkboxes are checked.

String formatting

You've already seen how you can convert any variable to a string using its ToString() method. If you pass "c" to ToString(), it converts it to the local currency. You can also pass it "f3" to format it as a decimal number with three decimal places, "0" (that's a zero) to convert it to a whole number, "0%" for a whole number percentage, and "n" to display it as a number with a comma separator for thousands. Take a minute and see how each of these looks in your program!

Kathleen's Test Drive

> This rocks! Estimating is about to get a whole lot easier.

Rob's one of Kathleen's favorite clients. She did his wedding last year, and now she's planning an important dinner party for him.

Rob (on phone): Hi Kathleen. How are the arrangements for my dinner party going?

Kathleen: Just great. We were out looking at decorations this morning and I think you'll love the way the party's going to look.

When you start the program, the Fancy Decorations box should already be checked because you set its Checked property to true. Setting the number of people to 10 gives a cost of $575.

Rob: That's awesome. Listen, we just got a call from my wife's aunt. She and her husband are going to be visiting for the next couple of weeks. Can you tell me what it does to the estimate to move from 10 to 12 people on the guest list?

Kathleen: Sure! I'll have that for you in just one minute.

Changing the Number of People value from 10 to 12 and hitting enter shows $665 as the total cost. Hmm, that seems a little low....

Kathleen: OK. It looks like the total cost for the dinner will go from $575 to $665.

Rob: Only $90 difference? That sounds like a great deal! What if we decide to cut the fancy decorations? What's the cost then?

Turning off the Fancy Decorations checkbox only reduces the amount by $5. That can't be right!

Kathleen: Um, it looks like…um, $660.

Rob: $660? I thought the decorations were $15 per person. Did you change your pricing or something? If it's only $5 difference, we might as well go with the fancy decorations. I've gotta tell you though, this pricing is confusing.

Kathleen: We just had this new program written to do the estimation for us. But it looks like there might be a problem. Just one second while I add the fancy decorations back to the bill.

When you turn the Fancy Decorations back on, the number shoots up to $770. These numbers are just wrong.

Kathleen: Rob, I think there's been a mistake. It looks like the cost with the fancy decorations just shot up to $770. That does seem to make more sense. But I am beginning not to trust this application. I'm going to send it back for some bug fixes and work up your estimate by hand. Can I get back to you tomorrow?

Rob: I am not paying $770 just to add two people to the party. The price you quoted me before was a lot more reasonable. I'll pay you the $665 you quoted me in the first place, but I just can't go higher than that!

BRAIN POWER

Why do you think the numbers are coming out wrong every time Kathleen makes a change?

Each option should be calculated **individually**

Even though we made sure to calculate all of the amounts according to what Kathleen said, we didn't think about what would happen when people made changes to just one of the options on the form.

When you launch the program, the form sets the number of people to 5 and Fancy Decorations to true. It leaves Healthy Option unchecked and it calculates the cost of the dinner party as $350. Here's how it comes up with the initial total cost:

We built a nasty little bug into the code we gave you to show you just how easy it is to have problems with how objects use one another's fields...and just how hard those problems are to spot.

5 people.

$20 per person for drinks ⟶ Total cost of drinks = $100

$25 per person for food ⟶ Total cost of food = $125

$15 per person for decorations plus $50 fee. ⟶ Total cost of decorations = $125

So far, so good!

$100 + $125 + 125 = $350

When you change the number of guests, the application should recalculate the total estimate the same way. But it doesn't:

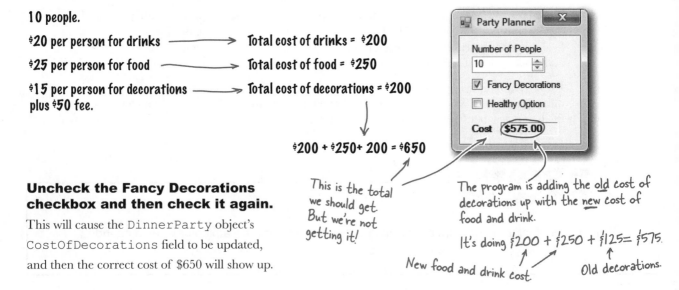

10 people.

$20 per person for drinks ⟶ Total cost of drinks = $200

$25 per person for food ⟶ Total cost of food = $250

$15 per person for decorations plus $50 fee. ⟶ Total cost of decorations = $200

$200 + $250 + 200 = $650

This is the total we should get. But we're not getting it!

The program is adding the old cost of decorations up with the new cost of food and drink.

It's doing $200 + $250 + $125 = $575.

New food and drink cost.   Old decorations.

Uncheck the Fancy Decorations checkbox and then check it again.

This will cause the `DinnerParty` object's `CostOfDecorations` field to be updated, and then the correct cost of $650 will show up.

The Problem Up Close

Take a look at the method that handles changes to the value in the `numericUpDown` control. It sets the value from the field to the `NumberofPeople` variable and then calls the `DisplayDinnerPartyCost()` method. Then it counts on that method to handle recalculating all the individual new costs.

```csharp
private void numericUpDown1_ValueChanged(
                    object sender, EventArgs e) {

    dinnerParty.NumberOfPeople = (int)numericUpDown1.Value;

    DisplayDinnerPartyCost();

}
```

> This line sets the value of NumberofPeople in this instance of DinnerParty to the value in the form.

> This method calls the CalculateCost() method, but _not_ the CalculateCostofDecorations() method.

So, when you make a change to the value in the `NumberofPeople` field, this method never gets called:

```csharp
public void CalculateCostOfDecorations(bool Fancy) {

    if (Fancy) {

        CostOfDecorations = (NumberOfPeople * 15.00M) + 50M;

    } else {

        CostOfDecorations = (NumberOfPeople * 7.50M) + 30M;

    }

}
```

> This variable is set to $125 from when the form first called it, and since this method doesn't get called again, it doesn't change.

> That's why the number corrects itself when you turn fancy decorations back on. Clicking the checkbox makes the program run CalculateCostOf Decorations() again.

o O

> Hold on! I assumed Kathleen would always set all three options at once!

People won't always use your classes in exactly the way you expect.

Luckily, C# gives you a powerful tool to make sure your program always works correctly—even when people do things you never thought of. It's called **encapsulation** and it's a really helpful technique for working with objects.

> ...and sometimes those "people" who are using your classes are you! You might be writing a class today that you'll be using tomorrow.

It's easy to accidentally misuse your objects

Kathleen ran into problems because her form ignored the convenient
`CalculateCostOfDecorations()` method that you set up and instead
went directly to the fields in the `DinnerParty` class. So even though your
`DinnerParty` class worked just fine, the form called it in an unexpected way...
and that caused problems.

1 **How the DinnerParty class expected to be called**
The `DinnerParty` class gave the form a perfectly good method to
calculate the total cost of decorations. All it had to do was set the number
of people and then call `CalculateCostOfDecorations()`, and then
`CalculateCost()` will return the correct cost.

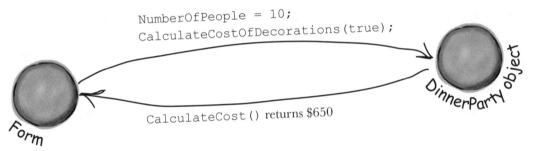

```
NumberOfPeople = 10;
CalculateCostOfDecorations(true);
```

`CalculateCost()` returns $650

2 **How the DinnerParty class was actually called**
The form set the number of people, but just called the `CalculateCost()`
method without first recalculating the cost of the decorations. That threw off
the whole calculation, and Kathleen ended up giving Rob the wrong price.

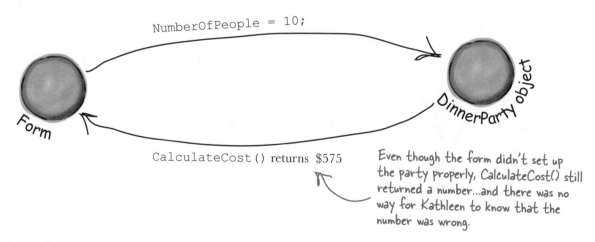

```
NumberOfPeople = 10;
```

`CalculateCost()` returns $575

Even though the form didn't set up
the party properly, CalculateCost() still
returned a number...and there was no
way for Kathleen to know that the
number was wrong.

Encapsulation means keeping some of the data in a class private

There's an easy way to avoid this kind of problem: make sure that there's only one way to use your class. Luckily, C# makes it easy to do that by letting you declare some of your fields as **private**. So far, you've only seen public fields. If you've got an object with a public field, any other object can read or change that field. But if you make it a private field, then **that field can only be accessed from inside that object** (or by another object *of the same class*).

Use your laziness to your own benefit—if you leave off the "private" or "public", then C# will just assume that your field is private.

Also, a class's static methods can access the private field in any instance of that class.

```
class DinnerParty {

    private int numberOfPeople;

    ...
```

If you want to make a field private, all you need to do is use the private keyword when you declare it. That tells C# that if you've got an instance of DinnerParty, its numberOfPeople field can only be read and written by that instance—or another instance of DinnerParty. Other objects won't even know it's there.

```
    public void SetPartyOptions(int people, bool fancy) {

        numberOfPeople = people;

        CalculateCostOfDecorations(fancy);

    }

    public int GetNumberOfPeople() {

        return numberOfPeople;

    }
```

Other objects still need a way to set the number of people for the dinner party. One good way to give them access to it is to add methods to set or get the number of people. That way you can make sure that the CalculateCostOfDecorations() method gets run every time the number of people is changed. That'll take care of that pesky bug.

By making the field that holds the number of party guests *private*, we only give the form one way to tell the DinnerParty class how many people are at the party—and we can make sure the cost of decorations is recalculated properly. When you make some data private and then write code to use that data, it's called *encapsulation*.

en-cap-su-la-ted, adj.
enclosed by a protective coating or membrane. *The divers were fully **encapsulated** by their submersible, and could only enter and exit through the airlock.*

Use encapsulation to control access to your class's methods and fields

When you make all of your fields and methods public, any other class can access them. Everything your class does and knows about becomes an open book for every other class in your program…and you just saw how that can cause your program to behave in ways you never expected. Encapsulation lets you control what you share and what you keep private inside your class. Let's see how this works:

SecretAgent

Alias
RealName
Password

AgentGreeting()

1 Super-spy Herb Jones is defending life, liberty, and the pursuit of happiness as an undercover agent in the USSR. His `ciaAgent` object is an instance of the `SecretAgent` class.

```
RealName: "Herb Jones"
Alias: "Dash Martin"
Password: "the crow flies at midnight"
```

ciaAgent

EnemyAgent

Borscht
Vodka

ContactComrades()
OverthrowCapitalists()

2 Agent Jones has a plan to help him evade the enemy KGB agents. He added an `AgentGreeting()` method that takes a password as its parameter. If he doesn't get the right password, he'll only reveal his alias, Dash Martin.

3 Seems like a foolproof way to protect the agent's identity, right? As long as the agent object that calls it doesn't have the right password, the agent's name is safe.

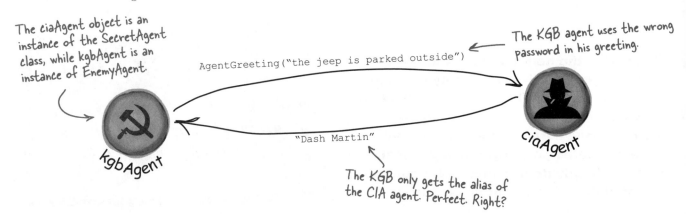

The ciaAgent object is an instance of the SecretAgent class, while kgbAgent is an instance of EnemyAgent.

The KGB agent uses the wrong password in his greeting.

```
AgentGreeting("the jeep is parked outside")
```

kgbAgent

```
"Dash Martin"
```

The KGB only gets the alias of the CIA agent. Perfect. Right?

ciaAgent

But is the realName field <u>REALLY</u> protected?

So as long as the KGB doesn't know any CIA agent passwords, the
CIA's real names are safe. Right? But what about the field declaration
for the realName field:

Setting your variables
public means they can be
accessed, and even changed,
from outside the class. →

public string RealName;

He left the field public...
Why go through all of
the trouble to guess his
password? I can just get
his name directly!

Setting your variables as public means
they can be accessed, and even changed,
from outside the class.

`string name = ciaAgent.RealName;`

kgbAgent

ciaAgent

There's no need to call any
method. The realName field is
wide open for everyone to see!

Agent Jones can use **private** fields to keep his identity secret from
enemy spy objects. Once he declares the realName field as private, the
only way to get to it is *by calling methods that have access to the
private parts of the class*. So the KGB agent is foiled!

The kgbAgent object can't
access the ciaAgent's private
fields because they're instances
of different classes.

Just replace public with
private, and boom, your
fields are now hidden
from the world.

private string realName;

Keeping your fields and methods
private makes sure no outside
code is going to make changes to
the values you're using when you
don't expect it.

You'd also want to make sure that the field
that stores the password is private, otherwise
the enemy agent can get to it.

Private fields and methods can only be accessed from <u>inside</u> the class

There's only one way that an object can get at the data stored inside another object's private fields: by using the public fields and methods that return the data. But while KGB and MI5 agents need to use the AgentGreeting() method, friendly spies can see everything—any class can **see private fields in other instances of the same class**.

Now that the fields are private, this is pretty much the only way the mi5Agent can get the ciaAgent's real name.

mi5agent is an instance of the BritishAgent class, so it doesn't have access to ciaAgent's private fields either.

Only another ciaAgent object can see them.

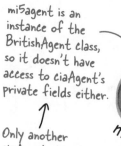

mi5Agent

AgentGreeting("the crow flies at midnight")

"Herb Jones"

ciaAgent

there are no Dumb Questions

Q: OK, so I need to access private data through public methods. What happens if the class with the private field doesn't give me a way to get at that data, but my object needs to use it?

A: Then you can't access the data from outside the object. When you're writing a class, you should always make sure that you give other objects some way to get at the data they need. Private fields are a very important part of encapsulation, but they're only part of the story. Writing a class with good encapsulation means giving a sensible, easy-to-use way for other objects to get the data they need, without giving them access to hijack data your class needs.

Q: Why would I ever want to keep a field with no way for another class to access?

A: Sometimes a class needs to keep track of information that is necessary for it to operate, but that no other object really needs to see. Here's an example. When computers generate random numbers, they use special values called *seeds*. You don't need to know how they work, but every instance of

Random actually contains an array of several dozen numbers that it uses to make sure that Next() always gives you a random number. If you create an instance of Random, you won't be able to see that array. That's because you don't need it—but if you had access to it, you might be able to put values in it that would cause it to give non-random values. So the seeds have been completely encapsulated from you.

Q: Hey, I just noticed that all of the event handlers I've been using have the `private` keyword. Why are they private?

A: Because C# forms are set up so that only the controls on the forms can trigger event handlers. When you put the `private` keyword in front of any method, then that method can only be used from inside your class. When the IDE adds an event handler method to your program, it declares it as private so other forms or objects can't get to it. But there's no rule that says that an event handler must be private. In fact, you can check this out for yourself—double-click on a button, then change its event handler declaration to `public`. The code will still compile and run.

> **The only way that one object can get to data stored in a private field inside another object is by using public methods that return the data.**

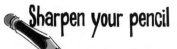 **Sharpen your pencil**

Here's a class with some private fields. Circle the statements below that **won't compile** if they're run from outside the class using **an instance of the object called mySuperChef.**

```
class SuperChef
{
      public string cookieRecipe;
      private string secretIngredient;
      private const int loyalCustomerOrderAmount = 60;
      public int Temperature;
      private string ingredientSupplier;

      public string GetRecipe (int orderAmount)
      {
            if (orderAmount >= loyalCustomerOrderAmount)
            {
                  return cookieRecipe + " " + secretIngredient;
            }
            else
            {
                  return cookieRecipe;
            }
      }
}
```

1. `string ovenTemp = mySuperChef.Temperature;`

2. `string supplier = mySuperChef.ingredientSupplier;`

3. `int loyalCustomerOrderAmount = 94;`

4. `mySuperChef.secretIngredient = "cardamom";`

5. `mySuperChef.cookieRecipe = "get 3 eggs, 2 1/2 cup flour, 1 tsp salt, 1 tsp vanilla and 1.5 cups sugar and mix them together. Bake for 10 minutes at 375. Yum!";`

6. `string recipe = mySuperChef.GetRecipe(56);`

7. After running all of the lines that will compile above, what's the value of `recipe`?

....

....

Sharpen your pencil
Solution

Here's a class with some private fields. Circle the statements below that **won't compile** if they're run from outside the class using **an instance of the object called mySuperChef**.

```
class SuperChef
{
        public string cookieRecipe;
        private string secretIngredient;
        private const int loyalCustomerOrderAmount = 60;
        public int Temperature;
        private string ingredientSupplier;

        public string GetRecipe (int orderAmount)
        {
                if (orderAmount >= loyalCustomerOrderAmount)
                {
                        return cookieRecipe + " " + secretIngredient;
                }
                else
                {
                        return cookieRecipe;
                }
        }
}
```

The only way to get the secret ingredient is to order a whole lot of cookies. Outside code can't access this field directly.

1. string ovenTemp = mySuperChef.Temperature;

#1 doesn't compile because you can't just assign an int to a string.

2. string supplier = mySuperChef.ingredientSupplier;

3. int loyalCustomerOrderAmount = 54;

#2 and #4 don't compile because ingredientSupplier and secretIngredient are private.

4. mySuperChef.secretIngredient = "cardamom";

5. mySuperChef.cookieRecipe = "Get 3 eggs, 2 1/2 cup flour, 1 tsp salt, 1 tsp vanilla and 1.5 cups sugar and mix them together. Bake for 10 minutes at 375. Yum!";

6. string recipe = mySuperChef.GetRecipe(56);

Even though you created a local variable called loyalCustomerAmount and set it to 54, that didn't change the object's loyalCustomerAmount value, which is still 60—so it won't print the secret ingredient.

7. After running all of the lines that will compile above, what's the value of recipe?

"Get 3 eggs, 2 1/2 cup flour, 1 tsp salt, 1 tsp vanilla and 1.5 cups sugar and mix them together. Bake for 10 minutes at 375. Yum!"

> Something's really not right here. If I make a field private, all that does is keep my program from compiling another class that tries to use it. But if I just change the "private" to "public" my program builds again! Adding "private" just broke my program. So why would I ever want to make a field private?

Because sometimes you want your class to hide information from the rest of the program.

A lot of people find encapsulation a little odd the first time they come across it because the idea of hiding one class's fields, properties, or methods from another class is a little counterintuitive. But there are some very good reasons that you'll want to think about what information in your class to expose to the rest of the program.

Encapsulation makes your classes...

★ **Easy to use**

You already know that classes use fields to keep track of their state. And a lot of them use methods to keep those fields up to date—methods that no other class will ever call. It's pretty common to have a class that has fields, methods, and properties that will never be called by any other class. If you make those members private, then they won't pop up in the IntelliSense window later when you need to use that class.

★ **Easy to maintain**

Remember that bug in Kathleen's program? It happened because the form accessed a field directly rather than using a method to set it. If that field had been private, you would have avoided that bug.

★ **Flexible**

A lot of times, you'll want to go back and add features to a program you wrote a while ago. If your classes are well encapsulated, then you'll know exactly how to use them later on.

> **Encapsulation means having one class hide information from another. It helps you prevent bugs in your programs.**

BRAIN POWER

How could building a poorly encapsulated class now make your programs harder to modify later?

Mike's navigator program could use better encapsulation

Remember Mike's street navigation program from Chapter 3? Mike joined a geocaching group, and he thinks his navigator will give him an edge. But it's been a while since he's worked on it, and now he's run into a little trouble. Mike's navigator program has a Route class that stores a single route between two points. But he's running into all sorts of bugs because he can't seem to figure out how it's supposed to be used! Here's what happened when Mike tried to go back to his navigator and modify the code:

Geocaching is a sport where people use their GPS navigators to hide and seek containers that can be hidden anywhere in the world. Mike is really into GPS stuff, so you can see why he likes it so much.

★ Mike set the StartPoint property to the GPS coordinates of his home and the EndPoint property to the coordinates of his office, and checked the Length property. It said the length was 15.3. When he called the GetRouteLength() method, it returned 0.

> Ugh, I can't remember if I was supposed to set the StartPoint field or use the SetStartPoint() method. I know I had this all working before!

★ He uses the SetStartPoint() property to set the start point to the coordinates of his home and the SetEndPoint() property to set the end point to his office. The GetRouteLength() method returned 9.51, and the Length property contained 5.91.

★ When he tried using the StartPoint property to set the starting point and the SetEndPoint() method to set the ending point, GetRouteLength() always returned 0 and the Length property always contained 0.

★ When he tried using the SetStartPoint() method to set the starting point and the EndPoint property to set the ending point, the Length property contained 0, and the GetRouteLength() method caused the program to crash with an error that said something about not being able to divide by zero.

Sharpen your pencil

Route
StartPoint
EndPoint
Length
GetRouteLength()
GetStartPoint()
GetEndPoint()
SetStartPoint()
SetEndPoint()
ChangeStartPoint()
ChangeEndPoint()

Here's the Route object from Mike's navigator program. Which properties or methods would *you* make **private** in order to make it easier to use?

....

....

....

....

....

There are lots of ways to solve this problem, all potentially correct! Write down the one you think is best.

Think of an object as a black box

Sometimes you'll hear a programmer refer to an object as a "black box," and that's a pretty good way of thinking about them. When you call an object's methods, you don't really care how that method works—at least, not right now. All you care about is that it takes the inputs you gave it and does the right thing.

> **When you come back to code that you haven't looked at in a long time, it's easy to forget how you intended it to be used. That's where encapsulation can make your life a lot easier!**

> I know my Route object works! What matters to me **now** is figuring out how to use it for my geocaching project.

Back in Chapter 3, Mike was thinking about how to build his navigator. That's when he really cared about how the Route object worked. But that was a while ago.

Since then, he got his navigator working, and he's been using it for a long time. He knows it works well enough to be really useful for his geocaching team. Now he wants to <u>reuse</u> his Route object.

If only Mike had thought about encapsulation when he originally built his Route object! If he had, then it wouldn't be giving him a headache today!

If you encapsulate your classes well <u>today</u>, that makes them a lot easier to reuse <u>tomorrow</u>.

Right now, Mike just wants to think about his Route object as a black box. He wants to feed his coordinates into it and get a length out of it. He doesn't want to think about how the Route calculates that length...at least, not right now.

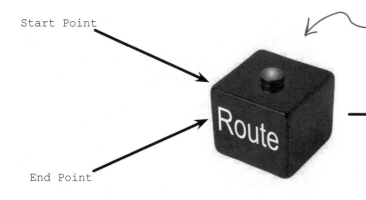

Start Point

End Point

Route

Length

So a well-encapsulated class does **exactly the same thing** as one that has poor encapsulation!

Exactly! The difference is that the well-encapsulated one is built in a way that prevents bugs and is easier to use.

It's easy to take a well-encapsulated class and turn it into a poorly encapsulated class: do a search-and-replace to change every occurrence of `private` to `public`.

And that's a funny thing about the `private` keyword: you can generally take any program and do that search-and-replace, and it will still compile and work in exactly the same way. That's one reason that encapsulation is difficult for some programmers to understand.

Until now, everything you've learned has been about making programs **do things**—perform certain behaviors. Encapsulation is a little different. It doesn't change the way your program behaves. It's more about the "chess game" side of programming: by hiding certain information in your classes when you design and build them, you set up a strategy for how they'll interact later. The better the strategy, the more flexible and maintainable your programs will be, and the more bugs you'll avoid.

And just like chess, there are an almost unlimited number of possible encapsulation strategies!

A few ideas for encapsulating classes

* **Think about ways the fields can be misused.**
  What can go wrong if they're not set properly?

* **Is everything in your class public?**
  If your class has nothing but public fields and methods, you probably need to spend a little more time thinking about encapsulation.

* **What fields require some processing or calculation to happen when they're set?**
  Those are prime candidates for encapsulation. If someone writes a method later that changes the value in any one of them, it could cause problems for the work your program is trying to do.

> The cost of decorations needs to be figured out first. Once you know that, you can just add it up with the cost of the food and drink to get the total cost.

* **Only make fields and methods public if you need to.**
  If you don't have a reason to declare something public, don't. You could make things really messy for yourself by making all of the fields in your program public—but don't just go making everything private, either. Spending a little time up front thinking about which fields really need to be public and which don't can save you a lot of time later.

Encapsulation keeps your data pristine

Sometimes the value in a field changes as your program does
what it's supposed to do. If you don't explicitly tell your program
to reset the value, you can do your calculations using the old
one. When this is the case, you want to have your program
execute some statements any time a field is changed—like
having Kathleen's program recalculate the cost every time
you change the number of people. We can avoid the problem
by encapsulating the data using private fields. We'll provide a
method to get the value of the field, and another method to set
the field and do all the necessary calculations.

A quick example of encapsulation

A `Farmer` class uses a field to store the number of cows, and
multiplies it by a number to figure out how many bags of cattle
feed are needed to feed the cows:

```
class Farmer
{
        private int numberOfCows;
}
```

*We'd better make this field private
so nobody can change it without also
changing bagsOfFeed—if they get
out of sync, that'll create bugs!*

When you create a form to let a user enter the number of cows into a numeric field,
you need to be able to change the value in the `numberOfCows` field. To do that,
you can create a method that returns the value of the field to the form object:

These accomplish the same thing!

```
public const int FeedMultiplier = 30;
public int GetNumberOfCows()
{
        return numberOfCows;
}

public void SetNumberOfCows(int newNumberOfCows)
{
        numberOfCows = newNumberOfCows;
        BagsOfFeed = numberOfCows * FeedMultiplier;
}
```

*The farmer
needs 30 bags
of feed for
each cow.*

*We'll add a method to give
other classes a way to get
the number of cows.*

*And here's a method to set the
number of cows that makes sure
the BagsOfFeed field is changed
too. Now there's no way for the
two to get out of sync.*

*We used camelCase for the private fields and PascalCase for the
public ones. PascalCase means capitalizing the first letter in every
word in the variable name. camelCase is similar to PascalCase,
except that the first letter is lowercase. That makes the
uppercase letters look like "humps" of a camel.*

Properties make encapsulation easier

You can use **properties**, which are methods that look just like fields to other objects. A property can be used to get or set a **backing field**, which is just a name for a field set by a property.

> We'll rename the private field to numberOfCows (notice the lowercase "n"). This will become the backing field for the NumberOfCows property.

```
private int numberOfCows;
```

> You'll often use properties by combining them with a normal field declaration. Here's the declaration for NumberOfCows.

```
public int NumberOfCows
{
```

> This is a **get accessor**. It's a method that's run any time the NumberOfCows property is **read**. It has a return value that matches the type of the variable—in this case it returns the value of the private numberOfCows property.

```
    get
    {
        return numberOfCows;
    }
```

> This is a **set accessor** that's called every time the NumberOfCows property is **set**. Even though the method doesn't look like it has any parameters, it actually has one called **value** that contains whatever value the field was set to.

```
    set
    {
        numberOfCows = value;
        BagsOfFeed = numberOfCows * FeedMultiplier;
    }
}
```

You **use** get and set accessors exactly like fields. Here's code for a button that sets the numbers of cows and then gets the bags of feed:

> When this line sets NumberOfCows to 10, the set accessor sets the private numberOfCows field and then updates the public BagsOfFeed field.

```
private void button1_Click(object sender, EventArgs e) {
    Farmer myFarmer = new Farmer();
    myFarmer.NumberOfCows = 10;

    int howManyBags = myFarmer.BagsOfFeed;

    myFarmer.NumberOfCows = 20;
    howManyBags = myFarmer.BagsOfFeed;
}
```

> Since the NumberOfCows set accessor updated BagsOfFeed, now you can get its value.

> Even though the code treats NumberOfCows like a field, it runs the set accessor, passing it 20. And when it queries the BagsOfFeed field it runs the get accessor, which returns 300.

Build an application to test the Farmer class

Create a new Windows Forms application that we can use to test the **Farmer** class and see properties in action. We'll use the `Console.WriteLine()` method to write the results to the output window in the IDE.

→ Do this ✳

❶ Add the `Farmer` class to your project:

```
class Farmer {
    public int BagsOfFeed;
    public const int FeedMultiplier = 30;

    private int numberOfCows;
    public int NumberOfCows {
        (add the get and set accessors from the previous page)
    }
}
```

❷ Build this form:

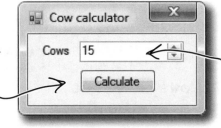

Name this button "calculate"—it uses the public Farmer data to write a line to the output.

Set the NumericUpDown control's Value to 15, its Minimum to 5, and its Maximum to 300.

❸ Here's the form for the code. It uses `Console.WriteLine()` to send its output to the **Output window** (which you can bring up by selecting "Output" from the Debug >> Windows menu). You can pass several parameters to `WriteLine()`—the first one is the string to write. If you include "`{0}`" inside the string, then `WriteLine()` replaces it with the first parameter. It replaces "`{1}`" with the second parameter, "`{2}`" with the third, etc.

```
public partial class Form1 : Form {
    Farmer farmer;
    public Form1() {
        InitializeComponent();
        farmer = new Farmer() { NumberOfCows = 15 };
    }
    private void numericUpDown1_ValueChanged(object sender, EventArgs e) {
        farmer.NumberOfCows = (int)numericUpDown1.Value;
    }
    private void calculate_Click(object sender, EventArgs e) {
        Console.WriteLine("I need {0} bags of feed for {1} cows",      ←
            farmer.BagsOfFeed, farmer.NumberOfCows);
    }
}
```

Use the Console.WriteLine() method to send a line of text to the IDE's Output window.

WriteLine() replaces "{0}" with the value in the first parameter, and "{1}" with the second parameter.

Use <u>automatic</u> <u>properties</u> to finish the class

It looks like the Cow Calculator works really well. Give it a shot—run it and click the button. Then change the number of cows to 30 and click it again. Do the same for 5 cows and then 20 cows. Here's what your Output window should look like:

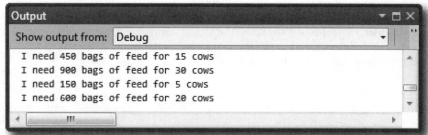

Can you see how this could lead you to accidentally add a really irritating bug in your program?

But there's a problem with the class. Add a button to the form that executes this statement:

```
farmer.BagsOfFeed = 5;
```

Now run your program again. It works fine until you press the new button. But press that button and then press the Calculate button again. Now your ouput tells you that you need 5 bags of feed—<u>no matter how many cows you have</u>! As soon as you change the NumericUpDown, the Calculate button should work again.

Fully encapsulate the Farmer class

The problem is that your class **isn't fully encapsulated**. You used properties to encapsulate NumberOfCows, but BagsOfFeed is still public. This is a common problem. In fact, it's so common that C# has a way of automatically fixing it. Just change the public BagsOfFeed field to an ***automatic property***. And the IDE makes it really easy for you to add automatic properties. Here's how:

The prop-tab-tab code snippet adds an automatic property to your code.

① Remove the BagsOfFeed field from the Farmer class. Put your cursor where the field used to be, and then type **prop** and press the tab key twice. The IDE will add this line to your code:

```
public int MyProperty { get; set; }
```

② Press the tab key—the cursor jumps to MyProperty. Change its name to BagsOfFeed:

```
public int BagsOfFeed { get; set; }
```

Now you've got a property instead of a field. When C# sees this, it works exactly the same as if you had used a backing field (like the private numberOfCows behind the public NumberOfCows property).

③ That hasn't fixed our problem yet. But there's an easy fix—just make it a **read-only property**:

```
public int BagsOfFeed { get; private set; }
```

Try to rebuild your code—you'll get an error on the line in the button that sets BagsOfFeed telling you that the **set accessor is inaccessible**. You can't modify BagsOfFeed from outside the Farmer class—you'll need to remove that line in order to get your code to compile, so remove the button from the form. Now your Farmer class is better encapsulated!

What if we want to change the feed multiplier?

We built the Cow Calculator to use a const for the feed multiplier. But what if we want to use the same Farmer class in different programs that need different feed multipliers? You've seen how poor encapsulation can cause problems when you make fields in one class too accessible to other classes. That's why you should **only make fields and methods public if you need to**. Since the Cow Calculator never updates FeedMultiplier, there's no need to allow any other class to set it. So let's change it to a read-only property that uses a backing field.

Do this!

❶ Remove this line from your program:

```
public const int FeedMultiplier = 30;
```

Use prop-tab-tab to add a read-only property. But instead of adding an automatic property, use a backing field:

```
private int feedMultiplier;
public int FeedMultiplier { get { return feedMultiplier; } }
```

This property acts just like an int field, except instead of storing a value it just returns the backing field, feedMultiplier. And since there's no set accessor, it's read-only. It has a public get, which means any other class can read the value of FeedMultiplier. But since its set is private, that makes it read-only— it can only be set by an instance of Farmer.

Since we changed FeedMultiplier from a public const to a private int field, we changed its name, so it starts with a lowercase "f". That's a pretty standard naming convention you'll see throughout the book.

❷ Go ahead and make that change to your code. Then run it. Uh-oh—something's wrong! BagsOfFeed **always returns 0 bags**.

Wait, that makes sense. FeedMultiplier never got initialized. It starts out with the default value of zero and never changes. When it's multiplied by the number of cows, it still gives you zero. So add an object initializer:

```
public Form1() {
    InitializeComponent();
    farmer = new Farmer() { NumberOfCows = 15, feedMultiplier = 30 };
```

Uh-oh—the **program won't compile!** You should get this error:

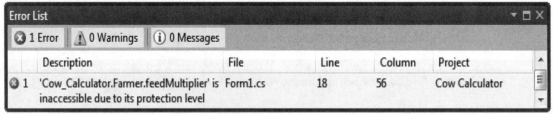

	Description	File	Line	Column	Project
❌ 1	'Cow_Calculator.Farmer.feedMultiplier' is inaccessible due to its protection level	Form1.cs	18	56	Cow Calculator

You can only initialize <u>public</u> fields and properties inside an object initializer. So how can you make sure your object gets initialized properly if some of the fields that need to be initialized are <u>private</u>?

Use a <u>constructor</u> to initialize private fields

If you need to initialize your object, but some of the fields that need to be initialized are private, then an object initializer just won't do. Luckily, there's a special method that you can add to any class called a **constructor**. If a class has a constructor, then that constructor is the **very first thing that gets executed** when the class is created with the new statement. You can pass parameters to the constructor to give it values that need to be initialized. But the constructor **does not have a return value**, because you don't actually call it directly. You pass its parameters to the new statement. And you already know that new returns the object—so there's no way for a constructor to return anything.

All you have to do to add a constructor to a class is add a method that has the same name as the class and no return value.

  Add a constructor to your Farmer class

This constructor only has two lines, but there's a lot going on here. So let's take it step by step. We already know that we need the number of cows and a feed multiplier for the class, so we'll add them as parameters to the constructor. Since we changed feedMultiplier from a const to an int, now we need an initial value for it. So let's make sure it gets passed into the constructor. We'll use the constructor to set the number of cows, too.

Notice how there's no "void" or "int" or another type after "public". That's because constructors don't have a return value.

"this" word in this. dMultiplier tells that you're king about the d, not the ameter with the e name.

```
public Farmer(int numberOfCows, int feedMultiplier) {
    this.feedMultiplier = feedMultiplier;
    NumberOfCows = numberOfCows;
}
```

The first thing we'll do is set the feed multiplier, because it needs to be set before we can call the NumberOfCows set accessor.

If we just set the private numberOfCows field, the NumberOfCows set accessor would never be called. Setting NumberOfCows makes sure it's called.

his is the error u'll get if ur constructor akes parameters t your new oesn't have any.

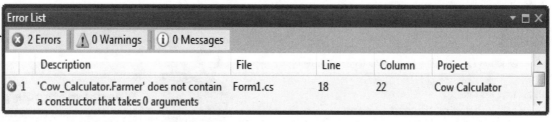

	Description	File	Line	Column	Project
⊗ 1	'Cow_Calculator.Farmer' does not contain a constructor that takes 0 arguments	Form1.cs	18	22	Cow Calculator

Error List — ⊗ 2 Errors — ⚠ 0 Warnings — ⓘ 0 Messages

  Now change the form so that it uses the constructor

The only thing you need to do now is change the form so that the new statement that creates the Farmer object uses the constructor instead of an object initializer. Once you replace the new statement, both errors will go away, and your code will work!

```
public Form1() {
    InitializeComponent();
    farmer = new Farmer(15, 30);
}
```

You already know that the form is an object. Well, it's got a constructor too! That's what this method is—notice how it's named Form1 (like the class) and it doesn't have a return value.

Here's where the new statement calls the constructor. It looks just like any other new statement, except that it has parameters that it passes into the constructor method. When you type it in, watch for the IntelliSense pop-up—it looks just like any other method.

Constructors
Way Up Close

Let's take a closer look at the Farmer constructor so we can get a good sense of what's really going on.

Constructors don't
return anything, so
there's no return type.

This constructor has two parameters, which work just like
ordinary parameters. The first one gives the number of cows,
and the second one is the feed multiplier.

```
public Farmer(int numberOfCows, int feedMultiplier) {
    this.feedMultiplier = feedMultiplier;
    NumberOfCows = numberOfCows;
}
```

We need to set the feed multiplier first,
because the second statement calls the
NumberOfCows set accessor, which needs
feedMultiplier to have a value in order to
set BagsOfFeed.

We need a way to differentiate the field called
feedMultiplier from the parameter with the
same name. That's where the "this" keyword
comes in really handy.

Since "this" is always a reference to the current object, this.feedMultiplier
refers to the field. If you leave "this" off, then feedMultiplier refers
to the parameter. So the first line in the constructor sets the private
feedMultiplier field equal to the second parameter of the constructor.

there are no
Dumb Questions

Q: Is it possible to have a constructor without any parameters?

A: Yes. It's actually very common for a class to have a constructor without a parameter. In fact, you've already seen an example of it—**your form's constructor**. Look inside a newly added Windows form and find its constructor's declaration:

```
public Form1() {
    InitializeComponent();
}
```

That's the constructor for your form object. It doesn't take any parameters, but it does have to do a lot. Take a minute and open up Form1.Designer.cs. Find the InitializeComponent() method by clicking on the plus sign next to "Windows Form Designer generated code".

That method initializes all of the controls on the form and sets all of their properties. If you drag a new control onto your form in the IDE's form designer and set some of its properties in the Properties window, you'll see those changes reflected inside the InitializeComponent() method.

The InitializeComponent() method is called inside the form's constructor so that the controls all get initialized as soon as the form object is created. (Remember, every form that gets displayed is just another object that happens to use methods that the .NET Framework provides in the System.Windows.Forms namespace to display windows, buttons, and other controls.)

When a method's parameter has the same name as a field, then it masks the field.

Watch it!

Did you notice how the constructor's feedMultiplier *parameter looks just like the backing field behind the* FeedMultiplier *property? If you wanted to use the backing field inside the constructor, you'd use the* this *keyword:* feedMultiplier *refers to the parameter, and* this.feedMultiplier *is how you'd access the private field.*

there are no
Dumb Questions

Q: Why would I need complicated logic in a get or set accessor? Isn't it just a way of creating a field?

A: Because sometimes you know that every time you set a field, you'll have to do some calculation or perform some action. Think about Kathleen's problem—she ran into trouble because the form didn't run the method to recalculate the cost of the decorations after setting the number of people in the `DinnerParty` class. If we replaced the field with a set accessor, then we could make sure that the set accessor recalculates the cost of the decorations. (In fact, you're about to do exactly that in just a couple of pages!)

Q: Wait a minute—so what's the difference between a method and a get or set accessor?

A: There is none! Get and set accessors are a special kind of method—one that looks just like a field to other objects, and is called whenever that field is set. Get accessors always return a value that's the same type as the field, and set accessors always take exactly one parameter called `value` whose type is the same as the field. Oh, and by the way, you can just say "property" instead of "get and set accessor."

Q: So you can have ANY kind of statement in a property?

A: Absolutely. Anything you can do in a method, you can do in a property. They can call other methods, access other fields, even create objects and instances. But they only get called when a property gets accessed, so it doesn't make sense to have any statements in them that don't have to do with getting or setting the property.

Q: If a set accessor always takes a parameter called `value`, why doesn't its declaration have `parentheses` with "`int value`" in them, like you'd have with any other method that takes a parameter called `value`?

A: Because C# was built to keep you from having to type in extra information that the compiler doesn't need. The parameter gets declared without you having to explicitly type it in, which doesn't sound like much when you're only typing one or two—but when you have to type a few hundred, it can be a real time saver (not to mention a bug preventer).

Every set accessor *always* has exactly one parameter called `value`, and the type of that parameter *always* matches the type of the property. C# has all the information it needs about the type and parameter as soon as you type "`set {`". So there's no need for you to type any more, and the C# compiler isn't going to make you type more than you have to.

Q: Wait a sec—is that why I don't add a return value to my constructor?

A: Exactly! Your constructor doesn't have a return value because *every* constructor is always `void`. It would be redundant to make you type "`void`" at the beginning of each constructor, so you don't have to.

Q: Can I have a get without a set or a set without a get?

A: Yes! When you have a get accessor but no set, you create a read-only property. For example, the `SecretAgent` class might have a `ReadOnly` field for the name:

```
string name = "Dash Martin";
public string Name {
    get { return name; }
}
```

And if you create a property with a set accessor but no get, then your backing field can only be written, not read. The `SecretAgent` class could use that for a `Password` property that other spies could write to but not see:

```
public string Password {
  set {
    if (value == secretCode) {
      name = "Herb Jones";
    }
  }
}
```

Both of those techniques can come in really handy when you're doing encapsulation.

Q: I've been using objects for a while, but I haven't written a constructor. Does that mean some classes don't need one?

A: No, it just means that C# automatically makes a zero-parameter constructor if there's none defined. If you define a constructor, then it doesn't do that. That's a valuable tool for encapsulation, because it means that you have the option—but not the requirement—to force anyone instantiating your class to use your constructor.

Properties (get and set accessors) are a special kind of method that's only run when another class reads or writes a property.

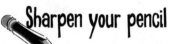
Sharpen your pencil

Take a look at the `get` and `set` accessors here. The form that is using this class has a new instance of `CableBill` called `thisMonth` and calls the `GetThisMonthsBill()` method with a button click. Write down the value of the `amountOwed` variable after the code below executed.

```
class CableBill {
    private int rentalFee;
    public CableBill(int rentalFee) {
        this.rentalFee = rentalFee;
        discount = false;
    }

    private int payPerViewDiscount;
    private bool discount;
    public bool Discount {
        set {
            discount = value;
            if (discount)
            payPerViewDiscount = 2;
            else
            payPerViewDiscount = 0;
        }
    }

    public int CalculateAmount(int payPerViewMoviesOrdered) {
        return (rentalFee - payPerViewDiscount) * payPerViewMoviesOrdered;
    }
}
```

1. ```
   CableBill january = new CableBill(4);
   MessageBox.Show(january.CalculateAmount(7).ToString());
   ```
   What's the value of amountOwed?

2. ```
   CableBill february = new CableBill(7);
   february.payPerViewDiscount = 1;
   MessageBox.Show(february.CalculateAmount(3).ToString());
   ```
   What's the value of amountOwed?

3. ```
   CableBill march = new CableBill(9);
   march.Discount = true;
   MessageBox.Show(march.CalculateAmount(6).ToString());
   ```
   What's the value of amountOwed?
   ```

there are no
Dumb Questions

Q: **I noticed that you used uppercase names for some fields but lowercase ones for others. Does that matter?**

A: Yes—it matters to you. But it doesn't matter to the compiler. C# doesn't care what you name your variables, but if you choose weird names then it makes your code hard to read. Sometimes it can get confusing when you have variables that are named the same, except one starts with an uppercase letter and the other starts with a lowercase one.

Case matters in C#. You can have two different variables called `Party` and `party` in the same method. It'll be confusing to read, but your code will compile just fine. Here are a few tips about variable names to help you keep it straight. They're not hard-and-fast rules—the compiler doesn't care whether a variable is uppercase or lowercase—but they're good suggestions to help make your code easier to read.

1. When you declare a private field, it should be in camelCase and start with a lowercase letter. (It's called camelCase because it starts with a lowercase letter and additional words are uppercase, so they resemble humps on a camel.)

2. Public properties and methods are in PascalCase (they start with an uppercase letter).

3. Parameters to methods should be in camelCase.

4. Some methods, especially constructors, will have parameters with the same names as fields. When this happens, the parameter **masks** the field, which means statements in the method that use the name end up referring to the parameter, not the field. Use the `this` keyword to fix the problem—add it to the variable to tell the compiler you're talking about the field, not the parameter.

Sharpen your pencil

This code has problems. Write down what you think is wrong with the code, and what you'd change.

```
class GumballMachine {
    private int gumballs;

    private int price;
    public int Price
    {
        get
        {
            return price;
        }
    }
    public GumballMachine(int gumballs, int price)
    {
        gumballs = this.gumballs;
        price = Price;
    }
    public string DispenseOneGumball(int price, int coinsInserted)
    {
        if (this.coinsInserted >= price) { // check the field
            gumballs -= 1;
            return "Here's your gumball";
        } else {
            return "Please insert more coins";
        }
    }
}
```

Sharpen your pencil
Solution

Write down the value of the `amountOwed` variable after the code below executed.

```
1. CableBill january = new CableBill(4);
   MessageBox.Show(january.CalculateAmount(7).ToString());
```

What's the value of amountOwed?

28

```
2. CableBill february = new CableBill(7);
   february.payPerViewDiscount = 1;
   MessageBox.Show(february.CalculateAmount(3).ToString());
```

What's the value of amountOwed?

won't compile

```
3. CableBill march = new CableBill(9);
   march.Discount = true;
   MessageBox.Show(march.CalculateAmount(6).ToString());
```

What's the value of amountOwed?

42

Sharpen your pencil
Solution

This code has problems. Write down what you think is wrong with the code, and what you'd change.

Lowercase price refers to the parameter to the constructor, not the field. This line sets the PARAMETER to the value returned by the Price get accessor, but Price hasn't even been set yet! So it doesn't do anything useful. If you change the constructor's parameter to uppercase Price, this line will work properly.

The "this" keyword is on the wrong "gumballs." this.gumballs refers to the property, while gumballs refers to the parameter.

This parameter masks the private field called Price, and the comment says the method is supposed to be checking the value of the price backing field.

```
public GumballMachine(int gumballs, int price)
{
    gumballs = this.gumballs;
    price = Price;
}

public string DispenseOneGumball(int price, int coinsInserted)
{
    if (this.coinsInserted >= price) { // check the field
        gumballs -= 1;
        return "Here's your gumball";
    } else {
        return "Please insert more coins";
    }
}
```

The "this" keyword is on a parameter, where it doesn't belong. It should be on price, because that field is masked by a parameter.

Use what you've learned about properties and constructors to fix Kathleen's Party Planner program.

ExeRcise

1 **How to fix the Dinner Party calculator**

To fix the `DinnerParty` class, we'll need to make sure the `CalculateCostOfDecorations()` method is called every time `NumberOfPeople` changes.

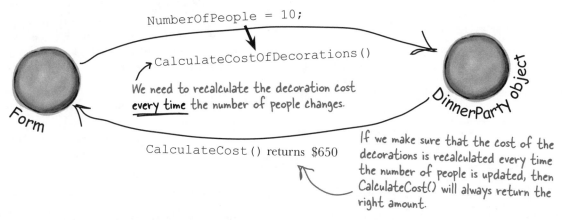

NumberOfPeople = 10;

CalculateCostOfDecorations()

We need to recalculate the decoration cost every time the number of people changes.

CalculateCost() returns $650

If we make sure that the cost of the decorations is recalculated every time the number of people is updated, then CalculateCost() will always return the right amount.

2 **Add properties and a constructor**

All you need to do to fix Kathleen's problem is make sure the `DinnerParty` class is well encapsulated. You'll start by **changing NumberOfPeople to a property** that calls `CalculateCostOfDecorations()` any time it's called. Then you'll **add a constructor** that makes sure the instance is initialized properly. Finally, you'll **change the form** so it uses the new constructor. If you do this right, that's the only change you'll need to make to the form.

★ You'll need to create a new property for `NumberOfPeople` that has a set accessor that calls `CalculateCostOfDecorations()`. It'll need a backing field called `numberOfPeople`.

★ The `NumberOfPeople` set accessor needs to have a value to pass as the parameter to the `CalculateCostOfDecorations()` method. So add a private `bool` field called `fancyDecorations` that you set every time `CalculateCostOfDecorations()` is called.

★ Add a constructor that sets up the class. It needs to take three parameters for the number of people, Healthy Option, and fancy decorations. The form currently calls two methods when it initializes the `DinnerParty` object—move them into the constructor:

```
dinnerParty.CalculateCostOfDecorations(fancyBox.Checked);
dinnerParty.SetHealthyOption(healthyBox.Checked);
```

★ Here's the constructor for the form—everything else in the form stays the same:

```
public Form1() {
    InitializeComponent();
    dinnerParty = new DinnerParty((int)numericUpDown1.Value,
                      healthyBox.Checked, fancyBox.Checked);
    DisplayDinnerPartyCost();
}
```

Exercise Solution

Use what you've learned about properties and constructors to fix Kathleen's Party Planner program.

```
class DinnerParty {
    const int CostOfFoodPerPerson = 25;

    private int numberOfPeople;
    public int NumberOfPeople {
        get { return numberOfPeople; }
        set {
            numberOfPeople = value;
            CalculateCostOfDecorations(fancyDecorations);
        }
    }
    private bool fancyDecorations;

    public decimal CostOfBeveragesPerPerson;
    public decimal CostOfDecorations = 0;

    public DinnerParty(int numberOfPeople, bool healthyOption, bool fancyDecorations) {
        NumberOfPeople = numberOfPeople;
        this.fancyDecorations = fancyDecorations;
        SetHealthyOption(healthyOption);
        CalculateCostOfDecorations(fancyDecorations);
    }

    public void SetHealthyOption(bool healthyOption) {
        if (healthyOption) {
            CostOfBeveragesPerPerson = 5.00M;
        } else {
            CostOfBeveragesPerPerson = 20.00M;
        }
    }

    public void CalculateCostOfDecorations(bool fancy) {
        fancyDecorations = fancy;
        if (fancy) {
            CostOfDecorations = (NumberOfPeople * 15.00M) + 50M;
        } else {
            CostOfDecorations = (NumberOfPeople * 7.50M) + 30M;
        }
    }

    public decimal CalculateCost(bool healthyOption) {
        decimal totalCost = CostOfDecorations
            + ((CostOfBeveragesPerPerson + CostOfFoodPerPerson) * NumberOfPeople);

        if (healthyOption) {
            return totalCost * .95M;
        } else {
            return totalCost;
        }
    }
}
```

Now that numberOfPeople is private, there's no way for the form to change it without also recalculating the cost of the decorations. That'll fix the bug that almost cost Kathleen one of her best clients!

By using a property, you can make sure that the cost of decorations is recalculated every time the number of people changes.

Be careful how you use "this." You'll need it to tell the difference between the parameter and private field named numberOfPeople.

So you'll need to put "this." in front of "fancyDecorations" because the fancyDecorations parameter masks the private field with the same name.

Make sure you store the fancy decorations in a field so the NumberOfPeople set accessor can use it.

Your object's family tree

So there I was riding my bicycle object down Dead Man's Curve when I realized it inherited from TwoWheeler and I forgot to add a Brakes() method...long story short, twenty-six stitches and Mom said I'm grounded for a month.

Sometimes you *DO* want to be just like your parents.

Ever run across an object that *almost* does exactly what you want *your* object to do? Found yourself wishing that if you could just *change a few things*, that object would be perfect? Well, that's just one reason that **inheritance** is one of the most powerful concepts and techniques in the C# language. Before you're through with this chapter, you'll learn how to **subclass** an object to get its behavior, but keep the **flexibility** to make changes to that behavior. You'll **avoid duplicate code**, **model the real world** more closely, and end up with code that's **easier to maintain**.

Kathleen does birthday parties, too

Now that you got your program working, Kathleen is using it all the time. But she doesn't just handle dinner parties—she does birthdays too, and they're priced a little differently. She'll need you to add birthdays to her program.

I just got a call for a birthday party for 10 people. Can your program handle that?

These are both the same as the dinner party.

Cost Estimate for a Birthday Party

- $25 per person.

- There are two options for the cost of decorations. If a client goes with the normal decorations, it's $7.50 per person with a $30 decorating fee. A client can also upgrade the party decorations to the "Fancy Option"—that costs $15 per person with a $50 one-time decorating fee.

- When the party has four people or less, use an 8-inch cake ($40). Otherwise, she uses a 16-inch cake ($75).

- Writing on the cake costs $.25 for each letter. The 8-inch cake can have up to 16 letters of writing, and the 16-inch one can have up to 40 letters of writing.

The application should handle both types of parties. Use a tab control, one tab for each kind of party.

Most of the changes have to do with cakes and writing.

We need a BirthdayParty class

Modifying your program to calculate the cost of Kathleen's
birthday parties means adding a new class and changing the
form to let you handle both kinds of parties.

*You'll do all this in a
minute—but first you'll
need to get a sense of
what the job involves.*

BirthdayParty
NumberOfPeople
CostOfDecorations
CakeSize
CakeWriting
CalculateCostOfDecorations()
CalculateCost()

Here's what we're going to do:

1 **Create a new BirthdayParty class**
Your new class will need to calculate the costs, deal with
decorations, and check the size of the writing on the cake.

2 **Add a TabControl to your form**
Each tab on the form is a lot like the `GroupBox` control you used
to choose which guy placed the bet in the Betting Parlor lab. Just
click on the tab you want to display, and drag controls into it.

3 **Label the first tab and move the Dinner Party controls into it**
You'll drag each of the controls that handle the dinner party into the new tab.
They'll work exactly like before, but they'll only be displayed when the dinner
party tab is selected.

4 **Label the second tab and add new Birthday Party controls to it**
You'll design the interface for handling birthday parties just like you did for the
dinner parties.

5 **Wire your birthday party class up to the controls**
Now all you need to do is add a `BirthdayParty` reference to the form's fields, and
add the code to each of your new controls so that it uses its methods and properties.

---
there are no
Dumb Questions

**Q: Why can't we just create a new instance of
`DinnerParty`, like Mike did when he wanted to compare
three routes in his navigation program?**

A: Because if you created another instance of the `DinnerParty`
class, you'd only be able to use it to plan extra dinner parties. Two
instances of the same class can be really useful if you need to manage
two different pieces of the same kind of data. But if you need to store
different kinds of data, you'll need **different classes** to do it.

Q: How do I know what to put in the new class?

A: Before you can start building a class, you need to know
what problem it's supposed to solve. That's why you had to talk to
Kathleen—she's going to be using the program. Good thing you took
a lot of notes! You can come up with your class's methods, fields, and
properties by thinking about its behavior (what it **needs to do**) and its
state (what it **needs to know**).

Build the Party Planner version 2.0

Start a new project—we're going to build Kathleen a new version of her program that handles birthdays *and* dinner parties. We'll start by creating a well-encapsulated `BirthdayParty` class to do the actual calculation.

> Make sure you use decimal as the type for the fields and properties that hold currency.

BirthdayParty
NumberOfPeople
CostOfDecorations
CakeSize
CakeWriting
CalculateCostOfDecorations()
CalculateCost()

Do this!

❶ Add the new BirthdayParty class to your program
You already know how you'll handle the `NumberOfPeople` property and the `CostOfDecorations` method—they're just like their counterparts in `DinnerParty`. We'll start by creating your new class and adding those, and then we'll add the rest of the behavior.

★ Add a public int field called `CakeSize`. You'll be adding a private method called `CalculateCakeSize()` that sets `CakeSize` to either 8 or 16 depending on the number of people. So first we'll add the constructor and the `NumberOfPeople` set accessor. We'll also add a couple more fields and a constant.

```
using System.Windows.Forms;
```
← Make sure you've added this using statement to the top of the class, because you'll be calling MessageBox.Show().

```
class BirthdayParty {
    public const int CostOfFoodPerPerson = 25;

    public decimal CostOfDecorations = 0;
    private bool fancyDecorations;
    public int CakeSize;

    public BirthdayParty(int numberOfPeople,
                    bool fancyDecorations, string cakeWriting)
    {
        this.numberOfPeople = numberOfPeople;
        this.fancyDecorations = fancyDecorations;
        CalculateCakeSize();
        this.CakeWriting = cakeWriting;
        CalculateCostOfDecorations(fancyDecorations);
    }
}
```

When the BirthdayParty object is initialized, it n to know the number of people, the kind of decora and the writing on the cake, so it can start out w the right cake cost when CalculateCost() is called.

The constructor's calling the set accessor to set the cake writing, in case the parameter is too long for the cake, so it's got to calculate the cake size first.

The constructor sets the properties and then runs the calculations.

★ You'll need a `CakeWriting` string property to hold the writing on the cake. The `CakeWriting` set accessor checks `CakeSize` because different sizes of cake can hold different numbers of letters. Then it uses `value.Length` to check how long the string is. If it's too long, instead of setting the private field, the set accessor pops up a message box that says, "Too many letters for a 16-inch cake" (or 8-inch cake).

★ And you'll need that `CalculateCakeSize()` method, too. Here it is:

```
private void CalculateCakeSize() {
    if (NumberOfPeople <= 4)
        CakeSize = 8;
    else
        CakeSize = 16;
}
```

The CalculateCakeSize() method sets the CakeSize field. It's called by the NumberOfPeople set accessor and the CalculateCost() method.

*This property is a little more complex than the ones you've seen before. It checks the cake size to see if it's too long for the cake, using the maxLength variable to store the maximum length. If it's too long, it gives an error message and then **cuts the backing field down** to the right size, so it can be reloaded into the text box.*

```
private string cakeWriting = "";
public string CakeWriting {
    get { return this.cakeWriting; }
    set {
        int maxLength;
        if (CakeSize == 8)
            maxLength = 16;
        else
            maxLength = 40;
        if (value.Length > maxLength) {
            MessageBox.Show("Too many letters for a " + CakeSize + " inch cake");
            if (maxLength > this.cakeWriting.Length)
                maxLength = this.cakeWriting.Length;
            this.cakeWriting = cakeWriting.Substring(0, maxLength);
        }
        else
            this.cakeWriting = value;
    }
}
```

Here's where the CakeWriting property makes sure that the cake's writing is never too long for the cake size. Its set accessor checks the cake size, then uses the backing field's Length property to make sure it's not too long. If it is, it cuts the string down to the right size.

you notice how left out some the brackets? en you only have statement in a e block, you don't d to add curly ckets around it.

Every string has a Substring() method that returns a portion of the string. This one cuts it down to the allowed length, so you'll need to reload the writing into the textbox when the text or cake size changes.

Curly brackets are optional for single-line blocks

A lot of times you'll have an if statement or while loop that's just got a single statement inside its block. When that happens a lot, you can end up with a whole lot of curly brackets—and that can be a real eyesore! C# helps you avoid that problem by letting you drop the curly brackets if there's just one statement. So this is perfectly valid syntax for a loop and an if statement:

```
for (int i = 0; i < 10; i++)
    DoTheJob(i);
```

```
if (myValue == 36)
    myValue *= 5;
```

Keep on going with the BirthdayParty class...

★ Finish off the `BirthdayParty` class by adding the `CalculateCost()` method. But instead of taking the decoration cost and adding the cost of beverages (which is what happens in `DinnerParty`), it'll add the cost of the cake.

> *We're using decimal because we're dealing with prices and currency.*

```
public decimal CalculateCost() {
    decimal TotalCost = CostOfDecorations + (CostOfFoodPerPerson * NumberOfPeople);
    decimal CakeCost;
    if (CakeSize == 8)
        CakeCost = 40M + CakeWriting.Length * .25M;
    else
        CakeCost = 75M + CakeWriting.Length * .25M;
    return TotalCost + CakeCost;
}
```

> *The CalculateCost() method is a lot like the one from DinnerParty, except that it adds the cost of the cake instead of the Healthy Choice option.*

```
private int numberOfPeople;
public int NumberOfPeople {
    get { return numberOfPeople; }
    set {
        numberOfPeople = value;
        CalculateCostOfDecorations(fancyDecorations);
        CalculateCakeSize();
        this.CakeWriting = cakeWriting;
    }
}
```

> *Making the CakeWriting method cut down the size of the cake is only half of the solution. The other half is making sure that the CakeWriting set accessor gets run every time the number of people changes.*

> *This method is just like the one in the DinnerParty class.*

> *So when the number of people changes, the class first recalculates the cake size, and then it uses its set accessor for CakeWriting to cut the text down—so if a 10-person party turns into a 4-person one, their 36-letter message will be cut down to one that'll fit on the smaller cake.*

```
public void CalculateCostOfDecorations(bool fancy) {
    fancyDecorations = fancy;
    if (fancy)
        CostOfDecorations = (NumberOfPeople * 15.00M) + 50M;
    else
        CostOfDecorations = (NumberOfPeople * 7.50M) + 30M;
}
```

② Use a TabControl to add tabs to the form

Drag a TabControl out of the toolbox and onto your form, and resize it so it takes up the entire form. Change the text of each tab using the TabPages property: a "…" button shows up in the Properties window next to the property. When you click it, the IDE pops up a window that lets you edit the properties of each tab. Set the Text property of the tabs to "Dinner Party" and "Birthday Party".

Click on the tabs to switch between them. Use the TabCollection property to change the text for each tab. Click the "…" button next to it and select each tab's Text property.

③ Paste the Dinner Party controls onto their tab

Open up the Party Planner program from Chapter 5 in another IDE window. Select the controls on the tab, copy them, and **paste them into the new Dinner Party tab**. You'll need to click **inside** the tab to make sure they get pasted into the right place (otherwise you'll get an error about not being able to add a component to a container of type TabControl).

One thing to keep in mind here: when you copy and paste a control into a form, you're only adding the control itself, **not the event handlers for the control**. And you'll need to check to make sure that the (Name) is set correctly in the Properties window for each of them. Make sure that each control has the same name as it did in your Chapter 5 project, and then double-click on each control after you add it to add a new empty event handler.

After you drag the Dinner Party controls onto the tab, they'll only be visible when the Dinner Party tab is selected.

④ Build the Birthday Party user interface

The Birthday Party GUI has a NumericUpDown control for the number of people, a CheckBox control for fancy decorations, and a Label control with a 3D border for the cost. Then you'll add a TextBox control for the cake writing.

This tab uses the NumericUpDown, CheckBox, and Label controls just like the Dinner Party tab does. Name them numberBirthday, fancyBirthday, and birthdayCost.

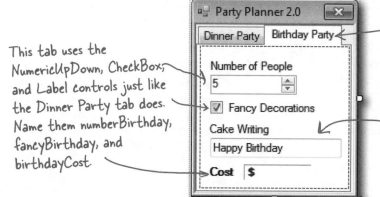

Click on the Birthday Party tab and add the new controls.

Add a TextBox control called cakeWriting for the writing on the cake (and a label above it so the user knows what it's for). Use its Text property to give it a default value of "Happy Birthday".

Keep on going with the code for the form...

❺ **Put it all together**

All the pieces are there—now it's just a matter of writing a little code to make the controls work.

★ You'll need fields in your form that have references to a `BirthdayParty` object and a `DinnerParty` object, and you'll need to instantiate them in the constructor.

★ You already have code for the dinner party controls' event handlers—they're in your Chapter 5 project. If you haven't double-clicked on the `NumericUpDown` and `CheckBox` controls in the Dinner Party tab to add the event handlers, do it now. Then copy the contents of each event handler from the Chapter 5 program and paste them in here. Here's the code for the form:

```
public partial class Form1 : Form {
    DinnerParty dinnerParty;
    BirthdayParty birthdayParty;
    public Form1() {
        InitializeComponent();
        dinnerParty = new DinnerParty((int)numericUpDown1.Value,
                            healthyBox.Checked, fancyBox.Checked);
        DisplayDinnerPartyCost();

        birthdayParty = new BirthdayParty((int)numberBirthday.Value,
                            fancyBirthday.Checked, cakeWriting.Text);
        DisplayBirthdayPartyCost();
    }


    // The fancyBox, healthyBox, and numericUpDown1 event handlers and
    // the DisplayDinnerCost() method are identical to the ones in the
    // Dinner Party exercise at the end of Chapter 5.


```

The BirthdayParty instance is initialized in the form's constructor, just like the instance of DinnerParty.

★ Add code to the `NumericUpDown` control's event handler method to set the object's `NumberOfPeople` property, and make the Fancy Decorations checkbox work.

```
private void numberBirthday_ValueChanged(object sender, EventArgs e) {
    birthdayParty.NumberOfPeople = (int)numberBirthday.Value;
    DisplayBirthdayPartyCost();
}
```

↖ The CheckBox and NumericUpDown controls' event handlers are just like the ones for the dinner party.

```
private void fancyBirthday_CheckedChanged(object sender, EventArgs e) {
    birthdayParty.CalculateCostOfDecorations(fancyBirthday.Checked);
    DisplayBirthdayPartyCost();
}
```

★ Use the Events page in the Properties window to add a new
TextChanged event handler to the cakeWriting TextBox. Click
on the lightning bolt button in the Properties window to switch to the
Events page. Then select the TextBox and scroll down until you find the
TextChanged event. Double-click on it to add a new event handler for it.

When you select the cakeWriting TextBox and double-click on the TextChanged row in the Events page of the Properties window, the IDE will add a new event handler that gets fired every time the text in the box changes.

```
private void cakeWriting_TextChanged(object sender, EventArgs e) {
    birthdayParty.CakeWriting = cakeWriting.Text;
    DisplayBirthdayPartyCost();
}
```

★ Add a DisplayBirthdayPartyCost() method and add it to
all of the event handlers so the cost label is updated automatically
any time there's a change.

The way that the form handles the cake writing can be really simple because the BirthdayParty class is **well encapsulated**. All the form has to do is use its controls to set the properties on the object, and the object takes care of the rest.

```
private void DisplayBirthdayPartyCost() {
    cakeWriting.Text = birthdayParty.CakeWriting;
    decimal cost = birthdayParty.CalculateCost();
    birthdayCost.Text = cost.ToString("c");
}
}
```

All the intelligence for dealing with the writing, the number of people, and the cake size is built into the NumberOfPeople and CakeWriting set accessors, so the form just has to set and display the values.

...and you're done with the form!

6 **Your program's done—time to run it**

Make sure the program works the way it's supposed to. Check that it pops up a message box if the writing is too long for the cake. Make sure the price is always right. If it's working, you're done!

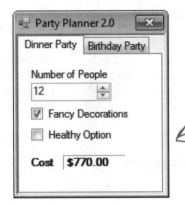

Start up the program and go to the Dinner Party tab. Make sure that it works just like your old Party Planner program.

Does the calculation work correctly? In this case, 10 people means $25 per person ($250) plus $75 for a 16" cake plus $7.50 per person ($75) for the non-fancy decorations plus a $30 decorating fee plus $.25 per letter for 21 letters on the cake ($5.25).

Click on the Birthday Party tab. Make sure the cost changes when you change the number of people or click the Fancy Decorations checkbox.

So $250 + $75 + $75 + $30 + $5.25 = $435.25. It works!

When you type in the Cake Writing text box, the TextChanged event handler should update the cost every time you add or remove a letter.

One more thing...can you add a $100 fee for parties over 12?

Kathleen's gotten so much business using your program that she can afford to charge a little more for some of her larger clients. So what would it take to change your program to add in the extra charge?

★ Change the `DinnerParty.CalculateCost()` to check `NumberOfPeople` and add $100 to the return value if it's over 12.

★ Do the exact same thing for `BirthdayParty.CalculateCost()`.

Take a minute and think about how you'd add a fee to both the `DinnerParty` and `BirthdayParty` classes. What code would you write? Where would it have to go?

Easy enough...but what happens if there are three similar classes? Or four? Or twelve? And what if you had to maintain that code and make more changes later? What if you had to make the *same exact change* to five or six *closely related* classes?

> Wow, I'd have to write the same code over and over again. That's a really inefficient way to work. There's got to be a better way!

You're right! Having the same code repeated in different classes is inefficient and error-prone.

Lucky for us, C# gives us a better way to build classes that are related to each other and share behavior: ***inheritance***.

When your classes use inheritance, you only need to write your code once

It's no coincidence that your `DinnerParty` and `BirthdayParty` classes have a lot of the same code. When you write C# programs, you often create classes that represent things in the real world—and those things are usually related to each other. Your classes have **similar code** because the things they represent in the real world—a birthday party and a dinner party—have **similar behaviors**.

Kathleen needs to figure out the cost of her parties, no matter what kind of parties they are.

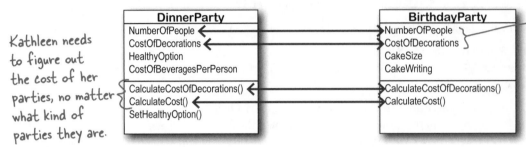

A birthday party handles the number of people and the cost of decorations in **almost** the same way as a dinner party.

Dinner parties and birthday parties are both parties

When you have two classes that are more specific cases of something more general, you can set them up to **inherit** from the same class. When you do that, each of them is a **subclass** of the same **base class**.

Both kinds of parties have to keep track of the number of people and the cost of decorations, so you can move that into the base class.

The way both parties handle the number of people and calculating the total cost is similar but **distinct**. We can break up the behavior for these things so the similar part is in the base class, while putting the distinct pieces in the two subclasses.

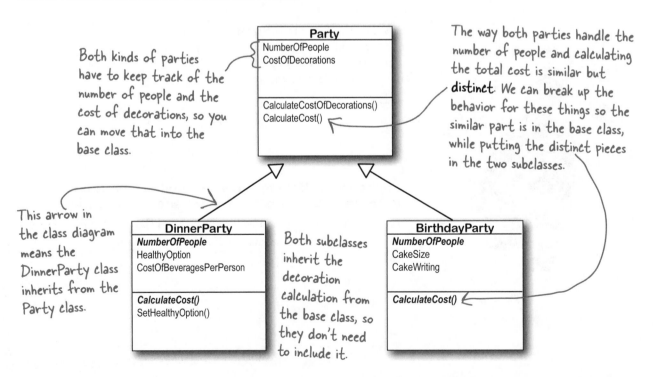

This arrow in the class diagram means the DinnerParty class inherits from the Party class.

Both subclasses inherit the decoration calculation from the base class, so they don't need to include it.

226 *Chapter 6*

Build up your class model by starting general and getting more specific

C# programs use inheritance because it mimics the relationship that the things they model have in the real world. Real-world things are often in a **hierarchy** that goes from more general to more specific, and your programs have their own **class hierarchy** that does the same thing. In your class model, classes further down in the hierarchy **inherit** from those above it.

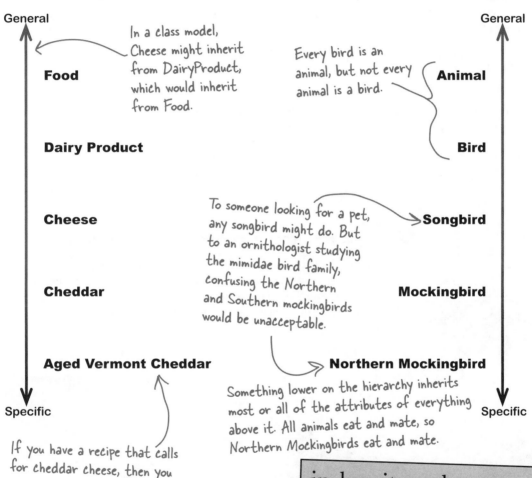

General

Food

In a class model, Cheese might inherit from DairyProduct, which would inherit from Food.

Dairy Product

Cheese

To someone looking for a pet, any songbird might do. But to an ornithologist studying the mimidae bird family, confusing the Northern and Southern mockingbirds would be unacceptable.

Cheddar

Aged Vermont Cheddar

Specific

If you have a recipe that calls for cheddar cheese, then you can use aged Vermont cheddar. But if it specifically needs aged Vermont, then you can't just use any cheddar—you need that specific cheese.

General

Every bird is an animal, but not every animal is a bird.

Animal

Bird

Songbird

Mockingbird

Northern Mockingbird

Something lower on the hierarchy inherits most or all of the attributes of everything above it. All animals eat and mate, so Northern Mockingbirds eat and mate.

Specific

in-her-it, verb.
to derive an attribute from one's parents or ancestors. *She wanted the baby to **inherit** her big brown eyes, and not her husband's beady blue ones.*

How would you design a zoo simulator?

Lions and tigers and bears…oh my! Also, hippos, wolves, and the occasional cat. Your job is to design a program that simulates a zoo. (Don't get too excited—we're not going to actually build the code, just design the classes to represent the animals.)

We've been given a list of some of the animals that will be in the program, but not all of them. We know that each animal will be represented by an object, and that the objects will move around in the simulator, doing whatever it is that each particular animal is programmed to do.

More importantly, we want the program to be easy for other programmers to maintain, which means they'll need to be able to add their own classes later on if they want to add new animals to the simulator.

So what's the first step? Well, before we can talk about **specific** animals, we need to figure out the **general** things they have in common—the abstract characteristics that **all** animals have. Then we can build those characteristics into a class that all animal classes can inherit from.

1 **Look for things the animals have in common**

Take a look at these six animals. What do a lion, a hippo, a tiger, a cat, a wolf, and a dalmatian have in common? How are they related? You'll need to figure out their relationships so you can come up with a class model that includes all of them.

Use inheritance to avoid duplicate code in subclasses

You already know that duplicate code sucks. It's hard to maintain, and always leads to headaches down the road. So let's choose fields and methods for an Animal base class that you **only have to write once**, and each of the animal subclasses can inherit from them. Let's start with the public fields:

★ Picture: an image that you can put into a PictureBox.

★ Food: the type of food this animal eats. Right now, there can be only two values: meat and grass.

★ Hunger: an int representing the hunger level of the animal. It changes depending on when (and how much) the animal eats.

★ Boundaries: a reference to a class that stores the height, width, and location of the pen that the animal will roam around in.

★ Location: the X and Y coordinates where the animal is standing.

In addition, the Animal class has four methods the animals can inherit:

★ MakeNoise(): a method to let the animal make a sound.

★ Eat(): behavior for when the animal encounters its preferred food.

★ Sleep(): a method to make the animal lie down and take a nap.

★ Roam(): the animals like to wander around their pens in the zoo.

② Build a base class to give the animals everything they have in common

The fields, properties, and methods in the base class will give all of the animals that inherit from it a common state and behavior. They're all animals, so it makes sense to call the base class Animal.

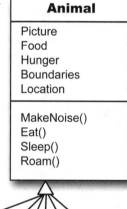

Animal
Picture Food Hunger Boundaries Location
MakeNoise() Eat() Sleep() Roam()

Choosing a base class is about making choices. You could have decided to use a ZooOccupant class that defines the feed and maintenance costs, or an Attraction class with methods for how the animals entertain the zoo visitors. But we think Animal makes the most sense here. Do you agree?

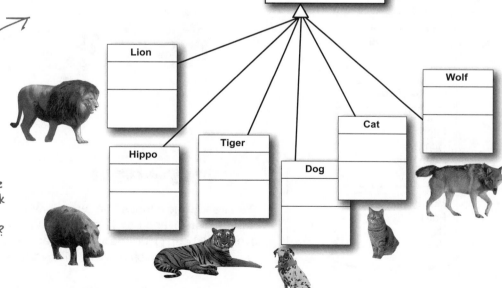

Different animals make different noises

Lions roar, dogs bark, and as far as *we* know hippos don't make any sound at all. Each of the classes that inherit from Animal will have a `MakeNoise()` method, but each of those methods will work a different way and will have different code. When a subclass changes the behavior of one of the methods that it inherited, we say that it **overrides** the method.

Just because a property or a method is in the Animal base class, that doesn't mean every subclass has to use it the same way...or at all!

Think about what you need to override

When a subclass changes the behavior of a method it inherited, we call it **overriding**. Every animal needs to eat. But a dog might take little bites of meat, while a hippo eats huge mouthfuls of grass. So what would the code for that behavior look like? Both the dog and the hippo would override the `Eat()` method. The hippo's method would have it consume, say, 20 pounds of hay each time it was called. The dog's `Eat()` method, on the other hand, would reduce the zoo's food supply by one 12-ounce can of dog food.

❸ Figure out what each animal does that the Animal class does differently—or not at all

What does each type of animal do that all the other animals don't? Dogs eat dog food, so the dog's `Eat()` method will need to override the `Animal.Eat()` method. Hippos swim, so a hippo will have a `Swim()` method that isn't in the Animal class at all.

So when you've got a subclass that inherits from a base class, it **must** inherit all of the base class's behaviors... but you can **modify** them in the subclass so they're not performed exactly the same way. That's what overriding is all about.

Grass is yummy! I could go for a good pile of hay right now.

I beg to differ.

Animal
Picture
Food
Hunger
Boundaries
Location
MakeNoise()
Eat()
Sleep()
Roam()

⚛ BRAIN POWER

We already know that some animals will override the **MakeNoise()** and **Eat()** methods. Which animals will override **Sleep()** or **Roam()**? Will any of them? What about the properties—which animals will override some properties?

Think about how to group the animals

Aged Vermont cheddar is a kind of cheese, which is a dairy product, which is a kind of food, and a good class model for food would represent that. Lucky for us, C# gives us an easy way to do it. You can create a chain of classes that inherit from each other, starting with the topmost base class and working down. So you could have a Food class, with a subclass called DairyProduct that serves as the base class for Cheese, which has a subclass called Cheddar, which is what AgedVermontCheddar inherits from.

4 **Look for classes that have a lot in common**

Don't dogs and wolves seem pretty similar? They're both canines, and it's a good bet that if you look at their behavior they have a lot in common. They probably eat the same food and sleep the same way. What about domestic cats, tigers, and lions? It turns out all three of them move around their habitats in exactly the same way. It's a good bet that you'll be able to have a Feline class that lives between Animal and those three cat classes that can help prevent duplicate code between them.

Animal
Picture Food Hunger Boundaries Location
MakeNoise() Eat() Sleep() Roam()

There's a pretty good chance that we'll be able to add a Canine class that the dogs and wolves both inherit from.

Lion
MakeNoise() Eat()

Hippo
MakeNoise() Eat()

Tiger
MakeNoise() Eat()

Dog
MakeNoise() Eat()

Cat
MakeNoise() Eat()

Wolf
MakeNoise() Eat()

The subclasses inherit all four methods from Animal, but we're only having them override MakeNoise() and Eat().

That's why we only show those two methods in the class diagrams.

Create the class hierarchy

When you create your classes so that there's a base class at the top with subclasses below it, and those subclasses have their own subclasses that inherit from them, what you've built is called a **class hierarchy**. This is about more than just avoiding duplicate code, although that is certainly a great benefit of a sensible hierarchy. But when it comes down to it, the biggest benefit you'll get is that your code becomes really easy to understand and maintain. When you're looking at the zoo simulator code, when you see a method or property defined in the Feline class, then you *immediately know* that you're looking at something that all of the cats share. Your hierarchy becomes a map that helps you find your way through your program.

5 **Finish your class hierarchy**

Now that you know how you'll organize the animals, you can add the Feline and Canine classes.

Animal

Picture
Food
Hunger
Boundaries
Location

MakeNoise()
Eat()
Sleep()
Roam()

Feline

Roam()

Since Feline overrides Roam(), anything that inherits from it gets its new Roam() and not the one in Animal.

Canine

Eat()
Sleep()

Hippo

MakeNoise()
Eat()

Lion

MakeNoise()
Eat()

Tiger

MakeNoise()
Eat()

Cat

MakeNoise()
Eat()

The three cats roam the same way, so they share an inherited Roam() method. But each one still eats and makes noise differently, so they'll all override the Eat() and MakeNoise() methods that they inherited from Animal.

Our wolves and dogs eat the same way, so we moved their common Eat() method up to the Canine class.

Wolf

MakeNoise()

Dog

MakeNoise()

Every subclass <u>extends</u> its base class

You're not limited to the methods that a subclass inherits from its base class...but you already know that! After all, you've been building your own classes all along. When you add inheritance to a class, what you're doing is taking the class you've already built and **extending** it by adding all of the fields, properties, and methods in the base class. So if you wanted to add a Fetch() method to the dog, that's perfectly normal. It won't inherit or override anything—only the dog will have that method, and it won't end up in Wolf, Canine, Animal, Hippo, or any other class.

> **hi-er-ar-chy, noun.**
> an arrangement or classification in which groups or things are ranked one above the other. *The president of Dynamco had worked his way up from the mailroom to the top of the corporate **hierarchy**.*

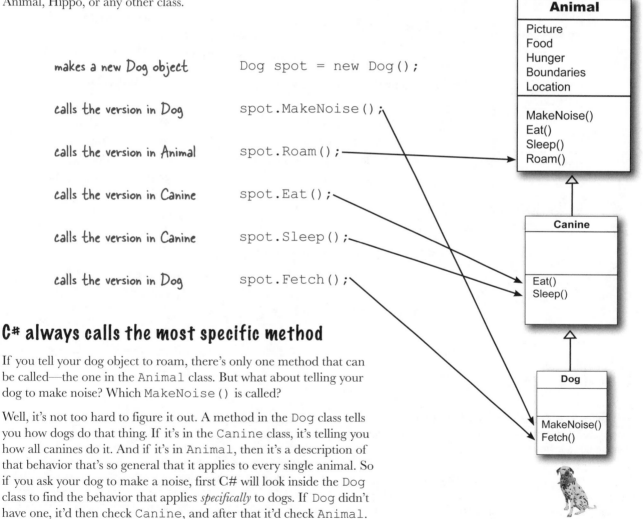

makes a new Dog object	`Dog spot = new Dog();`
calls the version in Dog	`spot.MakeNoise();`
calls the version in Animal	`spot.Roam();`
calls the version in Canine	`spot.Eat();`
calls the version in Canine	`spot.Sleep();`
calls the version in Dog	`spot.Fetch();`

Animal
Picture
Food
Hunger
Boundaries
Location

MakeNoise()
Eat()
Sleep()
Roam()

Canine

Eat()
Sleep()

Dog

MakeNoise()
Fetch()

C# always calls the most specific method

If you tell your dog object to roam, there's only one method that can be called—the one in the Animal class. But what about telling your dog to make noise? Which MakeNoise() is called?

Well, it's not too hard to figure it out. A method in the Dog class tells you how dogs do that thing. If it's in the Canine class, it's telling you how all canines do it. And if it's in Animal, then it's a description of that behavior that's so general that it applies to every single animal. So if you ask your dog to make a noise, first C# will look inside the Dog class to find the behavior that applies *specifically* to dogs. If Dog didn't have one, it'd then check Canine, and after that it'd check Animal.

Use a colon to inherit from a base class

When you're writing a class, you use a **colon (:)** to have it inherit from a base class. That makes it a subclass, and gives it **all of the fields, properties, and methods** of the class it inherits from.

When a subclass inherits from a base class, all of the fields, properties, and methods in the base class are automatically added to the subclass.

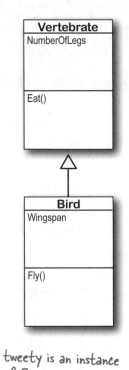

```
class Vertebrate
{
    public int NumberOfLegs;
    public void Eat() {
        // code to make it eat
    }
}
```

The Bird class uses a colon to inherit from the Vertebrate class. This means that it inherits all of the fields, properties, and methods from Vertebrate.

```
class Bird : Vertebrate
{
    public double Wingspan;
    public void Fly() {
        // code to make the bird fly
    }
}
```

You extend a class by adding a colon to the end of the class declaration, followed by the base class to inherit from.

tweety is an instance of Bird, so it's got the Bird methods and fields as usual.

```
public button1_Click(object sender, EventArgs e) {
    Bird tweety = new Bird();
    tweety.Wingspan = 7.5;
    tweety.Fly();
    tweety.NumberOfLegs = 2;
    tweety.Eat();
}
```

Since the Bird class inherits from Vertebrate, every instance of Bird also has the fields and methods defined in the Vertebrate class.

there are no Dumb Questions

Q: Why does the arrow point up, from the subclass to the base class? Wouldn't the diagram look better with the arrow pointing down instead?

A: It might look better, but it wouldn't be as accurate. When you set up a class to inherit from another one, you build that relationship into the subclass—the base class remains the same. And that makes sense when you think about it from the perspective of the base class.

Its behavior is completely unchanged when you add a class that inherits from it. The base class isn't even aware of this new class that inherited from it. Its methods, fields, and properties remain entirely intact. But the subclass definitely changes its behavior. Every instance of the subclass automatically gets all of the properties, fields, and methods from the base class, and it all happens just by adding a colon. That's why you draw the arrow on your diagram so that it's part of the subclass, and points to the base class that it inherits from.

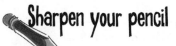 **Sharpen your pencil**

Take a look at these class models and declarations, and then circle the statements that won't work.

Aircraft
AirSpeed
Altitude
TakeOff()
Land()

```
class Aircraft {
    public double AirSpeed;
    public double Altitude;
    public void TakeOff() { ... };
    public void Land() { ... };
}

class FirePlane : Aircraft {
    public double BucketCapacity;
    public void FillBucket() { ... };
}

public void FireFightingMission() {
    FirePlane myFirePlane = new FirePlane();
    new FirePlane.BucketCapacity = 500;
    Aircraft.Altitude = 0;
    myFirePlane.TakeOff();
    myFirePlane.AirSpeed = 192.5;
    myFirePlane.FillBucket();
    Aircraft.Land();
}
```

FirePlane
BucketCapacity
FillBucket()

Sandwich
Toasted
SlicesOfBread
CountCalories()

```
class Sandwich {
    public boolean Toasted;
    public int SlicesOfBread;
    public int CountCalories() { ... }
}

class BLT : Sandwich {
    public int SlicesOfBacon;
    public int AmountOfLettuce;
    public int AddSideOfFries() { ... }
}

public BLT OrderMyBLT() {
    BLT mySandwich = new BLT();
    BLT.Toasted = true;
    Sandwich.SlicesOfBread = 3;
    mySandwich.AddSideOfFries();
    mySandwich.SlicesOfBacon += 5;
    MessageBox.Show("My sandwich has "
        + mySandwich.CountCalories + "calories".);
    return mySandwich;
}
```

BLT
SlicesOfBacon
AmountOfLettuce
AddSideOfFries()

i can think of one way to make a penguin fly...

Sharpen your pencil
Solution

Take a look at these class models and declarations, and then circle the statements that won't work.

Aircraft

AirSpeed
Altitude
TakeOff()
Land()

FirePlane

BucketCapacity
FillBucket()

```
class Aircraft {
    public double AirSpeed;
    public double Altitude;
    public void TakeOff() { ... };
    public void Land() { ... };
}

class FirePlane : Aircraft {
    public double BucketCapacity;
    public void FillBucket() { ... };
}

public void FireFightingMission() {
    FirePlane myFirePlane = new FirePlane();
    new FirePlane.BucketCapacity = 500;
    Aircraft.Altitude = 0;
    myFirePlane.TakeOff();
    myFirePlane.AirSpeed = 192.5;
    myFirePlane.FillBucket();
    Aircraft.Land();
}
```

That's not how you use the new keyword.

These statements all use the class names instead of the name of the instance, myFirePlane.

Sandwich

Toasted
SlicesOfBread
CountCalories()

BLT

SlicesOfBacon
AmountOfLettuce
AddSideOfFries()

```
class Sandwich {
    public boolean Toasted;
    public int SlicesOfBread;
    public int CountCalories() { ... }
}

class BLT : Sandwich {
    public int SlicesOfBacon;
    public int AmountOfLettuce;
    public int AddSideOfFries() { ... }
}

public BLT OrderMyBLT() {
    BLT mySandwich = new BLT();
    BLT.Toasted = true;
    Sandwich.SlicesOfBread = 3;
    mySandwich.AddSideOfFries();
    mySandwich.SlicesOfBacon += 5;
    MessageBox.Show("My sandwich has "
        + mySandwich.CountCalories + "calories".);
    return mySandwich;
}
```

These properties are part of the instance, but the statements are trying to call them incorrectly using the class names.

CountCalories is a method, but this statement doesn't include the parentheses () after the call to the method.

236   Chapter 6

We know that inheritance adds the base class fields, properties, and methods to the subclass...

Inheritance is simple when your subclass needs to inherit ***all*** of the base class methods, properties, and fields.

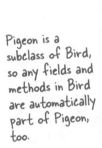

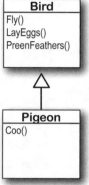

Pigeon is a subclass of Bird, so any fields and methods in Bird are automatically part of Pigeon, too.

```
class Bird {
    public void Fly() {
        // here's the code to make the bird fly
    }

    public void LayEggs() { ... };

    public void PreenFeathers() { ... };
}


class Pigeon : Bird {
    public void Coo() { ... }
}


class Penguin : Bird {
    public void Swim() { ... }
}


public void BirdSimulator() {
        Pigeon Harriet = new Pigeon();

        Penguin Izzy = new Penguin();

        Harriet.Fly();

        Harriet.Coo();

        Izzy.Fly();

}
```

...but some birds don't fly!

What do you do if your base class has a method that your subclass needs to ***modify***?

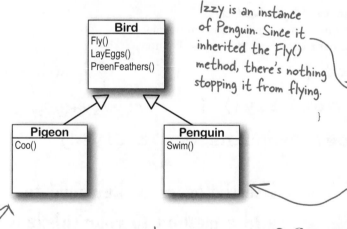

Izzy is an instance of Penguin. Since it inherited the Fly() method, there's nothing stopping it from flying.

Both Pigeon and Penguin inherit from Bird, so they both get the Fly(), LayEggs(), and PreenFeathers() methods.

Pigeons fly, lay eggs, and preen their feathers, so there's no problem with the Pigeon class inheriting from Bird.

Penguin objects shouldn't be able to fly! But if the Penguin class inherits from Bird, then you'll have penguins flying all over the place. So what do we do?

If this were your Bird Simulator code, what would you do to keep the penguins from flying?

A subclass can override methods to change or replace methods it inherited

Sometimes you've got a subclass that you'd like to inherit *most* of the behaviors from the base class, but *not all of them.* When you want to change the behaviors that a class has inherited, you can **override** the methods.

1 **Add the virtual keyword to the method in the base class**
A subclass can only override a method if it's marked with the **virtual** keyword, which tells C# to allow the subclass to override methods.

```
class Bird {

    public virtual void Fly() {

        // code to make the bird fly

    }

}
```

Adding the virtual keyword to the Fly() method tells C# that a subclass is allowed to override it.

2 **Add a method with the same name to the derived class**
You'll need to have exactly the same signature—meaning the same return value and parameters—and you'll need to use the **override** keyword in the declaration.

```
class Penguin : Bird {

    public override void Fly() {

        MessageBox.Show("Penguins can't fly!")

    }
}
```

To override the Fly() method, add an identical method to the subclass and use the override keyword.

When you override a method, your new method needs to have exactly the same signature as the method in the base class it's overriding. In this case, that means it needs to be called Fly, return void, and have no parameters.

Use the override keyword to add a method to your subclass that replaces one that it inherited. Before you can override a method, you need to mark it virtual in the base class.

Any place where you can use a base class, you can use one of its subclasses instead

One of the most useful things you can do with inheritance is use a subclass in place of the base class it inherits from. So if your `Recipe()` method takes a `Cheese` object and you've got an `AgedVermontCheddar` class that inherits from `Cheese`, then you can pass an instance of `AgedVermontCheddar` to the `Recipe()` method. `Recipe()` only has access to the fields, properties, and methods that are part of the `Cheese` class, though—it doesn't have access to anything specific to `AgedVermontCheddar`.

```
Sandwich
------------
Toasted
SlicesOfBread
------------
CountCalories()
```

```
        △
```

```
BLT
------------
SlicesOfBacon
AmountOfLettuce
------------
AddSideOfFries()
```

1 Let's say we have a method to analyze `Sandwich` objects:

```
public void SandwichAnalyzer(Sandwich specimen) {
    int calories = specimen.CountCalories();
    UpdateDietPlan(calories);
    PerformBreadCalculations(specimen.SlicesOfBread, specimen.Toasted);
}
```

2 You could pass a sandwich to the method—but you could also pass a BLT. Since a BLT is a *kind* of sandwich, we set it up so that it inherits from the `Sandwich` class:

```
public button1_Click(object sender, EventArgs e) {
    BLT myBLT = new BLT();
    SandwichAnalyzer(myBLT);
}
```

> We'll talk about this more in the next chapter!

3 You can always move ***down*** the class diagram—a reference variable can always be set equal to an instance of one of its subclasses. But you can't move ***up*** the class diagram.

```
public button2_Click(object sender, EventArgs e) {
    Sandwich mySandwich = new Sandwich();
    BLT myBLT = new BLT();
    Sandwich someRandomSandwich = myBLT;
    BLT anotherBLT = mySandwich;      // <--- THIS WON'T COMPILE!!!
}
```

> You can assign myBLT to any Sandwich variable because a BLT is a kind of sandwich.

> But you can't assign mySandwich to a BLT variable, because not every sandwich is a BLT! That's why this last line will cause an error.

MiXed Messages Exercise

```
a = 6;        56
b = 5;        11
a = 5;        65
```

A short C# program is listed below. One block of the program is missing! Your challenge is to match the candidate block of code (on the left) with the output—what's in the message box that the program pops up—that you'd see if the block were inserted. Not all the lines of output will be used, and some of the lines of output might be used more than once. Draw lines connecting the candidate blocks of code with their matching output.

Instructions:

1. **Fill in the four blanks in the code.**
2. **Match the code candidates to the output.**

```
class A {
  public int ivar = 7;
  public _____ string m1() {
    return "A's m1, ";
  }
  public string m2() {
    return "A's m2, ";
  }
  public _____ string m3() {
    return "A's m3, ";
  }
}

class B : A {
  public _____ string m1() {
    return "B's m1, ";
  }
}
```

```
class C : B {
  public _____ string m3() {
    return "C's m3, " + (ivar + 6);
  }
}
```

Here's the entry point for the program—it doesn't show a form, it just pops up a message box.

```
class Mixed5 {
  public static void Main(string[] args) {
    A a = new A();
    B b = new B();
    C c = new C();
    A a2 = new C();
    string q = "";
```

Hint: Think really hard about what this line really means.

```



```

candidate code goes here (three lines)

```
    System.Windows.Forms.MessageBox.Show(q);
  }
}
```

code candidates:

```
q += b.m1();
q += c.m2();
q += a.m3();
_____
q += c.m1();
q += c.m2();
q += c.m3();
_____
q += a.m1();
q += b.m2();
q += c.m3();
_____
q += a2.m1();
q += a2.m2();
q += a2.m3();
```

output:

```
A's m1, A's m2, C's m3, 6

B's m1, A's m2, A's m3,

A's m1, B's m2, A's m3,

B's m1, A's m2, C's m3, 13

B's m1, C's m2, A's m3,

B's m1, A's m2, C's m3, 6

A's m1, A's m2, C's m3, 13
```

(Don't just type this into the IDE—you'll learn a lot more if you figure this out on paper!)

Póol Puzzle

Your *job* is to take code snippets from the pool and place them into the blank lines in the code. You may use the same snippet more than once, and you might not need to use all the snippets. Your *goal* is to make a set of classes that will compile and run together as a program. Don't be fooled—this one's harder than it looks.

```
class Rowboat ..................... {
   public ............... rowTheBoat() {
      return "stroke natasha";
   }
}
```

```
class ............... {
   private int ............... ;
   ............. void.....................( ............. ) {
      length = len;
   }
   public int getLength() {
      ..................... ;
   }
   public ..................... move() {
      return    "................" ;
   }
}
```

```
class TestBoats {
   ..................... Main(){
      ............. xyz = "";
      .............b1 = new Boat();
      Sailboat b2 = new ................. ();
      Rowboat ........... = new Rowboat();
      b2.setLength(32);
      xyz = b1. ........... ();
      xyz += b3. ........... ();
      xyz += .........move();
      System.Windows.Forms.MessageBox.Show(xyz);
   }
}
```

Hint: This is the entry point for the program.

```
class ................. : Boat {
   public ............................. () {
      return " ................. ";
   }
}
```

OUTPUT:

```
                                    [x]

   drift    drift    hoist sail


                    [  OK  ]
```

Pool:

Rowboat   subclasses
Sailboat
Boat   Testboats   ;   override
                int len   drift   hoist sail
   return   virtual   stroke natasha   rowTheBoat
   continue   int length   string   move
b1   break   :   int b1   void   public   setLength
b2   b3   length   int b2   int b3   int   static   getLength
   len   int b2   private

MiXed MEssages

```
a = 6;        56
b = 5;        11
a = 5;        65
```

```
class A {
    public   virtual   string m1() {
    ...
    public   virtual   string m3() {
}
```

```
class B : A {
    public   override   string m1() {
    ...
class C : B {
    public   override   string m3() {
```

You can always substitute a reference to a subclass in place of a base class. In other words, you can always use something more specific in place of something more general—so if you've got a line of code that asks for a `Canine`, you can send it a reference to a `Dog`. So this line of code:

```
A a2 = new C();
```

means that you're instantiating a new C object, and then creating an A reference called a2 and pointing it at that object. Names like A, a2, and C make for a good puzzle, but they're a little hard to understand. Here are a few lines that follow the same pattern, but have names that you can understand:

```
Sandwich mySandwich = new BLT();

Cheese ingredient= new AgedVermontCheddar();

Songbird tweety = new NorthernMockingbird();
```

```
q += b.m1();
q += c.m2();
q += a.m3();
_____
q += c.m1();
q += c.m2();
q += c.m3();
_____
q += a.m1();
q += b.m2();
q += c.m3();
_____
q += a2.m1();
q += a2.m2();
q += a2.m3();
```

```
A's m1, A's m2, C's m3, 6

B's m1, A's m2, A's m3,

A's m1, B's m2, C's m3, 6

B's m1, A's m2, C's m3, 13

B's m1, C's m2, A's m3,

A's m1, B's m2, A's m3,

B's m1, A's m2, C's m3, 6

A's m1, A's m2, C's m3, 13
```

Pool Puzzle Solution

```
class Rowboat:    Boat    {
    public   string   rowTheBoat() {
        return "stroke natasha";
    }
}
class   Boat   {
    private int   length   ;
    public   void   setLength   (   int len   ) {
        length = len;
    }
    public int getLength() {
        return length   ;
    }
    public   virtual string   move() {
        return "   drift   ";
    }
}
```

```
class TestBoats {
    public static void Main(){
        string   xyz = "";
        Boat   b1 = new Boat();
        Sailboat b2 = new   Sailboat   ();
        Rowboat   b3   = new Rowboat();
        b2.setLength(32);
        xyz = b1.   move   ();
        xyz += b3.   move   ();
        xyz +=   b2   .move();
        System.Windows.Forms.MessageBox.Show(xyz);
    }
}
class   Sailboat   : Boat {
    public   override string move   () {
        return "   hoist sail   ";
    }
}
```

there are no Dumb Questions

Q: About the entry point that you pointed out in the Pool Puzzle—does this mean I can have a program that doesn't have a Form1 form?

A: Yes. When you create a new Windows Application project, the IDE creates all the files for that project for you, including Program.cs (which contains a static class with an entry point) and Form1.cs (which contains an empty form called Form1).

Try this: instead of creating a new Windows Application project, create an empty project by selecting "Empty Project" instead of "Windows Application" when you create a new project in the IDE. Then add a class file to it in the Solution Explorer and type in everything in the Pool Puzzle solution. Since your program uses a message box, you need to add a **reference** by right-clicking on "References" in the Solution Explorer, selecting "Add Reference", and choosing System.Windows.Forms from the .NET tab. (That's another thing the IDE does for you automatically when you create a Windows Application.) Finally, select "Properties" from the Project menu and choose the "Windows Application" output type.

Now run it...you'll see the results! Congratulations, you just created a C# program from scratch.

↑
Flip back to the beginning of Chapter 2 if you need a refresher on Main() and the entry point!

Q: Can I inherit from the class that contains the entry point?

A: Yes. The entry point ***must*** be a static method, but that method ***doesn't have to be*** in a static class. (Remember, the `static` keyword means that the class can't be instantiated, but that its methods are available as soon as the program starts. So in the Pool Puzzle program, you can call `TestBoats.Main()` from any other method without declaring a reference variable or instantiating an object using a `new` statement.)

Q: I still don't get why they're called "virtual" methods—they seem real to me!

A: The name "virtual" has to do with how .NET handles the virtual methods behind the scenes. It uses something called a virtual method table (or vtable). That's a table that .NET uses to keep track of which methods are inherited and which ones have been overridden. Don't worry—you don't need to know how it works to use virtual methods!

Q: What did you mean by only being able to move up the class diagram but not being able to move down?

A: When you've got a diagram with one class that's above another one, the class that's higher up is more *abstract* than the one that's lower down. More specific or concrete classes (like `Shirt` or `Car`) inherit from more abstract ones (like `Clothing` or `Vehicle`). When you think about it that way, it's easy to see how if all you need is a vehicle, a car or van or motorcycle will do. But if you need a car, a motorcycle won't be useful to you.

Inheritance works exactly the same way. If you have a method with `Vehicle` as a parameter, and if the `Motorcycle` class inherits from the `Vehicle` class, then you can pass an instance of `Motorcycle` to the method. But if the method takes `Motorcycle` as a parameter, you can't pass any `Vehicle` object, because it may be a `Van` instance. Then C# wouldn't know what to do when the method tries to access the `Handlebars` property!

You can always pass an instance of a subclass to any method whose parameters expect a class that it inherits from.

Look, I just don't see why I need to use those "virtual" and "override" keywords. If I don't use them, the IDE just gives me a warning, but the warning doesn't actually mean anything—my program still runs! I mean, I'll put the keywords in if it's the "right" thing to do, but it just seems like I'm jumping through hoops for no good reason.

There's an important reason for virtual and override!

The virtual and override keywords aren't just for decoration. They actually make a real difference in how your program works. But don't take our word for it—here's a real example to show you how they work.

Instead of creating a Windows Forms application, you're going to create a new console application instead! This means it won't have a form.

 Do this!

① **Create a new console application and add classes.**
Right-click on the project in the Solution Explorer and add classes, just like normal. Add the following five classes: Jewels, Safe, Owner, Locksmith, and JewelThief.

② **Add the code for the new classes.**
Here's the code for the five new classes you added:

```
class Jewels {
    public string Sparkle() {
        return "Sparkle, sparkle!";
    }
}
```

A Safe object keeps a Jewels reference in its contents field. It doesn't return that reference unless Open() is called with the right combination.

Notice how the private keyword hides the contents and combination.

```
class Safe {
    private Jewels contents = new Jewels();
    private string safeCombination = "12345";
    public Jewels Open(string combination)
    {
        if (combination == safeCombination)
            return contents;
        else
            return null;
    }
    public void PickLock(Locksmith lockpicker) {
        lockpicker.WriteDownCombination(safeCombination);
    }
}
```

> ## Console applications don't use forms
>
> If you create a console application instead of a Windows Forms application, all the IDE creates for you is a new class called Program with an empty Main() entry point method. When you run it, it pops up a command window to display the output. You can read more about console applications in Appendix A.

A locksmith can pick the combination lock and get the combination by calling the PickLock() method and passing in reference to himself. The safe calls his WriteDownCombination() method with the combination.

```
class Owner {
    private Jewels returnedContents;
    public void ReceiveContents(Jewels safeContents) {
        returnedContents = safeContents;
        Console.WriteLine("Thank you for returning my jewels! " + safeContents.Sparkle());
    }
}
```

❸ **The JewelThief class inherits from Locksmith.**
Jewel thieves are locksmiths gone bad! They can pick the lock on the safe, but instead of returning the jewels to the owner they steal them!

```
class Locksmith {
    public void OpenSafe(Safe safe, Owner owner) {
        safe.PickLock(this);
        Jewels safeContents = safe.Open(writtenDownCombination);
        ReturnContents(safeContents, owner);
    }

    private string writtenDownCombination = null;
    public void WriteDownCombination(string combination) {
        writtenDownCombination = combination;
    }

    public void ReturnContents(Jewels safeContents, Owner owner) {
        owner.ReceiveContents(safeContents);
    }
}
```

A Locksmith's OpenSafe() method picks the lock, opens the safe, and returns the contents to the owner.

Locksmith
OpenSafe() WriteDownCombination() ReturnContents()

△

JewelThief
private stolenJewels
ReturnContents()

```
class JewelThief : Locksmith {
    private Jewels stolenJewels = null;
    public void ReturnContents(Jewels safeContents, Owner owner) {
        stolenJewels = safeContents;
        Console.WriteLine("I'm stealing the contents! " + stolenJewels.Sparkle());
    }
}
```

A JewelThief object inherits the OpenSafe() and WriteDownCombination() methods. But when the OpenSafe() method calls ReturnContents() to return the jewels to the owner, the JewelThief steals them instead!

❹ **Here's the Main() method for the Program class.**
But ***don't run it just yet!*** Before you run the program, try to figure out what it's going to print to the console.

```
class Program {
    static void Main(string[] args) {
        Owner owner = new Owner();
        Safe safe = new Safe();

        JewelThief jewelThief = new JewelThief();
        jewelThief.OpenSafe(safe, owner);
        Console.ReadKey();
    }
}
```

adKey() its for the er to press key. It keeps e program om ending.

 Sharpen your pencil

Read through the code for your program. Before you run it, write down what you think it will print to the console. (Hint: Figure out what JewelThief inherits from Locksmith!)

A subclass can hide methods in the superclass

Go ahead and run the JewelThief program. Since it's a console application, instead of writing its console output to the Output window, it'll pop up a command window and print the output there. Here's what you should see:

Did you expect the program's output to be different? Maybe something like this:

```
I'm stealing the contents! Sparkle, sparkle!
```

It looks like the JewelThief acted just like a Locksmith! So what happened?

Hiding methods versus overriding methods

The reason the `JewelThief` object acted like a `Locksmith` object when its `ReturnContents()` method was called was because of the way the `JewelThief` class declared its `ReturnContents()` method. There's a big hint in that warning message you got when you compiled your program:

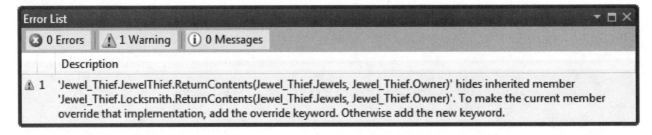

Since the `JewelThief` class inherits from `Locksmith` and replaces the `ReturnContents()` method with its own method, it looks like `JewelThief` is overriding Locksmith's `ReturnContents()` method. But that's not actually what's happening. You probably expected `JewelThief` to override the method (which we'll talk about in a minute), but instead `JewelThief` is hiding it.

There's a big difference. When a subclass hides the method, it replaces (technically, it "redeclares") a method in its base class that has the same name. So now our subclass really has two different methods that share a name: one that it inherits from its base class, and another brand-new one that's defined in its own class.

> **If a subclass just adds a method with the same name as a method in its superclass, it only hides the superclass method instead of overriding it.**

Use different references to call hidden methods

The JewelThief only hides the ReturnContents() method (as opposed to extending it), and that causes it to act like a Locksmith object whenever it's called like a Locksmith object. JewelThief inherits one version of ReturnContents() from Locksmith, and it defines a second version of it, which means that there are two different methods with the same name. That means your class needs two different ways to call it.

And, in fact, it has exactly that. If you've got an instance of JewelThief, you can use a JewelThief reference variable to call the new ReturnContents() method. But if you use a Locksmith reference variable to call it, it'll call the hidden Locksmith ReturnContents() method.

```
// The JewelThief subclass hides a method in the Locksmith base class,
// so you can get different behavior from the same object based on the
// reference you use to call it!

// Declaring your JewelThief object as a Locksmith reference causes it to
// call the base class ReturnContents() method
Locksmith calledAsLocksmith = new JewelThief();
calledAsLocksmith.ReturnContents(safeContents, owner);

// Declaring your JewelThief object as a JewelThief reference causes it to
// call the JewelThief's ReturnContents() method instead, because it hides
// the base class's method of the same name.
JewelThief calledAsJewelThief = new JewelThief();
calledAsJewelThief.ReturnContents(safeContents, owner);
```

Use the <u>new</u> keyword when you're hiding methods

Take a close look at that warning message. Sure, we never really read most of our warnings, right? But this time, actually read what it says: **To make the current member override that implementation, add the override keyword. Otherwise add the new keyword.**

So go back to your program and add the **new** keyword.

```
new public void ReturnContents(Jewels safeContents, Owner owner) {
```

As soon as you add new to your JewelThief class's ReturnContents() method declaration, that error message will go away. But your program still won't act the way you expect it to! It still calls the ReturnContents() method defined in the Locksmith object. Why? Because the ReturnContents() method is being called ***from a method defined by the Locksmith class***—specifically, from inside Locksmith.OpenSafe(), even though it's being initiated by a JewelThief object. If JewelThief only **hides** the ReturnContents() method, its own ReturnContents() will never be called.

Can you figure out how to get JewelThief to override the ReturnContents() method instead of just hiding it? See if you can do it before turning to the next page!

Use the <u>override</u> and <u>virtual</u> keywords to inherit behavior

We really want our JewelThief class to always use its own ReturnContents()
method, no matter how it's called. This is the way we expect inheritance to work most
of the time, and it's called **overriding**. And it's very easy to get your class to do it.
The first thing you need to do is use the **override** keyword when you declare the
ReturnContents() method, like this:

```
class JewelThief {

    . . .

    override public void ReturnContents
                (Jewels safeContents, Owner owner)
```

But that's not everything you need to do. If you just add that override and try to
compile, you'll get an error that looks like this:

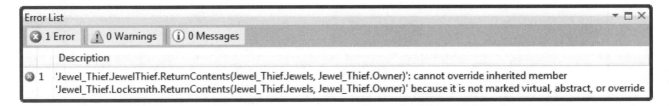

Again, take a really close look and actually read the error. JewelThief can't override the
inherited member ReturnContents() because it's not marked virtual, abstract,
or override in Locksmith. Well, that's an easy error to fix! Just mark Locksmith's
ReturnContents() with the virtual keyword:

```
class Locksmith {

    . . .

    virtual public void ReturnContents
                (Jewels safeContents, Owner owner)
```

Now run your program again. Here's what you should see:

And *that's* the output we were looking for.

When I come up with my class hierarchy, I usually want to override methods and not hide them. But if I do hide them, I'll always use the **new** keyword, right?

Exactly. Most of the time you want to override methods, but hiding them is an option.

When you're working with a subclass that extends a base class, you're much more likely to use overriding than you are to use hiding. So when you see that compiler warning about hiding a method, pay attention to it! Make sure you really want to hide the method, and didn't just forget to use the virtual and override keywords. If you always use the virtual, override, and new keywords correctly, you'll never run into a problem like this again!

If you want to override a method in a base class, always mark it with the virtual keyword, and always use the override keyword any time you want to override the method in a subclass. If you don't, you'll end up accidentally hiding methods instead.

A subclass can access its base class using the base keyword

Even when you override a method or property in your base class,
sometimes you'll still want to access it. Luckily, we can use **base**, which
lets us access any method in the base class.

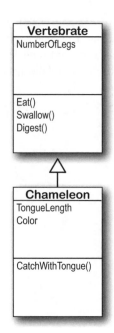

1 All animals eat, so the `Vertebrate` class has an `Eat()` method that
takes a `Food` object as its parameter.

```
class Vertebrate {
    public virtual void Eat(Food morsel) {
        Swallow(morsel);
        Digest();
    }
}
```

2 Chameleons eat by catching food with their tongues. So the `Chameleon` class inherits
from `Vertebrate` but overrides `Eat()`.

```
class Chameleon : Vertebrate {
    public override void Eat(Food morsel) {
        CatchWithTongue(morsel);
        Swallow(morsel);
        Digest();
    }
}
```

The chameleon needs to swallow and digest the food, just like any other animal. Do we really need to duplicate this code, though?

3 Instead of duplicating the code, we can use the **base** keyword to call the method that
was overridden. Now we have access to both the old and the new version of `Eat()`.

```
class Chameleon : Vertebrate {
    public override void Eat(Food morsel) {
        CatchWithTongue(morsel);
        base.Eat(morsel);
    }
}
```

This line calls the Eat() method in the base class that Chameleon inherited from.

Now that you've had a chance to absorb some of the ideas behind inheritance, here's something to think
about. While reusing code is a good way to save keystrokes, another valuable part of inheritance is that it
makes it easier to maintain your code later. **Can you think of a reason why that's true?**

When a base class has a constructor, your subclass needs one, too

If your class has constructors that take parameters, then any class that inherits from it **must call one of those constructors**. The subclass's constructor can have different parameters from the base class constructor.

Add this extra line to the end of your subclass's constructor declaration to tell C# that it needs to call the base class's constructor every time the subclass is instantiated.

```
class Subclass : BaseClass {

    public Subclass(parameter list)

        : base(the base class's parameter list) {
        // first the base class constructor is executed
        // then any statements here get executed
    }
}
```

Here's the constructor for the subclass.

The base class constructor is executed before the subclass constructor

But don't take our word for it—see for yourself!

Do this!

1 **Create a base class with a constructor that pops up a message box**
Then add a button to a form that instantiates this *base class* and shows a message box:

```
class MyBaseClass {
    public MyBaseClass(string baseClassNeedsThis) {
        MessageBox.Show("This is the base class: " + baseClassNeedsThis);
    }
}
```

This is a parameter that the base class constructor needs.

Keep an eye out for this slightly cryptic error. It means that your subclass didn't call the base constructor.

2 **Try adding a subclass, but don't call the constructor**
Then add a button to a form that instantiates this *subclass* and shows a message box:

Select Build >> Build Solution in the IDE and you'll get an error from this code.

```
class MySubclass : MyBaseClass{
    public MySubclass(string baseClassNeedsThis, int anotherValue) {
        MessageBox.Show("This is the subclass: " + baseClassNeedsThis
            + " and " + anotherValue);
    }
}
```

> ● 1 No overload for method 'MyBaseClass' takes '0' arguments

3 **Fix the error by making the constructor call the one from the base class**
Then instantiate the subclass and *see what order* the two message boxes pop up!

```
class MySubclass : MyBaseClass{
    public MySubclass(string baseClassNeedsThis, int anotherValue)
        : base(baseClassNeedsThis)
    {
        // the rest of the subclass is the same
```

This is how we send the base class the parameter its constructor needs.

Add this line to tell C# to call the constructor in the base class. It has a parameter list that shows what gets passed to the base class constructor. Then the error will go away and you can make a button to see the two message boxes pop up!

Now you're ready to finish the job for Kathleen!

When you last left Kathleen, you'd finished adding birthday parties to her program. She needs you to charge an extra $100 for parties over 12. It seemed like you were going to have to write the same exact code twice, once for each class. Now that you know how to use inheritance, you can have them inherit from the same base class that contains all of their shared code, so you only have to write it once.

DinnerParty
NumberOfPeople
CostOfDecorations
CostOfBeveragesPerPerson
HealthyOption
CalculateCostOfDecorations()
CalculateCost()
SetHealthyOption()

BirthdayParty
NumberOfPeople
CostOfDecorations
CakeSize
CakeWriting
CalculateCostOfDecorations()
CalculateCost()

Exercise

If we play our cards right, we should be able to change the two classes without making any changes to the form!

① **Let's create the new class model**

We'll still have the same DinnerParty and BirthdayParty classes, but now they'll inherit from a single Party class. We need them to have exactly the same methods, properties, and fields, so we don't have to make any changes to the form. But some of those methods, properties, and fields will be moved into the Party base class, and we may have to override a few of them.

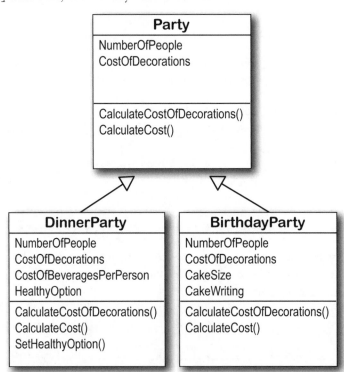

2 **Build the Party base class**

Create the `Party` class—make sure it's public. You'll need to look really closely at the properties and methods in the class diagram, and figure out what you need to move out of `DinnerParty` and `BirthdayParty` and into `Party`.

★ Move the `NumberOfPeople` and `CostOfDecorations` properties into it so that they're compatible with both `DinnerParty` and `BirthdayParty`.

Later on, you'll learn about the "protected" keyword. A protected field is public to a subclass, but private to everyone else.

★ Do the same for `CalculateCostOfDecorations()` and `CalculateCost()`. If those methods need any private fields, you'll need to move them, too. (Remember, subclasses can only see **public** fields—once you move a private field to `Party`, the `DinnerParty` and `BirthdayParty` classes won't have access to it.)

★ You'll also need a constructor. Take a close look at the `BirthdayParty` and `DinnerParty` constructors—anything they have in common should be moved to it.

★ Now **add the $100 bonus** for parties over 12 people. After all, that's why we're doing this! It's common to both birthday and dinner parties, so it belongs in Party.

3 **Make DinnerParty inherit from Party**

Now that `Party` does a lot of the things `DinnerParty` does, you can eliminate the overlap and only keep the part of `DinnerParty` that's unique to dinner parties.

★ Make sure the constructor is working properly. Does it do anything the `Party` constructor doesn't? If so, keep that and then leave everything else to the base class constructor.

★ Any logic that has to do with setting the Healthy Option should stay in `DinnerParty`.

★ Uh-oh—we can't override the `CalculateCost()` method here if we want to keep the form code the same, because our form needs to pass it a `bool` called `healthyOption`. So instead, we'll **overload** it—which just means adding a new `CalculateCost()` method to the class that takes different parameters. So you'll use exactly the same declaration for the method that you used at the beginning of the chapter. But you can still take advantage of inheritance by calling `base.CalculateCost()` to access the `CalculateCost()` method in the `Party` class.

You'll learn all about overloading in Chapter 8—this is just a sneak preview to give you a leg up on it later.

4 **Make BirthdayParty inherit from Party**

Do the same thing for `BirthdayParty`—leave anything not specific to birthdays to the base class, and only keep the birthday-specific functionality in `BirthdayParty`.

★ What does the `BirthdayParty` constructor need to do that's not part of `Party`?

★ You'll need to deal with the cost of the cake inside of `BirthdayParty`. That touches a method and a property, so you'll need to override them.

★ Yes, you can override a property! It's just like overriding a method. When you set the value of `base.NumberOfPeople`, it calls the property's set accessor in the base class. You'll need to use the `base` keyword to both get and set the value.

Exercise Solution

Check it out—you changed the DinnerParty and BirthdayParty classes so that they inherited from the same base class, Party. Then you were able to make the change to the cost calculation to add the $100 fee, and you didn't have to change the form at all. Neat!

```
class Party
{
    const int CostOfFoodPerPerson = 25;
    private bool fancyDecorations;
    public decimal CostOfDecorations = 0;

    public Party(int numberOfPeople, bool fancyDecorations) {
        this.fancyDecorations = fancyDecorations;
        this.NumberOfPeople = numberOfPeople;
    }

    private int numberOfPeople;
    public virtual int NumberOfPeople {
        get { return numberOfPeople; }
        set {
            numberOfPeople = value;
            CalculateCostOfDecorations(fancyDecorations);
        }
    }

    public void CalculateCostOfDecorations(bool fancy) {
        fancyDecorations = fancy;
        if (fancy)
            CostOfDecorations = (NumberOfPeople * 15.00M) + 50M;
        else
            CostOfDecorations = (NumberOfPeople * 7.50M) + 30M;
    }

    public virtual decimal CalculateCost() {
        decimal TotalCost = CostOfDecorations + (CostOfFoodPerPerson * NumberOfPeople);
        if (NumberOfPeople > 12)
        {
            TotalCost += 100M;
        }
        return TotalCost;
    }
}
```

This code was moved straight out of the DinnerParty and BirthdayParty classes and into Party.

The Party constructor does everything that was previously in both the DinnerParty and BirthdayParty constructors.

NumberOfPeople needs to be virtual because BirthdayParty needs to override it (so that a change to the number of people calculates a new cake size).

The decoration calculation is identical in both birthday and dinner parties, so it makes sense to move it to Party. That way none of the code is duplicated in multiple classes.

The cost calculation needs to be a virtual method because the birthday party overrides it (and also extends it by calling the base class method).

```
class BirthdayParty : Party {
    public int CakeSize;

    public BirthdayParty(int numberOfPeople, bool fancyDecorations, string cakeWriting)
        : base(numberOfPeople, fancyDecorations) {
        CalculateCakeSize();
        this.CakeWriting = cakeWriting;
        CalculateCostOfDecorations(fancyDecorations);
    }

    private void CalculateCakeSize() {
        if (NumberOfPeople <= 4)
            CakeSize = 8;
        else
            CakeSize = 16;
    }

    private string cakeWriting = "";
    public string CakeWriting {
        get { return this.cakeWriting; }
        set {
            int maxLength;
            if (CakeSize == 8)
                maxLength = 16;
            else
                maxLength = 40;
            if (value.Length > maxLength) {
                MessageBox.Show("Too many letters for a " + CakeSize + " inch cake");
                if (maxLength > this.cakeWriting.Length)
                    maxLength = this.cakeWriting.Length;
                this.cakeWriting = cakeWriting.Substring(0, maxLength);
            } else
                this.cakeWriting = value;
        }
    }

    public override decimal CalculateCost() {
        decimal CakeCost;
        if (CakeSize == 8)
            CakeCost = 40M + CakeWriting.Length * .25M;
        else
            CakeCost = 75M + CakeWriting.Length * .25M;
        return base.CalculateCost() + CakeCost;
    }

    public override int NumberOfPeople {
        get { return base.NumberOfPeople; }
        set {
            base.NumberOfPeople = value;
            CalculateCakeSize();
            this.CakeWriting = cakeWriting;
        }
    }
}
```

The constructor relies on the base class to do most of the work. Then it calls CalculateCakeSize(), just like the old BirthdayParty constructor did.

The CalculateCakeSize() method is specific to birthday parties, so it stays in the BirthdayParty class.

The CakeWriting property stays intact in the BirthdayParty class too.

CalculateCost() also needs to be overridden, because it needs to first calculate the cost of the cake, and then add it to the cost that's calculated in the Party class's CalculateCost() method.

The NumberOfPeople property has to override the one in Party because the set accessor needs to recalculate the cake size. The set accessor needs to call base.NumberOfPeople so that the set accessor in Party also gets executed.

Continues on page 256.

great job!

Exercise Solution continued from p.255

Here's the last class in Kathleen's solution.
(There's no change to the form code.)

```
class DinnerParty : Party
{
    public decimal CostOfBeveragesPerPerson;

    public DinnerParty(int numberOfPeople, bool healthyOption,
                    bool fancyDecorations)
        : base(numberOfPeople, fancyDecorations) {
        SetHealthyOption(healthyOption);
        CalculateCostOfDecorations(fancyDecorations);
    }

    public void SetHealthyOption(bool healthyOption) {
        if (healthyOption)
            CostOfBeveragesPerPerson = 5.00M;
        else
            CostOfBeveragesPerPerson = 20.00M;
    }

    public decimal CalculateCost(bool healthyOption) {
        decimal totalCost = base.CalculateCost()
                        + (CostOfBeveragesPerPerson * NumberOfPeople);

        if (healthyOption)
            return totalCost * .95M;
        else
            return totalCost;
    }
}
```

This public field is only used in dinner parties, not birthday parties, so it stays in the class.

To do what the old DinnerParty class did, the new constructor calls the Party constructor and then calls SetHealthyOption().

The SetHealthyOption() method stays exactly the same.

DinnerParty needs a different CalculateCost() that takes a parameter, so instead of overriding it we overloaded it. It calls the CalculateCost() method in Party using the base keyword, and then adds the cost of the beverages and adds in the healthy option discount.

You'll learn all about how overloading works in Chapter 8.

> The program's perfect. It's so much easier to run my business now—thanks so much!

Uh-oh—there's still a potential bug in the program!

Now the DinnerParty class has two CalculateCost() methods, one that it inherits from Party and this new one that we added. We haven't fully encapsulated the class—someone could easily misuse this code by calling the wrong CalculateCost() method. So if you do this:

```
DinnerParty dinner = new DinnerParty(5, true, true);
decimal cost1 = dinner.CalculateCost(true);
decimal cost2 = dinner.CalculateCost();
```

cost1 will be set to 261.25, while cost2 will be set to 250. This isn't an academic question—it's a real problem. Sometimes there's code in the base class that you don't want to call directly. Even worse, we never intended the Party class to be instantiated…but there's nothing stopping someone from doing it. Do we even know what will happen if someone creates an instance of Party? We can be pretty sure it'll do something we didn't plan for.

Luckily, C# gives us a really good solution to these problems, which you'll learn about in the next chapter!

Build a beehive management system

A queen bee needs your help! Her hive is out of control, and
she needs a program to help manage it. She's got a beehive full
of workers, and a whole bunch of jobs that need to be done
around the hive. But somehow she's lost control of which bee
is doing what, and whether or not she's got the beepower to do
the jobs that need to be done.

It's up to you to build a beehive management system to help
her keep track of her workers. Here's how it'll work:

① The queen assigns jobs to her workers
There are six possible jobs that the workers can do. Some
know how to collect nectar and manufacture honey, others
can maintain the hive and patrol for enemies. A few bees can
do every job in the hive. So your program will need to give
her a way to assign a job to any bee that's available to do it.

The bees work shifts,
and most jobs require
more than one shift.
So the queen enters
the number of shifts
the job will take, and
clicks the "Assign
this job" button.

This drop-down list shows all six jobs that the
workers can do. The queen knows what jobs need
to be done, and she doesn't really care which bee
does each job. So she just selects which job has to
be done—the program will figure out if there's a
worker available to do it and assign the job to him.

If there's a bee
available to do the job,
the program assigns
the job to the bee and
lets the queen know
it's taken care of.

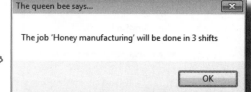

② When the jobs are all assigned, it's time to work
Once the queen's done assigning the work, she'll tell the bees to work the next
shift by clicking the "Work the next shift" button. The program then generates
a shift report that tells her which bees worked that shift, what jobs they did, and
how many more shifts they'll be working each job.

First you'll build the basic system

This project is divided into two parts. The first part is a bit of a review, where you'll create the basic system to manage the hive. It's got two classes, Queen and Worker. You'll build the form for the system, and hook it up to the two classes. And you'll make sure the classes are well encapsulated so they're easy to change when you move on to the second part.

Sometimes class diagrams list private fields and types.

Queen
private workers: Worker[] private shiftNumber: int
AssignWork() WorkTheNextShift()

The program has one Queen object that manages the work being done.

★ The Queen uses an array of Worker objects to track each of the worker bees and whether or not those bees have been assigned jobs. It's stored in a private Worker[] field called worker.

★ The form calls the AssignWork() method, passing a string for the job that needs to be performed and an int for the number of shifts. It'll return true if it finds a worker to assign the job to, or false if it couldn't find a worker to do that job.

★ The form's "Work the next shift" button calls WorkTheNextShift(), which tells the workers to work and returns a shift report to display. It tells each Worker object to work one shift, and then checks that worker's status so it can add a line to the shift report.

CurrentJob and ShiftsLeft are read-only properties.

Worker
CurrentJob: string ShiftsLeft: int
private jobsICanDo: string[] private shiftsToWork: int private shiftsWorked: int
DoThisJob() WorkOneShift()

The queen uses an array of Worker objects to keep track of all of the workers and what jobs they're doing.

★ CurrentJob is a read-only property that tells the Queen object what job the worker's doing ("Sting patrol", "Hive maintenance", etc.). If the worker isn't doing any job, it'll return an empty string.

★ The Queen object attempts to assign a job to a worker using its DoThisJob() method. If that worker is not already doing the job, and if it's a job that he knows how to do, then he'll accept the assignment and the method returns true. Otherwise, it returns false.

★ When the WorkOneShift() method is called, the worker works a shift. He keeps track of how many shifts are left in the current job. If the job is done, then he resets his current job to an empty string so that he can take on his next assignment.

String.IsNullOrEmpty()

Each bee stores his current job as a string. So a worker can figure out if he's currently doing a job by checking his CurrentJob property—it'll be equal to an empty string if he's waiting for his next job. C# gives you an easy way to do that: String.IsNullOrEmpty(CurrentJob) will return true if the CurrentJob string is either empty or null, and false otherwise.

Exercise

A queen bee needs your help! Use what you've learned about classes and objects to build a beehive management system to help her track her worker bees.

❶ Build the form

The form is pretty simple—all of the intelligence is in the `Queen` and `Worker` classes. The form has a private Queen field, and two buttons call its `AssignWork()` and `WorkTheNextShift()` methods. You'll need to add a `ComboBox` control for the bee jobs (flip back to the previous page to see its list items), a `NumericUpDown` control, two buttons, and a multiline text box for the shift report. You'll also need the form's constructor—it's below the screenshot.

This is a ComboBox control named "workerBeeJob". Use its Items property to set the list, and set its DropDownStyle property to "DropDownList" so the user is only allowed to choose items from the list. The Shifts box is a NumericUpDown control called "shifts."

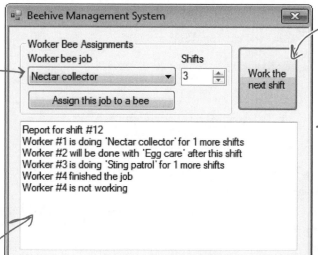

The nextShift button calls the queen's WorkTheNextShift() method, which returns a string that contains the shift report.

Look closely at this shift report, which the Queen object generates. It starts with a shift number, and then reports what each worker is doing. Use the escape sequences "\r\n" to add a line break in the middle of a string.

Name this TextBox "report" and set its MultiLine property to true.

```
public Form1() {
    InitializeComponent();
    Worker[] workers = new Worker[4];
    workers[0] = new Worker(new string[] { "Nectar collector", "Honey manufacturing" });
    workers[1] = new Worker(new string[] { "Egg care", "Baby bee tutoring" });
    workers[2] = new Worker(new string[] { "Hive maintenance", "Sting patrol" });
    workers[3] = new Worker(new string[] { "Nectar collector", "Honey manufacturing",
                "Egg care", "Baby bee tutoring", "Hive maintenance", "Sting patrol" });
    queen = new Queen(workers);
}
```

Each Worker object's constructor takes one parameter, an array of strings that tell it what jobs it knows how to do.

Your form will need a Queen field called queen. You'll pass that array of Worker object references to the Queen object's constructor.

❷ Build the Worker and Queen classes

You've got almost everything you need to know about the `Worker` and Queen classes. There are just a couple more details. `Queen.AssignWork()` loops through the Queen object's `worker` array and attempts to assign the job to each `worker` using its `DoThisJob()` method. The `Worker` object checks its `jobsICanDo` string array to see if it can do the job. If it can, it sets its private `shiftsToWork` field to the job duration, its `CurrentJob` to the job, and its `shiftsWorked` to zero. When it works a shift, it increases `shiftsWorked` by one. The read-only `ShiftsLeft` property returns `shiftsToWork` − `shiftsWorked`—the queen uses it to see how many shifts are left on the job.

Exercise Solution

ShiftsLeft is a read-only property that calculates how many shifts are left on the current job.

CurrentJob is a read-only property that tells the queen which job needs to be done.

The queen uses the worker's DoThisJob() method to assign work to him—he checks his JobsICanDo property to see if he knows how to do the job.

The constructor just sets the JobsICanDo property, which is a string array. It's private because we want the queen to ask the worker to do a job, rather than make her check whether he knows how to do it.

```csharp
class Worker {
    public Worker(string[] jobsICanDo) {
        this.jobsICanDo = jobsICanDo;
    }

    public int ShiftsLeft {
        get {
            return shiftsToWork - shiftsWorked;
        }
    }

    private string currentJob = "";
    public string CurrentJob {
        get {
            return currentJob;
        }
    }

    private string[] jobsICanDo;
    private int shiftsToWork;
    private int shiftsWorked;

    public bool DoThisJob(string job, int numberOfShifts) {
        if (!String.IsNullOrEmpty(currentJob))
            return false;
        for (int i = 0; i < jobsICanDo.Length; i++)
            if (jobsICanDo[i] == job) {
                currentJob = job;
                this.shiftsToWork = numberOfShifts;
                shiftsWorked = 0;
                return true;
            }
        return false;
    }

    public bool WorkOneShift() {
        if (String.IsNullOrEmpty(currentJob))
            return false;
        shiftsWorked++;
        if (shiftsWorked > shiftsToWork) {
            shiftsWorked = 0;
            shiftsToWork = 0;
            currentJob = "";
            return true;
        }
        else
            return false;
    }
}
```

We used !—the NOT operator—to check if the string is NOT null or empty. It's just like checking to see if something's false.

The queen uses the worker's WorkOneShift() method to tell him to work the next shift. The method only returns true if this is the very last shift that he's doing the job. That way the queen can add a line to the report that the bee will be done after this shift.

Take a close look at the logic here. First it checks the currentJob field: if the worker's not working on a job, it just returns false, which stops the method. If not, then it increments ShiftsWorked, and then checks to see if the job's done by comparing it with ShiftsToWork. If it is, the method returns true. Otherwise it returns false.

```
class Queen {
    public Queen(Worker[] workers) {
        this.workers = workers;
    }

    private Worker[] workers;
    private int shiftNumber = 0;

    public bool AssignWork(string job, int numberOfShifts) {
        for (int i = 0; i < workers.Length; i++)
            if (workers[i].DoThisJob(job, numberOfShifts))
                return true;
        return false;
    }

    public string WorkTheNextShift() {
        shiftNumber++;
        string report = "Report for shift #" + shiftNumber + "\r\n";
        for (int i = 0; i < workers.Length; i++)
        {
            if (workers[i].WorkOneShift())
                report += "Worker #" + (i + 1) + " finished the job\r\n";
            if (String.IsNullOrEmpty(workers[i].CurrentJob))
                report += "Worker #" + (i + 1) + " is not working\r\n";
            else
                if (workers[i].ShiftsLeft > 0)
                    report += "Worker #" + (i + 1) + " is doing '" + workers[i].CurrentJob
                        + "' for " + workers[i].ShiftsLeft + " more shifts\r\n";
                else
                    report += "Worker #" + (i + 1) + " will be done with '"
                        + workers[i].CurrentJob + "' after this shift\r\n";
        }
        return report;
    }
}
```

The queen keeps her array of workers private because once they're assigned, no other class should be able to change them...or even see them, since she's the only one who gives them orders. The constructor sets the field's value.

When she assigns work to her worker bees, she starts with the first one and tries assigning him the job. If he can't do it, she moves on to the next. When a bee who can do the job is found, the method returns (which stops the loop).

The queen's WorkTheNextShift() method tells each worker to work a shift and adds a line to the report depending on the worker's status.

We already gave you the constructor. Here's the rest of the code for the form:

```
Queen queen;

private void assignJob_Click(object sender, EventArgs e) {
    if (queen.AssignWork(workerBeeJob.Text, (int)shifts.Value) == false)
        MessageBox.Show("No workers are available to do the job '"
            + workerBeeJob.Text + "'", "The queen bee says...");
    else
        MessageBox.Show("The job '" + workerBeeJob.Text + "' will be done in "
            + shifts.Value + " shifts", "The queen bee says...");
}

private void nextShift_Click(object sender, EventArgs e) {
    report.Text = queen.WorkTheNextShift();
}
```

The form uses its queen field to keep a reference to the Queen object, which in turn has an array of references to the worker objects.

The assignJob button calls the queen's AssignWork() method to assign work to a worker, and displays a message box, depending on whether or not a worker's available to do the job.

The nextShift button tells the queen to work the next shift. She generates a report, which it displays in the report text box.

Inheritancecross

Before you move on to the next part of the exercise,
give your brain a break with a quick crossword.

Across

5. This method gets the value of a property.
7. This method returns true if you pass it "".
8. The constructor in a subclass doesn't need the same _____ as the constructor in its base class.
9. A control on a form that lets you create tabbed applications.
11. This type of class can't be instantiated.

Down

1. A _____ can override methods from its base class.
2. If you want a subclass to override a method, mark the method with this keyword in the base class.
3. A method in a class that's run as soon as it's instantiated.
4. What a subclass does to replace a method in the base class.
6. This contains base classes and subclasses.
7. What you're doing by adding a colon to a class declaration.
10. A subclass uses this keyword to call the members of the class it inherited from.

⟶ Answers on page 268.

Use inheritance to extend the bee management system

Now that you have the basic system in place, use inheritance to let it track how much honey each bee consumes. Different bees consume different amounts of honey, and the queen consumes the most honey of all. So you'll use what you've learned about inheritance to create a Bee base class that Queen and Worker inherit from.

The Bee class has the basic honey consumption behavior. Since honey consumption requires the number of shifts left, we'll move the ShiftsLeft property into it and mark it as virtual so the Worker can override it.

All bees consume honey, so we'll add a GetHoneyConsumption() method to the base class — the queen and workers can inherit it. But queens and workers consume honey differently. We'll make it a virtual method, so one of the subclasses can override it.

Bee

public ShiftsLeft: int

virtual
  GetHoneyConsumption():
  double

Sometimes we'll show you return values and private members in class diagrams.

The worker just needs to subclass Bee and override the ShiftsLeft method with the one you already wrote.

The queen needs to change her report to add honey consumption data. That means she needs to add each worker's honey consumption—and since she consumes honey herself, she'll need to inherit from Bee and override its virtual GetHoneyConsumption() method.

Queen

private workers: Worker[]
private shiftNumber: int

AssignWork()
WorkTheNextShift()

Worker

CurrentJob: string
ShiftsLeft: int

private jobsICanDo: string[]
private shiftsToWork: int
private shiftsWorked: int

DoThisJob()
WorkOneShift()

Add Existing Item

Whenever you have a two-part exercise, it's always a good idea to start a new project for the second part. That way you can always get back to the first solution if you need it. An easy way to do that is to right-click on the project name in the new project's Solution Explorer in the IDE, select "Add Existing Item" from the menu, navigate to the old project's folder, and select the files you want to add. The IDE will make new copies of those files in the new project's folder, and add them to the project. There are a few things to watch out for, though. The IDE will NOT change the namespace, so you'll need to edit each class file and change its namespace line by hand. And if you add a form, make sure to add its designer (.Designer.cs) and resource (.resx) files—and make sure you change their namespaces, too.

We're not done yet! The queen needs to keep track of how much honey the hive is spending on its workers. Here's a perfect chance to use your new inheritance skills!

1

The queen needs to know how much honey the hive uses

The queen just got a call from her accountant bees, who told her that the hive isn't producing enough honey. She'll need to know how much honey she and her workers are using so she can decide whether to divert workers from egg maintenance to honey production.

★ All bees eat honey, so the hive runs through a lot of honey. That's why they need to keep making more of it.

★ Worker bees use more honey when they're working. They need the most honey when the job starts, to give them plenty of energy for the job. They consume less and less as the job goes on. On the last shift the bee uses 10 units of honey; on the second-to-last shift he uses 11 units; on the shift before that he uses 12 units, etc. So if the bee is working (meaning his `ShiftsLeft` is greater than zero), then you can find out how many units of honey to consume by adding 9 to `ShiftsLeft`.

★ If a bee doesn't have a job (i.e., its `ShiftsLeft` is zero), he only uses 7.5 units of honey for the shift.

★ These numbers are all for normal bees. If a bee weighs over 150 milligrams, it uses 35% more honey. This doesn't include queens, though (see below).

★ Queens require a lot of honey. A queen uses more honey when she's got more workers doing jobs, because it's a lot of work overseeing them. She needs to consume as much honey as if she'd worked as many shifts as the worker with the most shifts left on his job.

★ Then she needs even more honey: she uses 20 extra units of honey per shift if there are 2 or fewer workers working, or 30 extra units of honey if there are 3 or more worker bees doing jobs. The queen's consumption isn't subject to the 35% rule, since all queens weigh 275 milligrams.

★ The queen needs all the honey consumption numbers added to the end of each shift report.

2

Create a Bee class to handle the honey calculations

Since the workers and queen all do their honey calculations in similar ways, you'll be able to avoid duplicating your code by having a `Bee` base class that `Worker` and `Queen` can inherit from. You know that each bee needs to know its weight (so it knows whether to multiply its honey expenditure by 35%).

★ Create a `GetHoneyConsumption()` method that calculates the amount of honey that a worker uses. Since the workers and queen all need to do this calculation but the queen needs to do extra calculations as well, it makes sense for the worker to inherit it and the queen to override it.

★ The `GetHoneyConsumption()` method needs the number of shifts left, so add a virtual read-only property called `ShiftsLeft` that returns zero. The worker's `ShiftsLeft` will override it.

★ The honey consumption calculation needs to know the bee's weight, so the `Bee` constructor will need to take the weight as a parameter and store it in a field. Since no other class needs to use it, you should make it private.

Here's a good rule of thumb. You should make fields and methods private by default, and only make them public if another class needs them. That way you avoid bugs in your programs caused by one class accessing another class's properties or methods incorrectly.

Hint: You can use the slightly cryptic "no overload" error message to your advantage! Have the Worker class inherit from Bee, then build your project. When the IDE displays the error, double-click on it and the IDE will jump right to the Worker constructor automatically. How convenient!

3 **Make the Worker class inherit from Bee**

You'll need to set up the constructor to call the base class constructor, like you did with Kathleen. You'll need to change the `Worker` constructor so that it takes the bee's weight as a parameter, and pass that parameter on to the base class constructor. Then, just add the `override` keyword to the `Worker`'s `ShiftLeft` method. Once you do that, each worker will be able to calculate his honey consumption for the queen…and you don't have to make any more changes to the `Worker` class!

4 **Make the Queen class inherit from Bee**

The `Queen` class needs a little more alteration than the `Worker` class, since she needs to actually do the honey calculation and add it to the shift report.

★ Override the `Bee.GetHoneyConsumption()` method and add the queen's extra calculation. She'll need to figure out whether she has 2 or fewer workers with jobs, so she knows whether she needs 20 or 30 units. Then she'll need to add that to the number of units she'd use if she had the same number of shifts left as the worker with the most shifts left.

★ Update the queen's `WorkTheNextShift()` method by adding the honey consumption line to the report. Add a loop to add up the honey consumption for each worker and also to find the worker with the largest honey consumption—do it **before** the queen tells each worker to work the shift (so she gets the consumption numbers for the current shift). She'll add those up, add her own consumption, and then add a line to the end of the shift report that says, "Total Honey Consumption: xxx units" (where xxx is the number of units of honey consumed).

★ You'll need to update the `Queen` constructor just like you did for `Worker`.

Go to the Queen class and type "public override"—when you press the space bar, the IDE automatically lists all the methods you can override. Select the method you want to override and it'll fill in the base method call automatically.

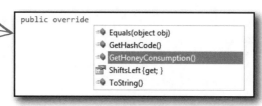

5 **Update the form to instantiate the bees properly**

Since you changed the `Queen` and `Worker` constructors, you'll also need to change the way they're called. Each constructor has a new `Weight` parameter, so you'll need the weights to use:

★ Worker Bee #1: 175mg; Worker Bee #2: 114mg; Worker Bee #3: 149mg; Worker Bee #4: 155mg; Queen Bee: 275mg

That's the only change you'll need to make to the form!

Here's the Bee class. It does the basic honey consumption calculation that's used by both the Worker and Queen classes.

The Bee class has a constructor that sets its Weight field and a HoneyConsumption() method that calculates how much honey a worker consumes.

```
class Bee {
    public Bee(double weight) {
        this.weight = weight;
    }

    public virtual int ShiftsLeft {
        get { return 0; }
    }

    private double weight;

    public virtual double GetHoneyConsumption() {
        double consumption;
        if (ShiftsLeft == 0)
            consumption = 7.5;
        else
            consumption = 9 + ShiftsLeft;
        if (weight > 150)
            consumption *= 1.35;
        return consumption;
    }
}
```

If a bee has 1 shift left, he consumes 10; if 2 left, he consumes 11, etc. If he has no job, then he consumes 7.5. If ShiftsLeft is zero, then the bee has no job.

If the bee weighs more than 150mg, then consumption goes up by 35%.

Inheritance made it easy for you to update your code and add the new honey consumption behavior to the Queen and Worker classes. It would have been a lot harder to make this change if you'd had a lot of duplicated code.

Only the form constructor changed—the rest of the form is exactly the same.

```
public Form1() {
  InitializeComponent();

  Worker[] workers = new Worker[4];
  workers[0] = new Worker(new string[] { "Nectar collector", "Honey manufacturing" }, 175);
  workers[1] = new Worker(new string[] { "Egg care", "Baby bee tutoring" }, 114);
  workers[2] = new Worker(new string[] { "Hive maintenance", "Sting patrol" }, 149);
  workers[3] = new Worker(new string[] { "Nectar collector", "Honey manufacturing",
            "Egg care", "Baby bee tutoring", "Hive maintenance", "Sting patrol" }, 155);
  queen = new Queen(workers);
}
```

The only change to the form is that the weights need to be added to the Worker constructors.

```
class Worker : Bee  {
    public Worker(string[] jobsICanDo, int weight)
        : base(weight) {
        this.jobsICanDo = jobsICanDo;
    }

    public override int ShiftsLeft {

    // ... the rest of the class is the same ...
```

All the Worker class needed was to inherit from Bee and have its constructor adjusted so that it takes a Weight parameter and passes it on to the base class constructor, and overrides the Bee.ShiftsLeft property by adding the override keyword to the property declaration.

The Queen class needed a few changes, starting with inheriting from Bee.

```
class Queen : Bee {
    public Queen(Worker[] workers)
        : base(275) {
        this.workers = workers;
    }
```

The queen weighs 275mg, so her constructor calls the base Bee constructor and passes it a weight of 275.

The WorkTheNextShift() has a loop added to the top that calls each worker's GetHoneyConsumption() method, and then calls her own GetHoneyConsumption() method to come up with a total consumption.

```
    public string WorkTheNextShift()
    {
        double totalConsumption = 0;
        for (int i = 0; i < workers.Length; i++)
            totalConsumption += workers[i].GetHoneyConsumption();
        totalConsumption += GetHoneyConsumption();

        // ... here's where the original code for this method goes, minus the return statement

        report += "Total honey consumption: " + totalConsumption + " units";
        return report;
    }
```

The rest of WorkTheNextShift() is the same, except that it adds the honey line to the report.

The queen overrides the Bee's GetHoneyConsumption() method to do her honey calculation. It finds the worker with the largest consumption and adds either 20 or 30 to it based on how many workers are working.

```
    public override double GetHoneyConsumption() {
        double consumption = 0;
        double largestWorkerConsumption = 0;
        int workersDoingJobs = 0;
        for (int i = 0; i < workers.Length; i++) {
            if (workers[i].GetHoneyConsumption() > largestWorkerConsumption)
                largestWorkerConsumption = workers[i].GetHoneyConsumption();
            if (workers[i].ShiftsLeft > 0)
                workersDoingJobs++;
        }
        consumption += largestWorkerConsumption;
        if (workersDoingJobs >= 3)
            consumption += 30;
        else
            consumption += 20;
        return consumption;
    }
}
```

This loop looks at the consumption of all the workers and finds the one with the largest consumption.

If there are 3 or more workers doing jobs, the queen needs 30 more units of honey; otherwise, she needs 20 more units.

 Inheritancecross Solution

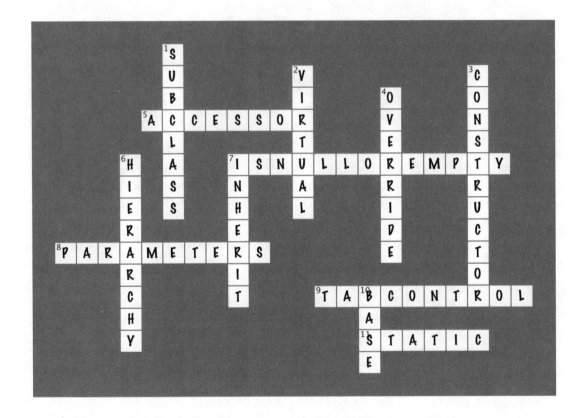

Making classes keep their promises

OK, OK, I know I implemented the BookieCustomer interface, but I can't code the PayMoney() method until next weekend.

You've got three days before I send some Thug objects by to make sure you implement the WalksWithALimp() method.

Actions speak louder than words.

Sometimes you need to group your objects together based on the **things they can do** rather than the classes they inherit from. That's where **interfaces** come in—they let you work with any class that can do the job. But with **great power comes great responsibility**, and any class that implements an interface must promise to **fulfill all of its obligations**…or the compiler will break their kneecaps, see?

Let's get back to bee-sics

The General Bee-namics corporation wants to make the
Beehive Management System you created in the last chapter
into a full-blown Hive Simulator. Here's an overview of the
specification for the new version of the program:

General Bee-namics Hive Simulator

To better represent life in the hive, we'll need to add specialized
capabilities to the worker bees.

- All bees consume honey and have a weight.

- Queens assign work, monitor shift reports, and tell workers to
  work the next shift.

- All worker bees work shifts.

- Sting patrol bees will need to be able to sharpen their stingers,
  look for enemies, and sting them.

- Nectar collector bees are responsible for finding flowers,
  gathering nectar, and then returning to the hive.

*The Bee and Worker
classes don't look like
they'll change much.
We can extend the
classes we already
have to handle these
new features.*

*Looks like we'll need to be able to
store different data for the worker
bees depending on the job they do.*

Lots of things are still the same

The bees in the new Hive Simulator will still consume honey
in the same way they did before. The queen still needs to be
able to assign work to the workers and see the shift reports
that tell who's doing what. The workers work shifts just like
they did before, too, it's just that the jobs they are doing have
been elaborated a little bit.

We can use inheritance to create classes for different types of bees

Here's a class hierarchy with `Worker` and `Queen` classes that inherit from `Bee`, and `Worker` has subclasses `NectarCollector` and `StingPatrol`.

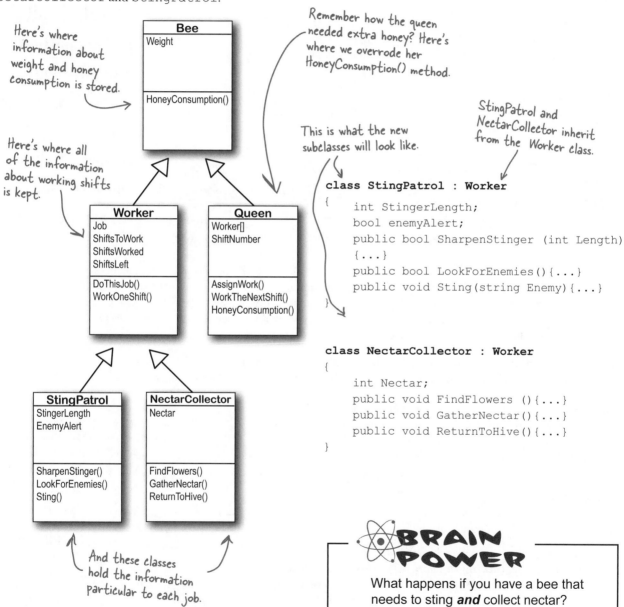

Here's where information about weight and honey consumption is stored.

Remember how the queen needed extra honey? Here's where we overrode her HoneyConsumption() method.

Here's where all of the information about working shifts is kept.

This is what the new subclasses will look like.

StingPatrol and NectarCollector inherit from the Worker class.

Bee
Weight

HoneyConsumption()

Worker
Job
ShiftsToWork
ShiftsWorked
ShiftsLeft

DoThisJob()
WorkOneShift()

Queen
Worker[]
ShiftNumber

AssignWork()
WorkTheNextShift()
HoneyConsumption()

StingPatrol
StingerLength
EnemyAlert

SharpenStinger()
LookForEnemies()
Sting()

NectarCollector
Nectar

FindFlowers()
GatherNectar()
ReturnToHive()

And these classes hold the information particular to each job.

```
class StingPatrol : Worker
{
    int StingerLength;
    bool enemyAlert;
    public bool SharpenStinger (int Length)
    {...}
    public bool LookForEnemies(){...}
    public void Sting(string Enemy){...}
}


class NectarCollector : Worker
{
    int Nectar;
    public void FindFlowers (){...}
    public void GatherNectar(){...}
    public void ReturnToHive(){...}
}
```

⊛**BRAIN**
POWER

What happens if you have a bee that needs to sting *and* collect nectar?

An interface tells a class that it **must** implement certain methods and properties

You use an interface to require a class to include all of the methods and properties listed inside the interface—if it doesn't, the compiler will throw an error.

A class can only inherit from one other class. So creating two separate subclasses for the `StingPatrol` and `NectarCollector` bees won't help us if we have a bee that can do **both** jobs.

The queen's `DefendTheHive()` method can only tell StingPatrol objects to keep the hive safe. She'd love to train the other bees to use their stingers, but she doesn't have any way to command them to attack:

```
class Queen {
  private void DefendTheHive(StingPatrol patroller) { ... }
}
```

I wish you guys could help defend the hive.

There are `NectarCollector` objects that know how to collect nectar from flowers, and instances of `StingPatrol` that can sharpen their stingers and patrol for enemies. But even if the queen could teach the `NectarCollector` to defend the hive by adding methods like `SharpenStinger()` and `LookForEnemies()` to its class definition, she still couldn't pass it into her `DefendTheHive()` method. She could use two different methods:

```
private void DefendTheHive(StingPatrol patroller);
private void AlternateDefendTheHive(NectarCollector patroller);
```

But that's not a particularly good solution. Both of those methods would be identical, because they'd call the same methods in the objects passed to them. The only difference is that one method would take a `StingPatrol`, and the other would take a `NectarCollector` that happens to have the methods necessary for patrolling the hive. And you already know how painful it is to maintain two identical methods.

Luckily, C# gives us **interfaces** to handle situations like that. Interfaces let you define a bunch of methods that a class **must** have.

An interface **requires** that a class has certain methods, and the way that it does that is by **making the compiler throw errors** if it doesn't find all the methods required by the interface in every class that implements it. Those methods can be coded directly in the class, or they can be inherited from a base class. The interface doesn't care how the methods or properties get there, as long as they're there when the code is compiled.

Even if the queen adds sting patrol methods to a NectarCollector object, she still can't pass it to her DefendTheHive() method because it expects a StingPatrol reference. She can't just set a StingPatrol reference equal to a NectarCollector object.

She could add a second method called AlternateDefendTheHive() that takes a NectarCollector reference instead, but that would be cumbersome and difficult to work with.

Plus, the DefendTheHive() and AlternateDefendTheHive() methods would be identical except for the type of the parameter. If she wanted to teach the BabyBeeCare or Maintenance objects to defend the hive, she'd need to keep adding new methods. What a mess!

Use the interface keyword to define an interface

Adding an interface to your program is a lot like adding a class, except you never write any methods. You just define the methods' return type and parameters, but instead of a block of statements inside curly brackets you just end the line with a semicolon.

Interfaces do not store data, so you **can't add any fields**. But you *can* add definitions for properties. The reason is that get and set accessors are just methods, and interfaces are all about forcing classes to have certain methods with specific names, types, and parameters. So if you've got a problem that looks like it could be solved by adding a field to an interface, try **using a property instead**—odds are, it'll do what you're looking for.

> **Interface names start with I**
>
> Whenever you create an interface, you should make its name start with an uppercase I. There's no rule that says you need to do it, but it makes your code a lot easier to understand. You can see for yourself just how much easier that can make your life. Just go into the IDE to any blank line inside any method and type "I"—IntelliSense shows .NET interfaces.

You declare an interface like this:

Interfaces don't store data. So they don't have fields...but they can have properties.

```
interface IStingPatrol
{
    int AlertLevel { get; }
    int StingerLength { get; set; }
    bool LookForEnemies();
    int SharpenStinger(int length);
}
```

Any class that implements this method must have all of these methods and properties, or the program won't compile.

Any class that implements this interface will need a SharpenStinger() method that takes an int parameter.

```
interface INectarCollector
{
    void FindFlowers();
    void GatherNectar();
    void ReturnToHive();
}
```

You don't write the code for the methods in the interface, just their names. You write the code in the class that implements it.

So how does this help the queen? Now she can make one single method that takes any object that knows how to defend the hive:

```
private void DefendTheHive(IStingPatrol patroller)
```

Since this takes an IStingPatrol reference, you can pass it ANY object that implements IStingPatrol.

This gives the queen a single method that can take a `StingPatrol`, `NectarStinger`, and any other bee that knows how to defend the hive—it doesn't matter which class she passes to the method. As long as it implements `IStingPatrol`, the `DefendTheHive()` method is guaranteed that the object has the methods and properties it needs to defend the hive.

Everything in a public interface is automatically public, because you'll use it to define the public methods and properties of any class that implements it.

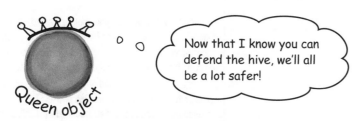

Now that I know you can defend the hive, we'll all be a lot safer!

Queen object

Now you can create an instance of NectarStinger that does both jobs

You use the **colon operator** to **implement** an interface, just like you do for inheritance. It works like this: the first thing after the colon is the class it inherits from, followed by a list of interfaces—unless it doesn't inherit from a class, in which case it's just a list of interfaces (in no particular order).

This class <u>inherits</u> from Worker and implements INectarCollector and IStingPatrol.

You <u>implement</u> an interface with a colon operator, just like you inherit.

```
class NectarStinger : Worker, INectarCollector,
IStingPatrol {
    public int AlertLevel {
        get { return alertLevel; }
    }
```

You can use more than one interface if you separate them with commas.

The NectarStinger sets the backing field for the AlertLevel property in its LookForEnemies() method.

```
    public int StingerLength {
        get { return stingerLength; }
        set {
            stingerLength = value;
        }
    }
```

```
    public bool LookForEnemies() {...}
    public int SharpenStinger(int length)
```

Every method in the interface has a method in the class. Otherwise it wouldn't compile

```
    {...}
    public void FindFlowers() {...}
    public void GatherNectar() {...}
    public void ReturnToHive() {...}
```

The bee retracts its stinger when there are no enemies around, so the backing field changes its value over time.

When you create a NectarStinger object, it will be able to do the job of both a NectarCollector and a StingPatrol worker bee.

When you've got a class that implements an interface, it acts just like any other class. You can instantiate it with new and use its methods:

```
NectarStinger bobTheBee = new NectarStinger();

bobTheBee.LookForEnemies();

bobTheBee.FindFlowers();
```

Q: **I still don't quite get how interfaces improve the beehive code. You'll still need to add a `NectarStinger` class, and it'll still have duplicate code...right?**

A: Interfaces aren't about preventing you from duplicating code. They're about letting you use one class in more than one situation. The goal is to create one worker bee class that can do two different jobs. You'll still need to create classes for them—that's not the point. The point of the interfaces is that now you've got a way to have a class that does any number of jobs. Say you have a `PatrolTheHive()` method that takes a `StingPatrol` object and a `CollectNectar()` method that takes a `NectarCollector` object. But you don't want `StingPatrol` to inherit from `NectarCollector` or vice versa—each class has public methods and properties that the other one shouldn't have. Now take a minute and try to think of a way to create one single class whose instances could be passed to both methods. Seriously, put the book down, take a minute and try to think up a way! How do you do it?

Interfaces fix that problem. Now you can create an IStingPatrol reference—and it can point to any object that implements `IStingPatrol`, no matter what the actual class is. It can point to a `StingPatrol`, or a `NectarStinger`, or even a totally unrelated object. If you've got an `IStingPatrol` reference pointing to an object, then you know you can use all of the methods and properties that are part of the `IStingPatrol` interface, regardless of the actual type of the object.

But the interface is only part of the solution. You'll still need to create a new class that implements it, since it doesn't actually come with any code. Interfaces aren't about avoiding the creation of extra classes or avoiding duplicate code. They're about making one class that can do more than one job without relying on inheritance, as inheritance brings a lot of extra baggage—you'll have to inherit every method, property, and field, not just those that have to do with the specific job.

Can you think of ways that you could still avoid duplicating code while using an interface? You could create a separate class called `Stinger` or `Proboscis` to contain the code that's specific to stinging or collecting nectar. `NectarStinger` and `NectarCollector` could both create a private instance of `Proboscis`, and any time they needed to collect nectar, they'd call its methods and set its properties.

Classes that implement interfaces have to include **ALL** of the interface's methods

Implementing an interface means that you have to have a method in the class for each and every property and method that's declared in the interface—if it doesn't have every one of them, it won't compile. If a class implements more than one interface, then it needs to include all of the properties and methods in each of the interfaces it implements. But don't take our word for it...

Do this!

1 **Create a new application and add a new class file called IStingPatrol.cs**
Instead of adding a class, type in the **IStingPatrol** interface from two pages ago. Your program should compile.

2 **Add a Bee class to the project**
Don't add any properties or methods yet. Just have it implement IStingPatrol:

```
class Bee : IStingPatrol
{
}
```

3 **Try to compile the program**
Select "Rebuild" from the Build menu. Uh-oh—the compiler won't let you do it:

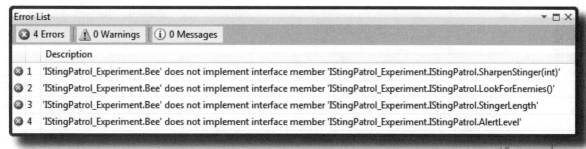

You'll see one of these "does not implement" errors for every member of IStingPatrol that's not implemented in the class. The compiler **really** wants you to implement every method in the interface.

4 **Add the methods and properties to the Bee class**
Add a LookForEnemies method and a SharpenStinger method—they don't have to do anything, they just need to compile. Then add a get accessor for an int called AlertLevel and get and set accessors for an int called StingerLength. Now the program will compile!

Get a little practice using interfaces

Interfaces are really easy to use, and the best way to understand them is to start using them. So create a new Windows Forms Application project, drag a button onto the form, and get started!

Do this!

1 Here's the `TallGuy` class, and the code for a button that creates it using an object initializer and calls its `TalkAboutYourself()` method. Nothing new here—we'll use it in a minute:

```
class TallGuy {
    public string Name;
    public int Height;

    public void TalkAboutYourself() {
        MessageBox.Show("My name is " + Name + " and I'm "
            + Height + " inches tall.");
    }
}

private void button1_Click(object sender, EventArgs e) {
    TallGuy tallGuy = new TallGuy() { Height = 74, Name = "Jimmy" };
    tallGuy.TalkAboutYourself();
}
```

2 Let's create an `IClown` interface for the class.

You already know that everything inside an interface has to be public. But don't take our word for it. Create a new project and declare an interface on your own, like this:

interface IClown

Now try to declare a private method inside the interface:

private void Honk();

Select Build>>Build Solution in the IDE. You'll see this error:

> ⊗ 1 | The modifier 'private' is not valid for this item

> You don't need to type "public" inside the interface, because it automatically makes every property and method public.

Now go ahead and **delete the private access modifier**—the error will go away and your program will compile just fine.

3 Before you go on to the next page, see if you can create the rest of the `IClown` interface, and modify the `TallGuy` class to implement this interface. Add your interface to your project just like you add a class: right-click on the project in the Solution Explorer and add a class file called `IClown.cs`.

Your new `IClown` interface should have a `void` method called `Honk` that doesn't take any parameters, and a `string` read-only property called `FunnyThingIHave` that has a `get` accessor but no `set` accessor.

4 Here's the interface—did you get it right?

```
interface IClown
{
    string FunnyThingIHave { get; }
    void Honk();
}
```

Here's an example of an interface that has a get accessor without a set accessor. Remember, interfaces can't contain fields, but when you implement this read-only property in a class, it'll look like a field to other objects.

OK, now modify the `TallGuy` class so that it implements `IClown`. Remember, the colon operator is always followed by the base class to inherit from (if any), and then a list of interfaces to implement, all separated by commas. Since there's no base class and only one interface to implement, the declaration looks like this:

TallGuy will implement the IClown interface.

```
class TallGuy : IClown
```

Then make sure the rest of the class is the same, including the two fields and the method. Select "Build Solution" from the Build menu in the IDE to compile and build the program. You'll see two errors, including this one:

What the IDE is telling you is that when you said TallGuy would implement IClown, you promised to add all of the properties and methods in that interface...and then you broke that promise!

> ⊗ `'TallGuy' does not implement interface`
>   `member 'IClown.Honk()'`

5 The errors will go away as soon as you add all of the methods and properties defined in the interface. So go ahead and implement the interface. Add a read-only string property called `FunnyThingIHave` with a get accessor that always returns the string "big shoes". Then add a `Honk()` method that pops up a message box that says, "Honk honk!"

Here's what it'll look like:

```
public string FunnyThingIHave {
    get { return "big shoes"; }
}

public void Honk() {
    MessageBox.Show("Honk honk!");
}
```

All the interface requires is that a class that implements it has a property called FunnyThingIHave with a get accessor. You can put any get accessor in there, even one that just returns the same string every time. Most get accessors won't do this, but this will work just fine if it does what you need it to do.

The interface says that you need a public void method called Honk, but it doesn't say what that method needs to do. It can do anything at all—no matter what it does, the code will compile as long as some method is there with the right signature.

6 Now your code will compile! Update your button so that it calls the `TallGuy` object's `Honk()` method.

You can't instantiate an interface, but you can <u>reference</u> an interface

Say you had a method that needed an object that could perform the FindFlowers() method. Any object that implemented the INectarCollector interface would do. It could be a Worker object, Robot object, or Dog object, as long as it implements the INectarCollector interface.

That's where **interface references** come in. You can use one to refer to an object that implements the interface you need and you'll always be sure that it has the right methods for your purpose—even if you don't know much else about it.

You can create an array of IWorker references, but you can't instantiate an interface. But what you can do is point those references at new instances of classes that implement IWorker. Now you can have an array that holds many different kinds of objects!

If you try to instantiate an interface, the compiler will complain.

This won't work...

```
IStingPatrol dennis = new IStingPatrol();
```

> ⊗ 1   Cannot create an instance of the abstract class or interface

You can't use the new keyword with an interface, which makes sense—the methods and properties don't have any implementation. If you could create an object from an interface, how would it know how to behave?

...but this will.

```
NectarStinger fred = new NectarStinger();
IStingPatrol george = fred;
```

Remember how you could pass a BLT reference into any class that expects a Sandwich, because BLT inherits from Sandwich? Well, this is the same thing—you can use a NectarStinger in any method or statement that expects an IStingPatrol.

Even though this object can do more, when you use an interface reference you only have access to the methods in the interface.

The first line is an ordinary new statement, creating a reference called Fred and pointing it to a NectarStinger object.

The second line is where things start to get interesting, because that line of code **creates a new reference variable using IStingPatrol**. That line may look a little odd when you first see it. But look at this:

```
NectarStinger ginger = fred;
```

You know what this third statement does—it creates a new NectarStinger reference called ginger and points it at whatever object fred is pointing to. The george statement uses IStingPatrol the same way.

So what happened?

There's only one new statement, so **only one object** was created. The second statement created a reference variable called george that can point to an instance of **any class that implements IStingPatrol**.

Interface references work just like object references

You already know all about how objects live on the heap.
When you work with an interface reference, it's just another
way to refer to the same objects you've already been dealing
with. Look—it's easy!

1 Create a couple of bees
This is totally familiar stuff by now.

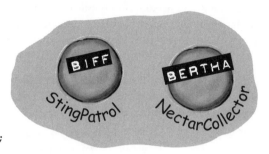

```
StingPatrol biff = new StingPatrol();
NectarCollector bertha = new NectarCollector();
```

*Let's assume that StingPatrol implements the
IStingPatrol interface and NectarCollector
implements the INectarCollector interface.*

2 Add IStingPatrol and INectarCollector references
You can use interface references just like you use any other
reference type.

```
IStingPatrol defender = biff;
INectarCollector cutiePie = bertha;
```

*These two statements use interfaces to
create new references to existing objects. You
can only point an interface reference at an
instance of a class that implements it.*

3 An interface reference will keep an object alive
When there aren't any references pointing to an object, it
disappears. But there's no rule that says those references all have
to be the same type! An interface reference is just as good as an
object reference when it comes to keeping track of objects.

```
biff = null;
```

*This object didn't disappear
because defender is still
pointing to it.*

4 Assign a new instance to an interface reference
You don't actually *need* an object reference—you can create a new
object and assign it straight to an interface reference variable.

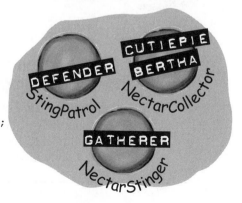

```
INectarCollector gatherer = new NectarStinger();
```

You can find out if a class implements a certain interface with "is"

Sometimes you need to find out if a certain class implements an interface. Suppose we have all our worker bees in an array, called `Bees`. We can make the array hold the type `Worker`, since all worker bees will be `Worker` classes, or subclasses of that type.

But which of the worker bees can collect nectar? In other words, we want to know if the class implements the `INectarCollector` interface. We can use the **is** keyword to find out exactly that.

> All the workers are in an array of Workers. We'll use "is" to sort out which type of worker each bee is.

> We've got an array of Worker bees who are all eligible to go on a nectar collecting mission. So we'll loop through the array, and use "is" to figure out which ones have the right methods and properties to do the job.

```
Worker[] bees = new Worker[3];

bees[0] = new NectarCollector();

bees[1] = new StingPatrol();

bees[2] = new NectarStinger();

for (int i = 0; i < bees.Length; i++)
{
    if (bees[i] is INectarCollector)
    {
        bees[i].DoThisJob("Nectar Collector", 3);
    }
}
```

> is lets you compare interfaces AND also other types, too!

> This is like saying, if this bee implements the INectarCollector interface...do this.

> Now that we know the bee is a nectar collector, we can assign it the job of collecting nectar.

BRAIN POWER

If you have some other class that doesn't inherit from `Worker` but **does** implement the `INectarCollector` interface, then it'll be able to do the job, too! But since it doesn't inherit from `Worker`, you can't get it into an array with other bees. Can you think of a way to get around the problem and create an array with both bees and this new class?

Interfaces can inherit from other interfaces

When one class inherits from another, it gets all of the methods and properties from the base class. **Interface inheritance** is even simpler. Since there's no actual method body in any interface, you don't have to worry about calling base constructors or methods. The inherited interfaces simply accumulate all of the methods and properties from the interfaces they inherit from.

When we draw an interface on a class diagram, we'll show inheritance using dashed lines.

```
interface IWorker
{
    string Job { get; }
    int ShiftsLeft { get; }
    void DoThisJob(string job, int shifts)
    void WorkOneShift()
}
```

We've created a new IWorker interface that the other interfaces inherit from.

(interface) IWorker
Job
ShiftsLeft
DoThisJob()
WorkOneShift()

(interface) IStingPatrol		(interface) INectarCollector
StingerLength		Nectar
EnemyAlert		
SharpenStinger()		FindFlowers()
LookForEnemies()		GatherNectar()
Sting()		ReturnToHive()

Any class that implements an interface that inherits from IWorker <u>must implement</u> its methods and properties

When a class implements an interface, it has to include every property and method in that interface. And if that interface inherits from another one, then all of *those* properties and methods need to be implemented, too.

```
interface IStingPatrol : IWorker
{
    int AlertLevel { get;}
    int StingerLength { get; set;}
    bool LookForEnemies();
    int SharpenStinger(int length);
}
```

Here's the same IStingPatrol interface, but now it inherits from the IWorker interface. It looks like a tiny change, but it makes a huge difference in any class that implements IStingPatrol.

A class that implements IStingPatrol must not only implement these methods...

...but the methods of the IWorker interface this interface inherits from, too.

(interface) IWorker
Job
ShiftsLeft
DoThisJob()
WorkOneShift()

The RoboBee 4000 can do a worker bee's job without using valuable honey

Let's create a new bee, a RoboBee 4000, that runs on gas. We can have it inherit from the `IWorker` interface, though, so it can do everything a normal worker bee can.

RoboBee
ShiftsToWork
ShiftsWorked
ShiftsLeft
Job
DoThisJob()

This is our basic Robot class, so robots can run on gasoline.

```
class Robot
{
    public void ConsumeGas() {...}
}

class RoboBee : Robot, IWorker
{
    private int shiftsToWork;
    private int shiftsWorked;
    public int ShiftsLeft
       {get {return shiftsToWork - shiftsWorked;}}
    public string Job { get; private set; }
    public bool DoThisJob(string job, int shiftsToWork){...}
    public void WorkOneShift() {...}
}
```

The RoboBee class inherits from Robot and implements IWorker. That means it's a robot, but can do the job of a worker bee. Perfect!

The RoboBee class implements all the methods from the IWorker interface.

If RoboBee didn't implement everything in the IWorker interface, the code wouldn't compile.

Remember, for other classes in the application, there's no functional difference between a RoboBee and a normal worker bee. They both implement the `IWorker` interface, so both act like worker bees as far as the rest of the program is concerned.

But, you could distinguish between the types by using `is`:

```
if (workerBee is Robot) {
  // now we know workerBee
  // is a Robot object
}
```

We can see what class or interface workerBee implements or subclasses with "is".

Any class can implement <u>ANY</u> interface as long as it keeps the promise of implementing the interface's methods and properties.

is tells you what an object implements, as tells the compiler how to treat your object

Sometimes you need to call a method that an object gets from an interface it implements. But what if you don't know if that object is the right type? You use **is** to find that out. Then, you can use **as** to treat that object—which you now know is the right type—as having the method you need to call.

```
IWorker[] bees = new IWorker[3];
    bees[0] = new NectarStinger();
    bees[1] = new RoboBee();
    bees[2] = new Worker();
```

All these bees implement IWorker, but we don't know which ones implement other interfaces, like INectarCollector.

We're looping through each bee...

```
for (int i = 0; i < bees.Length; i++) {
    if (bees[i] is INectarCollector) {
        INectarCollector thisCollector;
        thisCollector = bees[i] as INectarCollector;
        thisCollector.GatherNectar();
        ...
```

...and checking to see if it implements INectarCollector.

We can't call INectarCollector methods on the bees. They're of type IWorker, and don't know about INectarCollector methods.

NOW we can call INectarCollector methods.

We use "as" to say, treat this object AS an INectarCollector implementation.

Sharpen your pencil

Take a look at the array on the left. For each of these statements, write down which values of i would make it evaluate to true. Also, two of them won't compile—cross those lines out.

```
IWorker[] Bees = new IWorker[8];
Bees[0] = new NectarStinger();
Bees[1] = new RoboBee();
Bees[2] = new Worker();
Bees[3] = Bees[0] as IWorker;
Bees[4] = IStingPatrol;
Bees[5] = null;
Bees[6] = Bees[0];
Bees[7] = new INectarCollector();
```

1. (Bees[i] is INectarCollector)

....

2. (Bees[i] is IStingPatrol)

....

3. (Bees[i] is IWorker)

....

A CoffeeMaker is also an Appliance

If you're trying to figure out how to cut down your energy bill each month, you don't really care what each of your appliances does. You only really care that they consume power. So if you were writing a program to monitor your electricity consumption, you'd probably just write an `Appliance` class. But if you needed to be able to distinguish a coffee maker from an oven, you'd have to build a class hierarchy. So you'd add the methods and properties that are specific to a coffee maker or oven to some `CoffeeMaker` and `Oven` classes, and they'd inherit from an `Appliance` class that has their common methods and properties.

Appliance
PluggedIn
Color
ConsumePower()

CoffeeMaker	Oven
CoffeeLeft	Capacity
FillWithWater() MakeCoffee()	Preheat() HeatUp() Reheat()

```
public void MonitorPower(Appliance appliance) {
    // code to add data to a household
    // power consumption database
}

CoffeeMaker misterCoffee = new CoffeeMaker();
MonitorPower(misterCoffee);
```

Here's a method in the program to monitor the power consumption for a house.

This code would appear later on in the program to monitor the coffee maker's power consumption.

Even though the MonitorPower() method takes a reference to an Appliance object, you can pass it the misterCoffee reference because CoffeeMaker is a subclass of Appliance.

You already saw this in the last chapter, when you saw how you could pass a BLT reference to a method that expected a Sandwich.

Sharpen your pencil — Solution

Take a look at the array on the left. For each of these statements, write down which values of `i` would make it evaluate to `true`. Also, two of them won't compile—cross them out.

```
IWorker[] Bees = new IWorker[8];
Bees[0] = new NectarStinger();
Bees[1] = new RoboBee();
Bees[2] = new Worker();
Bees[3] = Bees[0] as IWorker;
Bees[4] = IStingPatrol;
Bees[5] = null;
Bees[6] = Bees[0];
Bees[7] = new INectarCollector();
```

NectarStinger() implements the IStingPatrol interface.

1. (Bees[i] is INectarCollector)
   0 and 6

2. (Bees[i] is IStingPatrol)
   0, 6

3. (Bees[i] is IWorker)
   0, 1, 2, 3, and 6

Upcasting works with both objects and interfaces

When you substitute a subclass for a base class—like substituting a coffee maker for an appliance or a BLT for a sandwich—it's called **upcasting**. It's a really powerful tool that you get when you build class hierarchies. The only drawback to upcasting is that you can only use the properties and methods of the base class. In other words, when you treat a coffee maker like an appliance, you can't tell it to make coffee or fill it with water. But you *can* tell whether or not it's plugged in, since that's something you can do with any appliance (which is why the `PluggedIn` property is part of the `Appliance` class).

① Let's create some objects

We can create a `CoffeeMaker` and `Oven` class as usual:

```
CoffeeMaker misterCoffee = new CoffeeMaker();

Oven oldToasty = new Oven();
```

> We'll start by instantiating an Oven object and a CoffeeMaker object as usual.

② What if we want to create an array of appliances?

You can't put a `CoffeeMaker` in an `Oven[]` array, and you can't put an `Oven` in a `CoffeeMaker[]` array. But you can put both of them in an `Appliance[]` array:

```
Appliance[] kitchenWare = new Appliance[2];

kitchenWare[0] = misterCoffee;

kitchenWare[1] = oldToasty;
```

> You can use upcasting to create an array of appliances that can hold both coffee makers and ovens.

③ But you can't treat an appliance like an oven

When you've got an `Appliance` reference, you can **only** access the methods and properties that have to do with appliances. You **can't** use the `CoffeeMaker` methods and properties through the `Appliance` reference *even if you know it's really a CoffeeMaker*. So these statements will work just fine, because they treat a `CoffeeMaker` object like an `Appliance`:

```
Appliance powerConsumer = new CoffeeMaker();

powerConsumer.ConsumePower();
```

> powerConsumer is an Appliance reference pointing to a CoffeeMaker object.

But as soon as you try to use it like a `CoffeeMaker`:

```
powerConsumer.MakeCoffee();
```

> This line won't compile because powerConsumer is an Appliance reference, so it can only be used to do Appliance things.

your code won't compile, and the IDE will display an error:

> ⊗ `'Appliance' does not contain a`
> `    definition for 'MakeCoffee'`

because once you upcast from a subclass to a base class, then you can only access the methods and properties that **match the reference** that you're using to access the object.

Downcasting lets you turn your appliance back into a coffee maker

Upcasting is a great tool, because it lets you use a coffee maker or an oven anywhere you just need an appliance. But it's got a big drawback—if you're using an `Appliance` reference that points to a `CoffeeMaker` object, you can only use the methods and properties that belong to `Appliance`. And that's where **downcasting** comes in: that's how you take your **previously upcast reference** and change it back. You can figure out if your `Appliance` is really a `CoffeeMaker` using the **is** keyword. And once you know that, you can convert the `Appliance` back to a `CoffeeMaker` using the **as** keyword.

Here's our Appliance reference that points to a CoffeeMaker object from the last page.

1 **We'll start with the CoffeeMaker we already upcast**
Here's the code that we used:

```
Appliance powerConsumer = new CoffeeMaker();
powerConsumer.ConsumePower();
```

2 **But what if we want to turn the Appliance back into a CoffeeMaker?**
The first step in downcasting is using the `is` keyword to check if it's even an option.

```
if (powerConsumer is CoffeeMaker)
    // then we can downcast!
```

3 **Now that we know it's a CoffeeMaker, let's use it like one**
The `is` keyword is the first step. Once you know that you've got an `Appliance` reference that's pointing to a `CoffeeMaker` object, you can use `as` to downcast it. And that lets you use the `CoffeeMaker` class's methods and properties. And since `CoffeeMaker` inherits from `Appliance`, it still has its `Appliance` methods and properties.

```
if (powerConsumer is CoffeeMaker) {
    CoffeeMaker javaJoe = powerConsumer as CoffeeMaker;
    javaJoe.MakeCoffee();
}
```

The javaJoe reference points to the same CoffeeMaker object as powerConsumer. But it's a CoffeeMaker reference, so it can call the MakeCoffee() method.

When downcasting fails, as returns null

So what happens if you try to use `as` to convert an `Oven` object into a `CoffeeMaker`? It returns null—and if you try to use it, .NET will cause your program to break.

Uh-oh, these don't match!

```
if (powerConsumer is CoffeeMaker) {
    Oven foodWarmer = powerConsumer as Oven;
    foodWarmer.Preheat();
}
```

powerConsumer is NOT an Oven object. So when you try to downcast it with "as", the foodWarmer reference ends up set to null. And when you try to use a null reference, this happens....

⚠ NullReferenceException was unhandled   ✕

Upcasting and downcasting work with interfaces, too

You already know that `is` and `as` work with interfaces. Well, so do all of the upcasting and downcasting tricks. Let's add an `ICooksFood` interface for any class that can heat up food. And we'll add a `Microwave` class—both `Microwave` and `Oven` implement the `ICooksFood` interface. Now there are three different ways that you can access an `Oven` object. And the IDE's `IntelliSense` can help you figure out exactly what you can and can't do with each of them:

> Any class that
> implements
> ICooksFood is
> an appliance
> that can heat
> up food.

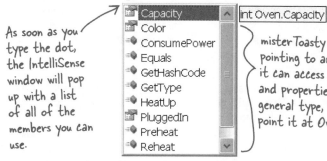

```
Oven misterToasty = new Oven();
misterToasty.
```

As soon as you type the dot, the IntelliSense window will pop up with a list of all of the members you can use.

misterToasty is an **Oven reference** pointing to an Oven object, so it can access all of the methods and properties...but it's the least general type, so you can only point it at Oven objects.

```
ICooksFood cooker;
if (misterToasty is ICooksFood)
    cooker = misterToasty as ICooksFood;
cooker.
```

cooker is an **ICooksFood reference** pointing to that same Oven object. It can only access ICooksFood members, but it can also point to a Microwave object.

```
Appliance powerConsumer;
if (misterToasty is Appliance)
    powerConsumer = misterToasty;
powerConsumer.
```

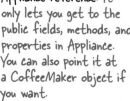

powerConsumer is an **Appliance reference**. It only lets you get to the public fields, methods, and properties in Appliance. You can also point it at a CoffeeMaker object if you want.

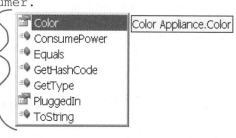

Three different references that point to the same object can access different methods and properties, depending on the reference's type.

there are no
Dumb Questions

Q: So back up—you told me that I can always upcast but I can't always downcast. Why?

A: Because the compiler can warn you if your upcast is wrong. The only time an upcast won't work is if you're trying to set an object equal to a class that it doesn't inherit from or an interface that it doesn't implement. And the compiler can figure out immediately that you didn't upcast properly, and will give you an error.

On the other hand, the compiler doesn't know how to check if you're downcasting *from* an object or interface reference *to* a reference that's not valid. That's because it's perfectly legal to put any class or interface name on the right-hand side of the `as` keyword. If the downcast is illegal, then the `as` statement will just return `null`. And it's a good thing that the compiler doesn't stop you from doing that, because there are plenty of times when you'd want to do it.

Q: Someone told me that an interface is like a contract, but I don't really get why. What does that mean?

A: Yes, we've heard that too—a lot of people like to say that an interface is like a contract. (That's a really common question on job interviews.) And it's true, to some extent. When you make your class implement an interface, you're telling the compiler that you promise to put certain methods into it. The compiler will hold you to that promise.

But we think that it's easier to remember how interfaces work if you think of an interface as a kind of checklist. The compiler runs through the checklist to make sure that you actually put all of the methods from the interface into your class. If you didn't, it'll bomb out and not let you compile.

Q: What if I want to put a method body into my interface? Is that OK?

A: No, the compiler won't let you do that. An interface isn't allowed to have any statements in it at all. Even though you use the colon operator to implement an interface, it's not the same thing as inheriting from a class. Implementing an interface doesn't add any behavior to your class at all, or make any changes to it. All it does is tell the compiler to make sure that your class has all of the methods that the interface says it should have.

Q: Then why would I want to use an interface? It seems like it's just adding restrictions, without actually changing my class at all.

A: Because when your class implements an interface, then an interface reference can point to any instance of that class. And that's really useful to you—it lets you create one reference type that can work with a whole bunch of different kinds of objects.

Here's a quick example. A horse, an ox, a mule, and a steer can all pull a cart. But in our zoo simulator, `Horse`, `Ox`, `Mule`, and `Steer` would all be different classes. Let's say you had a cart-pulling ride in your zoo, and you wanted to create an array of any animal that could pull carts around. Uh-oh—you can't just create an array that will hold all of those. If they all inherited from the same base class, then you could create an array of those. But it turns out that they don't. So what'll you do?

That's where interfaces come in handy. You can create an `IPuller` interface that has methods for pulling carts around. Now you could declare your array like this:

```
IPuller[] pullerArray;
```

Now you can put a reference to any animal you want in that array, as long as it implements the `IPuller` interface.

Q: Is there an easier way to implement interfaces? It's a lot of typing!

A: Why yes, there is! The IDE gives you a very powerful shortcut that automatically implements an interface for you. Just start typing your class:

```
class
    Microwave : ICooksFood
    { }
```

Click on ICooksFood—you'll see a small bar appear underneath the "I". Hover over it and you'll see an icon appear underneath it:

interface ICooksFood

ICooksFood

Sometimes it's hard to click on the icon, but Ctrl-peri will work, too.

Click on the icon and choose "Implement Interface 'ICooksFood'" from the menu. It'll automatically add any members that you haven't implemented yet. Each one has a single `throws` statement in it—they'll cause your program to halt, as a reminder in case you forget to implement one of them. (You'll learn about `throws` in Chapter 10.)

An interface is like a checklist that the compiler runs through to make sure your class implemented a certain set of methods.

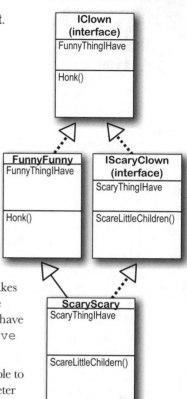

Extend the IClown interface and use classes that implement it.

Exercise

1 Start with the `IClown` interface from the last "Do This!" on page 277:

```
interface IClown {
    string FunnyThingIHave { get; }
    void Honk();
}
```

2 Extend `IClown` by creating a new interface, `IScaryClown`, that inherits from `IClown`. It should have an additional `string` property called `ScaryThingIHave` with a get accessor but no set accessor, and a `void` method called `ScareLittleChildren()`.

3 Create these classes:

★ A funny clown class called `FunnyFunny` that uses a private string variable to store a funny thing. Use a constructor that takes a parameter called `FunnyThingIHave` and uses it to set the private field. The `Honk()` method should say, "Honk honk! I have a " followed by the funny thing it has. The `FunnyThingIHave` set accessor should return the same thing.

★ A scary clown class called `ScaryScary` that uses a private variable to store an integer that was passed to it by its constructor in a parameter called `numberOfScaryThings`. The `ScaryThingIHave` get accessor should return a string consisting of the number from the constructor followed by "spiders". The `ScareLittleChildren()` pops up a message box that says, "Boo! Gotcha!"

4 Here's code for a button—but it's not working. Can you figure out how to fix it?

```
private void button1_Click(object sender, EventArgs e) {
    ScaryScary fingersTheClown = new ScaryScary("big shoes", 14);
    FunnyFunny someFunnyClown = fingersTheClown;
    IScaryClown someOtherScaryclown = someFunnyClown;
    someOtherScaryclown.Honk();
}
```

Fingers the Clown is scary.

You better get this one right...or else!

*no no! nooo! noo! **no more scary clowns!***

ExerciSe SoLutioN

Extend the IClown interface and use classes that implement it.

```
interface IClown {
    string FunnyThingIHave { get; }
    void Honk();
}

interface IScaryClown : IClown {
string ScaryThingIHave { get; }
    void ScareLittleChildren();
}

class FunnyFunny : IClown {
    public FunnyFunny(string funnyThingIHave) {
        this.funnyThingIHave = funnyThingIHave;
    }
    private string funnyThingIHave;
    public string FunnyThingIHave {
        get { return "Honk honk! I have " + funnyThingIHave; }
    }

    public void Honk() {
        MessageBox.Show(this.FunnyThingIHave);
    }
}

class ScaryScary : FunnyFunny, IScaryClown {
    public ScaryScary(string funnyThingIHave, int numberOfScaryThings)
            : base(funnyThingIHave) {
        this.numberOfScaryThings = numberOfScaryThings;
    }

    private int numberOfScaryThings;
    public string ScaryThingIHave {
        get { return "I have " + numberOfScaryThings + " spiders"; }
    }

    public void ScareLittleChildren() {
        MessageBox.Show("Boo! Gotcha!");
    }
}

private void button1_Click(object sender, EventArgs e) {
    ScaryScary fingersTheClown = new ScaryScary("big shoes", 14);
    FunnyFunny someFunnyClown = fingersTheClown;
    IScaryClown someOtherScaryclown = someFunnyClown as ScaryScary;
    someOtherScaryclown.Honk();
}
```

The Honk() method just uses this set accessor to display its message—no need to have the same code twice.

You could have implemented the IClown method and property again, but why not just inherit from FunnyFunny?

Since ScaryScary is a subclass of FunnyFunny and FunnyFunny implements IClown, ScaryScary implements IClown too.

You can set a FunnyFunny reference equal to a ScaryScary object because ScaryScary inherits from FunnyFunny. But you can't set any IScaryClown reference to just any clown, because you don't know if that clown is scary. That's why you need to use the as keyword.

You can also use the someOtherScaryClown reference to call ScareLittleChildren()—but you can't get to it from the someFunnyClown reference.

There's more than just public and private

You already know how important the `private` keyword is, how you use it, and how it's different from `public`. C# has a name for these keywords: they're called **access modifiers**. The name makes sense, because when you change an access modifier on a property, field, or method of a class—its **members**—or the entire class, you change the way other classes can access it. There are a few more access modifiers that you'll use, but we'll start with the ones you know:

> We call a class's methods, fields, and properties its **members**. Any member can be marked with the public or private access modifier.

⭐ **`public` means that anyone can access it** — (as long as they can access the declaring class)
When you mark a class or class member `public`, you're telling C# that any instance of any other class can access it. It's the least restrictive access modifier. And you've already seen how it can get you in trouble—only mark class members public if you have a reason. That's how you make sure your classes are well encapsulated.

⭐ **`private` means that only other members can access it**
When you mark a class member `private`, then it can only be accessed from other members inside that class or **other instances of that class**. You can't mark a class `private`—unless that class **lives inside another class**, in which case it's only available to instances of its container class. Then it's private by default, and if you want it to be public you need to mark it public.

> If you leave off the access modifier when you declare a class member, it defaults to private.

⭐ **`protected` means public to subclasses, private to everyone else**
You've already seen how a subclass can't access the private fields in its base class—it has to use the `base` keyword to get to the public members of the base object. Wouldn't it be convenient if the subclass could access those private fields? That's why you have the `protected` access modifier. Any class member marked `protected` can be accessed by any other member of its class, and any member of a subclass of its class.

⭐ **`internal` means public only to other classes in an assembly**
The built-in .NET Framework classes are **assemblies**—libraries of classes that are in your project's list of references. You can see a list of assemblies by right-clicking on "References" in the Solution Explorer and choosing "Add Reference…"—when you create a new Windows Forms application, the IDE automatically includes the references you need to build a Windows application. When you build an assembly, you can use the `internal` keyword to keep classes private to that assembly, so you can only expose the classes you want. You can combine this with `protected`—anything you mark `protected internal` can only be accessed from within the assembly **or** from a subclass.

> If you leave off the access modifier when you declare a class or an interface, then by default it's set to internal. And that's just fine for most classes—it means that any other class in the assembly can read it. If you're not using multiple assemblies, internal will work just as well as public for classes and interfaces. Give it a shot—go to an old project, change some of the classes to internal, and see what happens.

⭐ **`sealed` says that this class can't be subclassed**
There are some classes that you just can't inherit from. A lot of the .NET Framework classes are like this—go ahead, try to make a class that inherits from `String` (that's the class whose `IsEmptyOrNull()` method you used in the last chapter). What happens? The compiler won't let you build your code—it gives you the error "cannot derive from sealed type 'string'". You can do that with your own classes—just add `sealed` after the access modifier.

> Sealed is a modifier, but it's not an <u>access</u> modifier. That's because it only affects inheritance—it doesn't change the way the class can be accessed.

There's a little more to all of these definitions. Take a peek at leftover #2 in the appendix to learn more about them.

Access modifiers change visibility

Let's take a closer look at the access modifers and how they affect the **scope** of the various class members. We made two changes: the funnyThingIHave backing field is now protected, and we changed the ScareLittleChildren() method so that it uses the funnyThingIHave field:

Make these two changes to your own exercise solution. Then change the protected access modifier back to private and see what errors you get.

❶ Here are two interfaces. IClown defines a clown who honks his horn and has a funny thing. IScaryClown inherits from clown. A scary clown does everything a clown does, plus he has a scary thing and scares little children.

```
interface IClown {
    string FunnyThingIHave { get; }
    void Honk();
}

interface IScaryClown : IClown {
    string ScaryThingIHave { get; }
    void ScareLittleChildren();
}
```

The "this" keyword also changes what variable you're referring to. It says to C#, "Look at the current instance of the class to find whatever I'm connected to—even if that matches a parameter or local variable."

This is a really common way to use "this", since the parameter and backing field have the same name. funnyThingIHave refers to the parameter, while this.funnyThingIHave is the backing field.

❷ The FunnyFunny class implements the IClown interface. We made the funnyThingIHave field protected so that it can be accessed by any instance of a subclass of FunnyFunny.

By adding "this", we told C# that we're talking about the backing field, not the parameter that has the same name.

```
class FunnyFunny : IClown {
    public FunnyFunny(string funnyThingIHave) {
        this.funnyThingIHave = funnyThingIHave;
    }
    protected string funnyThingIHave;
    public string FunnyThingIHave {
        get { return "Honk honk! I have " + funnyThingIHave; }
    }

    public void Honk() {
        MessageBox.Show(this.FunnyThingIHave);
    }
}
```

We changed FunnyThingIHave to protected. Look and see how it affects the ScaryScary.ScareLittleChildren() method.

When you use "this" with a property, it tells C# to execute the set or get accessor.

❸ The ScaryScary class implements the IScaryClown interface. It also inherits from FunnyFunny, and since FunnyFunny implements IClown, that means ScaryScary does, too. Take a look at how the ScareLittleChildren() method accesses the funnyThingIHave backing field—it can do that because we used the protected access modifier. If we'd made it private instead, then this code wouldn't compile.

Access Modifiers Up Close

> numberOfScaryThings is private, which is typical of a backing field. So only another instance of ScaryScary would be able to see it.

```
class ScaryScary : FunnyFunny, IScaryClown {
    public ScaryScary(string funnyThingIHave,
                      int numberOfScaryThings)
        : base(funnyThingIHave) {
        this.numberOfScaryThings = numberOfScaryThings;
    }

    private int numberOfScaryThings;
    public string ScaryThingIHave {
        get { return "I have " + numberOfScaryThings + " spiders"; }
    }

    public void ScareLittleChildren() {
        MessageBox.Show("You can't have my "
                        + base.funnyThingIHave);
    }
}
```

> The "base" keyword tells C# to use the value from the base class. But we could also use "this" in this case. Can you figure out why?

> The protected keyword tells C# to make something private to everyone **except** instances of a subclass.

> If we'd left funnyThingIHave private, this would cause the compiler to give you an error. But when we changed it to protected, that made it visible to any subclass of FunnyFunny.

❹ Here's a button that instantiates FunnyFunny and ScaryScary. Take a look at how it uses as to downcast someFunnyClown to an IScaryClown reference.

```
private void button1_Click(object sender, EventArgs e) {
    ScaryScary fingersTheClown = new ScaryScary("big shoes", 14);
    FunnyFunny someFunnyClown = fingersTheClown;
    IScaryClown someOtherScaryclown = someFunnyClown as ScaryScary;
    someOtherScaryclown.Honk();
}
```

> Since this button click event handler is not part of FunnyFunny and ScaryScary, it can't access the protected funnyThingIHave field.

> We put in some extra steps to show you that you could upcast ScaryScary to FunnyFunny, and then downcast that to IScaryClown. But all three of those lines could be collapsed into a single line. Can you figure out how?

> It's outside of both classes, so the statements inside it only have access to the public members of any FunnyFunny or ScaryScary objects.

eww, *duplicate* **code!**

there are no
Dumb Questions

Q: Why would I want to use an interface instead of just writing all of the methods I need directly into my class?

A: You might end up with a lot of different classes as you write more and more complex programs. Interfaces let you group those classes by the kind of work they do. They help you be sure that every class that's going to do a certain kind of work does it using the same methods. The class can do the work however it needs to, and because of the interface, you don't need to worry about how it does it to get the job done.

Here's an example: you can have a truck class and a sailboat class that implement `ICarryPassenger`. Say the `ICarryPassenger` interface stipulates that any class that implements it has to have a `ConsumeEnergy()` method. Your program could use them both to carry passengers even though the sailboat class's `ConsumeEnergy()` method uses wind power and the truck class's method uses diesel fuel.

Imagine if you didn't have the `ICarryPassenger` interface. Then it would be tough to tell your program which vehicles could carry people and which couldn't. You would have to look through each class that your program might use and figure out whether or not there was a method for carrying people from one place to another. Then you'd have to call each of the vehicles your program was going to use with whatever method was defined for carrying passengers. And since there's no standard interface, they could be named all sorts of things or buried inside other methods. You can see how that'll get confusing pretty fast.

Q: Why do I need to use a property? Can't I just include a field?

A: Good question. An interface only defines the way a class should do a specific kind of job. It's not an object by itself, so you can't instantiate it and it can't store information. If you added a field that was just a variable declaration, then C# would have to store that data somewhere—and an interface can't store data by itself. A property is a way to make something that looks like a field to other objects, but since it's really a method, it doesn't actually store any data.

Q: What's the difference between a regular object reference and an interface reference?

A: You already know how a regular, everyday object reference works. If you create an instance of `Skateboard` called `VertBoard`, and then a new reference to it called `HalfPipeBoard`, they both point to the same thing. But if `Skateboard` implements the interface `IStreetTricks` and you create an interface reference to `Skateboard` called `StreetBoard`, it will only know the methods in the `Skateboard` class that are also in the `IStreetTricks` interface.

All three references are actually pointing to the same object. If you call the object using the `HalfPipeBoard` or `VertBoard` references, you'll be able to access any method or property in the object. If you call it using the `StreetBoard` reference, you'll only have access to the methods and properties in the interface.

Q: Then why would I ever want to use an interface reference if it limits what I can do with the object?

A: Interface references give you a way of working with a bunch of different kinds of objects that do the same thing. You can create an array using the interface reference type that will let you pass information to and from the methods in `ICarryPassenger` whether you're working with a truck object, a horse object, a unicycle object, or a car object. The way each of those objects does the job is probably a little different, but with interface references, you know that they all have the same methods that take the same parameters and have the same return types. So, you can call them and pass information to them in exactly the same way.

Q: Why would I make something protected instead of private or public?

A: Because it helps you encapsulate your classes better. There are a lot of times that a subclass needs access to some internal part of its base class. For example, if you need to override a property, it's pretty common to use the backing field in the base class in the get accessor, so that it returns some sort of variation of it. But when you build classes, you should only make something public if you have a reason to do it. Using the protected access modifier lets you expose it only to the subclass that needs it, and keep it private from everyone else.

> Interface references only know about the methods and properties that are defined in the interface.

Some classes should never be instantiated

Remember our zoo simulator class hierarchy? You'll definitely end up instantiating a bunch of hippos, dogs, and lions. But what about the Canine and Feline classes? How about the Animal class? It turns out that there are some classes that just don't need to be instantiated...and, in fact, don't make any sense if they are. Here's an example.

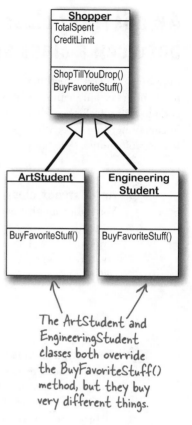

The ArtStudent and EngineeringStudent classes both override the BuyFavoriteStuff() method, but they buy very different things.

Let's start with a basic class for a student shopping at the student bookstore.

```
class Shopper {
    public void ShopTillYouDrop()
        while (TotalSpent < CreditLimit)
            BuyFavoriteStuff();
    }
    public virtual void BuyFavoriteStuff () {
        // No implementation here - we don't know
        // what our student likes to buy!
    }
}
```

Here's the ArtStudent class—it subclasses Shopper:

```
class ArtStudent : Shopper {
    public override void BuyFavoriteStuff () {
        BuyArtSupplies();
        BuyBlackTurtlenecks();
        BuyDepressingMusic();
    }
}
```

And the EngineeringStudent class also inherits from Shopper:

```
class EngineeringStudent : Shopper {
    public override void BuyFavoriteStuff () {
        BuyPencils();
        BuyGraphingCalculator();
        BuyPocketProtector();
    }
}
```

So what happens when you instantiate Shopper? Does it ever make sense to do it?

An abstract class is like a cross between a class and an interface

Suppose you need something like an interface, that requires classes to implement certain methods and properties. But you need to include some code in that interface, so that certain methods don't have to be implemented in each inheriting class. What you want is an **abstract class**. You get the features of an interface, but you can write code in it like a normal class.

⭐ **An abstract class is <u>like</u> a normal class**
You define an abstract class just like a normal one. It has fields and methods, and you can inherit from other classes, too, exactly like with a normal class. There's almost nothing new to learn here, because you already know everything that an abstract class does!

⭐ **An abstract class is <u>like</u> an interface**
When you create a class that implements an interface, you agree to implement all of the properties and methods defined in that interface. An abstract class works the same way—it can include declarations of properties and methods that, just like in an interface, must be implemented by inheriting classes.

⭐ **But an abstract class can't be instantiated**
The biggest difference between an **abstract** class and a **concrete** class is that you can't use new to create an instance of an abstract class. If you do, C# will give you an error when you try to compile your code.

> ⊗ Cannot create an instance of the abstract class or interface 'MyClass'

> A method that has a declaration but no statements or method body is called an **abstract method**. Inheriting classes must implement all abstract methods, just like when they inherit from an interface.

> Only abstract classes can have abstract methods. If you put an abstract method into a class, then you'll have to mark that class abstract or it won't compile. You'll learn more about how to mark a class abstract in a minute.

> The opposite of abstract is **concrete**. A concrete method is one that has a body, and all the classes you've been working with so far are concrete classes.

> This error is because you have abstract methods without any code! The compiler won't let you instantiate a class with missing code, just like it wouldn't let you instantiate an interface.

Wait, what? A class that I can't instantiate? Why would I even want something like that?

Because you want to provide some code, but still require that subclasses fill in the rest of the code.

Sometimes *bad things happen* when you create objects that should never be created. The class at the top of your class diagram usually has some fields that it expects its subclasses to set. An Animal class may have a calculation that depends on a Boolean called HasTail or Vertebrate, but there's no way for it to set that itself.

Here's a class that the Objectville Astrophysics Club uses to send their rockets to different planets.

Here's an example...

The astrophysicists have two missions—one to Mars, and one to Venus.

```
class PlanetMission {
  public long RocketFuelPerMile;
  public long RocketSpeedMPH;
  public int MilesToPlanet;

  public long UnitsOfFuelNeeded() {
    return MilesToPlanet * RocketFuelPerMile;
  }

  public int TimeNeeded() {
    return MilesToPlanet / (int) RocketSpeedMPH;
  }

  public string FuelNeeded() {
    return "You'll need "
      + MilesToPlanet * RocketFuelPerMile
      + " units of fuel to get there. It'll take "
      + TimeNeeded() + " hours.";
  }
}
```

It doesn't make sense to set these fields in the base class, because we don't know what rocket or planet we'll be using.

```
class Venus : PlanetMission {
    public Venus() {
        MilesToPlanet = 40000000;
        RocketFuelPerMile = 100000;
        RocketSpeedMPH = 25000;
    }
}

class Mars : PlanetMission {
    public Mars() {
        MilesToPlanet = 75000000;
        RocketFuelPerMile = 100000;
        RocketSpeedMPH = 25000;
    }
}
```

The constructors for the Mars and Venus subclasses set the three fields they inherited from Planet. But those fields **won't get set** if you instantiate Planet directly. So what happens when FuelNeeded() tries to use them?

```
private void button1_Click(object s, EventArgs e) {
  Mars mars = new Mars();
  MessageBox.Show(mars.FuelNeeded());
}

private void button2_Click(object s, EventArgs e) {
  Venus venus = new Venus();
  MessageBox.Show(venus.FuelNeeded());
}

private void button3_Click(object s, EventArgs e) {
  PlanetMission planet = new PlanetMission();
  MessageBox.Show(planet.FuelNeeded());
}
```

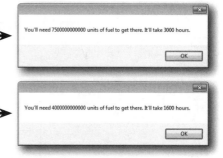

You'll need 7500000000000 units of fuel to get there. It'll take 3000 hours.

OK

You'll need 4000000000000 units of fuel to get there. It'll take 1600 hours.

OK

Before you flip the page, try to figure out what will happen when the user clicks the third button....

Like we said, some classes should never be instantiated

The problems all start when you create an instance of the `PlanetMission` class. Its `FuelNeeded()` method expects the fields to be set by the subclass. But when they aren't, they get their default values—zero. And when C# tries to divide a number by zero…

> The PlanetMission class wasn't written to be instantiated. We were only supposed to inherit from it. But we did instantiate it, and that's where the problems started.

```
private void button3_Click(object s, EventArgs e) {
    PlanetMission planet = new PlanetMission();
    MessageBox.Show(planet.FuelNeeded());
}
```

> When the FuelNeeded() method tried to divide by RocketSpeedMPH, it was zero. And when you divide by zero, this happens.

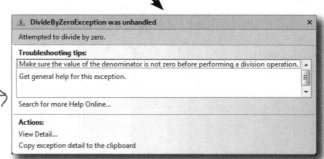

DivideByZeroException was unhandled
Attempted to divide by zero.

Troubleshooting tips:
Make sure the value of the denominator is not zero before performing a division operation.
Get general help for this exception.

Search for more Help Online…

Actions:
View Detail…
Copy exception detail to the clipboard

Solution: use an abstract class

When you mark a class `abstract`, C# won't let you write code to instantiate it. It's a lot like an interface—it acts like a template for the classes that inherit from it.

> Adding the abstract keyword to the class declaration tells C# this is an abstract class, and can't be instantiated.

> Now C# will refuse to compile our program until we remove the line that creates an instance of PlanetMission.

```
abstract class PlanetMission {
    public long RocketFuelPerMile;
    public long RocketSpeedMPH;
    public int MilesToPlanet;

    public long UnitsOfFuelNeeded() {
        return MilesToPlanet * RocketFuelPerMile;
    }

    // the rest of the class is defined here
}
```

BRAIN POWER

Flip back to the solution to Kathleen's party planning program in the previous chapter on pages 254–256, and take another look at the encapsulation problems that we left in the code. Can you figure out how you'd use an abstract class to solve them?

An abstract method doesn't have a body

You know how an interface only has declarations for methods and properties, but it doesn't actually have any method bodies? That's because every method in an interface is an **abstract method**. So let's implement it! Once we do, the error will go away. Any time you extend an abstract class, you need to make sure that you override all of its abstract methods. Luckily, the IDE makes this job easier. Just type "public override"—as soon as you press space, the IDE will display a drop-down box with a list of any methods that you can override. Select the SetMissionInfo() method and fill it in:

> **Every method in an interface is automatically abstract, so you don't need to use the abstract keyword in an interface, just in an abstract class. Only abstract classes can have abstract methods... but they can have concrete methods too.**

```
abstract class PlanetMission {

    public abstract void SetMissionInfo(
        int milesToPlanet, int rocketFuelPerMile,
        long rocketSpeedMPH);

    // the rest of the class...
```

This abstract method is just like what you'd see in an interface—it doesn't have a body, but any class that inherits from PlanetMission has to implement the SetMissionInfo() method or the program won't compile.

It really sucks to be an abstract method. You don't have a body.

If we add that method in and try to build the program, the IDE gives us an error:

> ⊗ 'VenusMission' does not implement inherited abstract member 'PlanetMission.SetMissionInfo(long, int, int)'

So let's implement it! Once we do, the error will go away.

```
class Venus : PlanetMission {
    public Venus() {
        SetMissinInfo(40000000, 100000, 25000);
    }
    public override SetMissionInfo(int milesToPlanet, long rocketFuelPerMile,
      int rocketSpeedMPH) {
        this.MilesToPlanet = milesToPlanet;
        this.RocketFuelPerMile = rocketFuelPerMile;
        this.RocketSpeedMPH = rocketSpeedMPH;
    }
}
```

When you inherit from an abstract class, you need to override all of its abstract methods.

Sharpen your pencil

Here's your chance to demonstrate your artistic abilities. On the left you'll find sets of class and interface declarations. Your job is to draw the associated class diagrams on the right. We did the first one for you. Don't forget to use a dashed line for implementing an interface and a solid line for inheriting from a class.

Given:

What's the Picture?

1)
```
interface Foo { }

class Bar : Foo { }
```

1)

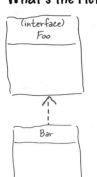

2)
```
interface Vinn { }

abstract class Vout : Vinn { }
```

2)

3)
```
abstract class Muffie : Whuffie { }

class Fluffie : Muffie { }

interface Whuffie { }
```

3)

4)
```
class Zoop { }

class Boop : Zoop { }

class Goop : Boop { }
```

4)

5)
```
class Gamma : Delta, Epsilon { }

interface Epsilon { }

interface Beta { }

class Alpha : Gamma,Beta { }

class Delta { }
```

5)

On the left you'll find sets of class diagrams. Your job is to turn these into valid C# declarations. We did number 1 for you.

What's the Declaration ?

Given:

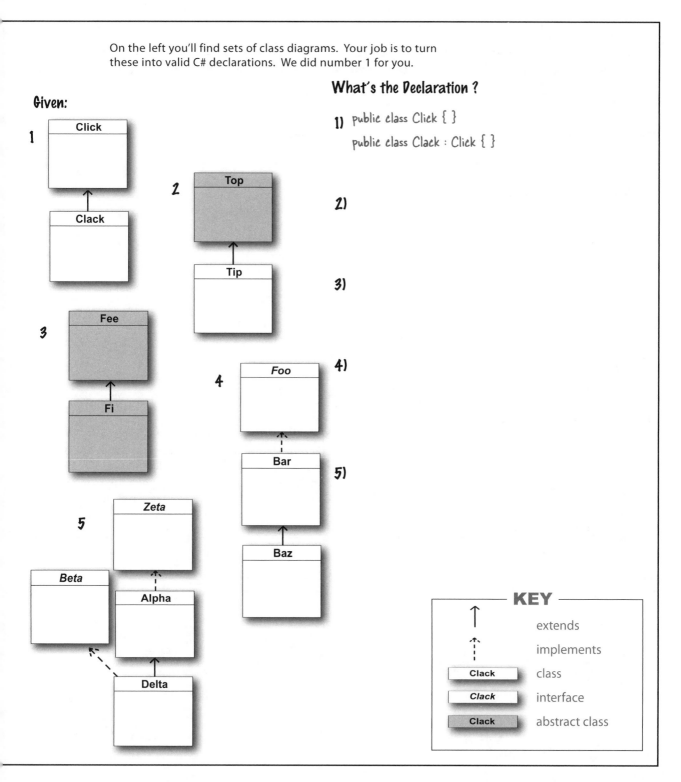

1) public class Click { }
   public class Clack : Click { }

2)

3)

4)

5)

Fireside Chats

Tonight's talk: **An abstract class and an interface butt heads over the pressing question, "Who's more important?"**

Abstract Class:	**Interface:**
I think it's obvious who's more important between the two of us. Programmers need me to get their jobs done. Let's face it. You don't even come close.	
	Nice. This oughta be good.
You can't really think you're more important than me. You don't even use real inheritance—you only get implemented.	
	Great, here we go again. Interfaces don't use real inheritance. Interfaces only implement. That's just plain ignorant. Implementation is as good as inheritance, in fact it's better!
Better? You're nuts. I'm much more flexible than you. I can have abstract methods or concrete ones. I can even have virtual methods if I want. Sure, I can't be instantiated but then, neither can you. And I can do pretty much anything else a regular class does.	
	Yeah? What if you want a class that inherits from you *and* your buddy? **You can't inherit from two classes.** You have to choose which class to inherit from. And that's just plain rude! There's no limit to the number of interfaces a class can implement. Talk about flexible! With me, a programmer can make a class do anything.

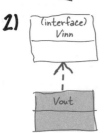 Sharpen your pencil
Solution

2)
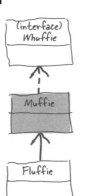

3)

4)
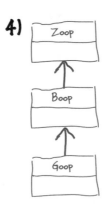

5)
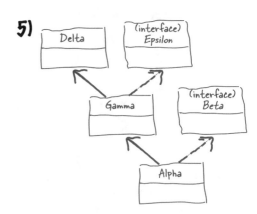

What's the Picture ?

Abstract Class:

You might be overstating your power a little bit.

That's exactly the kind of drivel I'd expect from an interface. Code is extremely important! It's what makes your programs run.

Really? I doubt that—programmers always care what's in their properties and methods.

Yeah, sure, tell a coder he can't code.

Interface:

You think that just because you can contain code, you're the greatest thing since sliced bread. But you can't change the fact that a program can only inherit from one class at a time. So you're a little limited. Sure, I can't include any code. But really, code is overrated.

Nine times out of ten, a programmer wants to make sure an object has certain properties and methods, but doesn't really care how they're implemented.

OK, sure. Eventually. But think about how many times you've seen a programmer write a method that takes an object that just needs to have a certain method, and it doesn't really matter right at that very moment exactly how the method's built. Just that it's there. So bang! The programmer just needs to write an interface. Problem solved!

What**ever**!

---

2) `abstract class Top { }`
`class Tip : Top { }`

3) `abstract class Fee { }`
`abstract class Fi : Fee { }`

4) `interface Foo { }`
`class Bar : Foo { }`
`class Baz : Bar { }`

5) `interface Zeta { }`
`class Alpha : Zeta { }`
`interface Beta { }`
`class Delta : Alpha, Beta { }`

Delta inherits from Alpha and implements Beta.

What's the Declaration ?

> I'm still hung up on not being able to inherit from two classes. I can't inherit from more than one class, so I have to use interfaces. That's a pretty big limitation of C#, right?

It's not a limitation, it's a protection.

If C# let you inherit from more than one base class, it would open up a whole can of worms. When a language lets one subclass inherit from two base classes, it's called **multiple inheritance**. And by giving you interfaces instead, C# saves you from a big fat mess that we like to call....

The Deadly Diamond of Death!

Television and MovieTheater both inherit from MoviePlayer, and both override the ShowAMovie() method. Both inherit the ScreenWidth property, too.

Imagine that the ScreenWidth property is used by both Television and MovieTheater, with different values. What happens if HomeTheater needs to use both values of ScreenWidth—say, to show both made-for-TV movies and feature films?

Which ShowAMovie() method runs when you call ShowAMovie() on the HomeTheater object?

Avoid ambiguity!

A language that allows the Deadly Diamond of Death can lead to some pretty ugly situations, because you need special rules to deal with this kind of ambiguous situation…which means extra work for you when you're building your program! C# protects you from having to deal with this by giving you interfaces. If `Television` and `MovieTheater` are interfaces instead of classes, then the same `ShowAMovie()` method can satisfy both of them. All the interface cares about is that there's some method called `ShowAMovie()`.

Pool Puzzle

Your *job* is to take code snippets from the pool and place them into the blank lines in the code and output. You may use the same snippet more than once, and you won't need to use all the snippets. Your *goal* is to make a set of classes that will compile and run and produce the output listed.

```
.................. Nose {
    .................. ;
    string Face { get; }
}

abstract class ..............: .............. {
    public virtual int Ear()
    {
        return 7;
    }
    public Picasso(string face)
    {
        .................. = face;
    }
    public virtual string Face {
        .......... { ........................ ; }
    }
    string face;
}

class ..............: .............. {
    public Clowns() : base("Clowns") { }
}
```

```
class .............. : .................. {
    public Acts() : base("Acts") { }
    public override .................. {
        return 5;
    }
}
```

Here's the entry point—this is a complete C# program.

```
class .................. : .............. {
    public override string Face {
        get { return "Of76"; }
    }
    public static void Main(string[] args) {
        string result = "";
        Nose[] i = new Nose[3];
        i[0] = new Acts();
        i[1] = new Clowns();
        i[2] = new Of76();
        for (int x = 0; x < 3; x++) {
            result += ( .................. + " "
                + .................. ) + "\n";
        }
        MessageBox.Show(result);
    }
}
```

Output

```
5 Acts
7 Clowns
7 Of76
```

OK

Note: Each snippet from the pool can be used more than once!

```
Acts( );
Nose( );
Of76( );
Clowns( );
Picasso( );
Of76 [ ] i = new Nose[3];
Of76 [ 3 ] i;
Nose [ ] i = new Nose( );
Nose [ ] i = new Nose[3];

            ;
class
abstract
interface
int Ear()
this
this.
face
this.face

            i
i( )
i(x)
i[x]
get
set
return

class
5 class
7 class
7 public class

i.Ear(x)
i[x].Ear()
i[x].Ear(
i[x].Face

Acts
Nose
Of76
Clowns
Picasso
```

Answers on page 324.

OK, I think I've got a pretty good handle on objects now!

The idea that you could combine your data and your code into classes and objects was a revolutionary one when it was first introduced—but that's how you've been building all your C# programs so far, so you can think of it as just plain programming.

You're an object oriented programmer.

There's a name for what you've been doing. It's called **object oriented programming**, or OOP. Before languages like C# came along, people didn't use objects and methods when writing their code. They just used functions (which is what they call methods in a non-OOP program) that were all in one place—as if each program were just one big static class that only had static methods. It made it a lot harder to create programs that modeled the problems they were solving. Luckily, you'll never have to write programs without OOP, because it's a core part of C#.

The four principles of object oriented programming

When programmers talk about OOP, they're referring to four important principles. They should seem very familiar to you by now because you've been working with every one of them. You'll recognize the first three principles just from their names: **inheritance**, **abstraction**, and **encapsulation**. The last one's called **polymorphism**. It sounds a little odd, but it turns out that you already know all about it too.

Encapsulation means creating an object that keeps track of its state internally using private fields, and uses public properties and methods to let other classes work with only the part of the internal data that they need to see.

This just means having one class or interface that inherits from another.

 **Inheritance**

 Encapsulation

The word "polymorphism" literally means "many forms". Can you think of a time when an object has taken on many forms in your code?

Abstraction

You're using abstraction when you create a class model that starts with more general—or abstract—classes, and then has more specific classes that inherit from it.

Polymorphism

Polymorphism means that one object can take many different forms

Any time you use a mockingbird in place of an animal or aged Vermont cheddar in a recipe that just calls for cheese, you're using **polymorphism**. That's what you're doing any time you upcast or downcast. It's taking an object and using it in a method or a statement that expects something else.

Keep your eyes open for polymorphism in the next exercise!

You're about to do a really big exercise—the biggest one you've seen so far—and you'll be using a lot of polymorphism in it, so keep your eyes open. Here's a list of four typical ways that you'll use polymorphism. We gave you an example of each of them (you won't see these particular lines in the exercise, though). As soon as you see similar code in what you write for the exercise, **check it off the following list**:

> **You're using polymorphism when you take an instance of one class and use it in a statement or a method that expects a different type, like a parent class or an interface that the class implements.**

☐ Taking any reference variable that uses one class and setting it equal to an instance of a different class.

```
NectarStinger bertha = new NectarStinger();

INectarCollector gatherer = bertha;
```

☐ Upcasting by using a subclass in a statement or method that expects its base class.

```
spot = new Dog();

zooKeeper.FeedAnAnimal(spot);
```

✓ *If FeedAnAnimal() expects an Animal object, and Dog inherits from Animal, then you can pass Dog to FeedAnAnimal().*

☐ Creating a reference variable whose type is an interface and pointing it to an object that implements that interface.

```
IStingPatrol defender = new StingPatrol();
```

← *This is upcasting, too!*

☐ Downcasting using the as keyword.

```
void MaintainTheHive(IWorker worker) {
    if (worker is HiveMaintainer) {
        HiveMaintainer maintainer = worker as HiveMaintainer;
        ...
```

The MaintainTheHive() method takes any IWorker as a parameter. It uses as to point a HiveMaintainer reference to the worker.

LONG EXERCISE

Let's build a house! Create a model of a house using classes to represent the rooms and locations, and an interface for any place that has a door.

Location

Name
Exits

Description()

Location is an abstract class. That's why we shaded it darker in the class diagram.

❶ Start with this class model

Every room or location in your house will be represented by its own object. The interior rooms all inherit from Room, and the outside places inherit from Outside, and both subclass the same base class, Location. It has two fields: Name is the name of the location ("Kitchen"), and Exits is an array of Location objects that the current location connects to. So diningRoom.Name will be equal to "Dining Room", and diningRoom.Exits will be equal to the array { LivingRoom, Kitchen }.

➔ **Create a Windows Application project and add Location, Room, and Outside classes to it.**

Room

Decoration

Outside

Hot

❷ You'll need the blueprint for the house

This house has three rooms, a front yard, a back yard, and a garden. There are two doors: the front door connects the living room to the front yard, and the back door connects the kitchen to the back yard.

Inside locations each have some kind of a decoration in a read-only property.

Outside locations can be hot, so the Outside class has a read-only Boolean property called Hot.

The living room connects to the dining room, which also connects to the kitchen.

Living Room

Dining Room

Front Yard

Kitchen

Back Yard

You can move between the back yard and the front yard, and both of them connect to the garden.

This symbol is an exterior door between the front yard and the living room. There's also an exterior door between the kitchen and back yard.

Garden

All rooms have doors, but only a few rooms have an exterior door that leads inside or outside the house.

❸ Use the IHasExteriorDoor interface for rooms with an exterior door

There are two exterior doors in the house, the front door and the back door. Every location that has one (the front yard, back yard, living room, and kitchen) should implement IHasExteriorDoor. The DoorDescription read-only property contains a description of the door (the front door is "an oak door with a brass knob", the back door is "a screen door"). The DoorLocation property contains a reference to the Location where the door leads (kitchen).

IHasExteriorDoor

DoorDescription
DoorLocation

❹ Here's the Location class

To get you started, here's the `Location` class:

```
abstract class Location {
    public Location(string name) {
        this.name = name;
    }
    public Location[] Exits;
    private string name;
    public string Name {
        get { return name; }
    }
    public virtual string Description {
        get {
            string description = "You're standing in the " + name
                + ". You see exits to the following places: ";
            for (int i = 0; i < Exits.Length; i++) {
                description += " " + Exits[i].Name;
                if (i != Exits.Length - 1)
                    description += ",";
            }
            description += ".";
            return description;
        }
    }
}
```

The constructor sets the name field, which is the read-only Name property's backing field.

Description is a virtual method. You'll need to override it.

The public Exits field is an array of Location references that keeps track of all of the other places that this location connects to.

The Description property returns a string that describes the room, including the name and a list of all of the locations it connects to (which it finds in the Exits[] field). Its subclasses will need to change the description slightly, so they'll override it.

The Room class will override and extend Description to add the decoration, and Outside will add the temperature.

Remember, Location is an abstract class—you can inherit from it and declare reference variables of type Location, but you can't instantiate it.

❺ Create the classes

First create the `Room` and `Outside` classes based on the class model. Then create two more classes: `OutsideWithDoor`, which inherits from `Outside` and implements `IHasExteriorDoor`, and `RoomWithDoor`, which subclasses `Room` and implements `IHasExteriorDoor`.

Here are the class declarations to give you a leg up:

Get the classes started now—we'll give you more details about them on the next page.

```
class OutsideWithDoor : Outside, IHasExteriorDoor
{
    // The DoorLocation property goes here
    // The read-only DoorDescription property goes here
}

class RoomWithDoor : Room, IHasExteriorDoor
{
    // The DoorLocation property goes here
    // The read-only DoorDescription property goes here
}
```

This one's going to be a pretty big exercise...but we promise it's a lot of fun! And you'll definitely know this stuff once you get through it.

We're not done yet—flip the page!

Long Exercise (continued)

Now that you've got the class model, you can create the objects for all of the parts of the house, and add a form to explore it.

6 **How your house objects work**

Here's the architecture for two of your objects, `frontYard` and `diningRoom`. Since each of them has a door, they both need to be instances of a class that implements `IHasExteriorDoor`. The `DoorLocation` property keeps a reference to the location on the other side of the door.

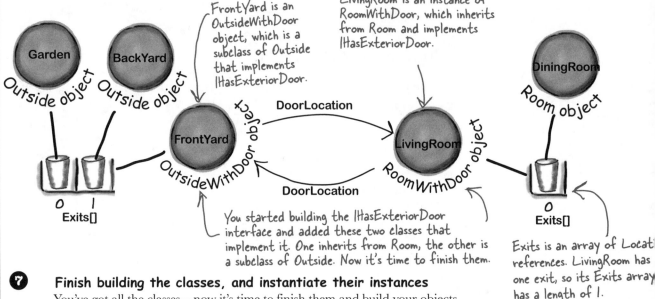

FrontYard is an OutsideWithDoor object, which is a subclass of Outside that implements IHasExteriorDoor.

LivingRoom is an instance of RoomWithDoor, which inherits from Room and implements IHasExteriorDoor.

DoorLocation

DoorLocation

You started building the IHasExteriorDoor interface and added these two classes that implement it. One inherits from Room, the other is a subclass of Outside. Now it's time to finish them.

Exits is an array of Locat references. LivingRoom has one exit, so its Exits array has a length of 1.

Exits[]

Exits[]

7 **Finish building the classes, and instantiate their instances**

You've got all the classes—now it's time to finish them and build your objects.

★ You'll need to make sure that the constructor for the `Outside` class sets the read-only `Hot` property and overrides the `Description` property to add the text "It's very hot here." if `Hot` is true. It's hot in the back yard but not the front yard or garden.

★ The constructor for `Room` needs to set the `Decoration`, and should override the `Description` property to add, "You see *(the decoration)* here." The living room has an antique carpet, the dining room has a crystal chandelier, and the kitchen has stainless steel appliances and a screen door that leads to the back yard.

★ Your form needs to create each of the objects and keep a reference to each one. So add a method to the form called `CreateObjects()` and call it from the form's constructor.

↖ Every location will have its own field in the form class.

★ Instantiate each of the objects for the six locations in the house. Here's one of those lines:

```
RoomWithDoor livingRoom = new RoomWithDoor("Living Room",
    "an antique carpet" , "an oak door with a brass knob");
```

Exits is an array of Location references, so this line creates one that has two references in it.

★ Your `CreateObjects()` method needs to populate the `Exits[]` field in each object:

```
frontYard.Exits = new Location[] { backYard, garden };
```

These are curly brackets. Anything else will cause an error.

8 **Build a form to explore the house**

Build a simple form to let you explore the house. It'll have a big multiline text box called `description` to show the description of the current room. A `ComboBox` called `exits` lists all of the exits in the current room. It's got two buttons: `goHere` moves to the room selected in the `ComboBox`, and `goThroughTheDoor` is only visible when there's an exterior door.

Here's where you'll set up what populates the ComboBox.

Explore the House

Click the goHere button to move to another location.

This is a multiline TextBox that displays the Description() of the current location. Its name is description.

The ComboBox contains a list of all of the exits, so name it exits. Make sure its DropDownStyle is set to DropDownList.

Go here: This is a ComboBox

Go through the door

This button is only visible when you're in a room with an exterior door. You can make it visible or invisible by setting its Visible property to true or false. It's called goThroughTheDoor.

9 **Now you just need to make the form work!**

You've got all the pieces, now you just need to put them together.

★ You'll need a field in your form called `currentLocation` to keep track of your current location.

★ Add a `MoveToANewLocation()` method that has a `Location` as its parameter. This method should first set `currentLocation` to the new location. Then it'll clear the combo box using its `Items.Clear()` method, and then add the name of each location in the `Exits[]` array using the combo box's `Items.Add()` method. Finally, reset the combo box so it displays the first item in the list by setting its `SelectedIndex` property to zero.

★ Set the text box so that it has the description of the current location.

★ Use the **is** keyword to check if the current location has a door. If it does, make the "Go through the door" button visible using its Visible property. If not, make it invisible.

★ If the "Go here:" button is clicked, move to the location selected in the combo box.

★ If the "Go through the door" button is clicked, move to the location that the door connects to.

Hint: When you choose an item in the combo box, its selected index in the combo box will be the same as the index of the corresponding location in the Exits[] array.

Another hint: Your form's currentLocation field is a Location reference. So even though it's pointing to an object that implements IHasExteriorDoor, you can't just type "currentLocation.DoorLocation" because DoorLocation isn't a field in Location. You'll need to downcast if you want to get the door location out of the object.

LONG EXERCISE SOLUTION

Here's the code to model the house. We used classes to represent the rooms and locations, and an interface for any place that has a door.

```csharp
interface IHasExteriorDoor {
    string DoorDescription { get; }
    Location DoorLocation { get; set; }
}
```

Here's the IHasExteriorDoor interface.

```csharp
class Room : Location {
    private string decoration;

    public Room(string name, string decoration)
        : base(name) {
        this.decoration = decoration;
    }

    public override string Description {
        get {
            return base.Description + " You see " + decoration + ".";
        }
    }
}
```

The Room class inherits from Location and adds a backing field for the read-only Decoration property. Its constructor sets the field.

```csharp
class RoomWithDoor : Room, IHasExteriorDoor {
    public RoomWithDoor(string name, string decoration, string doorDescription)
        : base(name, decoration)
    {
        this.doorDescription = doorDescription;
    }

    private string doorDescription;
    public string DoorDescription {
        get { return doorDescription; }
    }

    private Location doorLocation;
    public Location DoorLocation {
        get { return doorLocation; }
        set { doorLocation = value; }
    }
}
```

The RoomWithDoor class inherits from Room and implements IHasExteriorDoor. It does everything that the room does, but it adds a description of the exterior door to the constructor. It also adds DoorLocation, a reference to the location that the door leads to. DoorDescription and DoorLocation are required by IHasExteriorDoor.

```csharp
class Outside : Location {
    private bool hot;
    public bool Hot { get { return hot; } }

    public Outside(string name, bool hot)
        : base(name)
    {
        this.hot = hot;
    }

    public override string Description {
        get {
            string NewDescription = base.Description;
            if (hot)
                NewDescription += " It's very hot.";
            return NewDescription;
        }
    }
}

class OutsideWithDoor : Outside, IHasExteriorDoor {
    public OutsideWithDoor(string name, bool hot, string doorDescription)
        : base(name, hot)
    {
        this.doorDescription = doorDescription;
    }

    private string doorDescription;
    public string DoorDescription {
        get { return doorDescription; }
    }

    private Location doorLocation;
    public Location DoorLocation {
        get { return doorLocation; }
        set { doorLocation = value; }
    }

    public override string Description {
        get {
            return base.Description + " You see " + doorDescription + ".";
        }
    }
}
```

Outside is a lot like Room—it inherits from Location, and adds a backing field for the Hot property, which is used in the Description() method extended from the base class.

OutsideWithDoor inherits from Outside and implements IHasExteriorDoor, and it looks a lot like RoomWithDoor.

The base class's Description property fills in whether or not the location is hot. And that relies on the original Location class's Description property to add the main description and exits.

We're not done yet—flip the page!

Long Exercise
Solution (continued)

Here's the code for the form. It's all in the Form1.cs, inside the Form1 declaration.

```
public partial class Form1 : Form
{
    Location currentLocation;

    RoomWithDoor livingRoom;
    Room diningRoom;
    RoomWithDoor kitchen;

    OutsideWithDoor frontYard;
    OutsideWithDoor backYard;
    Outside garden;

    public Form1() {
        InitializeComponent();
        CreateObjects();
        MoveToANewLocation(livingRoom);
    }

    private void CreateObjects() {
        livingRoom = new RoomWithDoor("Living Room", "an antique carpet",
                "an oak door with a brass knob");
        diningRoom = new Room("Dining Room", "a crystal chandelier");
        kitchen = new RoomWithDoor("Kitchen", "stainless steel appliances", "a screen door");

        frontYard = new OutsideWithDoor("Front Yard", false, "an oak door with a brass knob");
        backYard = new OutsideWithDoor("Back Yard", true, "a screen door");
        garden = new Outside("Garden", false);

        diningRoom.Exits = new Location[] { livingRoom, kitchen };
        livingRoom.Exits = new Location[] { diningRoom };
        kitchen.Exits = new Location[] { diningRoom };
        frontYard.Exits = new Location[] { backYard, garden };
        backYard.Exits = new Location[] { frontYard, garden };
        garden.Exits = new Location[] { backYard, frontYard };

        livingRoom.DoorLocation = frontYard;
        frontYard.DoorLocation = livingRoom;

        kitchen.DoorLocation = backYard;
        backYard.DoorLocation = kitchen;
    }
```

This is how the form keeps track of which room is being displayed.

The form uses these reference variables to keep track of each of the rooms in the house.

The form's constructor creates the objects and then uses the MoveToANewLocation method.

When the form creates the objects, first it needs to instantiate the classes and pass the right information to each one's constructor.

Here's where we pass the door description to the OutsideWithDoor constructors.

Here's where the Exits[] array for each instance is populated. We need to wait to do this until after all the instances are created, because otherwise we wouldn't have anything to put into each array!

For the IHasExteriorDoor objects, we need to set their door locations.

```
private void MoveToANewLocation(Location newLocation) {
    currentLocation = newLocation;

    exits.Items.Clear();
    for (int i = 0; i < currentLocation.Exits.Length; i++)
        exits.Items.Add(currentLocation.Exits[i].Name);
    exits.SelectedIndex = 0;

    description.Text = currentLocation.Description;

    if (currentLocation is IHasExteriorDoor)
        goThroughTheDoor.Visible = true;
    else
        goThroughTheDoor.Visible = false;
}
```

The MoveToANewLocation() method displays a new location in the form.

First we need to clear the combo box, then we can add each of the locations' names to it. Finally, we set its selected index (or which line is highlighted) to zero so it shows the first item in the list. Don't forget to set the ComboBox's DropDownStyle property to "DropDownList"—that way the user won't be able to type anything into the combo box.

This makes the "Go through the door" button invisible if the current location doesn't implement IHasExteriorDoor.

```
private void goHere_Click(object sender, EventArgs e) {
    MoveToANewLocation(currentLocation.Exits[exits.SelectedIndex]);
}

private void goThroughTheDoor_Click(object sender, EventArgs e) {
    IHasExteriorDoor hasDoor = currentLocation as IHasExteriorDoor;
    MoveToANewLocation(hasDoor.DoorLocation);
}
}
```

When the user clicks the "Go here:" button, it moves to the location selected in the combo box.

We need to use the **as** keyword in order to downcast currentLocation to an IHasExteriorDoor so we can get access to the DoorLocation field.

But we're not done yet!

It's fine to create a model of a house, but wouldn't it be cool to turn it into a game? Let's do it! You'll play Hide and Seek against the computer. We'll need to add an Opponent class and have him hide in a room. And we'll need to make the house a lot bigger. Oh, and he'll need someplace to hide! We'll add a new interface so that some rooms can have a hiding place. Finally, we'll update the form to let you check the hiding places, and keep track of how many moves you've made trying to find your opponent. Sound fun? Definitely!

→ Let's get started!

build your opponent

Exercise

Time for hide and seek! Build on your original house program to add more rooms, hiding places, and an opponent who hides from you. *Create a new project, and use the IDE's "Add Existing Item" feature to add the classes from the first part of the exercise.*

❶ Add an IHidingPlace interface

We don't need to do anything fancy here. Any `Location` subclass that implements `IHidingPlace` has a place for the opponent to hide. It just needs a string to store the name of the hiding place ("in the closet", "under the bed", etc.).

★ Give it a get accessor, but no set accessor—we'll set this in the constructor, since once a room has a hiding place we won't ever need to change it.

❷ Add classes that implement IHidingPlace

You'll need two more classes: `OutsideWithHidingPlace` (which inherits from `Outside`) and `RoomWithHidingPlace` (which inherits from `Room`). Also, let's make any room with a door have a hiding place, so it'll have to inherit from `RoomWithHidingPlace` instead of `Room`. *So every room with an exterior door will also have a hiding place.*

❸ Add a class for your opponent

The Opponent object will find a random hiding place in the house, and it's your job to find him.

★ He'll need a private `Location` field (`myLocation`) so he can keep track of where he is, and a private `Random` field (`random`) to use when he moves to a random hiding place.

★ The constructor takes the starting location and sets `myLocation` to it, and sets `random` to a new instance of `Random`. He starts in the front yard (that'll be passed in by the form), and moves from hiding place to hiding place randomly. He moves 10 times when the game starts. When he encounters an exterior door, he flips a coin to figure out whether or not to go through it.

★ Add a `Move()` method that moves the opponent from his current location to a new location. First, if he's in a room with a door, then he flips a coin to decide whether or not to go through the door, so if `random.Next(2)` is equal to 1, he goes through it. Then he chooses one of the exits from his current location at random and goes through it. If that location doesn't have a hiding place, then he'll do it again—he'll choose a random exit from his current location and go there, and he'll keep doing it over and over until he finds a place to hide.

★ Add a `Check()` method that takes a location as a parameter and returns true if he's hiding in that location, or false otherwise.

❹ Add more rooms to the house

Update your `CreateObjects()` method to add more rooms:

★ Add **stairs** with a wooden bannister that connect the living room to the **upstairs hallway**, which has a picture of a dog and a closet to hide in.

★ The upstairs hallway connects to three rooms: a **master bedroom** with a large bed, a **second bedroom** with a small bed, and a **bathroom** with a sink and a toilet. Someone could hide under the bed in either bedroom or in the shower.

★ The front yard and back yard both connect to the **driveway**, where someone could hide in the garage. Also, someone could hide in the shed in the **garden**.

⑤ OK, time to update the form

You'll need to add a few buttons to the form. And we'll get a little more intricate with making them visible or invisible, depending on the state of the game.

The middle button's called check. You don't need to set its Text property.

You use the top two buttons and the combo box exactly the same way as before, except that they're only visible while the game is running.

When the game first starts, the hide button is the only one displayed. When you click it, the form counts to 10 in the text box, and calls the opponent's Move() method 10 times. Then it makes this button invisible.

This is the button you'll use to check the room's hiding place. It's only visible if you're in a room that has a place to hide. When it's shown, the Text property is changed from "check" to the word "Check" followed by the name of the hiding place—so for a room with a hiding place under the bed, the button will say, "Check under the bed".

⑥ Make the buttons work

There are two new buttons to add to the form.

Flip back to Chapter 2 for a refresher on DoEvents() and Sleep()—they'll come in handy.

★ The middle button checks the hiding place in the current room and is only visible when you're in a room with a place to hide using the opponent's Check() method. If you found him, then it resets the game.

★ The bottom button is how you start the game. It counts to 10 by showing "1...", waiting 200 milliseconds, then showing "2...", then "3...", etc., in the text box. After each number, it tells the opponent to move by calling his Move() method. Then it shows, "Ready or not, here I come!" for half a second, and then the game starts.

⑦ Add a method to redraw the form, and another one to reset the game

Add a RedrawForm() method that puts the right text in the description text box, makes the buttons visible or invisible, and puts the correct label on the middle button. Then add a ResetGame() method that's run when you find your opponent. It resets the opponent object so that he starts in the front yard again—he'll hide when you click the "Hide!" button. It should leave the form with nothing but the text box and "Hide!" button visible. The text box should say where you found the opponent, and how many moves it took.

⑧ Keep track of how many moves the player made

Make sure the text box displays the number of times you checked a hiding place or moved between rooms. When you find the opponent, he should pop up a mesage box that says, "You found me in X moves!"

⑨ Make it look right when you start the program

When you first start the program, all you should see is an empty text box and the "Hide!" button. When you click the button, the fun begins!

Build on your original house program to add more rooms, hiding places, and an opponent who hides from you.

Here's the new IHidingPlace interface. It just has one string field with a get accessor that returns the name of the hiding place.

```
interface IHidingPlace {
    string HidingPlaceName { get; }
}

class RoomWithHidingPlace : Room, IHidingPlace {
    public RoomWithHidingPlace(string name, string decoration, string hidingPlaceName)
        : base(name, decoration)
    {
        this.hidingPlaceName = hidingPlaceName;
    }
    private string hidingPlaceName;
    public string HidingPlaceName {
        get { return hidingPlaceName; }
    }
    public override string Description {
        get {
            return base.Description + " Someone could hide " + hidingPlaceName + ".";
        }
    }
}
```

The RoomWithHidingPlace class inherits from Room and implements IHidingPlace by adding the HidingPlaceName property. The constructor sets its backing field.

```
class RoomWithDoor : RoomWithHidingPlace, IHasExteriorDoor {
    public RoomWithDoor(string name, string decoration,
                        string hidingPlaceName, string doorDescription)
        : base(name, decoration, hidingPlaceName)
    {
        this.doorDescription = doorDescription;
    }

    private string doorDescription;
    public string DoorDescription {
        get { return doorDescription; }
    }

    private Location doorLocation;
    public Location DoorLocation {
        get { return doorLocation; }
        set { doorLocation = value; }
    }
}
```

Since we decided every room with a door also needed a hiding place, we made RoomWithDoor inherit from RoomWithHidingPlace. The only change to it is that its constructor takes a hiding place name and sends it on to the RoomWithHidingPlace constructor.

```
class OutsideWithHidingPlace : Outside, IHidingPlace {
    public OutsideWithHidingPlace(string name, bool hot, string hidingPlaceName)
        : base(name, hot)
    { this.hidingPlaceName = hidingPlaceName; }

    private string hidingPlaceName;
    public string HidingPlaceName {
        get { return hidingPlaceName; }
    }

    public override string Description {
        get {
            return base.Description + " Someone could hide " + hidingPlaceName + ".";
        }
    }
}

class Opponent {
    private Random random;
    private Location myLocation;
    public Opponent(Location startingLocation) {
        myLocation = startingLocation;
        random = new Random();
    }
    public void Move() {
        if (myLocation is IHasExteriorDoor) {
            IHasExteriorDoor LocationWithDoor =
                            myLocation as IHasExteriorDoor;
            if (random.Next(2) == 1)
                myLocation = LocationWithDoor.DoorLocation;
        }
        bool hidden = false;
        while (!hidden) {
            int rand = random.Next(myLocation.Exits.Length);
            myLocation = myLocation.Exits[rand];
            if (myLocation is IHidingPlace)
                hidden = true;
        }
    }
    public bool Check(Location locationToCheck) {
        if (locationToCheck != myLocation)
            return false;
        else
            return true;
    }
}
```

The OutsideWithHidingPlace class inherits from Outside and implements IHidingPlace just like RoomWithHidingPlace does.

The Opponent class constructor takes a starting location. It creates a new instance of Random, which it uses to move randomly between rooms.

The Move() method first checks if the current room has a door using the is keyword—if so, it has a 50% chance of going through it. Then it moves to a random location, and keeps moving until it finds a hiding place.

The guts of the Move() method is this while loop. It keeps looping until the variable hidden is true—and it sets it to true when it finds a room with a hiding place.

The Check() method just checks the opponent's location against the location that was passed to it using a Location reference. If they point to the same object, then he's been found!

We're not done yet—flip the page!

Exercise Solution (continued)

Here's all the code for the form. The only things that stay the same are the goHere_Click() and goThroughTheDoor_Click() methods.

Here are all the fields in the Form1 class. It uses them to keep track of the locations, the opponent, and the number of moves the player has made.

The Form1 constructor creates the objects, sets up the opponent, and then resets the game. We added a boolean parameter to ResetGame() so that it only displays its message when you win, not when you first start up the program.

```csharp
int Moves;

Location currentLocation;

RoomWithDoor livingRoom;
RoomWithHidingPlace diningRoom;
RoomWithDoor kitchen;
Room stairs;
RoomWithHidingPlace hallway;
RoomWithHidingPlace bathroom;
RoomWithHidingPlace masterBedroom;
RoomWithHidingPlace secondBedroom;

OutsideWithDoor frontYard;
OutsideWithDoor backYard;
OutsideWithHidingPlace garden;
OutsideWithHidingPlace driveway;

Opponent opponent;
```

```csharp
public Form1() {
    InitializeComponent();
    CreateObjects();
    opponent = new Opponent(frontYard);
    ResetGame(false);
}
private void MoveToANewLocation(Location newLocation) {
    Moves++;
    currentLocation = newLocation;
    RedrawForm();
}
```

The MoveToANewLocation() method sets the new location and then redraws the form.

```csharp
private void RedrawForm() {
    exits.Items.Clear();
    for (int i = 0; i < currentLocation.Exits.Length; i++)
        exits.Items.Add(currentLocation.Exits[i].Name);
    exits.SelectedIndex = 0;
    description.Text = currentLocation.Description + "\r\n(move #" + Moves + ")";
    if (currentLocation is IHidingPlace) {
        IHidingPlace hidingPlace = currentLocation as IHidingPlace;
        check.Text = "Check " + hidingPlace.HidingPlaceName;
        check.Visible = true;
    }
    else
        check.Visible = false;
    if (currentLocation is IHasExteriorDoor)
        goThroughTheDoor.Visible = true;
    else
        goThroughTheDoor.Visible = false;
}
```

We need the hiding place name but we've only got the CurrentLocation object, which doesn't have a HidingPlaceName property. So we can use **as** to copy the reference to an IHidingPlace variable.

RedrawForm() populates the combo box list, sets the text (adding the number of moves), and then makes the buttons visible or invisible depending on whether or not there's a door or the room has a hiding place.

Wow—you could add an entire wing onto the house just by adding a couple of lines! That's why well-encapsulated classes and objects are really useful.

```
private void CreateObjects() {
    livingRoom = new RoomWithDoor("Living Room", "an antique carpet",
            "inside the closet", "an oak door with a brass handle");
    diningRoom = new RoomWithHidingPlace("Dining Room", "a crystal chandelier",
            "in the tall armoire");
    kitchen = new RoomWithDoor("Kitchen", "stainless steel appliances",
            "in the cabinet", "a screen door");
    stairs = new Room("Stairs", "a wooden bannister");
    hallway = new RoomWithHidingPlace("Upstairs Hallway", "a picture of a dog",
            "in the closet");
    bathroom = new RoomWithHidingPlace("Bathroom", "a sink and a toilet",
            "in the shower");
    masterBedroom = new RoomWithHidingPlace("Master Bedroom", "a large bed",
            "under the bed");
    secondBedroom = new RoomWithHidingPlace("Second Bedroom", "a small bed",
            "under the bed");

    frontYard = new OutsideWithDoor("Front Yard", false, "a heavy-looking oak door");
    backYard = new OutsideWithDoor("Back Yard", true, "a screen door");
    garden = new OutsideWithHidingPlace("Garden", false, "inside the shed");
    driveway = new OutsideWithHidingPlace("Driveway", true, "in the garage");

    diningRoom.Exits = new Location[] { livingRoom, kitchen };
    livingRoom.Exits = new Location[] { diningRoom, stairs };
    kitchen.Exits = new Location[] { diningRoom };
    stairs.Exits = new Location[] { livingRoom, hallway };
    hallway.Exits = new Location[] { stairs, bathroom, masterBedroom, secondBedroom };
    bathroom.Exits = new Location[] { hallway };
    masterBedroom.Exits = new Location[] { hallway };
    secondBedroom.Exits = new Location[] { hallway };
    frontYard.Exits = new Location[] { backYard, garden, driveway };
    backYard.Exits = new Location[] { frontYard, garden, driveway };
    garden.Exits = new Location[] { backYard, frontYard };
    driveway.Exits = new Location[] { backYard, frontYard };

    livingRoom.DoorLocation = frontYard;
    frontYard.DoorLocation = livingRoom;

    kitchen.DoorLocation = backYard;
    backYard.DoorLocation = kitchen;
}
```

The new CreateObjects() method creates all the objects to build the house. It's a lot like the old one, but it has a whole lot more places to go.

We're still not done—flip the page!

**Exercise
Solution (continued)**

Here's the rest of the code for the form. The goHere and goThroughTheDoor button event handlers are identical to the ones in the first part of this exercise, so flip back a few pages to see them.

```
private void ResetGame(bool displayMessage) {
    if (displayMessage) {
        MessageBox.Show("You found me in " + Moves + " moves!");
        IHidingPlace foundLocation = currentLocation as IHidingPlace;
        description.Text = "You found your opponent in " + Moves
            + " moves! He was hiding " + foundLocation.HidingPlaceName + ".";
    }
    Moves = 0;
    hide.Visible = true;
    goHere.Visible = false;
    check.Visible = false;
    goThroughTheDoor.Visible = false;
    exits.Visible = false;
}

private void check_Click(object sender, EventArgs e) {
    Moves++;
    if (opponent.Check(currentLocation))
        ResetGame(true);
    else
        RedrawForm();
}

private void hide_Click(object sender, EventArgs e) {
    hide.Visible = false;

    for (int i = 1; i <= 10; i++) {
        opponent.Move();
        description.Text = i + "... ";
        Application.DoEvents();
        System.Threading.Thread.Sleep(200);
    }

    description.Text = "Ready or not, here I come!";
    Application.DoEvents();
    System.Threading.Thread.Sleep(500);

    goHere.Visible = true;
    exits.Visible = true;
    MoveToANewLocation(livingRoom);
}
```

The ResetGame() method resets the game. It displays the final message, then makes all the buttons except the "Hide!" one invisible.

We want to display the name of the hiding place, but CurrentLocation is a Location reference, so it doesn't give us access to the HidingPlaceName field. Luckily, we can use the **as** keyword to downcast it to an IHidingPlace reference that points to the same object.

When you click the check button, it checks whether or not the opponent is hiding in the current room. If he is, it resets the game. If not, it redraws the form (to update the number of moves).

Remember DoEvents() from FlashyThing in Chapter 2? Without it, the text box doesn't refresh itself and the program looks frozen.

The hide button is the one that starts the game. The first thing it does is make itself invisible. Then it counts to 10 and tells the opponent to move. Finally, it makes the first button and the combo box visible, and then starts off the player in the living room. The MoveToANewLocation() method calls RedrawForm().

 OOPcross

Across

3. What an abstract method doesn't have
4. C# doesn't allow _____ inheritance
6. When you pass a subclass to a method that expects its base class, you're using this OOP principle
8. The OOP principle where you hide private data and only expose those methods and fields that other classes need access to
10. One of the four principles of OOP that you implement using the colon operator
14. Every method in an interface is automatically _____
15. If your class implements an interface that _____ from another interface, then you need to implement all of its members, too
17. An access modifier that's not valid for anything inside an interface
18. Object _____ Programming means creating programs that combine your data and code together into classes and objects

Down

1. When you move common methods from specific classes to a more general class that they all inherit from, you're using this OOP principle
2. If a class that implements an interface doesn't implement all of its methods, getters, and setters, then the project won't _____
5. Everything in an interface is automatically _____
7. An abstract class can include both abstract and _____ methods
9. You can't _____ an abstract class
11. A class that implements this must include all of the methods, getters, and setters that it defines
12. What you do with an interface
13. The `is` keyword returns true if an _____ implements an interface
16. An interface can't technically include a _____, but it can define getters and setters that look just like one from the outside

Pool Puzzle Solution from page 305

Your *job* is to take code snippets from the pool and place them into the blank lines in the code and output. You may use the same snippet more than once, and you won't need to use all the snippets. Your *goal* is to make a set of classes that will compile and run and produce the output listed.

> Here's where the Acts class calls the constructor in Picasso, which it inherits from. It passes "Acts" into the constructor, which gets stored in the face property.

```
interface Nose {
    int Ear() ;
    string Face { get; }
}

abstract class Picasso : Nose {
    public virtual int Ear()
    {
        return 7;
    }
    public Picasso(string face)
    {
        this.face = face;
    }
    public virtual string Face {
        get { return face ; }
    }
    string face;
}

class Clowns : Picasso {
    public Clowns() : base("Clowns") { }
}
```

> Properties can appear anywhere in the class! It's easier to read your code if they're at the top, but it's perfectly valid to have the face property at the bottom of the Picasso class.

```
class Acts : Picasso {
    public Acts() : base("Acts") { }
    public override int Ear() {
        return 5;
    }
}

class Of76 : Clowns {
    public override string Face {
        get { return "Of76"; }
    }
    public static void Main(string[] args) {
        string result = "";
        Nose[] i = new Nose[3];
        i[0] = new Acts();
        i[1] = new Clowns();
        i[2] = new Of76();
        for (int x = 0; x < 3; x++) {
            result += ( i[x].Ear() + " "
                      + i[x].Face ) + "\n";
        }
        MessageBox.Show(result);
    }
}
```

> Face is a get accessor that returns the value of the face property. Both of them are defined in Picasso and inherited into the subclasses.

OOPcross solution

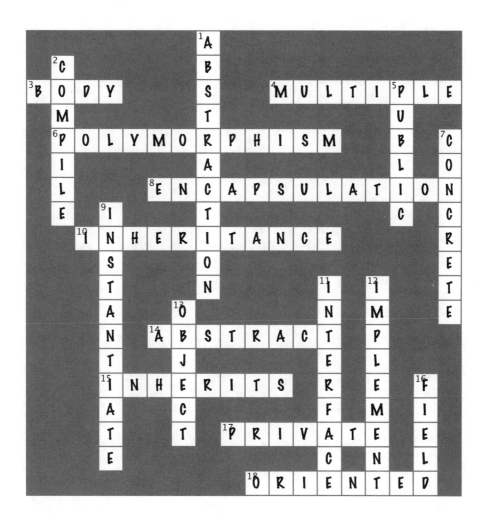

8 enums and collections

Storing lots of data

Finally, a way to organize my Boyfriend objects!

When it rains, it pours.

In the real world, you don't get to handle your data in tiny little bits and pieces. No, your data's going to come at you in **loads, piles, and bunches**. You'll need some pretty powerful tools to organize all of it, and that's where **collections** come in. They let you **store, sort, and manage** all the data that your programs need to pore through. That way, you can think about writing programs to work with your data, and let the collections worry about keeping track of it for you.

Strings don't always work for storing categories of data

Suppose you have several worker bees, all represented by `Worker` classes. How would you write a constructor that took a job as a parameter? If you use a string for the job name, you might end up with code that looks like this:

Our bee management software kept track of each worker's job using a string like "Sting Patrol" or "Nectar Collector".

Our code would allow these values to be passed in a constructor even though the program only supports Sting Patrol, Nectar Collector, and other jobs that a bee does.

```
Worker buzz = new Worker("Attorney General");
Worker clover = new Worker("Dog Walker");
Worker gladys = new Worker("Newscaster");
```

This code compiles, no problem. But these jobs don't make any sense for a bee. The Worker class really shouldn't allow these types as valid data.

You could probably add code to the `Worker` constructor to check each string and make sure it's a valid bee job. However, if you add new jobs that bees can do, you've got to change this code and recompile the `Worker` class. That's a pretty short-sighted solution. What if you have other classes that need to check for the types of worker bees they can be? Now you've got to duplicate code, and that's a bad path to go down.

What we need is a way to say, "Hey, there are only certain values that are allowed here." We need to **enumerate** the values that are OK to use.

Enums let you work with a set of valid values

An **enum** is a data type that only allows certain values for that piece of data. So we could define an enum called Jobs, and define the allowed jobs:

The stuff inside the brackets is called the enumerator list, and each item is an enumerator. The whole thing together is called an enumeration.

This is the name of the enum.

But most people just call them **enums**.

```
enum Job {
        NectarCollector,
        StingPatrol,
        HiveMaintenance,
        BabyBeeTutoring,
        EggCare,
        HoneyManufacturing,
}
```

The last enumerator doesn't have to end with a comma, but using one makes it easier to rearrange them using cut and paste.

Each of these is a valid job. Any can be used as a Jobs value.

Separate each value with a comma, and end the whole thing with a curly brace.

Now, you can reference these with types like this:

This is the name of the enum.

Finally, the value you want from the enum.

```
Worker nanny = new Worker(Job.EggCare);
```

We've changed the Worker constructor to accept Worker.Jobs as its parameter type.

But you can't just make up a new value for the enum! If you do, the program won't compile.

```
private void button1_Click(object sender EventArgs e)
{
        Worker buzz = new Worker(Jobs.AttorneyGeneral);
}
```

Here's the error you get from the compiler.

> ⊗ 'Jobs' does not contain a definition for 'AttorneyGeneral'

Enums let you represent numbers with names

Sometimes it's easier to work with numbers if you have names for them. You can assign numbers to the values in an enum and use the names to refer to them. That way, you don't have a bunch of unexplained numbers floating around in your code. Here's an enum to keep track of the scores for tricks at a dog competition:

You can cast an int to an enum, and you can cast an (int-based) enum back to an int.

```
public enum TrickScore {
    Sit = 7,
    Beg = 25,
    RollOver = 50,
    Fetch = 10,
    ComeHere = 5,
    Speak = 30,
}
```

These don't have to be in any particular order, and you can give multiple names to the same number.

Supply a name, then "=", then the number that name stands in for.

Some enums use a different type, like byte or long—like the one at the bottom of this page—and you can cast those back to their type.

Here's an excerpt from a method that uses the `TrickScore` enum by casting it to and from an `int`.

```
int value = (int)TrickScore.Fetch * 3;
MessageBox.Show(value.ToString());
TrickScore score = (TrickScore)value;
MessageBox.Show(score.ToString());
```

The (int) cast tells the compiler to turn this into the number it represents. So since TrickScore.Fetch has a value of 10, (int)TrickScore.Fetch turns it into the int value 10.

Since Fetch has a value of 10, this statement sets value to 30.

You can cast an int back to a TrickScore. Since value is equal to 30, score gets set to TrickScore.Fetch. So when you call score.ToString(), it returns "Fetch".

You can cast the enum as a number and do calculations with it, or you can use the `ToString()` method to treat the name as a string. If you don't assign any number to a name, the items in the list will be given values by default. The first item will be assigned a 0 value, the second a 1, etc.

But what happens if you want to use really big numbers for one of the enumerators? The default type for the numbers in an enum is `int`, so you'll need to specify the type you need using the `:` operator, like this:

```
public enum TrickScore : long {
    Sit = 7,
    Beg = 2500000000025
}
```

This tells the compiler to treat values in the TrickScore enum as longs, not ints.

If you tried to compile this code without specifying long as the type, you'd get this message:
`Cannot implicitly convert type 'long' to 'int'.`

Use what you've learned about enums to build a class that holds a playing card.

Card
Suit
Value
Name

Exercise

① Create a new project and add a Card class

You'll need two public fields: Suit (which will be Spades, Clubs, Diamonds, or Hearts) and Value (Ace, Two, Three...Ten, Jack, Queen, King). And you'll need a read-only property, Name ("Ace of Spades", "Five of Diamonds").

② Use two enums to define the suits and values

Use the familiar Add >> Class feature in the IDE to add them, replacing the word class with enum in the newly added files. Make sure that (int)Suits.Spades is equal to 0, followed by Clubs (equal to 1), Diamonds (2), and Hearts (3). Make the values equal to their face values: (int)Values.Ace should equal 1, Two should be 2, Three should be 3, etc. Jack should equal 11, Queen should be 12, and King should be 13.

③ Add a property for the name of the card

Name should be a read-only property. The get accessor should return a string that describes the card. This code will run in a form that calls the Name property from the card class and displays it:

```
Card card = new Card(Suits.Spades, Values.Ace);
string cardName = card.Name;
```

The value of cardName should be "Ace of Spades".

To make this work, your Card class will need a constructor that takes two parameters.

④ Add a form button that pops up the name of a random card

You can get your program to create a card with a random suit and value by casting a random number between 0 and 3 as a Suits and another random number between 1 and 13 as a Values. To do this, you can take advantage of a feature of the built-in Random class that gives it three different ways to call its Next() method:

When you've got more than one way to call a method, it's called overloading. More on that later....

```
Random random = new Random();
int numberBetween0and3 = random.Next(4);
int numberBetween1and13 = random.Next(1, 14);
int anyRandomInteger = random.Next();
```

This tells Random to return a value at least 1 but under 14.

Three of Clubs

OK

there are no Dumb Questions

Q: Hold on a second. When I was typing in that code, I noticed that an IntelliSense window popped up that said something about "3 of 3" when I used that Random.Next() **method. What was that about?**

A: What you saw was a method that was **overloaded**. When a class has a method that you can call more than one way, it's called overloading. When you're using a class with an overloaded method, the IDE lets you know all of the options that you have. In this case, the Random class has three possible Next() methods. As

soon as you type "random.Next(" into the code window, the IDE pops up its IntelliSense box that shows the parameters for the different overloaded methods. The up and down arrows next to the "3 of 3" let you scroll between them. That's really useful when you're dealing with a method that has dozens of overloaded definitions. So when you're doing it, make sure you choose the right overloaded Next() method! But don't worry too much now—we'll talk a lot about overloading later on in the chapter.

```
random.Next(
```

▲ 3 of 3 ▼ int Random.Next(int minValue, int maxValue)
    Returns a random number within a specified range.
    minValue: The inclusive lower bound of the random number returned.

Exercise Solution

A deck of cards is a great example of where limiting values is important. Nobody wants to turn over their cards and be faced with a Joker of Clubs, or a 13 of Hearts. Here's how we wrote the Card class.

```
enum Suits {
    Spades,
    Clubs,
    Diamonds,
    Hearts
}
```

When you don't specify values, the first item in the list is equal to zero, the second is 1, the third is 2, etc.

```
enum Values {
    Ace = 1,
    Two = 2,
    Three = 3,
    Four = 4,
    Five = 5,
    Six = 6,
    Seven = 7,
    Eight = 8,
    Nine = 9,
    Ten = 10,
    Jack = 11,
    Queen = 12,
    King = 13
}
```

Here's where we set the value of Values.Ace to 1.

The Card class has a Suit property of type Suits, and a Value property of type Values.

```
class Card {
    public Suits Suit { get; set; }
    public Values Value { get; set; }

    public Card(Suits suit, Values value) {
        this.Suit = suit;
        this.Value = value;
    }
    public string Name {
        get { return Value.ToString() + " of " + Suit.ToString(); }
    }
}
```

The get accessor for the Name property can take advantage of the way an enum's ToString() method returns its name converted to a string.

Here's the code for the button that pops up the name of a random card.

Here's where we use the overloaded Random.Next() method to generate a random number that we cast to the enum.

```
Random random = new Random();
private void button1_Click(object sender, EventArgs e) {
    Card card = new Card((Suits)random.Next(4), (Values)random.Next(1, 14));
    MessageBox.Show(card.Name);
}
```

We <u>could</u> use an array to create a deck of cards...

What if you want to create a class to represent a deck of cards? It would need a
way to keep track of every card in the deck, and it'd need to know what order they
were in. A Card array would do the trick—the top card in the deck would be at
value 0, the next card at value 1, etc. Here's a starting point—a Deck that starts
out with a full deck of 52 cards.

This array declaration would continue all the way through the deck. It's just abbreviated here to save space.

```
class Deck {
    private Card[] cards =  {
        new Card(Suits.Spades, Values.Ace),
        new Card(Suits.Spades, Values.Two),
        new Card(Suits.Spades, Values.Three),
        // ...
        new Card(Suits.Diamonds, Values.Queen),
        new Card(Suits.Diamonds, Values.King),
    };

    public void PrintCards() {
        for (int i = 0; i < cards.Length; i++)
            Console.WriteLine(cards[i].Name());
    }
}
```

...but what if you wanted to do more?

Think of everything you might need to do with a deck of cards, though. If
you're playing a card game, you routinely need to change the order of the
cards, and add and remove cards from the deck. You just can't do that with
an array very easily.

**BRAIN POWER**

How would you add a Shuffle() method to the Deck class that
rearranges the cards in random order? What about a method to deal the
first card off the top of the deck? How would you add a card to the deck?

Arrays are hard to work with

An array is fine for storing a fixed list of values or references. But once you need
to move array elements around, or add more elements than the array can hold,
things start to get a little sticky.

1 Every array has a length, and you need to know the length to work with it. You could use
null references to keep some array elements empty:

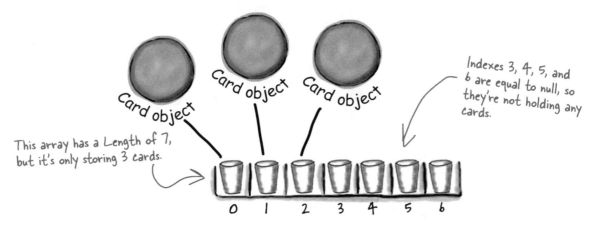

Indexes 3, 4, 5, and
6 are equal to null, so
they're not holding any
cards.

This array has a Length of 7,
but it's only storing 3 cards.

2 You'd need to keep track of how many cards are being held. So you'd need an `int` field,
which we could call `topCard` that would hold the index of the last card in the array. So
our 3-card array would have a `Length` of 7, but we'd set `topCard` equal to 3.

We'll add a topCard field to keep
track of how many cards are in the
array. Any index above topCard has a
null Card reference.

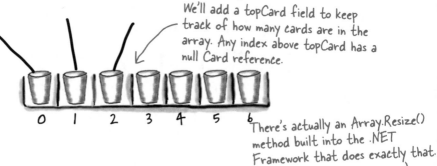

There's actually an Array.Resize()
method built into the .NET
Framework that does exactly that.

3 But now things get complicated. It's easy enough to add a `Peek()` method that just returns a
reference to the top card—so you can peek at the top of the deck. But what if you want to add
a card? If `topCard` is less than the array's `Length`, you can just put your card in the array at
that index and add 1 to `topCard`. But if the array's full, you'll need to create a new, bigger array
and copy the existing cards to it. Removing a card is easy enough—but after you subtract 1 from
`topCard`, you'll need to make sure to set the removed card's array index back to null. And what
if you need to remove a card **from the middle of the list**? If you remove card 4, you'll need to
move card 5 back to replace it, and then move 6 back, then 7 back…wow, what a mess!

Lists make it easy to store collections of...anything

The .NET Framework has a bunch of **collection** classes that handle all of those
nasty issues that come up when you add and remove array elements. The most
common sort of collection is a List<T>. Once you create a List<T> object, it's
easy to add an item, remove an item from any location in the list, peek at an item,
and even move an item from one place in the list to another. Here's how a list works:

*We'll sometimes
leave the <T> off
because it can
make the book a
little hard to read.
When you see List,
think List<T>!*

1 First you create a new instance of List<T>

Every array has a type—you don't just have an array, you have an int array, a Card
array, etc. Lists are the same way. You need to specify the type of object or value that the
list will hold by putting it in angle brackets <> when you use the new keyword to create it.

```
List<Card> cards = new List<Card>();
```

*You specified <Card> when you
created the list, so now this
list only holds references to
Card objects.*

List<Card> object

Relax

**The <T> at the end
of List<T> means
it's *generic*.**

The T gets replaced with a type—so
List<int> just means a List of
ints. You'll get plenty of practice with
generics over the next few pages.

2 Now you can add to your List<T>

Once you've got a List<T> object, you can add as many items to it as you want (as long as they're
polymorphic with whatever type you specified when you created your new List<T>).

*Which means
they're
assignable
to the type:
interfaces,
abstract classes,
base classes, etc.*

```
cards.Add(new Card(Suits.Diamonds, Values.King);
cards.Add(new Card(Suits.Clubs, Values.Three);
cards.Add(new Card(Suits.Hearts, Values.Ace);
```

*A list keeps its elements
in order, just like an
array. King of Diamonds
is first, 3 of Clubs
is second, and Ace of
Hearts is third.*

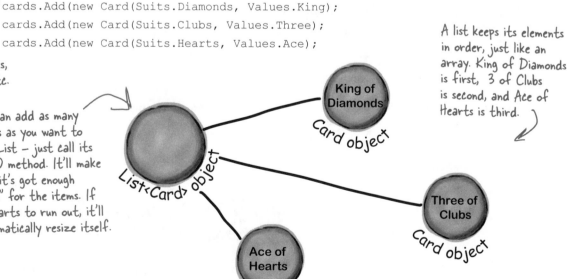

*You can add as many
cards as you want to
the List – just call its
Add() method. It'll make
sure it's got enough
"slots" for the items. If
it starts to run out, it'll
automatically resize itself.*

King of
Diamonds

Card object

Three of
Clubs

Card object

Ace of
Hearts

Card object

List<Card> object

Lists are more flexible than arrays

The List class is built into the .NET Framework, and it lets you do a lot of
things with objects that you can't do with a plain old array. Check out some
of the things you can do with a List<T>.

1 **You can make one.**
```
List<Egg> myCarton = new List<Egg>();
```

A new List object is
created on the heap. But
there's nothing in it yet.

2 **Add something to it.**
```
Egg x = new Egg();
myCarton.Add(x);
```

Now the List expands to hold
the Egg object...

3 **Add something else to it.**
```
Egg y = new Egg();

myCarton.Add(y);
```

...and expands again to hold
the second Egg object.

4 **Find out how many things are in it.**
```
int theSize = myCarton.Count;
```

5 **Find out if it has something in particular in it.**
```
bool Isin = myCarton.Contains(x);
```

Now you can search for any
Egg inside the list. This would
definitely come back true.

6 **Figure out where that thing is.**
```
int idx = myCarton.IndexOf(y);
```

The index for x would be 0 and the
index for y would be 1.

7 **Take something out of it.**
```
myCarton.Remove(y);
```

poof!

When we removed y, we left only x in
the List, so it shrank! And eventually
it will get garbage-collected.

Sharpen your pencil

Fill in the rest of the table below by looking at the `List` code on the left and putting in what you think the code might be if it were using a regular array instead. We don't expect you to get all of them exactly right, so just make your best guess.

Assume these statements are all executed in order, one after another.

We filled in a couple for you....

List	regular array
`List<String> myList = new List <String>();`	String [] myList = new String[2];
`String a = "Yay!";`	String a = "Yay!";
`myList.Add(a);`	
`String b = "Bummer";`	String b = "Bummer";
`myList.Add(b);`	
`int theSize = myList.Count;`	
`Guy o = myList[1];`	
`bool isIn = myList.Contains(b);`	

Hint: You'll need more than one line of code here.

Sharpen your pencil Solution

Your job was to fill in the rest of the table by looking at the `List` code on the left and putting in what you think the code might be if it were using a regular array instead.

List	regular array
`List<String> myList =` `    new List <String>();`	`String[] myList = new String[2];`
`String a = "Yay!"`	`String a = "Yay!";`
`myList.Add(a);`	`myList[0] = a;`
`String b = "Bummer";`	`String b = "Bummer";`
`myList.Add(b);`	`myList[1] = b;`
`int theSize = myList.Count;`	`int theSize = myList.Length;`
`Guy o = myList[1];`	`Guy o = myList[1];`

`bool isIn = myList.Contains(b);`	`bool isIn = false;`
	`  for (int i = 0; i < myList.`
	`    Length; i++) {`
	`  if (b == myList[i]) {`
	`      isIn = true;`
	`    }`
	`  }`

↑

Lists are objects that use methods just like every other class you've used so far. You can see the list of methods available from within the IDE just by typing a `.` next to the `List` name, and you pass parameters to them just the same as you would for a class you created yourself.

↑

With arrays you're a lot more limited. You need to set the size of the array when you create it, and any logic that'll need to be performed on it will need to be written on your own.

The .NET Framework does have an Array class, which makes some of these things a little easier to do, but we're concentrating on List objects because they're a lot easier to use.

Lists shrink and grow dynamically

The great thing about a List is that you don't need to know how long it'll be when you create it. A List automatically grows and shrinks to fit its contents. Here's an example of a few of the methods that make working with Lists a lot easier than arrays. **Create a new Console Application** and add this code to the Main() method. It won't print anything—**use the debugger** to step through the code and see what's going on.

We're declaring a List of Shoe objects called ShoeCloset.

```
List<Shoe> shoeCloset = new List<Shoe>();

shoeCloset.Add(new Shoe()
    { Style = Style.Sneakers, Color = "Black" });
shoeCloset.Add(new Shoe()
    { Style = Style.Clogs, Color = "Brown" });
shoeCloset.Add(new Shoe()
    { Style = Style.Wingtips, Color = "Black" });
shoeCloset.Add(new Shoe()
    { Style = Style.Loafers, Color = "White" });
shoeCloset.Add(new Shoe()
    { Style = Style.Loafers, Color = "Red" });
shoeCloset.Add(new Shoe()
    { Style = Style.Sneakers, Color = "Green" });

int numberOfShoes = shoeCloset.Count;
foreach (Shoe shoe in shoeCloset) {
    shoe.Style = Style.Flipflops;
    shoe.Color = "Orange";
}



shoeCloset.RemoveAt(4);


Shoe thirdShoe = shoeCloset[3];
Shoe secondShoe = shoeCloset[2];
shoeCloset.Clear();


shoeCloset.Add(thirdShoe);
if (shoeCloset.Contains(secondShoe))
    Console.WriteLine("That's surprising.");
```

You can use a new statement inside the List.Add() method.

foreach is a special kind of loop for Lists. It will execute a statement for each object in the List. This loop creates an identifier called shoe. As the loop goes through the items, it sets shoe equal to the first item in the list, then the second, then the third, until the loop is done.

foreach loops work on arrays, too! In fact, they work on any collection.

This returns the total number of Shoe objects in the List.

This foreach loop goes through each of the shoes in the closet.

The Remove() method will remove the object by its reference; RemoveAt() does it by index number.

The Clear() method removes all of the objects in a List.

We saved references to two shoes before we cleared the list. We added one back, but the other's still missing.

This line will never run, because Contains() will return false. We only added thirdShoe into the cleared list, not fifthShoe.

Here's the Shoe class we're using, and the Style enum it uses.

```
class Shoe {
    public Style Style;
    public string Color;
}

enum Style {
    Sneakers,
    Loafers,
    Sandals,
    Flipflops,
    Wingtips,
    Clogs,
}
```

Generics can store <u>any</u> type

You've already seen that a List can store strings or Shoes.
You could also make Lists of integers or any other object
you can create. That makes a List a **generic collection**.
When you create a new List object, you tie it to a specific
type: you can have a List of ints, or strings, or Shoe objects.
That makes working with Lists easy—once you've created
your list, you always know the type of data that's inside it.

> *This doesn't actually mean that you add the letter T. It's a
> notation that you'll see whenever a class or interface works
> with all types. The <T> part means you can put a type in
> there, like List<Shoe>, which limits its members to that type.*

List<T> name = new List<T>();

*Lists can be either very flexible (allowing any
type) or very restrictive. So they do what arrays
do, and then quite a few things more.*

The .NET Framework comes with some generic
interfaces that let the collections you're building work
with any and all types. The List class implement those
interfaces, and that's why you could create a List of
integers and work with it in pretty much the same way
that you would work with a List of Shoe objects.

→ ***Check it out for yourself.*** Type the word **List** into
the IDE, and then right-click on it and select "Go To
Definition". That will take you to the declaration for
the List class. It implements a few interfaces:

*This is where RemoveAt(), IndexOf(), and
Insert() come from.*

```
class List<T> : IList<T>,
ICollection<T>, IEnumerable<T>, IList,
ICollection, IEnumerable
```

*This is where Add(), Clear(),
CopyTo(), and Remove()
come from. It's the basis
for all generic collections.*

*This interface lets you use
foreach, among other things.*

BULLET POINTS

- **List** is a class in the .NET Framework.

- A List **resizes dynamically** to whatever
  size is needed. It's got a certain capacity—
  once you add enough data to the list, it'll grow
  to accommodate it.

- To put something into a List, use **Add()**.
  To remove something from a List, use
  Remove().

- You can remove objects using their <u>index</u>
  number using **RemoveAt()**.

- You declare the type of the List using a
  type argument, which is a type name in
  angle brackets. Example: List<Frog>
  means the List will be able to hold only
  objects of type Frog.

- To find out where something is (and if it is) in
  a List, use **IndexOf()**.

- To get the number of elements in a List,
  use the **Count** property.

- You can use the **Contains()** method to
  find out if a particular object is in a List.

- **foreach** is a special kind of loop that
  will iterate through all of the elements in a
  List and execute code on it. The syntax
  for a foreach loop is **foreach (string s in
  StringList)**. You don't have to tell the
  foreach loop to increment by one; it will go
  through the entire List all on its own.

Code Magnets

Can you reconstruct the code snippets to make a working Windows Form that will pop up the message box below when you click a button?

```
a.RemoveAt(2);
```

```
List<string> a = new List<string>();
```

```
public void printL (List<string> a){
```

```
if (a.Contains("two")) {
        a.Add(twopointtwo);
}
```

```
a.Add(zilch);
a.Add(first);
a.Add(second);
a.Add(third);
```

```
}
```

```
string result = "";
```

```
if (a.Contains("three")){
        a.Add("four");
        }
```

```
foreach (string element in a)
{
    result += "\n" + element;
}
```

```
MessageBox.Show(result);
```

```
if (a.IndexOf("four") != 4) {
        a.Add(fourth);
        }
```

```
}
```

```
printL(a);
```

```
private void button1_Click(object sender,
EventArgs e){




















}
```

Message box:
```
zero
one
three
four
4.2
```
OK

```
string zilch = "zero";
string first =  "one";
string second = "two";
string third = "three";
string fourth = "4.2";
string twopointtwo = "2.2";
```

Code Magnets Solution

Remember how we talked about using intuitive names back in Chapter 3? Well, that may make for good code, but it makes these puzzles way too easy. Just don't use cryptic names like "printL()" in real life!

```
private void button1_Click(object sender, EventArgs e)
{
    List<string> a = new List<string>();

    string zilch = "zero";
    string first = "one";
    string second = "two";
    string third = "three";
    string fourth = "4.2";
    string twopointtwo = "2.2";

    a.Add(zilch);
    a.Add(first);
    a.Add(second);
    a.Add(third);

    if (a.Contains("three")){
        a.Add("four");
    }

    a.RemoveAt(2);

    if (a.IndexOf("four") != 4) {
        a.Add(fourth);
    }

    if (a.Contains("two")) {
        a.Add(twopointtwo);
    }

    printL(a);
}

public void printL (List<string> a){
    string result = "";

    foreach (string element in a)
    {
        result += "\n" + element;
    }

    MessageBox.Show(result);
}
}
```

Message box displays:
```
zero
one
three
four
4.2
OK
```

Can you figure out why "2.2" never gets added to the list, even though it's declared here?

RemoveAt() removes the element at index #2—which is the third element in the list.

The printL() method uses a foreach loop to go through a list of strings, add each of them to one big string, and then show it in a message box.

The foreach loop goes through all of the elements in the list and prints them.

Q: **So why would I ever use an enum instead of a `List`? Don't they solve the same problem?**

A: Enums are a little different than `Lists`. First and foremost, enums are **types**, while `Lists` are **objects**.

You can think of enums as a handy way to store *lists of constants* so you can refer to them by name. They're great for keeping your code readable and making sure that you are always using the right variable names to access values that you use really frequently.

A `List` can store just about anything. Since it's a list of *objects*, each element in a list can have its own methods and properties. Enums, on the other hand, have to be assigned one of the **value types** in C# (like the ones on the first page of Chapter 4). So you can't store reference variables in them.

Enums can't dynamically change their size either. They can't implement interfaces or have methods, and you'll have to cast them to another type to store a value from an enum in another variable. Add all of that up and you've got some pretty big differences between the two ways of storing data. But both are really useful in their own right.

Q: **OK, it sounds like `Lists` are pretty powerful. So why would I ever want to use an array?**

A: If you know that you have a fixed number of items to work with, or if you want

> Arrays also take up less memory and CPU time for your programs, but that only accounts for a tiny performance boost. If you have to do the same thing, say, millions of times a second, you might want to use an array and not a list. But if your program is running slowly, it's pretty unlikely that switching from lists to arrays will fix the problem.

a fixed sequence of values with a fixed length, then an array is perfect. Luckily, you can easily convert any list to an array using the `ToArray()` method...and you can convert an array to a list using one of the overloaded constructors for the `List<T>` object.

Q: **I don't get the name "generic". Why is it called a generic collection? Why isn't an array generic?**

A: A generic collection is a collection object (or a built-in object that lets you store and manage a bunch of other objects) that's been set up to store only one type (or more than one type, which you'll see in a minute).

Q: **OK, that explains the "collection" part. But what makes it "generic"?**

A: Supermarkets used to carry generic items that were packaged in big white packages with black type that just said the name of what was inside ("Potato Chips", "Cola", "Soap", etc.). The generic brand was all about what was inside the bag, and not about how it was displayed.

The same thing happens with generic data types. Your `List<T>` will work exactly the same with whatever happens to be inside it. A list of `Shoe` objects, `Card` objects, ints, longs, or even other lists will still act at the container level. So you can always add, remove, insert, etc., no matter what's inside the list itself.

> The term "generic" refers to the fact that even though a specific instance of List can only store one specific type, the List class in general works with any type.
>
> That's what the <T> stuff is all about. It's the way that you tie a specific instance of a List to one type. But the List class as a whole is generic enough to work with ANY type. That's why generic collections are different from anything you've seen so far.

Q: **Can I have a list that doesn't have a type?**

A: No. Every list—in fact, every generic collection (and you'll learn about the other generic collections in just a minute)—must have a type connected to it. C# does have non-generic lists called `ArrayLists` that can store any kind of object. If you want to use an `ArrayList`, you need to include a "`using System.Collections;`" line in your code. But you really shouldn't ever need to do this, because a `List<object>` will work just fine!

When you create a new List object, you always supply a type—that tells C# what type of data it'll store. A list can store a value type (like int, bool, or decimal) or a class.

Collection initializers work just like object initializers

C# gives you a nice bit of shorthand to cut down on typing when you need to
create a list and immediately add a bunch of items to it. When you create a
new `List` object, you can use a **collection initializer** to give it a starting list
of items. It'll add them as soon as the list is created.

You saw this code a few pages ago—it creates a new List<Shoe> and fills it with new Shoe objects.

```
List<Shoe> shoeCloset = new List<Shoe>();
shoeCloset.Add(new Shoe() { Style = Style.Sneakers, Color = "Black" });
shoeCloset.Add(new Shoe() { Style = Style.Clogs, Color = "Brown" });
shoeCloset.Add(new Shoe() { Style = Style.Wingtips, Color = "Black" });
shoeCloset.Add(new Shoe() { Style = Style.Loafers, Color = "White" });
shoeCloset.Add(new Shoe() { Style = Style.Loafers, Color = "Red" });
shoeCloset.Add(new Shoe() { Style = Style.Sneakers, Color = "Green" });
```

The same code rewritten using a collection initializer

Notice how each Shoe object is initialized with its own object initializer? You can nest them inside a collection initializer, just like this.

You can create a collection initializer by taking each item that was being added using Add() and adding it to the statement that creates the list.

```
List<Shoe> shoeCloset = new List<Shoe>() {
    new Shoe() { Style = Style.Sneakers, Color = "Black" },
    new Shoe() { Style = Style.Clogs, Color = "Brown" },
    new Shoe() { Style = Style.Wingtips, Color = "Black" },
    new Shoe() { Style = Style.Loafers, Color = "White" },
    new Shoe() { Style = Style.Loafers, Color = "Red" },
    new Shoe() { Style = Style.Sneakers, Color = "Green" },
};
```

The statement to create the list is followed by curly brackets that contain separate new statements, separated by commas.

You're not limited to using new statements in the initializer—you can include variables, too.

A collection initializer makes your code more compact by letting you combine creating a list with adding an initial set of items.

Let's create a List of Ducks

 Do this!

Here's a Duck class that keeps track of your extensive duck collection. (You *do* collect ducks, don't you?) **Create a new Console Application** and add a new Duck class and KindOfDuck enum.

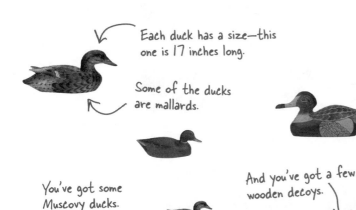

Each duck has a size—this one is 17 inches long.

Some of the ducks are mallards.

You've got some Muscovy ducks.

And you've got a few wooden decoys.

Duck
Size
Kind
Quack()
Swim()
Eat()
Walk()

```
class Duck {
    public int Size;
    public KindOfDuck Kind;
}
```

The class has two public fields. It's also got some methods, which we're not showing here.

```
enum KindOfDuck {
    Mallard,
    Muscovy,
    Decoy,
}
```

We'll use an enum called KindOfDuck to keep track of what sort of ducks are in your collection.

Add Duck and KindOfDuck to your project.

Here's the initializer for your List of Ducks

We've got six ducks, so we'll create a List<Duck> that has a collection initializer with six statements. Each statement in the initializer creates a new duck, using an object initializer to set each Duck object's Size and Kind field. **Add this code** to your Main() method in Program.cs:

```
List<Duck> ducks = new List<Duck>() {

    new Duck() { Kind = KindOfDuck.Mallard, Size = 17 },

    new Duck() { Kind = KindOfDuck.Muscovy, Size = 18 },

    new Duck() { Kind = KindOfDuck.Decoy, Size = 14 },

    new Duck() { Kind = KindOfDuck.Muscovy, Size = 11 },

    new Duck() { Kind = KindOfDuck.Mallard, Size = 14 },

    new Duck() { Kind = KindOfDuck.Decoy, Size = 13 },

};

// This keeps the output from disappearing before you can read it
Console.ReadKey();
```

You'll be adding code to your Main() method to print to the console. Make sure you keep this line at the end so the program stays open until you hit a key.

Lists are easy, but <u>SORTING</u> can be tricky

It's not hard to think about ways to sort numbers or letters. But what do you sort two objects on, especially if they have multiple fields? In some cases you might want to order objects by the value in the name field, while in other cases it might make sense to order objects based on height or date of birth. There are lots of ways you can order things, and lists support any of them.

You could sort a list of ducks by size...   *Sorted smallest to biggest....*

...or by kind. *Sorted by kind of duck....*

Lists know how to sort themselves

Every list comes with a Sort() method that rearranges all of the items in the list to put them in order. Lists already know how to sort most built-in types and classes, and it's easy to teach them how to sort your own classes.

Technically, it's not the List<T> that knows how to sort itself. It depends on an IComparer<T> object, which you'll learn about in a minute.

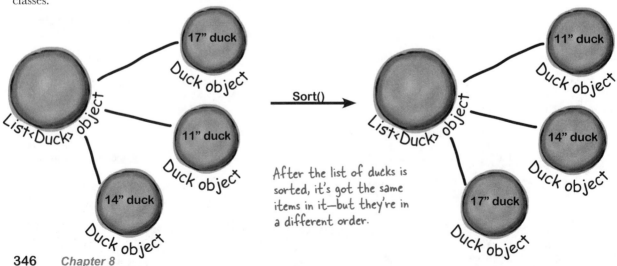

After the list of ducks is sorted, it's got the same items in it—but they're in a different order.

IComparable<Duck> helps your list sort its ducks

The `List.Sort()` method knows how to sort any type or class that **implements the IComparable<T> interface**. That interface has just one member—a method called `CompareTo()`. `Sort()` uses an object's `CompareTo()` method to compare it with other objects, and uses its return value (an int) to determine which comes first.

But sometimes you need to sort a list of objects that don't implement IComparable<T>, and .NET has another interface to help with that. You can pass `Sort()` an instance of a class that implements `IComparer<T>`. That interface also has one method. The `List` object's `Sort()` method uses the comparer object's `Compare()` method to compare pairs of objects, in order to figure out which one comes first in the sorted list.

An object's CompareTo() method compares it to another object

One way to let our `List` object sort is to modify the `Duck` class to implement IComparable<Duck>. To do that, we'd add a `CompareTo()` method that takes a `Duck` reference as a parameter. If the duck to compare should come after the current duck in the sorted list, `CompareTo()` returns a positive number.

Update your project's `Duck` class by implementing IComparable<Duck> so that it sorts itself based on duck size:

> **You can make any class work with the List's built-in Sort() method by having it implement IComparable<T> and adding a CompareTo() method.**

```
class Duck : IComparable<Duck> {
    public int Size;
    public KindOfDuck Kind;

    public int CompareTo(Duck duckToCompare) {
        if (this.Size > duckToCompare.Size)
            return 1;
        else if (this.Size < duckToCompare.Size)
            return -1;
        else
            return 0;
    }
}
```

When you implement IComparable<T>, you specify the type being compared when you have the class implement the interface.

Most CompareTo() methods look a lot like this. This method first compares the Size field against the other duck's Size field. If this duck is bigger, it returns 1. If it's smaller, it returns −1. And if they're the same size, it returns zero.

If you want to sort your list from smallest to biggest, have CompareTo() return a positive number if it's comparing to a smaller duck, and a negative number if it's comparing to a bigger one.

Add this code to the end of your `Main()` method above the call to `Console.ReadKey()` to tell your list of ducks to sort itself. Use the debugger to see this at work by **putting a breakpoint** in the `CompareTo()` method.

```
ducks.Sort();
```

Use IComparer to tell your List how to sort

Lists have a special interface built into the .NET Framework that lets you build a separate class to help the List<T> sort out its members. By **implementing the IComparer<T> interface**, you can tell your List exactly how you want it to sort your objects. You do that by implementing the Compare() method in the IComparer<T> interface. It takes two object parameters, x and y, and returns an int. If x is less than y, it should return a negative value. If they're equal, it should return zero. And if x is greater than y, it should return a positive value.

Here's an example of how you'd declare a comparer class to compare Duck objects by size. Add it to your project as a new class:

This class implements IComparer, and specifies the type of object it can sort: Duck objects.

```
class DuckComparerBySize : IComparer<Duck>
{
    public int Compare(Duck x, Duck y)
    {
        if (x.Size < y.Size)
            return -1;
        if (x.Size > y.Size)
            return 1;
        return 0;
    }
}
```

These will always match: the same type in each.

The Compare() method returns an int, and has two parameters: both of the type you're sorting.

You can do whatever types of comparisons you want in the method.

Any negative number means object x should go before object y. x is "less than" y.

Any positive value means object x should go after object y. x is "greater than" y.

0 means that these two objects should be treated as the same (using this comparison calculation).

Here's a method to print the ducks in a List<Duck>.

Add this PrintDucks method to your Program class in your project so you can print the ducks in a list.

Update your Main() method to call it before and after you sort the list so you can see the results!

```
public static void PrintDucks(List<Duck> ducks)
{
    foreach (Duck duck in ducks)
        Console.WriteLine(duck.Size.ToString() + "-inch " + duck.Kind.ToString());
    Console.WriteLine("End of ducks!");
}
```

Your List will sort differently depending on how you implement IComparer<T>.

Create an instance of your comparer object

When you want to sort using IComparer<T>, you need to create a new instance of the class that implements it. That object exists for one reason—to help List.Sort() figure out how to sort the array. But like any other (non-static) class, you need to instantiate it before you use it.

> We left out the code you already saw a few pages ago to initialize the list. Make sure you initialize your list before you try to sort it! If you don't, you'll get a null pointer exception.

```
DuckComparerBySize sizeComparer = new DuckComparerBySize();
ducks.Sort(sizeComparer);
PrintDucks(ducks);
```

> d this code to your program's
> ain() method to see how the
> cks get sorted.

> You'll pass Sort() a reference to the new DuckComparerBySize object as its parameter.

> Sorted smallest to biggest....

Multiple IComparer implementations, multiple ways to sort your objects

You can create multiple IComparer<Duck> classes with different sorting logic to sort the ducks in different ways. Then you can use the comparer you want when you need to sort in that particular way. Here's another duck comparer implementation to add to your project:

> This comparer sorts by duck type. Remember, when you compare the enum Kind, you're comparing their **index** values.

```
class DuckComparerByKind : IComparer<Duck> {
    public int Compare(Duck x, Duck y) {
        if (x.Kind < y.Kind)
            return -1;
        if (x.Kind > y.Kind)
            return 1;
        else
            return 0;
    }
}
```

> So Mallard comes before Muscovy, which comes before Decoy.

> We compared the ducks' Kind properties, so the ducks are sorted based on the index value of the KindOfDuck enum.

> Here's an example of how enums and Lists work together. Enums stand in for numbers, and are used in sorting of lists.

> Notice how "greater than" and "less than" have a different meaning here. We used < and > to compare enum index values, which lets us put the ducks in order.

```
DuckComparerByKind kindComparer = new DuckComparerByKind();
ducks.Sort(kindComparer);
PrintDucks(ducks);
```

> Sorted by kind of duck....

> More duck sorting code for your Main() method.

IComparer can do complex comparisons

> If you don't provide Sort() with an IComparer<T> object , it uses a default one that can sort value types or compare references. Flip to Leftover #5 in the Appendix to learn a little more about comparing objects.

One advantage to creating a separate class for sorting your ducks is that you can build more complex logic into that class—and you can add members that help determine how the list gets sorted.

```csharp
enum SortCriteria {
    SizeThenKind,
    KindThenSize,
}
```

This enum tells the object which way to sort the ducks.

Here's a more complex class to compare ducks. Its Compare() method takes the same parameters, but it looks at the public SortBy field to determine how to sort the ducks.

```csharp
class DuckComparer : IComparer<Duck> {
    public SortCriteria SortBy = SortCriteria.SizeThenKind;

    public int Compare(Duck x, Duck y) {
        if (SortBy == SortCriteria.SizeThenKind)
            if (x.Size > y.Size)
                return 1;
            else if (x.Size < y.Size)
                return -1;
            else
                if (x.Kind > y.Kind)
                    return 1;
                else if (x.Kind < y.Kind)
                    return -1;
                else
                    return 0;
        else
            if (x.Kind > y.Kind)
                return 1;
            else if (x.Kind < y.Kind)
                return -1;
            else
                if (x.Size > y.Size)
                    return 1;
                else if (x.Size < y.Size)
                    return -1;
                else
                    return 0;
    }
}
```

This if statement checks the SortBy field. If it's set to SizeThenKind, then it first sorts the ducks by size, and then within each size it'll sort the ducks by their kind.

Instead of just returning 0 if the two ducks are the same size, the comparer checks their kind, and only returns 0 if the two ducks are both the same size and the same kind.

If SortBy isn't set to SizeThenKind, then the comparer first sorts by the kind of duck. If the two ducks are the same kind, then it compares their size.

```csharp
DuckComparer comparer = new DuckComparer();

comparer.SortBy = SortCriteria.KindThenSize;
ducks.Sort(comparer);
PrintDucks(ducks);

comparer.SortBy = SortCriteria.SizeThenKind;
ducks.Sort(comparer);
PrintDucks(ducks);
```

Here's how we'd use this comparer object. First we'd instantiate it as usual. Then we can set the object's SortBy field before calling ducks.Sort(). Now you can change the way the list sorts its ducks just by changing one field in the object. Add this code to the end of your Main() method. Now it sorts and re-sorts the list a bunch of times!

Exercise

Create five random cards and then sort them.

① **Create code to make a jumbled set of cards**
Create a new Console Application and add code to the Main() method that creates five random
Card objects. After you create each object, use the built-in Console.WriteLine() method to
write its name to the output. Use Console.ReadKey() at the end of the program to keep your
window from disappearing when the program finishes.

② **Create a class that implements IComparer<Card> to sort the cards**
Here's a good chance to use that IDE shortcut to implement an interface:

```
class CardComparer_byValue : IComparer<Card>
```

Then click on IComparer<Card> and hover over the I. You'll see a box appear underneath it.
When you click on the box, the IDE pops up its "Implement interface" window:

Sometimes it's a little hard to
get this box to pop up, so the
IDE has a useful shortcut: just
press **ctrl-period**.

IComparer<Card>

Implement interface 'IComparer<Card>'

Explicitly implement interface 'IComparer<Card>'

Click on "Implement interface IComparer<Card>" in the box to tell the IDE to automatically fill
in all of the methods and properties that you need to implement. In this case, it creates an empty
Compare() method to compare two cards, x and y. Write the method so that it returns 1 if x is
bigger than y, –1 if it's smaller, and 0 if they're the same card. In this case, make sure that any king
comes after any jack, which comes after any four, which comes after any ace.

③ **Make sure the output looks right**
Here's what your output window should look like after you click the button.

When you use the built-in
Console.WriteLine()
method, it adds a line
to this output. Console.
ReadKey() waits for you
to press a key before the
program ends.

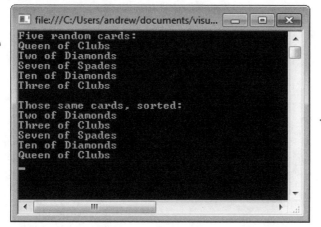

Your IComparer
object needs to sort
the cards by value,
so the cards with
the lowest values are
first in the list.

look it up

Create five random cards and then sort them.

Exercise Solution

Here's the "guts" of the card sorting, which uses the built-in List.Sort() method. Sort() takes an IComparer object, which has one method: Compare(). This implementation takes two cards and first compares their values, then their suits.

```csharp
class CardComparer_byValue : IComparer<Card> {
    public int Compare(Card x, Card y) {
        if (x.Value < y.Value) {
            return -1;
        }
        if (x.Value > y.Value) {
            return 1;
        }
        if (x.Suit < y.Suit) {
            return -1;
        }
        if (x.Suit > y.Suit) {
            return 1;
        }
        return 0;
    }
}
```

If x has a bigger value, return 1. If x's value is smaller, return –1. Remember, both return statements end the method immediately.

These statements only get executed if x and y have the same value—that means the first two return statements weren't executed.

If none of the other four return statements were hit, the cards must be the same—so return zero.

Here's a generic List of Card objects to store the cards. Once they're in the list, it's easy to sort them using an IComparer.

```csharp
static void Main(string[] args)
{
    Random random = new Random();
    Console.WriteLine("Five random cards:");
    List<Card> cards = new List<Card>();
    for (int i = 0; i < 5; i++)
    {
        cards.Add(new Card((Suits)random.Next(4),
                           (Values)random.Next(1, 14)));
        Console.WriteLine(cards[i].Name);
    }

    Console.WriteLine();
    Console.WriteLine("Those same cards, sorted:");
    cards.Sort(new CardComparer_byValue());
    foreach (Card card in cards)
    {
        Console.WriteLine(card.Name);
    }
    Console.ReadKey();
}
```

We're using Console.ReadKey() to keep console applications from exiting after they finish. This is great for learning, but not so great if you want to write real command-line applications. If you use Ctrl-F5 to start your program, the IDE runs it without debugging. When it finishes, it prints "Press any key to continue…" and waits for a keypress. But it doesn't debug your program (because it's running without debugging), so your breakpoints and watches won't work.

Overriding a ToString() method lets an object describe itself

Every .NET object has a **method called ToString() that converts it to a string**. By default, it just returns the name of your class (MyProject.Duck). The method is inherited from Object (remember, that's the base class for every object). This is a really useful method, and it's used a lot. For example, the + operator to concatenate strings **automatically calls an object's ToString()**. And Console.WriteLine() or String.Format() will automatically call it when you pass objects to them, which can really come in handy when you want to turn an object into a string.

Go back to your duck sorting program. Put a breakpoint in the Main() method anywhere after the list is initialized and debug your program. Then **hover over any ducks variable** so it shows the value in a window. Any time you look at a variable in the debugger that's got a reference to a List, you can explore the contents of it by clicking the + button:

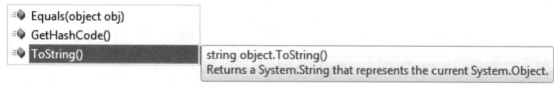

The IDE calls the ToString() method when it displays an object in its Watch window. But the ToString() method that Duck inherited from Object just returns its class name. It would be really useful if we could make ToString() more informative.

So instead of passing a value to Console.WriteLine(), String.Format(), etc., you can pass an object—its ToString() method is called automatically. That also works with value types like ints and enums, too!

Hmm, that's not as useful as we'd hoped. You can see that there are six Duck objects in the list ("MyProject" is the namespace we used). If you click the + button next to a duck, you can see its Kind and Size values. But wouldn't it be easier if you could see all of them at once?

Luckily, ToString() is a virtual method on Object, the base class of every object. So all you need to do is **override the ToString() method**—and when you do, you'll see the results immediately in the IDE's Watch window! Open up your Duck class and start adding a new method by typing **override**. As soon as you press space, the IDE will show you the methods you can override:

```
override
    ≡● Equals(object obj)
    ≡● GetHashCode()
    ≡● ToString()        string object.ToString()
                         Returns a System.String that represents the current System.Object.
```

Click on ToString() to tell the IDE to add a new ToString() method. Replace the contents so it looks like this:

```
public override string ToString()
{
    return "A " + Size + " inch " + Kind.ToString();
}
```

Run your program and look at the list again. Now the IDE shows you the contents of your Ducks!

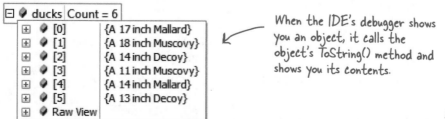

When the IDE's debugger shows you an object, it calls the object's ToString() method and shows you its contents.

Update your foreach loops to let your Ducks and Cards print themselves

You've seen two different examples of programs looping through a list of objects and calling `Console.WriteLine()` to print a line to the console for each object—like this `foreach` loop that prints every card in a `List<Card>`:

```
foreach (Card card in cards)
{
    Console.WriteLine(card.Name);
}
```

The `PrintDucks()` method did something similar for Duck objects in a `List`:

```
foreach (Duck duck in ducks)
{
    Console.WriteLine(duck.Size.ToString() + "-inch " + Kind);
}
```

The + operator automatically calls the KindOfDuck enum's ToString() method.

This is a pretty common thing to do with objects. But now that your Duck has a `ToString()` method, your `PrintDucks()` method should take advantage of it:

```
public static void PrintDucks(List<Duck> ducks) {
    foreach (Duck duck in ducks) {
        Console.WriteLine(duck);
    }
    Console.WriteLine("End of ducks!");
}
```

If you pass Console.WriteLine() a reference to an object, it will call that object's ToString() method automatically.

Add this to your Ducks program and run it again. It prints the same output. And now if you want to add, say, a `Gender` property to your Duck object, you just have to update the `ToString()` method, and everything that uses it (including the `PrintDucks()` method) will reflect that change.

Add a ToString() method to your Card object, too

Your Card object already has a Name property that returns the name of the card:

```
public string Name
{
    get { return Value.ToString() + " of " + Suit.ToString(); }
}
```

You're still allowed to call ToString() like this, but now you know it's not necessary in this case, because + calls it automatically.

That's exactly what its `ToString()` method should do. So add a `ToString()` method to the Card class:

```
public override string ToString()
{
    return Name;
}
```

ToString() is useful for a lot more than just making your objects easier to identify in the IDE. Keep your eyes open over the next few chapters, and you'll see how useful it is for every object to have a way to convert itself to a string. That's why every object has a ToString() method.

Now your programs that use Card objects will be easier to debug.

When you write a foreach loop, you're using IEnumerable<T>

foreach Loops
Up Close

Go to the IDE, find a List<Duck> variable, and use IntelliSense to take a look at its GetEnumerator() method. Start typing ".GetEnumerator" and see what comes up:

Collection initializers work with ANY IEnumerable<T> object!

```
ducks.GetEnumerator
```

GetEnumerator	List<Duck>.Enumerator List<Duck>.GetEnumerator()
	Returns an enumerator that iterates through the System.Collections.Generic.List<T>.

Add a line to create a new array of Duck objects:

```
Duck[] duckArray = new Duck[6];
```

Then type duckArray.GetEnumerator—the array also has a GetEnumerator() method. That's because all List, and arrays implement an interface called **IEnumerable<T>**, which contains one method. That method, GetEnumerator(), returns an **Enumerator object**.

It's the Enumerator object that provides the machinery that lets you loop through a list in order. Here's a foreach loop that loops through a List<Duck> with a variable called duck:

```
foreach (Duck duck in ducks) {
    Console.WriteLine(duck);
}
```

And here's what that loop is actually doing behind the scenes:

```
IEnumerator<Duck> enumerator = ducks.GetEnumerator();
while (enumerator.MoveNext()) {
    Duck duck = enumerator.Current;
    Console.WriteLine(duck);
}
IDisposable disposable = enumerator as IDisposable;
if (disposable != null) disposable.Dispose();
```

When a collection implements IEnumerable<T>, it's giving you a way to write a loop that goes through its contents in order.

(Don't worry about the last two lines for now. You'll learn about IDisposable in Chapter 9.)

Technically, there's a little more than this, but you get the idea....

Those two loops print out the same ducks. You can see this for yourself by running both of them; they'll both have the same output.

Here's what's going on. When you're looping through a list or array (or any other collection), the MoveNext() method returns true if there's another element in the list, or false if the enumerator has reached the end of the list. The Current property always returns a reference to the current element. Add it all together, and you get a foreach loop!

Try experimenting with this by changing your Duck's ToString() to increment the Size property. Debug your program and hover over a Duck. Then do it again. Remember, each time you do it, the IDE calls its ToString() method.

What do you think would happen during a foreach loop if your ToString() method changes one of the object's fields?

You can upcast an entire list using IEnumerable

Remember how you can upcast any object to its superclass? Well, when you've got a List of objects, you can upcast the entire list at once. It's called **covariance**, and all you need for it is an IEnumerable<T> interface reference.

Create a Console Application and add a base class, Bird (for Duck to extend), and a Penguin class. We'll use the ToString() method to make it easy to see which class is which.

```
class Bird {
    public string Name { get; set; }
    public void Fly() {
        Console.WriteLine("Flap, flap");
    }
    public override string ToString() {
        return "A bird named " + Name;
    }
}
```

```
class Penguin : Bird
{
    public void Fly() {
        Console.WriteLine("Penguins can't fly!");
    }
    public override string ToString() {
        return "A penguin named " + base.Name;
    }
}
```

Here's a Bird class, and a Penguin class that inherits from it. Add them to a new Console Application project, then copy your existing Duck class into it. Just change its declaration so that it extends Bird.

```
class Duck : Bird, IComparable<Duck> {
    // The rest of the class is the same
}
```

Here are the first few lines of your Main() method to initialize your list **and then upcast it**.

Copy the same collection initializer you've been using to initialize your List of ducks.

```
List<Duck> ducks = new List<Duck>() { // initialize your list as usual }
IEnumerable<Bird> upcastDucks = ducks;
```

Take a close look at that last line of code. You're taking a reference to your List<Duck> and assigning it to an IEnumerable<Bird> interface variable. Debug through it and you'll see it's pointing to the same object.

Combine your birds into a single list

Covariance is really useful when you want to take a collection of objects and add them to a more general list. Here's an example: if you have a list of Bird obects, you can add your Duck list to it in one easy step. Here's an example that uses the List.AddRange() method, which you can use to add the contents of one list into another.

```
List<Bird> birds = new List<Bird>();

birds.Add(new Bird() { Name = "Feathers" });
birds.AddRange(upcastDucks);
birds.Add(new Penguin() { Name = "George" });

foreach (Bird bird in birds) {
    Console.WriteLine(bird);
}
```

Once the ducks were upcast into an IEnumerable<Bird>, you could add them to a list of Bird objects.

You can build your own overloaded methods

You've been using **overloaded methods** and even an overloaded constructor that were part of the built-in .NET Framework classes and objects, so you can already see how useful they are. Wouldn't it be cool if you could build overloaded methods into your own classes? Well, you can—and it's easy! All you need to do is write two or more methods that have the same name but take different parameters.

You can also use a using statement instead of changing the namespace. If you want to learn more about namespaces, take a minute and flip to Leftover #2 in the Appendix.

Do this!

1 **Create a new project and add the Card class to it.**
You can do this easily by right-clicking on the project in the Solution Explorer and selecting "Existing Item" from the Add menu. The IDE will make a copy of the class and add it to the project. The file will **still have the namespace from the old project**, so go to the top of the Card.cs file and change the namespace line to <u>match the name of the new project</u> you created. Then do the same for the Values and Suits enums.

If you don't do this, you'll only be able to access the Card class by specifying its namespace (like oldnamespace.Card).

2 **Add some new overloaded methods to the card class.**
Create two static DoesCardMatch() methods. The first one should check a card's suit. The second should check its value. Both return true only if the card matches.

```
public static bool DoesCardMatch(Card cardToCheck, Suits suit) {
    if (cardToCheck.Suit == suit) {
        return true;
    } else {
        return false;
    }
}
public static bool DoesCardMatch(Card cardToCheck, Values value) {
    if (cardToCheck.Value == value) {
        return true;
    } else {
        return false;
    }
}
```

Overloaded methods don't have to be static, but it's good to get a little practice writing static methods.

You've seen overloading already. Flip back to the solution to Kathleen's party planning program in Chapter 6 on pages 253–256—you added an overloaded CalculateCost() method to the DinnerParty class.

3 **Add a button to the form to use the new methods.**
Add this code to the button:

```
Card cardToCheck = new Card(Suits.Clubs, Values.Three);
bool doesItMatch = Card.DoesCardMatch(cardToCheck, Suits.Hearts);
MessageBox.Show(doesItMatch.ToString());
```

Notice how you're using ToString() here. That's because MessageBox.Show() takes a string, not a bool or object.

As soon as you type "DoesCardMatch (" the IDE will show you that you really did build an overloaded method: `Card.DoesCardMatch(`

```
▲ 1 of 2 ▼  bool Card.DoesCardMatch(Card cardToCheck, Suits suit)
```

Take a minute and play around with the two methods so you can get used to overloading.

Get some practice using `List`s by building a class to store a deck of cards, along with a form that uses it.

Build a form that lets you move cards between two decks

You've built a card class already. Now it's time to build a class to hold any number of cards, which we'll call `Deck`. A real-life deck has 52 cards, but the `Deck` class can hold any number of cards—or no cards at all.

Then you'll build a form that shows you the contents of two `Deck` objects. When you first start the program, deck #1 has up to 10 random cards, and deck #2 is a complete deck of 52 cards, both sorted by suit and then value—and you can reset either deck to its initial state using two Reset buttons. The form also has buttons (labeled "<<" and ">>") to move cards between the decks.

These buttons are named moveToDeck2 (top) and moveToDeck1 (bottom). They move cards from one deck to the other.

Remember, you can use a control's Name property to give it a name to make your code easier to read. Then when you double-click on the button, its event handler is given a matching name.

Use two ListBox controls to show the two decks. When the moveToDeck1 button is clicked, it moves the selected card from deck #2 to deck #1.

The reset1 and reset2 buttons first call the ResetDeck() method and then the RedrawDeck() method.

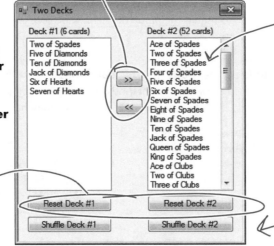

These buttons are named shuffle1 and shuffle2. They call the appropriate Deck.Shuffle() method, and then redraw the deck.

In addition to the event handlers for the six buttons, you'll need to add two methods for the form. First add a `ResetDeck()` method, which resets a deck to its initial state. It takes an int as a parameter: if it's passed 1, it resets the first `Deck` object by reinitializing it to an empty deck and a random number of up to 10 random cards; if it's passed 2, it resets the second `Deck` object so that it contains a full 52-card deck. Then add this method:

```
private void RedrawDeck(int DeckNumber) {
    if (DeckNumber == 1) {
        listBox1.Items.Clear();
        foreach (string cardName in deck1.GetCardNames())
            listBox1.Items.Add(cardName);
        label1.Text = "Deck #1 (" + deck1.Count + " cards)";
    } else {
        listBox2.Items.Clear();
        foreach (string cardName in deck2.GetCardNames())
            listBox2.Items.Add(cardName);
        label2.Text = "Deck #2 (" + deck2.Count + " cards)";
    }
}
```

Take a look at how we used the foreach loop to add each of the cards in the deck to the listbox.

The RedrawDeck() method shuffles the deck, draws random cards from it, and updates the two listbox controls with whatever happens to be in the two Deck objects.

Build the Deck class

⎯ When you have the declarations for a class
   without the implementation, it's called a "skeleton".

Here's the skeleton for the Deck class. We've filled in several of the methods for you. You'll need to finish it by writing the `Shuffle()` and `GetCardNames()` methods, and you'll have to get the `Sort()` method to work. We also added two useful **overloaded constructors**: one that creates a complete deck of 52 cards, and another that takes an array of `Card` objects and loads them into the deck.

```
                                    ⎯ The Deck stores its cards in a List—but it keeps
class Deck {                          it private to make sure it's well encapsulated.
    private List<Card> cards;
    private Random random = new Random();   If you don't pass parameters
                                             into the constructor, it creates
    public Deck() {                          a complete deck of 52 cards.
        cards = new List<Card>();
        for (int suit = 0; suit <= 3; suit++)
            for (int value = 1; value <= 13; value++)
                cards.Add(new Card((Suits)suit, (Values)value));
    }
                                                This overloaded constructor takes one
    public Deck(IEnumerable<Card> initialCards) {   parameter—an array of cards, which
        cards = new List<Card>(initialCards);       it loads as the initial deck.
    }

    public int Count { get { return cards.Count; } }

    public void Add(Card cardToAdd) {
        cards.Add(cardToAdd);
    }

    public Card Deal(int index) {
        Card CardToDeal = cards[index];
        cards.RemoveAt(index);
        return CardToDeal;
    }

    public void Shuffle() {
        // this method shuffles the cards by rearranging them in a random order
    }

    public IEnumerable<string> GetCardNames() {
        // this method returns a string array that contains each card's name
    }

    public void Sort() {
        cards.Sort(new CardComparer_bySuit());
    }
}
```

Deck

Count

Add()
Deal()
GetCardNames()
Shuffle()
Sort()

The parameter has the type IEnumerable<Card>, which lets you pass any collection into the constructor, not just a List<T> or an array.

Again, even though GetCardNames() returns an array, we expose IEnumerable<string>.

The Deal method deals one card out of the deck—it removes the Card object from the deck and returns a reference to it. You can deal from the top of the deck by passing it 0, or deal from the middle by passing it the index of the card to deal.

Hint: The ListBox control's SelectedIndex property will be the same as the index of the card in the list. You can pass it directly to the Deal() method. If no card is selected, it'll be less than zero. In that case, the moveToDeck button should do nothing.

You'll need to write the Shuffle() method and the GetCardNames() method, and add a class that implements IComparer to make the Sort() method work. And you'll need to add the Card class you already wrote. If you use "Add Existing Item" to add it, don't forget to change its namespace.

Another hint: The form makes it really easy to test your Shuffle() method. Keep clicking the "Reset Deck #1" button until you get a three-card deck. That'll make it easy to see if your shuffling code works.

Exercise Solution

Build a class to store a deck of cards, along with a form that uses it.

```
class Deck {
    private List<Card> cards;
    private Random random = new Random();
    public Deck() {
        cards = new List<Card>();
        for (int suit = 0; suit <= 3; suit++)
            for (int value = 1; value <= 13; value++)
                cards.Add(new Card((Suits)suit, (Values)value));
    }
    public Deck(IEnumerable<Card> initialCards) {
        cards = new List<Card>(initialCards);
    }
    public int Count { get { return cards.Count; } }
    public void Add(Card cardToAdd) {
        cards.Add(cardToAdd);
    }
    public Card Deal(int index) {
        Card CardToDeal = cards[index];
        cards.RemoveAt(index);
        return CardToDeal;
    }
    public void Shuffle() {
        List<Card> NewCards = new List<Card>();
        while (cards.Count > 0) {
            int CardToMove = random.Next(cards.Count);
            NewCards.Add(cards[CardToMove]);
            cards.RemoveAt(CardToMove);
        }
        cards = NewCards;
    }
    public IEnumerable<string> GetCardNames() {
        string[] CardNames = new string[cards.Count];
        for (int i = 0; i < cards.Count; i++)
            CardNames[i] = cards[i].Name;
        return CardNames;
    }
    public void Sort() {
        cards.Sort(new CardComparer_bySuit());
    }
}
```

Here's the constructor that creates a complete deck of 52 cards. It uses a nested for loop. The outside one loops through the four suits. That means the inside loop that goes through the 13 values runs four separate times, once per suit.

Here's the other constructor—this class has two overloaded constructors, each with different parameters.

The Add and Deal methods are pretty straightforward—they use the methods for the Cards list. The Deal method removes a card from the list, and the Add method adds a card to the list.

The Shuffle() method creates a new instance of List<Cards> called NewCards. Then it pulls random cards out of the Cards field and sticks them in NewCards until Cards is empty. Once it's done, it resets the Cards field to point to the new instance. The old instance won't have any more references pointing to it, so it'll get collected by the garbage collector.

Your GetCardNames() method needs to create an array that's big enough to hold all the card names. This one uses a for loop, but it could also use foreach.

```
class CardComparer_bySuit : IComparer<Card>
{
    public int Compare(Card x, Card y)
    {
        if (x.Suit > y.Suit)
            return 1;
        if (x.Suit < y.Suit)
            return -1;
        if (x.Value > y.Value)
            return 1;
        if (x.Value < y.Value)
            return -1;
        return 0;
    }
}


    Deck deck1;
    Deck deck2;
    Random random = new Random();

    public Form1() {
        InitializeComponent();
        ResetDeck(1);
        ResetDeck(2);
        RedrawDeck(1);
        RedrawDeck(2);
    }


    private void ResetDeck(int deckNumber) {
        if (deckNumber == 1) {
            int numberOfCards = random.Next(1, 11);
            deck1 = new Deck(new Card[] { });
            for (int i = 0; i < numberOfCards; i++)
                deck1.Add(new Card((Suits)random.Next(4),
                                   (Values)random.Next(1, 14)));
            deck1.Sort();
        } else
            deck2 = new Deck();
    }
```

Sorting by suit is a lot like sorting by value. The only difference is that in this case the suits are compared first, and then the values are compared only if the suits match.

Instead of using if/else if, we used a series of if statements. This works because each if statement only executes if the previous one didn't—otherwise the previous one would have returned.

The form's constructor needs to reset the two decks, and then it draws them.

To reset deck #1, this method first uses random.Next() to pick how many cards will go into the deck, and then creates a new empty deck. It uses a for loop to add that many random cards. It finishes off by sorting the deck. Resetting deck #2 is easy—just create a new instance of Deck().

You've already got the RedrawDeck() method from the instructions.

→ We're not done yet—flip the page!

Exercise Solution (continued)

Naming your controls makes it a lot easier to read your code. If these were called button1_Click, button2_Click, etc., you wouldn't know which button's code you were looking at!

Here's the rest of the code for the form.

```csharp
private void reset1_Click(object sender, EventArgs e) {
    ResetDeck(1);
    RedrawDeck(1);
}

private void reset2_Click(object sender, EventArgs e) {
    ResetDeck(2);
    RedrawDeck(2);
}

private void shuffle1_Click(object sender, EventArgs e) {
    deck1.Shuffle();
    RedrawDeck(1);
}

private void shuffle2_Click(object sender, EventArgs e) {
    deck2.Shuffle();
    RedrawDeck(2);
}

private void moveToDeck1_Click(object sender, EventArgs e) {
    if (listBox2.SelectedIndex >= 0)
        if (deck2.Count > 0) {
            deck1.Add(deck2.Deal(listBox2.SelectedIndex));
        }
    RedrawDeck(1);
    RedrawDeck(2);
}

private void moveToDeck2_Click(object sender, EventArgs e)
    if (listBox1.SelectedIndex >= 0)
        if (deck1.Count > 0)
            deck2.Add(deck1.Deal(listBox1.SelectedIndex));
    RedrawDeck(1);
    RedrawDeck(2);
}
}
```

These buttons are pretty simple—first reset or shuffle the deck, then redraw it.

You can use the ListBox control's SelectedIndex property to figure out which card the user selected and then move it from one deck to the other. (If it's less than zero, no card was selected, so the button does nothing.) Once the card's moved, both decks need to be redrawn.

Use a dictionary to store keys and values

A list is like a big long page full of names. But what if you also want, for each name, an address? Or for every car in the garage list, you want details about that car? You need a **dictionary**. A dictionary lets you take a special value—the **key**—and associate that key with a bunch of data—the **value**. And one more thing: a specific key can **only appear once** in any dictionary.

This is the key. It's how you look up a definition in (you guessed it) a dictionary.

dic·tion·ar·y

A book that lists the words of a language in alphabetical order and gives their meaning.

This is the value. It's the data associated with a particular key.

Here's how you declare a `Dictionary` in C#:

Dictionary <Tkey, TValue> kv = new Dictionary <TKey, TValue>();

These are like List<T>. The <T> means a type goes in there. So you can declare one type for the key, and another type for the value.

These represent types. The first type in the angle brackets is always the key, and the second is always the data.

And here's a `Dictionary` in action:

```
private void button1_Click(object sender, EventArgs e)
{
    Dictionary<string, string> wordDefinition =
        new Dictionary<string, string>();

    wordDefinition.Add ("Dictionary", "A book that lists the words of a "
                        + "language in alphabetical order and gives their meaning");
    wordDefinition.Add ("Key", "A thing that provides a means of gaining access to "
                        + "our understanding something.");
    wordDefinition.Add ("Value", "A magnitude, quantity, or number.");

    if (wordDefinition.ContainsKey("Key"))
        MessageBox.Show(wordDefinition["Key"]);
}
```

This dictionary has string values for keys, and strings as the value. It's like a real dictionary: <u>term</u>, and <u>definition</u>.

The Add() method is how you add keys and values to the dictionary.

Add() takes a key, and then the value.

ContainsKey() tells you if a key is in the dictionary. Handy, huh?

Here's how you get the value for a key. It looks kind of like an array index—get the value for the key at this index.

The Dictionary Functionality Rundown

Dictionaries are a lot like lists. Both types are flexible in letting you work with lots of data types, and also come with lots of built-in functionality. Here are the basic `Dictionary` methods:

✦ Add an item.

You can add an item to a dictionary by passing a key and a value to its `Add()` method.

```
Dictionary<string, string> myDictionary = new Dictionary<string, string>();
myDictionary.Add("some key", "some value");
```

✦ Look up a value using its key.

The most important thing you'll do with a dictionary is look up values—which makes sense, because you stored those values in a dictionary so you could look them up using their unique keys. For this `Dictionary<string, string>`, you'll look up values using a string key, and it'll return a string.

```
string lookupValue = myDictionary["some key"];
```

✦ Remove an item.

Just like a `List`, you can remove an item from a dictionary using the `Remove()` method. All you need to pass to the `Remove` method is the `Key` value to have both the key and the value removed.

```
myDictionary.Remove("some key");
```

> Keys are unique in a Dictionary; any key appears exactly once. Values can appear any number of times—two keys can have the same value. That way, when you look up or remove a key, the Dictionary knows what to remove.

✦ Get a list of keys.

You can get a list of all of the keys in a dictionary using its `Keys` property and loop through it using a `foreach` loop. Here's what that would look like:

```
foreach (string key in myDictionary.Keys) { ... };
```

> Keys is a property of your dictionary object. This particular dictionary has string keys, so Keys is a collection of strings.

✦ Count the pairs in the dictionary.

The `Count` property returns the number of key-value pairs that are in the dictionary:

```
int howMany = myDictionary.Count;
```

Your key and value can be different types

Dictionaries are really versatile and can hold just about anything, from strings to numbers and even objects. Here's an example of a dictionary that's storing an integer as a key and a duck object as a value.

> It's common to see a dictionary that maps integers to objects when you're assigning unique ID numbers to objects.

```
Dictionary<int, Duck> duckDictionary = new Dictionary<int, Duck>();
duckDictionary.Add(376, new Duck()
                { Kind = KindOfDuck.Mallard, Size = 15 });
```

Build a program that uses a Dictionary

Here's a quick program that any New York baseball fan will like. When an important player retires, the team retires the player's jersey number. Let's build a program that looks up who wore famous numbers and when those numbers were retired. Here's a class to keep track of a jersey number:

Do this!

```
class JerseyNumber {
    public string Player { get; private set; }
    public int YearRetired { get; private set; }

    public JerseyNumber(string player, int numberRetired) {
        Player = player;
        YearRetired = numberRetired;
    }
}
```

Yogi Berra was #8 for one team and Cal Ripken, Jr. was #8 for another. But in a Dictionary only one key can map to a single value, so we'll only include numbers from one team here. Can you think of a way to store retired numbers for multiple teams?

Here's the form:

And here's all of the code for the form:

```
public partial class Form1 : Form {
    Dictionary<int, JerseyNumber> retiredNumbers = new Dictionary<int, JerseyNumber>() {
        {3, new JerseyNumber("Babe Ruth", 1948)},
        {4, new JerseyNumber("Lou Gehrig", 1939)},
        {5, new JerseyNumber("Joe DiMaggio", 1952)},
        {7, new JerseyNumber("Mickey Mantle", 1969)},
        {8, new JerseyNumber("Yogi Berra", 1972)},
        {10, new JerseyNumber("Phil Rizzuto", 1985)},
        {23, new JerseyNumber("Don Mattingly", 1997)},
        {42, new JerseyNumber("Jackie Robinson", 1993)},
        {44, new JerseyNumber("Reggie Jackson", 1993)},
    };

    public Form1() {
        InitializeComponent();

        foreach (int key in retiredNumbers.Keys) {
            number.Items.Add(key);
        }
    }

    private void number_SelectedIndexChanged(object sender, EventArgs e) {
        JerseyNumber jerseyNumber = retiredNumbers[(int)number.SelectedItem] as JerseyNumber;
        nameLabel.Text = jerseyNumber.Player;
        yearLabel.Text = jerseyNumber.YearRetired.ToString();
    }
}
```

Use a collection initializer to populate your Dictionary with JerseyNumber objects.

Add each key from the dictionary to the ComboBox's Items collection.

The ComboBox's SelectedItem property is an Object. Since the Dictionary key is an int, we need to cast it to an int value before doing the lookup in the Dictionary.

Use the ComboBox's SelectedIndexChanged event to update the two labels on the form with the values from the JerseyNumber object retrieved from the Dictionary.

Long Exercise

Build a game of **Go Fish!** that you can play against the computer.

This exercise is a little different....

There's a good chance that you're learning C# because you want a job as a professional developer. That's why we modeled this exercise after a professional assignment. When you're working as a programmer on a team, you don't usually build a complete program from start to finish. Instead, you'll build a *piece* of a bigger program. So we're going to give you a puzzle that's got some of the pieces already filled in. The code for the form is given to you in step #3. You just have to type it in—which may seem like a great head start, but it means that your classes **have to work with that code**. And that can be a challenge!

1 Start with the spec

Every professional software project starts with a specification, and this one is no exception. You'll be building a game of the classic card game **Go Fish!** Different people play the game by slightly different rules, so here's a recap of the rules you'll be using:

★ The game starts with a deck of 52 cards. Five cards are dealt to each player. The pile of cards that's left after everyone's dealt a hand is called the **stock**. Each player takes turns asking for a value ("Do you have any sevens?"). Any other player holding cards with that value must hand them over. If nobody has a card with that value, then the player must "go fish" by taking a card from the stock.

★ The goal of the game is to make books, where a book is the complete set of all four cards that have the same value. The player with the most books at the end of the game is the winner. As soon as a player collects a book, he places it face-up on the table so all the other players can see what books everyone else has.

★ When placing a book on the table causes a player to run out of cards, then he has to draw five more cards from the stock. If there are fewer than five cards left in the stock, he takes all of them. The game is over as soon as the stock is out of cards. The winner is then chosen based on whoever has the most books.

★ For this computer version of Go Fish, there are two computer players and one human player. Every round starts with the human player selecting one of the cards in his hand, which is displayed at all times. He does this by choosing one of the cards and indicating that he will ask for a card. Then the two computer players will ask for their cards. The results of each round will be displayed. This will repeat until there's a winner.

★ The game will take care of all of the trading of cards and pulling out of books automatically. Once there's a winner, the game is over. The game displays the name of the winner (or winners, in case of a tie). No other action can be taken—the player will have to restart the program in order to start a new game.

> If you don't know what you're building before you start, then how would you know when you're done? That's why most professional software projects start with a specification that tells you what you're going to build.

② **Build the form**

Build the form for the Go Fish! game. It should have a `ListBox` control for the player's hand, two `TextBox` controls for the progress of the game, and a button to let the player ask for a card. To play the game, the user will select one of the cards from the hand and click the button to ask the computer players if they have that card.

This TextBox control should have its Name property set to textName. In this screenshot, it's disabled, but it should be enabled when the program starts.

Set this button's Name property to buttonStart. It's disabled in this screenshot, but it starts out enabled. It'll get disabled once the game is started.

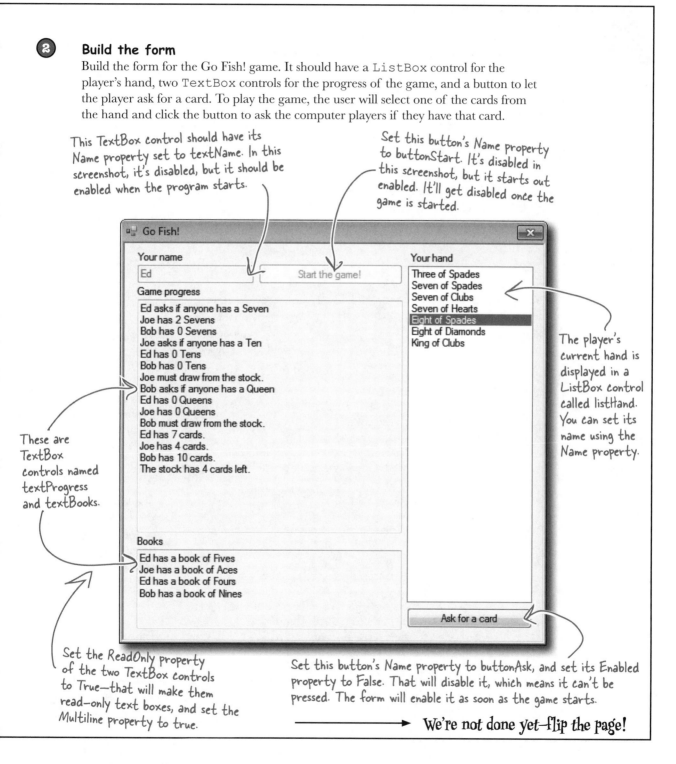

The player's current hand is displayed in a ListBox control called listHand. You can set its name using the Name property.

These are TextBox controls named textProgress and textBooks.

Set the ReadOnly property of the two TextBox controls to True—that will make them read-only text boxes, and set the Multiline property to true.

Set this button's Name property to buttonAsk, and set its Enabled property to False. That will disable it, which means it can't be pressed. The form will enable it as soon as the game starts.

→ We're not done yet—flip the page!

ℒⱺₙᵍ Exercise (continued)

③ Here's the code for the form

Enter it exactly like you see here. The rest of the code that you write will have to work with it.

```csharp
public partial class Form1 : Form {
    public Form1() {
        InitializeComponent();
    }

    private Game game;

    private void buttonStart_Click(object sender, EventArgs e) {
        if (String.IsNullOrEmpty(textName.Text)){
            MessageBox.Show("Please enter your name", "Can't start the game yet");
            return;
        }
        game = new Game(textName.Text, new List<string> { "Joe", "Bob" }, textProgress)
        buttonStart.Enabled = false;
        textName.Enabled = false;
        buttonAsk.Enabled = true;
        UpdateForm();
    }

    private void UpdateForm() {
        listHand.Items.Clear();
        foreach (String cardName in game.GetPlayerCardNames())
            listHand.Items.Add(cardName);
        textBooks.Text = game.DescribeBooks();
        textProgress.Text += game.DescribePlayerHands();
        textProgress.SelectionStart = textProgress.Text.Length;
        textProgress.ScrollToCaret();
    }

    private void buttonAsk_Click(object sender, EventArgs e) {
        textProgress.Text = "";
        if (listHand.SelectedIndex < 0) {
            MessageBox.Show("Please select a card");
            return;
        }
        if (game.PlayOneRound(listHand.SelectedIndex)) {
            textProgress.Text += "The winner is... " + game.GetWinnerName();
            textBooks.Text = game.DescribeBooks();
            buttonAsk.Enabled = false;
        } else
            UpdateForm();
    }
}
```

This is the only class that the form interacts with. It runs the whole game.

The Enabled property enables or disables a control on the form.

When you start a new game, it creates a new instance of the Game class, enables the "Ask" button, disables the "Start Game" button, and then redraws the form.

This method clears and repopulates the ListBox that holds the player's hand, and then updates the text boxes.

Using SelectionStart and ScrollToCaret() like this scrolls the text box to the end, so if there's too much text to display at once it scrolls down to the bottom.

The SelectionStart line moves the flashing text box cursor to the end, and once it's moved, the ScrollToCaret() method scrolls the text box down to the cursor.

The player selects one of the cards and clicks the "Ask" button to see if any of the other players have a card that matches its value. The Game class plays a round using the PlayOneRound() method.

④   **You'll need this code, too**

You'll need the code you wrote before for the Card class, the Suits and Values enums, the Deck class, and the CardComparer_byValue class. But you'll need to add a few more methods to the Deck class...and you'll need to understand them in order to use them.

```
public Card Peek(int cardNumber) {
    return cards[cardNumber];
}
```
The Peek() method lets you take a peek at one of the cards in the deck without dealing it.

```
public Card Deal() {
    return Deal(0);
}
```
Someone overloaded Deal() to make it a little easier to read. If you don't pass it any parameters, it deals a card off the top of the deck.

```
public bool ContainsValue(Values value) {
    foreach (Card card in cards)
        if (card.Value == value)
            return true;
    return false;
}
```
The ContainsValue() method searches through the entire deck for cards with a certain value, and returns true if it finds any. Can you guess how you'll use this in the Go Fish game?

```
public Deck PullOutValues(Values value) {
    Deck deckToReturn = new Deck(new Card[] { });
    for (int i = cards.Count - 1; i >= 0; i--)
        if (cards[i].Value == value)
            deckToReturn.Add(Deal(i));
    return deckToReturn;
}
```
You'll use the PullOutValues() method when you build the code to get a book of cards from the deck. It looks for any cards that match a value, pulls them out of the deck, and returns a new deck with those cards in it.

```
public bool HasBook(Values value) {
    int NumberOfCards = 0;
    foreach (Card card in cards)
        if (card.Value == value)
            NumberOfCards++;
    if (NumberOfCards == 4)
        return true;
    else
        return false;
}
```
The HasBook() method checks a deck to see if it contains a book of four cards of whatever value was passed as the parameter. It returns true if there's a book in the deck, false otherwise.

```
public void SortByValue() {
    cards.Sort(new CardComparer_byValue());
}
```
The SortByValue() method sorts the deck using the Comparer_byValue class.

→   Still not done—flip the page!

LONG EXERCISE (CONTINUED)

 5 Now comes the HARD part: Build the Player class

There's an instance of the `Player` class for each of the three players in the game. They get created by the `buttonStart` button's event handler.

Look closely at each of the comments—they tell you what the methods are supposed to do. Your job is to fill in the methods.

```
class Player
{
    private string name;
    public string Name { get { return name; } }
    private Random random;
    private Deck cards;
    private TextBox textBoxOnForm;

    public Player(String name, Random random, TextBox textBoxOnForm) {
        // The constructor for the Player class initializes four private fields, and then
        // adds a line to the TextBox control on the form that says, "Joe has just
        // joined the game" - but use the name in the private field, and don't forget to
        // add a line break at the end of every line you add to the TextBox.
    }

    public IEnumerable<Values> PullOutBooks() {  } // see the facing page for the code

    public Values GetRandomValue() {
        // This method gets a random value—but it has to be a value that's in the deck!
    }

    public Deck DoYouHaveAny(Values value) {
        // This is where an opponent asks if I have any cards of a certain value
        // Use Deck.PullOutValues() to pull out the values. Add a line to the TextBox
        // that says, "Joe has 3 sixes" - use the new Card.Plural() static method
    }

    public void AskForACard(List<Player> players, int myIndex, Deck stock) {
        // Here's an overloaded version of AskForACard() - choose a random value
        // from the deck using GetRandomValue() and ask for it using AskForACard()
    }

    public void AskForACard(List<Player> players, int myIndex, Deck stock, Values value) {
        // Ask the other players for a value. First add a line to the TextBox: "Joe asks
        // if anyone has a Queen". Then go through the list of players that was passed in
        // as a parameter and ask each player if he has any of the value (using his
        // DoYouHaveAny() method). He'll pass you a deck of cards - add them to my deck.
        // Keep track of how many cards were added. If there weren't any, you'll need
        // to deal yourself a card from the stock (which was also passed as a parameter),
        // and you'll have to add a line to the TextBox: "Joe had to draw from the stock"
    }
    // Here's a property and a few short methods that were already written for you
    public int CardCount { get { return cards.Count; } }

    public void TakeCard(Card card) { cards.Add(card); }

    public IEnumerable<string> GetCardNames() { return cards.GetCardNames(); }

    public Card Peek(int cardNumber) { return cards.Peek(cardNumber); }

    public void SortHand() { cards.SortByValue(); }
}
```

That Peek() method we added to the Deck class will come in handy. It lets the program look at one of the cards in the deck by giving its index number, but unlike Deal() it doesn't remove the card.

```
public IEnumerable<Values> PullOutBooks() {
    List<Values> books = new List<Values>();
    for (int i = 1; i <= 13; i++) {
        Values value = (Values)i;
        int howMany = 0;
        for (int card = 0; card < cards.Count; card++)
            if (cards.Peek(card).Value == value)
                howMany++;
        if (howMany == 4) {
            books.Add(value);
            for (int card = cards.Count - 1; card >= 0; card--)
                cards.Deal(card);
        }
    }
    return books;
}
```

You'll have to build TWO overloaded versions of the AskForACard() method. The first one is used by the opponents when they ask for cards—it'll look through their hands and find a card to ask for. The second one is used when the player asks for the card. Both of them ask EVERY other player (both computer and human) for any cards that match the value.

6 **You'll need to add this method to the Card class**

It's a static method to take a value and return its plural—that way a ten will return "Tens" but a six will return "Sixes" (with "es" on the end). Since it's static, you call it with the class name—Card.Plural()—and not from an instance.

```
public partial class Card {
    public static string Plural(Values value) {
        if (value == Values.Six)
            return "Sixes";
        else
            return value.ToString() + "s";
    }
}
```

We used a partial class to add this static method to Card to make it easy for you to see what's going on. But you don't need to use a partial class—if you want, you can just add it straight into the existing Card class.

Nearly there–keep flipping!

Long Exercise (continued)

⑦ **The rest of the job: Build the Game class**
The form keeps one instance of Game. It manages the game play. Look
closely at how it's used in the form.

> The Player and Game classes both use a reference to
> the multiline TextBox on the form to print messages
> for the user to read. Make sure you add "using
> System.Windows.Forms;" to the top of their files.

```
class Game {
    private List<Player> players;
    private Dictionary<Values, Player> books;
    private Deck stock;
    private TextBox textBoxOnForm;

    public Game(string playerName, IEnumerable<string> opponentNames, TextBox textBoxOnForm)
        Random random = new Random();
        this.textBoxOnForm = textBoxOnForm;
        players = new List<Player>();
        players.Add(new Player(playerName, random, textBoxOnForm));
        foreach (string player in opponentNames)
            players.Add(new Player(player, random, textBoxOnForm));
        books = new Dictionary<Values, Player>();
        stock = new Deck();
        Deal();
        players[0].SortHand();
    }
    private void Deal() {
        // This is where the game starts - this method's only called at the beginning
        // of the game. Shuffle the stock, deal five cards to each player, then use a
        // foreach loop to call each player's PullOutBooks() method.
    }
    public bool PlayOneRound(int selectedPlayerCard) {
        // Play one round of the game. The parameter is the card the player selected
        // from his hand - get its value. Then go through all of the players and call
        // each one's AskForACard() methods, starting with the human player (who's
        // at index zero in the Players list - make sure he asks for the selected
        // card's value). Then call PullOutBooks() - if it returns true, then the
        // player ran out of cards and needs to draw a new hand. After all the players
        // have gone, sort the human player's hand (so it looks nice in the form).
        // Then check the stock to see if it's out of cards. If it is, reset the
        // TextBox on the form to say, "The stock is out of cards. Game over!" and return
        // true. Otherwise, the game isn't over yet, so return false.
    }
    public bool PullOutBooks(Player player) {
        // Pull out a player's books. Return true if the player ran out of cards, otherwise
        // return false. Each book is added to the Books dictionary. A player runs out of
        // cards when he's used all of his cards to make books—and he wins the game.
    }
    public string DescribeBooks() {
        // Return a long string that describes everyone's books by looking at the Books
        // dictionary: "Joe has a book of sixes. (line break) Ed has a book of Aces."
    }
```

> It's great for encapsulation, too. If
> you expose an IEnumerable<T> instead
> of, say, a List<T>, then you can't
> accidentally write code that modifies it.

> **Using IEnumerable<T> in
> public class members is
> a great way to make your
> classes more <u>flexible</u>, and
> that's something you need
> to think about when your
> code needs to be reused.
> Now someone else can use
> a string[]. List<string>, or
> something else entirely to
> instantiate the Game class.**

Here's a hint for writing the GetWinnerName() method: You'll need to create a new Dictionary<string, int> called winners at the top of the method. The winners dictionary will let you use each player's name to look up the number of books he made during the game. First you'll use a foreach loop to go through the books that the players made and build the dictionary. Then you'll use another foreach loop to find the highest number of books associated with any player. But there might be a tie—more than one player might have the most books! So you'll need one more foreach loop to look for all the players in winners that have the number of books that you found in the second loop and build a string that says who won.

```
public string GetWinnerName() {
        // This method is called at the end of the game. It uses its own dictionary
        // (Dictionary<string, int> winners) to keep track of how many books each player
        // ended up with in the books dictionary. First it uses a foreach loop
        // on books.Keys -- foreach (Values value in books.Keys) -- to populate
        // its winners dictionary with the number of books each player ended up with.
        // Then it loops through that dictionary to find the largest number of books
        // any winner has. And finally it makes one last pass through winners to come
        // up with a list of winners in a string ("Joe and Ed"). If there's one winner,
        // it returns a string like this: "Ed with 3 books". Otherwise it returns a
        // string like this: "A tie between Joe and Bob with 2 books."
}

// Here are a couple of short methods that were already written for you:

public IEnumerable<string> GetPlayerCardNames() {
    return players[0].GetCardNames();
}

public string DescribePlayerHands() {
    string description = "";
    for (int i = 0; i < players.Count; i++) {
        description += players[i].Name + " has " + players[i].CardCount;
        if (players[i].CardCount == 1)
            description += " card." + Environment.NewLine;
        else
            description += " cards." + Environment.NewLine;
    }
    description += "The stock has " + stock.Count + " cards left.";
    return description;
}
```

Go to the Watch window and type (int)'\r' to cast the character \r to a number. It turns into 13. '\n' turns into 10. Every char turns into its own unique number called its Unicode value. You'll learn more about that in the next chapter.

Use Environment.NewLine to add line breaks

You've been using \n throughout the book to add line breaks to message boxes. .NET also gives you a convenient constant for addling line breaks: Environment.NewLine. It always contains the constant value "\r\n". If you actually look at the characters that make up a Windows-formatted text file, at the end of every line you'll see two characters: '\r' and '\n'. Other operating systems (like Unix) only use a '\n' to indicate the end of each line. The MessageBox.Show() method is smart enough to automatically convert '\n' characters to line breaks, but your code can be easier to read if you use Environment.NewLine instead of escape characters. Also, Environment.NewLine is what gets appended to the end of each line when you use Console.WriteLine().

Long Exercise Solution

Here are the filled-in methods in the `Game` class.

The Deal() method gets called when the game first starts—it shuffles the deck and then deals five cards to each player. Then it pulls out any books that the players happened to have been dealt.

```
private void Deal() {
    stock.Shuffle();
    for (int i = 0; i < 5; i++)
        foreach (Player player in players)
            player.TakeCard(stock.Deal());
    foreach (Player player in players)
        PullOutBooks(player);
}

public bool PlayOneRound(int selectedPlayerCard) {
    Values cardToAskFor = players[0].Peek(selectedPlayerCard).Value;
    for (int i = 0; i < players.Count; i++) {
        if (i == 0)
            players[0].AskForACard(players, 0, stock, cardToAskFor);
        else
            players[i].AskForACard(players, i, stock);
        if (PullOutBooks(players[i])) {
            textBoxOnForm.Text += players[i].Name
                            + " drew a new hand" + Environment.NewLine;
            int card = 1;
            while (card <= 5 && stock.Count > 0) {
                players[i].TakeCard(stock.Deal());
                card++;
            }
        }
    }
    players[0].SortHand();
    if (stock.Count == 0) {
        textBoxOnForm.Text =
            "The stock is out of cards. Game over!" + Environment.NewLine;
        return true;
    }
    return false;
}

public bool PullOutBooks(Player player)
{
    IEnumerable<Values> booksPulled = player.PullOutBooks();
    foreach (Values value in booksPulled)
        books.Add(value, player);
    if (player.CardCount == 0)
        return true;
    return false;
}
```

After the player or opponent asks for a card, the game pulls out any books that he made. If a player's out of books, he draws a new hand by dealing up to 5 cards from the stock.

As soon as the player clicks the "Ask for a card" button, the game calls AskForACard() with that card. Then it calls AskForACard() for each opponent.

After the round is played, the game sorts the player's hand to make sure it's displayed in order on the form. Then it checks to see if the game's over. If it is, PlayOneRound() returns true.

PullOutBooks() looks through a player's cards to see if he's got four cards with the same value. If he does, they get added to his books dictionary. And if he's got no cards left afterward, it returns true.

The form needs to display a list of books, so it uses DescribeTheBooks() to turn the player's books dictionary into words.

```csharp
public string DescribeBooks() {
    string whoHasWhichBooks = "";
    foreach (Values value in books.Keys)
        whoHasWhichBooks += books[value].Name + " has a book of "
            + Card.Plural(value) + Environment.NewLine;
    return whoHasWhichBooks;
}

public string GetWinnerName() {
    Dictionary<string, int> winners = new Dictionary<string, int>();
    foreach (Values value in books.Keys) {
        string name = books[value].Name;
        if (winners.ContainsKey(name))
            winners[name]++;
        else
            winners.Add(name, 1);
    }
    int mostBooks = 0;
    foreach (string name in winners.Keys)
        if (winners[name] > mostBooks)
            mostBooks = winners[name];
    bool tie = false;
    string winnerList = "";
    foreach (string name in winners.Keys)
        if (winners[name] == mostBooks)
        {
            if (!String.IsNullOrEmpty(winnerList))
            {
                winnerList += " and ";
                tie = true;
            }
            winnerList += name;
        }
    winnerList += " with " + mostBooks + " books";
    if (tie)
        return "A tie between " + winnerList;
    else
        return winnerList;
}
```

Once the last card's been picked up, the game needs to figure out who won. That's what the GetWinnerName() does. And it'll use a dictionary called winners to do it. Each player's name is a key in the dictionary; its value is the number of books that player got during the game.

Next the game looks through the dictionary to figure the number of books that the player with the most books has. It puts that value in a variable called mostBooks.

Now that we know which player has the most books, the method can come up with a string that lists the winner (or winners).

→ We're not done yet—flip the page!

Long Exercise
Solution (continued)

Here are the filled-in methods in the `Player` class.

```
public Player(String name, Random random, TextBox textBoxOnForm) {
    this.name = name;
    this.random = random;
    this.textBoxOnForm = textBoxOnForm;
    this.cards = new Deck( new Card[] {} );
    textBoxOnForm.Text += name +
                " has just joined the game" + Environment.NewLine;
}
```

Here's the constructor for the Player class. It sets its private fields and adds a line to the progress text box saying who joined.

```
public Values GetRandomValue() {
    Card randomCard = cards.Peek(random.Next(cards.Count));
    return randomCard.Value;
}
```

The GetRandomValue() method uses Peek() to look at a random card in the player's hand.

```
public Deck DoYouHaveAny(Values value) {
    Deck cardsIHave = cards.PullOutValues(value);
    textBoxOnForm.Text += Name + " has " + cardsIHave.Count + " "
            + Card.Plural(value) + Environment.NewLine;
    return cardsIHave;
}
```

DoYouHaveAny() uses the PullOutValues() method to pull out and return all cards that match the parameter.

```
public void AskForACard(List<Player> players, int myIndex, Deck stock) {
    Values randomValue = GetRandomValue();
    AskForACard(players, myIndex, stock, randomValue);
}
```

There are two overloaded AskForACard() methods. This one is used by the opponents—it gets a random card from the hand and calls the other AskForACard().

> **Bonus mini-exercise:** Can you figure out a way to improve encapsulation and design in your Player class by replacing `List<Player>` with `IEnumerable<Player>` in these two methods without changing the way the software works? Flip to Leftover #7 in the Appendix for a useful tool to help with that.

```
public void AskForACard(List<Player> players, int myIndex,
    Deck stock, Values value) {
    textBoxOnForm.Text += Name + " asks if anyone has a "
                            + value  + Environment.NewLine;
    int totalCardsGiven = 0;
    for (int i = 0; i < players.Count; i++) {
        if (i != myIndex) {
            Player player = players[i];
            Deck CardsGiven = player.DoYouHaveAny(value);
            totalCardsGiven += CardsGiven.Count;
            while (CardsGiven.Count > 0)
                cards.Add(CardsGiven.Deal());
        }
    }
    if (totalCardsGiven == 0) {
        textBoxOnForm.Text += Name +
            " must draw from the stock." + Environment.NewLine;
        cards.Add(stock.Deal());
    }
}
```

This AskForACard() method looks through every player (except for the one asking), calls its DoYouHaveAny() method, and adds any cards handed over to the hand.

If no cards were handed over, the player has to draw from the stock using its Deal() method.

And yet <u>MORE</u> collection types...

List and Dictionary objects are two of the **built-in generic collections** that are part of the .NET Framework. Lists and dictionaries are very flexible—you can access any of the data in them in any order. But sometimes you need to restrict how your program works with the data because the *thing* that you're representing inside your program works like that in the real world. For situations like this, you'll use a **Queue** or a **Stack**. Those are the other two generic collections that are similar to lists, but they're especially good at making sure that your data is processed in a certain order.

There are other types of collections, too—but these are the ones that you're most likely to come in contact with.

Use a Queue when the first object you store will be the first one you'll use, like:

★ Cars moving down a one-way street

★ People standing in line

★ Customers on hold for a customer service support line

★ Anything else that's handled on a first-come, first-served basis

A queue is first-in first-out, which means that the first object that you put into the queue is the first one you pull out of it to use.

Use a Stack when you always want to use the object you stored most recently, like:

★ Furniture loaded into the back of a moving truck

★ A stack of books where you want to read the most recently added one first

★ People boarding or leaving a plane

★ A pyramid of cheerleaders, where the ones on top have to dismount first... imagine the mess if the one on the bottom walked away first!

The stack is first in, last out: the first object that goes into the stack is the last one that comes out of it.

Generic collections are an important part of the .NET Framework

They're really useful—so much that the IDE automatically adds this statement to the top of every class you add to your project:

```
using System.Collections.Generic;
```

Almost every large project that you'll work on will include some sort of generic collection, because your programs need to store data. And when you're dealing with groups of similar things in the real world, they almost always naturally fall into a category that corresponds pretty well to one of these kinds of collections.

You can, however, use foreach to enumerate through a stack or queue, because they implement IEnumerable!

A queue is like a list that lets you put objects on the end of the list and use the ones in the front. A stack only lets you access the last object you put into it.

don't you hate waiting in line?

A queue is FIFO—First In, First Out

A **queue** is a lot like a list, except that you can't just add or remove items at any
index. To add an object to a queue, you **enqueue** it. That adds the object to the
end of the queue. You can **dequeue** the first object from the front of the queue.
When you do that, the object is removed from the queue, and the rest of the objects
in the queue move up a position.

Create a new queue of strings.

```
Queue<string> myQueue = new Queue<string>();
myQueue.Enqueue("first in line");
myQueue.Enqueue("second in line");
myQueue.Enqueue("third in line");
myQueue.Enqueue("last in line");
string takeALook = myQueue.Peek();①
string getFirst = myQueue.Dequeue();②
string getNext = myQueue.Dequeue();③
int howMany = myQueue.Count;④
myQueue.Clear();
MessageBox.Show("Peek() returned: " + takeALook + "\n"
    + "The first Dequeue() returned: " + getFirst + "\n"
    + "The second Dequeue() returned: " + getNext + "\n"
    + "Count before Clear() was " + howMany + "\n"
    + "Count after Clear() is now " + myQueue.Count);
                                                    ⑤
```

Here's where we add four items to the queue. When we pull them out of the queue, they'll come out in the same order they went in.

Peek() lets you take a "look" at the first item in the queue without removing it.

The first Dequeue() pulls the first item out of the queue. Then the second one shifts up into the first place—the next call to Dequeue() pulls that one out next.

The Clear() method removes all objects from the queue.

The queue's Count property returns the number of items in the queue.

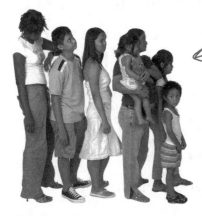

Objects in a queue need to wait their turn. The first one in the queue is the first one to come out of it.

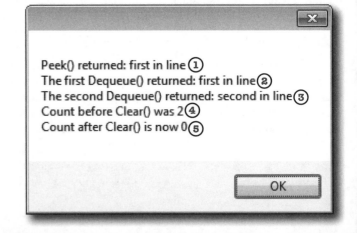

Peek() returned: first in line ①
The first Dequeue() returned: first in line②
The second Dequeue() returned: second in line③
Count before Clear() was 2④
Count after Clear() is now 0⑤

A stack is <u>LIFO</u>—Last In, First Out

A **stack** is really similar to a queue—with one big difference. You **push** each item onto a stack, and when you want to take an item from the stack, you **pop** one off of it. When you pop an item off of a stack, you end up with the most recent item that you pushed onto it. It's just like a stack of plates, magazines, or anything else— you can drop something onto the top of the stack, but you need to take it off before you can get to whatever's underneath it.

Creating a stack is just like creating any other generic collection.

en you push item onto a ck, it pushes e other items ck one notch d sits on top.

```
Stack<string> myStack = new Stack<string>();
myStack.Push("first in line");
myStack.Push("second in line");
myStack.Push("third in line");
myStack.Push("last in line");
①string takeALook = myStack.Peek();
②string getFirst = myStack.Pop();
③string getNext = myStack.Pop();
④int howMany = myStack.Count;
myStack.Clear();
MessageBox.Show("Peek() returned: " + takeALook + "\n"
    + "The first Pop() returned: " + getFirst + "\n"
    + "The second Pop() returned: " + getNext + "\n"
    + "Count before Clear() was " + howMany + "\n"
    + "Count after Clear() is now " + myStack.Count);
                                          ⑤
```

When you pop an item off the stack, you get the most recent item that was added.

You can also use Environment. NewLine instead of \n here, but we wanted the code to be easier to read.

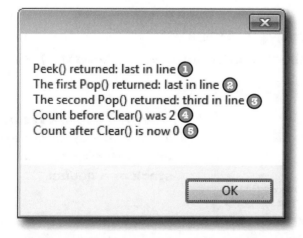

Peek() returned: last in line ①
The first Pop() returned: last in line ②
The second Pop() returned: third in line ③
Count before Clear() was 2 ④
Count after Clear() is now 0 ⑤

The last object you put on a stack is the first object that you pull off of it.

> Wait a minute, something's bugging me. You haven't shown me anything I can do with a stack or a queue that I can't do with a list—they just save me a couple of lines of code. But I can't get at the items in the middle of a stack or a queue. I can do that with a list pretty easily! So why would I give that up just for a little convenience?

Don't worry—you don't give up anything when you use a queue or a stack.

It's really easy to copy a Queue object to a List object. And it's just as easy to copy a List to a Queue, a Queue to a Stack...in fact, you can create a List, Queue, or Stack from any other object that implements the **IEnumerable** interface. All you have to do is use the overloaded constructor that lets you pass the collection you want to copy from as a parameter. That means you have the flexibility and convenience of representing your data with the collection that best matches the way you need it to be used. (But remember, you're making a copy, which means you're creating a whole new object and adding it to the heap.)

Let's set up a stack with four items—in this case, a stack of strings.

```
Stack<string> myStack = new Stack<string>();
myStack.Push("first in line");
myStack.Push("second in line");
myStack.Push("third in line");
myStack.Push("last in line");

Queue<string> myQueue = new Queue<string>(myStack);
List<string> myList = new List<string>(myQueue);
Stack<string> anotherStack = new Stack<string>(myList);
MessageBox.Show("myQueue has " + myQueue.Count + " items\n"
    + "myList has " + myList.Count + " items\n"
    + "anotherStack has " + anotherStack.Count + " items\n");
```

It's easy to convert that stack to a queue, then copy the queue to a list, and then copy the list to another stack.

All four items were copied into the new collections.

myQueue has 4 items
myList has 4 items
anotherStack has 4 items

...and you can always use a foreach loop to access all of the members in a stack or a queue!

Exercise

Write a program to help a cafeteria full of lumberjacks eat some flapjacks. Start with the `Lumberjack` class, filling in the missing code. Then design the form, and add the button event handlers to it.

1 Here's the **Lumberjack** class. Fill in the get accessor for `FlapjackCount` and the `TakeFlapjacks` and `EatFlapjacks` methods.

```
enum Flapjack {
    Crispy,
    Soggy,
    Browned,
    Banana
}
```

```
class Lumberjack {
    private string name;
    public string Name { get { return name; } }
    private Stack<Flapjack> meal;
    public Lumberjack(string name) {
        this.name = name;
        meal = new Stack<Flapjack>();
    }
    public int FlapjackCount { get { // return the count } }
    public void TakeFlapjacks(Flapjack Food, int HowMany) {
        // Add some number of flapjacks to the Meal stack
    }
    public void EatFlapjacks() {
        // Write this output to the console
    }
}
```

Output ▾ □ ✕

```
Ed's eating flapjacks
Ed ate a browned flapjack
Ed ate a soggy flapjack
Ed ate a soggy flapjack
Ed ate a soggy flapjack
Ed ate a crispy flapjack
Ed ate a soggy flapjack
Ed ate a banana flapjack
Ed ate a browned flapjack
```

2 Build this form. It lets you enter the names of lumberjacks into a text box so they get in the breakfast line. You can give the lumberjack at the front of the line a plate of flapjacks, and then tell him to move on to eat them using the "Next lumberjack" button. We've given you the click event handler for the "Add flapjacks" button. Use a queue called **breakfastLine** to keep track of the lumberjacks.

Breakfast for Lumberjacks ▯ ✕

Lumberjack name [   ]

[Add lumberjack]

Feed a Lumberjack

Breakfast line [1 ⬍]
```
1. Ed
2. Billy      ○ Crispy
3. Jones
4. Fred       ○ Soggy
5. Johansen
6. Bobby, Jr. ◉ Browned

This           ○ Banana
listbox
is called      [ Add flapjacks ]
line.          [ Ed has 8 flapjacks ]


            [ Next lumberjack ]
```

When the user clicks "Add Lumberjack", add the name in the name text box to the breakfastLine queue.

When you drag these RadioButton controls into the group box, the form automatically links them and only allows the user to check one of them at a time. Look at the addFlapjacks_Click method to figure out what they should be named.

```
private void addFlapjacks_Click(...) {
    Flapjack food;
    if (crispy.Checked == true)
        food = Flapjack.Crispy;
    else if (soggy.Checked == true)
        food = Flapjack.Soggy;
    else if (browned.Checked == true)
        food = Flapjack.Browned;
    else
        food = Flapjack.Banana;

    Lumberjack currentLumberjack = breakfastLine.Peek();
    currentLumberjack.TakeFlapjacks(food,
                    (int)howMany.Value);
    RedrawList();
}
```

Note the special "else if" syntax.

Peek() returns a reference to the first lumberjack in the queue.

This button should dequeue the next lumberjack, call his EatFlapjacks(), then redraw the list box.

You'll need to add a RedrawList() method to update the list box with the contents of the queue. All three buttons will call it. Here's a hint: it uses a foreach loop.

The NumericUpDown control is called howMany, and the label is called nextInLine.

> **Notice how the Flapjack enum uses uppercase letters ("Soggy"), but the output has lowercase letters ("soggy")? Here's a hint to help you get the output right. ToString() returns a string object, and one of its public members is a method called ToLower() that returns a lowercase version of the string.**

Exercise Solution

```
private Queue<Lumberjack> breakfastLine = new Queue<Lumberjack>();
private void addLumberjack_Click(object sender, EventArgs e) {
    breakfastLine.Enqueue(new Lumberjack(name.Text));
    name.Text = "";
    RedrawList();
}
private void RedrawList() {
    int number = 1;
    line.Items.Clear();
    foreach (Lumberjack lumberjack in breakfastLine) {
        line.Items.Add(number + ". " + lumberjack.Name);
        number++;
    }
    if (breakfastLine.Count == 0) {
        groupBox1.Enabled = false;
        nextInLine.Text = "";
    } else {
        groupBox1.Enabled = true;
        Lumberjack currentLumberjack = breakfastLine.Peek();
        nextInLine.Text = currentLumberjack.Name + " has "
            + currentLumberjack.FlapjackCount + " flapjacks";
    }
}
private void nextLumberjack_Click(object sender, EventArgs e) {
    Lumberjack nextLumberjack = breakfastLine.Dequeue();
    nextLumberjack.EatFlapjacks();
    nextInLine.Text = "";
    RedrawList();
}

class Lumberjack {
    private string name;
    public string Name { get { return name; } }
    private Stack<Flapjack> meal;

    public Lumberjack(string name) {
        this.name = name;
        meal = new Stack<Flapjack>();
    }

    public int FlapjackCount { get { return meal.Count; } }

    public void TakeFlapjacks(Flapjack food, int howMany) {
        for (int i = 0; i < howMany; i++) {
            meal.Push(food);
        }
    }

    public void EatFlapjacks() {
        Console.WriteLine(name + "'s eating flapjacks");
        while (meal.Count > 0) {
            Console.WriteLine(name + " ate a "
                + meal.Pop().ToString().ToLower() + " flapjack");
        }
    }
}
```

We called the list box "line", and the label between the two buttons "nextInLine".

The RedrawList() method uses a foreach loop to pull the lumberjacks out of their queue and add each of them to the list box.

This if statement updates the label with information about the first lumberjack in the queue.

The TakeFlapjacks method updates the Meal stack.

Here's where the Flapjack enum is made lowercase. Take a minute and figure out what's going on.

The EatFlapjacks method uses a while loop to print out the lumberjack's meal.

meal.Pop() returns an enum, whose ToString() method is called to return a string object, whose ToLower() method is called to return another string object.

Collectioncross

Across

3. An instance of a _____ collection only works with one specific type
6. A special kind of loop that works on IEnumerable<T>
9. The name of the method you use to send a string to the output
10. How you remove something from a stack
11. An object that's like an array but more flexible
13. Two methods in a class with the same name but different parameters are _____.
15. A method to figure out if a certain object is in a collection
19. An easy way to keep track of categories
20. All generic collections implement this interface
21. How you remove something from a queue

Down

1. The generic collection that lets you map keys to values
2. This collection is first-in, first-out
4. The built-in class that lets your program write text to the output
5. A method to find out how many things are in a collection
7. The only method in the IComparable interface
8. Most professional projects start with this
12. An object that implements this interface helps your list sort its contents
14. How you add something to a queue
16. This collection is first-in, last-out
17. How you add something to a stack
18. This method returns the next object to come off of a stack or queue

 Collectioncross solution

```
            ¹D                              ²Q
³G E N E R I C          ⁴C              ⁵C   U
         I              O          ⁶F O R E A C H  ⁷C
⁸S   ⁹W R I T E L I N E O          U   U      O
 P       I              S          N   E      M
 E     ¹⁰P O P          O    ¹¹L ¹²I S T       P
 C       N              L        C            A
 I       A         ¹³O V E R L O A D E D      R
 F       R              L        M            E
 I       Y         ¹⁴E           P            T
 C              ¹⁵C O N T A I N S             O
 A            ¹⁶S       Q        R
 T    ¹⁷P  ¹⁸P  T       U   ¹⁹E N U M
²⁰I E N U M E R A B L E U        R
 O    S    E    C       U
 N    H    K    K   ²¹D E Q U E U E
```

C# Lab

The Quest

This lab gives you a spec that describes a program for you to build, using the knowledge you've gained over the last few chapters.

This project is bigger than the ones you've seen so far. So read the whole thing before you get started, and give yourself a little time. And don't worry if you get stuck—there's nothing new in here, so you can move on in the book and come back to the lab later.

We've filled in a few design details for you, and we've made sure you've got all the pieces you need...and nothing else.

It's up to you to finish the job. You can download an executable for this lab from the website...but we won't give you the code for the answer.

The spec: build an adventure game

Your job is to build an adventure game where a mighty adventurer is on a quest to defeat level after level of deadly enemies. You'll build a **turn-based system**, which means the player makes one move and then the enemies make one move. The player can move **or** attack, and then each enemy gets a chance to move **and** attack. The game keeps going until the player either defeats all the enemies on all seven levels or dies.

The enemies get a bit of an advantage—they move every turn, and after they move they'll attack the player if he's in range.

The game window gives an overhead view of the dungeon where the player fights his enemies.

The player can pick up weapons and potions along the way.

The player and enemies move around in the dungeon.

The player moves using the four Move buttons.

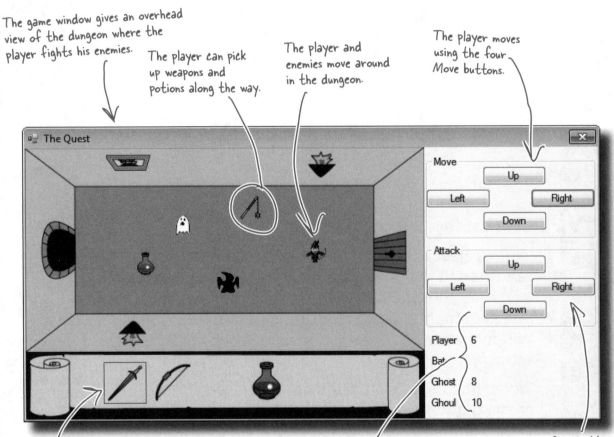

Here's the player's inventory. It shows what items the player's picked up, and draws a box around the item that they're currently using. The player clicks on an item to equip it, and uses the Attack button to use the item.

The game shows you the number of **hit points** for the player and enemies. When the player attacks an enemy, the enemy's hit points go down. Once the hit points get down to zero, the enemy or player dies.

These four buttons are used to attack enemies and drink potions. (The player can use any of the buttons to drink a potion.)

The player picks up weapons...

There are weapons and potions scattered around the dungeon that the player can pick up and use to defeat his enemies. All he has to do is move onto a weapon, and it disappears from the floor and appears in his inventory.

A black box around a weapon means it's currently equipped. Different weapons work differently—they have different ranges, some only attack in one direction while others have a wider range, and they cause different levels of damage to the enemies they hit.

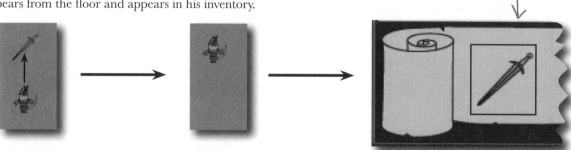

...and attacks enemies with them

Every level in the game has a weapon that the player can pick up and use to defeat his enemies. Once the weapon's picked up, it should disappear from the game floor.

The bat is to the right of the player, so he hits the Right attack button.

The attack causes the bat's hit points to drop, from 6 to 2 in this case.

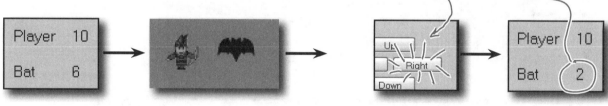

Higher levels bring more enemies

There are three different kinds of enemies: a bat, a ghost, and a ghoul. The first level has only a bat. The seventh level is the last one, and it has all three enemies.

A ghoul moves quickly toward the player, and causes heavy damage when it attacks.

The bat flies around somewhat randomly. When it's near the player, it causes a small amount of damage.

The ghost moves slowly toward the player. As soon as it's close to the player, it attacks and causes a medium amount of damage.

The design: building the form

The form gives the game its unique look. Use the form's
BackgroundImage property to display the image of the dungeon
and the inventory, and a series of PictureBox controls to show
the player, weapons, and enemies in the dungeon. You'll use a
TableLayoutPanel control to display the hit points for the player,
bat, ghost, and ghoul as well as the buttons for moving and attacking.

The dungeon itself is a static image,
displayed using the BackgroundImage
property of the form.

Make sure the
BackgroundImageLayout
property is set to None.

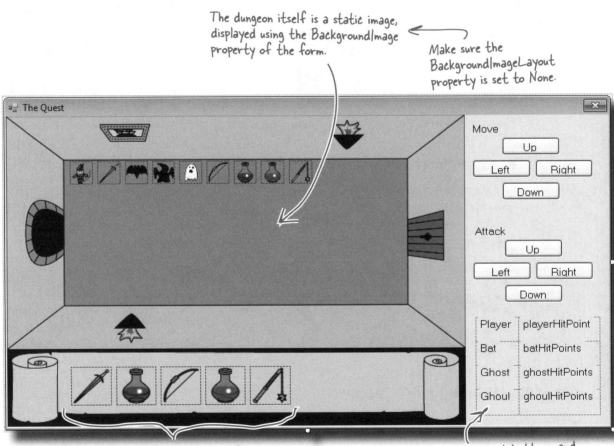

Each of these icons is a PictureBox.

Hit points, movement buttons, and
attack buttons are all displayed in a
TableLayoutPanel.

**Download the background image and the graphics for the
weapons, enemies, and player from the Head First Labs
website: www.headfirstlabs.com/books/hfcsharp**

Everything in the dungeon is a PictureBox

Players, weapons, and enemies should all be represented by icons. Add nine PictureBox controls, and set their Visible properties to False. Then, your game can move around the controls, and toggle their Visible properties as needed.

You can set a PictureBox's BackColor property to Color.Transparent to let the form's background picture or color show through any transparent pixels in the picture.

Add nine PictureBox controls to the dungeon. Use the Size property to make each one 30x30. It doesn't matter where you place them—the form will move them around. Use the little black arrow that shows up when you click on the PictureBox to set each to one of the images from the Head First Labs website.

After you've added the nine PictureBox controls, right-click on the player's icon and select "Bring to Front", then send the three weapon icons to the back. That ensures player icons stay "above" any items that are picked up.

Controls overlap each other in the IDE, so the form needs to know which ones are in front, and which are in back. That's what the "Bring to Front" and "Send to Back" form designer commands do.

The inventory contains PictureBox controls, too

You can represent the inventory of the player as five 50x50 PictureBox controls. Set the BackColor property of each to **Color. Transparent** (if you use the Properties window to set the property, just type it into the BackColor row). Since the picture files have a transparent background, you'll see the scroll and dungeon behind them:

You'll need five more 50x50 PictureBoxes for the inventory.

When the player equips one of the weapons, the form should set the BorderStyle of that weapon icon to FixedSingle and the rest of the icons' BorderStyle to None.

Build your stats window

The hit points are in a TableLayoutPanel, just like the attack and movement buttons. For the hit points, create two columns in the panel, and drag the column divider to the left a bit. Add four rows, each 25% height, and add in Label controls to each of the eight cells:

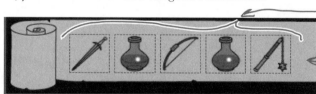

2 columns, 4 rows...8 cells for your hit point statistics.

Each cell has a Label in it, and you can update those values during the game.

The architecture: using the objects

You'll need several types of objects in your game: a `Player` object, several subtypes of an `Enemy` object, and several sub-types of a `Weapon` object. And you'll also need one object to keep up with everything that's going on: the `Game` object.

This is just the general overview. We'll give you a lot more details on how the player and enemies move, how the enemy figures out if it's near the player, etc.

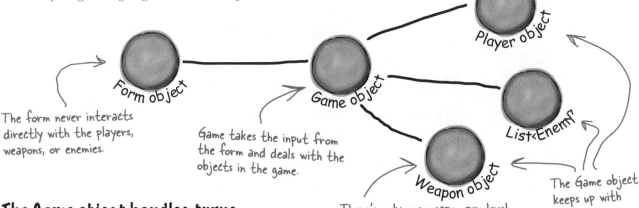

The form never interacts directly with the players, weapons, or enemies.

Game takes the input from the form and deals with the objects in the game.

There's only one weapon per level, so the game just needs a Weapon reference, not a List. The Player, however, has a List<Weapon> to hold the inventory.

The Game object keeps up with players, weapons, and a list of enemies.

The Game object handles turns

When one of your form's move buttons is clicked, the form will call the `Game` object's `Move()` method. That method will let the player take a turn, and then let all the enemies move. So it's up to `Game` to handle the turn-based movement portion of the game.

For example, here's how the move buttons work:

We left the parameters out of this diagram. Each Move() method takes a direction, and some of them take a Random object, too.

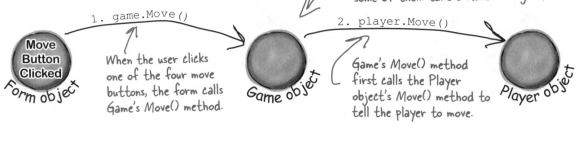

When the user clicks one of the four move buttons, the form calls Game's Move() method.

Game's Move() method first calls the Player object's Move() method to tell the player to move.

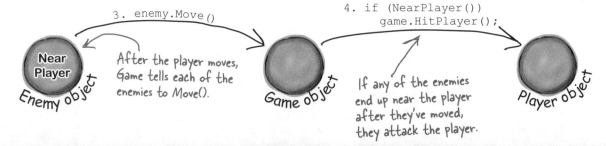

After the player moves, Game tells each of the enemies to Move().

If any of the enemies end up near the player after they've moved, they attack the player.

The form delegates activity to the Game object

Movement, attacking, and inventory all begin in the form. So clicking a movement or attack button, or an item in inventory, triggers code in your form. But it's the Game object that controls the objects in the game. So the form has to pass on anything that happens to the Game object, and then the Game object takes it from there:

Game.Move() calls the enemies' Move() methods, which all take a random reference.

The Form object calls the game's Move(), and then calls its own UpdateCharacters() method to update the screen.

How moving works

`1. Move(Direction.Right, random);`

Move Button Clicked — *Form object*

Use a Direction enum for the four button directions.

`2. UpdateCharacters();`

Game object

Game handles updating locations, so when UpdateCharacters() is called, things are moved to their new locations.

When the player hits an enemy, it causes a random amount of damage (up to a maximum damage limit).

This UpdateCharacters() method is part of the form. It reads the location of the player, enemies, and any weapons currently in the dungeon and moves the PictureBoxes to match them.

How attacking works

`1. Attack(Direction.Right, random);`

Attack Button Clicked — *Form object*

`2. UpdateCharacters();`

Game object

Attacking is like movement...the form calls Attack() on Game, and Game handles dealing with the attack.

The UpdateCharacters() method also checks the player's inventory and makes sure the correct icons are displayed on the inventory scroll.

The inventory scroll displays all of the icons for the items that the player has picked up.

How the inventory scroll works

`if (game.CheckPlayerInventory("Bow")) {`

Inventory Icon Clicked — *Form object*

`game.Equip("Bow");`

`inventoryBow.BorderStyle = BorderStyle.FixedSingle;`

`inventorySword.BorderStyle = BorderStyle.None;`

Game object

All the other weapons' borders should be turned off.

The BorderStyle property highlights the active item in the player's inventory.

The Quest

Building the Game class

We've gotten you started with the Game class in the code below.
There's a lot for you to do—so read through this code carefully, get
it into the IDE, and get ready to go to work:

```
using System.Drawing;
```
You'll need Rectangle and Point from System.Drawing, so be sure to add this to the top of your class.

```
class Game {
    public List<Enemy> Enemies;
    public Weapon WeaponInRoom;
```
These are OK as public properties if Enemy and Weapon are well encapsulated...in other words, just make sure the form can't do anything inappropriate with them.

The game keeps a private Player object. The form will only interact with this through methods on Game, rather than directly.
```
    private Player player;
    public Point PlayerLocation { get { return player.Location; } }
    public int PlayerHitPoints { get { return player.HitPoints; } }
    public List<string> PlayerWeapons { get { return player.Weapons; } }

    private int level = 0;
    public int Level { get { return level; } }
```
The Rectangle object has Top, Bottom, Left, and Right fields, and works perfectly for the overall game area.
```
    private Rectangle boundaries;
    public Rectangle Boundaries { get { return boundaries; } }

    public Game(Rectangle boundaries) {
        this.boundaries = boundaries;
        player = new Player(this,
            new Point(boundaries.Left + 10, boundaries.Top + 70));
    }
```
Game starts out with a bounding box for the dungeon, and creates a new Player object in the dungeon.
```
    public void Move(Direction direction, Random random) {
        player.Move(direction);
        foreach (Enemy enemy in Enemies)
            enemy.Move(random);
    }
```
Movement is simple: move the player in the direction the form gives us, and move each enemy in a random direction.
```
    public void Equip(string weaponName) {
        player.Equip(weaponName);
    }
    public bool CheckPlayerInventory(string weaponName) {
        return player.Weapons.Contains(weaponName);
    }
    public void HitPlayer(int maxDamage, Random random) {
        player.Hit(maxDamage, random);
    }
}
```
These are all great examples of encapsulation.... Game doesn't know how Player handles these actions, it just passes on the needed information and lets Player do the rest.

```
public void IncreasePlayerHealth(int health, Random random) {
  player.IncreaseHealth(health, random);
}
```

Attack() is almost exactly like Move(). The player attacks, and the enemies all get a turn to move.

```
public void Attack(Direction direction, Random random) {
  player.Attack(direction, random);
  foreach (Enemy enemy in Enemies)
    enemy.Move(random);
}
```

GetRandomLocation() will come in handy in the NewLevel() method, which will use it to determine where to place enemies and weapons.

```
private Point GetRandomLocation(Random random) {
  return new Point(boundaries.Left +
    random.Next(boundaries.Right / 10 - boundaries.Left / 10) * 10,
      boundaries.Top +
    random.Next(boundaries.Bottom / 10 - boundaries.Top / 10) * 10);
}
```

This is just a math trick to get a random location within the rectangle that represents the dungeon area.

```
public void NewLevel(Random random) {
  level++;
  switch (level) {
    case 1:
      Enemies = new List<Enemy>();
      Enemies.Add(new Bat(this, GetRandomLocation(random)));
      WeaponInRoom = new Sword(this, GetRandomLocation(random));
      break;
    }
  }
}
```

We only added the case for Level 1. It's your job to add cases for the other levels.

We've only got room in the inventory for one blue potion and one red potion. So if the player already has a red potion, then the game shouldn't add a red potion to the level (and the same goes for the blue potion).

So if the blue potion is still in the player's inventory from Level 2, nothing appears on this level.

Finish the rest of the levels

It's your job to finish the NewLevel() method. Here's the breakdown for each level:

Level	Enemies	Weapons
2	Ghost	Blue potion
3	Ghoul	Bow
4	Bat, Ghost	Bow, if not picked up on 3; otherwise, blue potion
5	Bat, Ghoul	Red potion
6	Ghost, Ghoul	Mace
7	Bat, Ghost, Ghoul	Mace, if not picked up on 6; otherwise, red potion
8	N/A	N/A – end the game with Application.Exit()

This only appears if the red potion from Level 5 has already been used up.

Finding common behavior: movement

You already know that duplicate code is bad, and duplicate code usually shows up when two or more objects share the same behavior. That's the case in the dungeon game, too…both enemies and players move.

Let's create a `Mover` class, to abstract that common behavior into a single place. `Player` and `Enemy` will inherit from `Mover`. And even though weapons don't move around, they inherit from `Mover`, too, because they need some of its properties and methods. `Mover` has a `Move()` method for moving around, and a read-only `Location` property that the form can use to position a subclass of `Mover`.

We added return values and parameters to this class diagram to make it easier for you to see what's going on.

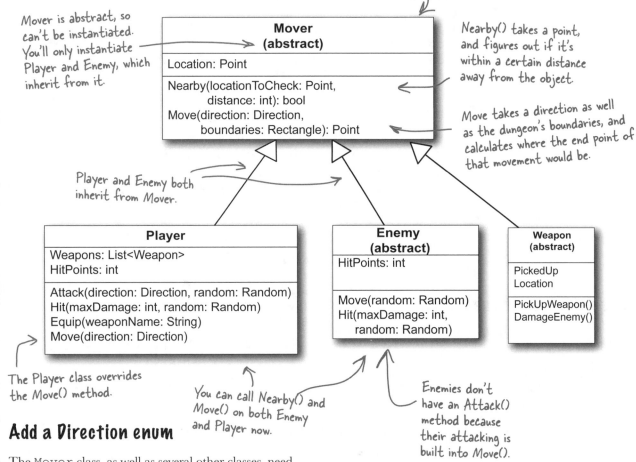

Mover is abstract, so can't be instantiated. You'll only instantiate Player and Enemy, which inherit from it.

Nearby() takes a point, and figures out if it's within a certain distance away from the object.

Move takes a direction as well as the dungeon's boundaries, and calculates where the end point of that movement would be.

Player and Enemy both inherit from Mover.

The Player class overrides the Move() method.

You can call Nearby() and Move() on both Enemy and Player now.

Enemies don't have an Attack() method because their attacking is built into Move().

Add a Direction enum

The `Mover` class, as well as several other classes, need a `Direction` enum. Create this enum, and give it four enumerated values: Up, Down, Left, and Right.

394

The Mover class source code

Here's the code for Mover:

Since protected properties are only available to subclasses, the form object can't set the location...only read it through the public get method we define.

```csharp
abstract class Mover {
  private const int MoveInterval = 10;
  protected Point location;
  public Point Location { get { return location; } }
  protected Game game;

  public Mover(Game game, Point location) {
    this.game = game;
    this.location = location;
  }

  public bool Nearby(Point locationToCheck, int distance) {
    if (Math.Abs(location.X - locationToCheck.X) < distance &&
        (Math.Abs(location.Y - locationToCheck.Y) < distance)) {
      return true;
    } else {
      return false;
    }
  }
  public Point Move(Direction direction, Rectangle boundaries) {
    Point newLocation = location;
    switch (direction) {
      case Direction.Up:
        if (newLocation.Y - MoveInterval >= boundaries.Top)
          newLocation.Y -= MoveInterval;
        break;
      case Direction.Down:
        if (newLocation.Y + MoveInterval <= boundaries.Bottom)
          newLocation.Y += MoveInterval;
        break;
      case Direction.Left:
        if (newLocation.X - MoveInterval >= boundaries.Left)
          newLocation.X -= MoveInterval;
        break;
      case Direction.Right:
        if (newLocation.X + MoveInterval <= boundaries.Right)
          newLocation.X += MoveInterval;
        break;
      default: break;
    }
    return newLocation;
  }
}
```

Instances of Mover take in the Game object and a current location.

The Nearby method checks a Point against this object's current location. If they're within distance of each other, then it returns true; otherwise, it returns false.

The Move() method tries to move one step in a direction. If it can, it returns the new Point. If it hits a boundary, it returns the original Point.

If the end location is outside the boundaries, the new location stays the same as the starting point.

Finally, this new location is returned (which might still be the same as the starting location!).

The Player class keeps track of the player

Here's a start on the Player class. Start with this code in the IDE, and then get ready to add to it.

The Player and Enemy objects need to stay inside the dungeon, which means they need to know the boundaries of the playing area. Use the Contains() method of the boundaries Rectangle to make sure they don't move out of bounds.

```
class Player : Mover {
  private Weapon equippedWeapon;
  private int hitPoints;
  public int HitPoints { get { return hitPoints; } }

  private List<Weapon> inventory = new List<Weapon>();
  public List<string> Weapons {
    get {
      List<string> names = new List<string>();
      foreach (Weapon weapon in inventory)
        names.Add(weapon.Name);
      return names;
    }
  }

  public Player(Game game, Point location);
          : base(game, location) {
    hitPoints = 10;
  }

  public void Hit(int maxDamage, Random random) {
    hitPoints -= random.Next(1, maxDamage);
  }

  public void IncreaseHealth(int health, Random random) {
    hitPoints += random.Next(1, health);
  }

  public void Equip(string weaponName) {
    foreach (Weapon weapon in inventory) {
      if (weapon.Name == weaponName)
        equippedWeapon = weapon;
    }
  }
}
```

All of the properties of Player are hidden from direct access.

A Player can hold multiple weapons in inventory, but can only equip one at a time.

Player inherits from Mover, so this passes in the Game and location to that base class.

The player's constructor sets its hitPoints to 10 and then calls the base class constructor.

When an enemy hits the player, it causes a random amount of damage. And when a potion increases the player's health, it increases it by a random amount.

The Equip() method tells the player to equip one of his weapons. The Game object calls this method when one of the inventory icons is clicked.

A Player object can only have one Weapon object equipped at a time.

Even though potions help the player rather than hurt the enemy, they're still **considered weapons** by the game. That way the inventory can be a List<Weapon>, and the game can point to one with its WeaponInRoom reference.

Write the Move() method for the Player

Game calls the Player's Move() method to tell a player to move in a certain direction. Move() takes the direction to move as an argument (using the Direction enum you should have already added). Here's the start of that method:

This happens when one of the movement buttons on the form is clicked.

```
public void Move(Direction direction) {
    base.location = Move(direction, game.Boundaries);
    if (!game.WeaponInRoom.PickedUp) {
        // see if the weapon is nearby, and possibly pick it up
    }
}
```

Move is in the Mover base class.

When the player picks up a weapon, it needs to disappear from the dungeon and appear in the inventory.

You've got to fill in the rest of this method. Check and see if the weapon is near the player (within a single unit of distance). If so, pick up the weapon and add it to the player's inventory.

If the weapon is the only weapon the player has, go ahead and equip it immediately. That way, the player can use it right away, on the next turn.

The Weapon and form will handle making the weapon's PictureBox invisible when the player picks it up... that's not the job of the Player class.

Add an Attack() method, too

The weapons all have an Attack() method that takes a Direction enum and a Random object. The player's Attack() will figure out which weapon is equipped and call its Attack().

Next up is the Attack() method. This is called when one of the form's attack buttons is clicked, and carries with it a direction (again, from the Direction enum). Here's the method signature:

```
public void Attack(Direction direction, Random random) {
    // Your code goes here
}
```

If the weapon is a potion, then Attack() removes it from the inventory after the player drinks it.

If the player doesn't have an equipped weapon, this method won't do anything. If the player does have an equipped weapon, this should call the weapon's Attack() method.

But potions are a special case. If a potion is used, remove it from the player's inventory, since it's not available anymore.

Potions will implement an IPotion interface (more on that in a minute), so you can use the "is" keyword to see if a Weapon is an implementation of IPotion.

Bats, ghosts, and ghouls inherit from the Enemy class

We'll give you another useful abstract class: Enemy. Each different sort of enemy has its own class that inherits from the Enemy class. The different kinds of enemies move in different ways, so the Enemy abstract class leaves the Move method as an abstract method—the three enemy classes will need to implement it differently, depending on how they move.

Enemy (abstract)
HitPoints: int
Move(random: Random) Hit(maxDamage: int, random: Random)

```
abstract class Enemy : Mover {
    private const int NearPlayerDistance = 25;
    private int hitPoints;
    public int HitPoints { get { return hitPoints; } }
    public bool Dead { get {
        if (hitPoints <= 0) return true;
        else return false;
    }
}
    public Enemy(Game game, Point location, int hitPoints)
            : base(game, location) { this.hitPoints = hitPoints; }

    public abstract void Move(Random random);

    public void Hit(int maxDamage, Random random) {
        hitPoints -= random.Next(1, maxDamage);
    }

    protected bool NearPlayer() {
        return (Nearby(game.PlayerLocation,
                    NearPlayerDistance));
    }
    protected Direction FindPlayerDirection(Point playerLocation) {
        Direction directionToMove;
        if (playerLocation.X > location.X + 10)
            directionToMove = Direction.Right;
        else if (playerLocation.X < location.X - 10)
            directionToMove = Direction.Left;
        else if (playerLocation.Y < location.Y - 10)
            directionToMove = Direction.Up;
        else
            directionToMove = Direction.Down;
        return directionToMove;
    }
}
```

The form can use this read-only property to see if the enemy should be visible in the game dungeon.

Each subclass of Enemy implements this.

When the player attacks an enemy, it calls the enemy's Hit() method, which subtracts a random number from the hit points.

The Enemy class inherited the Nearby() method from Mover, which it can use to figure out whether it's near the player.

If you feed FindPlayerDirection() the player's location, it'll use the base class's location field to figure out where the player is in relation to the enemy and return a Direction enum that tells you in which direction the enemy needs to move in order to move toward the player.

Write the different Enemy subclasses

The three Enemy subclasses are pretty straightforward. Each enemy has a
different number of starting hit points, moves differently, and does a different
amount of damage when it attacks. You'll need to have each one pass a different
startingHitPoints parameter to the Enemy base constructor, and you'll have
to write different Move() methods for each subclass.

Here's an example of how one of those classes might look:

```
class Bat : Enemy {
    public Bat(Game game, Point location)
        : base(game, location, 6)
    { }
    public override void Move(Random random) {
        // Your code will go here
    }
}
```

The bat starts with 6 hit points, so it
passes 6 to the base class constructor.

You probably won't need any constructor for
these; the base class handles everything.

Each of these subclasses the
Enemy base class, which in turn
subclasses Mover.

The bat flies around
somewhat randomly, so
it uses Random to fly
in a random direction
half the time.

Once an enemy has no more hit points,
the form will no longer display it. But
it'll still be in the game's Enemies list
until the player finishes the level.

Bat
Move()

The bat starts with 6 hit points. It'll keep moving toward the player
and attacking **as long as it has one or more hit points.** When it
moves, there's a 50% chance that it'll move toward the player, and a
50% chance that it'll move in a random direction. After the bat moves,
it checks if it's near the player—if it is, then it attacks the player with
up to 2 hit points of damage.

We'll have to make
sure the form
sees if an enemy
should be visible
at every turn.

Ghost
Move()

The ghost is harder to defeat than the bat, but like the bat, it will only
move and attack if its hit points are greater than zero. It starts with 8
hit points. When it moves, there's a 1 in 3 chance that it'll move toward
the player, and a 2 in 3 chance that it'll stand still. If it's near the player,
it attacks the player with up to 3 hit points of damage.

The ghost
and ghoul use
Random to make
them move more
slowly than the
player.

Ghoul
Move()

The ghoul is the toughest enemy. It starts with 10 hit points, and only
moves and attacks if its hit points are greater than zero. When it moves,
there's a 2 in 3 chance that it'll move toward the player, and a 1 in 3
chance that it'll stand still. If it's near the player, it attacks the player
with up to 4 hit points of damage.

Weapon inherits from Mover, each weapon inherits from Weapon

Weapon inherits from Mover because it uses its Nearby() and Move() methods in DamageEnemy().

We need a base Weapon class, just like we had a base Enemy class. And each weapon has a location, as well as a property indicating whether or not it's been picked up. Here's the base Weapon class:

```
abstract class Weapon : Mover {

  protected Game game;
  private bool pickedUp;
  public bool PickedUp { get { return pickedUp; } }
  private Point location;
  public Point Location { get { return location; } }

  public Weapon(Game game, Point location) {
    this.game = game;
    this.location = location;
    pickedUp = false;
  }

  public void PickUpWeapon() { pickedUp = true; }

  public abstract string Name { get; }

  public abstract void Attack(Direction direction, Random random);

  protected bool DamageEnemy(Direction direction, int radius,
                             int damage, Random random) {
    Point target = game.PlayerLocation;
    for (int distance = 0; distance < radius; distance++) {
      foreach (Enemy enemy in game.Enemies) {
        if (Nearby(enemy.Location, target, radius)) {
          enemy.Hit(damage, random);
          return true;
        }
      }
      target = Move(direction, target, game.Boundaries);
    }
    return false;
  }
}
```

A pickedUp weapon shouldn't be displayed anymore...the form can use this get accessor to figure that out.

Every weapon has a location in the game dungeon.

The constructor sets the game and location fields, and sets pickedUp to false (because it hasn't been picked up yet).

Each weapon class needs to implement a Name property and an Attack() method that determines how that weapon attacks.

Each weapon's Name property returns its name ("Sword", "Mace", "Bow").

Each weapon has a different range and pattern of attack, so the weapons implement the Attack() method differently.

The Nearby() method in the Mover class only takes two parameters, a Point and an int, and it compares the Point to the Mover field location. You'll need to add an overloaded Nearby() that's almost identical, except that it takes three parameters, two Points and a distance, which compares the first Point to the second Point (instead of location).

The DamageEnemy() method is called by Attack(). It attempts to find an enemy in a certain direction and radius. If it does, it calls the enemy's Hit() method and returns true. If no enemy's found, it returns false.

Different weapons attack in different ways

Each subclass of `Weapon` has its own name and attack logistic. Your job is to implement these classes. Here's the basic skeleton for a `Weapon` subclass:

```
class Sword : Weapon {

    public Sword(Game game, Point location)
        : base(game, location) { }

    public override string Name { get { return "Sword"; } }

    public override void Attack(Direction direction, Random random) {
        // Your code goes here
    }
}
```

Each subclass represents one of the three weapons: a sword, bow, or mace.

Each subclass relies on the base class to do the initialization work.

You're basically hardcoding in the name of each weapon.

The player can use the weapons over and over—they never get dropped or used up.

The Game object will pass on the direction to attack in.

Sword

Name
Attack()

The sword is the first weapon the player picks up. It's got a wide angle of attack: if he attacks up, then it first tries to attack an enemy that's in that direction—if there's no enemy there, it looks in the direction that's clockwise from the original attack and attacks any enemy there, and if it still fails to hit then it attempts to attack an enemy counterclockwise from the original direction of attack. It's got a radius of 10, and causes 3 points of damage.

Think carefully about this...what is to the right of the direction left? What is to the left of up?

Bow

Name
Attack()

The bow has a very narrow angle of attack, but it's got a very long range—it's got an attack radius of 30, but only causes 1 point of damage. Unlike the sword, which attacks in three directions (because the player swings it in a wide arc), when the player shoots the bow in a direction, it only shoots in that one direction.

Mace

Name
Attack()

The mace is the most powerful weapon in the dungeon. It doesn't matter in which direction the player attacks with it—since he swings it in a full circle, it'll attack any enemy within a radius of 20 and cause up to 6 points of damage.

The different weapons will call DamageEnemy() in various ways. The Mace attacks in all directions, so if the player's attacking to the right, it'll call DamageEnemy(Direction.Right, 20, 6, random). If that didn't hit an enemy, it'll attack Up. If there's no enemy there, it'll try Left, then Down—that makes it swing in a full circle.

401

Potions implement the IPotion interface

There are two potions, a blue potion and a red potion, which increase the player's health. They act just like weapons—the player picks them up in the dungeon, equips them by clicking on the inventory, and **uses them by clicking one of the attack buttons**. So it makes sense for them to inherit from the abstract Weapon class.

But potions act a little differently, too, so you'll need to add an IPotion interface so they can have extra behavior: increasing the player's health. The IPotion interface is really simple. Potions only need to add one read-only property called Used that returns false if the player hasn't used the potion, and true if he has. The form will use it to determine whether or not to display the potion in the inventory.

```
interface IPotion {
    bool Used { get; }
}
```

IPotion makes potions usable only once. It's also possible to find out if a Weapon is a potion with "if (weapon is IPotion)" because of this interface.

The potions inherit from the Weapon class because they're used just like weapons—the player clicks on the potion in the inventory scroll to equip it, and then clicks any of the attack buttons to use it.

Weapon (abstract)

PickedUp
Location

PickUpWeapon()
DamageEnemy()

IPotion (interface)

Used

RedPotion

Name

Attack()

BluePotion

Name

Attack()

You should be able to write these classes using this class diagram and the information below.

BluePotion

Name

Attack()

The BluePotion class's Name property should return the string "Blue Potion". Its Attack() method will be called when the player uses the blue potion—it should increase the player's health by up to 5 hit points by calling the IncreasePlayerHealth() method. After the player uses the potion, the potion's Used() method should return true.

If the player picks up a blue potion on level 2, uses it, and then picks up another one on level 4, the game will end up creating two different BluePotion instances.

RedPotion

Name

Attack()

The RedPotion class is very similar to BluePotion, except that its Name property returns the string "Red Potion", and its Attack() method increases the player's health by up to 10 hit points.

The form brings it all together

There's one instance of the Game object, and it lives as a private field of your form. It's created in the form's Load event, and the various event handlers in the form use the fields and methods on the Game object to keep the game play going.

Everything begins with the form's Load event handler, which passes the Game a Rectangle that defines the boundaries of the dungeon play area. Here's some form code to get you going:

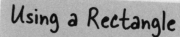

> ## Using a Rectangle
>
> You'll find a lot of Rectangles any time you work with forms. You can create one by passing it X, Y, Width, and Height values, or two Points (for opposite corners). Once you've got a rectangle instance, you can also access its Left, Right, Top, and Bottom, as well as its X, Y, Width, and Height values.

```
private Game game;
private Random random = new Random();
private void Form1_Load(object sender,
                        EventArgs e) {
    game = new Game(new Rectangle(78, 57, 420, 155));
    game.NewLevel(random);
    UpdateCharacters();
}
```

These are the boundaries of the dungeon in the background image you'll download and add to the form.

Remember to double-click on each PictureBox so the IDE adds a separate event handler method for each of them.

The form has a separate event handler for each of these PictureBox's Click events. When the player clicks on the sword, it first checks to make sure the sword is in the player's inventory using the Game object's CheckPlayerInventory() method. If the player's holding the sword, the form calls game.Equip() to equip it. It then sets each PictureBox's BorderStyle property to draw a box around the sword, and make sure none of the other icons has a box around it.

There's an event handler for each of the four movement buttons. They're pretty simple. First the button calls game.Move() with the appropriate Direction value, and then it calls the form's UpdateCharacters() method.

Make sure you change the buttons back when the player equips the sword, bow, or mace.

The four attack button event handlers are also really simple. Each button calls game.Attack(), and then calls the form's UpdateCharacters() method. If the player equips a potion, it's still used the same way—by calling game.Attack()—but potions have no direction. So make the Left, Right, and Down buttons invisible when the player equips a potion, and change the text on the Up button to say "Drink".

The form's UpdateCharacters() method moves the PictureBoxes into position

The last piece of the puzzle is the form's `UpdateCharacters()` method. Once all the objects have moved and acted on each other, the form updates everything…so weapons that been dropped have their `PictureBoxes`' `Visible` properties set to false, enemies and players are drawn in their new locations (and dead ones are made invisible), and inventory is updated.

Here's what you need to do:

 Update the player's position and stats

The first thing you'll do is update the player's `PictureBox` location and the label that shows his hit points. Then you'll need a few variables to determine whether you've shown each of the various enemies.

```
public void UpdateCharacters() {
   Player.Location = game.PlayerLocation;
   playerHitPoints.Text =
     game.PlayerHitPoints.ToString();

   bool showBat = false;
   bool showGhost = false;
   bool showGhoul = false;
   int enemiesShown = 0;
   // more code to go here...
```

> The showBat variable will be set to true if we made the bat's PictureBox visible. Same goes for showGhost and showGhoul.

② Update each enemy's location and hit points

Each enemy could be in a new location and have a different set of hit points. You need to update each enemy after you've updated the player's location:

```
foreach (Enemy enemy in game.Enemies) {
   if (enemy is Bat) {
     bat.Location = enemy.Location;
     batHitPoints.Text = enemy.HitPoints.ToString();
     if (enemy.HitPoints > 0) {
       showBat = true;
       enemiesShown++;
     }
   }
}
// etc...
```

> ← This goes right after the code from above.

> This will affect the visibility of the enemy PictureBox controls in just a bit.

> You'll need two more if statements like this in your foreach loop—one for the ghost and one for the ghoul.

Once you've looped through all the enemies on the level, check the `showBat` variable. If the bat was killed, then `showBat` will still be false, so make its `PictureBox` invisible and clear its hit points label. Then do the same for `showGhost` and `showGhoul`.

③ Update the weapon PictureBoxes

Declare a `weaponControl` variable and use a big `switch` statement to set it equal to the `PictureBox` that corresponds to the weapon in the room.

```
sword.Visible = false;
bow.Visible = false;
redPotion.Visible = false;
bluePotion.Visible = false;
mace.Visible = false;
Control weaponControl = null;
switch (game.WeaponInRoom.Name) {
    case "Sword":
        weaponControl = sword; break;
```

Make sure your controls' names match these names. It's easy to end up with bugs that are difficult to track down if they don't match.

You'll have more cases for each weapon type.

The rest of the cases should set the variable `weaponControl` to the correct control on the form. After the `switch`, set `weaponControl.Visible` to `true` to display it.

④ Set the Visible property on each inventory icon PictureBox

Check the Game object's `CheckPlayerInventory()` method to figure out whether or not to display the various inventory icons.

⑤ Here's the rest of the method

The rest of the method does three things. First it checks to see if the player's already picked up the weapon in the room, so it knows whether or not to display it. Then it checks to see if the player died. And finally, it checks to see if the player's defeated all of the enemies. If he has, then the player advances to the next level.

```
weaponControl.Location = game.WeaponInRoom.Location;
if (game.WeaponInRoom.PickedUp) {
    weaponControl.Visible = false;
} else {
    weaponControl.Visible = true;
}
if (game.PlayerHitPoints <= 0) {
    MessageBox.Show("You died");
    Application.Exit();
}
if (enemiesShown < 1) {
    MessageBox.Show("You have defeated the enemies on this level");
    game.NewLevel(random);
    UpdateCharacters();
}
```

Every level has one weapon. If it's been picked up, we need to make its icon invisible.

Application.Exit() immediately quits the program. It's part of System.Windows.Forms, so you'll need the appropriate using statement if you want to use it outside of a form.

If there are no more enemies on the level, then the player's defeated them all and it's time to go to the next level.

The fun's just beginning!

Seven levels, three enemies…that's a pretty decent game. But you can make it even better. Here are a few ideas to get you started.…

Make the enemies smarter
Can you figure out how to change the enemies' Move() methods so that they're harder to defeat? Then see if you can change their constants to properties, and add a way to change them in the game.

Add more levels
The game doesn't have to end after seven levels. See if you can add more…can you figure out how to make the game go on indefinitely? If the player does win, make a cool ending animation with dancing ghosts and bats! And the game ends pretty abruptly if the player dies. Can you think of a more user-friendly ending? Maybe you can let the user restart the game or retry his last level.

Add different kinds of enemies
You don't need to limit the dangers to ghouls, ghosts, and bats. See if you can add more enemies to the game.

Add more weapons
The player will definitely need more help defeating any new enemies you've added. Think of new ways that the weapons can attack, or different things that potions can do. Take advantage of the fact that Weapon is a subclass of Mover—make magic weapons the player has to chase around!

Add more graphics
You can go to **www.headfirstlabs.com/books/hfcsharp/** to find more graphics files for additional enemies, weapons, and other images to help spark your imagination.

Make it an action game
Here's an interesting challenge. Can you figure out how to use the KeyDown event and Timer you used in the Key Game in Chapter 4 to change this from a turn-based game into an action game?

This is your chance to show off! Did you come up with a cool new version of the game? Join the Head First C# forum and claim your bragging rights: www.headfirstlabs.com/books/hfcsharp/

9 reading and writing files

Save the byte array, save the world

> OK, go ahead with our shopping list...chicken wire...tequila...grape jelly...bandages...yes, dear, **I am** writing this down.

Sometimes it pays to be a little persistent.

So far, all of your programs have been pretty short-lived. They fire up, run for a while, and shut down. But that's not always enough, especially when you're dealing with important information. You need to be able to **save your work**. In this chapter, we'll look at how to **write data to a file**, and then how to **read that information back in** from a file. You'll learn about the .NET **stream classes**, and also take a look at the mysteries of **hexadecimal** and **binary**.

.NET uses streams to read and write data

A **stream** is the .NET Framework's way of getting data in and out of your program. Any time your program reads or writes a file, connects to another computer over a network, or generally does anything where it **sends or receives bytes** from one place to another, you're using streams.

Whenever you want to read data from a file or write data to a file, you'll use a Stream object.

Let's say you have a simple program—a form with an event handler that needs to read data from a file. You'll use a Stream object to do it.

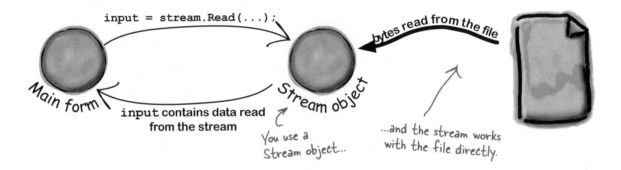

input = stream.Read(...);

input contains data read from the stream

Main form

Stream object

You use a Stream object...

...and the stream works with the file directly.

bytes read from the file

And if your program needs to write data out to the file, it can use another Stream object.

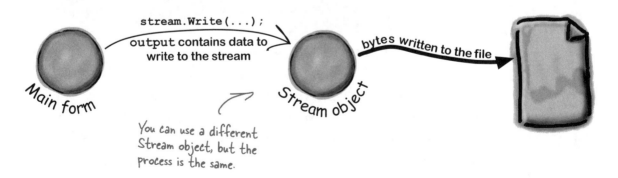

stream.Write(...);

output contains data to write to the stream

Main form

Stream object

You can use a different Stream object, but the process is the same.

bytes written to the file

Different streams read and write different things

Every stream is a subclass of the abstract **Stream** class, and there are a bunch of built-in stream classes to do different things. We'll be concentrating on reading and writing regular files, but everything you learn in this chapter will just as easily apply to compressed or encrypted files, or network streams that don't use files at all.

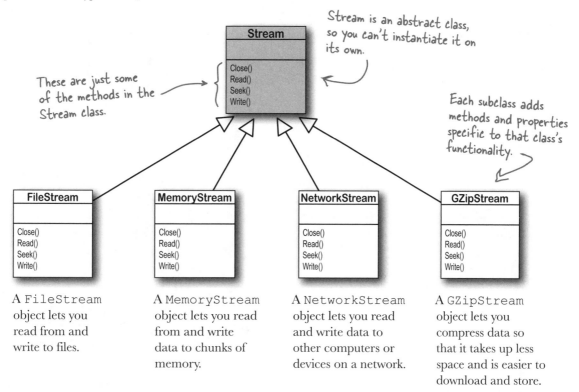

Stream is an abstract class, so you can't instantiate it on its own.

These are just some of the methods in the Stream class.

Each subclass adds methods and properties specific to that class's functionality.

A `FileStream` object lets you read from and write to files.

A `MemoryStream` object lets you read from and write data to chunks of memory.

A `NetworkStream` object lets you read and write data to other computers or devices on a network.

A `GZipStream` object lets you compress data so that it takes up less space and is easier to download and store.

Things you can do with a stream:

1 **Write to the stream.**
You can write your data to a stream through a stream's `Write()` method.

2 **Read from the stream.**
You can use the `Read()` method to get data from a file, or a network, or memory, or just about anything else, using a stream.

3 **Change your position within the stream.**
Most streams support a `Seek()` method that lets you find a position within the stream so you can read or insert data at a specific place.

Streams let you read and write data. Use the right kind of stream for the data you're working with.

A FileStream reads and writes bytes to a file

When your program needs to write a few lines of text
to a file, there are a lot of things that have to happen:

Make sure you add using System. IO; to any program that uses streams.

1 Create a new `FileStream` object and tell it to write to the file.

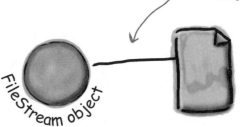

A FileStream can only be attached to one file at a time.

2 The `FileStream` attaches itself to a file.

3 Streams write bytes to files, so you'll need to convert the string that you
want to write to an array of `bytes`.

*This is called **encoding**, and we'll talk more about it later on...*

Eureka! →

```
69 117 114 101 107 97 33
 0   1   2   3   4  5  6
```

4 Call the stream's `Write()` method and pass it the `byte` array.

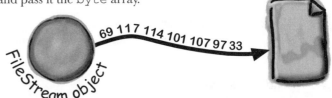

`69 117 114 101 107 97 33`

5 Close the stream so other programs can access the file.

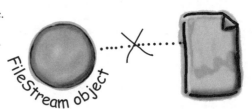

*Forgetting to close a stream is a **big deal**. Otherwise, the file will be locked, and other programs won't be able to use it until you close your stream.*

How to write text to a file in 3 simple steps

StreamWriter creates and manages a FileStream object for you automatically.

C# comes with a convenient class called **StreamWriter** that does all of those things in one easy step. All you have to do is create a new StreamWriter object and give it a filename. It **automatically** creates a FileStream and opens the file. Then you can use the StreamWriter's Write() and WriteLine() methods to write everything to the file you want.

① **Use the StreamWriter's constructor to open or create a file**

You can pass a filename to the StreamWriter() constructor. When you do, the writer automatically opens the file. StreamWriter also has an overloaded constructor that takes a bool: true if you want to add text to the end of an existing file (or append), or false if you want to delete the existing file and create a new file with the same name.

```
StreamWriter writer = new StreamWriter(@"C:\newfiles\toaster oven.txt", true);
```

Putting @ in front of the filename tells C# to treat this as a literal string without escape characters like \t for tab or \n for newline.

② **Use the Write() and WriteLine() methods to write to the file**

These methods work just like the ones in Console: Write() writes text, and WriteLine() writes text and adds a line break to the end. If you include "{0}", "{1}", "{2}", etc., inside the string you're writing, the methods include parameters in the strings being written: "{0}" is replaced with the first parameter after the string being written, "{1}" is replaced with the second, etc.

```
writer.WriteLine("The {0} is set to {1} degrees.", appliance, temp);
```

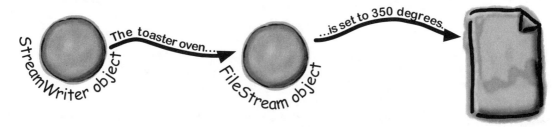

③ **Call the Close() method to release the file**

If you leave the stream open and attached to a file, then it'll keep the file locked open and no other program will be able to use it. So make sure you always close your files!

```
writer.Close();
```

The Swindler launches another diabolical plan

The citizens of Objectville have long lived in fear of the Swindler. Now he's using a `StreamWriter` to implement another evil plan. Let's take a look at what's going on. Create a new Console Application and add this to the `Main()` method::

> *It's probably not a good idea to write to your root folder, and your OS might not even let you do it. So pick another directory you want to write to.*

> *This line creates the StreamWriter object and tells it where the file will be.*

> *The path starts with an @ sign so that the StreamWriter doesn't interpret the "\" as the start of an escape sequence.*

```
StreamWriter sw = new StreamWriter(@"C:\secret_plan.txt");
sw.WriteLine("How I'll defeat Captain Amazing");
sw.WriteLine("Another genius secret plan by The Swindler");
sw.Write("I'll create an army of clones and ");
sw.WriteLine("unleash them upon the citizens of Objectville.");
string location = "the mall";
for (int number = 0; number <= 6; number++){
    sw.WriteLine("Clone #{0} attacks {1}", number, location);
    if (location == "the mall") { location = "downtown"; }
    else { location = "the mall"; }
}
sw.Close();
```

> *WriteLine() adds a new line after writing. Write() sends just the text, with no extra line feeds at the end.*

> *Can you figure out what's going on with the location variable in this code?*

> *Close() frees up any connections to the file and any resources the StreamWriter is using. The text doesn't get written if you don't close the stream.*

> *You can use the {} within the text to pass in variables to the string being written. {0} is replaced by the first parameter after the string, {1} by the second, and so on.*

> *This is what the above code produces.*

StreamWriter is in the System.IO namespace, so make sure you add "using System.IO;" to the top of your program.

```
secret_plan - Notepad
File  Edit  Format    Help
How I'll defeat Captain Amazing
Another genius secret plan by The Swindler
I'll create an army of clones and unleash them upon the citizens of Objectville.
Clone #0 attacks the mall
Clone #1 attacks downtown
Clone #2 attacks the mall
Clone #3 attacks downtown
Clone #4 attacks the mall
Clone #5 attacks downtown
Clone #6 attacks the mall
```

StreamWriter Magnets

Suppose you have the code for `button1_Click()` shown below. Your job is to use the magnets to build code for the Flobbo class so that when the event handler is called, it produces the output shown at the bottom of the page. Good luck!

```
private void button1_Click(object sender, EventArgs e) {
    Flobbo f = new Flobbo("blue yellow");
    StreamWriter sw = f.Snobbo();
    f.Blobbo(f.Blobbo(f.Blobbo(sw), sw), sw);
}
```

```
sw.WriteLine(Zap);
Zap = "red orange";
return true;
```

```
}
```

```
sw.WriteLine(Zap);
sw.Close();
return false;
```

```
public bool Blobbo
        (bool Already, StreamWriter sw) {
```

```
public bool Blobbo(StreamWriter sw) {
```

```
sw.WriteLine(Zap);
Zap = "green purple";
return false;
```

```
}
```

```
return new
    StreamWriter("macaw.txt");
```

```
}
```

```
}
```

```
}
```

```
private string Zap;

public Flobbo(string Zap) {
    this.Zap = Zap;
}
```

```
class Flobbo {
```

```
if (Already) {
```

```
} else {
```

```
public StreamWriter Snobbo() {
```

Output:

```
macaw.txt - Notepad
File  Edit  Format  View  Help
blue yellow
green purple
red orange
```

StreamWriter Magnets Solution

Your job was to construct the Flobbo class from the magnets
to create the desired output.

```
private void button1_Click(object sender, EventArgs e) {
    Flobbo f = new Flobbo("blue yellow");
    StreamWriter sw = f.Snobbo();
    f.Blobbo(f.Blobbo(f.Blobbo(sw), sw), sw);
}
```

Just a reminder: we picked
intentionally weird variable
names and methods in these
puzzles because if we used
really good names, the
puzzle would be too easy!
Don't use names like this in
your code, ok?

```
class Flobbo {

    private string Zap;

    public Flobbo(string Zap) {
        this.Zap = Zap;
    }

    public StreamWriter Snobbo() {

        return new
            StreamWriter("macaw.txt");
    }

    public bool Blobbo(StreamWriter sw) {

        sw.WriteLine(Zap);
        Zap = "green purple";
        return false;
    }

    public bool Blobbo
        (bool Already, StreamWriter sw) {

        if (Already) {

            sw.WriteLine(Zap);
            sw.Close();
            return false;

        } else {

            sw.WriteLine(Zap);
            Zap = "red orange";
            return true;
        }
    }
}
```

The Blobbo() method
is overloaded—it's got
two declarations with
different parameters.

Make sure you close
files when you're done
with them.

Output:

macaw - Notepad

File   Edit   Format   View   Help

blue yellow
green purple
red orange

Reading and writing using <u>two</u> objects

Let's read Swindler's secret plans with another stream, a `StreamReader`. `StreamReader` works just like `StreamWriter`, except instead of writing a file you give the reader the name of the file to read in its constructor. The `ReadLine()` method returns a string that contains the next line from the file. You can write a loop that reads lines from it until its `EndOfStream` field is true—that's when it runs out of lines to read:

```
StreamReader reader =
    new StreamReader(@"c:\secret_plan.txt");
StreamWriter writer =
    new StreamWriter(@"c:\emailToCaptainAmazing.txt");
```

Pass the file you want to read from into the StreamReader's constructor.

This program uses a StreamReader to read the Swindler's plan, and a StreamWriter to write a file that will get emailed to Captain Amazing.

```
writer.WriteLine("To: CaptainAmazing@objectville.net");
writer.WriteLine("From: Commissioner@objectiville.net");
writer.WriteLine("Subject: Can you save the day... again?");
writer.WriteLine();
writer.WriteLine("We've discovered the Swindler's plan:");
while (!reader.EndOfStream) {
    string lineFromThePlan = reader.ReadLine();
    writer.WriteLine("The plan -> " + lineFromThePlan);
}
writer.WriteLine();
writer.WriteLine("Can you help us?");
writer.Close();
reader.Close();
```

An empty WriteLine() method writes a blank line.

EndOfStream is the property that tells you if there's no data left unread in the file.

This loop reads a line from the reader and writes it out to the writer.

Make sure to close every stream that you open, even if you're just reading a file.

The StreamReader and StreamWriter opened up their own streams when you instantiated them. Calling their Close() methods tells them to close those streams.

```
emailToCaptainAmazing - Notepad
File  Edit       View  Help
To: CaptainAmazing@objectville.net
From: Commissioner@objectiville.net
Subject: Can you save the day... again?

We've discovered the Swindler's plan:
The plan -> How I'll defeat Captain Amazing
The plan -> Another genius secret plan by The Swindler
The plan -> I'll create an army of clones and unleash them upon the citizens of objectville.
The plan -> Clone #0 attacks the mall
The plan -> Clone #1 attacks downtown
The plan -> Clone #2 attacks the mall
The plan -> Clone #3 attacks downtown
The plan -> Clone #4 attacks the mall
The plan -> Clone #5 attacks downtown
The plan -> Clone #6 attacks the mall

Can you help us?
```

Data can go through <u>more</u> <u>than</u> <u>one</u> stream

One big advantage to working with streams in .NET is that you can have your data go through more than one stream on its way to its final destination. One of the many types of streams that .NET ships with is the CryptoStream class. This lets you encrypt your data before you do anything else with it:

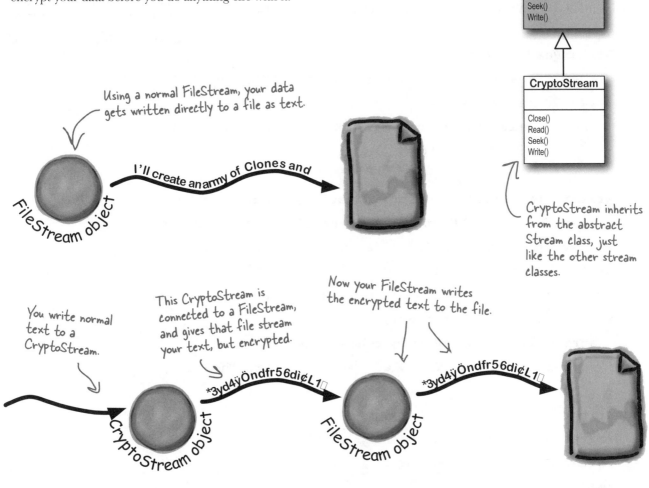

Using a normal FileStream, your data gets written directly to a file as text.

I'll create an army of Clones and

FileStream object

Stream

Close()
Read()
Seek()
Write()

CryptoStream

Close()
Read()
Seek()
Write()

CryptoStream inherits from the abstract Stream class, just like the other stream classes.

You write normal text to a CryptoStream.

This CryptoStream is connected to a FileStream, and gives that file stream your text, but encrypted.

Now your FileStream writes the encrypted text to the file.

*3yd4ÿÖndfr56di¢L1

CryptoStream object

FileStream object

*3yd4ÿÖndfr56di¢L1

You can <u>CHAIN</u> streams. One stream can write to another stream, which writes to another stream...often ending with a network or file stream.

Pool Puzzle

Your **job** is to take code snippets from the pool and place them into the blank lines in the program. You can use the same snippet more than once, and you won't need to use all the snippets. Your **goal** is to make the program produce the output shown to the right.

```
order - Notepad                    _ □ X
File  Edit  Format  View  Help
West
East
South
North
That's all folks!
```

```
class Pineapple {
  const _____ d = "delivery.txt";
  public _____ _____
       { North, South, East, West, Flamingo }
  public static void Main() {
       _____ o = new _____("order.txt");
    Pizza pz = new Pizza(new _____(d, true));
    pz._____(Fargo.Flamingo);
    for (_____ w = 3; w >= 0; w--) {
      Pizza i = new Pizza
             (new _____(d, false));
      i.Idaho((Fargo)w);
      Party p = new Party(new _____(d));
      p._____(o);
    }
    o._____("That's all folks!");
    o._____();
  }
}
```

Note: Each snippet from the pool can be used more than once!

```
class Pizza {
    private _____ _____;
    public Pizza(_____ _____) {
        _____.writer = writer;
    }
    public void _____(_____.Fargo f) {
      writer._____(f);
      writer._____();
    }
}


class Party {
    private _____ reader;
    public Party(_____ reader) {
        _____.reader = reader;
    }
    public void HowMuch(_____ q) {
        q._____(reader._____());
        reader._____();
    }
}
```

Pool snippets:

int
long
string
enum
class

HowMany
HowMuch
HowBig
HowSmall

ReadLine
WriteLine

Stream
reader
writer
StreamReader
StreamWriter
Open
Close

public
private
this
class
static

for
while
foreach

=
>=
<=
!=
==
++
--

Fargo
Utah
Idaho
Dakota
Pineapple

Pool Puzzle Solution

This enum (specifically, its ToString() method) is used to print a lot of the output.

```csharp
class Pineapple {
    const string d = "delivery.txt";
    public enum Fargo { North, South, East, West, Flamingo }
    public static void Main() {
        StreamWriter o = new StreamWriter("order.txt");
        Pizza pz = new Pizza(new StreamWriter(d, true));
        pz.Idaho(Fargo.Flamingo);
        for (int w = 3; w >= 0; w--) {
            Pizza i = new Pizza(new StreamWriter(d, false));
            i.Idaho((Fargo)w);
            Party p = new Party(new StreamReader(d));
            p.HowMuch(o);
        }
        o.WriteLine("That's all folks!");
        o.Close();
    }
}

class Pizza {
    private StreamWriter writer;
    public Pizza(StreamWriter writer) {
        this.writer = writer;
    }
    public void Idaho(Pineapple.Fargo f) {
        writer.WriteLine(f);
        writer.Close();
    }
}

class Party {
    private StreamReader reader;
    public Party(StreamReader reader) {
        this.reader = reader;
    }
    public void HowMuch(StreamWriter q) {
        q.WriteLine(reader.ReadLine());
        reader.Close();
    }
}
```

Here's the entry point for the program. It creates a StreamWriter that it passes to the Party class. Then it loops through the Fargo members, passing each of them to the Pizza.Idaho() method to print.

The Pizza class keeps a StreamWriter as a private field, and its Idaho() method writes Fargo enums to the file using their ToString() methods, which WriteLine() calls automatically.

The Party class has a StreamReader field, and its HowMuch() method reads a line from that StreamReader and writes it to a StreamWriter.

Use built-in objects to pop up standard dialog boxes

When you're working on a program that reads and writes files, there's a good chance that you'll need to pop up a dialog box at some point to prompt the user for a filename. That's why .NET ships with objects to pop up the standard Windows file dialog boxes.

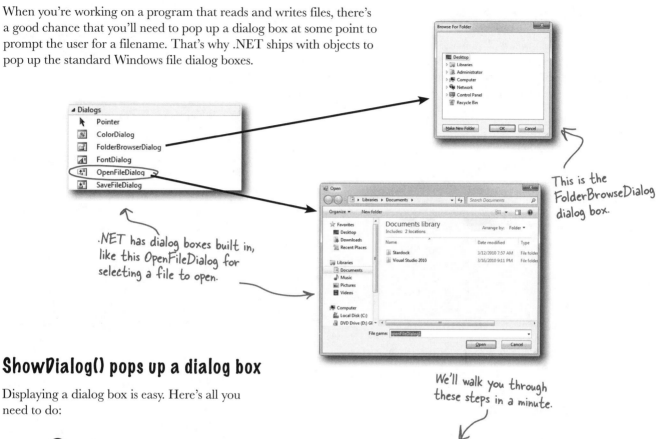

This is the FolderBrowseDialog dialog box.

.NET has dialog boxes built in, like this OpenFileDialog for selecting a file to open.

ShowDialog() pops up a dialog box

Displaying a dialog box is easy. Here's all you need to do:

We'll walk you through these steps in a minute.

1 Create an instance of the dialog box object. You can do this in code using new, or you can drag it out of the Toolbox and onto your form.

2 Set the dialog box object's properties. A few useful ones include Title (which sets the text in the title bar), InitialDirectory (which tells it which directory to open first), and FileName (for Open and Save dialog boxes).

3 Call the object's ShowDialog() method. That pops up the dialog box, and doesn't return until the user clicks the OK or Cancel button, or closes the window.

4 The ShowDialog() method returns a DialogResult, which is an enum. Some of its members are OK (which means the user clicked OK), Cancel, Yes, and No (for Yes/No dialog boxes).

Dialog boxes are just another .NET control

You can add Windows standard file dialog boxes to your program by dragging them to your form—just drag an OpenFileDialog control out of the Toolbox and drop it onto your form. Instead of showing up as a visual control, you'll see it appear in the space below your form. That's because it's a **component**, which is a special kind of **non-visual Toolbox control** that doesn't appear directly on the form, but which you can still use in your form's code just like you use any other control.

"Non-visual" just means it doesn't appear on your form when you drag it out of the Toolbox.

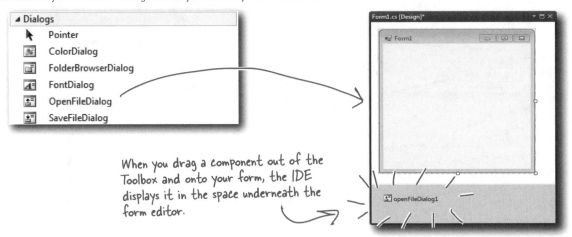

When you drag a component out of the Toolbox and onto your form, the IDE displays it in the space underneath the form editor.

The InitialDirectory property changes the folder that's first displayed when the dialog opens.

The Filter property lets you change the filters that show up on the bottom of the dialog box, such as what types of files to show.

```
openFileDialog1.InitialDirectory = @"c:\MyFolder\Default\";

openFileDialog1.Filter = "Text Files (*.txt)|*.txt|"

  + "Comma-Delimited Files (*.csv)|*.csv|All Files (*.*)|*.*";

openFileDialog1.FileName = "default_file.txt";

openFileDialog1.CheckFileExists = true;

openFileDialog1.CheckPathExists = false;

DialogResult result = openFileDialog1.ShowDialog();

if (result == DialogResult.OK){

    OpenSomeFile(openFileDialog1.FileName);

}
```

These properties tell the dialog box to display an error message if the user tries to open up a file or path that doesn't exist on the drive.

Display the dialog box using its ShowDialog() method, which returns a DialogResult. That's an enum that you can use to check whether or not the user hit the OK button. It'll be set to DialogResult.OK if the user clicked OK, and DialogResult.Cancel if he hit Cancel.

Dialog boxes are objects, too

An **OpenFileDialog** object shows the standard Windows "Open" window, and the **SaveFileDialog** shows the "Save" window. You can display them by creating a new instance, setting the properties on the object, and calling its ShowDialog() method. The ShowDialog() method returns a DialogResult enum (because some dialog boxes have more than two buttons or results, so a simple bool wouldn't be enough).

> When you drag a save dialog object out of the Toolbox and onto your form, the IDE just adds a line like this to your form's InitializeComponent() method.

```
saveFileDialog1 = new SaveFileDialog();

saveFileDialog1.InitialDirectory = @"c:\MyFolder\Default\";

saveFileDialog1.Filter = "Text Files (*.txt)|*.txt|"
   + "Comma-Delimited Files (*.csv)|*.csv|All Files (*.*)|*.*";

DialogResult result = saveFileDialog1.ShowDialog();

if (result == DialogResult.OK){

    SaveTheFile(saveFileDialog1.FileName);

}
```

> The Filter property isn't hard to figure out. Just compare what's between the | characters in the string with what shows up in the window.

> The ShowDialog() and FileName properties work exactly the same as on the OpenFileDialog object.

> The SaveFileDialog object pops up the standard Windows "Save as..." dialog box.

> The Title property lets you change this text.

> The ShowDialog() method pops up the dialog box and opens the folder specified in the InitialDirectory property.

> Change the "Save as type" list using the Filter property.

> When the user chooses a file, its full path is saved in the FileName property.

> The DialogResult returned by the ShowDialog() method lets you figure out which button the user clicked.

Use the built-in File and Directory classes to work with files and directories

Like `StreamWriter`, the `File` class creates streams that let you work with files behind the scenes. You can use its methods to do most common actions without having to create the `FileStreams` first. `Directory` objects let you work with whole directories full of files.

Things you can do with a File:

1 **Find out if the file exists**
You can check to see if a file exists using the `Exists()` method. It'll return true if it does and false if it doesn't.

2 **Read from and write to the file**
You can use the `OpenRead()` method to get data from a file, or the `Create()` or `OpenWrite()` method to write to the file.

3 **Append text to the file**
The `AppendAllText()` method lets you append text to an already-created file. It even creates the file if it's not there when the method runs.

4 **Get information about the file**
The `GetLastAccessTime()` and `GetLastWriteTime()` methods return the date and time when the file was last accessed and modified.

Things you can do with a Directory:

1 **Create a new directory**
Create a directory using the `CreateDirectory()` method. All you have to do is supply the path; this method does the rest.

2 **Get a list of the files in a directory**
You can create an array of files in a directory using the `GetFiles()` method; just tell the method which directory you want to know about and it will do the rest.

3 **Delete a directory**
Deleting a directory is really simple too. Just use the `Delete()` method.

FileInfo works just like File

If you're going to be doing a lot of work with a file, you might want to create an instance of the FileInfo class instead of using the File class's static methods.

The FileInfo class does just about everything the File class does except you have to instantiate it to use it. You can create a new instance of FileInfo and access its Exists() method or its OpenRead() method in just the same way.

The only difference is that the File class is faster for a small number of actions, and FileInfo is better suited for big jobs.

File is a static class, so it's just a set of methods that let you work with files. FileInfo is an object that you instantiate, and its methods are the same as the ones you see on File.

there are no
Dumb Questions

Q: I still don't get that {0} and {1} thing that was part of the `StreamWriter`.

A: When you're printing strings to a file, you'll often find yourself in the position of having to print the contents of a bunch of variables. For example, you might have to write something like this:

```
writer.WriteLine("My name is " + name +
    "and my age is " + age);
```

It gets really tedious and somewhat error-prone to have to keep using + to combine strings. It's easier to take advantage of {0} and {1}:

```
writer.WriteLine(
  "My name is {0} and my age is {1}",
  name, age);
```

It's a lot easier to read that code, especially when many variables are included in the same line.

Q: Why did you put an @ in front of the string that contained the filename?

A: When you add a string literal to your program, the compiler converts escape sequences like \n and \r to special characters. That makes it difficult to type filenames, which have a lot of backslash characters in them. If you put @ in front of a string, it tells C# not to interpret escape sequences. It also tells C# to include line breaks in your string, so you can hit Enter halfway through the string and it'll include that as a line break in the output:

```
string twoLine = @"this is a string
that spans two lines.";
```

Q: And what do \n and \t mean again?

A: Those are escape sequences. \n is a line feed and \t is a tab. \r is a return character, or half of a Windows return—in Windows text files, lines have to end with \r\n (like we talked about when we introduced `Environment.NewLine` from Chapter 8). If you want to use an *actual* backslash in your string and not have C# interpret it as the beginning of an escape sequence, just do a *double* backslash: \ \.

Q: What was that in the beginning about converting a string to a byte array? How would that even work?

A: You've probably heard many times that files on a disk are represented as bits and bytes. What that means is that when you write a file to a disk, the operating system treats it as one long sequence of bytes. The `StreamReader` and `StreamWriter` are converting from *bytes* to *characters* for you—that's called encoding and decoding. Remember from Chapter 4 how a `byte` variable can store any number between 0 and 255? Every file on your hard drive is one long sequence of numbers between 0 and 255. It's up to the programs that read and write those files to interpret those bytes as meaningful data. When you open a file in Notepad, it converts each individual byte to a character—for example, E is 69 and a is 97 (but this depends on the encoding…you'll learn more about encodings in just a minute). And when you type text into Notepad and save it, Notepad converts each of the characters back into a byte and saves it to disk. And if you want to write a `string` to a stream, you'll need to do the same.

Q: If I'm just using a `StreamWriter` to write to a file, why do I really care if it's creating a `FileStream` for me?

A: If you're only reading or writing lines to or from a text file in order, then all you need are `StreamReader` and `StreamWriter`. But as soon as you need to do anything more complex than that, you'll need to start working with other streams. If you ever need to write data like numbers, arrays, collections, or objects to a file, a `StreamWriter` just won't do. But don't worry, we'll go into a lot more detail about how that will work in just a minute.

Q: What if I want to create my own dialog boxes? Can I do that?

A: Yes, you definitely can. You can add a new form to your project and design it to look exactly how you want. Then you can create a new instance of it with `new` (just like you created an `OpenFileDialog` object). Then you can call its `ShowDialog()` method, and it'll work just like any other dialog box. We'll talk a lot more about adding other forms to your program in Chapter 13.

Q: Why do I need to worry about closing streams after I'm done with them?

A: Have you ever had a word processor tell you it couldn't open a file because it was "busy"? When one program uses a file, Windows locks it and prevents other programs from using it. And it'll do that for your program when it opens a file. If you don't call the `Close()` method, then it's possible for your program to keep a file locked open until it ends.

Sharpen your pencil

.NET has two built-in classes with a bunch of static methods for working with files and folders. The **File** class gives you methods to work with files, and the **Directory** class lets you work with directories. Write down what you think each of these lines of code does.

Code	What the code does

`if (!Directory.Exists(@"c:\SYP")) {`
`    Directory.CreateDirectory(@"c:\SYP");`
`}`	

`if (Directory.Exists(@"c:\SYP\Bonk")) {`
`    Directory.Delete(@"c:\SYP\Bonk");`
`}`	

`Directory.CreateDirectory(@"c:\SYP\Bonk");`	
`Directory.SetCreationTime(@"c:\SYP\Bonk",` `        new DateTime(1976, 09, 25));`	
`string[] files = Directory.GetFiles(@"c:\windows\",` `        "*.log", SearchOption.AllDirectories);`	

`File.WriteAllText(@"c:\SYP\Bonk\weirdo.txt",`
`        @"This is the first line`
`and this is the second line`
`and this is the last line");`	

`File.Encrypt(@"c:\SYP\Bonk\weirdo.txt");` See if you can guess what this one does—you haven't seen it yet.	
`File.Copy(@"c:\SYP\Bonk\weirdo.txt",` `        @"c:\SYP\copy.txt");`	
`DateTime myTime =` `        Directory.GetCreationTime(@"c:\SYP\Bonk");`	
`File.SetLastWriteTime(@"c:\SYP\copy.txt", myTime);`	
`File.Delete(@"c:\SYP\Bonk\weirdo.txt");`	

Use file dialogs to open and save files (all with just a few lines of code)

You can build a program that opens a text file. It'll let you make changes to the file and save your changes, with very little code, all using standard .NET controls. Here's how:

Do this

1 **Build a simple form.**
All you need is a TextBox and two Buttons. Drop the OpenFileDialog and SaveFileDialog controls onto the form, too. Double-click on the buttons to create their event handlers and **add a private string field called name to the form**. Don't forget to put a using statement up top for System.IO.

> Here's a trick to make your TextBox fill up the form. Drag a TableLayoutPanel from the Containers toolbox onto the form, set its Dock property to Fill, and use its Rows and Columns property editors to give it two rows and one column. Drag the TextBox into the top cell. Then drag a FlowLayoutPanel out of the Toolbox into the bottom cell, set its Dock to Fill, set its FlowDirection property to RightToLeft, and drag the two buttons onto it. Set the size of the top row in the TableLayoutPanel to 100%, and resize the bottom row so that the two buttons just fit. Now your editor will resize smoothly!

2 **Hook the Open button up to the openFileDialog.**
The Open button shows an OpenFileDialog and then uses File.ReadAllText() to read the file into the text box:

```
private void open_Click(object sender, EventArgs e) {
    if (openFileDialog1.ShowDialog() == DialogResult.OK) {
        name = openFileDialog1.FileName;
        textBox1.Clear();
        textBox1.Text = File.ReadAllText(name);
    }
}
```

Clicking Open shows the OpenFileDialog control.

3 **Now, hook up the Save button.**
The Save button uses the File.WriteAllText() method to save the file:

```
private void save_Click(object sender, EventArgs e) {
    if (saveFileDialog1.ShowDialog() == DialogResult.OK) {
        name = saveFileDialog1.FileName;
        File.WriteAllText(name, textBox1.Text);
    }
}
```

The ReadAllText() and WriteAllText() methods are part of the File class. That's coming up on the next page. We'll look at them in more detail in just a few pages.

4 **Play with the other properties of the dialog boxes.**
+ Use the Title property of the saveFileDialog to change the text in the title bar.

+ Set the initialFolder property to have the OpenFileDialog start in a specified directory.

+ Filter the OpenFileDialog so it will only show text files using the Filter property.

If you don't add a filter, then the drop-down lists at the bottom of the open and save dialog boxes will be empty. Try using this filter: "Text Files (*.txt)|*.txt".

dispose in the proper receptacle

Sharpen your pencil
Solution

.NET has two built-in classes with a bunch of static methods for working with files and folders. The **File** class gives you methods to work with files, and the **Directory** class lets you work with directories. Your job was to write down what each bit of code did.

Code	What the code does

`if (!Directory.Exists(@"c:\SYP")) {`
`    Directory.CreateDirectory(@"c:\SYP");`
`}`
	Check if the C:\SYP folder exists. If it doesn't, create it.

`if (Directory.Exists(@"c:\SYP\Bonk")) {`
`    Directory.Delete(@"c:\SYP\Bonk");`
`}`
	Check if the C:\SYP\Bonk folder exists. If it does, delete it.

`Directory.CreateDirectory(@"c:\SYP\Bonk");`	Create the directory C:\SYP\Bonk.
`Directory.SetCreationTime(@"c:\SYP\Bonk",` `    new DateTime(1976, 09, 25));`	Set the creation time for the C:\SYP\Bonk folder to September 25, 1976.
`string[] files = Directory.GetFiles(@"c:\windows\",` `    "*.log", SearchOption.AllDirectories);`	Get a list of all files in C:\Windows that match the *.log pattern, including all matching files in any subdirectory.

`File.WriteAllText(@"c:\SYP\Bonk\weirdo.txt",`
`    @"This is the first line`
`and this is the second line`
`and this is the last line");`
	Create a file called "weirdo.txt" (if it doesn't already exist) in the C:\SYP\Bonk folder and write three lines of text to it.

`File.Encrypt(@"c:\SYP\Bonk\weirdo.txt");` ↖ This is an alternative to using a CryptoStream.	Take advantage of built-in Windows encryption to encrypt the file "weirdo.txt" using the logged-in account's credentials.
`File.Copy(@"c:\SYP\Bonk\weirdo.txt",` `    @"c:\SYP\copy.txt");`	Copy the C:\SYP\Bonk\weirdo.txt file to C:\SYP\Copy.txt.
`DateTime myTime =` `    Directory.GetCreationTime(@"c:\SYP\Bonk");`	Declare the myTime variable and set it equal to the creation time of the C:\SYP\Bonk folder.
`File.SetLastWriteTime(@"c:\SYP\copy.txt", myTime);`	Alter the last write time of the copy.txt file in C:\SYP\ so it's equal to whatever time is stored in the myTime variable.
`File.Delete(@"c:\SYP\Bonk\weirdo.txt");`	Delete the C:\SYP\Bonk\weirdo.txt file.

IDisposable makes sure your objects are disposed of properly

A lot of .NET classes implement a particularly useful interface called
IDisposable. It **has only one member**: a method called **Dispose()**.
Whenever a class implements IDisposable, it's telling you that there
are important things that it needs to do in order to shut itself down, usually
because it's **allocated resources** that it won't give back until you tell it to.
The Dispose() method is how you tell the object to release those resources.

You can use the "Go To Definition" feature in the IDE to show you the
official C# definition of IDisposable. Go to your project and type
"IDisposable" anywhere inside a class. Then right-click on it and select "Go
To Definition" from the menu. It'll open a new tab with code in it. Expand all
of the code and this is what you'll see:

You'll learn more about "Go To Definition" later on.

Declare an object in a using block and that object's Dispose() method is called automatically.

```
namespace System
{
    // Summary:
    //      Defines a method to release allocated resources.
    public interface IDisposable
    {
        // Summary:
        //       Performs application-defined tasks
        //       associated with freeing, releasing, or
        //       resetting unmanaged resources.
        void Dispose();
    }
}
```

A lot of classes allocate important resources, like memory, files, and other objects. That means they take them over, and don't give them back until you tell them you're done with those resources.

Any class that implements IDisposable will immediately release any resources that it took over as soon as you call its Dispose() method. It's almost always the last thing you do before you're done with the object.

al-lo-cate, verb.
to distribute resources
or duties for a particular
purpose. *The programming
team was irritated at their project
manager because he **allocated**
all of the conference rooms for a
useless management seminar.*

Go To Definition
There's a handy feature in the IDE that lets you automatically jump to the
definition for any variable, object, or method. Just right-click on it and
select "Go To Definition", and the IDE will automatically jump right to the
code that defines it. You can also press F12 instead of using the menu.

Avoid file system errors with <u>using</u> statements

We've been telling you all chapter that you need to **close your streams**. That's because some of the most common bugs that programmers run across when they deal with files are caused when streams aren't closed properly. Luckily, C# gives you a great tool to make sure that never happens to you: IDisposable and the Dispose() method. When you **wrap your stream code in a using statement**, it automatically closes your streams for you. All you need to do is **declare your stream reference** with a using statement, followed by a block of code (inside curly brackets) that uses that reference. When you do that, the using statement **automatically calls the stream's Dispose() method** as soon as it finishes running the block of code. Here's how it works:

These "using" statements are different from the ones at the top of your code.

A using statement is always followed by an object declaration...

...and then a block of code within curly braces.

```
using (StreamWriter sw = new StreamWriter("secret_plan.txt")) {

    sw.WriteLine("How I'll defeat Captain Amazing");

    sw.WriteLine("Another genius secret plan");

    sw.WriteLine("by The Swindler");

}
```

These statements can use the object created in the using statement above like any normal object.

When the using statement ends, the Dispose() method of the object being used is run.

In this case, the object being used is pointed to by sw—which was declared in the using statement—so the Dispose() method of the Stream class is run...which closes the stream.

Every stream has a Dispose() method that closes the stream. So if you declare your stream in a using statement, it will always close itself!

Use multiple using statements for multiple objects

You can pile using statements on top of each other—you don't need extra sets of curly brackets or indents.

```
using (StreamReader reader = new StreamReader("secret_plan.txt"))

using (StreamWriter writer = new StreamReader("email.txt"))

{

    // statements that use reader and writer

}
```

You don't need to call Close() on the streams now, because the using statement will close them automatically.

Any time you use a stream, you should ALWAYS declare it inside a using statement. That makes sure it's always closed!

Trouble at work

Meet Brian. He likes his job as a C# developer, but he *loves* taking the occasional day off. His boss **hates** when people take vacation days, so Brian's got to come up with a good excuse.

> Sorry I've gotta leave early, boss. My cat's got a vet appointment.

> That's the ninth vet appointment you've had since March, son. If I find out you're lying to me, you'd better start looking for a new job!

You can help Brian out by building a program to manage his excuses

Use what you know about reading and writing files to build an excuse manager that Brian can use to keep track of which excuses he's used recently and how well they went over with the boss.

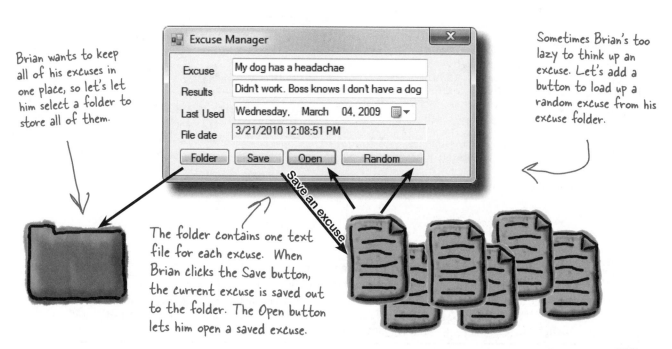

Brian wants to keep all of his excuses in one place, so let's let him select a folder to store all of them.

Sometimes Brian's too lazy to think up an excuse. Let's add a button to load up a random excuse from his excuse folder.

The folder contains one text file for each excuse. When Brian clicks the Save button, the current excuse is saved out to the folder. The Open button lets him open a saved excuse.

Save an excuse

Build the excuse manager so Brian can manage his excuses at work.

Excuse
Description: string
Results: string
LastUsed: DateTime
ExcusePath: string
OpenFile(string)
Save(string)

Exercise

1 **Build the form**

This form has a few special features:

★ When the form's first loaded, **only the Folder button should be enabled**—disable the other three buttons until the user selects a folder.

★ When the form opens or saves an excuse, it displays the file date for the excuse file using a `Label` control with `AutoSize` set to `False` and `BorderStyle` set to `Fixed3D`.

★ After an excuse is saved, the form pops up an "Excuse Written" message box.

★ The Folder button brings up a folder browser dialog box. If the user selects a folder, it enables the Save, Open, and Random Excuse buttons.

★ The form knows when there are unsaved changes. When there are no unsaved changes, the text on the form's title bar is "Excuse Manager". But when the user has changed any of the three fields, the form adds an asterisk (*) to the title bar. The asterisk goes away when the data is saved or a new excuse is opened.

★ The form will need to keep track of the current folder and whether or not the current excuse has been saved. You can figure out when the excuse hasn't been saved by **using the Changed event handlers** for the three input controls. ⟵ *When you drag a text box to a form and double-click on it, you create a Changed event handler for that field.*

2 **Create an `Excuse` class and store an instance of it in the form**

Now add a `CurrentExcuse` field to the form to hold the current excuse. You'll need **three overloaded constructors**: one for when the form's first loaded, one for opening up a file, and one for a random excuse. Add methods `OpenFile()` to open an excuse (for the constructors to use), and `Save()` to save the excuse. Then add this `UpdateForm()` method to update the controls (it'll give you some **hints** about the class):

```
private void UpdateForm(bool changed) {
    if (!changed) {
        this.description.Text = currentExcuse.Description;
        this.results.Text = currentExcuse.Results;
        this.lastUsed.Value = currentExcuse.LastUsed;
        if (!string.IsNullOrEmpty(currentExcuse.ExcusePath))
            FileDate.Text = File.GetLastWriteTime(currentExcuse.ExcusePath).ToString();
        this.Text = "Excuse Manager";
    }
    else
        this.Text = "Excuse Manager*";
    this.formChanged = changed;
}
```

This parameter indicates whether or not the form has changed. You'll need a field in your form to keep track of this status.

Remember, the ! means NOT—so this checks if the excuse path is NOT null or empty.

Double-click on the input controls so the IDE builds Changed event handlers for you. The event handlers for the three input controls will first change the Excuse instance and then call UpdateForm(true)—then it's up to you to change the fields on your form.

And make sure you initialize the excuse's `LastUsed` value in the form's constructor:

```
public Form1() {
    InitializeComponent();
    currentExcuse.LastUsed = lastUsed.Value;
}
```

3 **Make the Folder button open a folder browser**

When the user clicks on the Folder button, the form should pop up a "Browse for Folder" dialog box. The form will need to store the folder in a field so that the other dialog boxes can use it. When the form **first loads**, the Save, Open, and Random Excuse buttons are **disabled**, but if the user selects a folder then the Folder button enables them.

Make the Save button save the current excuse to a file

Clicking the Save button should bring up the Save As dialog box.

★ Each excuse is saved to a separate text file. The first line of the file is the excuse, the second is the result, and the third is the date last used (using the DateTimePicker's ToString() method). The Excuse class should have a Save() method to save an excuse out to a specified file.

★ When the Save As dialog box is opened, its folder should be set to the folder that the user selected using the Folder button, and the filename should be set to the excuse plus a ".txt" extension.

★ The dialog box should have two filters: Text Files (*.txt) and All Files (*.*).

★ If the user tries to save the current excuse but has left either the excuse or the result blank, the form should pop up a warning dialog box:

You can display this Exclamation icon by using the overloaded MessageBox.Show() method that allows you to specify a MessageBoxIcon parameter.

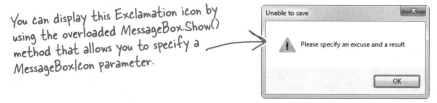

Make the Open button open a saved excuse

Clicking the Open button should bring up the Open dialog box.

★ When the Open dialog box is opened, its folder should be set to the folder that the user selected using the Folder button.

★ Add an Open() method to the Excuse class to open an excuse from a given file.

★ Use Convert.ToDateTime() to load the saved date into the DateTimePicker control.

★ If the user tries to open a saved excuse but the current excuse hasn't been saved, it pops up this dialog box:

Show a Yes/No dialog box by using the overloaded MessageBox.Show() method that lets you specify the MessageBoxButtons.YesNo parameter. If the user clicks "No", then Show() returns DialogResult.No.

Finally, make the Random Excuse button load a random excuse

When the user clicks the Random Excuse button, it looks in the excuse folder, chooses one of the excuses at random, and opens it.

★ The form will need to save a Random object in a field and pass it to one of the overloaded constructors of the Excuse object.

★ If the current excuse hasn't been saved, the button should pop up the same warning dialog box as the Open button.

Exercise Solution

Build the excuse manager so Brian can manage his excuses at work.

> The form uses fields to store the current Excuse object to the selected folder and remember whether or not the current excuse has changed, and to keep a Random object for the Random Excuse button.

```
private Excuse currentExcuse = new Excuse();
private string selectedFolder = "";
private bool formChanged = false;
Random random = new Random();

private void folder_Click(object sender, EventArgs e) {
    folderBrowserDialog1.SelectedPath = selectedFolder;
    DialogResult result = folderBrowserDialog1.ShowDialog();
    if (result == DialogResult.OK) {
        selectedFolder = folderBrowserDialog1.SelectedPath;
        save.Enabled = true;
        open.Enabled = true;
        randomExcuse.Enabled = true;
    }
}
```

> If the user selected a folder, the form saves the folder name and then enables the other three buttons.

> The two vertical bars mean OR—this is true if description is empty OR results is empty.

```
private void save_Click(object sender, EventArgs e) {
    if (String.IsNullOrEmpty(description.Text) || String.IsNullOrEmpty(results.Text)) {
        MessageBox.Show("Please specify an excuse and a result",
            "Unable to save", MessageBoxButtons.OK, MessageBoxIcon.Exclamation);
        return;
    }
    saveFileDialog1.InitialDirectory = selectedFolder;
    saveFileDialog1.Filter = "Text files (*.txt)|*.txt|All files (*.*)|*.*";
    saveFileDialog1.FileName = description.Text + ".txt";
    DialogResult result = saveFileDialog1.ShowDialog();
    if (result == DialogResult.OK) {
        currentExcuse.Save(saveFileDialog1.FileName);
        UpdateForm(false);
        MessageBox.Show("Excuse written");
    }
}
```

> Here's where the filters are set for the Save As dialog.

> This will cause two rows to show up in the "Files of Type" drop-down at the bottom of the Save dialog box: one for Text Files (*.txt), and one for All Files (*.*).

```
private void open_Click(object sender, EventArgs e) {
    if (CheckChanged()) {
        openFileDialog1.InitialDirectory = selectedFolder;
        openFileDialog1.Filter = "Text files (*.txt)|*.txt|All files (*.*)|*.*";
        openFileDialog1.FileName = description.Text + ".txt";
        DialogResult result = openFileDialog1.ShowDialog();
        if (result == DialogResult.OK) {
            currentExcuse = new Excuse(openFileDialog1.FileName);
            UpdateForm(false);
        }
    }
}
```

> Use the DialogResult enum returned by the Open and Save dialog boxes to make sure you only open or save if the user clicked "OK", and not "Cancel".

```
private void randomExcuse_Click(object sender, EventArgs e) {
    if (CheckChanged()) {
        currentExcuse = new Excuse(random, selectedFolder);
        UpdateForm(false);
    }
}
```

```
private bool CheckChanged() {
    if (formChanged) {
        DialogResult result = MessageBox.Show(
            "The current excuse has not been saved. Continue?",
            "Warning", MessageBoxButtons.YesNo, MessageBoxIcon.Warning);
        if (result == DialogResult.No)
            return false;
    }
    return true;
}
```

MessageBox.Show() also returns a
DialogResult enum that we can check.

```
private void description_TextChanged(object sender, EventArgs e) {
    currentExcuse.Description = description.Text;
    UpdateForm(true);
}
```

Here are the three
Changed event handlers
for the three input
fields on the form. If any
of them are triggered,
that means the excuse
has changed, so first
we update the Excuse
instance and then we
call UpdateForm(), add
the asterisk to the
form's title bar, and set
Changed to true.

```
private void results_TextChanged(object sender, EventArgs e) {
    currentExcuse.Results = results.Text;
    UpdateForm(true);
}

private void lastUsed_ValueChanged(object sender, EventArgs e) {
    currentExcuse.LastUsed = lastUsed.Value;
    UpdateForm(true);
}
```

Passing true to UpdateForm() tells it
to just mark the form as changed, but
not update the input controls.

```
class Excuse {
    public string Description { get; set; }
    public string Results { get; set; }
    public DateTime LastUsed { get; set; }
    public string ExcusePath { get; set; }
    public Excuse() {
        ExcusePath = "";
    }
    public Excuse(string excusePath) {
        OpenFile(excusePath);
    }
    public Excuse(Random random, string folder) {
        string[] fileNames = Directory.GetFiles(folder, "*.txt");
        OpenFile(fileNames[random.Next(fileNames.Length)]);
    }
    private void OpenFile(string excusePath) {
        this.ExcusePath = excusePath;
        using (StreamReader reader = new StreamReader(excusePath)) {
            Description = reader.ReadLine();
            Results = reader.ReadLine();
            LastUsed = Convert.ToDateTime(reader.ReadLine());
        }
    }
    public void Save(string fileName) {
        using (StreamWriter writer = new StreamWriter(fileName))
        {
            writer.WriteLine(Description);
            writer.WriteLine(Results);
            writer.WriteLine(LastUsed);
        }
    }
}
```

The Random Excuse button uses Directory.GetFiles() to
read all of the text files in the selected folder into an
array, and then chooses a random array index to open.

We made sure to use a using
statement every time we
opened a stream. That way
our files will always be closed.

Here's where the using
statement comes in. We
declared the StreamWriter
inside a using statement, so
its Close() method is called
for us automatically!

Did you call LastUsed.ToString()? Remember, WriteLine() calls it automatically!

Writing files usually involves making a lot of decisions

You'll write lots of programs that take a single input, maybe from a file, and have to decide what to do based on that input. Here's code that uses one long `if` statement—it's pretty typical. It checks the `part` variable and prints different lines to the file based on which enum it uses. There are lots of choices, so lots of `else if`s:

```
enum BodyPart {
    Head,
    Shoulders,
    Knees,
    Toes
}
```

> Here's an enum—we'll want to compare a variable against each of the four members and write a different line to the StreamWriter depending on which one it matches. We'll also write something different if none of them match.

```
private void WritePartInfo(BodyPart part, StreamWriter writer) {
    if (part == BodyPart.Head)
        writer.WriteLine("the head is hairy");
    else if (part == BodyPart.Shoulders)
        writer.WriteLine("the shoulders are broad");
    else if (part == BodyPart.Knees)
        writer.WriteLine("the knees are knobby");
    else if (part == BodyPart.Toes)
        writer.WriteLine("the toes are teeny");
    else
        writer.WriteLine("some unknown part is unknown");
}
```

> If we use a series of if/else statements, then we end up writing this "if (part ==[option])" over and over.

> We've got a final else in case we didn't find a match.

BRAIN POWER

What sort of things can go wrong when you write code that has this many if/else statements? Think about typos and bugs caused by brackets, a single equals sign, etc.

Use a <u>switch</u> statement to choose the right option

Comparing one variable against a bunch of different values is a really common pattern that you'll see over and over again. It's especially common when you're reading and writing files. It's so common, in fact, that C# has a special kind of statement designed specifically for this situation.

A **switch statement** lets you compare one variable against many values in a way that's compact and easy to read. Here's a switch statement that does exactly the same thing as the series of if/else statements on the opposite page:

> There's nothing about a switch statement that's specifically related to files. It's just a useful C# tool that we can use here.

A switch statement compares ONE variable against MULTIPLE possible values.

```csharp
enum BodyPart
{
    Head,
    Shoulders,
    Knees,
    Toes,
}
```

> You'll start with the switch keyword followed by the variable that's going to be compared against a bunch of different possible values.

```csharp
private void WritePartInfo(BodyPart part, StreamWriter writer)
{
    switch (part) {
        case BodyPart.Head:
            writer.WriteLine("the head is hairy");
            break;
        case BodyPart.Shoulders:
            writer.WriteLine("the shoulders are broad");
            break;
        case BodyPart.Knees:
            writer.WriteLine("the knees are knobby");
            break;
        case BodyPart.Toes:
            writer.WriteLine("the toes are teeny");
            break;
        default:
            writer.WriteLine("some unknown part is unknown");
            break;
    }
}
```

> Every case ends with "break;" so C# knows where one case ends and the next begins.

> You can also end a case with "return" — the program will compile as long as there's no way for one case to "fall through" to the next one.

> Switch statements can end with a "default:" block that gets executed if none of the other cases are matched.

> The body of the switch statement is a series of cases that compare whatever follows the switch keyword against a particular value.

> Each of these cases consists of the case keyword followed by the value to compare and a colon. After that is a series of statements followed by "break;". Those statements will be executed if the case matches the comparison value.

Use a switch statement to let your deck of cards read from a file or write itself out to one

The switch statement lets you test one value against a bunch of cases and execute different statements depending on which one it matches.

Writing a card out to a file is straightforward—just make a loop that writes the name of each card out to a file. Here's a method you can add to the Deck object that does exactly that:

```
public void WriteCards(string filename) {
    using (StreamWriter writer = new StreamWriter(filename)) {
        for (int i = 0; i < cards.Count; i++) {
            writer.WriteLine(cards[i].Name);
        }
    }
}
```

But what about reading the file in? It's not quite so simple. That's where the switch statement can come in handy.

```
Suits suit;
switch (suitString) {
    case "Spades":
        suit = Suits.Spades;
        break;
    case "Clubs":
        suit = Suits.Clubs;
        break;
    case "Hearts":
        suit = Suits.Hearts;
        break;
    case "Diamonds":
        suit = Suits.Diamonds;
        break;
    default:
        MessageBox.Show(suitString + " isn't a valid suit!");
}
```

The switch statement starts with a value to compare against. This switch statement is called from a method that has a suit stored in a string.

Each of these case lines compares some value against the value in the switch line. If they match, it executes all of the following statements until it hits a break.

The default line comes at the end. If none of the cases match, the statements after the default get executed instead.

Add an overloaded Deck() constructor that reads a deck of cards in from a file

You can use a switch statement to build a new constructor for the Deck class that you wrote in the last chapter. This constructor reads in a file and checks each line for a card. Any valid card gets added to the deck.

There's a method that you can find on every string that'll come in handy: Split(). It lets you split the string into an array of substrings by passing it a char[] array of separator characters that it'll use to split the string up.

This line tells C# to split the nextCard string using a space as a separator character. That splits the string "Six of Diamonds" into the array {"Six", "of", "Diamonds"}.

```csharp
public Deck(string filename) {
    cards = new List<Card>();
    StreamReader reader = new StreamReader(filename);
    while (!reader.EndOfStream) {
        bool invalidCard = false;
        string nextCard = reader.ReadLine();
        string[] cardParts = nextCard.Split(new char[] { ' ' });
        Values value = Values.Ace;
        switch (cardParts[0]) {
            case "Ace": value = Values.Ace; break;
            case "Two": value = Values.Two; break;
            case "Three": value = Values.Three; break;
            case "Four": value = Values.Four; break;
            case "Five": value = Values.Five; break;
            case "Six": value = Values.Six; break;
            case "Seven": value = Values.Seven; break;
            case "Eight": value = Values.Eight; break;
            case "Nine": value = Values.Nine; break;
            case "Ten": value = Values.Ten; break;
            case "Jack": value = Values.Jack; break;
            case "Queen": value = Values.Queen; break;
            case "King": value = Values.King; break;
            default: invalidCard = true; break;
        }
        Suits suit = Suits.Clubs;
        switch (cardParts[2]) {
            case "Spades": suit = Suits.Spades; break;
            case "Clubs": suit = Suits.Clubs; break;
            case "Hearts": suit = Suits.Hearts; break;
            case "Diamonds": suit = Suits.Diamonds; break;
            default: invalidCard = true; break;
        }
        if (!invalidCard) {
            cards.Add(new Card(suit, value));
        }
    }
}
```

This switch statement checks the first word in the line to see if it matches a value. If it does, the right value is assigned to the value variable.

We do the same thing for the third word in the line, except we convert this one to a suit.

> All that code just to read in one simple card? That's way too much work! What if my object has a whole bunch of fields and values? Are you telling me I need to write a switch statement for each of them?

There's an easier way to store your objects in files. It's called serialization.

Instead of painstakingly writing out each field and value to a file line by line, you can save your object the easy way by serializing it out to a stream. ***Serializing*** an object is like **flattening it out** so you can slip it into a file. And on the other end, you can ***deserialize*** it, which is like taking it out of the file and **inflating** it again.

Ok, just to come clean here: There's also a method called Enum.Parse() — you'll learn about it in Chapter 14 — that will convert the string "Spades" to the enum value Suits.Spades. But serialization still makes a lot more sense here. You'll find out more about that shortly....

What happens to an object when it's serialized?

It seems like something mysterious has to happen to an object in order to copy it off of the heap and put it into a file, but it's actually pretty straightforward.

① Object on the heap

When you create an instance of an object, it has a **state**. Everything that an object "knows" is what makes one instance of a class different from another instance of the same class.

② Object serialized

When C# serializes an object, it **saves the complete state of the object**, so that an identical instance (object) can be brought back to life on the heap later.

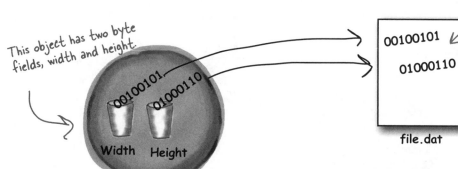

This object has two byte fields, width and height.

00100101
01000110

Width   Height

00100101

01000110

file.dat

The instance variable values for width and height are saved to the file "file.dat", along with a little more info that the CLR needs to restore the object later (like the type of the object and each of its fields).

Object on the heap again

③ And later on...

Later—maybe days later, and in a different program—you can go back to the file and **deserialize** it. That pulls the original class back out of the file and restores it **exactly as it was**, with all of its fields and values intact.

But what exactly IS an object's state? What needs to be saved?

We already know that **an object stores its state in its fields**. So when an object is serialized, every one of those fields needs to be saved to the file.

Serialization starts to get interesting when you have more complicated objects. 37 and 70 are bytes—those are value types, so they can just be written out to a file as-is. But what if an object has an instance variable that's an object *reference*? What about an object that has five instance variables that are object references? What if those object instance variables themselves have instance variables?

Think about it for a minute. What part of an object is potentially unique? Imagine what needs to be restored in order to get an object that's identical to the one that was saved. Somehow everything on the heap has to be written to the file.

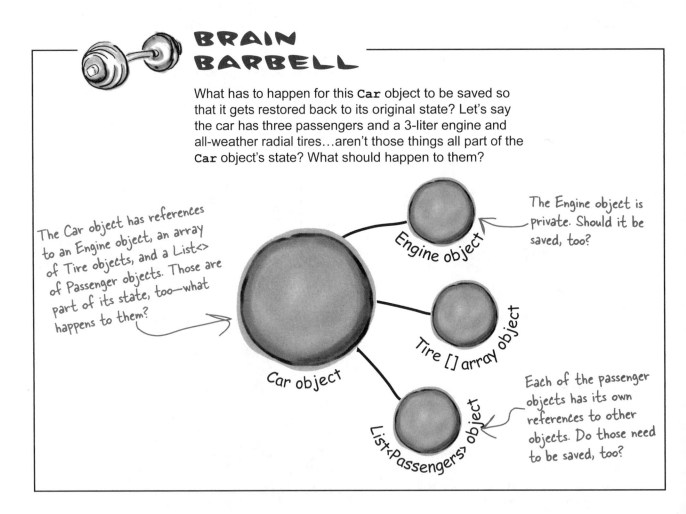

BRAIN BARBELL

What has to happen for this **Car** object to be saved so that it gets restored back to its original state? Let's say the car has three passengers and a 3-liter engine and all-weather radial tires…aren't those things all part of the **Car** object's state? What should happen to them?

The Car object has references to an Engine object, an array of Tire objects, and a List<> of Passenger objects. Those are part of its state, too—what happens to them?

The Engine object is private. Should it be saved, too?

Each of the passenger objects has its own references to other objects. Do those need to be saved, too?

Car object

Engine object

Tire [] array object

List<Passengers> object

When an object is serialized, all of the objects it refers to get serialized, too…

…and all of the objects *they* refer to, and all of the objects *those other objects* refer to, and so on and so on. But don't worry—it may sound complicated, but it all happens automatically. C# starts with the object you want to serialize and looks through its fields for other objects. Then it does the same for each of them. Every single object gets written out to the file, along with all the information C# needs to reconstitute it all when the object gets deserialized.

Some people call this whole group of connected objects a "graph."

When you ask C# to serialize the Kennel object, it looks for any field that has a reference to another object.

"Fido"

DoggyID object

Breed.Beagle
4 years old
32 pounds
14" tall

Collar object

Kennel object

Dog object

One of the fields of the Kennel object is this List<Dog> that contains two Dog objects, so C# will need to serialize them, too.

List<Dog> object

"Spike"

DoggyID object

Each of the two Dog objects has references to a DoggyID object and a Collar object. They'll need to get serialized along with each Dog.

Breed.Mutt
6 years old
18 pounds
11" tall

Collar object

Dog object

DoggyID and Collar are the end of the line—they don't have references to any other objects.

Serialization lets you read or write a whole object all at once

You're not just limited to reading and writing lines of text to your files. You can use **serialization** to let your programs copy entire objects to files and read them back in…all in just a few lines of code! There's a tiny amount of prep work you need to do—add one [Serializable] line to the top of the class to serialize—but once you do that, everything's ready to write.

> It's quick to copy an object out to a file or read it in from one. You can serialize or deserialize it.

You'll need a BinaryFormatter object

If you want to serialize an object—*any* object—the first thing you do is create an instance of BinaryFormatter. It's really straightforward to do—and all it takes is one line of code (and an extra using line at the top of the class file).

```
using System.Runtime.Serialization.Formatters.Binary;
    . . .
BinaryFormatter formatter = new BinaryFormatter();
```

Now just create a stream and read or write your objects

Use the Serialize() method from the BinaryFormatter object to write any object out to a stream.

The File.Create() method creates a new file. You can open an existing one using File.OpenWrite().

```
using (Stream output = File.Create(filenameString)) {
    formatter.Serialize(output, objectToSerialize);
}
```

The Serialize() method takes an object and writes it out to a stream. That's a whole lot easier than building a method to write it out yourself!

And once you've got an object serialized out to a file, use the BinaryFormatter object's Deserialize() method to read it back in. The method returns a reference, so you need to cast the output so that it matches the type of the reference variable you're copying it to.

```
using (Stream input = File.OpenRead(filenameString)) {
    SomeObj obj = (SomeObj)formatter.Deserialize(input)
}
```

When you use Deserialize() to read an object back from a stream, don't forget to cast the return value to match the type of object you're reading.

If you want your class to be serializable, mark it with the [Serializable] attribute

An **attribute** is a special tag that you can add to the top of any C# class. It's how C# stores **metadata** about your code, or information about how the code should be used or treated. When you **add [Serializable] to the top of a class just above the class declaration**, you're telling C# that your class is safe for serialization. And you only use it with classes that include fields that are either value types (like an int, decimal, or enum) or other serializable classes. If you don't add the attribute to the class you want to serialize, or if you include a field with a type that isn't serializable, then your program will have an error when you try to run it. ***See for yourself...***

Do this

 Create a class and serialize it

Remember the Guy class from Chapter 3? Let's serialize Joe so we can keep a file that knows how much money he's got in his pocket even after you close your program.

```
[Serializable]
 class Guy
```
You need to add this attribute to the top of any class in order to serialize it.

Here's code to serialize it to a file called Guy_file.dat—add a "Save Joe" button and a "Load Joe" button to the form:

```
using System.IO;
using System.Runtime.Serialization.Formatters.Binary;

...

private void saveJoe_Click(object sender, EventArgs e)
{
  using (Stream output = File.Create("Guy_File.dat")) {
    BinaryFormatter formatter = new BinaryFormatter();
    formatter.Serialize(output, joe);
  }
}
private void loadJoe_Click(object sender, EventArgs e)
{
  using (Stream input = File.OpenRead("Guy_File.dat")) {
    BinaryFormatter formatter = new BinaryFormatter();
    joe = (Guy)formatter.Deserialize(input);
  }
  UpdateForm();
}
```

You'll need these two using lines. The first one is for the file and stream methods, and the second is for serialization.

Run the program and play around with it

If Joe had two hundred dollars saved up from his transactions with Bob during your time running the program, it would be a pain to lose all that money just because you needed to exit. Now your program can save Joe out to a file and restore him whenever you want.

Let's serialize and deserialize a deck of cards

Take a deck of cards and write it out to a file. C# makes
serializing objects really easy. All you need to do is
create a stream and write out your objects.

Do this

❶ Create a new project and add the Deck and Card classes
Right-click on the project in the Solution Explorer and choose "Add/Existing Item", and add the
`Card` and `Deck` classes (and the `Suits` and `Values` enums and `CardComparer_bySuit` and
`CardComparer_byValue` interfaces) you used in Go Fish! in Chapter 8. You'll also need to add the two
card comparer classes, since `Deck` uses them. The IDE will copy the files into the new project—make sure
you change the `namespace` line at the top of each class file to match your new project's namespace.

❷ Mark the classes serializable
Add the `[Serializable]` attribute to both classes you added to the
project.

> If you don't do
> this, C# won't let
> you serialize the
> classes to a file.

❸ Add a couple of useful methods to the form
The `RandomDeck` method creates a random deck of cards, and the
`DealCards` method deals all of the cards and prints them to the console.

```
Random random = new Random();
private Deck RandomDeck(int number) {
    Deck myDeck = new Deck(new Card[] { });
    for (int i = 0; i < number; i++)
    {
        myDeck.Add(new Card(
            (Suits)random.Next(4),
            (Values)random.Next(1, 14)));
    }
    return myDeck;
}

private void DealCards(Deck deckToDeal, string title) {
    Console.WriteLine(title);
    while (deckToDeal.Count > 0)
    {
        Card nextCard = deckToDeal.Deal(0);
        Console.WriteLine(nextCard.Name);
    }
    Console.WriteLine("------------------");
}
```

> This creates an empty
> deck and then adds some
> random cards to it using
> the Card class from the
> last chapter.

> The DealCards()
> method deals each of
> the cards off of the
> deck and prints it to
> the console.

4 **OK, prep work's done.. now serialize that deck**

Start by adding buttons to serialize a random deck to a file and read it back. Check the console output to make sure the deck you wrote out is the same as the deck you read.

```
private void button1_Click(object sender, EventArgs e) {
    Deck deckToWrite = RandomDeck(5);
    using (Stream output = File.Create("Deck1.dat")) {
        BinaryFormatter bf = new BinaryFormatter();
        bf.Serialize(output, deckToWrite);
    }
    DealCards(deckToWrite, "What I just wrote to the file");
}

private void button2_Click(object sender, EventArgs e) {
    using (Stream input = File.OpenRead("Deck1.dat")) {
        BinaryFormatter bf = new BinaryFormatter();
        Deck deckFromFile = (Deck)bf.Deserialize(input);
        DealCards(deckFromFile, "What I read from the file");
    }
}
```

The BinaryFormatter object takes any object marked with the Serializable attribute—in this case a Deck object—and writes it out to a stream using its Serialize() method.

The BinaryFormatter's Deserialize() method returns an Object, which is just the general type that every C# object inherits from—which is why we need to cast it to a Deck object.

5 **Now serialize a bunch of decks to the same file**

Once you open a stream, you can write as much as you want to it. You can serialize as many objects as you need into the same file. So now add two more buttons to write out a random number of decks to the file. Check the output to make sure everything looks good.

```
private void button3_Click(object sender, EventArgs e) {
    using (Stream output = File.Create("Deck2.dat")) {
        BinaryFormatter bf = new BinaryFormatter();
        for (int i = 1; i <= 5; i++) {
            Deck deckToWrite = RandomDeck(random.Next(1,10));
            bf.Serialize(output, deckToWrite);
            DealCards(deckToWrite, "Deck #" + i + " written");
        }
    }
}

private void button4_Click(object sender, EventArgs e) {
    using (Stream input = File.OpenRead("Deck2.dat")) {
        BinaryFormatter bf = new BinaryFormatter();
        for (int i = 1; i <= 5; i++) {
            Deck deckToRead = (Deck)bf.Deserialize(input);
            DealCards(deckToRead, "Deck #" + i + " read");
        }
    }
}
```

You can serialize one object after another to the same stream.

Notice how the line that reads a single deck from the file uses (Deck) to cast the output of Deserialize() to a Deck. That's because Deserialize() returns an object, but doesn't necessarily know what type of object.

As long as you cast the objects you read off the stream to the right type, there's no limit to the number of objects you can serialize.

6 **Take a look at the file you wrote**

Open up Deck1.dat in Notepad (File.Create() created it in the bin\ Debug folder under your project folder). It may not be something you'd read on the beach, but it's got all the information to restore your whole deck of cards.

> Wait a minute. I'm not sure I like all this writing objects out to some weird file that looks like garbage when I open it up. When I wrote the deck of cards as strings, I could open up the output in Notepad and see everything in it. Isn't C# supposed to make it easy for me to understand everything I'm doing?

When you serialize objects out to a file, they're written in a binary format.

But that doesn't mean it's indecipherable—just compact. That's why you can recognize the strings when you open up a file with serialized objects in it: that's the most compact way C# can write strings to a file—as strings. But writing out a number as a string would be really wasteful. Any int can be stored in four bytes. So it would be odd if C# stored, say, the number 49,369,144 as an 8-character string that you could read—10 characters if you include commas. That would be a waste of space!

Behind the Scenes

.NET uses **Unicode** to encode a char or string into bytes. Luckily, Windows has a useful little tool to help us figure out how Unicode works. Open up the Character Map (it's in the Start menu under Accessories / System Tools, or do Start/Run and type "charmap.exe").

When you look at all the letters and symbols that are used in languages all around the world, you realize just how many different *things* need to be written to a file just to store text. That's why .NET **encodes** all of its strings and characters in a format called Unicode. Encoding just means taking the logical data (like the letter H) and turning it into bytes (the number 72). It needs to do that because letters, numbers, enums, and other data all end up in bytes on disk or in memory. And that's why Character Map is useful—it shows you how letters are encoded into numbers.

Select the Arial font and scroll down until you reach the Hebrew letters. Find the letter Shin and click on it.

As soon as you click on the letter, its Unicode number shows up in the status bar. The Hebrew letter Shin is number 05E9. That's a hexadecimal number—"**hex**" for short.

You can convert it to decimal using the Windows calculator: open it up, put it in Scientific mode, click the "Hex" radio button, enter "05E9", and then click "Dec"—it's 1,513.

Unicode is an industry standard developed by a non-profit group called the Unicode Consortium, and it works across programs and different computer platforms. Take a minute and look at their website: http://unicode.org/

Character Map

Font: *O* Arial

U+05E9: Hebrew Letter Shin

.NET uses Unicode to store characters and text

The two C# types for storing text and characters—`string` and `char`—keep their data in memory as Unicode. When that data's written out as bytes to a file, each of those Unicode numbers is written out to the file. So start a new project and drag three buttons onto a form, and we'll use the `File.WriteAllBytes()` and `ReadAllBytes()` methods to get a sense of exactly how Unicode data is written out to a file.

Do this!

1 **Write a normal string out to a file and read it back**

Use the same `WriteAllText()` method that you used in the text editor to have the first button write the string "Eureka!" out to a file called "eureka.txt". Then create a new byte array called `eurekaBytes`, read the file into it, and then print out all of the bytes read:

```
File.WriteAllText("eureka.txt", "Eureka!");
byte[] eurekaBytes = File.ReadAllBytes("eureka.txt");
foreach (byte b in eurekaBytes)
    Console.Write("{0} ", b);
Console.WriteLine();
```

↖ The ReadAllBytes() method returns a reference to a new array of bytes that contains all of the bytes that were read in from the file.

You'll see these bytes written to the output: `69 117 114 101 107 97 33`. Now **open up the file in the Simple Text Editor** that you wrote earlier in the chapter. It says "Eureka!"

2 **Make the second button display the bytes as hex numbers**

It's not just Character Map that shows numbers in hex. Almost anything you read that has to do with encoding data will show that data in hex, so it's useful to know how to work with it. Make the code for the second button's event handler in your program **identical to the first one**, except change the `Console.Write()` line so it looks like this instead:

```
Console.Write("{0:x2} ", b);
```

Hex uses the numbers 0 through 9 and letters A through F to represent numbers in base 16, so 6B is equal to 107.

That tells `Write()` to print parameter 0 (the first one after the string to print) as a two-character hex code. So it writes the same seven bytes in hex instead of decimal: `45 75 72 65 6b 61 21` ←

3 **Make the third button write out Hebrew letters**

Go back to Character Map and double-click on the Shin character (or click the Select button). It'll add it to the "Characters to copy" box. Then do the same for the rest of the letters in "Shalom": Lamed (U+05DC), Vav (U+05D5), and Final Mem (U+05DD). Now add the code for the third button's event handler. It'll look exactly like button 2, except for one change. Click the "Copy" button in Character Map, and then paste the letters over "Eureka!" and add the `Encoding.Unicode` parameter, so it looks like this:

```
File.WriteAllText("eureka.txt", "שלום", Encoding.Unicode);
```

Did you notice that the IDE pasted the letters in **backward**? That's because it knows that Hebrew is read right-to-left, so any time it encounters Hebrew Unicode letters, it displays them right-to-left. Put your cursor in the middle of the letters—the left and right arrow keys reversed! That makes it a lot easier if you need to type in Hebrew. Now run the code, and look closely at the output: `ff fe e9 05 dc 05 d5 05 dd 05`. The first two characters are "FF FE", which is the Unicode way of saying that we're going to have a string of two-byte characters. The rest of the bytes are the Hebrew letters—but they're reversed, so U+05E9 appears as **e9 05**. Now open the file up in your Simple Text Editor—it looks right!

C# can use byte arrays to move data around

Since all your data ends up encoded as **bytes**, it makes sense to think of a file as one **big byte array**. And you already know how to read and write byte arrays.

Here's the code to create a byte array, open an input stream, and read data into bytes 0 through 6 of the array.

```
byte[] greeting;
greeting = File.ReadAllBytes(filename);
```

7 byte variables

0	1	2	3	4	5	6
72	101	108	108	111	33	33

These numbers are the Unicode numbers for the characters in "Hello!!"

This is a static method for Arrays that reverses the order of the bytes. We're just using it to show that the changes you make to the byte array get written out to the file exactly.

```
Array.Reverse(greeting);
File.WriteAllBytes(filename, greeting);
```

When the program writes the byte array out to a file, the text is in reverse order too.

7 byte variables

0	1	2	3	4	5	6
33	33	111	108	108	101	72

Now the bytes are in reverse order.

Reversing the bytes in "Hello!!" only works because each of those characters is one byte long. Can you figure out why this won't work for שלום?

StreamWriter also encodes your data. It just specializes in text and text encoding.

Use a BinaryWriter to write binary data

You **could** encode all of your strings, chars, ints, and floats into byte arrays before writing them out to files, but that would get pretty tedious. That's why .NET gives you a very useful class called **BinaryWriter** that **automatically encodes your data** and writes it to a file. All you need to do is create a FileStream and pass it into the BinaryWriter's constructor. Then you can call its methods to write out your data. So add another button to your program, and we'll show you how to use BinaryWriter().

—Do this!

1 Start by creating a Console Application and setting up some data to write to a file.

```
int intValue = 48769414;
string stringValue = "Hello!";
byte[] byteArray = { 47, 129, 0, 116 };
float floatValue = 491.695F;
char charValue = 'E';
```

If you use File.Create(), it'll start a new file—if there's one there already, it'll blow it away and start a brand new one. There's also the File.OpenWrite() method, which opens the existing one and starts overwriting it from the beginning.

2 To use a BinaryWriter, first you need to open a new stream with File.Create():

```
using (FileStream output = File.Create("binarydata.dat"))
using (BinaryWriter writer = new BinaryWriter(output)) {
```

3 Now just call its Write() method. Each time you do, it adds new bytes onto the end of the file that contain an encoded version of whatever data you passed it as a parameter.

```
writer.Write(intValue);
writer.Write(stringValue);
writer.Write(byteArray);
writer.Write(floatValue);
writer.Write(charValue);
}
```

Each Write() statement encodes one value into bytes, and then sends those bytes to the FileStream object. You can pass it any value type, and it'll encode it automatically.

The FileStream writes the bytes to the end of the file.

Sharpen your pencil

4 Now use the same code you used before to read in the file you just wrote.

```
byte[] dataWritten = File.ReadAllBytes("binarydata.dat");
foreach (byte b in dataWritten)
    Console.Write("{0:x2} ", b);
Console.WriteLine(" - {0} bytes", dataWritten.Length);

Console.ReadKey();
```

Here's a hint: Strings can be different lengths, so the string has to start with a number to tell .NET how long it is. Also, you can look up the string and char Unicode values using Character Map.

Write down the output in the blanks below. Can you **figure out what bytes correspond** to each of the five Write() statements? Mark each group of bytes with the name of the variable.

_   - ___ bytes

an amalgam of data

float and int values take up 4 bytes when you write them to a file. If you'd used long or double, then they'd take up 8 bytes each.

Sharpen your pencil
Solution

86 29 e8 02 06 48 65 6c 6c 6f 21 2f 81 00 74 f6 d8 f5 43 45 — 20 bytes

intValue   stringValue   byteArray   charValue

The first byte in the string is 6—that's the length of the string. You can use Character Map to look up each of the characters in "Hello!"—it starts with U+0048 and ends with U+0021.

If you use the Windows calculator to convert these bytes from hex to decimal, you can see that these are the numbers in byteArray.

char holds a Unicode character, and 'E' only takes one byte—it's encoded as U+0045.

Use BinaryReader to read the data back in

The BinaryReader class works just like BinaryWriter. You create a stream, attach the BinaryReader object to it, and then call its methods. But the reader **doesn't know what data's in the file**! And it has no way of knowing. Your float value of 491.695F was encoded as d8 f5 43 45. But those same bytes are a perfectly valid int—1,140,185,334. So you'll need to tell the BinaryReader exactly what types to read from the file. Add one more button to your form, and have it read the data you just wrote.

Don't take our word for it. Replace the line that reads the float with a call to ReadInt32(). (You'll need to change the type of floatRead to int.) Then you can see for yourself what it reads from the file.

① Start out by setting up the FileStream and BinaryReader objects:

```
using (FileStream input = File.OpenRead("binarydata.dat"))
using (BinaryReader reader = new BinaryReader(input)) {
```

② You tell BinaryReader what type of data to read by calling its different methods.

```
int intRead = reader.ReadInt32();
string stringRead = reader.ReadString();
byte[] byteArrayRead = reader.ReadBytes(4);
float floatRead = reader.ReadSingle();
char charRead = reader.ReadChar();
```

Each value type has its own method in BinaryReader() that returns the data in the correct type. Most don't need any parameters, but ReadBytes() takes one parameter that tells BinaryReader how many bytes to read.

③ You tell BinaryReader what type of data to read by calling its different methods.

```
Console.Write("int: {0}  string: {1}  bytes: ", intRead, stringRead);
foreach (byte b in byteArrayRead)
    Console.Write("{0} ", b);
Console.Write(" float: {0}  char: {1} ", floatRead, charRead);
}
Console.ReadKey();
```

Here's the output that gets printed to the console:

```
int: 48769414  string: Hello!  bytes: 47 129 0 116  float: 491.695  char: E
```

You can read and write serialized files manually, too

Serialized files don't look so pretty when you open them up in Notepad. You'll find all the files you write in your project's `bin\Debug` folder—let's take a minute and get more acquainted with the inner workings of a serialized file.

Do this!

1 **Serialize two Card objects to different files**
Use the serialization code you've already written to serialize the **Three of Clubs** to `three-c.dat` and **Six of Hearts** to `six-h.dat`. Check to make sure that both files were written out and are now in a folder, and that they both have the same file size. Then open one of them in Notepad:

There are some words in the file, but it's mostly unreadable.

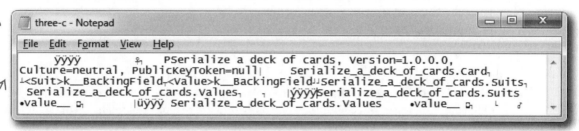

2 **Write a loop to compare the two binary files**
We used the ReadByte() method to read the next byte from a stream—it returns an int that contains the value of that byte. We also used the stream's Length field to make sure we read the whole file.

```
byte[] firstFile = File.ReadAllBytes("three-c.dat");
byte[] secondFile = File.ReadAllBytes("six-h.dat");
for (int i = 0; i < firstFile.Length; i++)
    if (firstFile[i] != secondFile[i])
        Console.WriteLine("Byte #{0}: {1} versus {2}",
            i, firstFile[i], secondFile[i]);
```

This loop examines the first byte from each of the files and compares them, then the second byte, then the third, etc. When it finds a difference, it writes a line to the console.

The two files are read into two different byte arrays, so they can be compared byte by byte. Since the same class was serialized to two different files, they'll be almost identical...but let's see just HOW identical they are.

Watch it!

When you write to a file, you don't always start from a clean slate!

Be careful if you use File.OpenWrite(). It doesn't delete the file—it just starts overwriting the data starting at the beginning. That's why we've been using File.Create()—it creates a new file.

→ We're not done yet—flip the page!

Find where the files differ, and use that information to alter them

The loop you just wrote pinpoints exactly where the two serialized `Card` files differ. Since the only difference between the two objects were their `Suit` and `Value` fields, then that should be the only difference in their files, too. So if we find the bytes that hold the suit and value, we should be able to **change them to make a new card** with whatever suit and value we want!

> ***You can also serialize your objects to XML. Flip to leftover #9 in the appendix to learn more about it.***

3 **Take a look at the console output to see how the two files differ**
The console should show that two bytes differ:

```
Byte #322: 1 versus 3
Byte #382: 3 versus 6
```

That should make a lot of sense! Go back to the `Suits` enum from the last chapter, and you'll find the value for Clubs is 1 and the value for Hearts is 3, so that's the first difference. And the second difference—six versus three—is pretty obviously the card's value. You might see different byte numbers, which isn't surprising: you might be using a different namespace, which would change the length of the file.

Remember how the namespace was included as part of the serialized file? If your namespace is different, then the byte numbers will be different, too.

Hmm, if byte #322 in the serialized file represents the suit, then we should be able to change the suit of the card by reading that file in, changing that one byte, and writing it out again. (Remember, your own serialized file might store the suit at a different location.)

4 **Write code to manually create a new file that contains the King of Spades**
We'll take one of the arrays that we read, alter it to contain a new card, and write it back out.

```
firstFile[322] = (byte)Suits.Spades;
firstFile[382] = (byte)Values.King;
File.Delete("king-s.dat");
File.WriteAllBytes("king-s.dat", firstFile);
```

If you found different byte numbers in step #3, substitute them in here.

Now **deserialize the card from king-s.dat** and see if it's the King of Spades!

Now that you know which bytes contain the suit and value, you can change just those bytes in the array before it gets written out to king-s.dat.

Working with binary files can be tricky

What do you do if you have a file and you aren't quite sure what's inside it? You don't know what application created it, and you need to know something about it—but when you open it in Notepad, it looks like a bunch of garbage. What if you've exhausted all your other options, and really need to just look inside? Looking at that picture, it's pretty clear that Notepad just isn't the right tool.

Here's the serialized card, opened up in Notepad. That's not going to be useful at all.

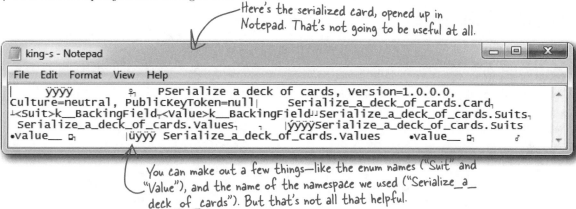

You can make out a few things—like the enum names ("Suit" and "Value"), and the name of the namespace we used ("Serialize_a_deck_of_cards"). But that's not all that helpful.

There's another option—it's a format called a "hex dump," and it's a pretty standard way to look at binary data. It's definitely more informative than looking at the file in Notepad. Hexadecimal—or "hex"—is a convenient way to display bytes in a file. Every byte takes 2 characters to display in hex, so you can see a lot of data in a really small space, and a format that makes it easy to spot patterns. Also, it's useful to display binary data in rows that are 8, 16, or 32 bytes long because most binary data tends to break down in chunks of 4, 8, 16, or 32…like all the types in C#. For example, an `int` takes up 4 bytes, and is 4 bytes long when serialized on disk. Here's what that same file looks like as a hex dump, using one of any number of free hex dump programs available for Windows:

You can immediately see the numeric value of each byte in the file.

The number at the beginning of each line is the offset (or distance into the file) of the first byte in the line.

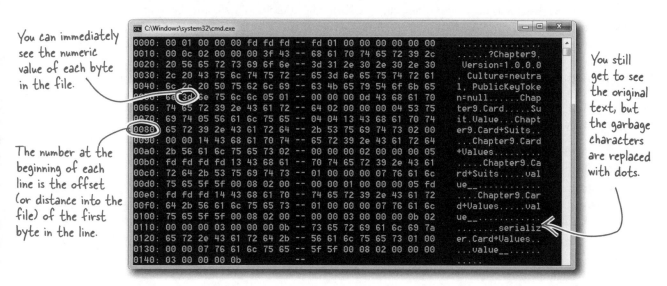

You still get to see the original text, but the garbage characters are replaced with dots.

Use file streams to build a hex dumper

A **hex dump** is a *hexadecimal* view of the contents of a file, and it's a really common way for programmers to take a deep look at a file's internal structure. Most operating systems ship with a built-in hex dump utility. Unfortunately, Windows doesn't. So let's build one!

How to make a hex dump

Start with some familiar text:

```
We the People of the United States, in Order to form a more perfect Union...
```

Here's what a hex dump of that text would look like:

Again, you can immediately see the numeric value of each byte in the file.

```
0000: 57 65 20 74 68 65 20 50 -- 65 6f 70 6c 65 20 6f 66    We the People of
0010: 20 74 68 65 20 55 6e 69 -- 74 65 64 20 53 74 61 74     the United Stat
0020: 65 73 2c 20 69 6e 20 4f -- 72 64 65 72 20 74 6f 20    es, in Order to
0030: 66 6f 72 6d 20 61 20 6d -- 6f 72 65 20 70 65 72 66    form a more perf
0040: 65 63 74 20 55 6e 69 6f -- 6e 2e 2e 2e                 ect Union...
```

And we'll need to replace the garbage characters with periods.

We'll add the number at the beginning of each line by using the offset of the first byte in the line.

Each of those numbers—57, 65, 6F—is the value of one byte in the file. The reason some of the "numbers" have letter values is that they're *hexadecimal* (or hex). That's just another way of writing a number. Instead of using ten digits from 0 to 9, it uses sixteen digits from 0 to 9 plus the letters A through F.

Each line in our hex dump represents sixteen characters in the input that was used to generate it. In our dump, the first four characters are the offset in the file—the first line starts at character 0, the next at character 16 (or hex 10), then character 32 (hex 20), etc. (Other hex dumps look slightly different, but this one will do for us.)

Working with hex

You can put hex numbers directly into your program—just add the characters 0x (a zero followed by an x) in front of the number:

```
int j = 0x20;
MessageBox.Show("The value is " + j);
```

When you use the + operator to concatenate a number into a string, it gets converted to decimal. You can use the static `String.Format()` method to convert your number to a hex-formatted string instead:

String.Format() uses parameters just like Console.WriteLine(), so you don't need to learn anything new to use it.

```
string h = String.Format("{0:x2}", j);
```

StreamReader and StreamWriter will do just fine (for now)

Our hex dumper will write its dump out to a file, and since it's just writing text a
`StreamWriter` will do just fine. But we can also take advantage of the **ReadBlock()**
method in `StreamReader`. It reads a block of characers into a `char` array—you
specify the number of characters you want to read, and it'll either read that many
characters or, if there are fewer than that many left in the file, it'll read the rest of the file.
Since we're displaying 16 characters per line, we'll read blocks of 16 characters.

> *The reason the method's called "ReadBlock()" is that when you call it, it "blocks" (which means it keeps executing and doesn't return to your program) until it's either read all the characters you asked for or run out of data to read.*

So add one more button to your program—add this hex dumper to it. Change the first
two lines so that they point to real files on your hard drive. Start with a serialized `Card`
file. Then see if you can modify it to use the Open and Save As dialog boxes.

```
using (StreamReader reader = new StreamReader(@"c:\files\inputFile.txt"))
using (StreamWriter writer = new StreamWriter(@"c:\files\outputFile.txt", false))
{
    int position = 0;

    while (!reader.EndOfStream) {
        char[] buffer = new char[16];
        int charactersRead = reader.ReadBlock(buffer, 0, 16);
        writer.Write("{0}: ", String.Format("{0:x4}", position));
        position += charactersRead;

        for (int i = 0; i < 16; i++) {
            if (i < charactersRead) {
                string hex = String.Format("{0:x2}", (byte)buffer[i]);
                writer.Write(hex + " ");
            }
            else
                writer.Write("   ");

            if (i == 7) { writer.Write("-- "); }
            if (buffer[i] < 32 || buffer[i] > 250) { buffer[i] = '.'; }
        }
        string bufferContents = new string(buffer);
        writer.WriteLine("   " + bufferContents.Substring(0, charactersRead));
    }
}
```

> *A StreamReader's EndOfStream property returns false if there are characters still left to read in the file.*

> *This **ReadBlock()** call reads up to 16 characters into a char array.*

> *The static **String.Format** method converts numbers to strings. "{0:x4}" tells Format() to print the second parameter—in this case, position—as a 4-character hex number.*

> *This loop goes through the characters and prints each of them to a line in the output.*

> *Some characters with a value under 32 don't print, so we'll replace all of them with a period.*

> *You can convert a char[] array to a string by passing it to the overloaded constructor for string.*

> *Every string has a Substring method that returns a piece of the string. In this case, it returns the first charactersRead characters starting at the beginning (position 0). (Look back at the top of the loop to see where charactersRead is set—the ReadBlock() method returns the number of characters that it read into the array.)*

Use Stream.Read() to read bytes from a stream ✳ ↙ Do this

The hex dumper works just fine for text files. But there's a problem. Try using `File.WriteAllBytes()` to write an array of bytes with values over 127 to a file and then run it through your dumper. Uh oh—they're all read in as "fd"! That's because **StreamReader is built to read text files**, which only contain bytes with values under 128. So let's do this right—by reading the bytes directly from the stream using the **Stream.Read()** method. And as a bonus, we'll build it just like a real hex dump utility: we'll make it take a filename as a **command-line argument**.

Create a new Console Application and **call it hexdumper**. The code for the program is on the facing page. Here's what it will look like when you run the program:

If you run hexdumper without any
arguments, it returns an error message
and exits with an error code.

It also exits with an error if you pass it
the name of a file that doesn't exist.

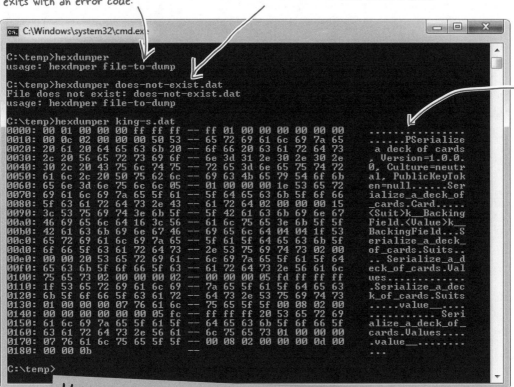

If you pass it a
valid filename, it'll
write a hex dump
of the contents
of the file to the
console.

Normally we use Console.
WriteLine() to print
to the console. But
we'll use **Console.Error.
WriteLine()** to print
error messages so they
don't get redirected
if we use > or >> to
redirect the output.

Using command-line arguments

Every time you create a new Console Application project, Visual Studio creates a Program class with an entry point method that has this declaration: **static void Main(string[] args)**. If you run your program with command-line arguments, the **args** parameter will contain those arguments. And it's not just for Console Applications, either: open up any Windows Forms Application project's Program.cs file, and you'll see the same thing.

You'll want to pass command-line arguments when you're debugging your program. To pass arguments when you run your program in the IDE's debugger, choose "Properties..." from the Project menu and enter them on the Debug tab.

Command-line arguments will be passed using the args parameter.

If args.Length is not equal to 1, then either zero or more than one argument was passed on the command line.

This Exit() method quits the program. If you pass it an int, it will return that error code (which is useful when writing command scripts and batch files).

```
static void Main(string[] args)
{
    if (args.Length != 1)
    {
        Console.Error.WriteLine("usage: hexdmper file-to-dump");
        System.Environment.Exit(1);
    }
    if (!File.Exists(args[0]))
    {
        Console.Error.WriteLine("File does not exist: {0}", args[0]);
        System.Environment.Exit(2);
    }
    using (Stream input = File.OpenRead(args[0]))
    {
        int position = 0;
        byte[] buffer = new byte[16];
        while (position < input.Length)
        {
            int charactersRead = input.Read(buffer, 0, buffer.Length);
            if (charactersRead > 0)
            {
                Console.Write("{0}: ", String.Format("{0:x4}", position));
                position += charactersRead;

                for (int i = 0; i < 16; i++)
                {
                    if (i < charactersRead)
                    {
                        string hex = String.Format("{0:x2}", (byte)buffer[i]);
                        Console.Write(hex + " ");
                    }
                    else
                        Console.Write("   ");

                    if (i == 7)
                        Console.Write("-- ");

                    if (buffer[i] < 32 || buffer[i] > 250) { buffer[i] = (byte)'.'; }
                }
                string bufferContents = Encoding.UTF8.GetString(buffer);
                Console.WriteLine("   " + bufferContents.Substring(0, charactersRead));
            }
        }
    }
}
```

Notice how we're using Console.Error.WriteLine() here.

Let's make sure that a valid file was passed. If it doesn't exist, print a different error message and return a different exit code.

We don't need a StreamReader because we're reading bytes directly from the stream.

Use the Stream.Read() method to read bytes directly into a buffer. Notice how this time the buffer is a byte array. That makes sense—we're reading bytes, not characters from a text file.

This part of the program is exactly the same, except the buffer contains bytes and not characters (but String.Format() does the right thing in either case).

This is an easy way to convert a byte array to a string. It's part of Encoding.UTF8 (or another Unicode encoding, or ASCII, or another encoding) because different encodings can map the same byte array to different strings.

there are no
Dumb Questions

Q: Why didn't I have to use the `Close()` method to close the file after I used `File.ReadAllText()` and `File.WriteAllText()`?

A: The `File` class has several very useful static methods that automatically open up a file, read or write data, and then **close it automatically**. In addition to the `ReadAllText()` and `WriteAllText()` methods, there are `ReadAllBytes()` and `WriteAllBytes()`, which work with byte arrays, and `ReadAllLines()` and `WriteAllLines()`, which read and write string arrays, where each string in the array is a separate line in the file. All of these methods automatically open and close the streams, so you can do your whole file operation in a single statement.

Q: If the `FileStream` has methods for reading and writing, why do I ever need to use `StreamReader` and `StreamWriter`?

A: The `FileStream` class is really useful for reading and writing bytes to binary files. Its methods for reading and writing operate with bytes and byte arrays. But a lot of programs work exclusively with text files—like the first version of the Excuse Generator, which only wrote strings out to files. That's where the `StreamReader` and `StreamWriter` come in really handy. They have methods that are built specifically for reading and writing lines of text. Without them, if you wanted to read a line of text in from a file, you'd have to first read a byte array and then write a loop to search through that array for a linebreak—so it's easy to see how they make your life easier.

Q: When should I use `File`, and when should I use `FileInfo`?

A: The main difference between the `File` and `FileInfo` classes is that the methods in `File` are static, so you don't need to create an instance of them. On the other hand, `FileInfo` requires that you instantiate it with a filename. In some cases, that would be more cumbersome, like if you only need to perform a single file operation (like just deleting or moving one file). On the other hand, if you need to do many file operations to the same file, then it's more efficient to use `FileInfo`, because you only need to pass it the filename once. You should decide which one to use based on the particular situation you encounter. In other words, if you're doing one file operation, use `File`. If you're doing a lot of file operations in a row, use `FileInfo`.

Q: Back up a minute. Why was "Eureka!" written out with one byte per character, but when I wrote out the Hebrew letters they took up two bytes? And what was that "FF FE" thing at the beginning of the bytes?

A: What you're seeing is the difference between two **closely related** Unicode encodings. Plain English letters, numbers, normal punctuation marks, and some standard characters (like curly brackets, ampersands, and other things you see on your keyboard) all have very low Unicode numbers—between 0 and 127. (If you've used ASCII before, they're the same as the ASCII characters.) If a file only contains those Unicode characters with low numbers, it just prints out their bytes.

Things get a little more complicated when you add higher-numbered Unicode characters into the mix. One byte can only hold a number between 0 and 255. But two bytes in a row can store numbers between 0 and 65,536—which, in hex, is FFFF. The file needs to be able to tell whatever program opens it up that it's going to contain these higher-numbered characters. So it puts a special reserved byte sequence at the beginning of the file: "FF FE". That's called the "byte order mark." As soon as a program sees that, it knows that all of the characters are encoded with two bytes each. (So an E is encoded as 00 45—with leading zeroes.)

Q: Why is it called a byte order mark?

A: Remember how your bytes were reversed? Shin's Unicode value of U+05E9 was written to the file as E9 05. That's called "little endian." Go back to the code that wrote out those bytes and change the third parameter to `WriteAllText()`: `Encoding.BigEndianUnicode`. That tells it to write the data out in "big endian," which doesn't flip the bytes around. You'll see the bytes come out as "05 E9" this time. You'll also see a different byte order mark: "FE FF". And your Simple Text Editor is smart enough to read both of them!

If you're writing a string that only has Unicode characters with low numbers, it writes one byte per character. But if it's got high-numbered characters, they'll be written using two or more bytes each.

The encoding is called UTF-8, which .NET uses by default. You can tell File.WriteAllText() to use a different encoding by passing it a different Encoding value. You can learn more about Unicode encodings at http://unicode.org.

Exercise

Change Brian's Excuse Manager so it uses binary files with serialized `Excuse` objects instead of text files.

1 **Make the `Excuse` class serializable**
Mark the Excuse class with the `[Serializable]` attribute to make it serializable. Also, you'll need to add the `using` line:
`using System.Runtime.Serialization.Formatters.Binary;`

2 **Change the `Excuse.Save()` method to serialize the excuse**
When the `Save()` method writes a file out to the folder, instead of using `StreamWriter` to write the file out, have it open a file and serialize itself out. You'll need to figure out how the current class can deserialize itself.

Hint: What keyword can you use inside of a class that returns a reference to itself?

3 **Change the `Excuse.OpenFile()` method to deserialize an excuse**
You'll need to create a temporary Excuse object to deserialize from the file, and then copy its fields into the current class.

4 **Now just change the form so it uses a new file extension**
There's just one very small change you need to make to the form. Since we're no longer working with text files, we shouldn't use the `.txt` extension anymore. Change the dialog boxes, default filenames, and directory search code so that they work with `*.excuse` files instead.

> Wow, that was really easy! All the code for saving and opening excuses was inside the Excuse class. I just had to change the class—I barely had to touch the form at all. It's like the form doesn't even care how the class saves its data. It just passes in the filename and knows everything will get saved properly.

That's right! Your code was very easy to change because the class was well encapsulated.

When you've got a class that hides its internal operations from the rest of the program and only exposes the behavior that needs to be exposed, it's called a **well-encapsulated class**. In the Excuse Manager program, the form doesn't have any information about how excuses are saved to files. It just passes a filename into the excuse class, and the class takes care of the rest. That makes it very easy to make big changes to how your class works with files. The better you encapsulate your classes, the easier they are to alter later on.

Remember how encapsulation was one of the four core OOP principles? Here's an example of how using those principles makes your programs better.

Exercise Solution

Change Brian's Excuse Manager so it uses binary files with serialized Excuse objects instead of text files.

You only need to change these three statements in the form: two in the Save button's Click event, and one in the Open button's—they just change the dialogs to use the .excuse extension, and set the default save filename.

```
private void save_Click(object sender, EventArgs e) {
  // existing code
  saveFileDialog1.Filter = "Excuse files (*.excuse)|*.excuse|All files (*.*)|*.*";
  saveFileDialog1.FileName = description.Text + ".excuse";
  // existing code
}
private void open_Click(object sender, EventArgs e) {
  // existing code
  openFileDialog1.Filter =
    "Excuse files (*.excuse)|*.excuse|All files (*.*)|*.*";
  // existing code
}

[Serializable]
class Excuse {
    public string Description { get; set; }
    public string Results { get; set; }
    public DateTime LastUsed { get; set; }
    public string ExcusePath { get; set; }

    public Excuse() {
        ExcusePath = "";
    }
    public Excuse(string excusePath) {
        OpenFile(excusePath);
    }
    public Excuse(Random random, string folder) {
        string[] fileNames = Directory.GetFiles(folder, "*.excuse");
        OpenFile(fileNames[random.Next(fileNames.Length)]);
    }
    private void OpenFile(string excusePath) {
        this.ExcusePath = excusePath;
        BinaryFormatter formatter = new BinaryFormatter();
        Excuse tempExcuse;
        using (Stream input = File.OpenRead(excusePath)) {
            tempExcuse = (Excuse)formatter.Deserialize(input);
        }
        Description = tempExcuse.Description;
        Results = tempExcuse.Results;
        LastUsed = tempExcuse.LastUsed;
    }
    public void Save(string fileName) {
        BinaryFormatter formatter = new BinaryFormatter();
        using (Stream output = File.OpenWrite(fileName)) {
            formatter.Serialize(output, this);
        }
    }
}
```

Standard save and open dialog boxes do the trick here.

Here's the entire Excuse class.

The only change to the form is to have it change the file extension it passes to the Excuse class.

The constructor for loading random excuses needs to look for the ".excuse" extension instead of ".txt" files.*

We pass in "this" because we want this class to be serialized.

 Filecross

Across

6. The method in the `File` class that checks whether or not a specific file is on the drive

9. This statement indicates the end of a case inside a switch statement

10. The abstract class that `FileStream` inherits from

11. A non-visual control that lets you pop up the standard Windows "Save As" dialog box

15. How you write numbers in base-16

16. If you don't call this method, your stream could be locked open so other methods or programs can't open it

17. The `StreamReader` method that reads data into a `char[]` array

18. An encoding system that assigns a unique number to each character

19. Use this statement to indicate which statements should be executed when the value being tested in a `switch` statement does not match any of the cases

Down

1. This class has a method that writes a type to a file

2. The static method in the `Array` class that turns an array backward

3. The event handler that gets run whenever someone modifies the data in an input control

4. This class has many static methods that let you manipulate folders

5. Using this OOP principle makes it a lot easier to maintain your code

7. If you don't use this attribute to indicate that a class can be written to a stream, BinaryFormatter will generate an error

8. This BinaryFormatter method reads an object from a stream

12. `\n` and `\r` are examples of this kind of sequence

13. This class lets you perform all the operations in the `File` class for a specific file

14. This method sends text to a stream followed by a line break

Filecross solution

Across and Down answers:

1	B	I	N	A	R	Y	W	R	I	T	E	R
2	R	E	V	E	R	S	E	R	S
3	C	H	A	N	G	E
4	D	E	S	E	R	I	A	L	I	Z	A	B	L	E
5	E	N	C	A	P	S	U	L	A	T	I	O	N
6	E	X	I	S	T
7	S	E	R	I	A	L	I	Z	A	B	L	E
8	D	E	S	E	R	I	A	L	I	Z	E
9	B	R	E	A	K
10	S	T	R	E	A	M
11	S	A	V	E	F	I	L	E
12	E	D	I	A	L	O	G	E	R	Y
13	F	I	L	I	N	F	I	N	F
14	W	R	I	T	E	L	I	N	E
15	H	E	X	A	D	E	C	I	M	A	L
16	C	L	O	S	E
17	R	E	A	D	B	L	O	C	K
18	U	N	I	C	O	D	E
19	D	E	F	A	U	L	T

10 exception handling

Putting out fires gets old

Good thing I wrote code to handle my HangoverException.

Programmers aren't meant to be firefighters.

You've worked your tail off, waded through technical manuals and a few engaging Head First books, and you've reached the pinnacle of your profession: **master programmer**. But you're still getting panicked phone calls in the middle of the night from work because **your program crashes**, or **doesn't behave like it's supposed to**. Nothing pulls you out of the programming groove like having to fix a strange bug...but with **exception handling**, you can write code to **deal with problems** that come up. Better yet, you can even react to those problems, and **keep things running**.

Brian needs his excuses to be mobile

Brian recently got reassigned to the international division. Now
he flies all over the world. But he still needs to keep track of his
excuses, so he installed the program you built on his laptop and
takes it with him everywhere.

Work's boring today. I want to
go scuba diving. Time to fire up
the Excuse Generator.

Brian's got the excuse
Generator running on
his laptop.

Same ol' Brian...
always looking for
an excuse to get
out of work.

But the program isn't working!

Brian clicks the "Random Excuse" button, and gets a pretty nasty
looking error. Something about not finding his excuses. What gives?

Excuse Manager

Unhandled exception has occurred in your application. If you click
Continue, the application will ignore this error and attempt to continue. If
you click Quit, the application will close immediately.

Index was outside the bounds of the array.

▼ Details   Continue   Quit

An unhandled
exception...must
have been a
problem we didn't
account for.

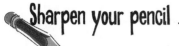

Sharpen your pencil

Here's another example of some broken code. There are five different exceptions that this code throws, and the error messages are shown on the right. It's your job to match the line of code that has a problem with the exception that line generates. Read the exception messages for a good hint.

```
public static void BeeProcessor() {
    object myBee = new HoneyBee(36.5, "Zippo");
    float howMuchHoney = (float)myBee;

    HoneyBee anotherBee = new HoneyBee(12.5, "Buzzy");
    double beeName = double.Parse(anotherBee.MyName);

    double totalHoney = 36.5 + 12.5;
    string beesWeCanFeed = "";
    for (int i = 1; i < (int) totalHoney; i++) {
        beesWeCanFeed += i.ToString();
    }
    float f =
      float.Parse(beesWeCanFeed);

    int drones = 4;
    int queens = 0;
    int dronesPerQueen = drones / queens;

    anotherBee = null;
    if (dronesPerQueen < 10) {
        anotherBee.DoMyJob();
    }
}
```

Calling double.Parse("32") will parse a string and return a double value, like 32.

When you have a reference that doesn't point to any object, it gets a special value called null. Setting a reference to null tells C# it doesn't point to anything.

⚠ OverflowException was unhandled ①
Value was either too large or too small for a Single.

⚠ NullReferenceException was unhandled ②
Object reference not set to an instance of an object.

⚠ InvalidCastException was unhandled ③
Specified cast is not valid.

⚠ DivideByZeroException was unhandled ④
Attempted to divide by zero.
Troubleshooting tips:
Make sure the value of the denominator is not zero before performing a division operation.
Get general help for this exception.

Search for more Help Online...

⚠ FormatException was unhandled ⑤
Input string was not in a correct format.
Troubleshooting tips:
Make sure your method arguments are in the right format.
When converting a string to DateTime, parse the string to take the date before putting each variable into the DateTime object.
Get general help for this exception.
Search for more Help Online...

Sharpen your pencil
Solution

Your job was to match the line of code that has a problem with the exception that line generates.

C# lets you cast myBee to a float—but there's no way to convert a HoneyBee object to a float value. When your code actually runs, the CLR has no idea how to actually d... that cast, so it throws an InvalidCastException.

```
object myBee = new HoneyBee(36.5, "Zippo");
float howMuchHoney = (float)myBee;
```

> ⚠ **InvalidCastException was unhandled**   ✕
> Specified cast is not valid.

The Parse() method wants you to give it a string in a certain format. "Buzzy" isn't a string it knows how to convert to a number. That's why it throws a FormatException.

```
HoneyBee anotherBee = new HoneyBee(12.5, "Buzzy");
double beeName = double.Parse(anotherBee.MyName);
```

> ⚠ **FormatException was unhandled**
> Input string was not in a correct format.
>
> **Troubleshooting tips:**
> Make sure your method arguments are in the right format.
> When converting a string to DateTime, parse the string to take the date before putting each variable into the DateTime object.
> Get general help for this exception.
>
> Search for more Help Online...

```
double totalHoney = 36.5 + 12.5;
string beesWeCanFeed = "";
for (int i = 1; i < (int) totalHoney; i++) {
    beesWeCanFeed += i.ToString();
}
float f = float.Parse(beesWeCanFeed);
```

The for loop will create a string called beesWeCanFeed that contains a number with over 60 digits in it. There's no way a float can hold a number that big, and trying to cram it into a float will throw an OverflowException.

> ⚠ **OverflowException was unhandled**
> Value was either too large or too small for a Single.

You'd never actually get all these exceptions in a row—the program would throw the first exception and then stop. You'd only get to the second exception if you fixed the first.

```
int drones = 4;
int queens = 0;
int dronesPerQueen = drones / queens;
```

It's really easy to throw a DivideByZeroException. Just divide any number by zero.

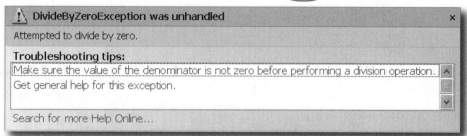

> ⚠ **DivideByZeroException was unhandled**   ✕
>
> Attempted to divide by zero.
>
> **Troubleshooting tips:**
>
> Make sure the value of the denominator is not zero before performing a division operation.
> Get general help for this exception.
>
> Search for more Help Online...

Dividing any integer by zero always throws this kind of exception. Even if you don't know the value of queens, you can prevent it just by checking the value to make sure it's not zero **before** you divide it into drones.

```
anotherBee = null;
if (dronesPerQueen < 10) {
    anotherBee.DoMyJob();
}
```

Setting the anotherBee reference variable equal to null tells C# that it doesn't point to anything. So instead of pointing to an object, it points to nothing. Throwing a NullReferenceException is C#'s way of telling you that there's no object whose DoMyJob() method can be called.

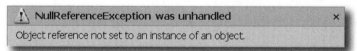

> ⚠ **NullReferenceException was unhandled**   ✕
>
> Object reference not set to an instance of an object.

That `DivideByZero` **error didn't have to happen. You can see just by looking at the code that there's something wrong. The same goes for the other exceptions. These problems were preventable—and the more you know about exceptions, the better you'll be at keeping your code from crashing.**

When your program throws an exception, .NET generates an Exception object.

You've been looking at .NET's way of telling you something went wrong in your program: an **exception**. In .NET, when an exception occurs, an object is created to represent the problem. It's called, no surprise here, Exception.

For example, suppose you have an array with four items. Then, you try and access the sixteenth item (index 15, since we're zero-based here):

> This code is obviously going to cause problems.

```
int[] anArray = {3, 4, 1, 11};
int aValue = anArray[15];
```

ex-cep-tion, noun.
a person or thing that is excluded from a general statement or does not follow a rule. *While Jim usually hates peanut butter, he made an* **exception** *for Ken's peanut butter fudge.*

As soon as your program runs into an exception, it generates an object with all the data it has about it.

Exception object

You can see this detail by clicking on the View Detail link in the unhandled exception window.

The exception object has a message that tells you what's wrong and a list of all of the calls that were made to the system's memory leading up to the event that caused the exception.

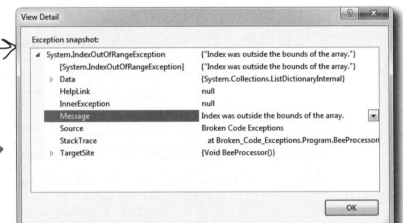

View Detail

Exception snapshot:

▲ System.IndexOutOfRangeException	{"Index was outside the bounds of the array."}
[System.IndexOutOfRangeException]	{"Index was outside the bounds of the array."}
▷ Data	{System.Collections.ListDictionaryInternal}
HelpLink	null
InnerException	null
Message	Index was outside the bounds of the array.
Source	Broken Code Exceptions
StackTrace	at Broken_Code_Exceptions.Program.BeeProcessor
▷ TargetSite	{Void BeeProcessor()}

OK

.NET goes to the trouble of creating an object because it wants to give you all the information about what caused the exception. You may have code to fix, or you may just need to make some changes to how you handle a particular situation in your program.

In this case, an **IndexOutOfRangeException** indicates you have a bug: you're trying to access an index in the array that's out of range. You've also got information about exactly where in the code the problem occurred, making it easy to track down (even if you've got thousands of lines of code).

Q: Why are there so many kinds of exceptions?

A: There are all sorts of ways that you can write code that C# simply doesn't know how to deal with. It would be difficult to troubleshoot your problems if your program simply gave a generic error message ("A problem occurred at line 37"). It's a lot easier to track down and fix problems in your code when you know specifically what kind of error occurred.

Q: So what *is* an exception, really?

A: It's an object that .NET creates when there's a problem. You can specifically generate exceptions in your code, too (more about that in a minute).

Q: Wait, what? It's an *object*?

A: Yes, an exception is an **object**. The properties in the object tell you information about the exception. For example, it's got a `Message` property that has a useful string like "Specified cast was invalid" or "Value was either too large or too small for a Single", which is what it used to generate the exception window. The reason that .NET generates it is to give you as much information as it can about exactly what was going on when it executed the statement that threw the exception.

Q: OK, I still don't get it. Sorry. Why are there so many different kinds of exceptions, again?

A: Because there are so many ways that your code can act in unexpected ways. There are a lot of situations that will cause your code to simply crash. It would be really hard to troubleshoot the problems if you didn't know why the crash happened. By throwing different kinds of exceptions under different circumstances, .NET is giving you a lot of really valuable information to help you track down and correct the problem.

Q: So exceptions are there to help me, not just cause a pain in my butt?

A: Yes! Exceptions are all about helping you expect the unexpected. A lot of people get frustrated when they see code throw an exception. But if you think about an exception as .NET's way of helping you track down and debug your program, it really helps out when you're trying to track down what's causing the code to bomb out.

Q: So when my code throws an exception, it's not necessarily because I did something wrong?

A: Exactly. Sometimes your data's different than you expected it to be—like you've got a method that's dealing with an array that's a lot longer or shorter than you anticipated when you first wrote it. And don't forget that human beings are using your program, and they almost always act in an unpredictable way. Exceptions are .NET's way to help you handle those unexpected situations so that your code still runs smoothly and doesn't simply crash or give a cryptic, useless error message.

Q: Once I knew what I was looking for, it was pretty clear that the code on the previous page was going to crash. Are all exceptions easy to spot?

A: No. Unfortunately, there will be times when your code will have problems, and it'll be really hard to figure out what's causing them just by looking at it. That's why the IDE gives you a really useful tool called the **debugger**. It lets you pause your program and execute it statement by statement, inspecting the value of each individual variable and field as you go. That makes it a lot easier for you to figure out where your code is acting in a way that's different from how you expect it to act. That's when you have the best chance of finding and fixing the exceptions—or, even better, preventing them in the first place.

> **Exceptions are all about helping you find and fix situations where your code behaves in ways you didn't expect.**

Brian's code did something unexpected

When Brian wrote his excuse manager, he never expected
the user to try to pull a random excuse out of an empty
directory.

1 The problem happened when Brian pointed his Excuse Manager program at an
empty folder on his laptop and clicked the Random button. Let's take a look at
it and see if we can figure out what went wrong. Here's the unhandled exception
window that popped up when he ran the program outside the IDE:

2 OK, that's a good starting point. It's telling us that the index was outside the
bounds of the array, right? So let's look for an array in the code for the Random
Excuse button's event handler:

```
private void randomExcuse_Click(object sender, EventArgs e) {
    if (CheckChanged()) {
        currentExcuse = new Excuse(random, selectedFolder);
        UpdateForm(false);
    }
}
```

3 Hmm, no arrays in there. But it creates a new `Excuse` object using one of the
overloaded constructors. Maybe there's an array in the constructor code:

```
public Excuse(Random random, string Folder) {
    string[] fileNames = Directory.GetFiles(Folder, "*.excuse");
    OpenFile(fileNames[random.Next(fileNames.Length)]);
}
```

*Bingo! There's the array.
We must be trying to use
an index that's past the
end of the array.*

4 It turns out that `Directory.GetFiles()` returns an empty array when you point it at a directory with no files in it. Hey, we can test for that! All we need to do is add a check to **make sure the directory's not empty** before we open a file, and the nasty unhandled exception window will be replaced with an informative message box.

```
private void randomExcuse_Click(object sender, EventArgs e) {
    string[] fileNames = Directory.GetFiles(selectedFolder,"*.excuse");
    if (fileNames.Length == 0) {
        MessageBox.Show("Please specify a folder with excuse files in it",
                        "No excuse files found");
    } else {
        if (CheckChanged() == true) {
            CurrentExcuse = new Excuse(random, Folder);
            UpdateForm(false);
        }
    }
}
```

*By checking for excuse files in the folder **before** we create the Excuse object, we can prevent the exception from being thrown—and pop up a helpful message box, too.*

> Oh, I get it. Exceptions aren't always bad. Sometimes they identify bugs, but a lot of the time they're just telling me that something happened that was different from what I expected.

That's right. Exceptions are a really useful tool that you can use to find places where your code acts in ways you don't expect.

A lot of programmers get frustrated the first time they see an exception. But exceptions are really useful, and you can use them to your advantage. When you see an exception, it's giving you a lot of clues to help you figure out when your code is reacting to a situation that you didn't anticipate. And that's good for you: it lets you know about a new scenario that your program has to handle, and it gives you an opportunity to **do something about it**.

All exception objects inherit from Exception

.NET has lots of different exceptions it may need to report. Since many of these have a lot of similar features, inheritance comes into play. .NET defines a base class, called `Exception`, that all specific exceptions types inherit from.

The `Exception` class has a couple of useful members. The `Message` property stores an easy-to-read message about what went wrong. And `StackTrace` tells you what code was being executed when the exception occurred, and what led up to the exception. (There are others, too, but we'll use those first.)

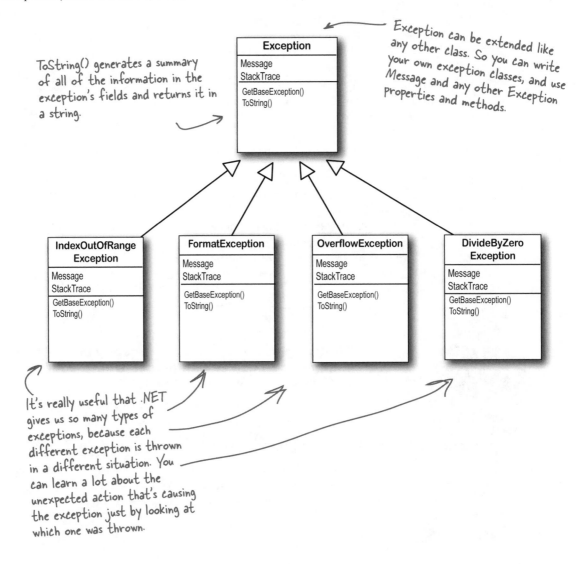

ToString() generates a summary of all of the information in the exception's fields and returns it in a string.

Exception can be extended like any other class. So you can write your own exception classes, and use Message and any other Exception Properties and methods.

It's really useful that .NET gives us so many types of exceptions, because each different exception is thrown in a different situation. You can learn a lot about the unexpected action that's causing the exception just by looking at which one was thrown.

The debugger helps you track down and prevent exceptions in your code

Before you can add exception handling to your program, you need to know which statements in your program are throwing the exception. That's where the **debugger** that's built into the IDE can be really helpful. You've been using the debugger throughout the book, but now let's take a few minutes and really dig into it. When you run the debugger, the IDE pops up a toolbar with some really useful buttons. Take a minute and hover your mouse cursor over each of them to see what it does:

The Debug toolbar only shows up when you're debugging your program in the IDE. So you'll have to run a program in order to hover over the toolbar icons.

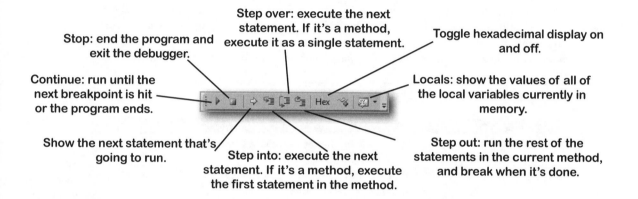

Stop: end the program and exit the debugger.

Step over: execute the next statement. If it's a method, execute it as a single statement.

Toggle hexadecimal display on and off.

Continue: run until the next breakpoint is hit or the program ends.

Locals: show the values of all of the local variables currently in memory.

Show the next statement that's going to run.

Step into: execute the next statement. If it's a method, execute the first statement in the method.

Step out: run the rest of the statements in the current method, and break when it's done.

Put your IDE into Expert mode to expand the Debug toolbar

When you first start using Visual Studio 2010 Express, it's set to Basic Settings mode, which is great for getting started. But now that you've been using it for a while, let's change it. Choose **Tools >> Settings >> Expert Settings** from the menu (it may take the IDE a minute to adjust its settings). Now take another look at the debug toolbar. You'll see that it added two new buttons (the other editions already have them turned on):

Break all causes the program to stop in its tracks as if it hit a breakpoint.

Restart stops the program and starts it up again.

Toggle hexadecimal mode on and off

Press the Hex button to turn hexadecimal mode on, then hover over any field or variable. Then press it again to turn off hexadecimal mode. The IDE automatically converts values to hex for you—and you learned last chapter how valuable that can be.

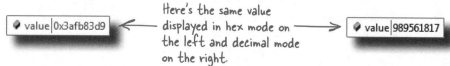

Here's the same value displayed in hex mode on the left and decimal mode on the right.

Use the IDE's debugger to ferret out exactly what went wrong in the Excuse Manager

Let's use the debugger to take a closer look at the problem that we ran into in the Excuse Manager. You've probably been using the debugger a lot over the last few chapters, but we'll go through it step by step anyway—to make sure we don't leave out any details.

 Add a breakpoint to the Random button's event handler

You've got a starting point—the exception happens when the Random Excuse button is clicked after an empty folder is selected. So open up the code for the button, click anywhere in the first line of the method (Debug >> Toggle Breakpoint or F9), and then run the program. Select an empty folder and click the Random button to make your program break at the breakpoint:

```csharp
private void randomExcuse_Click(object sender, EventArgs e)
{
    string[] fileNames = Directory.GetFiles(selectedFolder, "*.excuse");
    if (fileNames.Length == 0)        ● fileNames.Length == 0 │ true │
    {
        MessageBox.Show("Please specify a folder with excuse files in it",
                        "No excuse files found");
    }
    else
    {
        if (CheckChanged())
        {
            currentExcuse = new Excuse(random, selectedFolder);
            UpdateForm(false);
        }
    }
}
```

Hover over the fileNames.Length property to show the hovering expression window, then click the pushpin to pin it s[o] it doesn't disappe[ar]

② **Step through the event handler and into the** `Excuse` **constructor**

Use the **Step Into** command (using either the toolbar or the F11 key) to move through the application line by line. Since you selected an empty folder, you should see the program execute the `MessageBox.Show()` and then exit the event handler.

Now **select a folder with excuses in it** and click the Random button again, then keep stepping into the code. (Make sure you're using Step Into, *not Step Over*—although you might want to step over the `CheckChanged()` method.) When it gets to the line that creates the new `Excuse` object, it'll jump straight into the constructor. Step past the first line so it sets the `fileNames` variable. Then hover over the variable to see its value, too.

③ Use the Watch window to reproduce the problem

You've already seen how powerful the Watch window is. Now we'll use it to reproduce the exception. Right-click on `fileNames` and choose **Expression: 'fileNames' >> Add Watch** to add a watch to the Watch window. Then **click on the empty line below fileNames and enter the expression** `random.Next(fileNames.Length)` to tell the debugger to add a watch for it. Here's what the Watch window should look like for a folder with three excuses (so `fileNames` has length 3).

We'll use the Watch window to reproduce the problem that caused the exception. We'll start by adding the fileNames array.

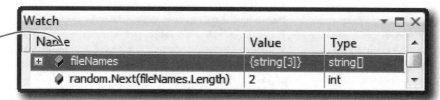

④ Set fileNames equal to an empty string array

The Watch window has another very useful feature—it lets you **change the value** of variables and fields that it's displaying. It even lets you **execute methods and create new objects**—and when you do, it displays its re-evaluate icon (⟳) that you can click to tell it to execute that line again, because sometimes running the same method twice will generate different results (like with Random).

Double-click on the value for `fileNames`—you'll see the text `{string[3]}` highlighted. Replace it with **new string[0]**. You should immediately see two things. First, you'll see the expand icon next to the `fileNames` variable disappear, because now it's empty. And second, the `random.Next()` line will become gray with a re-evaluate icon (⟳). Click the icon to execute the method again, which should return 0.

We know the problem happened with an empty fileNames array, so we'll use the Watch window to change its value to an empty string array.

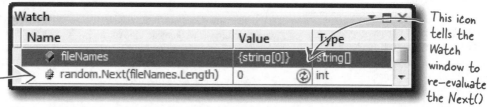

This icon tells the Watch window to re-evaluate the Next() method.

⑤ Reproduce the problem that threw Brian's original exception

Here's where debugging gets really interesting. Add one more line to the debugger—the statement that actually threw the exception: `fileNames[random.Next(fileNames.Length)]`. As soon as you type it in, the Watch window evaluates it…and that throws the exception. It tells you that it found the exception by displaying an exclamation point, and displays the text of the exception in the Value column.

This exclamation point is the Watch window's way of telling you it found an exception.

Watch			
Name	Value	Type	
⬦ fileNames	{string[0]}	string[]	
⬦ random.Next(fileNames.Length)	0	⟳ int	
❗ fileNames[random.Next(fileNames.Length)]	Out of bounds array index	⟳ string	

When you get an exception, you can go back and reproduce it in the debugger. That's another way that more descriptive exception messages can help you fix your code.

Q: How come Brian's unhandled exception window looked different from the one in the IDE?

A: Because when you run a program inside the IDE, you're running it in the debugger, which **breaks the program** (as if you'd pressed the Break All button or inserted a breakpoint) as soon as it intercepts an exception, and displays it in a useful window. That lets you inspect the `Exception` object and your program's fields and variables so you can track down the problem.

When Brian ran his program, he wasn't running it from inside the IDE. He'd published his program and installed it, just like you did back in Chapter 1 with the Contact List program. You can run your program outside the IDE any time without publishing it—just build your program, which causes Visual Studio to create an executable file. Look inside your project's folder for the `bin/` folder—one of its subdirectories should have the `exe` file for your application. If you run that, any exceptions that it throws will be unhandled and show the same window that Brian saw.

Q: So that's it? When an exception happens outside the IDE, my program just stops and there's nothing I can do about it?

A: Well, your program does stop when there's an *unhandled* exception. But that doesn't mean that all of your exceptions have to be unhandled! We'll talk a lot more about how you can handle exceptions in your code. There's no reason your users ever have to see an unhandled exception.

Q: How do I know where to put a breakpoint?

A: That's a really good question, and there's no one right answer. When your code throws an exception, it's always a good idea to start with the statement that threw it. But usually, the problem actually happened earlier in the program, and the exception is just fallout from it. For example, the statement that throws a divide by zero error could be dividing values that were generated 10 statements earlier but just haven't been used yet. So there's no one good answer to where you should put a breakpoint, because every situation is different. But as long as you've got a good idea how your code works, you should be able to figure out a good starting point.

Q: Can I run any method in the Watch window?

A: Yes. Any statement that's valid in your program will work inside the Watch window, even things that make absolutely no sense to run inside a Watch window. Here's an example. Bring up a program, start it running, break it, and then add this to the Watch window: `System.Threading.Thread.Sleep(2000)`. (Remember, that method causes your program to delay for two seconds.) There's no reason you'd ever do that in real life, but it's interesting to see what happens: you'll get an hourglass for two seconds while the method evaluates. Then, since `Sleep()` has no return value, the Watch window will display the value, "`Expression has been evaluated and has no value`" to let you know that it didn't return anything. But it did evaluate it. Not only that, but it displays IntelliSense pop ups to

help you type code into the window. That's useful because it'll tell you what methods are available to an object when your program is running.

Q: Wait, so isn't it possible for me to run something in the Watch window that'll change the way my program runs?

A: Yes! Not permanently, but it can definitely affect your program's output. But even better, just *hovering* over fields inside the debugger can cause your program to change its behavior, because hovering over a property *executes its get accessor*. If you have a property that has a get accessor that executes a method, then hovering over that property will cause that method to execute. And if that method sets a value in your program, then that value will stay set if you run the program again. And that can cause some pretty unpredictable results inside the debugger. Programmers have a name for results that seem to be unpredictable and random: they're called **heisenbugs** (which is a joke that makes sense to physicists and cats in boxes).

> **When you run your program inside the IDE, an unhandled exception will cause it to break as if it had run into a breakpoint.**

Uh oh—the code's still got problems...

Brian was happily using his Excuse Manager when he remembered that he had a folder full of excuses that he made when he first built the program—but he forgot that he made that folder **before** he added serialization to the program. Let's see what happens....

No, not again!

1 You can re-create Brian's problem—just create your own text-based Excuse file using Notepad. The first line should be the description, the second should be the results, and the third should be the last used date ("10/4/2007 12:08:13 PM").

2 Pop open the Excuse Manager and open up the excuse. It throws an exception! But this time, click on the Details button so we can take a closer look at what it says. Pay attention to the **call stack**—that's what it's called when a method is called by another method, which is called by another method, etc.

The program threw a SerializationException. Can we figure out what line threw it from the exception details?

Excuse Manager

Unhandled excepti
Continue, the applic
you click Quit, the a

Index was outside t

▼ Details

It looks like there was a problem with the BinaryFormatter—which makes sense, because it was trying to deserialize a text file.

You can learn a lot from the **call stack**, which tells you which methods were running. You can see that the Excuse class's OpenFile() method was being called from its constructor (".ctor"), which was called from the "Random Excuse" button's click event handler.

```
************** Exception Text **************

System.Runtime.Serialization.SerializationException: End of Stream encountered before parsing
was completed.

   at System.Runtime.Serialization.Formatters.Binary.__BinaryParser.Run()

   at System.Runtime.Serialization.Formatters.Binary.ObjectReader.Deserialize(HeaderHa
   ndler handler, __BinaryParser serParser, Boolean fCheck, Boolean isCrossAppDomain,
   IMethodCallMessage methodCallMessage)

   at System.Runtime.Serialization.Formatters.Binary.BinaryFormatter.Deserialize(Stream
   serializationStream, HeaderHandler handler, Boolean fCheck, Boolean isCrossAppDomain,
   IMethodCallMessage methodCallMessage)

   at System.Runtime.Serialization.Formatters.Binary.BinaryFormatter.Deserialize(Stream
   serializationStream)

   at Chapter10.Excuse.OpenFile(String ExcusePath) in C:\Documents and Settings\Administrator\
   My Documents\Visual Studio 2005\Projects\Chapter10\Chapter10\Excuse.cs:line 40

   at Chapter10.Excuse..ctor(Random random, String Folder) in C:\Documents and Settings\
   Administrator\My Documents\Visual Studio 2005\Projects\Chapter10\Chapter10\Excuse.cs:line 30

   at Chapter10.Form1.randomExcuse_Click(Object sender, EventArgs e) in C:\Documents and
   Settings\Administrator\My Documents\Visual Studio 2005\Projects\Chapter10\Chapter10\Form1.
   cs:line 146
```

3 So the Details button in the unhandled exception window tells you a lot about what caused this problem. **Can you think of anything you can do about it?**

> Wait a second. Of course the program's gonna crash—I gave it a bad file. Users screw up all the time. You can't expect me to do anything about that, right?

Actually, there is something you can do about it.

Yes, it's true that users screw up all the time. That's a fact of life. But that doesn't mean you can't do anything about it. There's a name for programs that deal with bad data, malformed input, and other unexpected situations gracefully: they're called **robust** programs. And C# gives you some really powerful exception handling tools to help you make your programs more robust. Because while you *can't* control what your users do, you *can* make sure that your program doesn't crash when they do it.

ro-bust, adj.
sturdy in construction; able to withstand or overcome adverse conditions. *After the Tacoma Narrows Bridge disaster, the civil engineering team looked for a more* **robust** *design for the bridge that would replace it.*

Watch it!

`BinaryFormatter` will throw an exception if there's anything at all wrong with a serialized file.

It's easy to get the Excuse Manager to throw a `SerializationException`—just feed it any file that's not a serialized Excuse object. When you try to deserialize an object from a file, `BinaryFormatter` expects the file to contain a serialized object that matches the class that it's trying to read. If the file contains anything else, anything at all, then the `Deserialize()` method will throw a `SerializationException`.

Handle exceptions with try and catch

In C#, you can basically say, "**Try** this code, and if an exception occurs, **catch** it with this *other* bit of code." The part of the code you're trying is the **try block**, and the part where you deal with exceptions is called the **catch block**. In the catch block, you can do things like print a friendly error message instead of letting your program come to a screeching halt:

```csharp
private void randomExcuse_Click(object sender, EventArgs e)
{
    // ... code you added a few pages ago goes here ...
    try {
        if (CheckChanged() == true) {
            currentExcuse = new Excuse(random, selectedFolder);
            UpdateForm(false);
        }
    }
    catch (SerializationException) {
        MessageBox.Show(
        "Your excuse file was invalid.",
        "Unable to open a random excuse");
    }
}
```

This is the try block. You start exception handling with try. In this case, we'll put the existing code in it.

The catch keyword means that the block immediately following it contains an exception handler.

Put the code that might throw an exception inside the try block. If no exception happens, it'll get run exactly as usual, and the statements in the catch block will be ignored. But if a statement in the try block throws an exception, the rest of the try block won't get executed.

When an exception is thrown, the program immediately jumps to the catch statement and starts executing the catch block.

This is the simplest kind of exception handling: stop the program, write out the exception message, and keep running.

> ⚛ **BRAIN POWER**
>
> If throwing an exception makes your code automatically jump to the catch block, what happens to the objects and data you were working with before the exception happened?

What happens when a method you want to call is risky?

Users are unpredictable. They feed all sorts of weird data into your program, and click on things in ways you never expected. And that's just fine, because you can handle unexpected input with good exception handling.

① **Let's say your user is using your code, and gives it some input that it didn't expect.**

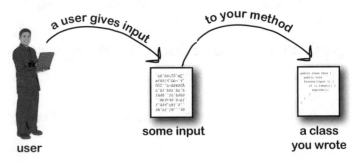

some input

a class you wrote

user

② **That method does something risky, something that might not work at <u>runtime</u>.**

a class you wrote

```
public void
    Process(Input i) {
        if (i.IsBad()) {
            explode();
        }
    }
```

"Runtime" just means "while your program is running." Some people refer to exceptions as "runtime errors."

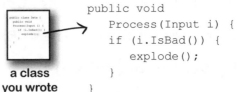

③ **You need to *know* that the method you're calling is risky.**

If you can come up with a way to do a less risky thing that avoids throwing the exception, that's the best possible outcome! But some risks just can't be avoided, and that's when you want to do this.

I wonder what happens if I click here...

My Process() method will blow up if it gets bad input data!

a class you wrote

user

④ **You then write code that can handle the failure if it *does* happen. You need to be prepared, just in case.**

Wow, this program's really stable!

now your program's more robust!

your class, now with exception handling

user

Q: So when do I use `try` and `catch`?

A: Any time you're writing risky code, or code that could throw an exception. The trick is figuring out which code is risky, and which code is safer.

You've already seen that code that uses input provided by a user can be risky. Users give you incorrect files, words instead of numbers, and names instead of dates, and they pretty much click everywhere you could possibly imagine. A good program will take all that input and work in a calm, predictable way. It might not give the users a result they can use, but it will let them know that it found the problem and hopefully suggest a solution.

Q: How can a program suggest a solution to a problem it doesn't even know about in advance?

A: That's what the `catch` block is for. A `catch` block is only executed when code in the `try` block throws an exception. It's your chance to make sure the user knows that something went wrong, and to let the user know that it's a situation that might be corrected.

If the Excuse Manager simply crashes when there's bad input, that's not particularly useful. But if it tries to read the input and displays garbage in the form, that's also not

useful—in fact, some people might say that it's worse. But if you have the program display an error message telling the user that it couldn't read the file, then the user has an idea of what went wrong, and information that he can use to fix the problem.

Q: So the debugger should really only be used to troubleshoot exceptions then?

A: No. As you've already seen many times throughout the book, the debugger's a really useful tool that you can use to examine any code you've written. Sometimes it's useful to step through your code and check the values of certain fields and variables—like when you've got a really complex method, and you want to make sure it's working properly.

But as you may have guessed from the name "debugger," its most common use is to track down and remove bugs. Sometimes those bugs are exceptions that get thrown. But a lot of the time, you'll be using the debugger to try to find other kinds of problems, like code that gives a result that you don't expect.

Q: I'm not sure I totally got what you did with the Watch window.

A: When you're debugging a program, you usually want to pay attention to how a few variables and fields change. That's where the Watch window comes in. If you

add watches for a few variables, the Watch window updates their values every time you step into, out of, or over code. That lets you monitor exactly what happens to them after every statement, which can be really useful when you're trying to track down a problem.

The Watch window also lets you type in any statement you want, and it'll evaluate it. If the statement updates any of the fields and variables in your program, then it does that, too. That lets you change values while your program is running, which can be another really useful tool for reproducing exceptions and other bugs.

Any changes you make in the Watch window just affect the data in memory, and only last as long as the program is running. Restart your program, and values that you changed will be undone.

The catch block is only executed when code in the try block throws an exception. It gives you a chance to make sure your user has the information to fix the problem.

Use the debugger to follow the try/catch flow

An important part of exception handling is that when a statement in
your `try` block throws an exception, the rest of the code in the block
gets **short-circuited**. The program's execution immediately jumps to
the first line in the `catch` block. ***But don't take our word for it....***

— Debug this

1   Make sure that you've incorporated all of the code from this chapter into the Random Excuse button's
Click event handler in your Excuse Manager. Place a breakpoint on the first line in the event handler.
Then run your program in the IDE. Click the Folder button and specify a folder with a single excuse
file in it—and make sure it's **not a valid excuse file** (but still has the ".excuse" extension). Press the
Random Excuse button. The debugger should break the program at the breakpoint you placed earlier.
Press the Step Over button (or F10) six times to get to the statement that calls the Excuse constructor.
Here's what your debugger screen should look like:

Here's the breakpoint we placed earlier on the first line of the event handler.

Step over the statements until your yellow "next statement" bar shows that the next statement to get executed will create the new Excuse object.

```
private void randomExcuse_Click(object sender, EventArgs e)
{
    string[] fileNames = Directory.GetFiles(selectedFolder, "*.excuse");
    if (fileNames.Length == 0)
    {
        MessageBox.Show("Please specify a folder with excuse files in it",
                        "No excuse files found");
    }
    try
    {
        if (CheckChanged() == true)
        {
            currentExcuse = new Excuse(random, selectedFolder);
            UpdateForm(false);
        }
    }
    catch (SerializationException)
    {
        MessageBox.Show(
            "Your excuse file was invalid.",
            "Unable to open a random excuse");
    }
}
```

Use the Step Over (F10) command in the debugger so it doesn't step into the CheckChanged() method.

2   Use Step Into (F11) to step into the `new` statement. The debugger will jump to the `Excuse` constructor, and
position its yellow "next statement" bar over the declaration line in the code. Keep hitting Step Into (F11) to
step into the `OpenFile()` method. Watch what happens when you hit the `Deserialize()` line.

As soon as you step into the new statement that creates the Excuse object, the debugger jumps to the constructor code.

```
public Excuse(Random random, string folder)
{
    string[] fileNames = Directory.GetFiles(folder, "*.excuse");
    OpenFile(fileNames[random.Next(fileNames.Length)]);
}
```

3 Keep stepping through the code. As soon as the debugger executes the Deserialize() statement, the exception is thrown and the program **short-circuits** right past the call to UpdateForm() and **jumps straight to the catch block**.

The debugger will highlight the catch statement with its yellow "next statement" block, but it shows the rest of the block in gray to show you that it's about to execute the whole thing.

```csharp
private void randomExcuse_Click(object sender, EventArgs e)
{
    string[] fileNames = Directory.GetFiles(selectedFolder, "*.excuse");
    if (fileNames.Length == 0)
    {
        MessageBox.Show("Please specify a folder with excuse files in it",
                        "No excuse files found");
    }
    try
    {
        if (CheckChanged() == true)
        {
            currentExcuse = new Excuse(random, selectedFolder);
            UpdateForm(false);
        }
    }
    catch (SerializationException)
    {
        MessageBox.Show(
            "Your excuse file was invalid.",
            "Unable to open a random excuse");
    }
}
```

4 Start the program again by pressing the Continue button (or F5). It'll begin running the program again, starting with whatever's highlighted by the yellow "next statement" block—in this case, the catch block.

Unable to open a random exc... ✕

Your excuse file was invalid.

OK

Here's a career tip: a lot of C# programming job interviews include a question about how you deal with exceptions in a constructor.

Watch it!

Be careful with exceptions in a constructor!

You've noticed by now that a constructor doesn't have a return value, not even void*. That's because a constructor doesn't actually return anything. Its only purpose is to initialize an object—which is a problem for exception handling inside the constructor. When an exception is thrown inside the constructor, then the statement that tried to instantiate the class **won't end up with an instance of the object**. That's why you had to move the* try/catch *block to the button's event handler. That way, if there's an exception in the constructor, the code won't expect* CurrentExcuse *to contain a valid* Excuse *object.*

If you have code that <u>ALWAYS</u> should run, use a finally block

When your program throws an exception, a couple of things can happen. If the exception ***isn't*** handled, your program will stop processing and crash. If the exception ***is*** handled, your code jumps to the `catch` block. But what about the rest of the code in your `try` block? What if you were closing a stream, or cleaning up important resources? That code needs to run, even if an exception occurs, or you're going to make a mess of your program's state. That's where the **finally** block comes in really handy. It comes after the `try` and `catch` blocks. The **finally block always runs**, whether or not an exception was thrown. Here's how you'd use it to finish the event handling in the Random Excuse button:

```csharp
private void randomExcuse_Click(object sender, EventArgs e) {
    string[] fileNames = Directory.GetFiles(selectedFolder, "*.excuse");
    if (fileNames.Length == 0) {
        MessageBox.Show("Please specify a folder with excuse files in it",
                        "No excuse files found");
    } else {
        try {
            if (CheckChanged() == true) {
                currentExcuse = new Excuse(random, selectedFolder);
            }
        }
        catch (SerializationException) {
            currentExcuse = new Excuse();
            currentExcuse.Description = "";
            currentExcuse.Results = "";
            currentExcuse.LastUsed = DateTime.Now;
            MessageBox.Show(
               "Your excuse file was invalid.",
               "Unable to open a random excuse");
        }
        finally {
            UpdateForm(false);
        }
    }
}
```

The finally block makes sure that UpdateForm() gets run whether or not an exception was thrown. So if the Excuse constructor successfully read an excuse, it'll call UpdateForm(), but it'll also call it if the constructor threw an exception and cleared out the excuse.

If the Excuse constructor throws an exception, w have **no way of knowing what's in CurrentExcuse.** But you **do** know that no instance of Excuse was created. So the catch block creates a new Excuse object and clears out all its fields.

> SerializationException is in the System.Runtime. Serialization namespace, so you'll need to add
> `using System.Runtime.Serialization;`
> to the top of your form's file.

Always catch specific exceptions like SerializationException. You typically follow a `catch` statement with a specific kind of exception telling it what to catch. It's valid C# code to just have "**catch (Exception)**" and you can even leave the exception type out and just use **catch**. When you do that, it **catches all exceptions**, no matter what type of exception is thrown. But it's a ***really bad practice to have a catch-all exception handler*** like that. Your code should always catch as specific an exception as possible.

Now debug this

1   Update the Random Excuse button's event handler with the code on the facing page. Then place a breakpoint on the first line in the method and debug the program.

2   Run the program normally, and make sure that the Random Excuse button works when you set the program's folder to one with a bunch of normal excuse files in it. The debugger should break at the breakpoint you set:

When the "next statement" bar and the breakpoint are on the same line, the IDE shows you the yellow arrow placed over the big red dot in the margin.

```
private void randomExcuse_Click(object sender, EventArgs e)
{
    string[] fileNames = Directory.GetFiles(selectedFolder, "*.excuse");
    if (fileNames.Length == 0)
    {
        MessageBox.Show("Please specify a folder with excuse files in it",
                            "No excuse files found");
    }
    else
    {
        try
        {
            if (CheckChanged() == true)
            {
                currentExcuse = new Excuse(random, selectedFolder);
            }
        }
        catch (SerializationException)
        {
            currentExcuse = new Excuse();
            currentExcuse.Description = "";
            currentExcuse.Results = "";
            currentExcuse.LastUsed = DateTime.Now;
            MessageBox.Show(
                "Your excuse file was invalid.",
                "Unable to open a random excuse");
        }
        finally
        {
            UpdateForm(false);
        }
    }
}
```

3   Step through the rest of the Random Excuse button's event handler and make sure it runs the way you expect it to. It should finish the `try` block, skip over the `catch` block (because no exceptions were thrown), and then execute the `finally` block.

4   Now set the program's folder so that it's pointed to the folder with one malformed excuse file in it and click the Random Excuse button. It should start executing the `try` block, and then jump to the `catch` block when it throws the exception. After it finishes all of the statements in the `catch` block, it'll execute the `finally` block.

there are no
Dumb Questions

Q: Back up a second. So every time my program runs into an exception, it's going to stop whatever it's doing unless I specifically write code to catch it. How is that a good thing?

A: One of the best things about exceptions is that they make it really obvious when you run into problems. Imagine how easy it could be in a complex application for you to lose track of all of the objects your program was working with. Exceptions call attention to your problems and help you root out their causes so that you always know that your program is doing what it's supposed to do.

Any time an exception occurs in your program, something you expected to happen didn't. Maybe an object reference wasn't pointing where you thought it was, or it was possible for a user to supply a value you hadn't considered, or a file you thought you'd be working with suddenly isn't available. If something like that happened and you didn't know it, it's likely that the output of your program would be wrong, and the behavior from that point on would be pretty different from you expected when you wrote the program.

Now imagine that you had no idea the error had occurred and your users started calling you up with incorrect data and telling you that your program was unstable. That's why it's a *good* thing that exceptions disrupt everything your program is doing. They force you to deal with the problem while it's easy to find and fix.

Q: OK, so now what's a handled exception and what's an unhandled exception?

A: Whenever your program throws an exception, the runtime environment will search through your code looking for a `catch` block that handles it. If you've written one, the `catch` block will execute and do whatever you specified for that particular exception. Since you wrote a `catch` block to deal with that error up front, that exception is considered handled. If the runtime can't find a `catch` block to match the exception, it stops everything your program is doing and raises an error. That's an *unhandled* exception.

Q: But isn't it easier to use a catch-all exception? Isn't it safer to write code that always catches every exception?

A: You should **always do your best to avoid catching `Exception`,** and instead catch specific exceptions. You know that old saying about how an ounce of prevention is better than a pound of cure? That's especially true in exception handling. Depending on catch-all exceptions is usually just a way to make up for bad programming. For example, you're much better off using `File.Exists()` to check for a file before you try to open it than catching a `FileNotFoundException`. While some exceptions are unavoidable, you'll find that a surprising number of them never have to be thrown in the first place.

It's sometimes really useful to leave exceptions unhandled. Real-life programs have complex logic, and it's often difficult to recover correctly when something goes wrong, especially when a problem occurs very far down in the program. By only handling specific exceptions, avoiding catch-all exception handlers, and letting those exceptions bubble up to get caught on a top level, you end up with much more robust code.

Q: What happens when you have a `catch` that doesn't specify a particular exception?

A: A `catch` block like that will catch any kind of exception the `try` block can throw.

Q: If a `catch` block with no specified exception will catch anything, why would I ever want to specify?

A: Good question. Because certain exceptions might require different actions to keep your program moving. An exception that happens when you divide by zero might have a `catch` block where you go back and set some number values to save some of the data you've been working with. A null reference exception might require that you create new instances of an object if you're going to recover.

Q: Does all error handling happen in a `try`/`catch`/`finally` sequence?

A: No. You can mix it up a bit. You could have **multiple `catch` blocks** if you wanted to deal with lots of different kinds of errors. You could also have no `catch` block at all. It's legal to have a `try`/`finally` block. That wouldn't handle any exceptions, but it would make sure that the code in the `finally` block ran even if you got stopped halfway through the `try` block. But we'll talk a lot more about that in a minute....

An unhandled exception means your program will run unpredictably. That's why the program stops whenever it runs into one.

Pool Puzzle

Your *job* is to take code snippets from the pool and place them into the blank lines in the program. You can use the same snippet more than once, and you won't need to use all the snippets. Your *goal* is to make the program produce the output.

Output: ────────────→ G'day Mate!

```
using System.IO;
public static void Main() {
    Kangaroo joey = new Kangaroo();
    int koala = joey.Wombat(
          joey.Wombat(joey.Wombat(1)));
    try {
        Console.WriteLine((15 / koala)
               + " eggs per pound");
    }
    catch (_____) {
        Console.WriteLine("G'Day Mate!");
    }
}
```

```
class Kangaroo {
    _____ fs;
    int croc;
    int dingo = 0;

    public int Wombat(int wallaby) {
        _____ __;
        try {
            if (_____ > 0) {
                __ = _____.OpenWrite("wobbiegong");
                croc = 0;
            } else if (_____ < 0) {
                croc = 3;
            } else {
                ___ = _____.OpenRead("wobbiegong");
                croc = 1;
            }
        }
        catch (IOException) {
            croc = -3;
        }
        catch {
            croc = 4;
        }
        finally {
            if (_____ > 2) {
                croc ___ dingo;
            }
        }
        _____ _____;
    }
}
```

Note: Each snippet from the pool can be used more than once!

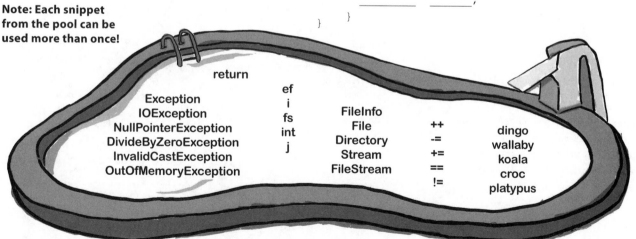

return

Exception
IOException
NullPointerException
DivideByZeroException
InvalidCastException
OutOfMemoryException

ef
i
fs
int
j

FileInfo
File
Directory
Stream
FileStream

++
-=
+=
==
!=

dingo
wallaby
koala
croc
platypus

The pool puzzles are getting harder, and the names are getting more obscure to give you fewer hints. You'll really need to work through the problem! Remember, the puzzles are optional, so don't worry if you need to move on and come back to this one...but if you really want to get this stuff into your brain, these puzzles will do the trick!

one object's trash is another's treasure

Pool Puzzle Solution

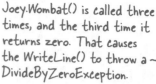

Joey.Wombat() is called three times, and the third time it returns zero. That causes the WriteLine() to throw a DivideByZeroException.

```csharp
public static void Main() {
    Kangaroo joey = new Kangaroo();
    int koala = joey.Wombat(joey.Wombat(joey.Wombat(1)));
    try {
        Console.WriteLine((15 / koala) + " eggs per pound");
    }
    catch (DivideByZeroException) {
        Console.WriteLine("G'Day Mate!");
    }
}
```

This catch block only catches exceptions where the code divides by zero.

The clue that this is a FileStream is that it has an OpenRead() method and throws an IOException.

```csharp
class Kangaroo {
    FileStream fs;
    int croc;
    int dingo = 0;
    public int Wombat(int wallaby) {
        dingo ++;
        try {
            if (wallaby > 0) {
                fs = File.OpenWrite("wobbiegong");
                croc = 0;
            } else if (wallaby < 0) {
                croc = 3;
            } else {
                fs = File.OpenRead("wobbiegong");
                croc = 1;
            }
        }
        catch (IOException) {
            croc = -3;
        }
        catch {
            croc = 4;
        }
        finally {
            if (dingo > 2) {
                croc -= dingo;
            }
        }
        return croc;
    }
}
```

This code opens a file called "wobbiegong" and keeps it open the first time it's called. Later on, it opens the file again. But it never closed the file, which causes it to throw an IOException.

Remember, you should avoid catch-all exceptions in your code. But you should also avoid other things we do to make puzzles more interesting, like using obfuscated variable names.

You already know that you always have to close files when you're done with them. If you don't, the file will be locked open, and if you try to open it again it'll throw an IOException.

Use the Exception object to get information about the problem

We've been saying all along that .NET generates an Exception object when an exception is thrown. When you write your catch block, you have access to that object. Here's how it works:

1 An object is humming along, doing its thing, when it encounters something unexpected and throws an exception.

2 Luckily, its try/catch block caught the exception. Inside the catch block, it gave the exception a name: **ex**.

```
try {
    DoSomethingRisky();
}
catch (RiskyThingException (ex) ){
    string message = ex.Message;
    MessageBox.Show(message, "I took too many risks!");
}
```

When you specify a type of exception in the catch block, if you provide a variable name, then your code can use it to access the Exception object.

3 The exception object stays around until the catch block is done. Then the **ex** reference disappears, and it's eventually garbage-collected.

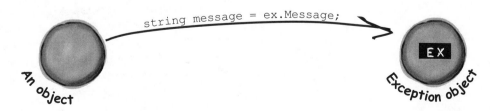

Use more than one catch block to handle multiple types of exceptions

You can also call the exception's ToString() method to get a lot o the pertinent data in your MessageBox.

You know that you can catch a specific type of exception…but what if you write code where more than one problem can occur? In these cases, you may want to write code that handles each different type of exception. That's where using more than one catch block comes in. Here's an example from the code in the beehive nectar processing plant. You can see how it catches several kinds of exceptions. In some cases it uses properties in the Exception object. It's pretty common to use the Message property, which usually contains a description of the exception that was thrown. You can also call throw; to **rethrow** the message, so it can be handled further up the call stack.

```
public void ProcessNectar(NectarVat vat, Bee worker, HiveLog log) {
    try {
        NectarUnit[] units = worker.EmptyVat(vat);
        for (int count = 0; count < worker.UnitsExpected, count++) {
            stream hiveLogFile = log.OpenLogFile();
            worker.AddLogEntry(hiveLogFile);
        }
    }

    catch (VatEmptyException) {
        vat.Emptied = true;
    }
    catch (HiveLogException ex) {
        throw;
    }
    catch (IOException ex) {
        worker.AlertQueen("An unspecified file error happened: "
            + "Message: " + ex.Message + "\r\n"
            + "Stack trace: " + ex.StackTrace + "\r\n"
            + "Data: " + ex.Data + "\r\n");
    }
    finally {
        vat.Seal();
        worker.FinishedJob();
    }
}
```

If you won't use the Exception object, there's no need to declare it.

When you have several catch blocks, they're examined in order. In this code, first it checks a VatEmptyException and then a HiveLogExcep The last catch block catches IOException. That's the base class for several different file exceptions, including FileNotFoundException and EndOfStreamException.

Sometimes you want to bubble an exception up to the method that called this one by using throw; to rethrow the exception.

This catch block assigns the exception to the variable ex, which it can use to get information from the Exception object.

It's fine for two blocks to use the same name ("ex") for the Exception.

This statement uses three properties in the Exception object: Message, which has the message you'd normally see in the excepti window in the IDE ("Attempted to divide by zero"); StackTrace which gives you a summary of the call stack; and Data, which sometimes contains pertinent data that's associated with the exception.

One class throws an exception, another class catches the exception

> Of course, one method in a single class can throw a method that's caught by another method in the same class.

When you're building a class, you don't always know how it's going to be used. Sometimes other people will end up using your objects in a way that causes problems—and sometimes you do it yourself! That's where exceptions come in.

The whole point behind throwing an exception is to see what might go wrong, so you can put in place some sort of contingency plan. You don't usually see a method that throws an exception and then catches it. An exception is usually thrown in one method and then caught in a totally different one—usually in a different object.

Instead of this...

Without good exception handling, one exception can halt the entire program. Here's how it would work in a program that manages bee profiles for a queen bee.

> This BeeProfile object's constructor expects the filename for a profile data file that it'll open using File.Open(). If there's a problem opening the file, the program bombs out.

```
stream = File.Open(profile);
```

new BeeProfile("prof.dat")

Hive object

The BeeProfile object tried to read a file but it wasn't there, so File.Open() threw an exception. The hive didn't catch it, so it went unhandled.

BeeProfile object

⚠ **FileNotFoundException was unhandled**
Unable to find the specified file.

> Notice how the BeeProfile object intercepts the exception, logs it using its WriteLogEntry() method, and then throws it again so it's passed along to the hive.

```
try {
    stream = File.Open(profile);
} catch (FileNotFoundException ex) {
    WriteLogEntry("unable to find " +
        profile + ": " + ex.Message());
    throw;
}
```

...we can do this.

The BeeProfile object can intercept the exception and add a log entry. Then it can turn around and throw the exception back to the hive, which catches it and recovers gracefully.

new BeeProfile("prof.dat")

Hive object

BeeProfile object

> Now when the hive tries to create a new BeeProfile object by passing it an invalid filename, it can trust BeeProfile to log the error and then alert it to the problem by throwing an exception. The hive can catch the exception and take some corrective action—in this case, recreating the bee profile.

```
try {
    prof = new BeeProfile("prof.dat");
} catch (FileNotFoundException) {
    Hive.RecreateBeeProfile("prof.dat");
}
```

Bees need an OutOfHoney exception

Your classes can throw their own exceptions. For example, if you get a null parameter in a method that was expecting a value, it's pretty common to throw the same exception a .NET method would:

```
throw new ArgumentException();
```

Your methods can throw this exception if they get invalid or unexpected values in their parameters.

But sometimes you want your program to throw an exception because of a special condition that could happen when it runs. The bees we created in the hive, for example, consume honey at a different rate depending on their weight. If there's no honey left to consume, it makes sense to have the hive throw an exception. You can create a custom exception to deal with that specific error condition just by creating your own class that inherits from `Exception` and then throwing the exception whenever you encounter a specific error.

```
class OutOfHoneyException : System.Exception {
    public OutOfHoneyException(string message) : base(message) { }
}
class HoneyDeliverySystem {
    ...
    public void FeedHoneyToEggs() {
        if (honeyLevel == 0) {
            throw new OutOfHoneyException("The hive is out of honey.");
        } else {
            foreach (Egg egg in Eggs) {
                ...
}
public partial class Form1 : Form {
...
    private void consumeHoney_Click(object sender, EventArgs e) {
        HoneyDeliverySystem delivery = new HoneyDeliverySystem();
        try {
            delivery.FeedHoneyToEggs()
        }
        catch (OutOfHoneyException ex){
            MessageBox.Show(ex.Message, "Warning: Resetting Hive");
            Hive.Reset();
        }
    }
}
```

You need to create a class for your exception and make sure that it inherits from System. Exception. Notice how we're overloading the constructor so we can pass an exception message.

This throws a new instance of the exception object.

If there's honey in the hive, the exception will never get thrown and this code will run.

You can catch a custom exception by name just like any other exception, and do whatever you need to do to handle it.

In this case, if the hive is out of honey none of the bees can work, so the simulator can't continue. The only way to keep the program working once the hive runs out of honey is to reset it, and we can do that by putting the code to reset it in the catch block.

The diagram on the right (top) shows:

Exception
Message
StackTrace
GetBaseException()
ToString()

△

your Exception
Message
StackTrace
GetBaseException()
ToString()

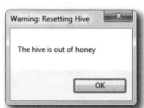

Exception Magnets

Arrange the magnets so the application writes the output to the console.

```
public static void Main() {
    Console.Write("when it ");
    ExTestDrive.Zero("yes");
    Console.Write(" it ");
    ExTestDrive.Zero("no");
    Console.WriteLine(".");
}

class MyException : Exception { }
```

output:

when it thaws it throws.

```
}
```

```
}
```

```
}
```

```
if (t == "yes") {
```

```
Console.Write("a");
```

```
Console.Write("o");
```

```
Console.Write("t");
```

```
Console.Write("w");
```

```
Console.Write("s");
```

```
try {
```

```
} catch (MyException) {
```

```
throw new MyException();
```

```
} finally {
```

```
doRisky(test);
```

```
Console.Write("r");
    }
}
```

```
class ExTestDrive {
    public static void Zero(string test) {
```

```
static void DoRisky(String t) {
    Console.Write("h");
```

```
public static void Main() {
    Console.Write("when it ");
    ExTestDrive.Zero("yes");
    Console.Write(" it ");
    ExTestDrive.Zero("no");
    Console.WriteLine(".");
}

class MyException : Exception { }
```

Exception Magnets Solution

Arrange the magnets so the application writes the output to the console.

output:

when it thaws it throws.

This line defines a custom exception called MyException, which gets caught in a catch block in the code.

```
class ExTestDrive {
    public static void Zero(string test) {
```
```
        try {
```
```
            Console.Write("t");
```
```
            doRisky(test);
```
```
            Console.Write("o");
```
```
        } catch (MyException) {
```
```
            Console.Write("a");
```
```
        } finally {
```
```
            Console.Write("w");
```
```
        }
```
```
        Console.Write("s");
    }
```
```
    static void DoRisky(String t) {
        Console.Write("h");
```
```
        if (t == "yes") {
```
```
            throw new MyException();
```
```
        }
```
```
        Console.Write("r");
    }
}
```

The Zero() method either prints "thaws" or "throws", depending on whether it was passed "yes" or something else as its test parameter.

The finally block makes sure that the method always prints "w". And the "s" is printed outside the exception handler, so it always prints, too.

This line only gets executed if doRisky() doesn't throw the exception.

The doRisky() method only throws an exception if it's passed the string "yes".

BULLET POINTS

- Any statement can throw an exception if something fails at runtime.

- Use a `try`/`catch` block to handle exceptions. Unhandled exceptions will cause your program to stop execution and pop up an error window.

- Any exception in the block of code after the `try` statement will cause the program's execution to immediately jump to the first statement in the block of code after `catch`.

- The `Exception` object gives you information about the exception that was caught. If you specify an `Exception` variable in your `catch` statement, that variable will contain information about any exception thrown in the `try` block:

  ```
  try {
    // statements that might
    // throw exceptions
  } catch (IOException ex) {
    // if an exception is thrown,
    // ex has information about it
  }
  ```

- There are many different kinds of exceptions that you can catch. Each has its own object that inherits from `Exception`. Really try to avoid just catching `Exception`—catch specific exceptions instead.

- Each `try` can have more than one `catch`:

  ```
  try { ... }
  catch (NullReferenceException ex) {
     // these statements will run if a
     // NullReferenceException is thrown
  }
  catch (OverflowException ex) { ... }
  catch (FileNotFoundException) { ... }
  catch (ArgumentException) { ... }
  ```

- Your code can throw an exception using `throw`:

  ```
  throw new Exception("Exception message");
  ```

- Your code can also **rethrow** an exception using `throw`; but this only works inside of a `catch` block. Rethrowing an exception preserves the call stack.

- You can create a custom exception by inheriting from the `Exception` base class.

  ```
  class CustomException : Exception;
  ```

- Most of the time, you only need to throw exceptions that are built into .NET, like `ArgumentException`. The reason you use different kinds of exceptions is so that you can **give more information to your users**. Popping up a window with the text "An unknown error has occurred" is not nearly as useful as an error message that says "The excuse folder is empty. Please select a different folder if you want to read excuses."

An easy way to avoid a lot of problems: using gives you try and finally for free

Remember, when you declare a reference in a "using" statement, its Dispose() method is automatically called at the end of the block.

You already know that `using` is an easy way to make sure that your files always get closed. But what you didn't know is that it's really **just a C# shortcut** for `try` and `finally`!

```
using (YourClass c
       = new YourClass() ) {

   // code

}
```

is like this

```
YourClass c = new YourClass();

try {

   // code

} finally {

   c.Dispose();
}
```

When you use a using statement, you're taking advantage of finally to make sure its Dispose() method is always called.

Exception avoidance: implement IDisposable to do your own cleanup

IDisposable is a really effective way to avoid common exceptions and problems. Make sure you use using statements any time you're working with any class that implements it.

Streams are great, because they already have code written to close themselves when the object is disposed of. But what if you have your own custom object, and it always needs to do something when it's disposed of? Wouldn't it be great if you could write your own code that got run if your object was used in a using statement?

C# lets you do just that with the IDisposable interface. Implement IDisposable, and write your cleanup code in the Dispose() method, like this:

You can only use a class in a "using" statement if it implements IDisposable; otherwise, your program won't compile.

Your object must implement IDisposable if you want to use your object within a using statement.

```
class Nectar : IDisposable {
    private double amount;
    private BeeHive hive;
    private Stream hiveLog;
    public Nectar(double amount, BeeHive hive, Stream hiveLog) {
        this.amount = amount;
        this.hive = hive;
        this.hiveLog = hiveLog;
    }
    public void Dispose() {
        if (amount > 0) {
            hive.Add(amount);
            hive.WriteLog(hiveLog, amount + " mg nectar added to the hive");
            amount = 0;
        }
    }
}
```

The IDisposable interface only has one member: the Dispose() method. Whatever you put in this method will get executed at the end of the using statement...or whenever Dispose() is called manually.

This Dispose() method was written so it could be called many times, not just once.

This particular code empties any remaining nectar into the hive and logs a message. It's important, and must happen, so we put it in the Dispose() method.

> **One of the guidelines for implementing IDispose is that your Dispose() method can be called multiple times without side effects. Can you think of why that's an important guideline?**

We can use multiple using statements now. First, let's use a built-in object Stream, which implements IDisposable. Then, we'll work with our updated Nectar object, which also implements IDisposable:

You'll see nested using statements like this when you need to declare two IDisposable references in the same block of code.

```
using (Stream log = new File.Write("log.txt"))
using (Nectar nectar = new Nectar(16.3, hive, log)) {
    Bee.FlyTo(flower);
    Bee.Harvest(nectar);
    Bee.FlyTo(hive);
}
```

The Nectar object uses the log stream, which will close automatically at the end of the outer using statement.

Then the Bee object uses the Nectar object, which will add its nectar to the hive automatically at the end of the inner using statement.

there are no Dumb Questions

Q: Can I only use objects that implement IDisposable with a using statement?

A: Yes. IDisposable is tailor-made to work with using statements, and adding a using statement is just like creating a new instance of a class, except that it always calls its Dispose() method.

Q: Can you put any statement inside a using block?

A: Definitely. The whole idea with using is that it helps you make sure that every object you create with it is disposed. But what you do with those objects is entirely up to you. In fact, you can create an object with a using statement and never even use it inside the block. But that would be pretty useless, so we don't recommend doing that.

Q: Can you call Dispose() outside of a using statement?

A: Yes. You don't ever actually **need** to use a using statement. You can call Dispose() yourself when you're done with the object. Or you can do whatever cleanup is necessary—like calling a stream's Close() method manually. But if you use a using statement, it'll make your code easier to understand and prevent problems that happen if you don't dispose of your objects.

Q: You mentioned a "try/finally" block. Does that mean it's OK to have a try and finally without a catch?

A: Yes! You can definitely have a try block without a catch, and just a finally. It looks like this:

```
try {
    DoSomethingRisky();
    SomethingElseRisky();
}
finally {
    AlwaysExecuteThis();
}
```

If DoSomethingRisky() throws an exception, then the finally block will immediately run.

Q: Does Dispose() only work with files and streams?

A: No, there are a lot of classes that implement IDisposable, and when you're using one you should always use a using statement. (You'll see some of them in the next few chapters.) And if you write a class that has to be disposed of in a certain way, then you can implement IDisposable, too.

> If try/catch is so great, why doesn't the IDE just put it around everything? Then we wouldn't have to write all these try/catch blocks on our own, right?

You want to know what <u>type</u> of exception is thrown, so you can handle <u>that</u> exception.
There's more to exception handling than just printing out a generic error message. For instance, in the excuse finder, if we know we've got a FileNotFoundException, we might print an error that suggested where the right files should be located. If we have an exception related to databases, we might send an email to the database administrator. All that depends on you catching *specific* exception types.

This is why there are so many classes that inherit from Exception, and why you may even want to write your own classes to inherit from Exception.

The worst catch block **EVER**: catch-all plus comments

A catch block will let your program keep running if you want. An exception gets thrown, you catch the exception, and instead of shutting down and giving an error message, you keep going. But sometimes, that's not such a good thing.

Take a look at this Calculator class, which seems to be acting funny all the time. What's going on?

```
class Calculator {

...

    public void Divide(int dividend, int divisor) {

        try {

            this.quotient = dividend / divisor;

        } catch {

            // Note from Jim: we need to figure out a way to prevent

            // people from entering in zero in a division problem.

        }
    }
}
```

Here's the problem. If divisor is zero, this will create a DivdeByZeroException.

But there's a catch block. So why are we still getting errors?

The programmer thought that he could **bury** his exceptions by using an empty catch block, but he just caused a headache for whoever had to track down problems with it later.

You should **handle** your exceptions, not **bury** them

Just because you can keep your program running doesn't mean you've *handled* your exceptions. In the code above, the calculator won't crash...at least, not in the Divide() method. But what if some other code calls that method, and tries to print the results? If the divisor was zero, then the method probably returned an incorrect (and unexpected) value.

Instead of just adding a comment and burying the exception, you need to **handle the exception**. And if you're not able to handle the problem, ***don't leave empty or commented catch blocks!*** That just makes it harder for someone else to track down what's going on. It's better to let the program continue to throw exceptions, because then it's easy to figure out what's going wrong.

Remember, when your code doesn't handle an exception, the exception bubbles up the call stack. Letting an exception bubble up is a perfectly valid way of handling an exception.

Temporary solutions are OK (temporarily)

Sometimes you find a problem, and know it's a problem, but aren't sure what to do about it. In these cases, you might want to log the problem and note what's going on. That's not as good as handling the exception, but it's better than doing nothing.

...but in real life, "temporary" solutions have a nasty habit of becoming permanent.

Here's a temporary solution to the calculator:

```
class Calculator {

...

  public void Divide(int dividend, int divisor) {

    try {

      this.quotient = dividend / divisor;

    } catch (Exception ex) {

      using (StreamWriter sw = new StreamWriter(@"C:\Logs\errors.txt");

        sw.WriteLine(ex.getMessage());

      };

    }

  }

}
```

This still needs to be fixed, but short-term, this makes it clear where the problem occurred. Still, wouldn't it be better to figure out why your Divide method is being called with a zero divisor in the first place?

> I get it. It's sort of like using exception handling to place a marker in the problem area.

Handling exceptions doesn't always mean the same thing as FIXING exceptions.

It's never good to have your program bomb out. But it's way worse to have no idea why it's crashing or what it's doing to users' data. That's why you need to be sure that you're always dealing with the errors you can predict and logging the ones you can't.

A few simple ideas for exception handling

Design your code to handle failures GRACEFULLY.

Give your users USEFUL error messages.

Throw built-in .NET exceptions where you can. Only throw custom exceptions if you need to give custom information.

Think about code in your try block that COULD get short-circuited.

...and most of all...

Avoid unnecessary file system errors...ALWAYS USE A USING BLOCK ANY TIME YOU USE A STREAM! ALWAYS ALWAYS ALWAYS!

Or anything else that implements IDisposable.

Use what you know about `try/catch/finally` to improve the exception handling in Brian's Excuse Manager.

1 Add exception handling to the Open button's Click event handler. Just make a simple `try/catch` block that pops up a message box. Here's what it should pop up if you try to open up a file that's not a real excuse file:

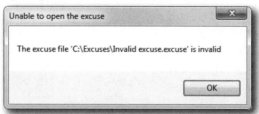

2 You're not done yet. Let's build a particularly devious little invalid excuse file. Put a breakpoint on the first line of the `Excuse.Save()` method, then run the program and save an excuse. When the program breaks, add a watch for the **LastUsed** property. Then edit its value in the Watch window and set it to **DateTime.Parse("October 14, 1066")** — you should see the value of the property update to that date. Tell the debugger to continue (F5). Did you get this `ArgumentOutOfRange` exception?

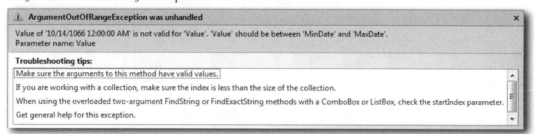

You're getting that exception because the form tried to set the `DateTimePicker` control's `Value` property to a value that's lower than its `MinDate`. But more importantly, before it threw the exception, the `Excuse` class wrote out a file. This is a **really useful technique** that you should keep in mind: generating files with known bad data so you can use them later to test your program.

3 Load the file you just created with bad data. You should get the same exception. You'll get a different exception if you try to open a file that's not a valid excuse file. Add an exception handling block ***nested inside the one you added in step 2*** so it doesn't fail when you try to load an invalid excuse file (which can happen in several situations). Here's what to do:

1. Declare a Boolean variable called `clearForm` above the `try/catch` block. You'll set this to `true` if there's an exception, and check it later to see if the form should be cleared.

2. Add another `try/catch` block inside the one you just added to the Open button.

3. Add a `finally` block to the outer `try/catch` to reset the form to its original empty state. Reset `LastUsed.Value` to `DateTime.Now` (which returns the current date) if the `clearForm` variable is set to `true`.

Exercise Solution

Use what you know about `try/catch/finally` to improve the exception handling to Brian's Excuse Manager.

```
private void open_Click(object sender, EventArgs e) {
    if (CheckChanged()) {
        openFileDialog1.InitialDirectory = selectedFolder;
        openFileDialog1.Filter =
          "Excuse files (*.excuse)|*.excuse|All files (*.*)|*.*";
        openFileDialog1.FileName = description.Text + ".excuse";
        DialogResult result = openFileDialog1.ShowDialog();
        if (result == DialogResult.OK) {
            bool clearForm = false;
            try {
                currentExcuse = new Excuse(openFileDialog1.FileName);
                try {
                    UpdateForm(false);
                }
                catch (ArgumentOutOfRangeException) {
                    MessageBox.Show("The excuse file '"
                        + openFileDialog1.FileName + "' had a invalid data",
                        "Unable to open the excuse");
                    clearForm = true;
                }
            }
            catch (SerializationException ex) {
                MessageBox.Show("An error occurred while opening the excuse '"
                    + openFileDialog1.FileName + "'\n" + ex.Message,
                    "Unable to open the excuse", MessageBoxButtons.OK,
                    MessageBoxIcon.Error);
                clearForm = true;
            }
            finally {
                if (clearForm) {
                    description.Text = "";
                    results.Text = "";
                    lastUsed.Value = DateTime.Now;
                }
            }
        }
    }
}
```

Here's the try/catch block to create a pop-up error, in case problems occur when the form calls the Excuse constructor to load an excuse.

Here's a nested try/catch. It handles exceptions that happen if the file that gets loaded has data that is out of range. That's not the same as problems arising from the Excuse constructor.

We're not using the exception object, so the catch statement doesn't need a variable name after the exception type.

Here's the message box from the outer try/catch block. It prints the exception message.

Both catch blocks set clearForm to true so that this finally block knows that the form should be reset. It's OK to have code that interacts with your finally block, since you know finally blocks will always run.

Exceptioncross

Across

5. The base class that `DivideByZeroException` and `FormatException` inherit from
8. An _____ exception happens when you try to cast a value to a variable that can't hold it
10. If the next statement is a method, "Step _____" tells the debugger to execute all the statements in the method and break immediately afterward
12. If you ____ your exceptions, it can make them hard to track down
13. This method is always called at the end of a `using` block
14. The field in the `Exception` object that contains a string with a description
15. One `try` block can have multiple _____ blocks
17. The _____ block contains any statements that absolutely must be run after an exception is handled
18. An _____ exception means you tried to cram a number that was too big into a variable that couldn't hold it

Down

1. The window in the IDE that you can use to check your variables' values
2. You'll get an exception if you try to divide by this
3. Toggle this if you want the debugger to stop execution when it hits a specific line of code
4. "Step ____" tells the debugger to execute the rest of the statements in the current method and then break
6. What a reference contains if it doesn't point to anything
7. You can only declare a variable with a `using` statement if it implements this interface
9. When a statement has a problem, it _____ an exception
11. A program that handles errors well
16. If the next statement is a method, "Step _____" tells the debugger to execute the first statement in that method

 # Exceptioncross Solution

```
          1W              2Z
  3B      A       4O      E
   R      T        U      R
  5E  X   C   E   P   T  I   O  6N              7I
   A      H                     U      D  A  S  9T
   K          8I  N  V  A  L  I  D  C  A  S   T H
   P                     L       I             H
 10O   V   E 11R                 S       12B U  R  Y
   I        O                            R   O
   N        B          13D  I  S  P  O  S  E   W
   T        U                    S             S
         14M  E  S  S  A  G  E  15C  A  T  C  H
            T             16I    B
                      17F  I  N  A  L  L  Y
                          T     E
         18O  V  E  R  F  L  O  W
```

Brian <u>finally</u> gets his vacation...

Now that Brian's got a handle on his exceptions, his job's going smoothly and he can take that well-deserved (and boss-approved!) vacation day.

...and things are looking up back home!

Your exception handling skills did more than just prevent problems. They ensured that Brian's boss has no idea anything went wrong in the first place!

Good ol' Brian. Never misses a day of work unless he's got a **real** problem.

Good exception handling is <u>invisible</u> to your users. The program never crashes, and if there are problems, they are handled gracefully, without confusing error messages.

11 events and delegates

What your code does when you're not looking

I'd better subscribe to that TreePopsUpOutOfNowhere event, or I'll have to call my OnBrokenLeg() method.

Your objects are starting to think for themselves.

You can't always control what your objects are doing. Sometimes things…happen. And when they do, you want your objects to be smart enough to **respond to anything** that pops up. And that's what events are all about. One object *publishes* an event, other objects *subscribe*, and everyone works together to keep things moving. Which is great, until you want your object to take control over who can listen. That's when **callbacks** will come in handy.

Ever wish your objects could think for themselves?

Suppose you're writing a baseball simulator. You're going to model a game, sell the software to the Yankees (they've got deep pockets, right?), and make a million bucks. You create your `Ball`, `Pitcher`, `Umpire`, and `Fan` objects, and a whole lot more. You even write code so that the `Pitcher` object can catch a ball.

Now you just need to connect everything together. You add an `OnBallInPlay()` method to `Ball`, and now you want your `Pitcher` object to respond with its event handler method. Once the methods are written, you just need to tie the separate methods together:

That's a commonly used way of naming methods—we'll talk more about it later.

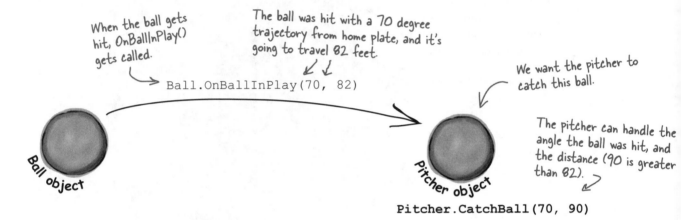

When the ball gets hit, OnBallInPlay() gets called.

The ball was hit with a 70 degree trajectory from home plate, and it's going to travel 82 feet.

`Ball.OnBallInPlay(70, 82)`

We want the pitcher to catch this ball.

The pitcher can handle the angle the ball was hit, and the distance (90 is greater than 82).

Ball object

Pitcher object

`Pitcher.CatchBall(70, 90)`

But how does an object <u>KNOW</u> to respond?

Here's the problem. You really want your `Ball` object to only worry about getting hit, and your `Pitcher` object to only worry about catching balls that come its way. In other words, you really don't want the `Ball` telling the `Pitcher`, "I'm coming to you."

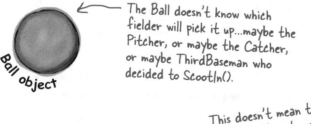

The Ball doesn't know which fielder will pick it up...maybe the Pitcher, or maybe the Catcher, or maybe ThirdBaseman who decided to ScootIn().

This doesn't mean that objects can't interact. It just means that a Ball shouldn't determine who fields it. That's not the Ball's job.

Ball object

> You want an object to worry about itself, not other objects. You're <u>separating</u> <u>the concerns</u> of each object.

When an <u>EVENT</u> occurs...objects listen

What you need to do when the ball is hit is to use an **event**. An event is simply *something that's happened* in your program. Then, other objects can respond to that event—like our `Pitcher` object.

Even better, more than one object can listen for events. So the `Pitcher` could listen for a ball-being-hit event, as well as a `Catcher`, `ThirdBaseman`, an `Umpire`, even a `Fan`. And each object can respond to the event differently.

So what we want is a `Ball` object that can **raise an event**. Then, we want to have other objects to **subscribe to that particular type of event**...that just means listen for it, and get notified when that event occurs.

> event, noun.
> a **thing** that happens, especially something of importance. *The solar eclipse was an amazing **event** to behold.*

Any object can <u>subscribe</u> to this event...and the Ball object doesn't need to know what objects are subscribed.

When a Ball gets hit, it <u>raises</u> a BallInPlay event.

BallInPlay event raised

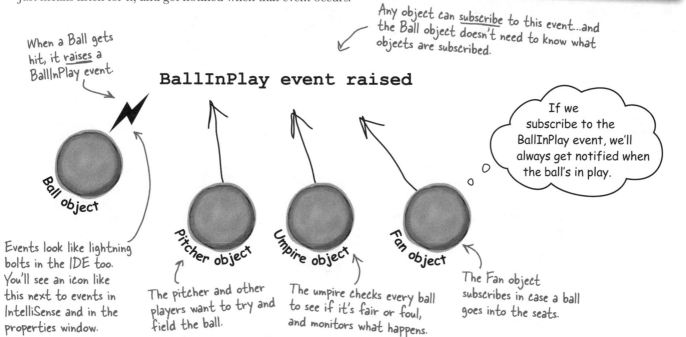

If we subscribe to the BallInPlay event, we'll always get notified when the ball's in play.

Events look like lightning bolts in the IDE too. You'll see an icon like this next to events in IntelliSense and in the properties window.

The pitcher and other players want to try and field the ball.

The umpire checks every ball to see if it's fair or foul, and monitors what happens.

The Fan object subscribes in case a ball goes into the seats.

Want to DO SOMETHING with an event? You need an <u>event handler</u>

Once your object "hears" about an event, you can set up some code to run. That code is called an **event handler**. An event handler gets information about the event, and runs every time that event occurs.

Remember, all this happens *without your intervention* at runtime. So you write code to raise an event, and then you write code to handle those events, and fire up your application. Then, whenever an event is raised, your handler kicks into action...*without you doing anything*. And, best of all, your objects have <u>separate</u> <u>concerns</u>. They're worrying about themselves, not other objects.

We've been doing this all along. Every time you click a button, an event is raised, and your code responds to that event.

if a tree falls in the woods...

One object <u>raises</u> its event, others listen for it...

Let's take a look at how events, event handlers, and subscriptions
works in C#:

①   First, other objects subscribe to the event

Before the `Ball` can raise its `BallInPlay` event, other objects need to
subscribe to it. That's their way of saying, any time a `BallInPlay` event
occurs, we want to know about it.

Every object adds its own
event handler to listen for
the event—just like you add
button1_Click() to your
programs to listen for Click
events.

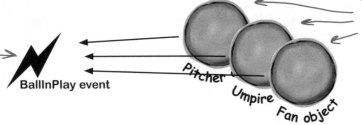

These objects are saying they
want to know any time a
BallInPlay event is raised.

②   Something triggers an event

The ball gets hit. It's time for the `Ball` object to raise a new event.

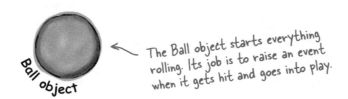

The Ball object starts everything
rolling. Its job is to raise an event
when it gets hit and goes into play.

Sometimes we'll talk
about raising an event,
or firing it, or invoking
it—they're all the same
thing. People just use
different names for it.

③   The ball raises an event

A new event gets raised (we'll talk about exactly how that works in just a minute). That
event also has some arguments, like the velocity of the ball, as well as its trajectory.
Those arguments are attached to the event as an instance of an `EventArgs` object,
and then the event is sent off, available to anyone listening for it.

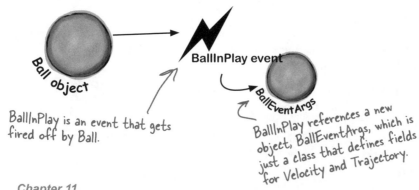

BallInPlay is an event that gets
fired off by Ball.

BallInPlay references a new
object, BallEventArgs, which is
just a class that defines fields
for Velocity and Trajectory.

Then, the other objects <u>handle</u> the event

Once an event is raised, all the objects subscribed to that event get notification, and can do something:

④ **Subscribers get notification**

Since the `Pitcher`, `Umpire`, and `Fan` object subscribed to the `Ball` object's `BallInPlay` event, they all get notified—all of their event handler methods get called one after another.

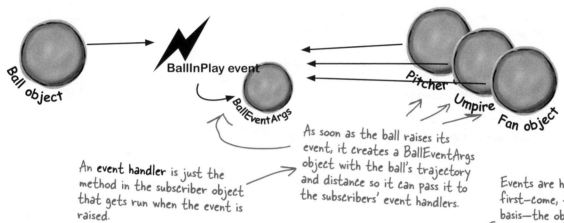

An **event handler** is just the method in the subscriber object that gets run when the event is raised.

As soon as the ball raises its event, it creates a BallEventArgs object with the ball's trajectory and distance so it can pass it to the subscribers' event handlers.

Events are handled on a first-come, first-served basis—the object that subscribes first gets notified first.

⑤ **Each object handles the event**

Now, `Pitcher`, `Umpire`, and `Fan` can all handle the `BallInPlay` event in their own way. But they don't all run at the same time—their event handlers get called one after another, with a reference to a `BallEventArgs` object as its parameter.

Here's what each object that handles the event gets to work with. It should also get a reference to the object that raised the event.

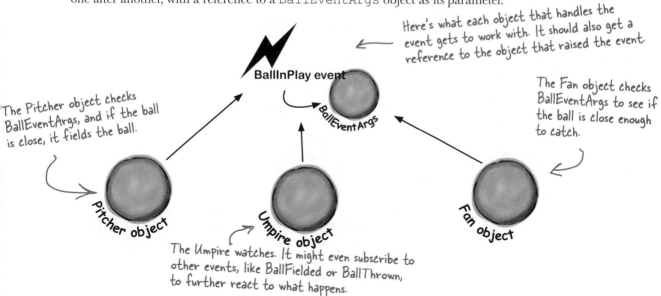

The Pitcher object checks BallEventArgs, and if the ball is close, it fields the ball.

The Fan object checks BallEventArgs to see if the ball is close enough to catch.

The Umpire watches. It might even subscribe to other events, like BallFielded or BallThrown, to further react to what happens.

Connecting the dots

Now that you've got a handle on what's going on,
let's take a closer look at how the pieces fit together.
Luckily, there are only a few moving parts.

It's a good idea (although not required) for your event argument objects to inherit from EventArgs. That's an empty class—it has no public members.

It means that you can upcast your EventArgs object in case you need to send it to an event that doesn't handle it in particular.

EventArgs

BallEventArgs
Trajectory
Distance

(1) **We need an object for the event arguments**
Remember, our `BallInPlay` event has a few arguments that it carries along. So we need a very simple object for those arguments. .NET has a standard class for it called **EventArgs**, but that class **has no members.** Its sole purpose is to allow your event arguments object to be passed to the event handlers that use it. Here's the class declaration:

```
class BallEventArgs : EventArgs
```

The ball will use these properties to pass information to the event handlers about where the ball's been hit.

(2) **Next we'll need to define the event in the class that'll raise it**
The ball class will have a line with the **event keyword**—this is how it informs other objects about the event, so they can subscribe to it. This line can be anywhere in the class—it's usually near the property declarations. But as long as it's in the `Ball` class, other objects can subscribe to a ball's event. It looks like this:

```
public event EventHandler BallInPlay;
```

Events are usually public. This event is defined in the Ball class, but we'll want Pitcher, Umpire, etc., to be able to reference it. You could make it private if you only wanted other instances of the same class to subscribe to it.

*After the event keyword comes EventHandler. That's **not a reserved C# keyword**—it's defined as part of .NET. The reason you need it is to tell the objects subscribing to the event what their event handler methods should look like.*

When you use EventHandler, you're telling other methods that their event handlers need to take two parameters: an object named sender and an EventArgs reference named e. sender is a reference to the object that raised the event, and e is a reference to an EventArgs object.

③ The subscribing classes need event handler methods

Every object that has to subscribe to the Ball's BallInPlay event needs to have an event handler. You already know how event handlers work—every time you added a method to handle a button's Click event or a NumericUpDown's ValueChanged event, the IDE added an **event handler method** to your class. The Ball's BallInPlay event is no different, and an event handler for it should look pretty familiar:

```
void ball_BallInPlay(object sender, EventArgs e)
```

There's no C# rule that says your event handlers need to be named a certain way, but there's a pretty standard naming convention: the name of the object reference, followed by an underscore, followed by the name of the event.

The BallInPlay event declaration listed its event type as EventHandler, which means that it needs to take two parameters—an object called sender and an EventArgs called e—and have no return value.

The class that has this particular event handler method has a Ball reference variable called ball, so its BallInPlay event handler starts with "ball_", followed by the name of the event being handled, "BallInPlay".

④ Each individual object subscribes to the event

Once we've got the event handler set up, the various Pitcher, Umpire, ThirdBaseman, and Fan objects need to hook up their own event handlers. Each one of them will have its own specific ball_BallInPlay method that responds differently to the event. So if there's a Ball object reference variable or field called ball, then the += operator will hook up the event handler:

```
ball.BallInPlay += new EventHandler(ball_BallInPlay);
```

This tells C# to hook the event handler up to the BallInPlay event of whatever object the ball reference is pointing to.

The += operator tells C# to subscribe an event handler to an event.

This part specifies which event handler method to subscribe to the event.

The event handler method's signature (its parameters and return value) has to match the one defined by EventHandler or the program won't compile.

Turn the page, there's a little more.... ⟶

⑤ **A `Ball` object raises its event to notify subscribers that it's in play**
Now that the events are all set up, the `Ball` can **raise its event** in response to something else that happens in the simulator. Raising an event is easy—it just calls the `BallInPlay` event.

```
EventHandler ballInPlay = BallInPlay;
if (ballInPlay != null)
    ballInPlay(this, e);
```

BallInPlay is copied to a variable, ballInPlay, which is null-checked and used to raise the event.

e is a new BallEventArgs object.

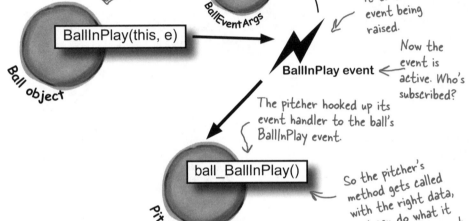

The ball gets hit, and the Ball object goes into action...

BallInPlay(this, e)

Ball object

BallEventArgs

...by creating a new BallEventArgs object with the right data...

...and passing it to the event being raised.

BallInPlay event

Now the event is active. Who's subscribed?

The pitcher hooked up its event handler to the ball's BallInPlay event.

ball_BallInPlay()

Pitcher object

So the pitcher's method gets called with the right data, and can do what it wants with the event.

Watch it!

If you raise an event with no handlers, it'll throw an exception.

If no other objects have added their event handlers to an event, it'll be null. So always check to make sure your event handler isn't equal to null before you raise it. If you don't, it'll throw a `NullReferenceException`. *That's also why you should* **copy the event to a variable** *before you check to see if it's null—in extremely rare cases, the event can become null between the the null check and the time that it's called.*

Use a standard name when you add a method to raise an event

Take a minute and go to the code for any form, and type the keyword **override** any place you'd declare a method. As soon as you press space, an IntelliSense window pops up:

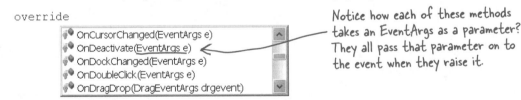

```
override
```

- OnCursorChanged(EventArgs e)
- OnDeactivate(EventArgs e)
- OnDockChanged(EventArgs e)
- OnDoubleClick(EventArgs e)
- OnDragDrop(DragEventArgs drgevent)

Notice how each of these methods takes an EventArgs as a parameter? They all pass that parameter on to the event when they raise it.

There are a huge number of events that a `Form` object can raise, and every one of them has its own method that raises it. The form's `OnDoubleClick()` raises the `DoubleClick` event, and that's the whole reason it's there. So the `Ball` event will follow the same convention: we'll make sure it **has a method called OnBallInPlay** that takes a `BallEventArgs` object as a parameter. The baseball simulator will call that method any time it needs the ball to raise its `BallInPlay` event—so when the simulator detects that the bat hit the ball, it'll create a new instance of `BallEventArgs` with the ball's trajectory and distance and pass it to `OnBallInPlay()`.

there are no
Dumb Questions

Q: Why do I need to include the word **EventHandler** when I declare an event? I thought the event handler was what the other objects used to subscribe to the events.

A: That's true—when you need to subscribe to an event, you write a method called an event handler. But did you notice how we used EventHandler in the the event declaration (step #2) **and** in the line to subscribe the event handler to it (step #4)? What EventHandler does is define the **signature** of the event—it tells the objects subscribing to the event exactly how they need to define their event handler methods. Specifically, it says that if you want to subscribe a method to this event, it needs to take two parameters (an object and an EventArgs reference) and have a void return value.

Q: What happens if I try to use a method that doesn't match the ones that are defined by **EventHandler**?

A: Then your program won't compile. The compiler will make sure that you don't ever accidentally subscribe an incompatible event handler method to an event. That's why the standard event handler, EventHandler, is so useful—as soon as you see it, you know exactly what your event handler method needs to look like.

Q: Wait, "standard" event handler? There are other kinds of event handlers?

A: Yes! Your events don't **have to** send an object and an EventArgs.

In fact, they can send anything at all—or nothing at all! Look at the last line in the IntelliSense window at the bottom of the facing page. Notice how the OnDragDrop method takes a DragEventArgs reference instead of an EventArgs reference? DragEventArgs inherits from EventArgs, just like BallEventArgs does. The form's DragDrop event doesn't use EventHandler. It uses something else, DragEventArgs, and if you want to handle it, your event handler method needs to take an object and a DragEventArgs reference.

The parameters of the event are defined by a *delegate*—EventHandler and DragEventArgs are two examples of delegates. But we'll talk more about that in a minute.

Q: So I can probably have my event handlers return something other than void, too, right?

A: Well, you can, but it's often a bad idea. If you don't return void from your handler, you can't *chain* event handlers. That means you can't connect more than one handler to each event. Since chaining is a handy feature, you'd do best to always return void from your event handlers.

Q: Chaining? What's that?

A: It's how more than one object can subscribe to the same event—they chain their event handlers onto the event, one after another. We'll talk a lot more about that in a minute, too.

Q: Is that why I used += when when I added my event handler? Like I'm somehow adding a new handler to existing handlers?

A: Exactly! Any time you add an event handler, you want to use +=. That way, your handler doesn't replace existing handlers. It just becomes one in what may be a very long chain of other event handlers, all of which are listening to the same event.

Q: Why does the ball use "this" when it raises the **BallInPlay()** event?

A: Because that's the first parameter of the standard event handler. Have you noticed how every Click event handler method has a parameter "object sender"? That parameter is a **reference to the object that's raising the event**. So if you're handling a button click, sender points to the button that was clicked. And if you're handling a BallInPlay event, sender will point to the Ball object that's in play—and the ball sets that parameter to this when it raises the event.

A <u>SINGLE</u> event is always raised by a <u>SINGLE</u> object.

But a <u>SINGLE</u> event can be responded to by <u>MULTIPLE</u> objects.

that'll save you some typing

The IDE creates event handlers for you automatically

Most programmers follow the same convention for naming their event handlers. If there's a `Ball` object that has a `BallInPlay` event and the name of the reference holding the object is called `ball`, then the event handler would typically be named `ball_BallInPlay()`. That's not a hard-and-fast rule, but if you write your code like that, it'll be a lot easier for other programmers to read.

Luckily, the IDE makes it really easy to name your event handlers properly. It has a feature that **automatically adds event handler methods for you** when you're working with a class that raises an event. It shouldn't be too surprising that the IDE can do this for you—after all, this is exactly what it does when you double-click on a button in your form.

Do this

1 **Start a new Windows application and add the `Ball` and `BallEventArgs`**
Here's the `Ball` class:

```
class Ball {
    public event EventHandler BallInPlay;
    public void OnBallInPlay(BallEventArgs e) {
        EventHandler ballInPlay = BallInPlay;
        if (ballInPlay != null)
            ballInPlay(this, e);
    }
}
```

And here's the `BallEventArgs` class:

```
class BallEventArgs : EventArgs {
    public int Trajectory { get; private set; }
    public int Distance { get; private set; }
    public BallEventArgs(int trajectory, int distance) {
        this.Trajectory = trajectory;
        this.Distance = distance;
    }
}
```

2 **Start adding the `Pitcher`'s constructor**
Add a new `Pitcher` class to your project. Then give it a constructor that takes a `Ball` reference called `ball` as a parameter. There will be one line of code in the constructor to add its event handler to `ball.BallInPlay`. Start typing the statement, but **don't type += yet**.

```
public Pitcher(Ball ball) {
    ball.BallInPlay
}
```

③ Type += and the IDE will finish the statement for you

As soon as you type += in the statement, the IDE displays a very useful little box:

```
public Pitcher(Ball ball) {
    ball.BallInPlay +=
}
```
```
new EventHandler(ball_BallInPlay);      (Press TAB to insert)
```

As soon as you press the tab key, the IDE will finish the statement for you. It'll look like this:

```
public Pitcher(Ball ball) {
    ball.BallInPlay += new EventHandler(ball_BallInPlay);
}
```

When you double-click on a button in the form designer, the IDE does the exact same trick—adding an event handler automatically—except that it adds the code to the form's InitializeComponent() method in the Form1.Designer.cs file instead of just adding it to the end of the class file.

④ The IDE will add your event handler, too

You're not done—you still need to add a method to chain onto the event. Luckily, the IDE takes care of that for you, too.

```
new EventHandler(ball_BallInPlay);
```
```
Press TAB to generate handler 'ball_BallInPlay' in this class
```

Hit the tab key again to make the IDE add this event handler method to your Pitcher class. The IDE will always follow the objectName_HandlerName() convention:

```
void ball_BallInPlay(object sender, EventArgs e) {
    throw new NotImplementedException();
}
```

The IDE always fills in this NotImplementedException() as a placeholder so if you run the code it'll throw an exception that tells you that you still need to implement something it filled in automatically.

⑤ Finish the pitcher's event handler

Now that you've got the event handler's skeleton added to your class, fill in the rest of its code. The pitcher should catch any low balls; otherwise, he covers first base. *Since BallEventArgs is a subclass of EventArgs, we'll downcast it using the as keyword so we can use its properties.*

```
void ball_BallInPlay(object sender, EventArgs e) {
    if (e is BallEventArgs) {
        BallEventArgs ballEventArgs = e as BallEventArgs;
        if ((ballEventArgs.Distance < 95) && (ballEventArgs.Trajectory < 60))
            CatchBall();
        else
            CoverFirstBase();
    }
}
```

You'll add these methods in a minute.

Exercise

It's time to put what you've learned so far into practice. Your job is to complete the `Ball` and `Pitcher` classes, add a `Fan` class, and make sure they all work together with a very basic version of your baseball simulator.

1 **Complete the `Pitcher` class.**

Below is what we've got for `Pitcher`. Add the `CatchBall()` and `CoverFirstBase()` methods. Both should print out that the catcher has either caught the ball or run to first base.

```
class Pitcher {
    public Pitcher(Ball ball) {
        ball.BallInPlay += new EventHandler(ball_BallInPlay);
    }

    void ball_BallInPlay(object sender, EventArgs e) {
        if (e is BallEventArgs){
            BallEventArgs ballEventArgs = e as BallEventArgs;
            if ((ballEventArgs.Distance < 95) && (ballEventArgs.Trajectory < 60))
                CatchBall();
            else
                CoverFirstBase();
        }
    }
}
```

You'll need to implement these two methods to write a line of output to the console.

Pitcher object

2 **Write a `Fan` class.**

Create another class called `Fan`. `Fan` should also subscribe to the `BallInPlay` event in its constructor. The fan's event handler should see if the distance is greater than 400 feet and the trajectory is greater than 30 (a home run), and grab for a glove to try and catch the ball if it is. If not, the fan should scream and yell. Write out what's going on with the fan to the console.

Look at the output window on the facing page to see exactly what it should print.

Fan object

3 **Build a very simple simulator.**
Create a new application. The application should have two NumericUpDown controls: one for the ball's distance, and one for its trajectory. Add a button labeled "Play ball!" When "Play ball!" is clicked, a ball is hit with the values in the two NumericUpDowns. Your form should look something like this:

The value for trajectory can range from 0 to 100, so set its Minimum property to 0, Maximum to 100, and Value to 20.

Don't forget to cast the Value properties to ints before you use them.

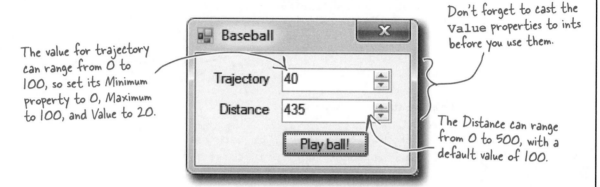

The Distance can range from 0 to 500, with a default value of 100.

4 **Create the following output.**
See if you can make your simulator generate this output with three successive balls put into play. Write down the values you used to get the result below:

```
Output                                            ▼ ☐ ✕
Show output from: Debug                                 ▼
  Pitcher: I covered first base                         ▲
  Fan: Woo-hoo! Yeah!
  Pitcher: I caught the ball                            ≡
  Fan: Woo-hoo! Yeah!
  Pitcher: I covered first base
  Fan: Home run! I'm going for the ball!                ▼
◄                                              ►
```

Ball 1:

Trajectory: ....

Distance: ....

Ball 2:

Trajectory: ....

Distance: ....

Ball 3:

Trajectory: ....

Distance: ....

Exercise Solution

It's time to put what you've learned so far into practice. Your job is to complete the `Ball` and `Pitcher` classes, add a `Fan` class, and make sure they all work together with a very basic version of your baseball simulator.

```
class Ball
{
    public event EventHandler BallInPlay;
    public void OnBallInPlay(BallEventArgs e) {
        EventHandler ballInPlay = BallInPlay;
        if (ballInPlay != null)
            ballInPlay(this, e);
    }
}
```

> The OnBallInPlay() method just raises the BallInPlay event—but it has to check to make sure it's not null, otherwise it'll throw an exception.

Read-only automatic properties work really well in event arguments because the event handlers only read the data passed to them.

```
class BallEventArgs : EventArgs
{
    public int Trajectory { get; private set; }
    public int Distance { get; private set; }
    public BallEventArgs(int trajectory, int distance)
    {
        this.Trajectory = trajectory;
        this.Distance = distance;
    }
}
```

> The Fan object's constructor chains its event handler onto the BallInPlay event.

```
class Fan {
    public Fan(Ball ball)
    {
        ball.BallInPlay += new EventHandler(ball_BallInPlay);
    }

    void ball_BallInPlay(object sender, EventArgs e)
    {
        if (e is BallEventArgs) {
            BallEventArgs ballEventArgs = e as BallEventArgs;
            if (ballEventArgs.Distance > 400 && ballEventArgs.Trajectory > 30)
                Console.WriteLine("Fan: Home run! I'm going for the ball!");
            else
                Console.WriteLine("Fan: Woo-hoo! Yeah!");
        }
    }
}
```

> The fan's BallInPlay event handler looks for any ball that's high and long.

```
class Pitcher {
    public Pitcher(Ball ball) {
        ball.BallInPlay += new EventHandler(ball_BallInPlay);
    }
    void ball_BallInPlay(object sender, EventArgs e) {
        if (e is BallEventArgs) {
            BallEventArgs ballEventArgs = e as BallEventArgs;
            if ((ballEventArgs.Distance < 95) && (ballEventArgs.Trajectory < 60))
                CatchBall();
            else
                CoverFirstBase();
        }
    }

    private void CatchBall() {
        Console.WriteLine("Pitcher: I caught the ball");
    }

    private void CoverFirstBase() {
        Console.WriteLine("Pitcher: I covered first base");
    }
}

public partial class Form1 : Form {
    Ball ball = new Ball();
    Pitcher pitcher;
    Fan fan;

    public Form1() {
        InitializeComponent();
        pitcher = new Pitcher(ball);
        fan = new Fan(ball);
    }

    private void playBallButton_Click(object sender, EventArgs e) {
        BallEventArgs ballEventArgs = new BallEventArgs(
            (int)trajectory.Value, (int)distance.Value);
        ball.OnBallInPlay(ballEventArgs);
    }
}
```

You already have the pitcher's BallInPlay event handler. It looks for any low balls.

The form needs one ball, one fan, and one pitcher. It hooks the fan and pitcher up to the ball in its constructor.

When the button's clicked, the form tells the pitcher to pitch the ball to the batter, which tells the ball to fire off its BallInPlay event, which calls the event handlers in the Pitcher and Fan objects.

Here are the values we used to get the output. Yours might be a little different.

Ball 1:
Trajectory: 75
Distance: 105

Ball 2:
Trajectory: 48
Distance: 80

Ball 3:
Trajectory: 40
Distance: 435

Generic EventHandlers let you define your own event types

Take a look at the event declaration in your Ball class:

```
public event EventHandler BallInPlay;
```

Now take a look at the Click event declaration from a button, form, and most of the other controls you've been using:

```
public event EventHandler Click;
```

Notice anything? They have different names, but they're declared exactly the same way. And while that works just fine, someone looking at your class declaration doesn't necessarily know that the BallEventHandler will always pass it a BallEventArgs when the event is fired. Luckily, .NET gives us a great tool to communicate that information very easily: a generic EventHandler. Change your ball's BallInPlay event handler so it looks like this:

> The generic argument to EventHandler has to be a subclass of EventArgs.

```
public event EventHandler<BallEventArgs> BallInPlay;
```

Now rebuild your code. You should see two errors in the Error List window:

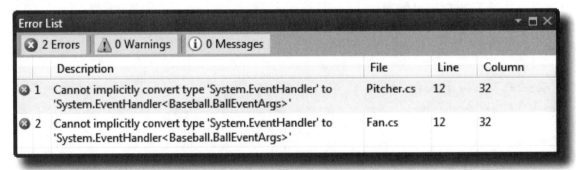

	Description	File	Line	Column
⊗ 1	Cannot implicitly convert type 'System.EventHandler' to 'System.EventHandler<Baseball.BallEventArgs>'	Pitcher.cs	12	32
⊗ 2	Cannot implicitly convert type 'System.EventHandler' to 'System.EventHandler<Baseball.BallEventArgs>'	Fan.cs	12	32

Now that you changed the event declaration, your Pitcher and Fan classes need to be updated so that they hook up to the events by passing the generic argument to EventHandler:

```
ball.BallInPlay += new EventHandler<BallEventArgs>(ball_BallInPlay);
```

Use implicit conversion by leaving out the <u>new</u> keyword and the event type

If you use the IDE to automatically create the event handler method like you did a few pages ago, it will always contain the new keyword followed by the event handler type. But if you leave out the new keyword and the event handler type, C# will do an **implicit conversion** and figure out the type for you:

```
ball.BallInPlay += ball_BallInPlay;
```

Try replacing the code in the Pitcher and Fan constructors with the line above. When you run the program, it will still work just fine.

The forms you've been building all use events

Every time you've created a button, double-clicked on it in the designer, and written code for a method like button1_Click(), you've been working with events.

Do this

① Create a new Windows Application project. Go to the Properties window for the form. Remember those icons at the top of the window? Click on the Events button (it's the one with the lightning bolt icon) to bring up **the events page in the Properties window**:

You can see all of the events for a control: just click on it and then click on this events button in the Properties window.

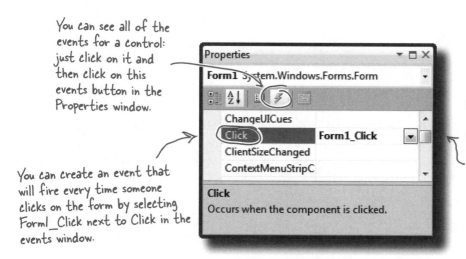

Scroll down to Click and double-click on the word "Click". When you do, the IDE will add a new click event handler to your form that gets fired every time you click on it. And it'll add a line to Form1.Designer.cs to hook the event handler up to the event.

You can create an event that will fire every time someone clicks on the form by selecting Form1_Click next to Click in the events window.

② Double-click on the "Click" row in the events page. The IDE will automatically add an event handler method to your form called Form1_Click. Add this line of code to it:

```
private void Form1_Click(object sender, EventArgs e) {
    MessageBox.Show("You just clicked on the form");
}
```

③ Visual Studio did more than just write a little method declaration for you, though. It also hooked the event handler up to the Form object's Click event. Open up Form1.Designer.cs and use the Quick Find (Edit >> Find and Replace >> Quick Find) feature in the IDE to search for the text Form1_Click in the current project. You'll find this line of code:

```
this.Click += new System.EventHandler(this.Form1_Click);
```

Now run the program and make sure your code works!

You're not done yet—flip the page! ⟶

One event, multiple handlers

Here's a really useful thing that you can do with events: you can **chain** them so that one event or delegate calls many methods, one after another. Let's add a few buttons to your application to see how it works.

4 Add these two methods to your form:

```
private void SaySomething(object sender, EventArgs e) {
    MessageBox.Show("Something");
}
private void SaySomethingElse(object sender, EventArgs e) {
    MessageBox.Show("Something else");
}
```

5 Now add two buttons to your form. Double-click on each button to add its event handler. Here's the code for both event handlers:

```
private void button1_Click(object sender, EventArgs e) {
    this.Click += new EventHandler(SaySomething);
}
private void button2_Click(object sender, EventArgs e) {
    this.Click += new EventHandler(SaySomethingElse);
}
```

Before you go on, take a minute and think about what those two buttons do. Each button **hooks up a new event handler to the form's Click event**. In the first three steps, you used the IDE to add an event handler as usual to pop up a message box every time the form fired its Click event—it added code to `Form1.Designer.cs` that used the += operator to hook up its event handler.

Now you added two buttons that use the exact same syntax to chain additional event handlers onto the same Click event. So **before you go on**, try to guess what will happen if you run the program, click the first button, then click the second button, and then click on the form. Can you figure it out before you run the program?

there are no Dumb Questions

Q: When I added a new event handler to the Pitcher object, why did the IDE make it throw an exception?

A: It added code to throw a NotImplementedException to remind you that you still need to implement code there. That's a really useful exception, because you can use it as a placeholder just like the IDE did. For example, you'll typically use it when you need to build the skeleton of a class but you don't want to fill in all the code yet. That way, if your program throws that exception, you know it's because you still need to finish the code, and not because your program is broken.

Watch it!

Event handlers always need to be "hooked up."

*If you drag a button onto your form and add a method called `button1_Click()` that has the right parameters but **isn't registered to listen to your button**, the method won't ever get called. Double-click on the button in the designer—the IDE will see the default event handler name is taken, so it'll add an event handler for the button called `button1_Click_1()`.*

Now run your program and do this:

★ **Click the form**—you'll see a message box pop up that says, "You just clicked on the form".

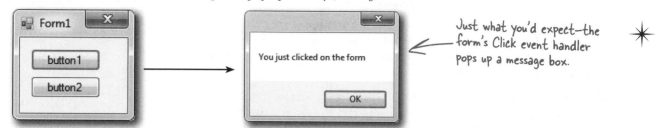

> Just what you'd expect—the form's Click event handler pops up a message box.

★ Now **click button1** and then **click on the form again**. You'll see two message boxes pop up: "You just clicked on the form" and then "Something".

> But every time you click a button, it causes yet another message box to pop up the next time you click on the form!

★ **Click button2 twice** and then **click on the form again**. You'll see four message boxes: "You just clicked on the form", "Something", "Something else", and "Something else".

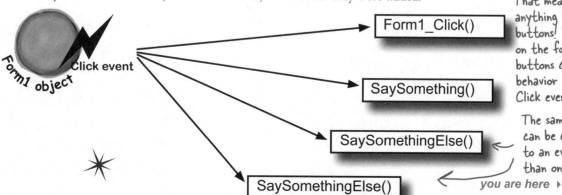

So what happened?

Every time you clicked one of the buttons, you chained another method—either Something() or SomethingElse()—onto the form's Click event. You can keep clicking the buttons, and they'll keep **chaining the same methods** onto the event. The event doesn't care how many methods are chained on, or even if the same method is in the chain more than once. It'll just call them all every time the event fires, one after another, in the order they were added.

> When you click these buttons, they chain different event handlers onto the form's Click event.

> That means you won't see anything when you click the buttons! You'll need to click on the form, because the buttons change the form's behavior by modifying its Click event.

> The same method can be chained on to an event more than once.

Connecting event senders with event receivers

One of the trickiest things about events is that the **sender** of the event has to know what kind of event to send—including the arguments to pass to the event. And the **receiver** of the event has to know about the return type and the arguments its handler methods must use.

But—and here's the tricky part—you can't tie the sender and receiver *together*. You want the sender to send the event and *not worry about who receives it*. And the receiver cares about the event, *not the object that raised the event*. So both sender and receiver focus on the event, not each other.

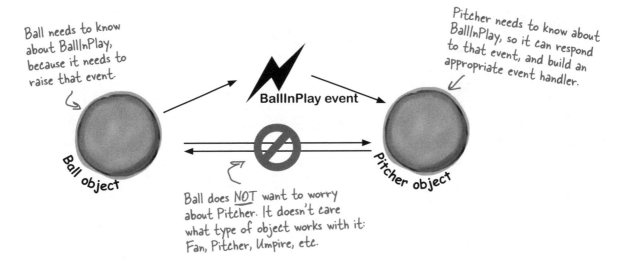

Ball needs to know about BallInPlay, because it needs to raise that event.

Pitcher needs to know about BallInPlay, so it can respond to that event, and build an appropriate event handler.

BallInPlay event

Ball object

Pitcher object

Ball does <u>NOT</u> want to worry about Pitcher. It doesn't care what type of object works with it: Fan, Pitcher, Umpire, etc.

"My people will get in touch with your people."

You know what this code does:

```
Ball currentBall;
```

It creates a **reference variable** that can point to any Ball object. It's not tied to a single Ball. Instead, it can point to any ball object—or it can be null, and not point to anything at all.

An event needs a similar kind of reference—except instead of pointing to an object, it needs one that **points to a method**. Every event needs to keep track of a list of methods that are subscribed to it. You've already seen that they can be in other classes, and they can even be private. So how does it keep track of all of the event handler methods that it needs to call? It uses something called a **delegate**.

> del-e-gate, noun.
> a person sent or authorized to represent others. *The president sent a **delegate** to the summit.*

A delegate <u>STANDS</u> <u>IN</u> for an actual method

When you create a delegate, all you need to do is specify the signature of methods that it can point to.

One of the most useful aspects of events is that when an event fires, it **has no idea** whose event handler methods it's calling. Anyone who happens to subscribe to an event gets his event handler called. So how does the event manage that?

It uses a C# type called a **delegate**. A delegate is a special kind of reference type that lets you **refer to a method inside a class**…and delegates are the basis for events.

You've actually already been using delegates throughout this chapter! When you created the `BallInPlay` event, you used `EventHandler`. Well, an `EventHandler` is just a delegate. If you right-click on `EventHandler` in the IDE and select "Go to definition", this is what you'll see (try it yourself):

So this delegate can be used to reference any method that takes an object and an EventArgs and has no return value.

```
public delegate void EventHandler(object sender, EventArgs e);
```

This specifies the return value of the delegate's signature—which means an EventHandler can only point to methods with void return values.

The name of this delegate is EventHandler.

Do this

A delegate adds a <u>new type</u> to your project

When you add a delegate to your project, you're adding a **delegate type**. And when you use it to create a field or variable, you're creating an **instance** of that delegate type. **So create a new Console Application project**. Then add a new class file to the project called `ConvertsIntToString.cs`. But instead of putting a class inside it, add a single line:

```
delegate string ConvertsIntToString(int i);
```

ConvertsIntToString is a delegate type that you've added to your project. Now you can use it to declare variables. This is just like how you can use a class or interface as a type to define variables.

Next, add a method called `HiThere()` to your `Program` class:

```
private static string HiThere(int i)
{
    return "Hi there! #" + (i * 100);
}
```

This method's signature matches ReturnsAString.

Finally, fill in the `Main()` method:

someMethod is a variable whose type is ConvertsIntToString. It's a lot like a reference variable, except instead of putting a label on an object on the heap you're putting a label on a method.

```
static void Main(string[] args)
{
    ConvertsIntToString someMethod = new ConvertsIntToString(HiThere);
    string message = someMethod(5);
    Console.WriteLine(message);
    Console.ReadKey();
}
```

You can set someMethod just like any other variable. When you call it like a method, it calls whatever method it happens to point to.

The `someMethod` variable is pointing to the `HiThere()` method. When your program calls `someMethod(5)`, it calls `HiThere()` and passes it the argument 5, which causes it to return the string value "Hi there! #500"—exactly as if it were called directly. Take a minute and step through the program in the debugger to see exactly what's going on.

Delegates in action

There's nothing mysterious about delegates—in fact, they
don't take much code at all to use. Let's use them to help a
restaurant owner sort out his top chef's secret ingredients.

 *Do this*

 Create a new Windows project and add a delegate

Delegates usually appear outside of any other classes, so add a new class file to your project and
call it GetSecretIngredient.cs. It will have exactly one line of code in it:

```
delegate string GetSecretIngredient(int amount);
```

(Make sure you delete the class declaration entirely.) This delegate can be used to create a variable
that can point to any method that takes one int parameter and returns a string.

Add a class for the first chef, Suzanne

Suzanne.cs will hold a class that keeps track of the first chef's secret ingredient. It has a
private method called SuzannesSecretIngredient() with a signature that matches
GetSecretIngredient. But it also has a read-only property—and check out that property's
type. It returns a GetSecretIngredient. So other objects can use that property to get a
reference to her SuzannesIngredientList() method.

*Suzanne's secret
ingredient method
takes an int
called amount and
returns a string
that describes her
secret ingredient.*

```
class Suzanne {
    public GetSecretIngredient MySecretIngredientMethod {
        get {
            return new GetSecretIngredient(SuzannesSecretIngredient);
        }
    }
    private string SuzannesSecretIngredient(int amount) {
        return amount.ToString() + " ounces of cloves";
    }
}
```

Then add a class for the second chef, Amy

Amy's method works a lot like Suzanne's:

*Amy's GetSecretIngredient property
returns a new instance of the
GetSecretIngredient delegate that's
pointing to her secret ingredient method.*

*Amy's secret
ingredient method
also takes an int
called amount and
returns a string,
but it returns a
different string
from Suzanne's.*

```
class Amy {
    public GetSecretIngredient AmysSecretIngredientMethod {
        get {
            return new GetSecretIngredient(AmysSecretIngredient);
        }
    }
    private string AmysSecretIngredient(int amount) {
        if (amount < 10)
            return amount.ToString()
                    + " cans of sardines -- you need more!";
        else
            return amount.ToString() + " cans of sardines";
    }
}
```

④ Create a new Windows project and add a delegate
Build this form. ━━━━━━━━━━━━━━━━━━━━━━━━━━━━━▶

Here's the code for the form:

```
GetSecretIngredient ingredientMethod = null;
Suzanne suzanne = new Suzanne();
Amy amy = new Amy();

private void useIngredient_Click(object sender, EventArgs e) {
    if (ingredientMethod != null)
        Console.WriteLine("I'll add " + ingredientMethod((int)amount.Value));
    else
        Console.WriteLine("I don't have a secret ingredient!");
}

private void getSuzanne_Click(object sender, EventArgs e) {
    ingredientMethod = new GetSecretIngredient(suzanne.MySecretIngredientMethod);
}

private void getAmy_Click(object sender, EventArgs e) {
    ingredientMethod = new GetSecretIngredient(amy.AmysSecretIngredientMethod);
}
```

⑤ Use the debugger to explore how delegates work
You've got a great tool—the IDE's debugger—that can really help you get a handle on how delegates work. Do the following steps:

★ Start by running your program. First click the "Get the ingredient" button—it should write a line to the console that says, "I don't have a secret ingredient!"

★ Click the "Get Suzanne's delegate" button—that takes the form's ingredientMethod field (which is a GetSecretIngredient delegate)—and sets it equal to whatever Suzanne's GetSecretIngredient property returns. That property returns a new instance of the GetSecretIngredient type that's pointing to the SuzannesSecretIngredient() method.

★ Click the "Get the ingredient" button again. Now that the form's ingredientMethod field is pointing to SuzannesSecretIngredient(), it calls that, passing it the value in the numericUpDown control (make sure it's named **amount**) and writing its output to the console.

★ Click the "Get Amy's delegate" button. It uses the Amy.GetSecretIngredient property to set the form's ingredientMethod field to point to the AmysSecretIngredient() method.

★ Click the "Get the ingredient" button one more time. Now it calls Amy's method.

★ Now **use the debugger** to see exactly what's going on. Place a breakpoint on the first line of each of the three methods in the form. Then **restart the program** (which resets the ingredientMethod so that it's equal to null), and start over with the above five steps. Use the Step Into (F11) feature of the debugger to step through every line of code. Watch what happens when you click "Get the ingredient". It steps right into the Suzanne and Amy classes, depending on which method the ingredientMethod field is pointing to.

Pool Puzzle

Your **job** is to take snippets from the pool and place them into the blank lines in the code. You can use the same snippet more than once, and you won't need to use all the snippets. Your **goal** is to complete the code for a form that writes this output to the console when its **button1** button is clicked.

Output

```
Fingers is coming to get you!
```

Note: Each thing from the pool can be used more than once

```csharp
public Form1() {
    InitializeComponent();

    this._____ += new EventHandler(Minivan);

    this._____ += new EventHandler(_____);
}

void Towtruck(object sender, EventArgs e) {
    Console.Write("is coming ");
}

void Motorcycle(object sender, EventArgs e) {
    button1._____ += new EventHandler(_____);
}

void Bicycle(object sender, EventArgs e) {
    Console.WriteLine("to get you!");
}

void _____(object sender, EventArgs e) {
    button1._____ += new EventHandler(Dumptruck);

    button1._____ += new EventHandler(_____);
}

void _____(object sender, EventArgs e) {
    Console.Write("Fingers ");
}
```

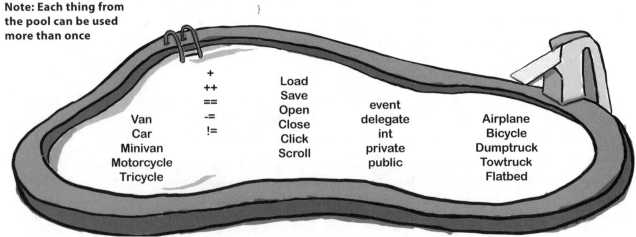

+	Load
++	Save
==	Open
-=	Close
!=	Click
	Scroll

Van
Car
Minivan
Motorcycle
Tricycle

event
delegate
int
private
public

Airplane
Bicycle
Dumptruck
Towtruck
Flatbed

An object can <u>subscribe</u> to an event...

Suppose we add a new class to our simulator, a `Bat` class, and that class adds a `HitTheBall` event into the mix. Here's how it works: if the simulator detects that the player hit the ball, it calls the `Bat` object's `OnHitTheBall()` method, which raises a `HitTheBall` event.

So now we can add a `bat_HitTheBall` method to the `Ball` class that subscribes to the `Bat` object's `HitTheBall` event. Then when the ball gets hit, its own event handler calls its `OnBallInPlay()` method to raise its own event, `BallInPlay`, and the chain reaction begins. Fielders field, fans scream, umpires yell...we've got a ball game.

Now its event handler can take information about how hard the swing was, figure out the distance and trajectory, and raise a BallInPlay event.

The simulator detects that the bat collided with the ball, so it calls the bat object's OnHitTheBall() method.

Ball subscribed to the HitTheBall event.

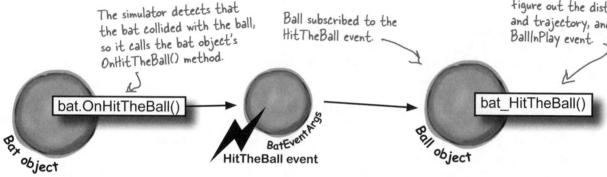

...but that's not always a good thing!

There's only ever going to be one ball in play at any time. But if the Bat object uses an event to announce to the ball that it's been hit, then any Ball object can subscribe to it. And that means we've set ourselves up for a nasty little bug—what happens if a programmer accidentally adds three more `Ball` objects? Then the batter will swing, hit, and **four different balls will fly** out into the field!

Uh-oh! These balls were supposed to be held in reserve in case the first one was hit out of the park.

But a careless programmer subscribed them all to the bat's HitTheBall event...so when the bat hit the ball that the pitcher threw, all four of them flew out into the field!

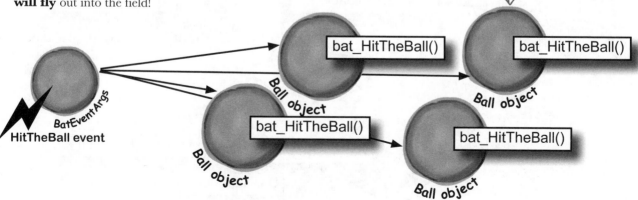

Use a callback to control who's listening

Our system of events only works if we've got one `Ball` and one `Bat`. If you've got several `Ball` objects, and they all subscribe to the public event `HitTheBall`, then they'll all go flying when the event is raised. But that doesn't make any sense…it's really only one `Ball` object that got hit. We need to let the one ball that's being pitched hook itself up to the bat, but we need to do it in a way that doesn't allow any other balls to hook themselves up.

That's where a **callback** comes in handy. It's a technique that you can use with delegates. Instead of exposing an event that anyone can subscribe to, an object uses a method (often a constructor) that takes a delegate as an argument and holds onto that delegate in a private field. We'll use a callback to make sure that the `Bat` notifies exactly one `Ball`:

① **The `Bat` will keep its delegate field private**
The easiest way to keep the wrong `Ball` objects from chaining themselves onto the `Bat`'s delegate is for the bat to make it private. That way, it has control over which `Ball` object's method gets called.

② **The `Bat`'s constructor takes a delegate that points to a method in the ball**
When the ball is in play, it creates the new instance of the bat, and it passes the `Bat` object a pointer to its `OnBallInPlay()` method. This is called a **callback method** because the `Bat` is using it to call back to the object that instantiated it.

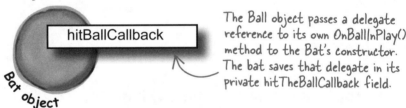

The Ball object passes a delegate reference to its own OnBallInPlay() method to the Bat's constructor. The bat saves that delegate in its private hitTheBallCallback field.

③ **When the bat hits the ball, it calls the callback method**
But since the bat kept its delegate private, it can be 100% sure that no other ball has been hit. That solves the problem!

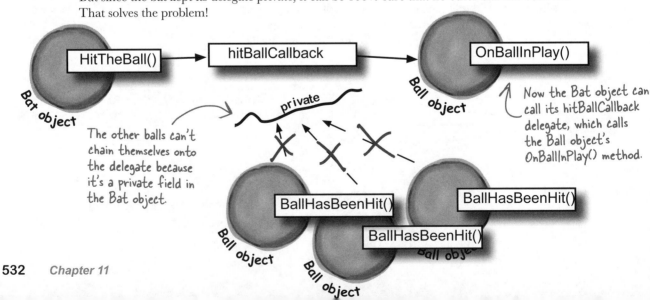

The other balls can't chain themselves onto the delegate because it's a private field in the Bat object.

Now the Bat object can call its hitBallCallback delegate, which calls the Ball object's OnBallInPlay() method.

The Case of the Golden Crustacean

Henry "Flatfoot" Hodgkins is a TreasureHunter. He's hot on the trail of one of the most prized possessions in the rare and unusual aquatic-themed jewelry markets: a jade-encrusted translucent gold crab. But so are lots of other TreasureHunters. They all got a reference to the same crab in their constructor, but Henry wants to claim the prize *first*.

Five Minute Mystery

In a stolen set of class diagrams, Henry discovers that the GoldenCrab class raises a RunForCover event every time anyone gets close to it. Even better, the event includes NewLocationArgs, which detail where the crab is moving to. But none of the other treasure hunters know about the event, so Henry figures he can cash in.

Henry adds code to his constructor to register his treasure_RunForCover() method as an event handler for the RunForCover event on the crab reference he's got. Then, he sends a lowly underling after the crab, knowing it will run away, hide, and raise the RunForCover event—giving Henry's treasure_RunForCover() method all the information he needs.

Everything goes according to plan, until Henry gets the new location and rushes to grab the crab. He's stunned to see three other TreasureHunters already there, fighting over the crab.

How did the other treasure hunters beat Henry to the crab?

⟶ Answers on page 537.

Pool Puzzle Solution

The constructor chains two event handlers onto the load events. They get fired off as soon as the form is loaded.

```
public Form1() {
    InitializeComponent();
    this.Load += new EventHandler(Minivan);
    this.Load += new EventHandler(Motorcycle);
}
void Towtruck(object sender, EventArgs e) {
    Console.Write("is coming ");
}
void Motorcycle(object sender, EventArgs e) {

    button1.Click += new EventHandler(Bicycle);
}
void Bicycle(object sender, EventArgs e) {
    Console.WriteLine("to get you!");
}
void Minivan(object sender, EventArgs e) {
    button1.Click += new EventHandler(Dumptruck);
    button1.Click += new EventHandler(Towtruck);
}
void Dumptruck(object sender, EventArgs e) {
    Console.Write("Fingers ");
}
```

The two Load event handlers hook up three separate event handlers to the button's Click event handler.

When the button is clicked, it calls the three event handlers that are chained to it.

A callback is just a way to <u>use</u> delegates

A callback is a **different way of using a delegate**. It's not a new keyword or operator. It just describes a **pattern**—a way that you use delegates with your classes so that one object can tell another object, "Notify me when this happens—if that's OK with you!"

Do this

(1) Define another delegate in your baseball project

Since the Bat will have a private delegate field that points to the Ball object's OnBallInPlay() method, we'll need a delegate that matches its signature:

```
delegate void BatCallback(BallEventArgs e);
```

Delegates don't always need to live in their own files. Try putting this one in the same file as Bat.

The Bat object's callback will point to a Ball object's OnBallInPlay() method, so the callback's delegate needs to match the signature of OnBallInPlay()—so it needs to take a BallEventArgs parameter and have a void return value.

(2) Add the Bat class to the project

The Bat class is simple. It's got a HitTheBall() method that the simulator will call every time a ball is hit. That HitTheBall() method uses the hitBallCallback() delegate to call the ball's OnBallInPlay() method (or whatever method is passed into its constructor).

```
         class Bat {
Make sure you    private BatCallback hitBallCallback;
check every      public Bat(BatCallback callbackDelegate) {
delegate to          this.hitBallCallback = new BatCallback(callbackDelegate);
make sure        }
it's not null,
otherwise it     public void HitTheBall(BallEventArgs e) {
could throw a ──→     if (hitBallCallback != null)
null reference           hitBallCallback(e);
exception.       }
         }
```

> We used = instead of += because in this case, we only want one bat to listen to any one ball, so this delegate only gets set once. But there's nothing stopping you from writing a callback that uses += to call back to multiple methods. The point of the callback is that the object doing the calling is <u>in control of who's listening</u>. In an event, other objects demand to be notified by adding event handlers. In a callback, other objects simply turn over their delegates and politely ask to be notified.

(3) We'll need to hook the bat up to a ball

So how does the Bat's constructor get a reference to a particular ball's OnBallInPlay() method? Easy—just call that Ball object's GetNewBat() method, which you'll have to add to Ball:

```
public Bat GetNewBat()
{
    return new Bat(new BatCallback(OnBallInPlay));
}
```

We set the callback in the Bat object's constructor. But in some cases, it makes more sense to set up the callback method using a public method or property's set accessor.

The Ball's GetNewBat() method creates a new Bat object, and it uses the BatCallBack delegate to pass a reference to its own OnBallInPlay() method to the new bat. That's the callback method the bat will use when it hits the ball.

④ Now we can encapsulate the `Ball` class a little better

It's unusual for one of the `On...` methods that raise an event to be `public`. You can check this for yourself—go to the form and try to call the `playBall` button's `OnClick()` event. You won't be able to, because it's `protected` (so a subclass can override it). So let's follow that pattern with our ball, too, by making its `OnBallInPlay()` method `protected`:

```
protected void OnBallInPlay(BallEventArgs e) {
    EventHandler<BallEventArgs> ballInPlay = BallInPlay;
    if (ballInPlay != null)
        ballInPlay(this, e);
}
```

This is a really standard pattern that you'll see over and over again when you work with .NET classes. When a .NET class has an event that gets fired, you'll almost always find a protected method that starts with "On".

⑤ All that's left to do is hook up the form

The form can't call the `Ball` object's `OnBallInPlay()` method anymore—which is exactly what we wanted. That's why we set up the `Ball.GetNewBat()` method. Now the form needs to ask the `Ball` for a new bat in order to hit the ball. And when it does, the `Ball` object will make sure that its `OnBallInPlay()` method is hooked up to the bat's callback.

```
private void playBallButton_Click(object sender, EventArgs e)
{
    Bat bat = ball.GetNewBat();
    BallEventArgs ballEventArgs = new BallEventArgs(
        (int)trajectory.Value, (int)distance.Value);
    bat.HitTheBall(ballEventArgs);
}
```

If the form (or the simulator) wants to hit a Ball object, it needs to get a new Bat object from that ball. The ball will make sure that the callback is hooked up to the bat. Now when the form calls the bat's HitTheBall() method, it calls the ball's OnBallInPlay() method, which fires its BallInPlay event.

Now **run the program**—it should work exactly like it did before. But it's now **protected** from any problems that would be caused by more than one ball listening for the same event.

But don't take our word for it—pop it open in the debugger!

BULLET POINTS

- When you add a delegate to your project, you're **creating a new type** that stores references to methods.

- Events use delegates to notify objects that actions have occurred.

- Objects subscribe to an object's event if they need to react to something that happened in that object.

- An `EventHandler` is a kind of delegate that's really common when you work with events.

- You can chain several event handlers onto one event. That's why you use += to assign a handler to an event.

- Always check that an event or delegate is not null before you use it to avoid a `NullReferenceException`.

- All of the controls in the toolbox use events to make things happen in your programs.

- When one object passes a reference to a method to another object so it—and only it—can return information, it's called a callback.

- Events let any method subscribe to your object's events anonymously, while callbacks let your objects exercise more control over which delegates they accept.

- Both callbacks and events use delegates to reference and call methods in other objects.

- The debugger is a really useful tool to help you understand how events, delegates, and callbacks work. Take advantage of it!

there are no
Dumb Questions

Q: How are callbacks different from events?

A: Events and delegates are part of .NET. They're a way for one object to announce to other objects that something specific has happened. When one object publishes an event, any number of other objects can subscribe to it without the publishing object knowing or caring. When an object fires off an event, if anyone happens to have subscribed to it then it calls each of their event handlers.

Callbacks are not part of .NET at all—instead, "callback" is just a name for the way we use delegates (or events—there's nothing stopping you from using a private event to build a callback). A callback is just a relationship between two classes where one object requests that it be notified. Compare this to an event, where one object **demands** that it be notified of that event.

Q: So a callback isn't an actual type in .NET?

A: No, it isn't. A callback is a *pattern*—it's just a novel way of using the existing types, keywords, and tools that C# comes with. Go back and take another look at the callback code you just wrote for the bat and ball. Did you see any new keywords that we haven't used before? Nope! But it does use a delegate, which **is** a .NET type.

It turns out that there are a lot of patterns that you can use. In fact, there's a whole area of programming called *design patterns*. A lot of problems that you'll run into have been solved before, and the ones that pop up over and over again have their own design patterns that you can benefit from.

Q: So callbacks are just private events?

A: Not quite. It seems easy to think about it that way, but private events are a different beast altogether. Remember what the `private` access modifier really means? When you mark a class member `private`, only instances of that same class can access it. So if you mark an event `private`, then other instances of the same class can subscribe to it. That's different from a callback, because it still involves one or more objects anonymously subscribing to an event.

Q: But it looks just like an event, except with the event keyword, right?

A: The reason a callback looks so much like an event is that they both use **delegates**. And it makes sense that they both use delegates, because that's C#'s tool for letting one object pass another object a reference to one of its methods.

But the big difference between normal events and callbacks is that an event is a way for a class to publish to the world that some specific thing has happened. A callback, on the other hand, is never published. It's private, and the method that's doing the calling keeps tight control over who it's calling.

Check out "Head First Design Patterns" at the Head First Labs website. It's a great way to learn about different patterns that you can apply to your own programs.

www.headfirstlabs.com/books/hfdp/

The first one you'll learn about is called the "Observer" (or "Publisher–Subscriber") pattern, and it'll look really familiar to you. One object publishes information, and other objects subscribe to it. Hmmm....

The Case of the Golden Crustacean

How did the other treasure hunters beat Henry to the crab?

The crux of the mystery lies in how the treasure hunter seeks his quarry. But first we'll need to see exactly what Henry found in the stolen diagrams.

In a stolen set of class diagrams, Henry discovers that the GoldenCrab class raises a RunForCover event every time anyone gets close to it. Even better, the event includes NewLocationArgs, which detail where the crab is moving to. But none of the other treasure hunters know about the event, so Henry figures he can cash in.

```
class GoldenCrab {
    public delegate void Escape(NewLocationArgs e);
    public event Escape RunForCover;
    public void SomeonesNearby() {
        NewLocationArgs e = new NewLocationArgs("Under the rock");
        RunForCover(e);
    }
}
class NewLocationArgs {
    public NewLocationArgs(HidingPlace newLocation) {
        this.newLocation = newLocation;
    }
    private HidingPlace newLocation;
    public HidingPlace NewLocation { get { return newLocation; } }
}
```

Any time someone comes close to the golden crab, its SomeonesNearby() method fires off a RunForCover event, and it finds a place to hide.

So how did Henry take advantage of his newfound insider information?

Henry adds code to his constructor to register his treasure_RunForCover() method as an event handler for the RunForCover event on the crab reference he's got. Then, he sends a lowly underling after the crab, knowing it will run away, hide, and raise the RunForCover event—giving Henry's treasure_RunForCover() method all the information he needs.

```
class TreasureHunter {
    public TreasureHunter(GoldenCrab treasure) {
        treasure.RunForCover += new GoldenCrab.Escape(treasure_RunForCover);
    }
    void treasure_RunForCover(NewLocationArgs e) {
        MoveHere(e.NewLocation);
    }
    void MoveHere(HidingPlace Location) {
        // ... code to move to a new location ...
    }
}
```

Henry thought he was being clever by altering his class's constructor to add an event handler that calls his MoveHere() method every time the crab raises its RunForCover event. But he forgot that the other treasure hunters inherit from the same class, and his clever code adds their event handlers to the chain, too!

And that explains why Henry's plan backfired. When he added the event handler to the TreasureHunter constructor, he was inadvertently ***doing the same thing for all of the treasure hunters!*** And that meant that every treasure hunter's event handler got chained onto the same RunForCover event. So when the Golden Crustacean ran for cover, everyone was notified about the event. And all of that that would have been fine if Henry were the first one to get the message. But Henry had no way of knowing when the other treasure hunters would have been called—if they subscribed before he did, they'd get the event first.

whack that mole!

Sharpen your pencil

Fill in the blanks to make this game of Whack-a-mole work. You need to supply the code that does the callbacks. Once you've got it filled in, go ahead and type it into the IDE. Or you can try to get it working in the IDE, and then fill in the blanks afterward. It's fun!

```
public partial class Form1 : Form {
    Mole mole;
    Random random = new Random();
    public Form1() {
        InitializeComponent();

        mole = new Mole(random, new Mole._____ (_____));
        timer1.Interval = random.Next(500, 1000);
        timer1.Start();
    }
    private void timer1_Tick(object sender, EventArgs e) {
        timer1.Stop();
        ToggleMole();
    }
    private void ToggleMole() {
        if (mole.Hidden == true)
            mole.Show();
        else
            mole.HideAgain();
        timer1.Interval = random.Next(500, 1000);
        timer1.Start();
    }
    private void MoleCallBack(int moleNumber, bool show) {
        if (moleNumber < 0) {
            timer1.Stop();
            return;
        }
        Button button;
        switch (moleNumber) {
            case 0: button = button1; break;
            case 1: button = button2; break;
            case 2: button = button3; break;
            case 3: button = button4; break;
            default: button = button5; break;
        }
        if (show == true)   {
            button.Text = "HIT ME!";
            button.BackColor = Color.Red;
        } else {
            button.Text = "";
            button.BackColor = SystemColors.Control;
        }
        timer1.Interval = random.Next(500, 1000);
        timer1.Start();
    }
    private void button1_Click(object sender, EventArgs e) {
        mole.Smacked(0);
    }
}
```

The form passes a delegate pointing to a callback method into the mole's constructor. Fill it in.

When you double-click on the timer in the form (after you drag it out of the toolbox), the IDE will create this event handler for it. Timers fire the Tick event over and over again. You'll learn all about them in the next chapter.

This method's called to pop up or hide the mole when the timer's elapsed.

This switch makes sure that the right button changes its color and text.

Form1.cs [Design] ▾ ✕

Whack-a-mole ⊠

Remember the Timer control? Drag it out of the toolbox, then **double-click** on it.

🕐 timer1

When you type in the code, add five button event handlers. Have button2_click() call mole.Smacked(1), and then make button3 call mole.Smacked(2), and make button4 call mole.Smacked(3) and button5 call mole.Smacked(4).

Just add these event handlers the usual way by double-clicking on the buttons in the form designer.

538 Chapter 11

```
using System.Windows.Forms;
class Mole {

    public _____ void PopUp(int hole, bool show);

    private _____ popUpCallback;
    private bool hidden;
    public bool Hidden { get { return hidden; } }
    private int timesHit = 0;
    private int timesShown = 0;
    private int hole = 0;
    Random random;

    public Mole(Random random, PopUp popUpCallback) {
        if (popUpCallback == null)
            throw new ArgumentException("popUpCallback can't be null");
        this.random = random;

        this._____ = _____;
        hidden = true;
    }

    public void Show() {
        timesShown++;
        hidden = false;
        hole = random.Next(5);

        _____ (hole, true);
    }

    public void HideAgain() {
        hidden = true;

        _____ (hole, false);
        CheckForGameOver();
    }

    public void Smacked(int holeSmacked) {
        if (holeSmacked == hole) {
            timesHit++;
            hidden = true;
            CheckForGameOver();

            _____ (hole, false);
        }
    }

    private void CheckForGameOver() {
        if (timesShown >= 10) {
            popUpCallback(-1, false);
            MessageBox.Show("You scored " + timesHit, "Game over");
            Application.Exit();
        }
    }
}
```

Fill in the delegate and field to hold the delegate—they're both at the top of the Mole class.

Here's where we make sure the callback is not null—if it is, the Mole object throws an ArgumentException.

When the form creates a new Mole object, it passes it a reference to its callback method. Take a look in the form to see how the constructor is called, and then fill in this blank.

After the mole shows itself, it needs to call the method on the form that displays the mole by turning the button red and showing the text "HIT ME!"

The HideAgain() and Smacked() methods also use the callback delegate to call the method on the form.

The way the game works is that it uses the timer to wait a random period of time between half a second and 1.5 seconds. Once that time has elapsed, it tells the mole to show itself. The form gives the Mole object a callback that it uses to tell the form to show or hide the mole in one of the five holes. The form uses its timer to wait between .5 and 1.5 seconds again, and then tells the mole to hide itself.

The game's over after the mole shows itself 10 times. Your score is the number of times you hit it.

Sharpen your pencil
Solution

Fill in the blanks to make this game of Whack-a-mole work. You need to supply the code that does the callbacks. Once you've got it filled in, go ahead and type it into the IDE. It's fun!

```
public partial class Form1 : Form {
    private void Form1_Load(object sender, EventArgs e)   {

        mole = new Mole(random, new Mole.___PopUp___(___MoleCallBack___));
        timer1.Interval = random.Next(500, 1000);
        timer1.Start();
    }
}
```

This is where the form passes a reference to its MoleCallBack() method into the Mole object. That lets the mole call its method.

```
class Mole {

    public ___delegate___ void PopUp(int hole, bool show);

    private ___PopUp___ popUpCallback;
```

Here's where the mole defines its delegate and uses it to set up a private field to hold a reference to the method on the form that changes the colors of the buttons.

```
    ...

    public Mole(Random random, PopUp popUpCallback) {
        this.random = random;

        this.___popUpCallback___ = ___popUpCallback___;
        hidden = true;
    }
```

When the form creates a new instance of the Mole object, it passes a reference to its MoleCallBack() method to the constructor as a parameter. This line in the constructor copies that reference to its popUpCallback field. Its methods can use that field to call the MoleCallBack() method in the form.

```
    public void Show() {
        timesShown++;
        hidden = false;
        hole = random.Next(5);
        ___popUpCallback___(hole, true);
    }

    public void HideAgain() {
        hidden = true;
        ___popUpCallback___(hole, false);
        CheckForGameOver();
    }
```

When the mole shows itself, hides again, or gets smacked, the Mole object uses its popUpCallback delegate field to call the method on the form that changes the color and text of one of the buttons.

```
    public void Smacked(int holeSmacked) {
        if (holeSmacked == hole) {
            timesHit++;
            hidden = true;
            CheckForGameOver();
            ___popUpCallback___(hole, false);
        }
```

12 review and preview

* **Knowledge, power, and building cool stuff**

> I just know I read about how upcasting and downcasting make event handling easier somewhere....

Learning's no good until you BUILD something.

Until you've actually written working code, it's hard to be sure if you really *get* some of the tougher concepts in C#. In this chapter, we're going to use what we've learned to do just that. We'll also get a preview of some of the new ideas coming up soon. And we'll do all that by building phase I of a **really complex application** to make sure you've got a good handle on what you've already learned from earlier chapters. So buckle up…it's time to **build some software**!

You've come a long way, ~~baby~~

[note from human resources: "baby" is no longer politically correct. Please use age-challenged or infant to avoid offending readers.]

We've come a long way since we first used the IDE to help us rescue the Objectville Paper Company. Here's just a few of the things you've done over the last several hundred pages:

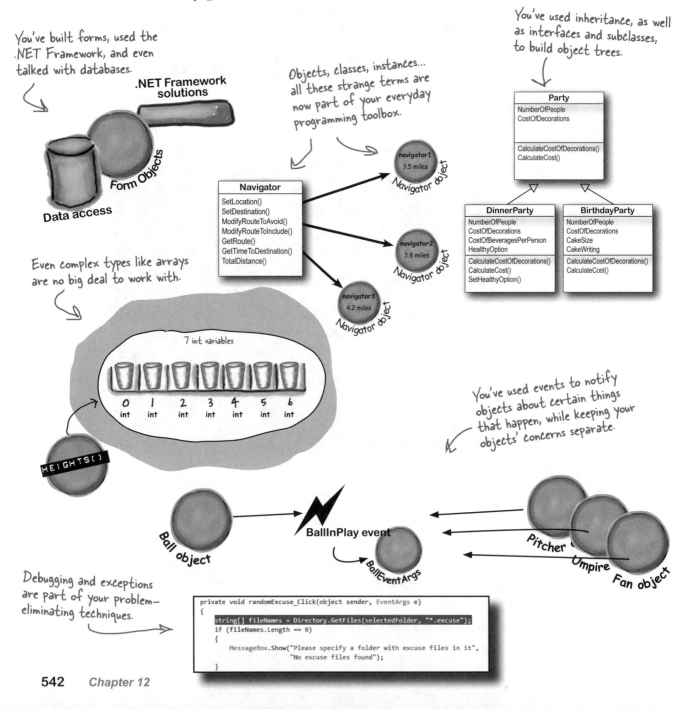

You've built forms, used the .NET Framework, and even talked with databases.

.NET Framework solutions

Form Objects

Data access

Objects, classes, instances... all these strange terms are now part of your everyday programming toolbox.

You've used inheritance, as well as interfaces and subclasses, to build object trees.

Party
NumberOfPeople
CostOfDecorations

CalculateCostOfDecorations()
CalculateCost()

DinnerParty
NumberOfPeople
CostOfDecorations
CostOfBeveragesPerPerson
HealthyOption

CalculateCostOfDecorations()
CalculateCost()
SetHealthyOption()

BirthdayParty
NumberOfPeople
CostOfDecorations
CakeSize
CakeWriting

CalculateCostOfDecorations()
CalculateCost()

Navigator
SetLocation()
SetDestination()
ModifyRouteToAvoid()
ModifyRouteToInclude()
GetRoute()
GetTimeToDestination()
TotalDistance()

navigator1 3.5 miles — Navigator object
navigator2 3.8 miles — Navigator object
navigator3 4.2 miles — Navigator object

Even complex types like arrays are no big deal to work with.

7 int variables

0 1 2 3 4 5 6
int int int int int int int

HEIGHTS[]

You've used events to notify objects about certain things that happen, while keeping your objects' concerns separate.

Ball object — BallInPlay event — BallEventArgs — Pitcher, Umpire, Fan object

Debugging and exceptions are part of your problem-eliminating techniques.

```
private void randomExcuse_Click(object sender, EventArgs e)
{
    string[] fileNames = Directory.GetFiles(selectedFolder, "*.excuse");
    if (fileNames.Length == 0)
    {
        MessageBox.Show("Please specify a folder with excuse files in it",
                        "No excuse files found");
    }
}
```

We've also become beekeepers

Back in Chapter 6, we built some bee classes. Remember these?

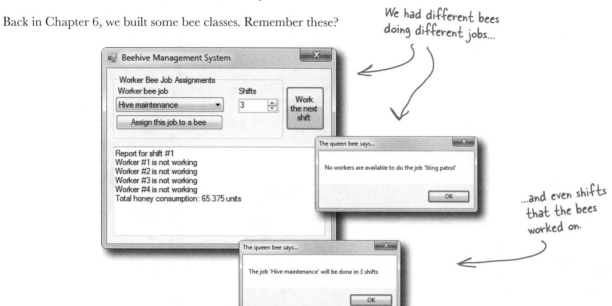

We had different bees doing different jobs...

...and even shifts that the bees worked on.

But we can do a lot better now...

You've learned a lot since Chapter 6, though. So let's start from scratch, and build an **animated beehive simulator** over the next few chapters. We'll end up with a user interface that shows us the hive and the field the bees are flying around, and even a stats window letting users know what their bees are doing.

The stats window lets us monitor the simulation in detail.

The Hive window shows us what's happening.

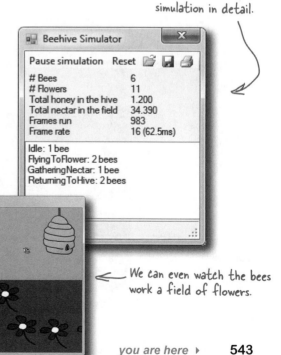

We can even watch the bees work a field of flowers.

The beehive simulator architecture

Here's the architecture for the bee simulator. Even
though the simulator will be controlling a lot of different
bees, the overall object model is pretty simple.

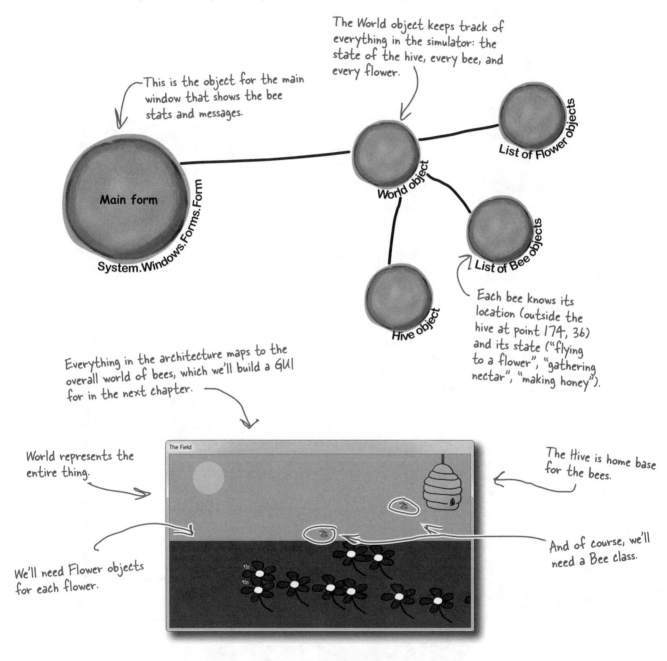

The World object keeps track of
everything in the simulator: the
state of the hive, every bee, and
every flower.

This is the object for the main
window that shows the bee
stats and messages.

Main form

System.Windows.Forms.Form

World object

List of Flower objects

List of Bee objects

Each bee knows its
location (outside the
hive at point 174, 36)
and its state ("flying
to a flower", "gathering
nectar", "making honey").

Hive object

Everything in the architecture maps to the
overall world of bees, which we'll build a GUI
for in the next chapter.

World represents the
entire thing.

The Hive is home base
for the bees.

We'll need Flower objects
for each flower.

And of course, we'll
need a Bee class.

The Field

Building the beehive simulator

Of course, we've never built anything this complex before, so it's going to take us a couple of chapters to put all the pieces together. Along the way, you'll add timers, LINQ, and a lot of graphical skill to your toolkit.

Here's what you're going to do in this chapter (more to come in the next):

1 **Build a Flower class that ages, produces nectar, and eventually wilts and dies.**

2 **Build a Bee class that has several different states (gathering nectar from a flower, returning to the hive), and knows what to do based on its state.**

3 **Build a Hive class that has an entrance, exit, nursery for new bees, and honey factory for turning collected nectar into honey.**

4 **Build a World class that manages the hive, flowers, and bees at any given moment.**

5 **Build a main form that collects statistics from the other classes and keeps the world going.**

stop and smell the flowers

Exercise

Let's jump right into some code. First up, we need a `Flower` class. The `Flower` class has a location defined by a point, an age, and a lifespan. As time goes on, the flower gets older. Then, when its age reaches its lifespan, the flower dies. It's your job to put all this into action.

A class "skeleton" is just its field, property, and method declarations, with no implementation.

1 **Write the skeleton code for `Flower`**

Below is the class diagram for `Flower`. Write the basic class skeleton. `Location`, `Age`, `Alive`, `Nectar`, and `NectarHarvested` are **automatic properties**. `NectarHarvested` is writable; the other four are **read-only**. For now, leave the methods blank; we'll come back to those in a minute.

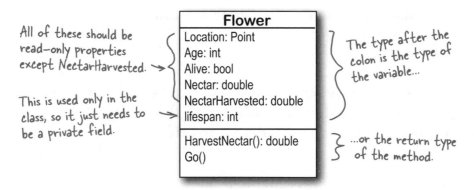

All of these should be read-only properties except NectarHarvested.

This is used only in the class, so it just needs to be a private field.

Flower

Location: Point
Age: int
Alive: bool
Nectar: double
NectarHarvested: double
lifespan: int

HarvestNectar(): double
Go()

The type after the colon is the type of the variable...

...or the return type of the method.

2 **Add several constants to the class**

We need lots of constants for flowers. Add six to your `Flower` class:

* `LifeSpanMin`, the shortest flower lifespan

* `LifeSpanMax`, the longest flower lifespan

* `InitialNectar`, how much nectar a flower starts with

* `MaxNectar`, how much nectar a flower can hold

* `NectarAddedPerTurn`, how much nectar gets added each time the flower grows older

* `NectarGatheredPerTurn`, how much nectar gets collected during a cycle

FYI, you don't usually show constants in a class diagram.

You should be able to figure out the types for each constant based on their values. Flowers live between 15,000 and 30,000 cycles, and have 1.5 units of nectar when they start out. They can store up to 5 units of nectar. In each cycle of life, a flower adds 0.01 units of nectar, and in a single cycle, 0.3 units can be collected.

Since this simulator will be animated, we'll be drawing it frame by frame. We'll use the words "frame," "cycle," and "turn" interchangeably.

You'll need to add `using System.Drawing;` to the top of any class file that uses a `Point`.

③ Build the constructor

The constructor for `Flower` should take in a `Point`, indicating the flower's location, and an instance of the `Random` class. You should be able to use those arguments to set the location of the flower, and then set its age to 0, set the flower to alive, and set its nectar to the initial amount of nectar for a flower. Since no nectar has been harvested yet, set that variable correctly, as well. Finally, figure out the flower's lifespan. Here's a line of code to help you:

```
lifeSpan = random.Next(LifeSpanMin, LifeSpanMax + 1);
```

This will only work if you've got your variables and constants named right, as well as the argument to the Flower constructor.

④ Write code for the `HarvestNectar()` method

Every time this method is called, it should check to see if the nectar gathered every cycle is larger than the amount of nectar left. If so, return 0. Otherwise, you should remove the amount collected in a cycle from the nectar the flower has left, and return how much nectar was collected. Oh, and don't forget to add that amount to the `NectarHarvested` variable, which keeps up with the total nectar collected from this particular flower.

Hint: You'll use NectarGatheredPerTurn, Nectar, and NectarHarvested in this method, but nothing else.

⑤ Write code for the `Go()` method

This is the method that makes the flower go. Assume every time this method is called, one cycle passes, so update the flower's age appropriately. You'll also need to see if the age is greater than the flower's lifespan. If so, the flower dies.

Assuming the flower stays alive, you'll need to add the amount of nectar each flower gets in a cycle. Be sure and check against the maximum nectar your flower can store, and don't overrun that.

*The final product will be **animated**, with little pictures of bees flying around. The Go() method will be called once every **frame**, and there will be several frames run per second.*

Answers on the next page...try and finish your code and compile it before peeking.

Exercise Solution

Your job was to build the `Flower` class for our beehive simulator.

Flower
Location: Point
Age: int
Alive: bool
Nectar: double
NectarHarvested: double
lifespan: int
HarvestNectar(): double
Go()

```
class Flower {
    private const int LifeSpanMin = 15000;
    private const int LifeSpanMax = 30000;
    private const double InitialNectar = 1.5;
    private const double MaxNectar = 5.0;
    private const double NectarAddedPerTurn = 0.01;
    private const double NectarGatheredPerTurn = 0.3;
    public Point Location { get; private set; }
    public int Age { get; private set; }
    public bool Alive { get; private set; }
    public double Nectar { get; private set; }
    public double NectarHarvested { get; set; }
    private int lifeSpan;

    public Flower(Point location, Random random) {
        Location = location;
        Age = 0;
        Alive = true;
        Nectar = InitialNectar;
        NectarHarvested = 0;
        lifeSpan = random.Next(LifeSpanMin, LifeSpanMax + 1);
    }

    public double HarvestNectar() {
        if (NectarGatheredPerTurn > Nectar)
            return 0;
        else {
            Nectar -= NectarGatheredPerTurn;
            NectarHarvested += NectarGatheredPerTurn;
            return NectarGatheredPerTurn;
        }
    }

    public void Go() {
        Age++;
        if (Age > lifeSpan)
            Alive = false;
        else {
            Nectar += NectarAddedPerTurn;
            if (Nectar > MaxNectar)
                Nectar = MaxNectar;
        }
    }
}
```

Location, Age, Alive, and Nectar are all read-only automatic properties.

NectarHarvested will need to be accessible to other classes.

Flowers have random lifespans, so the field of flowers doesn't all change at once.

A bee calls HarvestNectar() to get nectar out of a flower. A bee can only harvest a little bit of nectar at a time, so he'll have to sit near the flower for several turns until the nectar's all gone.

As part of the simulator's animation, the Go() method will be called each frame. This makes the flower age just a tiny little bit per frame. As the simulator runs, those tiny bits will add up over time.

Make sure the flower stops adding nectar after it's dead.

Point lives in the `System.Drawing` namespace, so make sure you added `using System.Drawing;` to the top of the class file.

Life and death of a flower

Our flower goes through a basic turn, living, adding nectar, having nectar harvested, and eventually dying:

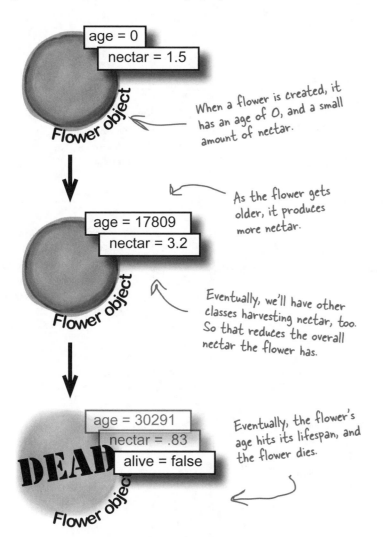

age = 0
nectar = 1.5

Flower object

When a flower is created, it has an age of 0, and a small amount of nectar.

age = 17809
nectar = 3.2

Flower object

As the flower gets older, it produces more nectar.

Eventually, we'll have other classes harvesting nectar, too. So that reduces the overall nectar the flower has.

age = 30291
nectar = .83
alive = false

DEAD

Flower object

Eventually, the flower's age hits its lifespan, and the flower dies.

there are no Dumb Questions

Q: It doesn't look like NectarHarvested is used anywhere in the class, except where we increment it. What's that variable for?

A: Good catch! We're planning ahead a bit. Eventually, the simulator will keep an eye on flowers, and how much total nectar has been harvested, for our statistics monitor. So leave it in, and our other classes will use it shortly.

Q: Why all the read-only automatic properties?

A: Remember Chapter 5, and hiding our privates? Always a good practice. Flowers can take care of those values, so we've made them read-only. Other objects, like bees and the hive, should be able to read those properties, but not change them. But remember, they're only read-only outside of the class—code inside the class can access the private set accesor.

Q: My code looks different. Did I do something wrong?

A: You might have your code in each method in a different order, but as long as your code *functions* the same way as ours does, you'll be OK. That's another aspect of encapsulation: the internals of each class aren't important to other classes, as long as each class does what it's supposed to do.

BRAIN POWER

If Go() increases the age of the Flower by 1, and the lifespan range is between 15,000 and 30,000, that means Go() will get called at least 15,000 times for each flower before it dies. How would you handle calling the method that many times? What if there are 10 flowers? 100? 1,000?

Now we need a Bee class

With flowers ready to be harvested, we need a Bee class. Below is
the basic code for Bee. The Bee knows its age, whether or not it's
in the hive, and how much nectar it can collect. We've also added a
method to move the bee toward a specific destination point.

```
class Bee {
    private const double HoneyConsumed = 0.5;
    private const int MoveRate = 3;
    private const double MinimumFlowerNectar = 1.5;
    private const int CareerSpan = 1000;

    public int Age { get; private set; }
    public bool InsideHive { get; private set; }
    public double NectarCollected { get; private set; }

    private Point location;
    public Point Location { get { return location; } }

    private int ID;
    private Flower destinationFlower;

    public Bee(int id, Point location) {
        this.ID = id;
        Age = 0;
        this.location = location;
        InsideHive = true;
        destinationFlower = null;
        NectarCollected = 0;
    }

    public void Go(Random random) {
        Age++;
    }
}
```

Like the Flower class, there are several bee-specific constants we need to define.
MinimumFlowerNectar is how the bee figures out which flowers are eligible for harvesting.

We used a backing field for location. If we'd used an automatic property, MoveTowardsLocation() wouldn't be able to set its members directly ("Location.X -= MoveRate").

Each bee will be assigned its own unique ID number.

A bee needs an ID and an initial location.

Bees start out inside the hive, they don't have a flower to go to, and they don't have any nectar.

We'll have to add a lot more code to Go() before we're done, but this will get us started.

Here we used Math.Abs() to calculate the absolute value of the difference between the destination and the current location.

```
private bool MoveTowardsLocation(Point destination) {
    if (Math.Abs(destination.X - location.X) <= MoveRate &&
        Math.Abs(destination.Y - location.Y) <= MoveRate)
        return true;

    if (destination.X > location.X)
        location.X += MoveRate;
    else if (destination.X < location.X)
        location.X -= MoveRate;

    if (destination.Y > location.Y)
        location.Y += MoveRate;
    else if (destination.Y < location.Y)
        location.Y -= MoveRate;

    return false;
}
```

This method starts by figuring out if we're already within our MoveRate of being at the destination.

If the bee reached its destination, the method returns true; otherwise, it returns false.

If we're not close enough, then we move toward the destination by our move rate.

We return false, since we're not yet at the destination point. We need to keep moving.

The MoveTowardsLocation() destination moves the bee's current location by changing the X and Y values of its location field. It returns true if the bee's reached its destination.

Exercise

Bees have lots of things they can do. Below is a list. Create a new enum that Bee uses called BeeState. You should also create a read-only automatic property called CurrentState for each Bee to track that bee's state. Set a bee's initial state to idle, and in the Go() method, add a switch statement that has an option for each item in the enum.

The enum item	What the item means
Idle	The bee isn't doing anything
FlyingToFlower	The bee's flying to a flower
GatheringNectar	The bee's gathering nectar from a flower
ReturningToHive	The bee's heading back to the hive
MakingHoney	The bee's making honey
Retired	The bee's hung up his wings

Exercise Solution

Bees have lots of things they can do. Below is a list. Create a new enum that Bee uses called BeeState. You should also create a private currentState field for each Bee to track that bee's state. Set a bee's initial state to idle, and in the Go() method, add a switch statement that has an option for each item in the enum.

```
enum BeeState {
   Idle,
   FlyingToFlower,
   GatheringNectar,
   ReturningToHive,
   MakingHoney,
   Retired
}
```

Here's the enum with all the different bee states.

```
class Bee {
   // constant declarations
   // variable declarations
```

We also need a variable to track the state of each bee.

```
   public BeeState CurrentState { get; private set; }

   public Bee(int ID, Point initialLocation) {
      this.ID = ID;
      Age = 0;
      location = initialLocation;
      InsideHive = true;
      CurrentState = BeeState.Idle;
      destinationFlower = null;
      NectarCollected = 0;
   }
}
```

The bee starts out idle.

Did you remember to add using System.Drawing; to the top of the class file (because it uses Point)?

```
public void Go(Random random) {                    Here's the switch() statement to
    Age++;                                          handle each bee's state.
    switch (CurrentState) {
        case BeeState.Idle:
            if (Age > CareerSpan) {
                CurrentState = BeeState.Retired;    If the age reaches the bee's lifespan,
            } else {                                the bee retires. But he'll finish the
                // What do we do if we're idle?      current job before he does.
            }
            break;
        case BeeState.FlyingToFlower:               We'll fill this code in
            // move towards the flower we're heading to   a bit later.
            break;
        case BeeState.GatheringNectar:              Here, we harvest
            double nectar = destinationFlower.HarvestNectar();   nectar from the
            if (nectar > 0)                                       flower we're working....
                NectarCollected += nectar;          ...and if there's nectar
            else                                    left, add it to what
                                                    we've already collected...
                CurrentState = BeeState.ReturningToHive;
            break;                                  ...but if there's no nectar
                                                    left, head for the hive.
        case BeeState.ReturningToHive:
            if (!InsideHive) {                      Returning to the hive is
                // move towards the hive            different based on whether
            } else {                                we're already in the hive or not.
                // what do we do if we're inside the hive?
            } break;
                                                    The bee adds half a unit of
        case BeeState.MakingHoney:                  nectar to the honey factory
            if (NectarCollected < 0.5) {            at a time. If there's not
                NectarCollected = 0;                enough nectar to add, the
                CurrentState = BeeState.Idle;       factory can't use it so the
            } else {                                bee just discards it.
                // once we have a Hive, we'll turn the nectar into honey
            }
            break;
        case BeeState.Retired:
            // Do nothing! We're retired!
            break;
    }
  }
}
```

We've filled out a few of the states. It's OK if you didn't come up with this code, but go ahead and add it in now.

You should have each of these states covered.

P. A. H. B. (Programmers Against Homeless Bees)

We've got bees, and flowers full of nectar. We need to write code so the bees can collect nectar, but before that happens, where do the bees get created in the first place? And where do they take all that nectar? That's where a `Hive` class comes in.

The hive isn't just a place for bees to come back to, though. It has several locations within it, all with different points in the world. There's the entrance and the exit, as well as a nursery for birthing more bees and a honey factory for turning nectar into honey.

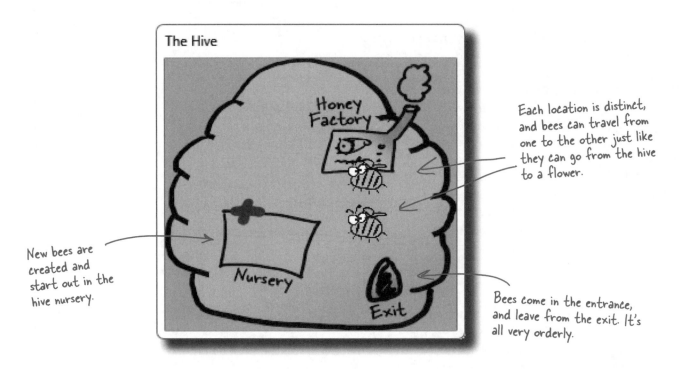

New bees are created and start out in the hive nursery.

Each location is distinct, and bees can travel from one to the other just like they can go from the hive to a flower.

Bees come in the entrance, and leave from the exit. It's all very orderly.

The hive runs on honey

The other big part that the hive plays is keeping up with how much honey it has stored up. It takes honey for the hive to keep running, and if new bees need to be created, that takes honey, too. On top of that, the honey factory has to take nectar that bees collect and turn that into honey. For every unit of nectar that comes in, .25 units of honey can be created.

Think about this for a second...as time passes, the hive uses honey to run, and to create more bees. Meanwhile, other bees are bringing in nectar, which gets turned into honey, which keeps things going longer.

It's up to you (with some help) to model all of this in the simulator code.

Exercise

It's up to you to write the code for `Hive`.

Hive
Honey: double
locations: Dictionary<string, Point>
beeCount: int
InitializeLocations()
AddHoney(Nectar: double): bool
ConsumeHoney(amount: double): bool
AddBee(random: Random)
Go(random: Random)
GetLocation(location: string): Point

① Write the skeleton code for `Hive`

Like we did with the `Flower` class, you should start with a basic skeleton for `Hive`. The class diagram is shown to the right. Make `Honey` a read-only automatic property, `locations` should be private, and `beeCount` is only used internally, so can be a private field.

② Define the constants for the `Hive`

You need a constant for the initial number of bees (6), the amount of honey the hive starts with (3.2), the maximum amount of honey the hive can store (15), the ratio of units of nectar produced from units of honey (.25), the maximum number of bees (8), and the minimum honey required for the hive to birth new bees (4). ←

You'll have to figure out good names for each, as well as the types. For types, don't just think about initial values, but also the values these constants will be used with. Doubles pair best with other doubles, and ints with other ints.

③ Write the code to work with `Locations`

First, write the `GetLocation()` method. It should take in a string, look up that string in the `locations` dictionary, and return the associated point. If it's not there, throw an `ArgumentException`.

Then, write the `InitializeLocations()` method. This method should set up the following locations in the hive:

- Entrance, at (600, 100)
- Nursery, at (95, 174)
- HoneyFactory, at (157, 98)
- Exit, at (194, 213)

Each of these maps to a location within the 2D space that our hive takes up. Later on, we'll have to make sure the simulator makes the hive cover all these points.

In this simulation, we're just assuming one hive, with fixed points. If you wanted multiple hives, you might make the points relative to the hive, instead of the overall world.

④ Build the `Hive` constructor

When a hive is constructed, it should set its honey to the initial amount of honey all hives have. It should set up the locations in the hive, and also create a new instance of `Random`. Then, `AddBee()` should be called—passing in the `Random` instance you just created—once for each bee that starts out in the hive.

AddBee() needs a Random object because it adds a random value to the Nursery location—that way the bees don't start on top of each other.

Your job was to start building the `Hive` class.

Make sure you add "using System.
Drawing;" because this code uses
Point.
↓

You might have different names
for your constants. That's OK, as
long as you're consistent in the
rest of your code.

```
class Hive {
  private const int InitialBees = 6;
  private const double InitialHoney = 3.2;
  private const double MaximumHoney = 15.0;
  private const double NectarHoneyRatio = .25;
  private const double MinimumHoneyForCreatingBees = 4.0;
  private const int MaximumBees = 8;

  private Dictionary<string, Point> locations;
  private int beeCount = 0;

  public double Honey { get; private set; }

  private void InitializeLocations() {
    locations = new Dictionary<string, Point>();
    locations.Add("Entrance", new Point(600, 100));
    locations.Add("Nursery", new Point(95, 174));
    locations.Add("HoneyFactory", new Point(157, 98));
    locations.Add("Exit", new Point(194, 213));
  }

  public Point GetLocation(string location) {
    if (locations.Keys.Contains(location))
      return locations[location];
    else
      throw new ArgumentException("Unknown location: " + location);
  }

  public Hive() {
    Honey = InitialHoney;
    InitializeLocations();
    Random random = new Random();
    for (int i = 0; i < InitialBees; i++)
      AddBee(random);
  }

  public bool AddHoney(double nectar) { return true; }
  public bool ConsumeHoney(double amount) { return true; }
  private void AddBee(Random random) { }
  public void Go(Random random) { }
}
```

We made MaximumHoney
a double, since it can
range from InitialHoney
(3.2) to this value. Since
InitialHoney will need to
be a double, it's best to
make this a double, too.

Remember dictionaries?
Ours stores a location,
keyed with a string value.

Don't forget to create a
new instance of Dictionary,
or this won't work.

The rest of this
method is pretty
straightforward.

This method protects other classes from
working with our locations dictionary
and changing something they shouldn't.
It's an example of **encapsulation**.

You should have called
AddBee() once for each bee
that a hive starts with.

We don't have code
for these yet, but
you should have built
empty methods as
placeholders.

You could also throw a NotImplementedException in any method you
haven't implemented yet. That's a great way to keep track of code you
still have to build.

Isn't this sort of a weird way to build code? Our bees don't know about flowers yet, and our hive is full of empty method declarations. Nothing actually works yet, right?

Real code is built bit by bit

It would be nice if you could write all the code for a single class at one time, compile it, test it, and put it away, and **then** start on your next class. Unfortunately, that's almost never possible.

More often than not, you'll write code just the way we are in this chapter: piece by piece. We were able to build pretty much the entire `Flower` class, but when it came to `Bee`, we've still got some work to do (mostly telling it what to do for each state).

And now, with `Hive`, we've got lots of empty methods to fill in. Plus, we haven't hooked any `Bees` up to the `Hive`. And there's still that nagging problem about how to call the `Go()` method in all these objects thousands of times....

But we didn't **really** start out by putting the classes together! We figured out the architecture first, and **then** started building.

First you design, <u>then</u> you build

We started out the project knowing exactly what we wanted to build: a beehive simulator. And we know a lot about how the bees, flowers, hive, and world all work together. That's why we started out with the **architecture**, which told us how the classes would work with each other. Then we could move on to each class, designing them individually.

Projects always go a lot more smoothly if you have a good idea of what you're building **before** you start building it. That seems pretty straightforward and common-sense. But it makes all the difference in the final product.

Filling out the Hive class

Let's get back to the Hive class, and fill in a few of
those missing methods:

```
class Hive {
  // constant declarations
  // variable declarations

  // InitializeLocations()
  // GetLocation()
  // Hive constructor

  public bool AddHoney(double nectar) {
    double honeyToAdd = nectar * NectarHoneyRatio;
    if (honeyToAdd + Honey > MaximumHoney)
      return false;
    Honey += honeyToAdd;
    return true;
  }
  public bool ConsumeHoney(double amount) {
    if (amount > Honey)
      return false;
    else {
      Honey -= amount;
      return true;
    }
  }
  private void AddBee(Random random) {
    beeCount++;
    int r1 = random.Next(100) - 50;
    int r2 = random.Next(100) - 50;
    Point startPoint = new Point(locations["Nursery"].X + r1,
                                 locations["Nursery"].Y + r2);
    Bee newBee = new Bee(beeCount, startPoint);
    // Once we have a system, we need to add this bee to the system
  }
  public void Go(Random random) { }
}
```

First, we figure out how
much honey this nectar can
be converted to...

...and then see if there's
room in the hive for that
much more honey.

If there's room, we add the
honey to the hive.

This method takes an amount of
honey, and tries to consume it
from the hive's stores.

If there's not enough honey in the hive
to meet the demand, we return false.

If there's enough, remove it from the
hive's stores and return true.

This creates a point within
50 units in both the X
and Y direction from the
nursery location.

This is
private...
only Hive
instances
can create
bees.

Add a new
bee, at the
designated
location.

We'll finish AddBee() and fill in
the Go() method soon....

The hive's Go() method

We've already written a Go() method for Flower, and a Go() method for Bee (even though we've got some additional code to add in). Here's the Go() method for Hive:

```
public void Go(Random random) {

   if (Honey > MinimumHoneyForCreatingBees)

      AddBee(random);

}
```

The only constraint (at least for now) is the hive must have enough honey to create more bees.

The same instance of Random that got passed to Go() gets sent to the AddBee() method.

Unfortunately, this isn't very realistic. Lots of times in a busy hive, the queen doesn't have time to create more bees. We don't have a QueenBee class, but let's assume that when there's enough honey to create bees, a new bee actually gets created 10% of the time. We can model that like this:

```
public void Go(Random random) {

   if (Honey > MinimumHoneyForCreatingBees

      && random.Next(10) == 1)  {

      AddBee(random);

   }

}
```

This is an easy way to simulate a 1 in 10 chance of a bee getting created. It comes up with a random number between 0 and 9. If the number is 1, then create the bee.

One reason to leave it out is so that you can save the Random seed—that way you can rerun a specific simulation...if you feel like doing that later!

---

there are no Dumb Questions

Q: So the hive can create an infinite number of bees?

A: Right now it can—or, at least, it's got a very large limit—but you're right, that's not very realistic. Later on, we'll come back to this, and add a constraint that only lets so many bees exist in our simulator world at one time.

Q: Couldn't we assign that instance of **Random** to a property of the class, instead of passing it on to **AddBee ()** ?

A: You sure could. Then AddBee could use that property, rather than a parameter passed in. There's not really a right answer to this one; it's up to you.

Q: I still don't understand how all of these **Go ()** methods are getting called.

A: That's OK, we're just about to get to that. First, though, we need one more object: the World class, which will keep track of everything that's going on in the hive, track all the bees, and even keep up with flowers.

We're ready for the World

With the Hive, Bee, and Flower classes in place, we can
finally build the World class. World handles coordination
between all the individual pieces of our simulator: keeping
up with all the bees, telling the hive if there is room for
more bees, locating flowers, etc.:

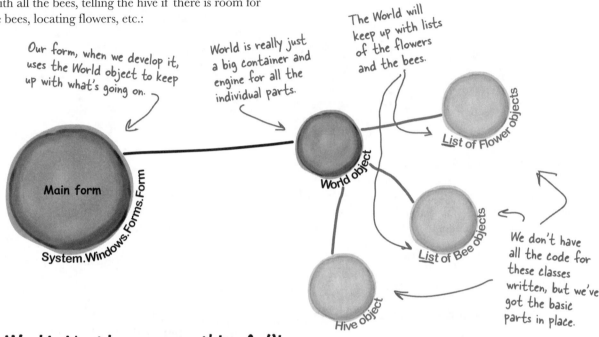

Our form, when we develop it,
uses the World object to keep
up with what's going on.

World is really just
a big container and
engine for all the
individual parts.

The World will
keep up with lists
of the flowers
and the bees.

We don't have
all the code for
these classes
written, but we've
got the basic
parts in place.

The World object keeps everything Go()ing

One of the biggest tasks of the World object is, for each turn in
the simulator, to call Go() on every Flower, Bee, and Hive
instance. In other words, World makes sure that life continues
in the simulator world.

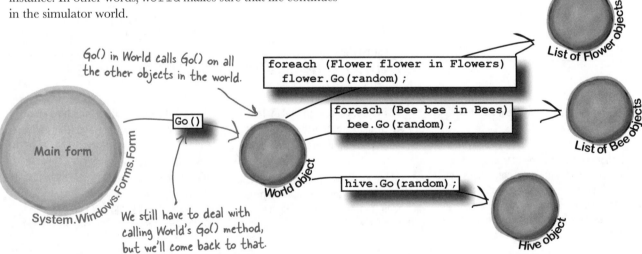

Go() in World calls Go() on all
the other objects in the world.

```
foreach (Flower flower in Flowers)
    flower.Go(random);
```

```
foreach (Bee bee in Bees)
    bee.Go(random);
```

```
hive.Go(random);
```

We still have to deal with
calling World's Go() method,
but we'll come back to that.

We're building a <u>turn-based</u> system

Our Go() methods in each object are supposed to run each **turn**, or **cycle**, of our simulator. A turn in this case just means an arbitrary amount of time: for instance, a turn could be every 10 seconds, or every 60 seconds, or every 10 minutes.

The main thing is that a turn affects every object in the world. The hive ages by one "turn," checking to see if it needs to add more bees. Then each bee takes a turn, moving a very small distance toward its destination or doing one small action, and getting older. Then each flower takes a turn, manufacturing a little nectar and getting older too. And that's what World does: it makes sure that every time its Go() method is called, every object in the world gets a turn to act.

Each "turn" will be drawn as a single frame of animation, so the world only needs to change a tiny little bit each turn.

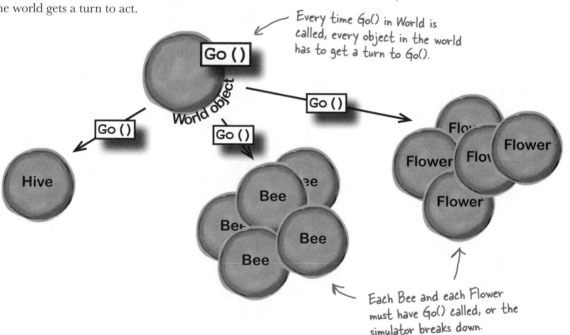

Every time Go() in World is called, every object in the world has to get a turn to Go().

Each Bee and each Flower must have Go() called, or the simulator breaks down.

Sharpen your pencil

One of the big object-oriented principles we've been using in the simulator is encapsulation (flip back to Chapter 5 for a refresher). See if you can look over the code we've developed so far and come up with two examples of encapsulation for each class you've built.

<u>Hive</u>	<u>Bee</u>	<u>Flower</u>
1.	1.	1. ....
....	....	....
2.	2.	2. ....
....	....	....

what in the world are you doing?

Here's the code for World

The World class is actually one of the simpler classes in our simulator. Here's a starting point for the code. But if you look closely, you'll notice that it's missing a few things (which you'll add in just a minute).

Encapsulation alert!

Take a look at the public Hive, Bees, and Flowers fields. Another class could accidentally reset any of those to null, which would cause serious problems! Can you think of a way to use properties or methods to encapsulate them better?

```csharp
using System.Drawing;
class World {
    private const double NectarHarvestedPerNewFlower = 50.0;
    private const int FieldMinX = 15;
    private const int FieldMinY = 177;
    private const int FieldMaxX = 690;
    private const int FieldMaxY = 290;

    public Hive Hive;
    public List<Bee> Bees;
    public List<Flower> Flowers;

    public World() {
        Bees = new List<Bee>();
        Flowers = new List<Flower>();
        Random random = new Random();
        for (int i = 0; i < 10; i++)
            AddFlower(random);
    }

    public void Go(Random random) {
        Hive.Go(random);

        for (int i = Bees.Count - 1; i >= 0; i--) {
            Bee bee = Bees[i];
            bee.Go(random);
            if (bee.CurrentState == BeeState.Retired)
                Bees.Remove(bee);
        }

        double totalNectarHarvested = 0;
        for (int i = Flowers.Count - 1; i >= 0; i--) {
            Flower flower = Flowers[i];
            flower.Go();
            totalNectarHarvested += flower.NectarHarvested;
            if (!flower.Alive)
                Flowers.Remove(flower);
        }
```

These define the bounds of the field, which is where flowers can live.

Every world has one hive, a list of bees, and a list of flowers.

When we create a new world, we initialize our lists, create a new hive, and then add 10 initial flowers.

This is easy...we just tell the Hive to Go(), passing in a Random instance.

We run through all the current bees and tell them Go().

If a bee's retired, we need to take it out of the world.

We run through each flower and tell it to Go().

We need to keep up with how much nectar's been collected this turn, too. So we get that by summing up the nectar collected from each flower.

Just like bees, we remove any flowers that die during this turn.

Sharpen your pencil
Solution

Here are the ones we came up with. Did you come up with any others?

One of the big object-oriented principles we've been using in the simulator is encapsulation (flip back to Chapter 5 for a refresher). See if you can look over the code we've developed so far and come up with two examples of encapsulation for each class you've built.

Hive

1. The hive's Locations dictionary is private

2. It gives the bees a method to add honey

Bee

1. The bee's location is read-only

2. So is its age. So other classes can't write to them

Flower

1. The flower provides a method to gather nectar

2. And it keeps its alive boolean private

```
    if (totalNectarHarvested > NectarHarvestedPerNewFlower) {
        foreach (Flower flower in Flowers)
            flower.NectarHarvested = 0;
        AddFlower(random);
    }
}

private void AddFlower(Random random)
{
    Point location = new Point(random.Next(FieldMinX, FieldMaxX),
                               random.Next(FieldMinY, FieldMaxY));
    Flower newFlower = new Flower(location, random);
    Flowers.Add(newFlower);
}
}
```

Bees **pollinate** flowers as they harvest nectar. Once they've harvested enough nectar from the flowers, they've pollinated enough for the world to add a new flower.

If there's enough nectar in the field, the world adds a new flower.

This handles coming up with a random location in the field...

...and then adding a new flower in that location.

there are no Dumb Questions

Q: Why don't you use `foreach` loops to remove dead flowers and retired bees?

A: Because you **can't remove items** from a collection from inside a `foreach` loop that's iterating on it. If you do, .NET will throw an exception.

Q: OK, then why does each of those `for` loops start at the end of the list and count down to 0?

A: Because each loop needs to preserve the numbering of the list. Let's say you started at the beginning of a list of five flowers, and your loop discovered that one of the flowers in the middle was dead. If it

removes the flower at index #3, now the list only has 4 flowers in it, and there's a new flower at index #3—and that flower will end up getting skipped, because the next time through the loop it'll look at index #4.

If the loop starts at the end, then the flower that moves into the empty slot will already have been looked at by the loop, so there's no chance of missing a flower.

Exercise

With all four of our core classes in place, we've got some work to do to tie them all together. Follow the steps below, and you should have working Bee, Hive, Flower, and World classes. But beware: you'll have to make changes to almost every class, in several places, before you're done.

1 **Update Bee to take in a Hive and World reference.**
Now that we've got a class for Hive and a class for World, Bee objects need to know about both. Update your code to take in references to a bee's hive and world as parameters to its constructor and save those references for later use.

2 **Update Hive to take in a World reference.**
Just as a Bee needs to know about its Hive, a Hive needs to know about its World. Update Hive to take in a World reference in its constructor, and save that reference. You should also update the code in Hive that creates new bees to pass into the Bee a reference to itself (the Hive) and the World.

3 **Update World to pass itself into a new Hive.**
Update your World class so that when it creates a new Hive, it passes in a reference to itself.

STOP! At this point, you should be able to compile all of your code. If you can't, check through it and correct any mistakes before continuing on.

4 **Place an upper limit on the bees that Hive can create.**
The Hive class has a MaximumBees constant that determines how many bees the Hive can support (inside and outside the hive, combined). Now that the Hive has access to the World, you should be able to enforce that constraint.

Hint: Look at code near where you create or add bees. There are two places where code related to this occurs in Hive, so be careful.

5 **When the Hive creates bees, let the World know.**
The World class uses a List of bee objects to keep up with all the bees that exist. When the Hive creates a new Bee, make sure that Bee gets added to the overall list that the World is keeping up with.

there are no
Dumb Questions

Q: **Why did you throw an exception in the `Hive` class's `GetLocation()` method?**

A: Because we needed a way to deal with bad data passed into the parameter. The hive has a few locations, but the parameter to `GetLocations()` can pass any string. What happens if there's a bug in the program that causes an invalid string (like an empty string, or the name of a location that's not in the locations dictionary) to be sent as the parameter? What should the method return?

When you've got an invalid parameter and it's not clear what to do with it, it's always a good idea to throw a new `ArgumentException`. Here's how the `GetLocation()` method does it:

```
throw new ArgumentException(
      "Unknown location: " + location);
```

This statement causes the `Hive` class to throw an `ArgumentException` with the message "Unknown location:" that contains the location that it couldn't find.

The reason this is useful is that it immediately alerts you if a bad location parameter is passed to the method. And by including the parameter in the exception message, you're giving yourself some valuable information that will help you debug the problem.

Q: **What's the point of storing all the locations in a `Point` if we're not drawing anything?**

A: Every bee has a location, whether or not you draw it on the screen in that location. The job of the `Bee` object is to keep track of where it is in the world. Each time its `Go()` method is called, it needs to move a very small distance toward its destination.

Now, even though we may not be drawing a picture of the bee yet, the bee still needs to keep track of where it is inside the hive or in the field, because it needs to know if it's arrived at its destination.

Q: **Then why use `Point` to store the location, and not something else? Aren't `Points` specifically for drawing?**

A: Yes, a `Point` is what all of the visual controls use for their `Location` properties. Plus, it'll come in handy when we do the animation. However, just because .NET uses them that way, that doesn't mean it's not also useful for us to keep track of locations. Yes, we could have created our own `BeeLocation` class with integer fields called X and Y. But why reinvent the wheel when C# and .NET give us `Point` for free?

It's almost always easier to repurpose or extend an existing class that does MOSTLY what you want it to do, rather than creating an all-new class from scratch.

ExeRciSe SoLutioN

With all four of our core classes in place, we've got some work to do to tie them all together. Follow the steps below, and you should have working Bee, Hive, Flower, and World classes. Here's how we made the changes to put this into place.

❶ Update Bee to take in a Hive and World reference.

Now that we've got a class for Hive and a class for World, Bee objects need to know about both. Update your code to take in references to a bee's hive and world in the constructor and save those references for later use.

```
class Bee {
   // existing constant declarations
   // existing variable declarations
   private World world;
   private Hive hive;

   public Bee(int ID, Point InitialLocation, World world, Hive hive) {
      // existing code
      this.world = world;
      this.hive = hive;
   }
}
```

This is pretty straightforward...take these in, assign them to private fields.

❷ Update Hive to take in a World reference.

Just as a Bee needs to know about its Hive, a Hive needs to know about its World. Update Hive to take in a World reference in its constructor, and save that reference. You should also update the code in Hive that creates new bees to pass into the Bee a reference to itself (the Hive) and the World.

```
class Hive {
   private World world;

   public Hive(World world) {
      this.world = world;
      // existing code
   }
   public void AddBee(Random random) {
      // other bee creation code
      Bee newBee = new Bee(beeCount, startPoint, world, this);
   }
}
```

More basic code...get the reference, set a private field. You want to assign the world FIRST because the rest of the constructor needs to use it.

New bees need a reference to the world, and to the hive, now.

If you're having trouble getting this running, you can download the code for this exercise (and all the others, too) from:
http://www.headfirstlabs.com/books/hfcsharp/

❸ **Place an upper limit on the bees that Hive can create.**
The Hive class has a MaximumBees constant that determines
how many bees the Hive can support (inside and outside the hive,
combined). Now that the Hive has access to the World, you should
be able to enforce that constraint.

We can use the World object to see how many total bees there are, and compare that to the maximum bees for this hive.

```
public void Go(Random random) {
   if (world.Bees.Count < MaximumBees
      && Honey > MinimumHoneyForCreatingBees
      && random.Next(10) == 1) {
     AddBee(random);
   }
}
```

We put that comparison first. If there's no room for bees, no sense in seeing if there's enough honey to create bees.

❹ **When the Hive creates bees, let the World know.**
The World class keeps up with all the bees that exist. When the
Hive creates a new Bee, make sure that Bee gets added to the
overall list that the World is keeping up with.

```
private void AddBee(Random random) {
   beeCount++;
   // Calculate the starting point
   Point startPoint = // start the near the nursery
   Bee newBee = new Bee(beeCount, startPoint, world, this);
   world.Bees.Add(newBee);
}
```

We add the new bee to the world's overall bee list.

This demonstrates one of the reasons we need a World reference in the Hive class.

❺ **Update World to pass itself into a new Hive.**
Update your World class so that when it creates a new Hive, it
passes in a reference to itself.

```
public World() {
   Bees = new List<Bee>();
   Flowers = new List<Flower>();
   Hive = new Hive(this);
   Random random = new Random();
     for (int i = 0; i < 10; i++)
       AddFlower(random);
}
```

This passes in the reference to the Hive.

Giving the bees behavior

The one big piece of code that's missing in our current classes is the Bee's Go() method. We were able to code a few of the states earlier, but there are plenty left (Idle is incomplete, FlyingToFlower, and part of MakingHoney).

Let's finish up those remaining states now:

```
public void Go(Random random) {
    Age++;
    switch (CurrentState) {
        case BeeState.Idle:
            if (Age > CareerSpan) {
                CurrentState = BeeState.Retired;
            } else if (world.Flowers.Count > 0
                   && hive.ConsumeHoney(HoneyConsumed)) {
                Flower flower =
                    world.Flowers[random.Next(world.Flowers.Count)];
                if (flower.Nectar >= MinimumFlowerNectar && flower.Alive) {
                    destinationFlower = flower;
                    CurrentState = BeeState.FlyingToFlower;
                }
            }
            break;
        case BeeState.FlyingToFlower:
            if (!world.Flowers.Contains(destinationFlower))
                CurrentState = BeeState.ReturningToHive;
            else if (InsideHive) {
                if (MoveTowardsLocation(hive.GetLocation("Exit"))) {
                    InsideHive = false;
                    location = hive.GetLocation("Entrance");
                }
            }
            else
                if (MoveTowardsLocation(destinationFlower.Location))
                    CurrentState = BeeState.GatheringNectar;
            break;
        case BeeState.GatheringNectar:
            double nectar = destinationFlower.HarvestNectar();
            if (nectar > 0)
                NectarCollected += nectar;
            else
                CurrentState = BeeState.ReturningToHive;
            break;
```

If we're idle, we want to go find another flower to harvest from.

See if there are flowers left, and then consume enough honey to keep on going. Otherwise, we're stuck.

We need another living flower with nectar.

Assuming that all works out, go to the new flower.

Make sure the flower hasn't died as we're heading toward it.

That's why we passed a reference to the hive to the Bee constructor.

If we can get to the exit, then we're out of the hive. Update our location. Since we're now on the field form, we should fly out near the entrance.

If we're out of the hive, and the flower is alive, get to it and start gathering nectar.

This is the exit. When the hive stores its "Exit" location, it corresponds to the point on the Hive form that shows the picture of the exit.

This is the entrance. When the bees fly back to the hive, they fly toward the entrance of the hive on the field form.

That's why the location dictionary stores two separate "Exit" and "Entrance" locations.

```
case BeeState.ReturningToHive:
    if (!InsideHive) {
        if (MoveTowardsLocation(hive.GetLocation("Entrance"))) {
            InsideHive = true;
            location = hive.GetLocation("Exit");
        }
    }
    else
        if (MoveTowardsLocation(hive.GetLocation("HoneyFactory")))
            CurrentState = BeeState.MakingHoney;
    break;
case BeeState.MakingHoney:
    if (NectarCollected < 0.5) {
        NectarCollected = 0;
        CurrentState = BeeState.Idle;
    }
    else
        if (hive.AddHoney(0.5))
            NectarCollected -= 0.5;
        else
            NectarCollected = 0;
    break;
case BeeState.Retired:
    // Do nothing! We're retired!
    break;
    }
}
```

If we've made it to the hive, update our location and the insideHive status.

If we're already in the hive, head to the honey factory.

Try and give this nectar to the hive.

If the hive could use the nectar to make honey...

...remove it from the bee.

If the hive's full, AddHoney() will return false, so the bee just dumps the rest of the nectar so he can fly out on another mission.

Once the bee's retired, he just has to wait around until the Hive removes him from the list. Then he's off to Miami!

BRAIN POWER

Suppose you wanted to change the simulator so it took two turns to reach a flower, and two turns to go from a flower back to the hive. Without writing any code, which *methods* of which classes would you have to change to put this new behavior into place?

The main form tells the world to Go()

OK, so you know that the world advances by one frame every time its Go() method is called. But what calls that Go() method? Why, the main form, of course! Time to lay it out.

Go ahead and add a new form to your project. Make it look like the form below. We're using some new controls, but we'll explain them all over the next several pages.

The labels in the right-hand column will show the stats. Name them "Bees", "Flowers", "HoneyInHive", etc.

The ToolStrip control puts a toolstrip at the top of your form. You can add the two buttons using the drop-down that appears on the ToolStrip when you're in the form designer. Set each button's DisplayStyle to Text.

Each of these labels lives in one cell of a TableLayoutPanel control. You lay it out just like a table in Microsoft Word. Click on the little black arrow to add, remove, and resize columns and rows.

Add a StatusStrip to put a status bar on the bottom. Use the drop-down that appears on the StatusStrip in the designer to add a StatusLabel to it.

Add a Timer control to the form. It doesn't show up at all—it's a non-visual component that the form designer displays as an icon in the space below the form.

The ToolStrip control adds a toolbar to the top of your form, and StatusStrip adds a status bar to the bottom. But they also appear as icons in the area below the form, so you can edit their properties.

We're finally getting to the code that moves the World object along.

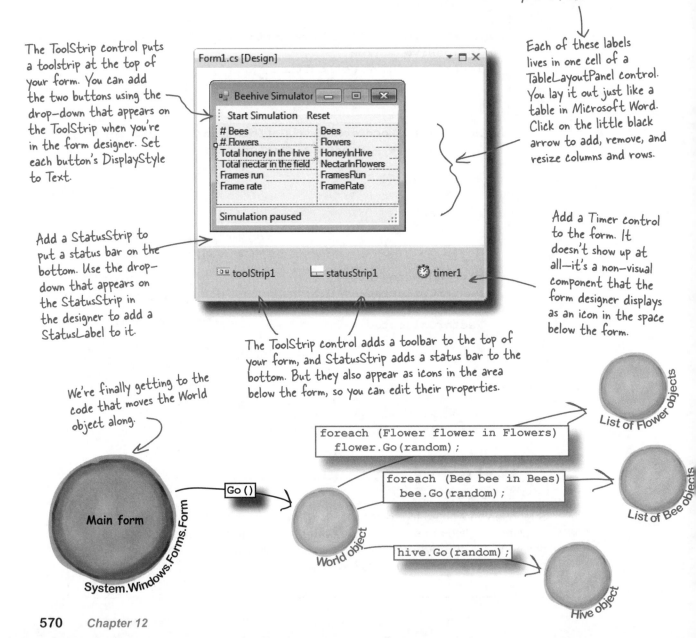

```
foreach (Flower flower in Flowers)
    flower.Go(random) ;
```

```
foreach (Bee bee in Bees)
    bee.Go(random) ;
```

```
hive.Go(random) ;
```

List of Flower objects

List of Bee objects

Main form
System.Windows.Forms.Form

Go()

World object

Hive object

We can use World to get statistics

Now we want to update all these controls. But we don't need click handlers for each one; instead, let's use a single method that will update the different statistics in the simulator window (we'll explain framesRun shortly):

> This indicates how long passes for a turn...we'll have to send this parameter in from somewhere else, in just a few pages.

```
private void UpdateStats(TimeSpan frameDuration) {
    Bees.Text = world.Bees.Count.ToString();
    Flowers.Text = world.Flowers.Count.ToString();
    HoneyInHive.Text = String.Format("{0:f3}", world.Hive.Honey);
    double nectar = 0;
    foreach (Flower flower in world.Flowers)
        nectar += flower.Nectar;
    NectarInFlowers.Text = String.Format("{0:f3}", nectar);
    FramesRun.Text = framesRun.ToString();
    double milliSeconds = frameDuration.TotalMilliseconds;
    if (milliSeconds != 0.0)
        FrameRate.Text = string.Format("{0:f0} ({1:f1}ms)",
                            1000 / milliSeconds, milliSeconds);
    else
        FrameRate.Text = "N/A";
}
```

> Most of this just involves getting data from the world and updating labels.

> Be sure you match your label names on the form with your code.

> Print the first parameter as a number with no decimals, then a space, then print the second parameter with one decimal followed by the letters "ms" (in parentheses)

> The frame rate is the number of frames run per second. We're using a TimeSpan object to store how long it took to run the frame. We divide 1000 by the number of milliseconds it took to run the frame—that gives us the total number of milliseconds it took to run the last frame.

> Add this method into Form1.

> This code uses the same String.Format() method you used in the hex dump. But instead of printing in hex using "x2", you use "f3" to display a number with three decimal places.

> **Whoa! Where did that World object come from...we haven't created that yet, have we? And what's all that time and frame stuff?**

> We'll talk more about this when we create that TimeSpan object.

Let's create a World

You're right, we need to create the World object. Add this line to your form's constructor:

```
public Form1() {
    InitializeComponent();
    world = new World();
}
```

Go ahead and add a private World field to your form called world.

That just leaves all the time-related code. We've always said we needed a way to run Go() in World over and over... sounds like we need some sort of timer.

Take a minute and create a new project so you can see how timers work. Then we'll get back to the simulator and put your new knowledge to work.

Timers fire events over and over again

Remember how you used a loop to animate the greyhounds? Well, there's a better way to do it. A **timer** is an especially useful component that triggers an event over and over again, up to a thousand times a second.

Do this

① Create a new project with a timer and three buttons

You don't have to close your current project—just pop open a new instance of Visual Studio and start up a new project. Drag a timer and three buttons onto the form. Click on the timer icon at the bottom of the designer and set its Interval property to 1000. That number is measured in milliseconds—it tells the timer to fire its tick event once a second.

You can also just double-click on the Timer icon to add the event handler instead of using the Properties window.

② Open the IDE's Properties window and click on the Events button.

(Remember, the Events button looks like a lightning bolt, and it lets you manage the events for any of your form's controls.) The timer control has exactly one event, Tick. **Click on the Timer** icon in the designer, then **double-click on its row** in the Events page and the IDE will create a new event handler method for you and hook it up to the property automatically.

The Events button in the Properties window lets you work with all the events for each of your controls.

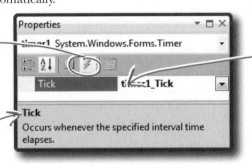

The bottom of the window has a description of the event.

The Timer control has one event called Tick. If you double-click here, the IDE creates an event handler method for you automatically.

③ Add code to the Tick event and to your buttons

Here's some code that will help you get a sense of how the timer works:

```
private void timer1_Tick(object sender, EventArgs e) {
    Console.WriteLine(DateTime.Now.ToString());
}
```

This statement writes the current date and time to the output. Check the output window to make sure the tick event is fired once a second (every 1000 milliseconds).

These buttons let you play with the Enabled property and the Start() and Stop() methods. The first one switches Enabled between true and false, and the other two call the Start() and Stop() methods.

```
private void toggleEnabled_Click(object sender, EventArgs e) {
    if (timer1.Enabled)
        timer1.Enabled = false;
    else
        timer1.Enabled = true;
}
```

The timer's Enabled property starts and stops the timer.

```
private void startTimer_Click(object sender, EventArgs e){
    timer1.Start();
    Console.WriteLine("Enabled = " + timer1.Enabled);
}
```

The timer's Start() method starts the timer and sets Enabled to true. The Stop() method stops the timer and sets Enabled to false.

```
private void stopTimer_Click(object sender, EventArgs e) {
    timer1.Stop();
    Console.WriteLine("Enabled = " + timer1.Enabled);
}
```

The timer's using an event handler behind the scenes

The timer's Tick event is an average, everyday event handler, just like the ones to handle button clicks.

Behind the Scenes

How do C# and .NET tell the timer what to do every tick? How does the `timer1_Tick()` method get run every time your timer ticks? Well, we're back to **events** and **delegates**, just like we talked about in the last chapter. Use the IDE's "Go To Definition" feature to remind yourself how the `EventHandler` delegate works:

4 **Right-click on your timer1 variable and select "Go To Definition"**
The "Go To Definition" feature will cause the IDE to automatically jump to the location in the code where the `timer1` variable is defined. The IDE will jump you to the code it created to add `timer1` as a property in the `Form1` object in `Form1.Designer.cs`. Scroll up in the file until you find this line:

```
this.timer1.Tick += new System.EventHandler(this.timer1_Tick);
```

This is the Tick event of your timer control. You've set this to occur every 1000 milliseconds.

Here's one of the System's delegates: the basic event handler. It's a delegate...a pointer to one or more methods.

Here's the method you just wrote, timer1_Tick(). You're telling the delegate to point to that method.

5 **Now right-click on EventHandler and select "Go To Definition"**
The IDE will automatically jump to the code that defines `EventHandler`. Take a look at the name of the new tab that it opened to show you the code: "EventHandler [from metadata]". This means that the code to define `EventHandler` isn't in your code. It's built into the .NET Framework, and the IDE generated a "fake" line of code to show you how it's represented:

```
public delegate void EventHandler(object sender, EventArgs e);
```

Each event is of type EventHandler. So our Tick event now points to the timer1_Tick() method.

Here's why every event in C# generally takes an Object and EventArgs parameter—that's the form of the delegate that C# defines for event handling.

BRAIN POWER

What code would you write to run the World's Go() method 10 times a second in our beehive simulator?

Add a timer to the simulator

Let's add a timer to the simulator. You've already got a timer control, probably called `timer1`. Instead of using the IDE to generate a `timer1_Tick()` method, though, we can wire the timer to an event handler method called `RunFrame()` manually:

> **DateTime & TimeSpan**
>
> .NET uses the DateTime class to store information about a time, and its Now property returns the current date and time. If you want to find the difference between two times, use a TimeSpan object: just subtract one DateTime object from another, and that'll return a TimeSpan object that holds the difference between them.

TimeSpan has properties like Days, Hours, Seconds, and Milliseconds that let you measure the span in different units.

```
public partial class Form1 : Form {
   World world;                              You should have a World
   private Random random = new Random();     property from earlier.
   private DateTime start = DateTime.Now;    These will be used to figure out
   private DateTime end;                     how long the simulator's been
   private int framesRun = 0;                running at any given point.
                                             We want to keep up with
                                             how many frames—or
                                             turns—have passed.
   public Form1() {
      InitializeComponent();
      world = new World();
                                                      Run every 50 milliseconds.
      timer1.Interval = 50;                    We set the handler to our own
      timer1.Tick += new EventHandler(RunFrame);   method, RunFrame().
      timer1.Enabled = false;   Timer starts off.                      A second
      UpdateStats(new TimeSpan());                                     is 1000
   }                          We also start out by updating stats, with a    milliseconds, so
                              new TimeSpan (0 time elapsed).               our timer will
   private void UpdateStats(TimeSpan frameDuration) {                     tick 20 times a
      // Code from earlier to update the statistics                      second.
   }


   public void RunFrame(object sender, EventArgs e) {
      framesRun++;              Increase the frame count, and
      world.Go(random);         tell the world to Go().
      end = DateTime.Now;
      TimeSpan frameDuration = end - start;   Next, we figure out the
      start = end;                            time elapsed since the last
      UpdateStats(frameDuration);             frame was run.
   }
}
```

Finally, update the stats again, with the new time duration.

Exercise

If you haven't dragged a ToolStrip and StatusStrip out of the toolbox and onto your form, do it now.

Your job is to write the event handlers for the **Start Simulation** and **Reset** buttons in the ToolStrip. Here's what each button should do:

1. Initially, the first button should read "Start Simulation." Pressing it causes the simulation to start, and the label to change to "Pause Simulation." If the simulation is paused, the button should read, "Resume simulation."

2. The second button should say "Reset." When it's pressed, the world should be recreated. If the timer is paused, the text of the first button should change from "Resume simulation" to "Start Simulation."

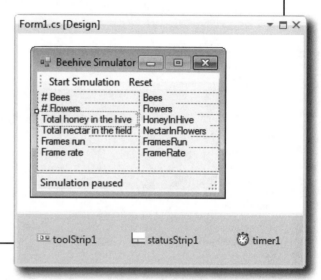

There's no single answer to this question—we just want you to think about what's left to do.

Just double-click on a ToolStrip button in the designer to make the IDE add its event handler, just like a normal button.

Sharpen your pencil

What do you think is left to be done in this phase of the simulator? Try running the program. Write down everything you think we still need to take care of before moving on to the graphical stuff.

....
....
....
....
....
....
....

there are no Dumb Questions

Q: We've been using the term "turn," but now you're talking about frames. What's the difference?

A: Semantics, really. We're still dealing in turns: little chunks of time where every object in the world gets to act. But since we'll soon be putting some heavy-duty graphics in place, we've started using "frame," as in a graphical game's frame-rate.

Exercise SOLUTION

Your job was to write the event handlers for the Start Simulation and Reset buttons.

Form1.cs [Design] ▼ ☐ ✕

Beehive Simulator ⊟ ◻ ✕

Start Simulation Reset

# Bees	Bees
# Flowers	Flowers
Total honey in the hive	HoneyInHive
Total nectar in the field	NectarInFlowers
Frames run	FramesRun
Frame rate	FrameRate

Simulation paused

🔲 toolStrip1   ⊏ statusStrip1   ⏱ timer1

```csharp
public partial class Form1 : Form {
  // variable declarations

  public Form1() {
    InitializeComponent();
    world = new World();
  }
  private void Form1_Load(object sender, tArgs e) {
    // code to start simulator
  }
  private void UpdateStats(TimeSpan frameDuration) {
    // Code from earlier to update the statistics
  }
  public void RunFrame(object sender, EventArgs e) {
    // event handler for timer
  }

  private void startSimulation_Click(object sender, EventArgs e) {
    if (timer1.Enabled) {
      toolStrip1.Items[0].Text = "Resume simulation";
      timer1.Stop();
    } else {
      toolStrip1.Items[0].Text = "Pause simulation";
      timer1.Start();
    }
  }

  private void reset_Click(object sender, EventArgs e) {
    framesRun = 0;
    world = new World();
    if (!timer1.Enabled)
      toolStrip1.Items[0].Text = "Start simulation";
  }
}
```

Be sure your form's control names match up with what you use in your code.

Toggle the timer, and update the message.

Resetting the simulator is just a matter of recreating the World instance and resetting framesRun.

The only time we need to change the first button's label is if it says, "Resume simulation." If it says, "Pause simulation," it doesn't need to change.

Test drive

You've done a ton of work. Compile your
code, fix any typos, and run the simulator.
How's it look?

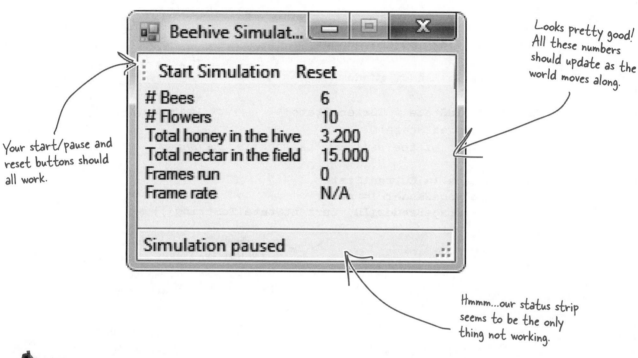

Looks pretty good!
All these numbers
should update as the
world moves along.

Your start/pause and
reset buttons should
all work.

Hmmm...our status strip
seems to be the only
thing not working.

Exercise

Here's your chance to put together everything you've learned. We need to
allow bees to tell our simulator what they're doing. When they do, we want
our simulator to update the status message in the simulator.

This time, it's up to you to not only write most of the code, but to figure out
what code you need to write. How can you have a method in your simulator
that gets called every time a bee changes its state?

To give you a little help, we've written the method to add to the form. The
Bee class should call this method any time its state changes:

```
private void SendMessage(int ID, string Message) {
    statusStrip1.Items[0].Text = "Bee #" + ID + ": " + Message;
}
```

* OK, one more
hint. You'll need to
make changes to
all <u>but</u> <u>one</u> of your
classes to make
this work.

Exercise Solution

Your job was to come up with a way for bees to let the simulator know about what they're doing.

Here's what we added to the Bee class.

```
class Bee {
   // all our existing code
   public BeeMessage MessageSender;

   public void Go(Random random) {
     Age++;
     BeeState oldState = CurrentState;
     switch (currentState) {
      // the rest of the switch statement is the same
     }
     if (oldState != CurrentState
        && MessageSender != null)
           MessageSender(ID, CurrentState.ToString());
   }
}
```

We used a **callback** to hook each individual bee object up to the form's SendMessage() method.

It uses a delegate called BeeMessage that takes a bee ID and a message. The bee uses it to send messages back to the form.

If the status of the Bee changed, we call back the method our BeeMessage delegate points to, and let that method know about the status change.

Here are the changes we made to the Hive.

```
class Hive {
   // all our existing code
   public BeeMessage MessageSender;

   public Hive(World world, BeeMessage MessageSender) {
     this.MessageSender = MessageSender;
     // existing constructor code
   }

   public void AddBee(Random random) {
     // existing AddBee() code
     Bee newBee = new Bee(beeCount, startPoint, world, this);
     newBee.MessageSender += this.MessageSender;
     world.Bees.Add(newBee);
   }
}
```

Hive needs a delegate too, so it can pass on the methods for each bee to call when they're created in AddBee().

AddBee() now has to make sure that each new bee gets the method to point at.

```
public delegate void BeeMessage(int ID, string Message);
```

BeeMessage is our delegate. It's also a match with the SendMessage() method we wrote in the form. Add it to its own file called BeeMessage.cs—it should be in the namespace, but outside of any class.

The World class required some changes as well.

```
class World {
   // all our existing code

   public World(BeeMessage messageSender) {
      Bees = new List<Bee>();
      Flowers = new List<Flower>();
      Hive = new Hive(this, messageSender);
      Random random = new Random();
      for (int i = 0; i < 10; i++)
          AddFlower(random);
   }
}
```

World doesn't need to have a delegate of its own. It just passes on the method to call to the Hive instance.

Last but not least, here's the updated form. Anything not shown stayed the same.

```
public partial class Form1 : Form {
   // variable declarations

   public Form1() {
      InitializeComponent();
      world = new World(new BeeMessage(SendMessage));
      // the rest of the Form1 constructor
   }

   private void reset_Click(object sender, EventArgs e) {
      framesRun = 0;
      world = new World(new BeeMessage(SendMessage));
      if (!timer1.Enabled)
          toolStrip1.Items[0].Text = "Start simulation";
   }

   private void SendMessage(int ID, string Message) {
      statusStrip1.Items[0].Text = "Bee #" + ID + ": " + Message;
   }
}
```

We create a new delegate from the Bee class (make sure you declared BeeMessage public), and point it at our SendMessage() method.

Same thing here...create the world with the method for bees to call back.

This is the method we gave you...be sure to add it in, too.

Let's work with groups of bees

Your bees should be buzzing around the hive and the field, and your simulation should be running! How cool is that? But since we don't have the visual part of the simulator working yet—that's what we're doing in the next chapter—all the information we have so far is the messages that the bees are sending back to the main form with their callbacks. So let's add more information about what the bees are doing.

You already have the form updating these stats and displaying the messages that the bees send as they do their jobs.

Go ahead and add a ListBox to your form. We'll use it to display some extra stats about the bees in the world.

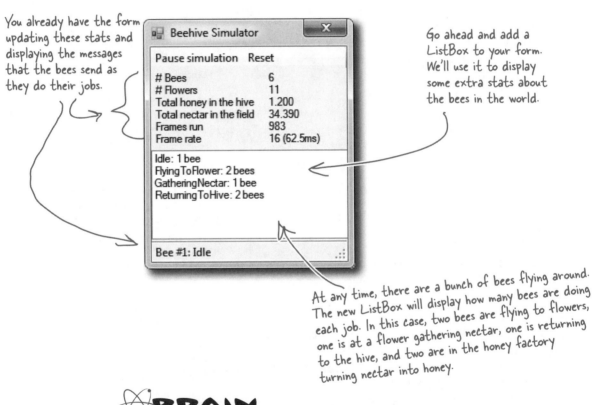

At any time, there are a bunch of bees flying around. The new ListBox will display how many bees are doing each job. In this case, two bees are flying to flowers, one is at a flower gathering nectar, one is returning to the hive, and two are in the honey factory turning nectar into honey.

⚛ BRAIN POWER

You know enough to gather the information you'd need to populate that ListBox—take a minute and think through how that would work. But it's a little more complex than it seems at first. What would you need to do to figure out how many bees are in each of the various Bee.State states?

A collection collects...<u>DATA</u>

Our bees are stored in a List<Bee>, which is one of the collection types. And collection types really just store data...a lot like a database does. So each bee is like a row of data, complete with a state, and ID, and so on. Here's how our bees look as a collection of objects:

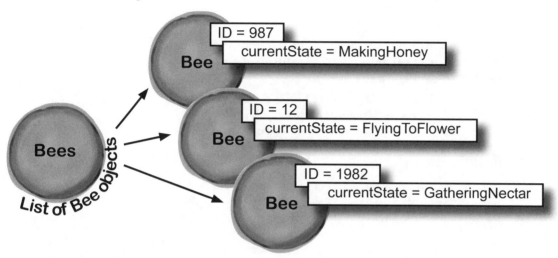

There's a lot of data in the Bee objects' fields. You can *almost* think of a collection of objects the same way you think of rows in a database. Each object holds data in its fields, the same way each row in a database holds data in its columns.

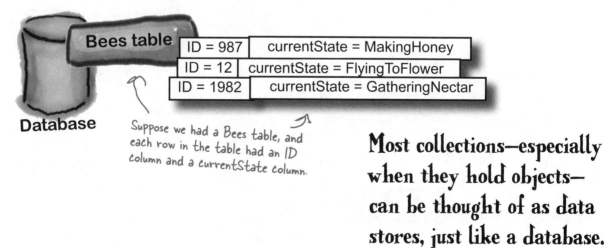

Suppose we had a Bees table, and each row in the table had an ID column and a currentState column.

Most collections—especially when they hold objects— can be thought of as data stores, just like a database.

> Who cares if you can **think** about a collection as a database if you can't **use** a collection like a database? What a total waste of time....

What if you could query collections, databases, and even XML documents with the same basic syntax?

C# has a really useful feature called **LINQ** (which stands for **Language INtegrated Query**). The idea behind LINQ is that it gives you a way to take an array, list, stack, queue, or other collection and work with all the data inside it all at once in a single operation.

But what's really great about LINQ is that you can use the same syntax that works with collections as you can for working with databases.

We'll spend most of Chapter 15 working with LINQ.

This LINQ query works essentially the same with data in a collection or a database.

```
var beeGroups =
  from bee in world.Bees
  group bee by bee.CurrentState
  into beeGroup
  orderby beeGroup.Key
  select beeGroup;
```

LINQ

Bees
List of Bee objects

Bee ID = 987 | currentState = MakingHoney
Bee ID = 12 | currentState = FlyingToFlower
Bee ID = 1982 | currentState = GatheringNectar

Bees table

ID = 987	currentState = MakingHoney
ID = 12	currentState = FlyingToFlower
ID = 1982	currentState = GatheringNectar

Database

If we had our bee data in a database— or even an XML file—LINQ could work with them in exactly the same way.

XML
```
<bee id="987" currentState="MakingHoney" />
<bee id="12" currentState="FlyingToFlower" />
<bee id="1982" currentState="GatheringNectar" />
```

LINQ makes working with data in collections and databases easy

We're going to spend an entire chapter on LINQ before long, but we can use LINQ and some Ready Bake Code to add some extra features to our simulator. Ready Bake Code is code you should type in, and it's OK if you don't understand it all. You'll learn how it all works in Chapter 15.

Ready Bake Code

```csharp
private void SendMessage(int ID, string Message) {
    statusStrip1.Items[0].Text = "Bee #" + ID + ": " + Message;
    var beeGroups =
        from bee in world.Bees
        group bee by bee.CurrentState into beeGroup
        orderby beeGroup.Key
        select beeGroup;
    listBox1.Items.Clear();
    foreach (var group in beeGroups) {
        string s;
        if (group.Count() == 1)
            s = "";
        else
            s = "s";
        listBox1.Items.Add(group.Key.ToString() + ": "
                           + group.Count() + " bee" + s);
        if (group.Key == BeeState.Idle
            && group.Count() == world.Bees.Count()
            && framesRun > 0) {
            listBox1.Items.Add("Simulation ended: all bees are idle");
            toolStrip1.Items[0].Text = "Simulation ended";
            statusStrip1.Items[0].Text = "Simulation ended";
            timer1.Enabled = false;
        }
    }
}
```

This is a LINQ query. It takes all the bees in the Bees collection, and groups them by their CurrentState property.

The group's Key is the bee's CurrentState, so that's the order the states will be displayed on the form.

Make sure this matches the list box control's name on your form.

beeGroups is from the LINQ query. We can count the members, and iterate over them.

This bit of code makes sure it says, "1 bee" and "3 bees", keeping the plural right.

Finally, add the group status (its key) and count to the list box.

Here's another nice feature. Since we know how many bees are idle...

...we can see if ALL bees are idle. If so, the hive's out of honey, so let's stop the simulation.

Relax

We'll learn a lot more about LINQ in upcoming chapters.

You don't need to memorize LINQ syntax or try to drill all of this into your head right now. You'll get a lot more practice working with LINQ in Chapter 15.

Test drive (Part 2)

Go ahead and compile your code and run your project. If
you get any errors, double-check your syntax, especially
with the new LINQ code. Then, fire up your simulator!

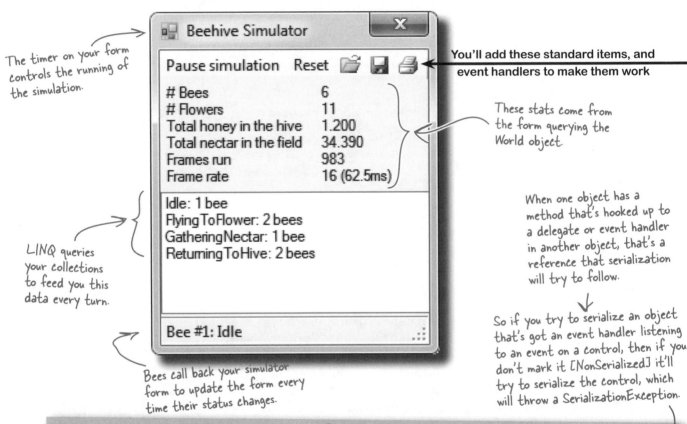

The timer on your form controls the running of the simulation.

You'll add these standard items, and event handlers to make them work

These stats come from the form querying the World object.

LINQ queries your collections to feed you this data every turn.

When one object has a method that's hooked up to a delegate or event handler in another object, that's a reference that serialization will try to follow.

So if you try to serialize an object that's got an event handler listening to an event on a control, then if you don't mark it [NonSerialized] it'll try to serialize the control, which will throw a SerializationException.

Bees call back your simulator form to update the form every time their status changes.

[NonSerialized] keeps data from getting serialized

Sometimes you want to serialize part of an object, not all of it. It might have data that you don't want written to the disk. Let's say you're building a system that a user logs into, and you want to save an object that stores the user's options and settings to a file. You might mark the password field with the [NonSerialized] attribute. That way, when you Serialize() the object, it will skip that field.

The [NonSerialized] attribute is especially useful when your object has a reference to an object that is not serializable. For example, if you try to serialize a Form, Serialize() will throw a SerializationException. So if our object has a reference to a Form object, then when you try to serialize it the serializer will follow that link and try to serialize the Form, too...which will throw that exception. But if you mark the field that holds the reference with the [NonSerialized] attribute, then Serialize() won't follow the reference at all.

One final challenge: Open and Save

We're almost ready to take on graphics, and add some visual eye candy to our simulator. First, though, let's do one more thing to this version: allow loading, saving, and printing of bee statistics.

 Add the Open, Save, and Print icons

The ToolStrip control has a really useful feature—it can automatically insert picture buttons for standard icons: new, open, save, print, cut, copy, paste, and help. Just right-click on the ToolStrip icon at the bottom of the Form Designer window and select "**Insert Standard Items**". Then click on the first item—that's the "new" icon—and delete it. Keep the next three items, because they're the ones we need (open, save, and print). After that comes a separator; you can either delete it or move it between the Reset button and the save buton. Then delete the rest of the buttons. Make sure you set its **CanOverflow** property to false (so it doesn't add an overflow menu button to the right-hand side of the toolbar) and its **GripStyle** property to Hidden (so it removes the sizing grip from the left-hand side).

> You'll add the Print button now—we'll make it print a status page for the hive in the next chapter.

 Add the button event handlers

The new standard buttons are named `openToolStripButton`, `saveToolStripButton`, and `printToolStripButton`. Just double-click on them to add their event handlers.

Exercise

Add code to make the save and open buttons work.

1. Make the save button serialize the world to a file. The save button should stop the timer (it can restart it after saving if the simulator was running). It should display a Save dialog box, and if the user specifies a filename then it should serialize the `World` object, and the number of frames that have been run.

When you try to serialize the `World` object, it will throw a `SerializationException` with this message: `Type 'Form1' is not marked as serializable`. That's because the serializer found one of the `BeeMessage` fields and tried to follow it. Since the delegate was hooked up to a field on the form, the serializer tried to serialize the form, too.

Fix this problem by adding the **[NonSerialized]** attribute to the **MessageSender** fields in the Hive and Bee classes, so .NET doesn't try and serialize the code your delegates point to.

2. Make the open button deserialize the world from a file. Take care of the timer just like in the save button: pop up an Open dialog box, and deserialize the world and the number of frames run from the selected file. Then you can hook up the `MessageSender` delegates again and restart the timer (if necessary).

3. Don't forget about exception handling! Make sure the world is intact if there's a problem reading or writing the file. Consider popping up a human-readable error message indicating what went wrong.

Your job was to make the Save and Open buttons work.

Don't forget the extra using statements.

```
using System.IO;
using System.Runtime.Serialization.Formatters.Binary;
```

You'll need to make the World, Hive, Flower, and Bee classes serializable. When you serialize the world, .NET will find its references to Hive, Flower, and Bee objects and serialize them, too.

```
[Serializable]              [Serializable]
class World {               class Flower {

[Serializable]              [Serializable]
class Hive {                class Bee {
```

And make sure the MessageSender fields in the Hive and Bee classes are marked [NonSerialized].

```
[NonSerialized]
public BeeMessage MessageSender;
```

Here's the code for the Save button.

```
private void saveToolStripButton_Click(object sender, EventArgs e) {
    bool enabled = timer1.Enabled;
    if (enabled)
        timer1.Stop();

    SaveFileDialog saveDialog = new SaveFileDialog();
    saveDialog.Filter = "Simulator File (*.bees)|*.bees";
    saveDialog.CheckPathExists = true;
    saveDialog.Title = "Choose a file to save the current simulation";
    if (saveDialog.ShowDialog() == DialogResult.OK) {
        try {
            BinaryFormatter bf = new BinaryFormatter();
            using (Stream output = File.OpenWrite(saveDialog.FileName)) {
                bf.Serialize(output, world);
                bf.Serialize(output, framesRun);
            }
        }
        catch (Exception ex) {
            MessageBox.Show("Unable to save the simulator file\r\n" + ex.Message,
                "Bee Simulator Error", MessageBoxButtons.OK, MessageBoxIcon.Error);
        }
    }
    if (enabled)
        timer1.Start();
}
```

We decided to use ".bees" as the extension for simulator save files.

Here's where the world is written out to a file.

Remember, when we serialize World, everything it references gets serialized...all the bees, flowers, and the hive.

After we save the file, we can restart the timer (if we stopped it).

Here's the code for the Open button.

```
private void openToolStripButton_Click(object sender, EventArgs e) {
    World currentWorld = world;
    int currentFramesRun = framesRun;

    bool enabled = timer1.Enabled;
    if (enabled)
        timer1.Stop();

    OpenFileDialog openDialog = new OpenFileDialog();
    openDialog.Filter = "Simulator File (*.bees)|*.bees";
    openDialog.CheckPathExists = true;
    openDialog.CheckFileExists = true;
    openDialog.Title = "Choose a file with a simulation to load";
    if (openDialog.ShowDialog() == DialogResult.OK) {
        try {
            BinaryFormatter bf = new BinaryFormatter();
            using (Stream input = File.OpenRead(openDialog.FileName)) {
                world = (World)bf.Deserialize(input);
                framesRun = (int)bf.Deserialize(input);
            }
        }
        catch (Exception ex) {
    MessageBox.Show("Unable to read the simulator file\r\n" + ex.Message,
    "Bee Simulator Error", MessageBoxButtons.OK, MessageBoxIcon.Error);
            world = currentWorld;
            framesRun = currentFramesRun;
        }
    }

    world.Hive.MessageSender = new BeeMessage(SendMessage);
    foreach (Bee bee in world.Bees)
        bee.MessageSender = new BeeMessage(SendMessage);
    if (enabled)
        timer1.Start();
}
```

Before opening the file and reading from it, save a reference to the current world and framesRun. If there's a problem, you can revert to these and keep running.

Set up the Open File dialog box and pop it up.

using ensures the stream gets closed.

Here's where we deserialize the world and the number of frames run to the file.

If the file operations throw an exception, we restore the current world and framesRun.

Once everything is loaded, we hook up the delegates and restart the timer.

You'll need to get your simulator up and running before you move on to the next chapter. You can download a working version from the Head First Labs website: www.headfirstlabs.com/books/hfcsharp/

13 controls and graphics

Make it pretty

Sometimes you have to take graphics into your own hands.

We've spent a lot of time relying on controls to handle everything visual in our applications. But sometimes that's not enough—like when you want to **animate a picture**. And once you get into animation, you'll end up **creating your own controls** for your .NET programs, maybe adding a little **double buffering**, and even **drawing directly onto your forms**. It all begins with the **Graphics** object, **bitmap**s, and a determination to not accept the graphics status quo.

You've been using controls all along to interact with your programs

TextBoxes, PictureBoxes, Labels...you've got a pretty good handle by now on how you can use the controls in the IDE's toolbox. But what do you *really* know about them? There's a lot more to a control than just dragging an icon onto your form.

⭐ **You can create your own controls**
The controls in the toolbox are really useful for building forms and applications, but there's nothing magical about them. They're just classes, like the classes that you've been writing on your own. In fact, C# makes it really easy for you to create controls yourself, just by inheriting from the right base class.

⭐ **Your custom controls show up in the IDE's toolbox**
There's also nothing mysterious about the toolbox in the IDE. It just looks in your project's classes and the built-in .NET classes for any controls. If it finds a class that implements the right interface, then it displays an icon for it in the toolbox. If you add your own custom controls, they'll show up in the toolbox, too.

You can create a class that inherits from any of the existing control classes—even if it doesn't have any other code in it—and it'll automatically show up in the toolbox.

⭐ **You can write code to add controls to your form, and even remove controls, while your program's running**
Just because you lay out a form in the IDE's form designer, it doesn't mean that it has to stay like that. You've already moved plenty of PictureBox controls around (like when you built the greyhound race). But you can add or remove controls, too. In fact, when you build a form in the IDE, all it's doing is writing the code that adds the controls to the form...which means you can write similar code, and run that code whenever you want.

Form controls are just objects

You already know how important **controls** are to your forms. You've been using buttons, text boxes, picture boxes, checkboxes, group boxes, labels, and other forms since Chapter 1. Well, it turns out that those controls are just objects, just like everything else you've been working with.

A control is just an object, like any other object—it just happens to know how to draw itself. The Form object keeps track of its controls using a special collection called **Controls**, which you can use to add or remove controls in your own code.

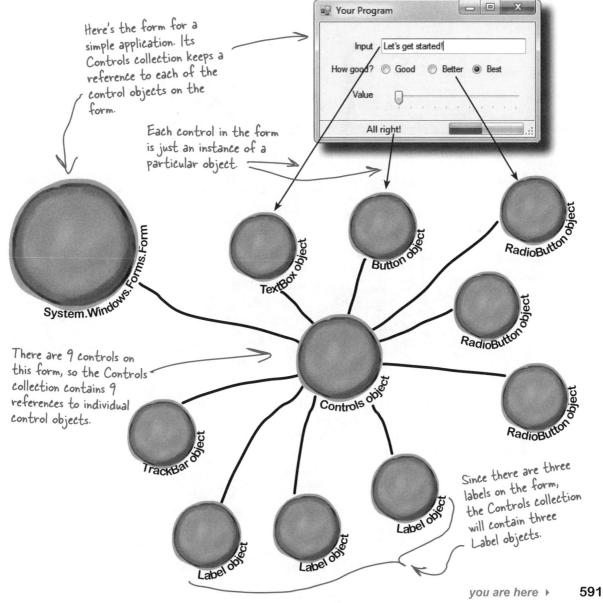

Here's the form for a simple application. Its Controls collection keeps a reference to each of the control objects on the form.

Each control in the form is just an instance of a particular object.

System.Windows.Forms.Form

TextBox object

Button object

RadioButton object

RadioButton object

RadioButton object

Controls object

There are 9 controls on this form, so the Controls collection contains 9 references to individual control objects.

TrackBar object

Label object

Label object

Label object

Since there are three labels on the form, the Controls collection will contain three Label objects.

Use controls to animate the beehive simulator

You've built a cool simulator, but it's not much to look at. It's time to create a
really stunning visualization that shows those bees in action. You're about to
build a renderer that animates the beehive…and controls are the key.

1 **The user interface shows you everything that's going on**

Your simulator will have three different windows. You've already built the main "heads-up display"
stats window that shows stats about the current simulation and updates from the bees. Now you'll
add a window that shows you what's going in inside the hive, and a window that shows the field of
flowers where the bees gather nectar.

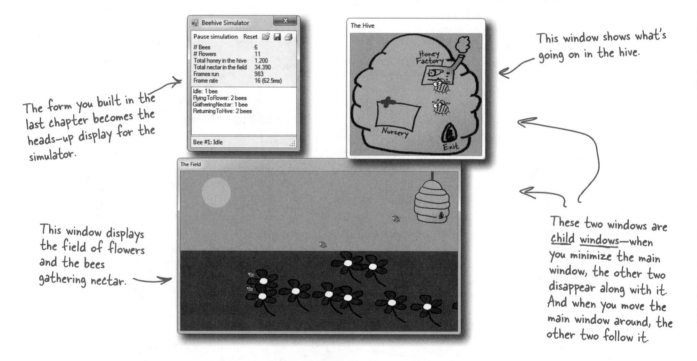

The form you built in the last chapter becomes the heads-up display for the simulator.

This window shows what's going on in the hive.

This window displays the field of flowers and the bees gathering nectar.

These two windows are <u>child</u> windows—when you minimize the main window, the other two disappear along with it. And when you move the main window around, the other two follow it.

2 **We'll make the Print button in the stats window work**

The stats window has working Open and Save buttons, but the Print button
doesn't work yet. We'll be able to reuse a lot of the graphics code to get the Print
button on the ToolStrip to print an info page about what's going on.

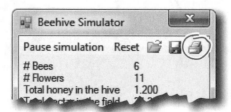

3 **The hive window shows you what's going on inside the hive**
As the bees fly around the world, you'll need to animate each one. Sometimes they're inside the hive, and when they are, they show up in this window.

The hive has three important locations in it. The bees are born in the nursery, they have to fly to the exit to leave the hive to gather nectar from the flowers, and when they come back they need to go to the honey factory to make honey.

The hive exit is on the hive form, and the entrance is on the field form. (That's why we put both of them in the hive's locations dictionary.)

Here's the entrance to the hive. When bees fly into it, they disappear from the field form and reappear near the exit in the hive form.

4 **The field window is where the bees collect the nectar**
Bees have one big job: to collect nectar from the flowers, and bring it back to the hive to make honey. Then they eat honey to give them energy to fly out and get more nectar.

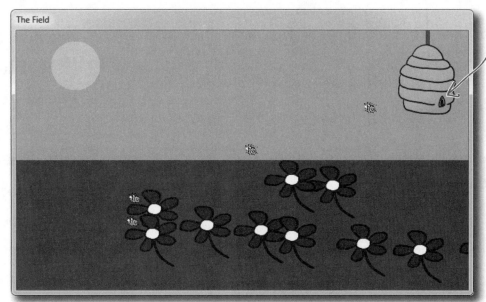

Add a renderer to your architecture

We need another class that reads the information in the
world and uses it to draw the hive, bees, and flowers on
the two new forms. We'll add a class called **Renderer**
to do exactly that. And since your other classes are well
encapsulated, this won't require a lot of changes to your
existing code.

You've already built these objects.

The World object keeps track of
everything in the simulator: the
state of the hive, every bee, and
every flower.

This is the object for the main
window that you've already built.

List of Flower objects

Main form

System.Windows.Forms.Form

World object

List of Bee objects

Each bee knows its
location—and we can use
that location to draw
the bee on the form.

Hive object

Renderer object

The Hive and
Field objects are
forms, tied to
your main form.

Hive form

The renderer reads the
information from the
World object and uses
that information to
update the <u>two</u> forms. It
keeps a reference to the
World object, as well as
the Hive form object and
the Field form object.

Field form

ren-der, verb.
to represent or depict artistically.
*Sally's art teacher asked the class to look
at all of the shadows and lines in the
model and **render** them on the page.*

**Because Bee,
Hive, Flower, and
World are <u>well
encapsulated</u>, a
class that renders
those objects can
be added <u>without</u>
lots of changes to
existing code.**

The renderer draws everything in the world on the two forms

The World object keeps track of everything in the simulation: the hive, the bees, and the flowers. But it doesn't actually draw anything or produce any output. That's the job of the Renderer object. It reads all of the information in the World, Hive, Bee, and Flower objects and draws them on the forms.

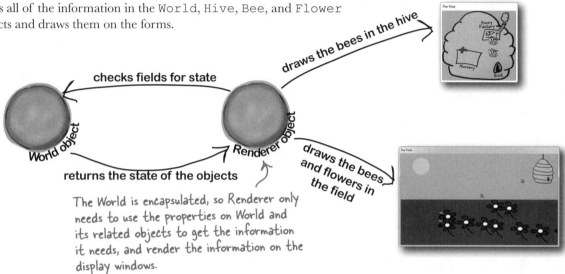

The World is encapsulated, so Renderer only needs to use the properties on World and its related objects to get the information it needs, and render the information on the display windows.

The simulator renders the world after <u>each frame</u>

After the main form calls the world's Go() method, it should call the renderer's Render() method to redraw the display windows. For example, each flower will be displayed using a PictureBox control. But let's go further with bees and create an animated control. You'll create this new control, called BeeControl, and define its behavior yourself.

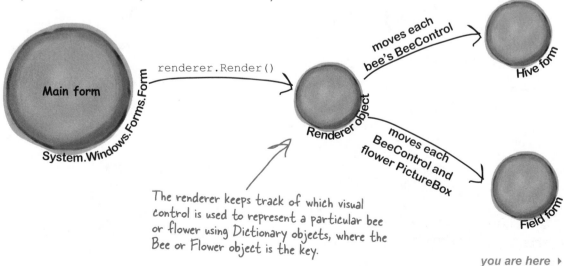

The renderer keeps track of which visual control is used to represent a particular bee or flower using Dictionary objects, where the Bee or Flower object is the key.

Controls are well suited for visual display elements

When a new bee is added to the hive, we'll want our simulator to add a new BeeControl to the Hive form and change its location as it moves around the world. When that bee flies out of the hive, our simulator will need to remove the control from the Hive form and add it to the Field form. And when it flies back to the hive with its load of nectar, its control needs to be removed from the Field form and added back to the Hive form. And all the while, we'll want the animated bee picture to flap its wings. Controls will make it easy to do all of that.

1 The world adds a new bee, and the renderer creates a new BeeControl and adds it to the Hive form's Controls collection.

2 When the bee flies out of the hive and enters the field, the renderer removes the BeeControl from the hive's Controls collection and adds it to the Field form's Controls collection.

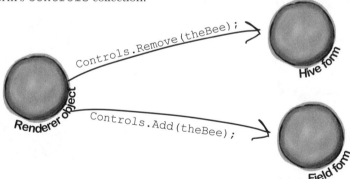

3 A bee will retire if it's idle and it's gotten too old. If the renderer checks the world's Bees list and finds that the bee is no longer there, it removes the control from the Hive form.

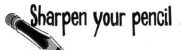
Sharpen your pencil

Can you figure out what each of these code snippets does? Assume each snippet is inside a form, and write down your best guess.

```
this.Controls.Add(new Button());
```
....
....
....

```
Form2 childWindow = new Form2();
childWindow.BackgroundImage =
         Properties.Resources.Mosaic;
childWindow.BackgroundImageLayout =
         ImageLayout.Tile;
childWindow.Show();
```
....
....
....
....
....
....

If you've got a ListBox on your form, you can use its AddRange() method to add list items.

```
Label myLabel = new Label();
myLabel.Text = "What animal do you like?";
myLabel.Location = new Point(10, 10);
ListBox myList = new ListBox();
myList.Items.AddRange( new object[]
     { "Cat", "Dog", "Fish", "None" } );
myList.Location = new Point(10, 40);
Controls.Add(myLabel);
Controls.Add(myList);
```
....
....
....
....
....
....

You don't need to write down each line, as much as summarize what's going on in the code block.

```
Label controlToRemove = null;
foreach (Control control in Controls) {
    if (control is Label
         && control.Text == "Bobby")
      controlToRemove = control as Label;
}
Controls.Remove(controlToRemove);
controlToRemove.Dispose();
```
....
....
....
....
....

Bonus question: Why do you think we didn't put the Controls.Remove() **statement inside the foreach loop?**
....
....
....

Try it out if you want, and write why you think you got the result that .NET gave you.

Sharpen your pencil
Solution

Can you figure out what each of these code snippets does? Assume each snippet is inside a form, and write down what you think it does.

```
this.Controls.Add(new Button());
```

Create a new button and add it to the form. It'll have default values (e.g., the Text property will be empty).

```
Form2 childWindow = new Form2();
childWindow.BackgroundImage =
          Properties.Resources.Mosaic;
childWindow.BackgroundImageLayout =
          ImageLayout.Tile;
childWindow.Show();
```

There's a second Form in the application called Form2, so this creates it, sets its background image to a resource image called "Mosaic", makes the background image so it's tiled instead of stretched, and then displays the window to the user.

```
Label myLabel = new Label();
myLabel.Text = "What animal do you like?";
myLabel.Location = new Point(10, 10);
ListBox myList = new ListBox();
myList.Items.AddRange( new object[]
      { "Cat", "Dog", "Fish", "None" } );
myList.Location = new Point(10, 40);
Controls.Add(myLabel);
Controls.Add(myList);
```

This code creates a new label, sets its text, and moves it to a new position. Then it creates a new list box, adds four items to the list, and moves it just underneath the label. It adds the label and list box to the form, so they both get displayed immediately.

What happens if there's no control named "Bobby" in the Controls collection?

```
Label controlToRemove = null;
foreach (Control control in Controls) {
    if (control is Label
        && control.Text == "Bobby")
        controlToRemove = control as Label;
}
Controls.Remove(controlToRemove);
controlToRemove.Dispose();
```

This loop searches through all the controls on the form until it finds a label with the text "Bobby". Once it finds the label, it removes it from the form.

If you try, .NET will throw an exception. It needs the collection intact, otherwise it'll lose its place and give you unpredictable results. That's why you'd use a for loop for this instead.

Bonus question: Why do you think we didn't put the Controls.Remove() statement inside the foreach loop?

You can't modify the Controls collection (or any other collection) in the middle of a foreach loop that's iterating through it.

Build your first animated control

You're going to **build your own control** that draws an animated bee picture. If you've never done animation, it's not as hard as it sounds: you draw a sequence of pictures one after another, and produce the illusion of movement. Lucky for us, the way C# and .NET handle resources makes it really easy for us to do animation.

Once you download the four bee animation pictures (Bee animation 1.png through Bee animation 4.png) from Head First Labs, you'll add them to your project's resources. When you flash these four bees quickly one after another, it'll look like their wings are flapping.

We want a control in the toolbox

If you build BeeControl right, it'll appear as a control that you can drag out of your toolbox and onto your form. It'll look just like a PictureBox showing a picture of a bee, except that it'll have animated flapping wings.

Download the images for this chapter from the Head First Labs website: www.headfirstlabs.com/books/hfcsharp/

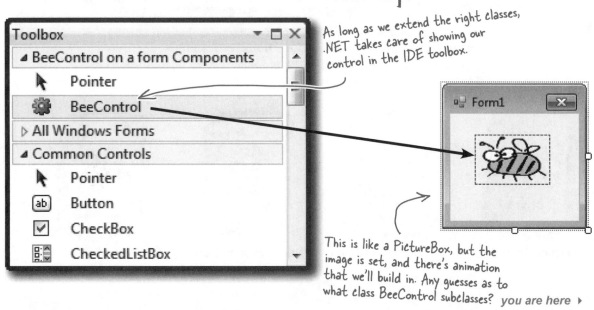

As long as we extend the right classes, .NET takes care of showing our control in the IDE toolbox.

This is like a PictureBox, but the image is set, and there's animation that we'll build in. Any guesses as to what class BeeControl subclasses?

BeeControl is LIKE a PictureBox...so let's start by INHERITING from PictureBox

Since every control in the toolbox is just an object, it's easy to make a new control. All you need to do is add a new class to your project that inherits from an existing control, and add any new behavior you want your control to perform.

We want a control—let's call it a **BeeControl**—that shows an animated picture of a bee flapping its wings, but we'll start with a control that shows a *non*-animated picture, and then just add animation. So we'll start with a PictureBox, and then we'll add code to draw an animated bee on it.

Animate this!

1 **Create a new project** and add the four animation cells to the project's resources, just like you added the Objectville Paper Company logo to your project way back in Chapter 1. But instead of adding them to the *form* resources, add them to the *project's* resources. Find **your project's Resources.resx file** in the Solution Explorer (it's under Properties). Double-click on it to bring up the project's Resources page.

In Chapter 1, we added the logo graphic to the form's Resources file. This time we're adding the resources to the project's global collection of resources, which makes them available to every class in the project (through the Properties.Resources collection).

Take a minute and flip back to Chapter 1 to remind yourself how you did this.

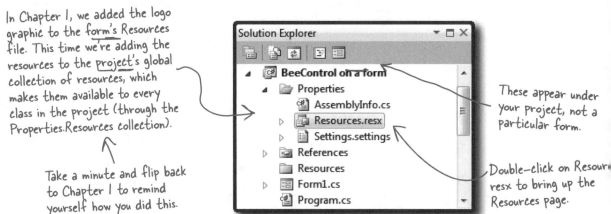

These appear under your project, not a particular form.

Double-click on Resources.resx to bring up the Resources page.

2 We've drawn a four-cell bee animation to import into your resources that you can download from **http://www.headfirstlabs.com/books/hfcsharp/**. Then, go to the Resources page, select "Images" from the first drop-down at the top of the screen, and select "Add Existing File…" from the "Add Resource" drop-down.

Bee animation 1.png   Bee animation 2.png   Bee animation 3.png   Bee animation 4.png

Import each of these images into your project's resources.

❸ When you add images or other resources to the project's Resources file, you can access them using the `Properties.Resources` class. Just go to any line in your code and type `Properties.Resources.` as soon as you do, IntelliSense pops up a drop-down list that shows all of the pictures you've imported.

When the program's running, each picture is stored in memory as a Bitmap object.

Note that "." at the end...that's what tells the IDE to pop up the properties and methods of the class you typed in.

| Application |
| Build |
| Build Events |
| Debug |
| Resources |
| Settings |
| Reference Paths |
| Signing |
| Security |

Images ▾ | Add Resource ▾ | ✕ Remove Resource | ▦ ▾

Bee_animation_1   Bee_animation_2

Bee_animation_3   Bee_animation_4

```
pictureBox1.Image =
    Properties.Resources.Bee_animation_1;
```

This sets the image used for a particular PictureBox's image (and for our starting image).

These images are stored as public properties of the Properties.Resources class.

You'll need to add a "using System.Windows.Forms" line for the PictureBox and Timer.

❹ **Now add your BeeControl!** Just add this `BeeControl` class to your project:

```
class BeeControl : PictureBox {
    private Timer animationTimer = new Timer();
    public BeeControl() {
        animationTimer.Tick += new EventHandler(animationTimer_Tick);
        animationTimer.Interval = 150;
        animationTimer.Start();
        BackColor = System.Drawing.Color.Transparent;
        BackgroundImageLayout = ImageLayout.Stretch;
    }

    private int cell = 0;
    void animationTimer_Tick(object sender, EventArgs e) {
        cell++;
        switch (cell) {
            case 1: BackgroundImage = Properties.Resources.Bee_animation_1; break;
            case 2: BackgroundImage = Properties.Resources.Bee_animation_2; break;
            case 3: BackgroundImage = Properties.Resources.Bee_animation_3; break;
            case 4: BackgroundImage = Properties.Resources.Bee_animation_4; break;
            case 5: BackgroundImage = Properties.Resources.Bee_animation_3; break;
            default: BackgroundImage = Properties.Resources.Bee_animation_2;
            cell = 0; break;
        }
    }
}
```

Make sure you add "using System.Windows.Forms" to the top of the class file.

Here's where you initialize the timer by instantiating it, setting its Interval property, and then adding its tick event handler.

Once we get back to frame #1, we'll reset cell back to 0.

Each time the timer's tick event fires, it increments cell, and then does a switch based on it to assign the right picture to the Image property (inherited from PictureBox).

When you change the code for a control, you need to rebuild your program to make your changes show up in the designer.

Then **rebuild your program**. Go back to the form designer and look in the toolbox, and the BeeControl is there. Drag it onto your form—you get an **animated** bee!

Create a button to add the BeeControl to your form

It's easy to add a control to a form—just add it to the Controls collection. And it's just as easy to remove it from the form by removing it from Controls. But controls implement IDisposable, so make sure you **always dispose your control** after you remove it.

Now do this

❶ Remove the BeeControl from your form, and then add a button
Go to the form designer and **delete the BeeControl from the form**. Then add a button. We'll make the button add and remove a BeeControl.

> You can use an object initializer to set the BeeControl properties after it's instantiated.

❷ Add a button to add and remove the bee control
Here's the event handler for it:

> When you add a control to the Controls collection, it appears on the form immediately.

```
BeeControl control = null;
private void button1_Click(object sender, EventArgs e) {
    if (control == null) {
        control = new BeeControl() { Location = new Point(100, 100) };
        Controls.Add(control);
    } else {
        using (control) {
            Controls.Remove(control);
        }
        control = null;
    }
}
```

> We're taking advantage of a using statement to make sure the control is disposed after it's removed from the Controls collection.

Now when you run your program, if you click the button once it'll add a new BeeControl to the form. Click it again and it'll delete it. It uses the private control field to hold the reference to the control. (It sets the reference to null when there's no control on the form.)

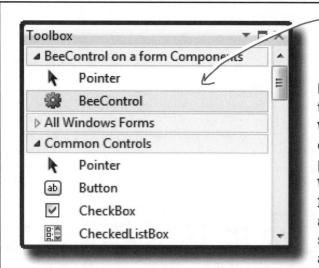

> You can add your own control to the toolbox just by creating a class that inherits from Control.

Behind the Scenes

Every visual control in your toolbox inherits from **System. Windows.Forms.Control.** That class has members that should be pretty familiar by now: **Visible, Width, Height, Text, Location, BackColor, BackgroundImage...** all of those familiar properties you see in the Properties window for any control.

Your controls need to dispose <u>their</u> controls, too!

There's a problem with the `BeeControl`. Controls need to be disposed after they're done. But the `BeeControl` creates a new instance of `Timer`, which is a control that shows up in the toolbox…and it never gets disposed! That's a problem. Luckily, it's easy to fix—just override the `Dispose()` method.

> *The control class implements IDisposable, so you need to make sure every control you use gets disposed.*

 Override the Dispose() method and dispose of the timer

Since `BeeControl` inherits from a control, then that control must have a `Dispose()` method. So we can just override and extend that method to dispose our timer. Just go into the control and type `override`:

```
class BeeControl : PictureBox {
    override
```

> *When you type "override" inside a class, the IDE pops up an IntelliSense window with all of the methods you can override. Select the Dispose() method and it'll fill one in for you!*

As soon as you click on `Dispose()`, the IDE will fill in the method with a call to `base.Dispose()`:

```
protected override void Dispose(bool disposing) {
    base.Dispose(disposing);
}
```

 Add the code to dispose the timer

Add code to the end of the new `Dispose()` method that the IDE added for you so that it calls `animationTimer.Dispose()` if the `disposing` argument is true.

```
protected override void Dispose(bool disposing) {
    base.Dispose(disposing);
    if (disposing) {
        animationTimer.Dispose();
    }
}
```

> *Here we're overriding a protected Dispose() method that's called by the control's implementation of IDisposable.Dispose(). It should only dispose the timer if the disposing argument is true.*

Now the `BeeControl` will dispose of its timer as part of its own `Dispose()` method. It cleans up after itself!

But don't take our word for it—**set a breakpoint** on the line you added and run your program. Every time a `BeeControl` object is removed from the form's `Controls` collection, its `Dispose()` method is called.

> **Any control that you write from scratch is responsible for disposing any other controls (or disposable objects) that it creates.**

We won't go into any more detail about this particular disposal pattern. But if you plan on building custom controls, you definitely should read this: <u>http://msdn.microsoft.com/en-us/library/system.idisposable.aspx</u>

A UserControl is an easy way to build a control

There's an easier way to build your own toolbox controls. Instead of creating a class that inherits from an existing control, all you need to do is **use the IDE to add a UserControl to your project**. You work with a `UserControl` just like a form. You can drag other controls out of the toolbox and onto it—it uses the normal form designer in the IDE. And you can use its events just like you do with a form. So let's rebuild the `BeeControl` using a `UserControl`.

Do this

1 Create a brand-new Windows Forms Application project. Add the four bee images to its resources. Drag a button to the form and give it exactly the same code as to add and remove a `BeeControl`.

2 Right-click on the project in the Solution Explorer and select "Add >> User Control...". Have the IDE **add a user control called BeeControl**. The IDE will open up the new control in the form designer.

Use the animationTimer_Tick() method and the cell field from the old bee control.

3 Drag a Timer control onto your user control. It'll show up at the bottom of the designer, just like with a form. Use the Properties window to **name it animationTimer and set its Interval to 150 and its Enabled to true**. Then double-click on it—the IDE will add its Tick event handler. Just use the same Tick event handler that you used earlier to animate the first bee control.

4 Now update the `BeeControl`'s constructor:

```
public BeeControl() {
    InitializeComponent();
    BackColor = System.Drawing.Color.Transparent;
    BackgroundImageLayout = ImageLayout.Stretch;
}
```

You can also do this from the Properties page in the IDE, instead of using code.

5 Now **run your program**—the button code should still work exactly the same as before, except now it's creating your new `UserControl`-based `BeeControl`. The button now adds and removes your `UserControl`-based `BeeControl`.

A UserControl is an easy way to add a control to the toolbox. Edit a UserControl just like a form—you can drag other controls out of the toolbox onto it, and you can use its events exactly like a form's events.

> But I've been using controls all this time, and I've never disposed a single one of them! Why should I start now?

You didn't dispose your controls because your forms did it for you.

But don't take our word for it. Use the IDE's search function to search your project for the word "Dispose", and you'll find that the IDE added a method in `Form1.Designer.cs` to override the `Dispose()` method that calls its own `base.Dispose()`. When the form is disposed, **it automatically disposes everything in its Controls collection** so you don't have to worry about it. But once you start removing controls from that collection or creating new instances of controls (like the `Timer` in the `BeeControl`) outside of the `Controls` collection, then you need to do the disposal yourself.

there are no
Dumb Questions

Q: Why does the form code for the PictureBox-based BeeControl work exactly the same with the UserControl-based BeeControl?

A: Because the code doesn't care how the BeeControl object is implemented. It just cares that it can add the object to the form's Controls method.

Q: I double-clicked on my OldBeeControl class in the Solution Explorer, and it had a message about adding components to my class. What's that about?

A: When you create a control by adding a class to your project that inherits from PictureBox or another control, the IDE does some clever things. One of the things it does is let you work with **components**, those non-visual controls like Timer and OpenFileDialog that show up in the space beneath your form when you work with them.

Give it a try—create an empty class that inherits from PictureBox. Then rebuild your project and double-click on it in the IDE. You'll get this message:

To add components to your class, drag them from the Toolbox and use the Properties window to set their properties.

Drag an OpenFileDialog out of the toolbox and onto your new class. It'll appear as an icon. You can click on it and set its properties. Set a few of them. Now go back to the code for your class. Check out the constructor—the IDE added code to instantiate the OpenFileDialog object and set its properties.

Q: When I changed the properties in the OpenFileDialog, I noticed an error message in the IDE: "You must rebuild your project for the changes to show up in any open designers." Why did I get this error?

A: Because the designer runs your control, and until you rebuild your code it's not running the latest version of the control.

Remember how the wings of the bee were flapping when you first created your BeeControl, even when you dragged it out of the toolbox and into the designer? You weren't running your program yet, but the code that you wrote was being executed. The timer was firing its Tick event, and your event handler was changing the picture. The only way the IDE can make that happen is if the code were actually compiled and running in memory somewhere. So it's reminding you to update your code so it can display your controls properly.

Your simulator's renderer will use your BeeControl to draw animated bees on your forms

Now you've got the tools to start adding animation to your simulator. With a `BeeControl` class and two forms, you just need a way to position bees, move them from one form to the other, and keep up with the bees. You'll also need to position flowers on the `FieldForm`, although since flowers don't move, that's pretty simple. All of this is code that we can **put into a new class, Renderer**. Here's what that class will do:

You'll want the hive and field forms "linked" to the stats form—that does useful things like minimizing the hive and field forms when you minimize the stats form. You can do this by telling Windows that the stats form is their owner.

 The <u>stats</u> form will be the <u>parent</u> of the hive and field forms

We'll build the renderer in a minute. But before we jump in and start coding, let's take a minute and come up with a plan for how the Renderer class will work...

The first step in adding graphics to the beehive simulator will be adding two forms to the project. You'll add one called `HiveForm` (to show the inside of the hive) and one called `FieldForm` (which will show the field of flowers). Then you'll add lines to the main form's constructor to show its two child forms. Pass a reference to the main form to tell Windows that the stats form is their **owner**:

```
public Form1() {
    // other code in the Form1 constructor
    hiveForm.Show(this);
    fieldForm.Show(this);
}
```

Every form object has a Show() method. If you want to set another form as its owner, just pass a reference to that form to Show().

The renderer keeps a reference to the world and each child form

At the very top of the `Renderer` class you'll need a few important fields. The class has to know the location of each bee and flower, so it needs a reference to the `World`. And it'll need to add, move, and remove controls in the two forms, so it needs a reference to each of those forms:

```
class Renderer {
    private World world;
    private HiveForm hiveForm;
    private FieldForm fieldForm;
```

Start your Renderer class with these lines. We'll add to this class throughout the chapter.

The renderer uses dictionaries to keep track of the controls

`World` keeps track of its `Bee` objects using a `List<Bee>` and a `List<Flower>` to store its flowers. The renderer needs to be able to look at each of those `Bee` and `Flower` objects and figure out what `BeeControl` and `PictureBox` they correspond to—or, if it can't find a corresponding control, it needs to create one. So here's a perfect opportunity to use dictionaries. We'll need two more private fields in `Renderer`:

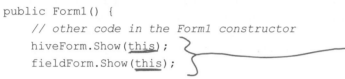

```
private Dictionary<Flower, PictureBox> flowerLookup =
    new Dictionary<Flower, PictureBox>();
private Dictionary<Bee, BeeControl> beeLookup =
    new Dictionary<Bee, BeeControl>();
```

These dictionaries become one-to-one mappings between a bee or flower and the control for that bee or flower.

These two dictionary collections let the renderer store exactly one control for each bee or flower in the world.

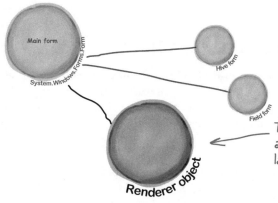

The renderer is acting on the two forms, as well as all the objects you built in the last chapter for the simulator.

4 The bees and flowers already know their locations

There's a reason we stored each bee and flower location using a Point. Once we have a Bee object, we can easily look up its BeeControl and set its location.

```
beeControl = beeLookup[bee];
beeControl.Location = bee.Location;
```

For each bee or flower, we can look up the matching control. Then, set that control's location to match the location of the bee or flower object.

5 If a bee doesn't have a control, the renderer adds it to the hive form

It's easy enough for the renderer to figure out if a particular bee or flower has a control. If the dictionary's ContainsKey() method returns false for a particular Bee object, that means there's no control on the form for that bee. So Renderer needs to create a BeeControl, add it to the dictionary, and then add the control to the form. (It also calls the control's BringToFront() method, to make sure the control doesn't get hidden behind the flower PictureBoxes.)

```
if (!beeLookup.ContainsKey(bee)) {
    beeControl = new BeeControl() { Width = 40, Height = 40 };
    beeLookup.Add(bee, beeControl);
    hiveForm.Controls.Add(beeControl);
    beeControl.BringToFront();
} else
    beeControl = beeLookup[bee];
```

ContainsKey() tells us if the bee exists in the dictionary. If not, then we need to add that bee, along with a corresponding control.

Remember how a dictionary can use anything as a key? Well, this one uses a Bee object as a key. The renderer needs to know which BeeControl on the form belongs to a particular bee. So it looks up that bee's object in the dictionary, which spits out the correct control. Now the renderer can move it around.

BringToFront() ensures the bee appears "on top of" any flowers on the FieldForm, and on top of the background of the HiveForm.

Add the hive and field forms to the project

Now you need forms to put bees on. So **start with your existing beehive simulator project**, and use "Add >> Existing Item…" to **add your new BeeControl user control**. The UserControl has a .cs file, a .designer.cs file, and a .resx file—you'll need to add all three. Then open up the code for both the .cs and .designer.cs files, and change the namespace lines so they match the namespace of your new project. Rebuild your project; the BeeControl should now show up in the toolbox. You'll also need to add the graphics to the new project's resources. Then add two more Windows forms to the project by **right-clicking on the project** in the Solution Explorer and choosing "Windows Form…" from the Add menu. If you name the files HiveForm.cs and FieldForm.cs, the IDE will automatically set their Name properties to HiveForm and FieldForm. You already know that forms are just objects, so HiveForm and FieldForm are really just two more classes.

> This is a PictureBox control with its BackgroundImage set to the outside hive picture and BackgroundImageLayout set to Stretch. When you load the hive pictures into the Resource Designer, they'll show up in the list of resources when you click the "…" button next to BackgroundImage in the Properties window.

Make sure you resize both forms so they look like these screenshots.

> You'll need the inside and outside hive images—"Hive (inside).png" and "Hive (outside).png"—loaded into your resources. Then add these two forms. Set each form's FormBorderStyle property to FixedSingle (so the user can't resize it), the ControlBox property to false (to take away its minimize and maximize controls), and StartPosition to Manual (so its Location property is settable).

Set the form's BackgroundImage property to the inside hive picture, and its BackgroundImageLayout property to Stretch.

Figure out where _your_ locations are

> Remember, go to the Properties window, click on the lightning-bolt icon to bring up the Events window, scroll down to the MouseClick row and double-click on it. The IDE will add the event handler for you.

You need to figure out where the hive is on your FieldForm. Using the Properties window, create a handler for the **MouseClick event for the Hive form**, and add this code:

```
private void HiveForm_MouseClick(object sender, MouseEventArgs e) {
    MessageBox.Show(e.Location.ToString());
}
```

We'll get your form running on the next few pages. Once it's running, click on the exit of the hive in the picture. The event handler will show you the exact coordinates of the spot that you clicked.

Add the same handler to the Field form, too. Then, by clicking, get the coordinates of the exit, the nursery, and the honey factory. Using all these locations, you'll be able to update the InitializeLocations() method you wrote in the Hive class in the last chapter:

Once you get your simulator running, you can use this to tweak the Hive's locations collection.

```
private void InitializeLocations()
{
    locations = new Dictionary<string, Point>();
    locations.Add("Entrance", new Point(626, 110));
    locations.Add("Nursery", new Point(77, 162));
    locations.Add("HoneyFactory", new Point(157, 78));
    locations.Add("Exit", new Point(175, 180));}
```

Remove the mouse click handler when you're done… you just needed it to get the locations on your forms.

These are the coordinates that worked for us, but if your form is a little bigger or smaller, your coordinates will be different.

Build the renderer

Here's the complete `Renderer` class. The main form calls this class's `Render()` method right after it calls `World.Go()` to draw the bees and flowers on the forms. You'll need to make sure that the flower graphic (`Flower.png`) is loaded into the project, just like the animated bee images.

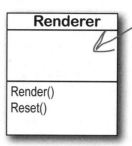

Renderer

Render()
Reset()

All fields in the renderer are private because no other class needs to update any of its properties. It's fully encapsulated. The world just calls Render() to draw the world to the forms, and Reset() to clear the controls on the forms if it needs to reset.

```
class Renderer {
    private World world;
    private HiveForm hiveForm;
    private FieldForm fieldForm;

    private Dictionary<Flower, PictureBox> flowerLookup =
        new Dictionary<Flower, PictureBox>();
    private List<Flower> deadFlowers = new List<Flower>();

    private Dictionary<Bee, BeeControl> beeLookup =
        new Dictionary<Bee, BeeControl>();
    private List<Bee> retiredBees = new List<Bee>();

    public Renderer(World world, HiveForm hiveForm, FieldForm fieldForm) {
        this.world = world;
        this.hiveForm = hiveForm;
        this.fieldForm = fieldForm;
    }

    public void Render() {
        DrawBees();
        DrawFlowers();
        RemoveRetiredBeesAndDeadFlowers();
    }

    public void Reset() {
        foreach (PictureBox flower in flowerLookup.Values) {
            fieldForm.Controls.Remove(flower);
            flower.Dispose();
        }
        foreach (BeeControl bee in beeLookup.Values) {
            hiveForm.Controls.Remove(bee);
            fieldForm.Controls.Remove(bee);
            bee.Dispose();
        }
        flowerLookup.Clear();
        beeLookup.Clear();
    }
```

The renderer keeps references to the world and the two forms it draws the bees on.

The world uses Bee and Flower objects to keep track of every bee and flower in the world. The forms use a PictureBox to display each flower and a BeeControl to display each bee. The renderer uses these dictionaries to connect each bee and flower to its own BeeControl or PictureBox.

When a flower dies or a bee retires, it uses the deadFlowers and retiredBees lists to clean out the dictionaries.

The timer on the main form that runs the animation calls the Render() method, which updates the bees and the flowers, and then cleans out its dictionaries.

If the simulator is reset, it calls each form's Controls.Remove() method to completely clear out the controls on the two forms. It finds all of the controls in each of its two dictionaries and removes them from the forms, calling Dispose() on each of them. Then it clears the two dictionaries.

here's the *renderer class*

It takes two foreach loops to draw the flowers. The first looks for new flowers and adds their PictureBoxes. The second looks for dead flowers and removes their PictureBoxes.

The first foreach loop uses the flowerLookup dictionary to check each flower to see if it's got a control on the form. If it doesn't, it creates a new PictureBox using an object initializer, adds it to the form, and then adds it to the flowerLookup dictionary.

```
private void DrawFlowers() {
    foreach (Flower flower in world.Flowers)
        if (!flowerLookup.ContainsKey(flower)) {
            PictureBox flowerControl = new PictureBox() {
                Width = 45,
                Height = 55,
                Image = Properties.Resources.Flower,
                SizeMode = PictureBoxSizeMode.StretchImage,
                Location = flower.Location
            };
            flowerLookup.Add(flower, flowerControl);
            fieldForm.Controls.Add(flowerControl);
        }

    foreach (Flower flower in flowerLookup.Keys) {
        if (!world.Flowers.Contains(flower)) {
            PictureBox flowerControlToRemove = flowerLookup[flower];
            fieldForm.Controls.Remove(flowerControlToRemove);
            flowerControlToRemove.Dispose();
            deadFlowers.Add(flower);
        }
    }
}

private void DrawBees() {
    BeeControl beeControl;
    foreach (Bee bee in world.Bees) {
        beeControl = GetBeeControl(bee);
        if (bee.InsideHive) {
            if (fieldForm.Controls.Contains(beeControl))
                MoveBeeFromFieldToHive(beeControl);
        } else if (hiveForm.Controls.Contains(beeControl))
            MoveBeeFromHiveToField(beeControl);
        beeControl.Location = bee.Location;
    }

    foreach (Bee bee in beeLookup.Keys) {
        if (!world.Bees.Contains(bee)) {
            beeControl = beeLookup[bee];
            if (fieldForm.Controls.Contains(beeControl))
                fieldForm.Controls.Remove(beeControl);
            if (hiveForm.Controls.Contains(beeControl))
                hiveForm.Controls.Remove(beeControl);
            beeControl.Dispose();
            retiredBees.Add(bee);
        }
    }
}
```

DrawFlowers() uses the Location property in the Flower object to set the PictureBox's location on the form.

The second foreach loop looks for any PictureBox in the flowerLookup dictionary that's no longer on the form and removes it.

After it removes the PictureBox, it calls its Dispose() method. Then it adds the Flower object to deadFlowers so it'll get cleared later.

DrawBees() also uses two foreach loops, and it does the same basic things as DrawFlowers(). But it's a little more complex, so we split some of its behavior out into separate methods to make it easier to understand.

DrawBees() checks if a bee is in the hive but its control is on the FieldForm, or vice versa. It uses two extra methods to move the BeeControls between the forms.

Once the BeeControl is removed, we need to call its Dispose() method—the user control will dispose of its timer for us.

The second foreach loop works just like in DrawFlowers(), except it needs to remove the BeeControl from the right form.

You'll need to make sure you've got using System.Drawing and using System.Windows.Forms at the top of the Renderer class file.

GetBeeControl() looks up a bee in the beeLookup dictionary and returns it. If it's not there, it creates a new 40 x 40 BeeControl and adds it to the hive form (since that's where bees are born).

```
private BeeControl GetBeeControl(Bee bee) {
    BeeControl beeControl;
    if (!beeLookup.ContainsKey(bee)) {
        beeControl = new BeeControl() { Width = 40, Height = 40 };
        beeLookup.Add(bee, beeControl);
        hiveForm.Controls.Add(beeControl);
        beeControl.BringToFront();
    }
    else
        beeControl = beeLookup[bee];
    return beeControl;
}
```

Don't forget that the ! means NOT.

MoveBeeFromHiveToField() takes a specific BeeControl out of the hive form's Controls collection and adds it to the field form's Controls collection.

```
private void MoveBeeFromHiveToField(BeeControl beeControl) {
    hiveForm.Controls.Remove(beeControl);
    beeControl.Size = new Size(20, 20);
    fieldForm.Controls.Add(beeControl);
    beeControl.BringToFront();
}
```

The bees on the field form are smaller than the ones on the hive form, so the method needs to change BeeControl's Size property.

```
private void MoveBeeFromFieldToHive(BeeControl beeControl) {
    fieldForm.Controls.Remove(beeControl);
    beeControl.Size = new Size(40, 40);
    hiveForm.Controls.Add(beeControl);
    beeControl.BringToFront();
}
```

MoveBeeFromFieldToHive() moves a BeeControl back to the hive form. It has to make it bigger again.

```
private void RemoveRetiredBeesAndDeadFlowers() {
    foreach (Bee bee in retiredBees)
        beeLookup.Remove(bee);
    retiredBees.Clear();
    foreach (Flower flower in deadFlowers)
        flowerLookup.Remove(flower);
    deadFlowers.Clear();
}
```

Whenever DrawBees() and DrawFlowers() found that a flower or bee was no longer in the world, it added them to the deadFlowers and retiredBees lists to be removed at the end of the frame.

After all the controls are moved around, the renderer calls this method to clear any dead flowers and retired bees out of the two dictionaries.

Now connect the main form to your two new forms, HiveForm and FieldForm

It's great to have a renderer, but so far, there aren't any forms to render onto. We can fix that by going back to the main Form class (probably called Form1) and making some code changes:

When the main form loads, it creates an instance of each of the other two forms. They're just objects in the heap for now—they won't be displayed until their Show() methods are called.

```
public partial class Form1 : Form {
    private HiveForm hiveForm = new HiveForm();
    private FieldForm fieldForm = new FieldForm();
    private Renderer renderer;

    // the rest of the fields

    public Form1() {
        InitializeComponent();

        MoveChildForms();
        hiveForm.Show(this);
        fieldForm.Show(this);
        ResetSimulator();

        timer1.Interval = 50;
        timer1.Tick += new EventHandler(RunFrame);
        timer1.Enabled = false;
        UpdateStats(new TimeSpan());
    }

    private void MoveChildForms() {
        hiveForm.Location = new Point(Location.X + Width + 10, Location.Y);
        fieldForm.Location = new Point(Location.X,
            Location.Y + Math.Max(Height, hiveForm.Height) + 10);
    }

    public void RunFrame(object sender, EventArgs e) {
        framesRun++;
        world.Go(random);
        renderer.Render();
        // previous code
    }

    private void Form1_Move(object sender, EventArgs e) {
        MoveChildForms();
    }
```

The code to reset the world moved to the ResetSimulator() method.

Move the code to instantiate the World into the ResetSimulator() method.

The form passes a reference to itself into Form.Show() so it becomes the parent form.

The main form's constructor moves the two child forms in place, then displays them. Then it calls ResetSimulator(), which instantiates Renderer.

Since both child forms have StartPosition set to Manual, the main form can move them using the Location property.

This code moves the two forms so that the hive form is next to the main stats form and the field form is below both of them.

Adding this one line to RunFrame makes the simulator update the graphics each time the world's Go() method is called.

The Move event is fired every time the main form is moved. Calling MoveChildForms() makes sure the child forms always move along with the main form.

Use the Events button in the Properties window to add the Move event handler.

Make sure you've set the field and hive forms' StartPosition property to Manual, or else MoveChildForms() won't work.

Here's where we **create new instances of** the World and Renderer classes, which resets the simulator.

```
private void ResetSimulator() {
    framesRun = 0;
    world = new World(new Bee.BeeMessage(SendMessage));
    renderer = new Renderer(world, hiveForm, fieldForm);
}

private void reset_Click(object sender, EventArgs e) {
    renderer.Reset();
    ResetSimulator();
    if (!timer1.Enabled)
        toolStrip1.Items[0].Text = "Start simulation";
}

private void openToolStripButton_Click(object sender, EventArgs e) {
    // The rest of the code in this button stays exactly the same.

    renderer.Reset();
    renderer = new Renderer(world, hiveForm, fieldForm);
}
}
```

The Reset button needs to call Reset() to clear out all the BeeControls and flower PictureBoxes, and then reset the simulator.

Finally, you'll need to add code to the Open button on the ToolStrip to use the Reset() method to remove the bees and flowers from the two forms' Controls collections, and then create a new renderer using the newly loaded world.

---

there are no
Dumb Questions

Q: I saw that you showed the form using a Show() method, but I don't quite get what was going on with passing this as a parameter.

A: This all comes down to the idea that a form is just another class. When you display a form, you're just instantiating that class and calling its Show() method. There's an overloaded version of Show() that takes one parameter, a parent window. When one form is a parent of another, it causes Windows to set up a special relationship between them—for example, when you minimize the parent window, it automatically minimizes all of that form's child windows, too.

Q: Can you alter the preexisting controls and muck around with their code?

A: No, you can't actually access the code inside the controls that ship with Visual Studio. However, every single one of those controls is a class that you can inherit, just like you inherited from PictureBox to create your BeeControl. If you want to add or change behavior in any of those controls, you add your own methods and properties that manipulate the ones in the base class.

Test drive...ahem...buzz

Compile all your code, chase down any errors you're
getting, and run your simulator.

Your bees should be happily
flapping their wings now.

Try changing the
constants on your
simulator, and seeing how
the renderer handles more
bees or flowers.

Looks great, but something's not quite right...

Look closely at the bees buzzing around the hive and the flowers, and you'll notice some problems with the way they're being rendered. Remember how you set each BeeControl's BackColor property to Color. Transparent? Unfortunately, that wasn't enough to keep the simulator from having some problems that are actually pretty typical of graphics programs.

1 **There are some <u>serious</u> performance issues**
Did you notice how the whole simulator slows down when all the bees are inside the hive? If not, try adding more bees by increasing the constants in the Hive class. Keep your eye on the frame rate—add more bees, and it starts to drop significantly.

2 **The flowers' "transparent" backgrounds aren't really transparent**
And there's another, completely *separate* problem. When we saved the graphics files for the flowers, we gave them transparent backgrounds. But while that made sure that each flower's background matched the background of the form, it doesn't look so nice when flowers overlap each other.

When you set a PictureBox's background color to Transparent, it draws any transparent pixels in the image so they match the background of the <u>form</u>...which isn't always the right thing to do.

When one PictureBox overlaps another, C# draws the transparent pixels so they match the form, not the other control that it overlaps, causing weird rectangular "cut-outs" any time two flowers overlap.

3 **The bees' backgrounds aren't transparent, either**
It turns out that Color.Transparent really does have some limitations. When the bees are hovering over the flowers, the same "cut-out" glitch happens. Transparency works a little better with the hive form, where the form's background image does show through the transparent areas of the bee graphics. But when the bees overlap, the same problems occur. And if you watch closely as the bees move around the hive, you'll see some glitches where the bee images are sometimes distorted when they move.

Let's take a closer look at those performance issues

Each bee picture you downloaded is big. Really big. Pop one of them open in Windows Picture Viewer and see for yourself. That means the `PictureBox` needs to shrink it down every time it changes the image, and scaling an image up or down takes time. The reason the bees move a lot slower when there's a lot of them flying around inside the hive is that the inside hive picture is HUGE. And when you made the background for the `BeeControl` transparent, it needs to do double work: first it has to shrink the bee picture down, and then it needs to shrink a portion of the form's background down so that it can draw it in the transparent area behind the bee.

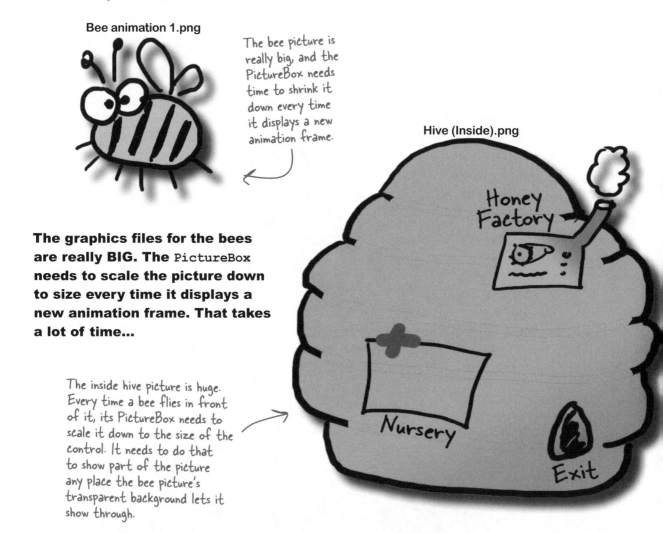

Bee animation 1.png

The bee picture is really big, and the PictureBox needs time to shrink it down every time it displays a new animation frame.

Hive (Inside).png

Honey Factory

Nursery

Exit

The graphics files for the bees are really BIG. The `PictureBox` needs to scale the picture down to size every time it displays a new animation frame. That takes a lot of time...

The inside hive picture is huge. Every time a bee flies in front of it, its PictureBox needs to scale it down to the size of the control. It needs to do that to show part of the picture any place the bee picture's transparent background lets it show through.

...so all we need to do to speed up the simulator's performance is to shrink down all the pictures *before* we try to display them.

All we need to do to speed up the graphics performance is add a method to the renderer that scales any image to a different size. Then we can **resize each picture once when it's loaded**, and only use the scaled-down version in the bee control and for the hive form's background.

1 **Add the `ResizeImage` method to the renderer**

All of the pictures in your project (like `Properties.Resources.Flower`) are stored as `Bitmap` objects. Here's a static method that resizes bitmaps—add it to the `Renderer` class:

```
public static Bitmap ResizeImage(Bitmap picture, int width, int height) {
    Bitmap resizedPicture = new Bitmap(width, height);
    using (Graphics graphics = Graphics.FromImage(resizedPicture)) {
        graphics.DrawImage(picture, 0, 0, width, height);
    }
    return resizedPicture;
}
```

> We'll take a closer look at what this Graphics object is and how this method works in the next few pages

2 **Add this `ResizeCells` method to your `BeeControl`**

Your `BeeControl` can store its own `Bitmap` objects—in this case, an array of four of them. Here's a control that'll populate that array, resizing each one so that it's exactly the right size for the control:

```
private Bitmap[] cells = new Bitmap[4];
private void ResizeCells() {
  cells[0] = Renderer.ResizeImage(Properties.Resources.Bee_animation_1, Width, Height);
  cells[1] = Renderer.ResizeImage(Properties.Resources.Bee_animation_2, Width, Height);
  cells[2] = Renderer.ResizeImage(Properties.Resources.Bee_animation_3, Width, Height);
  cells[3] = Renderer.ResizeImage(Properties.Resources.Bee_animation_4, Width, Height);
}
```

> These lines take each of the Bitmap objects that store the bee pictures and shrink them down using the ResizeImage() method we wrote.

3 **Change the `switch` statement so that it uses the cells array, not the resources**

The BeeControl's `Tick` event handler has a switch statement that sets its `BackgroundImage`:

```
BackgroundImage = Properties.Resources.Bee_animation_1;
```

Replace `Properties.Resources.Bee_animation_1` with `cells[0]`. Now replace the rest of the **case** lines, so that case 2 uses `cells[1]`, case 3 uses `cells[2]`, case 4 uses `cells[3]`, case 5 uses `cells[2]`, and the default case uses `cells[1]`. That way only the resized image is displayed.

4 **Add calls to `ResizeCells()` to the `BeeControl`**

You'll need to add two calls to the new `ResizeCells()` method. First, **add it** to the bottom of the constructor. Then go back to the IDE designer by double-clicking on the `BeeControl` in the Properties window. Go over to the Events page in the Properties window (by clicking on the lightning-bolt icon), scroll down to Resize, and double-click on it to **add a Resize event handler**. Make the new `Resize` event handler call `ResizeCells()`, too—that way it'll resize its animation pictures every time the form is resized.

5 **Set the form's background image manually**

Go to the Properties window and set the hive form's background image to `(none)`. Then go to its constructor and set the image to one that's sized properly.

```
public partial class HiveForm : Form {
    public HiveForm() {
        InitializeComponent();
        BackgroundImage = Renderer.ResizeImage(
            Properties.Resources.Hive__inside_,
            ClientRectangle.Width, ClientRectangle.Height);
    }
}
```

> Your form has a ClientRectangle property that contains a Rectangle that has the dimensions of its display area.

Now run the simulator—it's much faster!

You resized your Bitmaps using a <u>Graphics</u> object

Forms and controls have a CreateGraphics() method that returns a new Graphics object. You'll see a lot more about that shortly.

Let's take a closer look at that ResizeImage() method you added to the renderer. The first thing it does is create a new Bitmap object that's the size that the picture will be resized to. Then it uses Graphics.FromImage() to **create a new Graphics object**. It uses that Graphics object's DrawImage() method to draw the picture onto the Bitmap. Notice how you passed the width and height parameters to DrawImage()—that's how you tell it to scale the image down to the new size. Finally you returned the new Bitmap you created, so it can be used as the form's background image or one of the four animation cells.

You pass a picture into the method, along with a new width and height that it'll be resized to.

```
public static Bitmap ResizeImage(Bitmap picture, int width, int height) {

    Bitmap resizedPicture = new Bitmap(width, height);

    using (Graphics graphics = Graphics.FromImage(resizedPicture)) {

        graphics.DrawImage(picture, 0, 0, width, height);

    }

    return resizedPicture;

}
```

The FromImage() method returns a new Graphics object that lets you draw graphics onto that image. Take a minute and use the IDE's IntelliSense to look at the methods in the Graphics class. When you call DrawImage(), it copies the image into the resizedPicture bitmap at the location (0, 0) and scaled to the width and height parameters.

Let's see image resizing in action

Just do this temporarily. Delete the button and code when you're done.

Drag a button onto the Field form and add this code. It creates a new PictureBox control that's 100 ×100 pixels, setting its border to a black line so you can see how big it is. Then it uses ResizeImage() to make a bee picture that's squished down to 80×40 pixels and assigns that new picture to its Image property. Once the PictureBox is added to the form, the bee is displayed.

```
private void button1_Click(object sender, EventArgs e)
{
    PictureBox beePicture = new PictureBox();
    beePicture.Location = new Point(10, 10);
    beePicture.Size = new Size(100, 100);
    beePicture.BorderStyle = BorderStyle.FixedSingle;
    beePicture.Image = Renderer.ResizeImage(
        Properties.Resources.Bee_animation_1, 80, 40);
    Controls.Add(beePicture);
}
```

You can see the image resizing in action—the squished bee image is much smaller than the PictureBox. ResizeImage() squished it down.

The ResizeImage() method creates a Graphics object to draw on an invisible Bitmap object. It returns that Bitmap so it can be displayed on a form or in a PictureBox.

Your image resources are stored in Bitmap objects

If you don't see any performance problems, keep adding bees until the program slows down!

When you import graphics files into your project's resources, what happens to them? You already know that you can access them using Properties.Resources. But what, exactly, is your program doing with them once they're imported?

.NET turns your image into a new Bitmap object:

The Bitmap class has several overloaded constructors. This one loads a graphics file from disk. You can also pass it integers for width and height—that'll create a new Bitmap with no picture.

`Bitmap bee = new Bitmap("Bee animation 1.png")`

Bitmap object

Bee animation 1.png

Then each Bitmap is drawn to the screen

Once your images are in Bitmap objects, your form draws them to the screen with a call like this:

This call gets a Graphics object to draw on the form. We use a using statment to make sure the Graphics object is disposed.

```
using (Graphics g = CreateGraphics()) {
    g.DrawImage(myBitmap, 30, 30, 150, 150);
}
```

DrawImage() takes a Bitmap, the image to draw...

...a starting X, Y coordinate...

...and a size, 150x150 pixels.

The bigger they are...

Did you notice those last two parameters to DrawImage()? What if the image in the Bitmap is 175 by 175? The graphics library must then resize the image to fit 150 by 150. What if the Bitmap contains an image that's 1,500 by 2,025? Then the scaling becomes even slower....

Resizing images takes a lot of processing power! If you do it once, it's no big deal. But if you do it EVERY FRAME, your program will slow down. We gave you REALLY BIG images for the bees and the hive. When the renderer moves the bees around (especially in front of the inside hive picture), it has to resize them over and over again. And that was causing the performance problems!

This image, which is 300x300 pixels...

← 150 →

150

...gets shrunk to this size, which is (for example) 150x150 pixels. And that slows your simulator down!

Use System.Drawing to <u>TAKE</u> <u>CONTROL</u> of graphics yourself

The Graphics object is part of the System.Drawing namespace. The .NET Framework comes with some pretty powerful graphics tools that go a lot further than the simple PictureBox control that's in the toolbox. You can draw shapes, use fonts, and do all sorts of complex graphics…and it all starts with a Graphics object. Any time you want to add or modify any object's graphics or images, you'll create a Graphics object that's **linked to the object you want to draw on**, and then use the Graphics object's methods to draw on your target.

> ## System.Drawing
> The graphics methods in the System.Drawing namespace are sometimes referred to as GDI+, which stands for Graphics Device Interface. When you draw graphics with GDI+, you start with a Graphics object that's hooked up to a Bitmap, form, control, or another object that you want to draw on using the Graphics object's methods.

1 **Start with the object you want to draw on**
For instance, think about a form. When you call the form's CreateGraphics() method, it returns an instance of Graphics that's set up to draw on itself.

> The form can call its own CreateGraphics() method, or another object can call it. Either way, the method returns a reference to a Graphics object whose methods will draw on it.

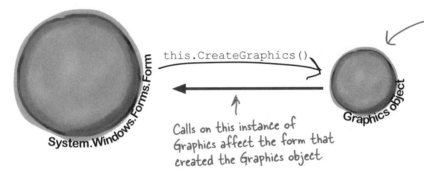

this.CreateGraphics()

System.Windows.Forms.Form

Calls on this instance of Graphics affect the form that created the Graphics object.

Graphics object

You don't draw on the Graphics object itself. You only use it to draw on other objects.

2 **Use the Graphics object's methods to draw on your object**
Every Graphics object has methods that let you draw on the object that created it. When you call methods in the Graphics object to draw lines, circles, rectangles, text, and images, they appear on the form.

Even though you're calling methods in this Graphics object, the actual graphics appear on the object that created it.

Graphics object

g.DrawLines()

The DrawLines() method, for example, draws a bunch of lines on whatever object created the Graphics instance.

System.Windows.Forms.Form

A 30-second tour of GDI+ graphics

There are all sorts of shapes and pictures that you can draw once you've created a Graphics object. All you need to do is call its methods, and it'll draw directly onto the object that created it.

> *You'll need to make sure you've got a* using System.Drawing; *line at the top of your class to use these methods. Or, when you add a form to your project, the IDE adds that line to your form class automatically.*

❶ The first step is always to grab yourself a Graphics object. Use a form's CreateGraphics() method, or have a Graphics object passed in. Remember, Graphics implements the IDisposable() interface, so if you create a new one, use a using statement:

```
using (Graphics g = this.CreateGraphics()) {
```

> *Remember, this draws on the object that created this instance.*

❷ If you want to draw a line, call DrawLine() with a starting point and ending point, each represented by X and Y coordinates:

```
g.DrawLine(Pens.Blue, 30, 10, 100, 45);
```

> *The start coordinate...*
>
> *...and the end coordinate.*

or you can do it using a couple of Points:

```
g.DrawLine(Pens.Blue, new Point(30, 45), new Point(100, 10));
```

❸ Here's code that draws a filled slate gray rectangle, and then gives it a sky blue border. It uses a Rectangle to define the dimensions—in this case, the upper left-hand corner is at (150, 15), and it's 140 pixels wide and 90 pixels high.

```
g.FillRectangle(Brushes.SlateGray, new Rectangle(150, 15, 140, 90));
g.DrawRectangle(Pens.SkyBlue, new Rectangle(150, 15, 140, 90));
```

> *There are a whole lot of colors you can use—just type "Color", "Pens", or "Brushes" followed by a dot, and the IntelliSense window will display them.*

❹ You can draw an ellipse or a circle using the DrawCircle() or FillCircle() methods, which also use a Rectangle to specify how big the shape should be. This code draws two ellipses that are slightly offset to give a shadow effect:

```
g.FillEllipse(Brushes.DarkGray, new Rectangle(45, 65, 200, 100));
g.FillEllipse(Brushes.Silver, new Rectangle(40, 60, 200, 100));
```

❺ Use the DrawString() method to draw text in any font and color. To do that, you'll need to create a Font object. It implements IDisposable, so use a using statement:

```
using (Font arial24Bold = new Font("Arial", 24, FontStyle.Bold)) {
    g.DrawString("Hi there!", arial24Bold, Brushes.Red, 50, 75);
}
```

> *If the above statements are executed in order, this is what will end up on the form. Each of the statements above matches up with the numbers here. The upper left-hand corner is coordinate (0, 0).*

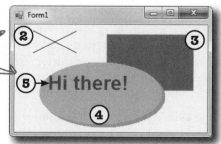

> *There's no step 1 on this picture, since that was creating the actual Graphics object.*

Use graphics to draw a picture on a form

Draw this

Let's create a new Windows application that draws a picture on a form **when you click on it**.

① Start by adding a `Click` event to the form

Go to the **Events page in the Properties window** (by clicking on the lightning-bolt icon), scroll down to the Click event, and double-click on it.

Start the event handler with a `using` line to create the `Graphics` object. When you work with GDI+, you use a lot of objects that implement `IDisposable`. If you don't dispose of them, they'll slowly suck up your computer's resources until you quit the program. So you'll end up using a lot of `using` statements:

```
using (Graphics g = CreateGraphics()) {
```

> Here's the first line in your Form1_Click() event handler method. We'll give you all the lines for the event handler—put them together to draw the picture.

② Pay attention to the order you draw things on our form

We want a sky blue background for this picture, so you'll draw a big blue rectangle first—then anything else you draw afterward will be drawn **on top of it**. You'll take advantage of one of the form's properties called `ClientRectangle`. It's a `Rectangle` that defines the boundaries of the form's drawing area. `Rectangle`s are really useful—you can create a `new` rectangle by specifying a `Point` for its upper left-hand corner, and its width and height. Once you do that, it'll automatically calculate its `Top`, `Left`, `Right`, and `Bottom` properties for you. And it's got **useful methods like `Contains()`, which will return true if a given point is inside it**.

```
g.FillRectangle(Brushes.SkyBlue, ClientRectangle);
```

> This will come in really handy later on in the book! What do you think you'll be doing with Contains()?

③ Draw the bee and the flower

You already know how the `DrawImage()` method works. Make sure you add the image resources.

```
g.DrawImage(Properties.Resources.Bee_animation_1, 50, 20, 75, 75);
g.DrawImage(Properties.Resources.Flower, 10, 130, 100, 150);
```

> Pens are for drawing lines, and they have a width. If you want to draw a filled shape or some text, you'll need a Brush.

④ Add a pen that you can draw with

Every time you draw a line, you use a `Pen` object to determine its color and thickness. There's a built-in `Pens` class that gives you plenty of pens (`Pens.Red` is a thin red pen, for example). But you can create your own pen using the `Pen` class constructor, which takes a `Brush` object and a thickness (it's a float, so make sure it ends with F). Brushes are how you draw filled graphics (like filled rectangles and ellipses), and there's a `Brushes` class that gives you brushes in various colors.

```
using (Pen thickBlackPen = new Pen(Brushes.Black, 3.0F)) {
```

This goes inside the inner using statement that created the Pen.

⑤ Add an arrow that points to the flower

There are some Graphics methods that take an array of Points, and connect them using a series of lines or curves. We'll use the DrawLines() method to draw the arrow head, and the DrawCurve() method to draw its shaft. There are other methods that take point arrays, too (like DrawPolygon(), which draws a closed shape, and FillPolygon(), which fills it in).

```
g.DrawLines(thickBlackPen, new Point[] {
    new Point(130, 110), new Point(120, 160), new Point(155, 163) });
g.DrawCurve(thickBlackPen, new Point[] {
    new Point(120, 160), new Point(175, 120), new Point(215, 70) });
}
```

Here's where the using block ends—we don't need the thickBlackPen any more, so it'll get disposed.

When you pass an array of points to DrawCurve(), it draws a smooth curve that connects them all in order.

⑥ Add a font to draw the text

Whenever you work with drawing text, the first thing you need to do is create a Font object. Again, use a using statement because Font implements IDisposable. Creating a font is straightforward. There are several overloaded constructors—the simplest one takes a font name, font size, and FontStyle enum.

```
using (Font font = new Font("Arial", 16, FontStyle.Italic)) {
```

⑦ Add some text that says "Nectar here"

Now that you've got a font, you can figure out where to put the string by measuring how big it will be when it's drawn. The MeasureString() method returns a SizeF that defines its size. (SizeF is just the float version of Size—and both of them just define a width and height.) Since we know where the arrow ends, we'll use the string measurements to position its center just above the arrow.

```
SizeF size = g.MeasureString("Nectar here", font);
g.DrawString("Nectar here", font, Brushes.Red, new Point(
    215 - (int)size.Width / 2, 70 - (int)size.Height));
}
}
```

Make sure you close out both using blocks.

You can create a Rectangle by giving it a point and a Size (or width and height). Once you've got it, you can find its boundaries and check its Contains() method to see if it contains a Point.

Sharpen your pencil

1. Most of your work with **Graphics** will involve thinking about your forms as a grid of X, Y coordinates. Here's the code to build the grid shown below; your job is to fill in the missing parts.

```
using (Graphics g = this.CreateGraphics())
using (Font f = new Font("Arial", 6, FontStyle.Regular)) {
    for (int x = 0; x < this.Width; x += 20) {

        ..................................................................

    }   ..................................................................
    for (int y = 0; y < this.Height; y += 20) {

        ..................................................................

    }   ..................................................................
}
```

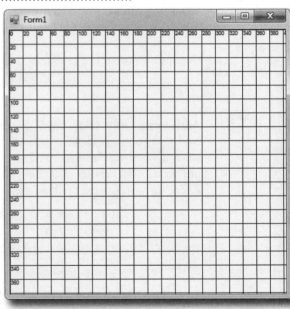

2. Can you figure out what happens when you run the code below? Draw the output onto the form, using the grid you just rendered for locating specific points.

```
using (Pen pen =
        new Pen(Brushes.Black, 3.0F)) {
    g.DrawCurve(pen, new Point[] {
        new Point(80, 60),
        new Point(200,40),
        new Point(180, 60),
        new Point(300,40),
    });
    g.DrawCurve(pen, new Point[] {
        new Point(300,180), new Point(180, 200),
        new Point(200,180), new Point(80, 200),
    });
    g.DrawLine(pen, 300, 40, 300, 180);
    g.DrawLine(pen, 80, 60, 80, 200);
    g.DrawEllipse(pen, 40, 40, 20, 20);
    g.DrawRectangle(pen, 40, 60, 20, 300);
    g.DrawLine(pen, 60, 60, 80, 60);
    g.DrawLine(pen, 60, 200, 80, 200);
}
```

FillPolygon(), DrawLines(), and a few other graphics methods have a constructor that takes an array of Points that define the vertices of a series of connected lines.

3. Here's some more graphics code, dealing with irregular shapes. Figure out what's drawn using the grid we've given you below.

```
g.FillPolygon(Brushes.Black, new Point[] {
      new Point(60,40), new Point(140,80), new Point(200,40),
      new Point(300,80), new Point(380,60), new Point(340,140),
      new Point(320,180), new Point(380,240), new Point(320,300),
      new Point(340,340), new Point(240,320), new Point(180,340),
      new Point(20,320), new Point(60, 280), new Point(100, 240),
      new Point(40, 220), new Point(80,160),
   });

using (Font big = new Font("Times New Roman", 24, FontStyle.Italic)) {
    g.DrawString("Pow!", big, Brushes.White, new Point(80, 80));
    g.DrawString("Pow!", big, Brushes.White, new Point(120, 120));
    g.DrawString("Pow!", big, Brushes.White, new Point(160, 160));
    g.DrawString("Pow!", big, Brushes.White, new Point(200, 200));
    g.DrawString("Pow!", big, Brushes.White, new Point(240, 240));
}
```

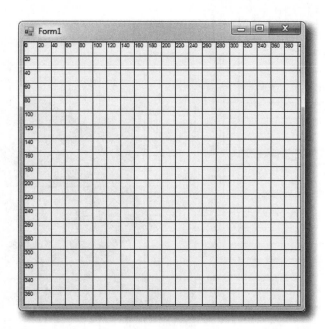

Sharpen your pencil
Solution

Your job was to fill in the missing code to draw a grid, and plot two chunks of code on the grids.

```
using (Graphics g = this.CreateGraphics())
using (Font f = new Font("Arial", 6, FontStyle.Regular)) {
    for (int x = 0; x < this.Width; x += 20) {
        g.DrawLine(Pens.Black, x, 0, x, this.Height);
        g.DrawString(x.ToString(), f, Brushes.Black, x, 0);
    }
    for (int y = 0; y < this.Height; y += 20) {
        g.DrawLine(Pens.Black, 0, y, this.Width, y);
        g.DrawString(y.ToString(), f, Brushes.Black, 0, y);
    }
}
```

First we draw the vertical lines and the numbers along the Y axis. There's a vertical line every 20 pixels along the X axis.

We used using statements to make sure the Graphics and Font objects get disposed after the form's drawn.

Next we draw the horizontal lines and X axis numbers. To draw a horizontal line, you choose a Y value and draw a line from (0, y) on the left-hand side of the form to (0, this.Width) on the right-hand side of the form.

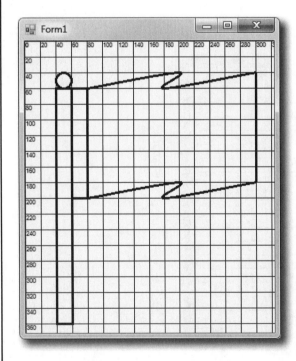

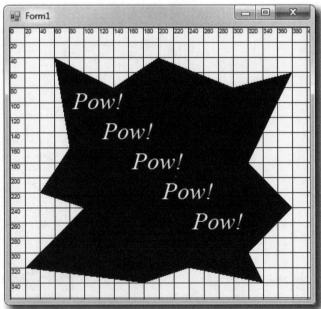

Graphics can fix our transparency problem...

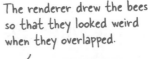

The renderer drew the bees so that they looked weird when they overlapped.

Remember those pesky graphics glitches? Let's tackle them! DrawImage() is the key to fixing the problem in the renderer where the images were drawing those boxes around the bees and flowers that caused the overlap issues. We'll start out by going back to our Windows application with the picture and changing it to draw a bunch of bees that overlap each other without any graphics glitches.

Do this

1 Add a DrawBee() method that draws a bee on any Graphics object. It uses the overloaded DrawImage() constructor that takes a Rectangle to determine where to draw the image, and how big to draw it.

```
public void DrawBee(Graphics g, Rectangle rect) {
    g.DrawImage(Properties.Resources.Bee_animation_1, rect);
}
```

2 Here's the new **Click event handler for the form**. Take a close look at how it works—it draws the hive so that its upper left-hand corner is way off the form, at location (-Width, -Height), and it draws it at twice the width and height of the form—so you can resize the form and it'll still draw OK. Then it draws four bees using the DrawBee() method.

Much better—click on the form and the bees overlap just fine.

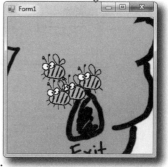

```
private void Form1_Click(object sender, EventArgs e) {
    using (Graphics g = CreateGraphics()) {
        g.DrawImage(Properties.Resources.Hive__inside_,
            -Width, -Height, Width * 2, Height * 2);
        Size size = new Size(Width / 5, Height / 5);
        DrawBee(g, new Rectangle(
                new Point(Width / 2 - 50, Height / 2 - 40), size));
        DrawBee(g, new Rectangle(
                new Point(Width / 2 - 20, Height / 2 - 60), size));
        DrawBee(g, new Rectangle(
                new Point(Width / 2 - 80, Height / 2 - 30), size));
        DrawBee(g, new Rectangle(
                new Point(Width / 2 - 90, Height / 2 - 80), size));
    }
}
```

First we'll draw the hive background, with its corner far off the page so we only see a small piece of it. Then we'll draw four bees so that they overlap—if they don't, make your form bigger and then click on it again so they do.

...but there's a catch

But look what happens if you drag it off the side of the screen and back! <u>Oh no!</u>

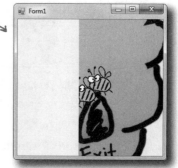

3 Run your program and click on the form, and watch it draw the bees! But something's wrong. When you drag the form off the side of the screen and back again, **the picture disappears!** Now go back and check the "Nectar here" program you wrote a few pages ago—**it's got the same problem!**

What do you think happened?

Use the Paint event to make your graphics stick

Forms and controls have a **Paint** event that gives you a **Graphics** object. Anything you draw on it is repainted automatically.

What good are graphics if they disappear from your form as soon as part of your form gets covered up? They're no good at all. Luckily, there's an easy way to make sure your graphics stay on your form: just **write a Paint event handler**. Your form fires a Paint event every time it needs to redraw itself—like when it's dragged off the screen. One of the properties of its PaintEventArgs parameter is a Graphics object called Graphics, and anything that you draw with it will "stick."

1 **Add a Paint event handler**

Double-click on "Paint" in the Events page in the Properties window to add a Paint event handler. The Paint event is fired any time the image on your form gets "dirty." So drawing your graphics inside of it will make your image stick around.

Double-click on Paint to add a Paint event handler. Its PaintEventArgs has a property called Graphics—and anything you draw with it will stick to your form.

Properties

Form1 System.Windows.Forms.Form

Paint — Form1_Paint

Paint
Occurs when a control needs repainting.

2 **Use the Graphics object from the Paint event's EventArgs**

Instead of starting with a using statement, make your event handler start like this:

```
private void Form1_Paint(object sender, PaintEventArgs e) {
    Graphics g = e.Graphics;
```

You **don't** have to use a using statement—since you didn't create it, **you don't have to dispose it**.

3 **Copy the code that draws the overlapping bees and hive**

Add the new DrawBee() method from the previous page into your new user control. Then copy the code from the Click event into your new Paint event—**except for the first line with the using statement**, since you already have a Graphics object called g. (Since you don't have the using statement anymore, make sure you take out its closing curly bracket.) Now run your program. **The graphics stick!**

Do the same with your "Nectar here" drawing to make it stick, too.

Forms and controls redraw themselves all the time

It may not look like it, but your forms have to redraw themselves all the time. Any time you have controls on a form, they're displaying graphics—labels display text, buttons display a picture of a button, checkboxes draw a little box with an X in it. You work with them as controls that you drag around, but each control actually draws its own image. Any time you drag a form off the screen or under another form and then drag it back or uncover it, the part of the form that was covered up is now invalid, which means that it no longer shows the image that it's supposed to. That's when .NET sends a message to the form telling it to redraw itself. The form fires off a Paint event any time it's "dirty" and needs to be redrawn. If you ever want your form or user control to redraw itself, you can tell .NET to make it "dirty" by calling its Invalidate() method.

See if you can combine your knowledge of forms and user controls—and get a little more practice using Bitmap objects and the DrawImage() method—by building a user control that uses TrackBars to zoom an image in and out.

1 **Add two TrackBar controls to a new user control**
Create a new Windows Application project. **Add a UserControl**—call it Zoomer—and set its Size property to (300, 300). Drag two TrackBar controls out of the toolbox and onto it. Drag trackBar1 to the bottom of the control. Then drag trackBar2 to the right-hand side of the control and set its Orientation property to Vertical. Both should have the Minimum property set to 1, Maximum set to 175, Value set to 175, and TickStyle set to None. Set each TrackBar's background color to white. Finally, double-click on each TrackBar to add a Scroll event handler. Make both event handlers call the control's Invalidate() method.

Your user control has a Paint event, and it works just like the one you just used in the form. Just use its PaintEventArgs parameter e. It has a property called Graphics, and anything that you draw with that Graphics object will be painted onto any instance of the user control you drag out of the toolbox.

Give the two trackbars white backgrounds because you'll be drawing a white rectangle behind everything, and you want them to blend in.

2 **Load a picture into a Bitmap object and draw it on the control**
Add a private Bitmap field called photo to your Zoomer user control. When you create the instance of Bitmap, use its constructor to load your favorite image file—we used a picture of a fluffy dog. Then add a Paint event to the control. The event handler should create a graphics object to draw on the control, draw a white filled rectangle over the entire control, and then use DrawImage() to draw the contents of your photo field onto your control so its upper left-hand corner is at (10, 10), its width is trackBar1.Value, and its height is trackBar2.Value. Then drag your control onto the form—make sure to resize the form so the trackbars are at the edges.

When you move the trackbars, the picture will shrink and grow!

Whenever the user scrolls one of the TrackBars, they call the user control's Invalidate() method. That will cause the user control to fire its Paint event and resize the photo. Remember, since you didn't create the Graphics object—it was passed to you in PaintEventArgs—you don't need to dispose it. So you don't have to use a using statement with it. Just draw the image inside the Paint event handler.

EXERCISE
SOLUTION

Get a little more practice using `Bitmap` objects and the `DrawImage()` method by building a form that uses them to load a picture from a file and zoom it in and out.

This particular Bitmap constructor loads its picture from a file. It's got other overloaded constructors, including one that lets you specify a width and height—that one creates an empty bitmap.

```
public partial class Zoomer : UserControl {

   Bitmap photo = new Bitmap("c:\Graphics\fluffy_dog.jpg");

   public Zoomer() {
      InitializeComponent();
   }

   private void Zoomer_Paint(object sender, PaintEventArgs e) {
      Graphics g = e.Graphics;
      g.FillRectangle(Brushes.White, 0, 0, Width, Height);
      g.DrawImage(photo, 10, 10, trackBar1.Value, trackBar2.Value);
   }

   private void trackBar1_Scroll(object sender, EventArgs e) {
      Invalidate();
   }

   private void trackBar2_Scroll(object sender, EventArgs e) {
      Invalidate();
   }
}
```

Substitute your own file—the Bitmap constructor can take many file formats. Even better, see if you can use an OpenFileDialog to zoom any image you want!

First we draw a big white rectangle so it fills up the whole control, then we draw the photo on top of it. The last two parameters determine the size of the image being drawn—trackBar1 sets the width, trackBar2 sets the height.

Every time the user slides one of the trackbar controls, it fires off a Scroll event. By making the event handlers call the control's Invalidate() method, we cause the form to repaint itself...and when it does, it draws a new copy of the image with a different size.

Each drag here is causing another image resize from DrawImage().

```
g.DrawImage(myBitmap, 30, 30, 150, 150);
```

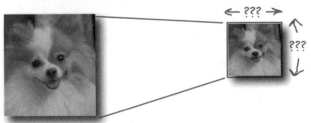

← ??? →

↑ ??? ↓

A closer look at how forms and controls repaint themselves

Behind the Scenes

Earlier, we said that when you start working with `Graphics` objects, you're really taking control of graphics. It's like you tell .NET, "Hey, I know what I'm doing, I can handle the extra responsibility." In the case of drawing and redrawing, you may not want to redraw when a form is minimized and maximized…or you may want to redraw ***more often***. Once you know what's going on behind the scenes with your form or control, you can take control of redrawing yourself:

① **Every form has a Paint event that draws the graphics on the form**

Go to the event list for any form and find the event called **Paint**. Whenever the form has to repaint itself, this event is fired. Every form and control uses a `Paint` event internally to decide when to redraw itself. But what fires that event? It's called by a method called **OnPaint** that the form or user control inherits from the `Control` class. (That method follows the pattern you saw in Chapter 11, where methods that fire an event are named "On" followed by the event name.) Go to any form and override `OnPaint`: *Do this just like you did earlier with Dispose()*

Override OnPaint on any form and add this line.

```
protected override void OnPaint(PaintEventArgs e) {
    Console.WriteLine("OnPaint {0} {1}", DateTime.Now, e.ClipRectangle);
    base.OnPaint(e);
}
```

Drag your form around—drag it halfway off the screen, minimize it, hide it behind other windows. Look closely at the output that it writes. You'll see that your `OnPaint` method fires off a `Paint` event any time part of it is "dirty"—or **invalid**—and needs to be redrawn. And if you look closely at the `ClipRectangle`, you'll see that it's a rectangle that describes the part of the form that needs to be repainted. That gets passed to the `Paint` event's `PaintEventArgs` so it can improve performance by only redrawing the portion that's invalid.

② **Invalidate() controls when to redraw, and WHAT to redraw**

.NET fires the `Paint` event when something on a form is interfered with, covered up, or moved offscreen, and then shown again. It calls `Invalidate()`, and passes the method a `Rectangle`. The `Rectangle` tells the `Invalidate()` method what part of the form needs to be redrawn…i.e., what part of the form is "dirty." Then .NET calls `OnPaint` to tell your form to fire a `Paint` event and repaint the dirty area.

Invalidate() essentially says that some part of the form might be "invalid," so redraw that part to make sure it's got the right things showing.

③ **The Update() method gives your Invalidate request top priority**

You may not realize it, but your form is getting messages all the time. The same system that tells it that it's been covered up and calls `OnPaint` has all sorts of other messages it needs to send. See for yourself: type `override` and scroll through all the methods that start with "On"—every one of them is a message your form responds to. The `Update()` method moves the Invalidate message to the top of the message list.

So when you call it yourself, you're telling .NET that your whole form or control is invalid, and the whole thing needs to be redrawn. You can pass it your own clip rectangle if you want—that'll get passed along to the Paint event's PaintEventArgs.

④ **The form's Refresh() method is Invalidate() plus Update()**

Forms and controls give you a shortcut. They have a `Refresh()` method that first calls `Invalidate()` to invalidate the whole client area (the area of the form where graphics appear), and then calls `Update()` to make sure that message moves to the top of the list.

Q: It still seems like just resizing the graphics in a program like Paint or PhotoShop would be better. Why can't I do that?

A: You can, if you're in control of the images you work with in your applications, and if they'll always stay the same size. But that's not often the case. Lots of times, you'll get images from another source, whether it's online or a co-worker in the design group. Or, you may be pulling an image from a read-only source, and you'll have to size it in code.

Q: But if I can resize it outside of .NET, that's better, right?

A: If you're sure you'll never need a larger size, it could be. But if your program might need to display the image in multiple sizes during the program, you'll have to resize at some point anyway. Plus, if your image ever needs to be displayed larger than the resize, you'll end up in real trouble. It's much easier to size down than it is to size up.

More often than not, it's better to be able to resize an image programmatically, than to be limited by an external program or constraints like read-only files.

Q: I get that `CreateGraphics()` gets the `Graphics` object for drawing on a form, but what was that `FromImage()` call in the `ResizeImage()` method about?

A: `FromImage()` retrieves the `Graphics` object for a `Bitmap` object. And just as `CreateGraphics()` called on a form returns the `Graphics` object for drawing on that form, `FromImage()` retrieves a `Graphics` object for drawing on the `Bitmap` the method was called on.

Q: So a `Graphics` object isn't just for drawing on a form?

A: Actually, a `Graphics` object is for drawing on, well, anything that gives you a `Graphics` object. The `Bitmap` gives you a `Graphics` object that you can use to draw onto an invisible image that you can use later. And you'll find `Graphics` objects on a lot more than forms. Drag a button onto a form, then go into your code and type its name followed by a period. Check out the IntelliSense window that popped up—it's got a `CreateGraphics()` method that returns a `Graphics` object. Anything you draw on it will show up on the button! Same goes for `Label`, `PictureBox`, `StatusStrip`...almost every toolbox control has a `Graphics` object.

Q: Wait, I thought `using` was just something I used with streams. Why am I using `using` with graphics?

A: The `using` keyword comes in handy with streams, but it's something that you use with *any* class that implements the `IDisposable` interface. When you instantiate a class that implements `IDisposable`, you should always call its `Dispose()` method when you're done with the object. That way it knows to clean up after itself. With streams, the `Dispose()` method makes sure that any file that was opened gets closed.

`Graphics`, `Pen`, and `Brush` objects are also disposable. When you create any of them, they take up some small amount of memory and other resources, and they don't always give them back immediately. If you're just drawing something once, you won't notice a difference. But most of the time, your graphics code will be called over and over and over again—like in a

Paint event handler, which could get called many times a second for a particularly busy form. That's why you should always `Dispose()` of your graphics-related objects. And the easiest way to make sure that you do is to use a `using` line, and let .NET worry about disposal. Any object you create with `using` will automatically have its `Dispose()` method called at the end of the block following the `using` statement. That will guarantee that your program won't slowly take up more and more memory if it runs for a long time.

Q: If I'm creating a new control, should I use a `UserControl` or should I create a class that inherits from one of the toolbox controls?

A: That depends on what you want your new control to do. If you're building a control that's really similar to one that's already in the toolbox, then you'll probably find it easiest to inherit from that control. But most of the time, when programmers create new controls in C#, they use user controls. One advantage of a user control is that you can **drag toolbox controls onto it**. It works a lot like a `GroupBox` or another container control—you can drag a button or checkbox onto your user control, and work with them just like you'd work with controls on a form. The IDE's form designer becomes a powerful tool to help you design user controls.

> **A user control can host other controls. The IDE's form designer lets you drag controls out of the toolbox and onto your new user control.**

I noticed a whole lot of flickering in my Zoomer control. With all this talk of taking control of graphics, I'll bet there's something we can do about that! But why does it happen?

Even without resizing, it takes time to draw an image onto a form.

Suppose you've got every image in the simulator resized. It still takes time to draw all those bees and flowers and the hive. And right now, we're drawing right to the `Graphics` object on the form. So if your eye catches the tail end of a render, you're going to perceive it as a little flicker.

The problem is that a lot of drawing is happening, so there's a good chance that some flickering will occur, even with our resizing. And that's why you run into problems with some amateur computer games, for example: the human eye catches the end of a rendering cycle, and perceives it as a little bit of flickering on the screen.

BRAIN POWER

How could you get rid of this flicker? If drawing lots of images onto the form causes flickering, and you have to draw lots of images, how do you think you might be able to avoid all the flickering?

Double buffering makes animation look a lot smoother

Go back to your image zoomer and fiddle with the trackbars. Notice how there's a whole lot of flickering when you move the bars? That's because the `Paint` event handler first has to draw the white rectangle and then draw the image every time the trackbar moves a tiny little bit. When your eyes see alternating white rectangles and images many times a second, they interpret that as a flicker. It's irritating…and it's avoidable using a technique called **double buffering**. That means drawing each frame or cell of animation to an invisible bitmap (a "buffer"), and only displaying the new frame once it's been drawn entirely. Here's how it would work with a `Bitmap`:

1 Here's a typical program that draws some graphics on a form using its `Graphics` object.

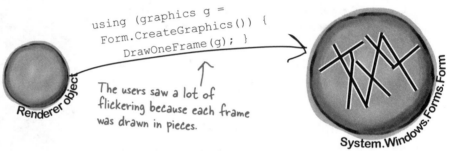

```
using (graphics g =
    Form.CreateGraphics()) {
        DrawOneFrame(g); }
```

The users saw a lot of flickering because each frame was drawn in pieces.

Renderer object

System.Windows.Forms.Form

2 To do double buffering, we can add a `Bitmap` object to the program to act as a buffer. Every time our form or control needs to be repainted, instead of drawing the graphics directly on the form, we draw on the buffer instead.

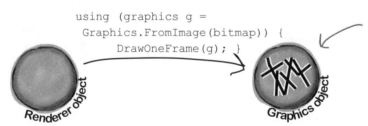

```
using (graphics g =
    Graphics.FromImage(bitmap)) {
        DrawOneFrame(g); }
```

Renderer object

Graphics object

By drawing each frame to an invisible bitmap, the users won't see the flicker any more. They'll only see the finished frame when we copy it from the bitmap back to the form.

3 Now that the frame is completely drawn out to the invisible `Bitmap` object, we can use `DrawImageUnscaled()` to copy the object back to the form's `Graphics`. It all gets copied at once, and that eliminates the flicker.

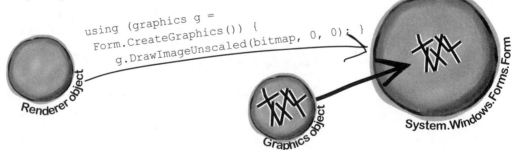

```
using (graphics g =
    Form.CreateGraphics()) {
        g.DrawImageUnscaled(bitmap, 0, 0); }
```

Renderer object

Graphics object

System.Windows.Forms.Form

Double buffering is <u>built into</u> forms and controls

You can do double buffering yourself using a `Bitmap`, but C# and .NET make it even easier with built-in support for double buffering. **All you need to do is set its `DoubleBuffered` property to true.** Try it out on your Zoomer user control—go to its Properties window, set `DoubleBuffered` to true, and your control will stop flickering! Now **go back to your `BeeControl`** and do the same. That won't fix all of the graphics problems—we'll do that in a minute—but it *will* make a difference.

Now you're ready to fix the graphics problems in the simulator!

Overhaul the beehive simulator

In the next exercise, you'll take your beehive simulator and completely overhaul it. You'll probably want to create a whole new project and use "Add >> Existing Item…" to add the current files to it so you have a backup of your current simulator. (Don't forget to change their namespace to match your new project.)

Here's what you're going to do:

> *When you use the Paint event for all your graphics, you can turn on double buffered painting simply by changing one property.*

1 **You'll start by removing the `BeeControl` user control**
There won't be any controls on the hive and field at all. No `BeeControls`, no `PictureBoxes`, nothing. The bees, flowers, and hive pictures will all be drawn using GDI+ graphics. So right-click on `BeeControl.cs` in the Solution Explorer and click Delete—they'll be removed from the project and permanently deleted.

2 **You'll need a timer to handle the bee wing flapping**
The bees flap their wings much more slowly than the simulator's frame rate, so you'll need a second, slower timer. This shouldn't be too surprising, since the `BeeControl` had its own timer to do the same thing.

3 **The big step: overhaul the renderer**
You'll need to throw out the current renderer entirely, because it does everything with controls. You won't need those lookup dictionaries, because there won't be any `PictureBoxes` or `BeeControls` to look up. Instead, it'll have two important methods: `DrawHive(g)` will draw a `Hive` form on a graphics object, and `DrawField(g)` will draw a `Field` form.

4 **Last of all, you'll hook up the new renderer**
The `Hive` and `Field` forms will need `Paint` event handlers. Each of them will call the `Renderer` object's `DrawField(g)` or `DrawHive(g)` methods. The two timers—one for telling the simulator to draw the next frame, and the other to flap the bees' wings—will call the two forms' `Invalidate()` methods to repaint themselves. When they do, their `Paint` event handlers will render the frame.

Let's get started! ⟶

Exercise

It's time to get rid of the graphics glitches in the beehive simulator. Use graphics and double buffering to make the simulator look polished.

① Change the main form's `RunFrame()` method

You'll need to remove the call to `Renderer.Render()` and add two `Invalidate()` statements.

```
public void RunFrame(object sender, EventArgs e) {
    framesRun++;
    world.Go(random);
    end = DateTime.Now;
    TimeSpan frameDuration = end - start;
    start = end;
    UpdateStats(frameDuration);
    hiveForm.Invalidate();
    fieldForm.Invalidate();
}
```

You'll need to remove the call to renderer.Render(), since that method will go away.

As long as you keep the world up to date and both forms have a reference to the renderer object, all you need to do to animate them is call their Invalidate() methods. Their Paint event handlers will take care of the rest.

② Add a second timer to the main form to make the bees' wings flap

Drag a new timer onto the main form and set its `Interval` to 150ms and `Enabled` to true. Then double-click on it and add this event handler:

```
private void timer2_Tick(object sender, EventArgs e) {
    renderer.AnimateBees();
}
```

Then add this `AnimateBees()` method to the renderer to make the bees' wings flap:

```
private int cell = 0;
private int frame = 0;
public void AnimateBees() {
    frame++;
    if (frame >= 6)
    frame = 0;
    switch (frame) {
        case 0: cell = 0; break;
        case 1: cell = 1; break;
        case 2: cell = 2; break;
        case 3: cell = 3; break;
        case 4: cell = 2; break;
        case 5: cell = 1; break;
        default: cell = 0; break;
    }
    hiveForm.Invalidate();
    fieldForm.Invalidate();
}
```

The whole idea here is to set a field called Cell that you can use when you're drawing the bees in the renderer. Make sure you're always drawing BeeAnimationLarge[Cell] in the hive form and BeeAnimationSmall[Cell] in the field form. The timer will constantly call the AnimateBees() method, which will cause the cell field to keep changing, which will cause your bees to flap their wings.

If your bees are flying to the wrong places, make sure your locations are correct! Use the `MouseClick` event trick from earlier in the chapter to find the right coordinates.

③ The hive form and field form both need a public `Renderer` property

Add a public `Renderer` property to the hive form and the field form:

```
public Renderer Renderer { get; set; }
```
←——Add this to both forms.

Don't forget to add these access modifiers!

To make this work, you'll need to **change the declaration** of your `Renderer` to add the `public` modifier: `public class Renderer`. You'll also need to **do the same** for the `World`, `Hive`, `Bee`, and `Flower` classes and the `BeeState` enum—add the `public` access modifier to each of their declarations. *(See **Leftover #2 in the Appendix** to understand why!)*

There are two places where you create a new `Renderer()`: in the open button (underneath a call to `renderer.Reset()` and in the `ResetSimulator()` method. **Remove all calls to `renderer.Reset()`.** Then update your `Renderer`'s constructor to set each form's `Renderer` property:

```
hiveForm.Renderer = this;
fieldForm.Renderer = this;
```

All the Reset() method did was remove the controls from the forms, and there won't be any controls to remove.

④ Set up the hive and field forms for double-buffered animation

Remove the code from the hive form's constructor that sets the background image. Then remove all controls from both forms and **set their `DoubleBuffered` properties to true**. Finally, add a `Paint` event handler to each of them. Here's the handler for the hive form—the field form's `Paint` event handler is identical, except that it calls `Renderer.PaintField()` instead of `Renderer.PaintHive()`:

```
private void HiveForm_Paint(object sender, PaintEventArgs e) {
    Renderer.PaintHive(e.Graphics);
}
```

Make sure you turn on double buffering, or your forms will flicker!

⑤ Overhaul the renderer by removing control-based code and adding graphics

Here's what you need to do to fix the renderer:

★ Remove the two dictionaries, since there aren't any more controls. And while you're at it, you don't need the `BeeControl` anymore, or the `Render()`, `DrawBees()`, or `DrawFlowers()` methods.

★ Add some `Bitmap` fields called `HiveInside`, `HiveOutside`, and `Flower` to store the images. Then create two `Bitmap[]` arrays called `BeeAnimationLarge` and `BeeAnimationSmall`. Each of them will hold four bee pictures—the large ones are 40×40 and the small are 20×20. Create a method called `InitializeImages()` to resize the resources and store them in these fields, and call it from the `Renderer` class constructor.

★ Add the `PaintHive()` method that takes a `Graphics` object as a parameter and paints the hive form onto it. First draw a sky blue rectangle, then use `DrawImageUnscaled()` to draw the inside hive picture, then use `DrawImageUnscaled()` to draw each bee that is inside the hive.

★ Finally, add the `PaintField()` method. It should draw a sky blue rectangle on the top half of the form, and a green rectangle on the bottom half. You'll find two form properties helpful for this: `ClientSize` and `ClientRectangle` tell you how big the drawing area is, so you can find half of its height using `ClientSize.Height / 2`. Then use `FillEllipse()` to draw a yellow sun in the sky, `DrawLine()` to draw a thick line for a branch the hive can hang from, and `DrawImageUnscaled()` to draw the outside hive picture. Then draw each flower onto the form. Finally, draw each bee (using the small bee pictures)—draw them last so they're in front of the flowers.

★ When you're drawing the bees, remember that `AnimateBees()` sets the `cell` field.

Exercise SoLution

It's time to get rid of the graphics glitches in the beehive simulator. Use graphics and double buffering to make the simulator look polished.

> Here's the complete Renderer class, including the AnimateBees() method that we gave you. Make sure you make all the modifications to the three forms—especially the Paint event handlers in the hive and field forms. Those event handlers call the renderer's PaintHive() and PaintField() methods, which do all of the animation.

```csharp
using System.Drawing;

public class Renderer {
    private World world;
    private HiveForm hiveForm;
    private FieldForm fieldForm;

    public Renderer(World TheWorld, HiveForm hiveForm, FieldForm fieldForm) {
        this.world = TheWorld;
        this.hiveForm = hiveForm;
        this.fieldForm = fieldForm;
        fieldForm.Renderer = this;
        hiveForm.Renderer = this;
        InitializeImages();
    }

    public static Bitmap ResizeImage(Image ImageToResize, int Width, int Height) {
        Bitmap bitmap = new Bitmap(Width, Height);
        using (Graphics graphics = Graphics.FromImage(bitmap)) {
            graphics.DrawImage(ImageToResize, 0, 0, Width, Height);
        }
        return bitmap;
    }

    Bitmap HiveInside;
    Bitmap HiveOutside;
    Bitmap Flower;
    Bitmap[] BeeAnimationSmall;
    Bitmap[] BeeAnimationLarge;
    private void InitializeImages() {
        HiveOutside = ResizeImage(Properties.Resources.Hive__outside_, 85, 100);
        Flower = ResizeImage(Properties.Resources.Flower, 75, 75);
        HiveInside = ResizeImage(Properties.Resources.Hive__inside_,
            hiveForm.ClientRectangle.Width, hiveForm.ClientRectangle.Height);
        BeeAnimationLarge = new Bitmap[4];
        BeeAnimationLarge[0] = ResizeImage(Properties.Resources.Bee_animation_1, 40, 40);
        BeeAnimationLarge[1] = ResizeImage(Properties.Resources.Bee_animation_2, 40, 40);
        BeeAnimationLarge[2] = ResizeImage(Properties.Resources.Bee_animation_3, 40, 40);
        BeeAnimationLarge[3] = ResizeImage(Properties.Resources.Bee_animation_4, 40, 40);
        BeeAnimationSmall = new Bitmap[4];
        BeeAnimationSmall[0] = ResizeImage(Properties.Resources.Bee_animation_1, 20, 20);
        BeeAnimationSmall[1] = ResizeImage(Properties.Resources.Bee_animation_2, 20, 20);
        BeeAnimationSmall[2] = ResizeImage(Properties.Resources.Bee_animation_3, 20, 20);
        BeeAnimationSmall[3] = ResizeImage(Properties.Resources.Bee_animation_4, 20, 20);
    }
```

> * Don't forget to change the class declaration in Renderer.cs from class Renderer to public class Renderer, and then do the same for World, Hive, Flower, and Bee; otherwise, you'll get a **build error** about field and type accessibility. Flip to Leftover #2 in the Appendix to learn about why you need to do this.

> The InitializeImages() method resizes all of the image resources and stores them in Bitmap fields inside the Renderer object. That way the PaintHive() and PaintForm() methods can draw the images unscaled using the forms' Graphics objects' DrawImageUnscaled() methods.

```
public void PaintHive(Graphics g) {
    g.FillRectangle(Brushes.SkyBlue, hiveForm.ClientRectangle);
    g.DrawImageUnscaled(HiveInside, 0, 0);
    foreach (Bee bee in world.Bees) {
        if (bee.InsideHive)
            g.DrawImageUnscaled(BeeAnimationLarge[cell],
                            bee.Location.X, bee.Location.Y);
    }
}

public void PaintField(Graphics g) {
    using (Pen brownPen = new Pen(Color.Brown, 6.0F)) {
        g.FillRectangle(Brushes.SkyBlue, 0, 0,
                fieldForm.ClientSize.Width, fieldForm.ClientSize.Height / 2);
        g.FillEllipse(Brushes.Yellow, new RectangleF(50, 15, 70, 70));
        g.FillRectangle(Brushes.Green, 0, fieldForm.ClientSize.Height / 2,
                fieldForm.ClientSize.Width, fieldForm.ClientSize.Height / 2);
        g.DrawLine(brownPen, new Point(593, 0), new Point(593, 30));
        g.DrawImageUnscaled(HiveOutside, 550, 20);
        foreach (Flower flower in world.Flowers) {
            g.DrawImageUnscaled(Flower, flower.Location.X, flower.Location.Y);
        }
        foreach (Bee bee in world.Bees) {
            if (!bee.InsideHive)
                g.DrawImageUnscaled(BeeAnimationSmall[cell],
                                bee.Location.X, bee.Location.Y);
        }
    }
}


private int cell = 0;
private int frame = 0;
public void AnimateBees() {
    frame++;
    if (frame >= 6)
    frame = 0;
    switch (frame) {
        case 0: cell = 0; break;
        case 1: cell = 1; break;
        case 2: cell = 2; break;
        case 3: cell = 3; break;
        case 4: cell = 2; break;
        case 5: cell = 1; break;
        default: cell = 0; break;
    }
    hiveForm.Invalidate();
    fieldForm.Invalidate();
}

}
```

A form's ClientSize property is a Rectangle that tells you how big its drawing area is.

The PaintField() method looks at the bees and flowers in the world and draws a field using their locations. First it draws the sky and the ground, then it draws the sun, and then the beehive. After that, it draws the flowers and the bees. It's important that everything is drawn in the right order—if it were to draw the flowers before the bees, then the bees would look like they were flying behind the flowers.

Here's the same AnimateBees() method from the exercise. It cycles through the animations using the Frame field—first it shows cell 0, then cell 1, then 2, then 3, and then back to 2, then 1 again. That way the wing flapping animation is smooth.

Use a Graphics object and an event handler for printing

The Graphics methods you've been using to draw on your forms are **the same ones you use to print**. .NET's printing objects in System.Drawing.Printing make it really easy to add printing and print preview to your applications. All you need to do is **create a PrintDocument object**. It's got an event called PrintPage, which you can use exactly like you use a timer's Tick event. Then call the PrintDocument object's Print() method, and it prints the document. And remember, the IDE makes it especially easy to add the event handler. Here's how:

Print this

1 **Start a new Windows application** and add a button to the form. Go to the form code and add a **using System.Drawing.Printing;** line to the top. Double-click on the button and add the event handler. Watch what happens as soon as you type **+=**:

```
private void button1_Click(object sender, EventArgs e) {
    PrintDocument document = new PrintDocument();
    document.PrintPage +=
```
`new PrintPageEventHandler(document_PrintPage);     (Press TAB to insert)`

2 Press Tab and the IDE automatically fills in the rest of the line. This is just like how you added event handlers in Chapter 11:

```
private void button1_Click(object sender, EventArgs e) {
    PrintDocument document = new PrintDocument();
    document.PrintPage += new PrintPageEventHandler(document_PrintPage);
```
`Press TAB to generate handler 'document_PrintPage' in this clas`

3 As soon as you press Tab, the IDE generates an event handler method and adds it to the form.

```
void document_PrintPage(object sender, PrintPageEventArgs e) {
    throw new NotImplementedException();
}
```

Now you can put ANY graphics code here—just replace the throw line and use e.Graphics for all of the drawing. We'll show you how in a minute....

The PrintPageEventArgs parameter e has a Graphics property. Just replace the throw statement with code that calls the e.Graphics object's drawing methods.

4 Now finish off the button1_Click event handler by calling **document.Print()**. When that method is called, the PrintDocument object creates a Graphics object and then fires off a PrintPage event with the Graphics object as a parameter. Anything that the event handler draws onto the Graphics object will get sent to the printer.

```
private void button1_Click(object sender, EventArgs e) {
    PrintDocument document = new PrintDocument();
    document.PrintPage += new PrintPageEventHandler(document_PrintPage);
    document.Print();
}
```

PrintDocument works with the print dialog and print preview window objects

Adding a print preview window or a print dialog box is a lot like adding an open or save dialog box. All you need to do is create a `PrintDialog` or `PrintPreviewDialog` object, set its `Document` property to your `Document` object, and then call the dialog's `Show()` method. The dialog will take care of sending the document to the printer—no need to call its `Print()` method. So let's add this to the button you created in Step 1:

> Once you've got a PrintDocument and an event handler to print the page, you can pop up a print preview window just by creating a new PrintPreviewDialog object.

5
```csharp
private void button1_Click(object sender, EventArgs e) {
    PrintDocument document = new PrintDocument();
    document.PrintPage += new PrintPageEventHandler(document_PrintPage);
    PrintPreviewDialog preview = new PrintPreviewDialog();    ←
    preview.Document = document;
    preview.ShowDialog(this);
}

void document_PrintPage(object sender,
                               PrintPageEventArgs e) {
    DrawBee(e.Graphics, new Rectangle(0, 0, 300, 300));
}
```
We'll reuse our DrawBee() method from a few pages ago.

Use e.HasMorePages to print multipage documents

If you need to print more than one page, all you need to do is have your `PrintPage` event handler set `e.HasMorePages` to true. That tells the `Document` that you've got another page to print. It'll call the event handler over and over again, once per page, as long as the event handler keeps setting `e.HasMorePages` to true. So modify your `Document`'s event handler to print two pages:

6
```csharp
bool firstPage = true;
void document_PrintPage(object sender, PrintPageEventArgs e) {
    DrawBee(e.Graphics, new Rectangle(0, 0, 300, 300));
    using (Font font = new Font("Arial", 36, FontStyle.Bold)) {
        if (firstPage) {
            e.Graphics.DrawString("First page", Font, Brushes.Black, 0, 0);
            e.HasMorePages = true;
            firstPage = false;
        } else {
            e.Graphics.DrawString("Second page", Font, Brushes.Black, 0, 0);
            firstPage = true;
        }
    }
}
```
If you set e.HasMorePages to true, the Document object will call the event handler again to print the next page.

Now run your program again, and make sure it's displaying two pages in the print preview.

print the world

Exercise

Write the code for the `Print` button in the simulator so that it pops up a print preview window showing the bee stats and pictures of the hive and the field.

① **Make the button pop up a print preview window**

Add an event handler for the button's click event that pauses the simulator, pops up the print preview dialog, and then resumes the simulator when it's done. (If the simulator is paused when the button is clicked, make sure it stays paused after the preview is shown.)

② **Create the document's `PrintPage` event handler**

It should create a page that looks exactly like the one on the facing page. We'll start you off:

```
private void document_PrintPage(object sender, PrintPageEventArgs e) {
    Graphics g = e.Graphics;
    Size stringSize;
    using (Font arial24bold = new Font("Arial", 24, FontStyle.Bold)) {
        stringSize = Size.Ceiling(
            g.MeasureString("Bee Simulator", arial24bold));
        g.FillEllipse(Brushes.Gray,
            new Rectangle(e.MarginBounds.X + 2, e.MarginBounds.Y + 2,
            stringSize.Width + 30, stringSize.Height + 30));
        g.FillEllipse(Brushes.Black,
            new Rectangle(e.MarginBounds.X, e.MarginBounds.Y,
            stringSize.Width + 30, stringSize.Height + 30));
        g.DrawString("Bee Simulator", arial24bold,
            Brushes.Gray, e.MarginBounds.X + 17, e.MarginBounds.Y + 17);
        g.DrawString("Bee Simulator", arial24bold,
            Brushes.White, e.MarginBounds.X + 15, e.MarginBounds.Y + 15);
    }
    int tableX = e.MarginBounds.X + (int)stringSize.Width + 50;
    int tableWidth = e.MarginBounds.X + e.MarginBounds.Width - tableX - 20;
    int firstColumnX = tableX + 2;
    int secondColumnX = tableX + (tableWidth / 2) + 5;
    int tableY = e.MarginBounds.Y;
    // Your job: fill in the rest of the method to make it print this
```

We created the oval with text in it using the MeasureString() method, which returns a Size that contains the size of a string. We drew the oval and text twice to give it a shadow effect.

You'll need these to build the table.

③ **This `PrintTableRow()` method will come in handy**

You'll find this method useful when you create the table of bee stats at the top of the page.

```
private int PrintTableRow(Graphics printGraphics, int tableX,
                int tableWidth, int firstColumnX, int secondColumnX,
                int tableY, string firstColumn, string secondColumn) {
    Font arial12 = new Font("Arial", 12);
    Size stringSize = Size.Ceiling(printGraphics.MeasureString(firstColumn, arial12)
    tableY += 2;
    printGraphics.DrawString(firstColumn, arial12, Brushes.Black,
                firstColumnX, tableY);
    printGraphics.DrawString(secondColumn, arial12, Brushes.Black,
                secondColumnX, tableY);
    tableY += (int)stringSize.Height + 2;
    printGraphics.DrawLine(Pens.Black, tableX, tableY, tableX + tableWidth, tableY);
    arial12.Dispose();
    return tableY;
}
```

Each time you call PrintTableRow(), it adds the height of the row it printed to tableY and returns the new value.

Take a close look at the notes we wrote on the printout. This is a little complex—take your time!

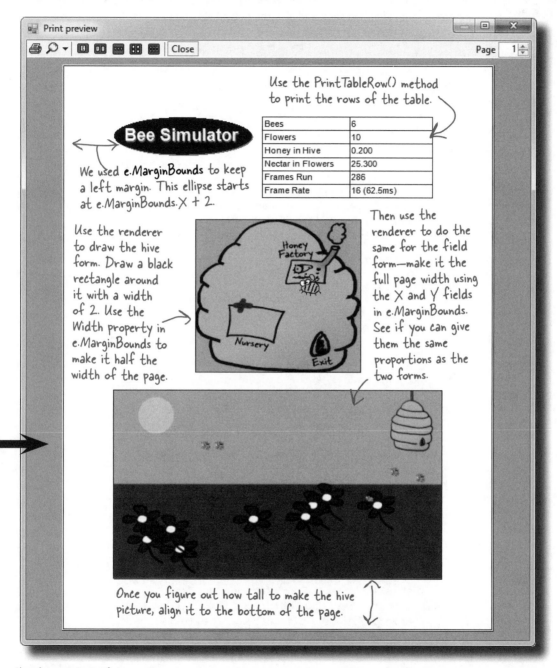

Use the PrintTableRow() method to print the rows of the table.

Bees	6
Flowers	10
Honey in Hive	0.200
Nectar in Flowers	25.300
Frames Run	286
Frame Rate	16 (62.5ms)

We used **e.MarginBounds** to keep a left margin. This ellipse starts at e.MarginBounds.X + 2.

Use the renderer to draw the hive form. Draw a black rectangle around it with a width of 2. Use the Width property in e.MarginBounds to make it half the width of the page.

Then use the renderer to do the same for the field form—make it the full page width using the X and Y fields in e.MarginBounds. See if you can give them the same proportions as the two forms.

Once you figure out how tall to make the hive picture, align it to the bottom of the page.

Here's a hint: To find the height of each form, find the ratio of its height divided by its width and multiply that by the final width. You can locate the top of the field form by subtracting its height from the bottom margin of the page: (e.MarginBounds.Y + e.MarginBounds.Height – fieldHeight).

Exercise Solution

Write the code for the Print button in the simulator so that it pops up a print preview window showing the bee stats and pictures of the hive and the field.

Here's the event handler for the Document's PrintPage event. It goes in the form.

```csharp
using System.Drawing.Printing;

private void document_PrintPage(object sender, PrintPageEventArgs e) {
    Graphics g = e.Graphics;

    Size stringSize;
    using (Font arial24bold = new Font("Arial", 24, FontStyle.Bold)) {
        stringSize = Size.Ceiling(
                g.MeasureString("Bee Simulator", arial24bold));
        g.FillEllipse(Brushes.Gray,
            new Rectangle(e.MarginBounds.X + 2, e.MarginBounds.Y + 2,
            stringSize.Width + 30, stringSize.Height + 30));
        g.FillEllipse(Brushes.Black,
            new Rectangle(e.MarginBounds.X, e.MarginBounds.Y,
            stringSize.Width + 30, stringSize.Height + 30));
        g.DrawString("Bee Simulator", arial24bold,
            Brushes.Gray, e.MarginBounds.X + 17, e.MarginBounds.Y + 17);
        g.DrawString("Bee Simulator", arial24bold,
            Brushes.White, e.MarginBounds.X + 15, e.MarginBounds.Y + 15);
    }

    int tableX = e.MarginBounds.X + (int)stringSize.Width + 50;
    int tableWidth = e.MarginBounds.X + e.MarginBounds.Width - tableX - 20;
    int firstColumnX = tableX + 2;
    int secondColumnX = tableX + (tableWidth / 2) + 5;
    int tableY = e.MarginBounds.Y;

    tableY = PrintTableRow(g, tableX, tableWidth, firstColumnX,
        secondColumnX, tableY, "Bees", Bees.Text);
    tableY = PrintTableRow(g, tableX, tableWidth, firstColumnX,
        secondColumnX, tableY, "Flowers", Flowers.Text);
    tableY = PrintTableRow(g, tableX, tableWidth, firstColumnX,
        secondColumnX, tableY, "Honey in Hive", HoneyInHive.Text);
    tableY = PrintTableRow(g, tableX, tableWidth, firstColumnX,
        secondColumnX, tableY, "Nectar in Flowers", NectarInFlowers.Text);
    tableY = PrintTableRow(g, tableX, tableWidth, firstColumnX,
        secondColumnX, tableY, "Frames Run", FramesRun.Text);
    tableY = PrintTableRow(g, tableX, tableWidth, firstColumnX,
        secondColumnX, tableY, "Frame Rate", FrameRate.Text);

    g.DrawRectangle(Pens.Black, tableX, e.MarginBounds.Y,
        tableWidth, tableY - e.MarginBounds.Y);
    g.DrawLine(Pens.Black, secondColumnX, e.MarginBounds.Y,
        secondColumnX, tableY);
```

We gave you this part already. It draws the oval header, and sets up variables that you'll use to draw the table of bee stats.

Did you figure out how the PrintTableRow() method works? All you need to do is call it once per row, and it prints whatever text you want in the two columns. The trick is that it returns the new tableY value for the next row.

Don't forget to draw the rectangle around the table and the line between the columns.

```
           using (Pen blackPen = new Pen(Brushes.Black, 2))
           using (Bitmap hiveBitmap = new Bitmap(hiveForm.ClientSize.Width,
                                            hiveForm.ClientSize.Height))
           using (Bitmap fieldBitmap = new Bitmap(fieldForm.ClientSize.Width,
                                            fieldForm.ClientSize.Height))

           using (Graphics hiveGraphics = Graphics.FromImage(hiveBitmap))
           {
               renderer.PaintHive(hiveGraphics);
           }

           int hiveWidth = e.MarginBounds.Width / 2;
           float ratio = (float)hiveBitmap.Height / (float)hiveBitmap.Width;
           int hiveHeight = (int)(hiveWidth * ratio);
           int hiveX = e.MarginBounds.X + (e.MarginBounds.Width - hiveWidth) / 2;
           int hiveY = e.MarginBounds.Height / 3;
           g.DrawImage(hiveBitmap, hiveX, hiveY, hiveWidth, hiveHeight);
           g.DrawRectangle(blackPen, hiveX, hiveY, hiveWidth, hiveHeight);

           using (Graphics fieldGraphics = Graphics.FromImage(fieldBitmap))
           {
               renderer.PaintField(fieldGraphics);
           }
           int fieldWidth = e.MarginBounds.Width;
           ratio = (float)fieldBitmap.Height / (float)fieldBitmap.Width;
           int fieldHeight = (int)(fieldWidth * ratio);
           int fieldX = e.MarginBounds.X;
           int fieldY = e.MarginBounds.Y + e.MarginBounds.Height - fieldHeight;
           g.DrawImage(fieldBitmap, fieldX, fieldY, fieldWidth, fieldHeight);
           g.DrawRectangle(blackPen, fieldX, fieldY, fieldWidth, fieldHeight);
       }
   }


   private void printToolStripButton1_Click(object sender, EventArgs e) {
       bool stoppedTimer = false;
       if (timer1.Enabled) {
           timer1.Stop();
           stoppedTimer = true;
       }
       PrintPreviewDialog preview = new PrintPreviewDialog();
       PrintDocument document = new PrintDocument();
       preview.Document = document;
       document.PrintPage += new PrintPageEventHandler(document_PrintPage);
       preview.ShowDialog(this);
       if (stoppedTimer)
           timer1.Start();
   }
```

There's so much more to be done...

You've built a pretty neat little simulator, but why stop now?
There's a whole lot more that you can do on your own. Here are
some ideas—see if you can implement some of them.

Add a control panel

Convert the constants in the World and Hive classes to properties. Then
add a new form with a control panel that has sliders to control them.

Add enemies

Add enemies that attack the hive. The more flowers there are, the more
enemies are attracted to the hive. Then add Sting Patrol bees to defend
against the enemies, and Hive Maintenance bees to defend and repair
the hive. Those bees take extra honey.

Add hive upgrades

If the hive gets enough honey, it gets bigger. A bigger hive can hold more
bees, but takes more honey and attracts more enemies. If enemies cause
too much damage, the hive gets smaller again.

> A good
> simulation will
> have lots of
> tradeoffs, and
> will give the
> user ways to
> decide which
> tradeoffs
> to make to
> influence the
> progress of
> the hive.

Add a queen bee who lays eggs

The eggs need Baby Bee Care worker bees to take care of them. More
honey in the hive causes the queen to lay more eggs, which need more
workers to care for them, who consume more honey.

Add animation

Animate the background of the Hive form so the sun slowly travels
across the sky. Make it get dark at night, and draw stars and a moon.
Add some perspective—make the bees get smaller the further they get
from the hive in the field of flowers.

Use your imagination!

Try to think of other ways you can make the simulation more interesting
or more interactive.

**Did you come up with a cool modification to the simulator? Show off
your skills—upload your project's source code to the Head First C#
forums at www.headfirstlabs.com/books/hfcsharp/.**

CAPTAIN AMAZING

THE DEATH OF THE OBJECT

Head First Labs

$2.98 Chapter 14

Captain Amazing backs Swindler into a corner...

...but ends up trapped himself.

A FEW MINUTES FROM NOW, YOU **AND** MY ARMY WILL BE GARBAGE (COLLECTED, THAT IS)

Is this the end of Captain Amazing...?

Sharpen your pencil

Below is the code detailing the fight between Captain Amazing and Swindler (not to mention his clone army). Your job is to draw out what's going on in memory when the FinalBattle class is instantiated.

You can assume that Clones was set using a collection initializer.

```
class FinalBattle {
  public CloneFactory Factory = new CloneFactory();
  public List<Clone> Clones = new List<Clone>() { ... };
  public SwindlersEscapePlane escapePlane;

  public FinalBattle() {
    Villain swindler = new Villain(this);
    using (Superhero captainAmazing = new Superhero()) {
      Factory.PeopleInFactory.Add(captainAmazing);
      Factory.PeopleInFactory.Add(swindler);      ❶
      captainAmazing.Think("I'll take down each clone's reference,
                              one by one");
      captainAmazing.IdentifyTheClones(Clones);
      captainAmazing.RemoveTheClones(Clones);
      swindler.Think("A few minutes from now, you AND my army will be garbage");
      swindler.Think("(collected, that is!)");
      escapePlane = new SwindlersEscapePlane(swindler);   ❷
      swindler.TrapCaptainAmazing(Factory);
      MessageBox.Show("The Swindler escaped");
    }
  }
}                      ❸
```

We've gotten you started here, with what's going on in the factory object.

Draw what's going on right here, when the SwindlersEscapePlane object is instantiated.

Draw a picture of what the heap will look like exactly one second after the FinalBattle constructor runs.

```
[Serializable]
class Superhero : IDisposable {
    private List<Clone> clonesToRemove = new List<Clone>();
    public void IdentifyTheClones(List<Clone> clones) {
        foreach (Clone clone in clones)
            clonesToRemove.Add(clone);
    }
    public void RemoveTheClones(List<Clone> clones) {
        foreach (Clone clone in clonesToRemove)
            clones.Remove(clone);
        ...
    }
    ...
}
```

There's more code here (including the Dispose() method to implement IDisposable) that we aren't showing you, but you don't need it to answer this.

```
class Villain {
  private FinalBattle finalBattle;
  public Villain(FinalBattle finalBattle) {
    this.finalBattle = finalBattle;
  }
  public void TrapCaptainAmazing(CloneFactory factory) {
    factory.SelfDestruct.Tick += new EventHandler(SelfDestruct_Tick);
    factory.SelfDestruct.Interval = 600;
    factory.SelfDestruct.Start();
  }
  private void SelfDestruct_Tick(object sender, EventArgs e) {
    finalBattle.Factory = null;
  }
}
```

```
class SwindlersEscapePlane {
  public Villain PilotsSeat;
  public SwindlersEscapePlane(Villain escapee) {
    PilotsSeat = escapee;
  }
}

class CloneFactory {
  public Timer SelfDestruct = new Timer();
  public List<object> PeopleInFactory = new List<object>();
  ...
}
```

There's a Clone class that we're not showing you in this code, too. You don't need it to answer the questions.

Make sure you add labels to your objects to show the reference variables that are pointing to them.

We started the first one for you. Make sure you draw in lines showing the architecture—we drew a line from the clone factory to the Villain object, because the factory has references to it (via its PeopleInFactory field).

❶

FACTORY
CloneFactory

SWINDLER
Villain object

We've left space, as there is more to be drawn at this stage.

Don't worry about drawing the Clone and List objects—just add the objects for the Captain, the Swindler, the clone factory, and Swindler's escape plane.

❷

Your job is to draw what's going on in these two bits of memory, too.

❸

Based on your diagrams, where in the code did Captain Amazing die?

....
....
....
....

Be sure and annotate that on your diagram, too.

Sharpen your pencil
Solution

Draw what's happening in memory with the `FinalBattle` program.

① The captainAmazing reference points to a Superhero object, and the swindler reference points to a Villain object, and the clone factory's PeopleInFactory list contains references to both of them.

Here's the object you should have added to this diagram.

FACTORY
CloneFactory

CAPTAIN AMAZING
Superhero object

SWINDLER
Villain object

② The escapePlane reference now points to a new instance of the SwindlersEscapePlane object, and its PilotSeat field points to the Villain object.

As long as there's a reference to swindler from the escapePlane, he won't get garbage-collected.

FACTORY
CloneFactory

CAPTAIN AMAZING
Superhero object

SWINDLER
Villain object

ESCAPE PLANE
SwindlersEscapePlane

When the selfDestruct fires, the factory reference variable is set to null, and eligible for garbage collection. So it's gone in this drawing.

③ As soon as the factory reference was gone, it took the CloneFactory object with it—and that caused the List object referenced by its PeopleInFactory field to disappear...and that was the only thing keeping the SuperHero object alive. Now he'll be destroyed the next time the garbage collector runs.

ESCAPE PLANE
SwindlersEscapePlane

SWINDLER
Villain

SELF DESTRUCT
Timer

Based on your diagrams, where in the code did Captain Amazing die?

```
void SelfDestruct_Tick(object sender, EventArgs e) {
    finalBattle.factory = null;
}
```

One second after the FinalBattle constructor ran, the hero was gone.

Once `finalBattleFactory` was set to null, it was ready for garbage collection. And it took the last reference to the Captain with it!

Once the Superhero instance had no clone factory referencing it, it was marked for garbage collection too.

653

Your last chance to DO something... your object's finalizer

Sometimes you need to be sure something happens **before** your object gets garbage-collected, like **releasing unmanaged resources**. ◄

A special method in your object called the **finalizer** allows you to write code that will always execute when your object is destroyed. Think of it as your object's personal `finally` block: it gets executed last, no matter what.

Here's an example of a finalizer in the `Clone` class:

> In general, you'll never write a finalizer for an object that only owns <u>managed resources</u>. Everything you've encountered so far in this book has been managed—meaning managed by the CLR (including any object that ends up on the heap). But occasionally programmers need to access an underlying Windows resource that isn't part of the .NET Framework. If you find code on the Internet that uses the `[DllImport]` attribute, you might be using an <u>unmanaged resource</u>. And some of those non-.NET resources might leave your system unstable if they're not "cleaned up" somehow (maybe by calling a method). And that's what finalizers are for.

```
[Serializable]
class Clone {
  string Location;
  int CloneID;

  public Clone (int cloneID, string location){
    this.CloneID = cloneID;
    this.Location = location;
  }

  public void TellLocation(string location, int cloneID){
    Console.WriteLine("My Identification number is {0} and " +
                      "you can find me here: {1}.", cloneID, location);
  }

  public void WreakHavoc(){...}

  ~Clone() {
    TellLocation(this.Location, this.CloneID);
    Console.WriteLine ("{0} has been destroyed", CloneID);
  }
}
```

Here's the constructor. It looks like the CloneID and Location fields are populated any time a Clone gets created.

This ~ (or "tilde") character says that the code in this block gets run when the object is garbage-collected.

This is the finalizer. It sends a message to the villain telling the ill-fated clone's location and ID. But it will only run when the object is garbage-collected.

You write a finalizer method just like a constructor, but instead of an access modifier, you put a ~ in front of the class name. That tells .NET that the code in the finalizer block should be run right before it garbage-collects the object.

Also, finalizers can't have parameters, because .NET doesn't need to tell it anything other than "you're done!"

Watch it!

Some of this code is for <u>learning purposes only</u>, not for your real programs.

*Throughout the book we've made reference to how objects "eventually" get garbage-collected, but we never really specified exactly when that happens...just that it happens sometime after the reference to the object disappears. We're about to show you some code that automatically triggers garbage collection **using GC.Collect()** and **pops up a MessageBox in a finalizer**. These things mess with the "guts" of the CLR. We're doing this to teach you about garbage collection. **Never do this outside of toy programs.***

When **<u>EXACTLY</u>** does a finalizer run?

The finalizer for your object runs **after** all references are gone, but **before** that object gets garbage-collected. And garbage collection happens after **all** references to your object go away. But garbage collection doesn't always happen *right after* the references are gone.

Suppose you have an object with a reference to it. .NET sends the garbage collector to work, and it checks out your object. But since there are references to your object, the garbage collector ignores it and moves along. Your object keeps living on in memory.

Then, something happens. That last object holding a reference to *your* object decides to move on. Now, your object is sitting in memory, with no references. It can't be accessed. It's basically a **dead object**.

But here's the thing. ***Garbage collection is something that .NET controls,*** not your objects. So if the garbage collector isn't sent out again for, say, a few seconds, or maybe even a few minutes, your object still lives on in memory. It's unusable, but it hasn't been garbage-collected. **And any finalizer your object has does not (yet) get run.**

Finally, .NET sends the garbage collector out again. Your finalizer runs…possibly several minutes after the last reference to the object was removed or changed. Now that it's been finalized, your object is dead, and the collector tosses it away.

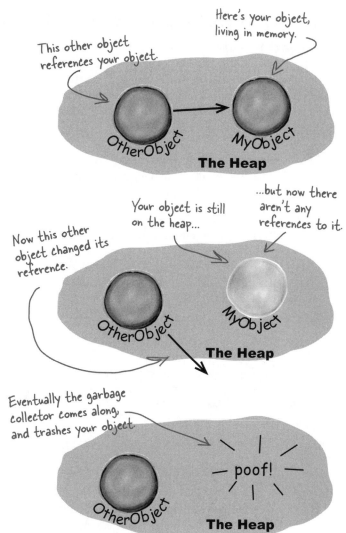

This other object references your object.

Here's your object, living in memory.

OtherObject → MyObject

The Heap

Your object is still on the heap…

…but now there aren't any references to it.

Now this other object changed its reference.

OtherObject   MyObject

The Heap

Eventually the garbage collector comes along, and trashes your object.

— poof! —

OtherObject

The Heap

You can **<u>SUGGEST</u>** to .NET that it's time to collect the garbage

.NET does let you *suggest* that garbage collection would be a good idea. **Most times, you'll never use this method, because garbage collection is tuned to respond to a lot of conditions in the CLR and calling it *isn't really a good idea.*** But just to see how a finalizer works, you could call for garbage collection on your own. If that's what you want to do, just call `GC.Collect()`.

Be careful, though. That method doesn't *force* .NET to garbage-collect things immediately. It just says, "Do garbage collection as soon as possible."

```
public void RemoveTheClones(
              List<Clone> clones) {
   foreach (Clone clone in clonesToRemove)
      clones.Remove(clone);
   GC.Collect();
}
```

We can't emphasize enough just how bad an idea it is to use GC.Collect() in a program that's not just a toy, because it can really confuse the CLR's garbage collector. It's an excellent tool for **learning** about garbage collection and finalizers, so we'll build a toy to play with it.

out.

Dispose() works with using, finalizers work with garbage collection

And like you saw earlier, Dispose() works without using as well. When you write a Dispose() method, it shouldn't have any side effects that cause problems if it's run many times.

`Dispose()` runs whenever an object that is created in a `using` statement is set to null or loses all of its references. If you don't use a `using` statement, then just setting the reference to null won't cause `Dispose()` to be called—you'll need to call it directly. An object's finalizer runs at garbage collection for that particular object. Let's create a couple of objects, and see how these two methods differ:

Do this!

1 **Create a `Clone` class and make sure it implements `IDisposable`**
The class should have one `int` automatic property called Id. It has a constructor, a `Dispose()` method, and a finalizer:

```
class Clone : IDisposable {
    public int Id { get; private set; }

    public Clone(int Id) {
        this.Id = Id;
    }

    public void Dispose() {
        MessageBox.Show("I've been disposed!",
                "Clone #" + Id + " says...");
    }

    ~Clone() {
        MessageBox.Show("Aaargh! You got me!",
                "Clone #" + Id + " says...");
    }
}
```

Since the class implements IDisposable, it has to have a Dispose() method.

Just a reminder: popping up a MessageBox in a finalizer can mess with the "guts" of the CLR. Don't do it outside of a toy program for learning about garbage collection.

Here's the finalizer. It will run when the object gets garbage-collected.

2 **Create a `Form` with three buttons**
Create one instance of `Clone` inside the `Click` handler for the first button with a `using` statement. Here's the first part of the code for the button:

Here's the form you should create.

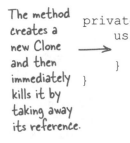

```
private void clone1_Click(object sender, EventArgs e) {
    using (Clone clone1 = new Clone(1)) {
        // Do nothing!
    }
}
```

The method creates a new Clone and then immediately kills it by taking away its reference.

Since we declared clone1 with a using statement, its Dispose() method gets run.

As soon as the using block is done and the Clone object's Dispose() method is called, there's no more reference to it and it gets marked for garbage collection.

3 **Implement the other two buttons**

Create another instance of `Clone` in the second button's `Click` handler, and set it to null manually:

```
private void clone2_Click(object sender, EventArgs e) {
    Clone clone2 = new Clone(2);
    clone2 = null;
}
```

Since this doesn't use a using statement, Dispose() won't ever get run, but the finalizer will.

For the third button, add a call to `GC.Collect()` to suggest garbage collection occur.

```
private void gc_Click(object sender, EventArgs e) {
    GC.Collect();
}
```

This suggests that garbage collection run.

Remember, normally it's not a great idea to do this. But it's fine here, because it's a good way to learn about garbage collection.

4 **Run the program and play with `Dispose()` and finalizers**

Click on the first button and check out the message box: `Dispose()` runs first.

Even though the Clone1 object has been set to null and its Dispose method has run, it's still on the heap waiting for garbage collection.

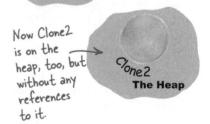

Garbage is collected...***eventually***. In most cases, you ***won't*** see the garbage collection message box, because your object is set to null, but garbage collection hasn't run yet.

Now click on the second button...nothing happens, right? That's because we didn't use a `using` statement, so there's no `Dispose()` method. And until the garbage collector runs, you won't see the message boxes from the finalizer.

Now click the third button, to suggest garbage collection. You should see the finalizer from both `Clone1` and `Clone2` fire up and display message boxes.

Now Clone2 is on the heap, too, but without any references to it.

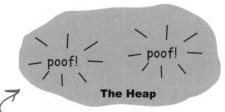

When GC.Collect() is run, both objects run their finalizers and disappear.

Play around with the program. Click the Clone #1 button, then the Clone #2 button, then the GC button. Do it a few times. Sometimes Clone #1 is collected first, and sometimes Clone #2 is. And once in a while, the garbage collector runs even though you didn't ask it to using `GC.Collect()`.

Finalizers <u>can't</u> depend on stability

When you write a finalizer, you can't depend on it running at any one time. Even if you call GC.Collect()—which you should avoid, unless you have a really good reason to do it—you're only *suggesting* that the garbage collector is run. It's not a guarantee that it'll happen right away. And when it does, you have no way of knowing what order the objects will be collected in.

So what does that mean, in practical terms? Well, think about what happens if you've got two objects that have references to each other. If object #1 is collected first, then object #2's reference to it is pointing to an object that's no longer there. But if object #2 is collected first, then object #1's reference is invalid. So what that means is that *you can't depend on references in your object's finalizer*. Which means that it's a really bad idea to try to do something inside a finalizer that depends on references being valid.

Serialization is a really good example of something that you **shouldn't do inside a finalizer**. If your object's got a bunch of references to other objects, serialization depends on *all* of those objects still being in memory… and all of the objects they reference, and the ones those objects reference, and so on. So if you try to serialize when garbage collection is happening, you could end up **missing** vital parts of your program because some objects might've been collected *before* the finalizer ran.

Luckily, C# gives us a really good solution to this: IDisposable. Anything that could modify your core data or that depends on other objects being in memory needs to happen as part of a Dispose() method, not a finalizer.

Some people like to think of a finalizers as a kind of fail-safe for the Dispose() method. And that makes sense—you saw with your Clone object that just because you implement IDisposable, that doesn't mean the object's Dispose() method will get called. But you need to be careful—if your Dispose() method depends on other objects that are on the heap, then calling Dispose() from your finalizer can cause trouble. The best way around this is to make sure you **always use a using statement** any time you're creating an IDisposable object.

Let's say you've got two objects that have references to each other...

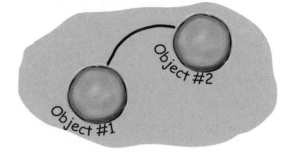

...if they're both marked for garbage collection at the same time, then object #1 could disappear first...

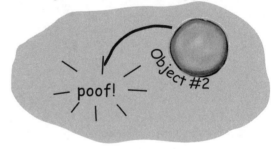

...on the other hand, object #2 could disappear before object #1. You've got no way of knowing the order...

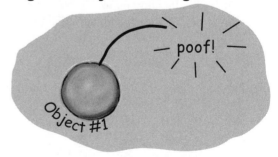

...and that's why one object's finalizer can't rely on any other object still being on the heap.

Make an object serialize itself in its Dispose()

Once you understand the difference between `Dispose()` and a finalizer, it's pretty easy to write objects that serialize themselves out automatically when they're disposed of.

Do this!

1 Make the `Clone` class (from page 656) serializable
Just add the `Serializeable` attribute on top of the class so that we can save the file

```
[Serializable]
class Clone : IDisposable
```

2 Modify `Clone`'s `Dispose()` method to `Serialize` itself out to a file
Let's use a `BinaryFormatter` to write `Clone` out to a file in `Dispose()`:

```csharp
using System.IO;
using System.Runtime.Serialization.Formatters.Binary;

// existing code

public void Dispose() {
   string filename = @"C:\Temp\Clone.dat";
   string dirname = @"C:\Temp\";
   if (File.Exists(filename) == false) {
     Directory.CreateDirectory(dirname);
   }
   BinaryFormatter bf = new BinaryFormatter();
   using (Stream output = File.OpenWrite(filename)) {
     bf.Serialize(output, this);
   }
   MessageBox.Show("Must...serialize...object!",
                  "Clone #" + ID + " says...");
}
```

You'll need a few more using directives to access the I/O classes we'll use.

The Clone will create the C:\Temp directory and serialize itself out to a file called Clone.dat.

We hardcoded the filename—we included them as string literals in the code. That's fine for a small toy program like this, but it's not problem-free. Can you think of problems this might cause, and how you could avoid them?

3 Run the application.
You'll see the same behavior you saw on the last few pages...but before the Clone1 object is garbage-collected, it's serialized to a file. Look inside the file and you'll see the binary representation of the object.

And is this Dispose() method really side-effect free? What happens if it's called more than once? These are all things you need to think about when you implement IDisposable.

**BRAIN POWER**

What do you think the rest of the `SuperHero` object's code looked like? We showed you part of it on page 650. Could you write the rest now?

Fireside Chats

Tonight's talk: **The Dispose() method and a finalizer spar over who's more valuable.**

| **Dispose():** | **Finalizer:** |

Dispose():

To be honest, I'm a little surprised I was invited here. I thought the programming world had come to a consensus. I mean, I'm way more valuable than you are. Really, you're pretty feeble. You can't even serialize yourself out, alter core data, anything. Pretty unstable, aren't you?

Finalizer:

Excuse me? That's rich. I'm feeble…OK. Well, I didn't want to get into this, but since we're already stooping this low…at least I don't need an interface to get started. Without IDisposable, you're just another useless method.

There's an interface specifically **because** I'm so important. In fact, I'm the only method in it!

Right, right…keep telling yourself that. And what happens when someone forgets to use a using statement when they instantiate their object? Then you're nowhere to be found.

OK, you're right, programmers need to know they're going to need me and either call me directly or use a using statement to call me. But they always know when I'm gonna run, and they can use me to do whatever they need to do to clean up after their object. I'm powerful, reliable, and easy to use. I'm a triple threat. And you? Nobody knows exactly when you'll run or what the state of the application will be when you finally do decide to show up.

> Handles are what your programs use w
> they go around .NET and the CLR a
> interact directly with Windows. Since
> .NET doesn't know about them, it can
> clean them up for you.

OK, but if you need to do something at the very last moment when an object is garbage-collected, there's no way to do it without me. I can free up network resources and Windows handles and streams and anything else that might cause a problem for the rest of the program if you don't clean it up. I can make sure that your objects deal with being trashed more gracefully, and that's nothing to sneeze at.

So there's basically nothing you can do that I can't do. But you think you're a big shot because you run when garbage collection happens.

I'll take that over your flash and attitude any day, pal.

Q: Can a finalizer use all of an object's fields and methods?

A: Sure. While you can't pass parameters to a finalizer method, you can use any of the fields in an object, either directly or using `this`—but be careful, because if those fields reference other objects, then the other objects may have already been garbage-collected. But you can definitely call other methods in the object being finalized (as long as those methods don't depend on other objects).

Q: What happens to exceptions that get thrown in a finalizer?

A: Good question. It's totally legal to put a `try`/`catch` block inside a finalizer method. Give it a try yourself. Create a divide-by-zero exception inside a `try` block in the `Clone` program we just wrote. Catch it and throw up a message box that says "I just caught an exception." right before the "...I've been destroyed." box we'd already written. Now run the program and click on the first button and then the GC button. You'll see both the exception box and the destroyed box pop up. (Of course, it's generally a **really bad idea** to pop up message boxes in finalizers for objects that are more than just toys...and those message boxes may never actually pop up.)

Q: How often does the garbage collector run automatically?

A: There's no good answer to that one. It doesn't run on an easily predictable cycle, and you don't have any firm control over it. You can be sure it will be run when your program exits. But if you want to be sure it'll run, you have to use `GC.Collect()` to set it off...and even then, timing is an issue.

Q: How soon after I call `GC.Collect()` will .NET start garbage collection?

A: When you run `GC.Collect()`, you're telling .NET to garbage collect as soon as possible. That's *usually* as soon as .NET finishes whatever it's doing. That means it'll happen pretty soon, but you can't actually control when.

Q: If I absolutely need something to run, I put it in a finalizer, right?

A: It's possible that your finalizer won't run. It's possible to suppress finalizers when garbage collection happens. Or the process could end entirely. But as a general rule, your finalizer should run.

A struct <u>looks</u> like an object...

One of the types in .NET we haven't talked about much is the `struct`. `struct` is short for **structure**, and `struct`s look a lot like objects. They have fields and properties, just like objects. And you can even pass them into a method that takes an `object` type parameter:

```
public struct AlmostSuperhero : IDisposable {
    public int SuperStrength;
    public int SuperSpeed { get; private set; }

    public void RemoveVillain(Villain villain)
    {
        Console.WriteLine("OK, " + villain.Name +
            " surrender and stop all the madness!");
        if (villain.Surrendered)
            villain.GoToJail();
        else
            villain.Kill();
    }

    public void Dispose() { ... }
}
```

Structs can implement interfaces but can't subclass other classes. And structs are sealed, so they can't be subclassed.

A struct can have properties and fields...

...and define methods.

...but <u>isn't</u> an object

But `struct`s **aren't** objects. They can have methods and fields, but they can't have finalizers. They also can't inherit from other classes or `struct`s, or have classes or `struct`s inherit from them.

All structs inherit from System.ValueType, which in turn inherits from System. Object. That's why every struct has a ToString() method — it gets it from Object. But that's all the inheriting that structs are allowed to do.

SuperHero

Structs can't inherit from other objects.

struct

You can mimic a standalone object with a struct, but structs don't stand in very well for complex inheritance hierarchies.

That's why you use classes a lot more than structs. But that doesn't mean they don't have their uses!

The power of objects lies in their ability to mimic real-world behavior, through inheritance and polymorphism.

Structs are best used for storing data, but the lack of inheritance and references can be a serious limitation.

But the thing that sets structs apart from objects more than almost anything else is that you **copy them by value, not by reference**. Flip the page to see what this means....

Values get copied; references get assigned

You already have a sense of how some types are different than others. On one hand you've got **value types** like int, bool, and decimal. On the other hand, you've got **objects** like List, Stream, and Exception. And they don't quite work exactly the same way, do they?

> Here's a quick refresher on value types vs. objects.

When you use the equals sign to set one value type variable to another, it **makes a copy of the value**, and afterward the two variables aren't connected to each other. On the other hand, when you use the equals sign with references, what you're doing is **pointing both references at the same object**.

★ Variable declaration and assignment works the same with value types or object types:

> Remember when we said that methods and statements ALWAYS live in classes? Well, it turns out that's not 100% accurate -- they can also live in structs.

```
int howMany = 25;
bool Scary = true;
List<double> temperatures = new List<double>();
Exception ex = new Exception("Does not compute");
```

> int and bool are value types, List and Exception are object types.

> These are all initialized in the same basic way.

★ Differences creep in when you start to assign values, though. Value types all are handled with copying. Here's an example:

> This line copies the value that's stored in the fifteenMore variable into the howMany variable and adds 15 to it.

> Changing the fifteenMore variable has no *effect* on howMany, and vice versa.

```
int fifteenMore = howMany;
fifteenMore += 15;
Console.WriteLine("howMany has {0}, fifteenMore has {1}",
                  howMany, fifteenMore);
```

The output here shows that fifteenMore and howMany are **not** connected:

```
howMany has 25, fifteenMore has 40
```

★ With object assignments, though, you're assigning references, not actual values:

> This line sets the differentList reference to point to the same object as the temperatures reference.

```
temperatures.Add(56.5D);
temperatures.Add(27.4D);
List<float> differentList = temperatures;
differentList.Add(62.9D);
```

> Both references point at the same actual object.

> TEMPERATURES
> DIFFERENTLIST
> List<double>

So changing the List means both references see the update…since they both point to a single List object.

```
Console.WriteLine("temperatures has {0}, differentlist has {1}",
                  temperatures.Count(), differentList.Count());
```

The output here demonstrates that differentList and temperatures are actually pointing to the **same** object:

```
temperatures has 3, differentList has 3
```

> When you called differentList.Add(), it added a new temperature to the object that both differentList and temperatures point to.

Structs are <u>value</u> types; objects are <u>reference</u> types

When you create a `struct`, you're creating a **value type**. What that means is when you use equals to set one `struct` variable equal to another, you're creating a fresh *copy* of the struct in the new variable. So even though a `struct` *looks* like an object, it doesn't act like one.

Do this

① **Create a struct called `Dog`**

Here's simple struct to keep track of a dog. It looks just like an object, but it's not. Add it to a **new console application**.

```
public struct Dog {
   public string Name;
   public string Breed;

   public Dog(string name, string breed) {
      this.Name = name;
      this.Breed = breed;
   }

   public void Speak() {
       Console.WriteLine("My name is {0} and I'm a {1}.", Name, Breed);
   }
}
```

> Yes, this is not good encapsulation. Bear with us—we're making a point.

② **Create a class called `Canine`**

Make an exact copy of the Dog struct, except **replace `struct` with `class`** and then **replace `Dog` with `Canine`**. (Don't forget to rename Dog's constructor.) Now you'll have a Canine class that you can play with, which is almost exactly equivalent to the Dog struct.

③ **Add a button that makes some copies of `Dogs` and `Canines`**

Here's the code for the `Main()` method:

```
Canine spot = new Canine("Spot", "pug");
Canine bob = spot;
bob.Name = "Spike";
bob.Breed = "beagle";
spot.Speak();

Dog jake = new Dog("Jake", "poodle");
Dog betty = jake;
betty.Name = "Betty";
betty.Breed = "pit bull";
jake.Speak();

Console.ReadKey();
```

> **You've already used structs in your programs. Remember `Point` from Chapters 12 and 13 or `DateTime` from chapter 9? Those are structs!**

Sharpen your pencil

④ **Before you press that button...**

Write down what you think will be written to the console when you run this code:

....

....

Sharpen your pencil Solution

What did you think would get written to the console?

My name is Spike and I'm a beagle.

My name is Jake and I'm a poodle.

Here's what happened...

A new Canine object was created and the spot reference points to it.

The bob and spot references both point to the same object, so both changed the same fields and accessed the same Speak() method. But structs don't work that way. When you created betty, you made a fresh copy of the data in jake. The two structs are completely independent of each other.

```
Canine spot = new Canine("Spot", "pug"); ①

Canine bob = spot; ②

bob.Name = "Spike";

bob.Breed = "beagle";

spot.Speak(); ③
```

The new reference variable bob was created, but no new object was added to the heap—the bob variable points to the same object as spot.

Since spot and bob both point to the same object, spot.Speak() and bob.Speak() both call the same method, and both of them produce the same output with "Spike" and "beagle".

```
Dog jake = new Dog("Jake", "poodle"); ④

Dog betty = jake; ⑤

betty.Name = "Betty";

betty.Breed = "pit bull";

jake.Speak(); ⑥
```

When you create a new struct, it looks really similar to creating an object—you've got a variable that you can use to access its fields and methods.

Here's the big difference. When ⑤ you added the betty variable, you created a *whole new* value.

When you set one struct equal to another, you're creating a fresh COPY of the data inside the struct. That's because struct is a VALUE TYPE.

Since you created a fresh copy of the data, jake was unaffected when you changed betty's fields.

The stack vs. the heap: more on memory

It's easy to understand how a struct differs from an object—you can make a fresh copy of a struct just using equals, which you can't do with an object. But what's really going on behind the scenes?

The .NET CLR divides your data into two places in memory. You already know that objects live on the **heap**. It also keeps another part of memory called the **stack** to store all of the local variables you declare in your methods, and the parameters that you pass into those methods. You can think of the stack as a bunch of slots that you can stick values in. When a method gets called, the CLR adds more slots to the top of the stack. When it returns, its slots are removed.

Even though you can assign a struct to an object variable, structs and objects are different.

The Code

Here's code that you might see in a program.

Here's what the stack looks like after these two lines of code run.

The Stack

This is where structs and local variables hang out.

```
Canine spot = new Canine("Spot", "pug");
Dog jake = new Dog("Jake", "poodle");
```

Dog jake
SPOT

```
Canine spot = new Canine("Spot", "pug");
Dog jake = new Dog("Jake", "poodle");
Dog betty = jake;
```

When you create a new struct—or any other value type variable—a new "slot" gets added onto the stack. That slot is a *copy* of the value in your type.

Dog betty
Dog jake
SPOT

```
Canine spot = new Canine("Spot", "pug");
Dog jake = new Dog("Jake", "poodle");
Dog betty = jake;
SpeakThreeTimes(jake);

public SpeakThreeTimes(Dog dog) {
    int i;
    for (i = 0; i < 5; i++)
        dog.Speak();
}
```

When you call a method, the CLR puts its local variables on the top of the stack. It takes them off when it's done.

int i
Dog dog
Dog betty
Dog jake
SPOT

> Wait a minute. Why do I even need to know this stuff? I can't control any of it directly, right?

You definitely want to understand how a struct you copy by value is different from an object you copy by reference.

There are times when you need to be able to write a method that can take either a value type **or** a reference type—perhaps a method that can work with either a Dog struct or a Canine object. If you find yourself in that situation, you can use the object keyword:

```
public void WalkDogOrCanine(object getsWalked) { ... }
```

If you send this method a struct, the struct gets **boxed** into a special object "wrapper" that allows it to live on the heap. While the wrapper's on the heap, you can't do much with the struct. You have to "unwrap" the struct to work with it. Luckily, all of this happens *automatically* when you set an object equal to a value type, or pass a value type into a method that expects an object.

You can also use the "is" keyword to see if an object is a struct, or any other value type, that's been boxed and put on the heap.

1 Here's what the stack and heap look like after you create an object variable and set it equal to a Dog struct.

```
Dog sid = new Dog("Sid", "husky");
Object obj = sid;
```

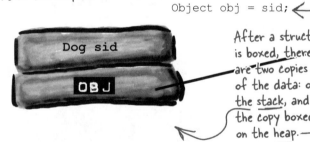

After a struct is boxed, there are two copies of the data: on the stack, and the copy boxed on the heap.

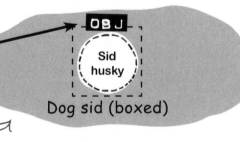

Dog sid (boxed)

2 If you want to unbox the object, all you need to do is cast it to the right type, and it gets unboxed automatically. You **can't use the as keyword with value types**, so you'll need to cast to Dog.

These are structs, so unless they're boxed, they don't live on the heap.

```
Dog happy = (Dog) obj;
```

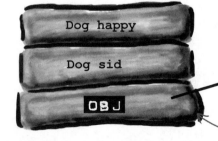

After this line runs, you've got a third copy of the data in a new struct called happy, which gets its own slot on the stack.

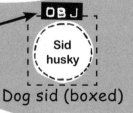

Dog sid (boxed)

When a method is called, it looks for its arguments on the stack

The stack plays an important part in how the CLR runs your programs. One thing we take for granted is the fact that you can write a method that calls another method, which in turn calls another method. In fact, a method can call itself (which is called *recursion*). The stack is what gives your programs the ability to do that.

Here are a couple of methods from a dog simulator program. They're pretty simple: FeedDog() calls Eat(), which calls CheckBowl().

```
public void FeedDog(Canine dogToFeed, Bowl dogBowl) {
    double eaten = Eat(dogToFeed.MealSize, dogBowl);
    return eaten + .05d; // A little is always spilled
}

public void Eat(double mealSize, Bowl dogBowl) {
    dogBowl.Capacity -= mealSize;
    CheckBowl(dogBowl.Capacity);
}

public void CheckBowl(double capacity) {
    if (capacity < 12.5d) {
        string message = "My bowl's almost empty!";
        Console.WriteLine(message);
    }
}
```

Remember the terminology here: a parameter is what you call the part of the method declaration that specifies the values it needs; an argument is the actual value or reference that you pass into a method when you call it.

Here's what the stack looks like as the FeedDog() method calls Eat(), which calls CheckBowl(), which calls Console.WriteLine():

1 The FeedDog() method takes two parameters, a Canine reference and a Bowl reference. So when it's called, the two arguments passed to it are on the stack.

2 FeedDog() needs to pass two arguments to the Eat() method, so they're pushed onto the stack as well.

3 As the method calls pile up and the program goes deeper into methods that call methods that call other methods, the stack gets bigger and bigger.

4 When Console.WriteLine() exits, its arguments will be popped off of the stack. That way, Eat() can keep going as if nothing had happened. That's why the stack is so useful!

Use out parameters to make a method return more than one value

Speaking of parameters and arguments, there are a few more ways that you can get values in and out of your programs, and they all involve adding **modifiers** to your method declarations. One of the most common ways of doing this is by using the **out modifier** to specify an output parameter. Here's how it works. Create a new Windows Forms application and add this empty method declaration to the form. Note the out modifiers on both parameters:

```
public int ReturnThreeValues(out double half, out int twice)
{
    return 1;
}
```

When you try to build your code, you'll see two errors: **The out parameter 'half' must be assigned a value before control leaves the current method** (and you'll get an identical message for the 'twice' parameter). Any time you use an out parameter, you *always* need to set it before the method returns—just like you always need to use a return statement if your method is declared with a return value. Here's the whole method:

```
Random random = new Random();

public int ReturnThreeValues(out double half, out int twice) {
    int value = random.Next(1000);
    half = ((double)value) / 2;
    twice = value * 2;
    return value;
}
```

This method needs to set all of its out parameters before it returns, otherwise it won't compile.

> A method can return more than one value by using out parameters.

Now that you've set the two out parameters, it compiles. So let's use them. Add a button with this event handler:

```
private void button1_Click(object sender, EventArgs e) {
    int a;
    double b;
    int c;
    a = ReturnThreeValues(b, c);
    Console.WriteLine("value = {0}, half = {1}, double = {2}", a, b, c);
}
```

Did you notice how you didn't need to initialize b and c? You don't need to initialize a variable before you use it as an argument to an out parameter.

Uh oh! There are more build errors: **Argument 1 must be passed with the out keyword**. Every time you call a method with an out parameter, you need to use the out keyword when you pass the argument to it. Here's what that line should look like:

```
a = ReturnThreeValues(out b, out c);
```

Now your program will build. When you run it, the ReturnThreeValues() methods sets the three values and returns all three of them: a gets the method's return value, b gets the value returned by the half parameter, and c gets the value returned by the twice parameter.

Pass by reference using the ref modifier

One thing you've seen over and over again is that every time you pass an `int`, `double`, `struct`, or any other value type into a method, you're passing a copy of that value to that method. There's a name for that: **pass by value**, which means that the entire value of the argument is copied.

But there's another way to pass arguments into methods, and it's called **pass by reference**. You can use the **ref** keyword to allow a method to work directly with the argument that's passed to it. Just like the `out` modifier, you need to use **ref** when you declare the method and also when you call it. It doesn't matter if it's a value type or a reference type, either—any variable that you pass to a method's `ref` parameter will be directly altered by that method.

You can see how it works—add this method to your program:

```
public void ModifyAnIntAndButton(ref int value, ref Button button) {
    int i = value;
    i *= 5;
    value = i - 3;
    button = button1;
}
```

When this method sets value and button parameters, what it's really doing is changing the values of the q and b variables in the button2_Click() method that called it.

Under the hood, an out argument is just like a ref argument, except that it doesn't need to be assigned before going into the method, and must be assigned before the method returns.

And add a button with this event handler to call the method:

```
private void button2_Click(object sender, EventArgs e) {
    int q = 100;
    Button b = button3;
    ModifyAnIntAndButton(ref q, ref b);
    Console.WriteLine("q = {0}, b.Text = {1}", q, b.Text);
}
```

This prints "q = 497, b.Text = button1" because the method actually altered the q and b variables.

When `button2_Click()` calls the `ModifyAnIntAndButton()` method, it passes its q and b variables by reference. The `ModifyAnIntAndButton()` method works them just like any other variable. But since they were passed by reference, the method was actually updating the q and b variables all along, and not just a copy of them. So when the method exits, the q and b variables are updated with the modified value.

Run the program and debug through it, adding a watch for the q and b variables to see how this works.

Built-in value types' TryParse() method uses out parameters

There's a great example of out parameters built right into some of the built-in value types. There are a lot of times that you'll want to convert a string like "35.67" into a double. And there's a method to do exactly that: double.Parse("35.67") will return the double value 35.67. But double.Parse("xyz") will throw a FormatException. Sometimes that's exactly what you want, but other times you want to check if a string can be parsed into a value. That's where the TryParse() method comes in: double.TryParse("xyz", out d) will return false and set i to 0, but double.TryParse("35.67", out d) will return true and set d to 35.67.

Also, remember back in Chapter 9 when we used a switch statement to convert "Spades" into Suits.Spades? Well, there are static methods Enum.Parse() and Enum.TryParse() that do the same thing, except for enums!

Use optional parameters to set default values

A lot of times, your methods will be called with the same arguments over and over again, but the method still needs the parameter because sometimes it's different. It would be useful if you could set a default value, so you only needed to specify the argument when calling the method if it was different.

That's exactly what optional parameters do. You can specify an optional parameter in a method declaration by using an equals sign followed by the default value for that parameter. You can have as many optional parameters as you want, but all of the optional parameters have to come after the required parameters.

Here's an example of a method that uses optional parameters to check if someone has a fever:

```
void CheckTemperature(double temperature, double tooHigh = 99.5, double tooLow = 96.5)
{
    if (temperature < tooHigh && temperature > tooLow)
        Console.WriteLine("Feeling good!");
    else
        Console.WriteLine("Uh-oh -- better see a doctor!");
}
```

This method has two optional parameters: `tooHigh` has a default value of 99.5, and `tooLow` has a default value of 96.5. Calling `CheckTemperature()` with one argument uses default values for both `tooHigh` and `tooLow`. If you call it with two arguments, it will use the second argument for the value of `tooHigh`, but still use the default value for `tooLow`. You can specify all three arguments to pass values for all three parameters.

There's another option as well. If you want to use some (but not all) of the default values, you can use **named arguments** to pass values for just those parameters that you want to pass. All you need to do is give the name of each parameter followed by a colon and its values. If you use more than one named argument, make sure you separate them with commas, just like any other argument.

Add the `CheckTemperature()` method to your form, and then add a button with the following event handler. Debug through it to make sure you understand exactly how this works:

```
private void button3_Click(object sender, EventArgs e)
{
    // Those values are fine for your average person
    CheckTemperature(101.3);

    // A dog's temperature should be between 100.5 and 102.5 Fahrenheit
    CheckTemperature(101.3, 102.5, 100.5);

    // Bob's temperature is always a little low, so set tooLow to 95.5
    CheckTemperature(96.2, tooLow: 95.5);
}
```

Use optional parameters and named arguments when you want your methods to have default values.

Use nullable types when you need nonexistent values

Take a minute and flip back to the contact cards you converted to a database way back in Chapter 1. Remember how you set up your table to allow nulls for each of its columns? That way, if someone left out a value or wrote something illegible, the database could use null to **represent that it doesn't have a value**. Normally, you could just use null. But for `structs` (and `ints`, `booleans`, and other value types), you can't set them to null. These statements:

```
bool myBool = null;
DateTime myDate = null;
```

will cause errors when you try to compile your program!

Let's say your program needs to work with a date and time value. Normally you'd use a `DateTime` variable. But what if that variable doesn't always have a value? That's where nullable types comes in really handy. All you need to do is add a question mark (?) to the end of any value type, and it becomes a **nullable type** that you can set to null.

bool? myNulableInt = null;

DateTime? myNullableDate = null;

Every nullable type has a property called `Value` that gets or sets the value. A `DateTime?` will have a `Value` of type `DateTime`, an `int?` will have one of type int, etc. They'll also have a property called `HasValue` that returns true if it's not null.

You can always convert a value type to a nullable type:

```
DateTime myDate = DateTime.Now;
DateTime? myNullableDate = myDate;
```

But you need to cast the nullable type in order to assign it back to a value type:

```
myDate = (DateTime) myNullableDate;
```

If `HasValue` is false, the `Value` property will throw an `InvalidOperationException`, and so will the cast (because that cast is equivalent to using the `Value` property).

> Did it seem odd that even the Client column was set to allow nulls? Someone's either a client or not, right? But there was no guarantee that every card has the Client blank filled in, and the database needed a way to represent that we might not know if someone's a client or not.

```
┌─────────────────────────────┐
│ Nullable<DateTime>          │
├─────────────────────────────┤
│ Value: DateTime             │
│ HasValue: bool              │
│ ...                         │
├─────────────────────────────┤
│ GetValueOrDefault(): DateTime│
│ ...                         │
│                             │
└─────────────────────────────┘
```

> Nullable<T> is a struct that lets you store a value type OR a null value. Here are some of the methods and properties on Nullable<DateTime>.

The question mark T? is an alias for Nullable<T>

When you add a question mark to any value type (like int? or decimal?), the compiler translates that to the Nullable<T> struct (Nullable<int> or Nullable<decimal>). You can see this for yourself: add a Nullable<DateTime> variable to a program, put a breakpoint on it, and add a watch for it in the debugger. You'll see System.DateTime? displayed in the watch window in the IDE. This is an example of an alias, and it's not the first one you've encountered. Hover your cursor over any int. You'll see that it translates to a struct called System.Int32:

int.Parse() and int.TryParse() are members of this struct ⟶

```
int value;
┌──────────────────────────────────────────┐
│ struct System.Int32                       │
│ Represents a 32-bit signed integer.       │
└──────────────────────────────────────────┘
```

Take a minute and do that for each of the types at the beginning of Chapter 4. Notice how all of them are aliases for structs—except for string, which is a class called System.String (it's a reference type, not a value type).

Nullable types help you make your programs more <u>robust</u>

Users do all sorts of crazy things. You think you know how people will use a program you're writing, but then someone clicks buttons in an unexpected order, or enters 256 spaces in a text box, or uses the Windows Task Manager to quit your program halfway through writing data to a file, and suddenly it's popping up all manner of errors. Remember in chapter 10 when we talked about how a program that can gracefully handle badly formatted, unexpected, or just plain bizarre input is called **robust**? Well, when you're processing raw input from your users, nullable types can be very useful in making your programs more robust. Now see for yourself— **create a new console application** and add this RobustGuy class to it:

When you add RobustGuy. ToString(), take a look at the IntelliSense window when you enter Birthday. Value. Since the Value property is a DateTime, you'll see all the usual DateTime members.

```
class RobustGuy {
    public DateTime? Birthday { get; private set; }
    public int? Height { get; private set; }

    public RobustGuy(string birthday, string height) {
        DateTime tempDate;
        if (DateTime.TryParse(birthday, out tempDate))
            Birthday = tempDate;
        else
            Birthday = null;

        int tempInt;
        if (int.TryParse(height, out tempInt))
            Height = tempInt;
        else
            Height = null;
    }

    public override string ToString() {
        string description;
        if (Birthday != null)
            description = "I was born on " + Birthday.Value.ToLongDateString();
        else
            description = "I don't know my birthday";
        if (Height != null)
            description += ", and I'm " + Height + " inches tall";
        else
            description += ", and I don't know my height";
        return description;
    }
}
```

Use the ToLongDateString() method to convert it to a human-readable string.

Use the DateTime and int TryParse() methods to attempt to convert the user input into values.

```
Ticks
TimeOfDay
ToBinary
ToFileTime
ToFileTimeUtc
ToLocalTime
ToLongDateString
ToLongTimeString
ToOADate
ToShortDateString
ToShortTimeString
ToString
ToUniversalTime
Year
```

If the user entered garbage, the Nullable types won't have values, so their HasValue() methods will return false.

Try experimenting with the other DateTime methods that start with "To" to see how they affect your program's output.

And here's the Main() method for the program. It uses **<u>Console.ReadLine()</u>** to get input from the user:

```
static void Main(string[] args) {
    Console.Write("Enter birthday: ");
    string birthday = Console.ReadLine();
    Console.Write("Enter height in inches: ");
    string height = Console.ReadLine();
    RobustGuy guy = new RobustGuy(birthday, height);
    Console.WriteLine(guy.ToString());
    Console.ReadKey();
}
```

Console.ReadLine() lets the user enter text into the console window. When the user hits enter, it returns the input as a string.

When you run the program, see what happens when you enter different values for dates. DateTime.TryParse() can figure out a lot of them. When you enter a date it can't parse, the RobustGuy's Birthday property will have no value.

Pool Puzzle

Your **job** is to take snippets from the pool and place them into the blank lines in the code. You **may** use the same snippet more than once, and you won't need to use all the snippets. Your **goal** is to make the code write this output to the console when a **new instance of the Faucet class is created**:

```
public class Faucet {
    public Faucet() {
        Table wine = new Table();
        Hinge book = new Hinge();
        wine.Set(book);
        book.Set(wine);
        wine.Lamp(10);
        book.garden.Lamp("back in");
        book.bulb *= 2;
        wine.Lamp("minutes");
        wine.Lamp(book);
    }
}
```

Output when you create a new Faucet object:

> back in 20 minutes

Here's the goal...to get this output.

```
public _____ Table {
    public string stairs;
    public Hinge floor;
    public void Set(Hinge b) {
        floor = b;
    }
    public void Lamp(object oil) {
        if (oil ____ int)
            _____.bulb = (int)oil;
        else if (oil ____ string)
            stairs = (string)oil;
        else if (oil ____ Hinge) {
            _____ vine = oil ____ _____;
            Console.WriteLine(vine.Table()
                + " " + _____.bulb + " " + stairs);
        }
    }
}


public _____ Hinge {
    public int bulb;
    public Table garden;
    public void Set(Table a) {
        garden = a;
    }
    public string Table() {
        return _____.stairs;
    }
}
```

Bonus points: Circle the lines where boxing happens.

Note: Each thing from the pool can be used more than once.

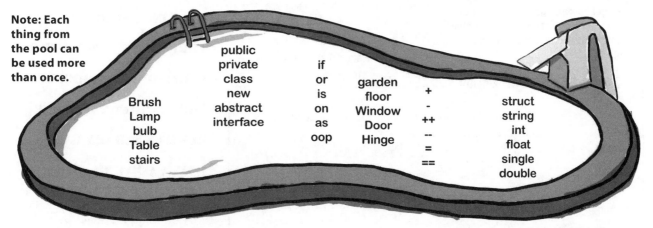

public
private
class
new
abstract
interface

Brush
Lamp
bulb
Table
stairs

if
or
is
on
as
oop

garden
floor
Window
Door
Hinge

+
-
++
--
=
==

struct
string
int
float
single
double

Answers on page 684.

Q: OK, back up a minute. Why do I care about the stack?

A: Because understanding the difference between the stack and the heap helps you keep your reference types and value types straight. It's easy to forget that structs and objects work very differently—when you use the equals sign with both of them, they look really similar. Having some idea of how .NET and the CLR handle things under the hood helps you understand *why* reference and value types are different.

Q: And boxing? Why is that important to me?

A: Because you need to know when things end up on the stack, and you need to know when data's being copied back and forth. Boxing takes extra memory and more time. When you're only doing it a few times (or a few hundred times) in your program, then you won't notice the difference. But let's say you're writing a program that does the same thing over and over again, millions of times a second. That's not too far-fetched, since that's exactly what your beehive simulator did. If you find that your program's taking up more and more memory, or going slower and slower, then it's possible that you can make it more efficient by avoiding boxing in the part of the program that repeats.

Q: I get how you get a fresh copy of a struct when you set one struct variable equal to another one. But why is that useful to me?

A: One place that's really helpful is with **encapsulation**. Take a look at this familiar code from a class that knows its location:

```
private Point location;
public Point Location {
   get { return location; }
}
```

If `Point` were a class, then this would be terrible encapsulation. It wouldn't matter that `location` is private, because you made a public read-only property that returns a reference to it, so any other object would be able to access it.

Lucky for us, `Point` is actually a struct. And that means that the public `Location` property returns a fresh copy of the point. The object that uses it can do whatever it wants to that copy—none of those changes will make it to the private `location` field.

Q: If `Point` is a struct, does that mean there are *other* structs that I've been working with all along?

A: Yes! One struct that's really useful and very common when you're working with graphics and forms is **Rectangle**. It's got some very useful methods that come in really handy when you need to figure out boundaries and check whether points are inside or outside of the rectangle. All you need to do is set its location and size, and it'll automatically compute its top, bottom, left, right, width, and height.

Another useful struct that you'll run into is **Size**. You've already seen it

in action—you used it when you were determining the size of a string using the `MeasureString()` method. It's a struct, too.

Q: How do I know whether to use a struct or a class?

A: Most of the time, programmers use classes. Structs have a lot of limitations that can really make it hard to work with them for large jobs. They don't support inheritance, abstraction, or polymorphism, and you already know how important those things are for building programs easily.

Where structs come in really handy is if you have a small, limited type of data that you need to work with repeatedly. Rectangles and points are good examples—there's not much you'll do with them, but you'll use them over and over again. Structs tend to be relatively small and limited in scope. If you find that you have a small chunk of a few different kinds of data that you want to store in a field in a class or pass to a method as a parameter, that's probably a good candidate for a struct.

> **A struct can be very valuable when you want to add good encapsulation to your class, because a read-only property that returns a struct always makes a fresh copy of it.**

Sharpen your pencil

This method is supposed to kill a Clone object, but it doesn't work. Why not?

```
private void SetCloneToNull(Clone clone) {
    clone = null;
}
```

← *Pop quiz, hotshot! Answer's on page 678.*

Captain Amazing...not so much

With all this talk of boxing, you should have a pretty good idea of what was going on with the less-powerful, more-tired Captain Amazing. In fact, it wasn't Captain Amazing at all, but a boxed struct:

VS.

That's one big advantage of structs (and other value types)—you can easily make copies of them.

1 **Structs can't inherit from classes or implement interfaces**
No wonder the Captain's superpowers seemed a little weak! He didn't get any inherited behavior.

2 **Structs are copied by value**
This is one of the most useful things about them. It's especially useful for encapsulation.

1 **You can't create a fresh copy of an object**
When you set one object variable equal to another, you're copying a **reference** to the **same** variable.

2 **You can use the "as" keyword with an object**
Objects allow for polymorphism by allowing an object to function as any of the objects it inherits from.

Back at the Lab

I THINK I'VE FOUND A WAY TO GIVE HIS POWERS TO A NORMAL CITIZEN!

ESSENCE OF AMAZING

Extension methods add new behavior to EXISTING classes

Remember the sealed access modifier from Chapter 7? It's how you set up a class that can't be extended.

Sometimes you need to extend a class that you can't inherit from, like a `sealed` class (a lot of the .NET classes are sealed, so you can't inherit from them). And C# gives you a powerful tool for that: **extension methods**. When you add a class with extension methods to your project, it **adds new methods that appear on classes** that already exist. All you have to do is create a static class, and add a **static** method that accepts an instance of the class as its first parameter using the `this` keyword.

So let's say you've got a `sealed OrdinaryHuman` class (remember, that means you can't extend it):

```
sealed class OrdinaryHuman {
    private int age;
    int weight;

    public OrdinaryHuman(int weight){
        this.weight = weight;
    }

    public void GoToWork() { /* code to go to work */ }
    public void PayBills() { /* code to pay bills */ }
}
```

The OrdinaryHuman class is sealed, so it can't be subclassed. But what if we want to add a method to it?

You use an extension method by specifying the first parameter using the "this" keyword.

Since we want to extend the OrdinaryHuman class, we make the first parameter this OrdinaryHuman.

The `SuperSoldierSerum` method adds an extension method to `OrdinaryHuman`:

```
static class SuperSoldierSerum {
    public static string BreakWalls(this OrdinaryHuman h, double wallDensity) {
        return ("I broke through a wall of " + wallDensity + " density.");
    }
}
```

Extension methods are always static methods, and they have to live in static classes.

When the program creates an instance of the OrdinaryHuman class, it can access the BreakWalls() method directly—as long as it has access to the SuperSoldierSerum class.

As soon as the `SuperSoldierSerum` class is added to the project, `OrdinaryHuman` gets a `BreakWalls` method. So now a form can use it:

```
static void Main(string[] args){
    OrdinaryHuman steve = new OrdinaryHuman(185);
    Console.WriteLine(steve.BreakWalls(89.2));
}
```

*Go ahead, try it out! **Create a new console application** and add the tw[o] classes and the Main() method to [it.] Debug into the BreakWalls() metho[d] and see what's going on.*

Sharpen your pencil Solution

So the clone parameter is just on the stack, so setting it to null doesn't do anything to the heap.

This method is supposed to kill a `Clone` object, but it doesn't work. Why not?

```
private void SetCloneToNull(Clone clone) {
    clone = null;
}
```

All this method does is set its own parameter to null, but that parameter's just a reference to a Clone. It's like sticking a label on an object and peeling it off again.

there are no
Dumb Questions

Q: **Tell me again why I wouldn't add the new methods I need directly to my class code, instead of using extensions?**

A: You could do that, and you probably should if you're just talking about adding a method to one class. Extension methods should be used pretty sparingly, and only in cases where you absolutely can't change the class you're working with for some reason (like it's part of the .NET Framework or another third party). Where extension methods really become powerful is when you need to extend the behavior of something you **wouldn't normally have access to**, like a type or an object that comes for free with the .NET Framework or another library.

Q: **Why use extension methods at all? Why not just extend the class with inheritance?**

A: If you can extend the class, then you'll usually end up doing that—extension methods aren't meant to be a replacement for inheritance. But they come in really handy when you've got classes that you can't extend. With extension methods, you can change the behavior of whole groups of objects, and even add functionality to some of the most basic classes in the .NET Framework.

Extending a class gives you new behavior, but requires that you use the new subclass if you want to use that new behavior.

Q: **Does my extension method affect all instances of a class, or just a certain instance of the class?**

A: It will affect all instances of a class that you extend. In fact, once you've created an extension method, the new method will show up in your IDE alongside the extended class's normal methods.

One more point to remember about extension methods: you don't gain access to any of the class's internals by doing an extension method, so it's still acting as an outsider!

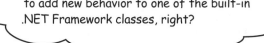

Oh, I get it! So you'd use extension methods to add new behavior to one of the built-in .NET Framework classes, right?

That's another thing you just can't do with inheritance—there's no way to inherit from an interface.

Exactly! There are some classes that you can't inherit from.

Pop open any project, add a class, and try typing this:

```
class x : string { }
```

Try to compile your code—the IDE will give you an error. The reason is that some .NET classes are **sealed**, which means that you can't inherit from them. (You can do this with your own classes, too! Just add the `sealed` keyword to your class after the `public` access modifier, and no other class will be allowed to inherit from it.) Extension methods give you a way to extend it, even if you can't inherit from it.

But that's not all you can do with extension methods. In addition to extending classes, you can also extend **interfaces**. All you have to do is use an interface name in place of the class, after the `this` keyword in the extension method's first parameter. When you do, the extension method is added to **every class that implements that interface**. Remember that LINQ code you added to your simulator in Chapter 12? LINQ was built entirely with extension methods, extending the `IEnumerable<T>` interface. (You'll learn a lot more about LINQ in Chapter 15.)

Extending a fundamental type: string

You don't often get to change the behavior of a language's
most fundamental types, like strings. But with extension
methods, you can do just that! Create a new project, and
add a file called `HumanExtensions.cs`.

Do this!

1 **Put all of your extension methods in a separate namespace**

It's a good idea to keep all of your extensions in a different namespace than the rest of
your code. That way, you won't have trouble finding them for use in other programs. Set
up a static class for your method to live in, too.

*Using a separate namespace is a good
organizational tool.*

```
namespace MyExtensions {
    public static class HumanExtensions {
```

*The class your extension method is
defined in must be static.*

2 **Create the static extension method, and define its first parameter as
`this` and then the type you're extending**

The two main things you need to know when you declare an extension method are that
the method needs to be static and it takes the class it's extending as its first parameter.

*"this string" says we're
extending the string class.*

```
public static bool IsDistressCall (this string s){
```

*The extension method must
be static, too.*

3 **Put the code to evaluate the string in the method**

*You want this class to be
accessed by code in the
other namespace, so make
sure you mark it public!*

```
public static class HumanExtensions {
    public static bool IsDistressCall(this string s){
        if (s.Contains("Help!"))
            return true;
        else
            return false;
    }
}
```

*This checks the string for a certain value...something
definitely not in the default string class.*

4 **Create a form and add a string**

Now go to your form code and add `using MyExtensions;` to the top, and add a button to the form so
you can try out your new extension method inside its event handler. Now, when you use a string, you get the
extension methods for free. You can see this for yourself by typing the name of a string variable and a period:

```
string message = "Clones are wreaking havoc at the factory. Help!";
message.
```

*As soon as you type
the dot, the IDE
pops up a helper
window with all of
string's methods...
including your
extension method.*

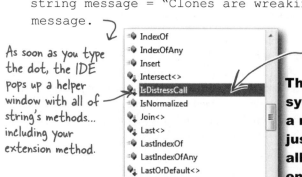

*Comment out the using line, and the
extension method will disappear from
the IntelliSense window.*

**This toy example just shows you the
syntax of extension methods. To get
a real sense of how useful they are,
just wait until the next chapter. It's
all about LINQ, which is implemented
entirely with extension methods.**

Extension Magnets

Arrange the magnets to produce this output:

a buck begets more bucks

```
namespace Upside {
```

```
public static class Margin {
```

```
public static void SendIt
```

```
using Upside;
namespace Sideways {
```

```
class Program {
```

```
}
```

```
public static string ToPrice
```

```
}
```

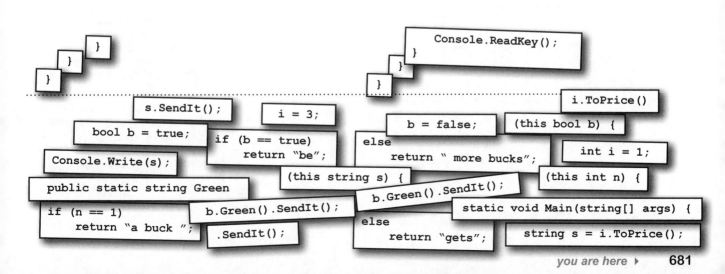

```
}
```

```
}
```

```
}
```

```
Console.ReadKey();
}
```

```
}
```

```
}
```

```
s.SendIt();
```

```
i = 3;
```

```
b = false;
```

```
i.ToPrice()
```

```
bool b = true;
```

```
if (b == true)
    return "be";
```

```
else
```

```
(this bool b) {
```

```
return " more bucks";
```

```
int i = 1;
```

```
Console.Write(s);
```

```
(this string s) {
```

```
b.Green().SendIt();
```

```
(this int n) {
```

```
public static string Green
```

```
b.Green().SendIt();
```

```
static void Main(string[] args) {
```

```
if (n == 1)
    return "a buck ";
```

```
.SendIt();
```

```
else
    return "gets";
```

```
string s = i.ToPrice();
```

Extension Magnets

Your job was to arrange the magnets to produce this output:

a buck begets more bucks

The Upside namespace has the extensions. The Sideways namespace has the entry point.

The Margin class extends string by adding a method called SendIt() that just writes the string to the console, and it extends int by adding a method called ToPrice() that returns "a buck" if the int's equal to 1, or "more bucks" if it's not.

The entry point method uses the extensions that you added in the Margin class.

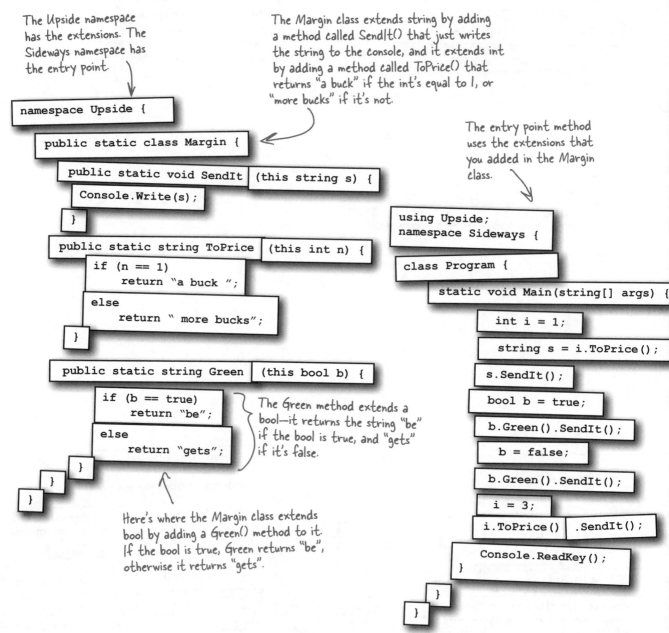

```
namespace Upside {

    public static class Margin {

        public static void SendIt (this string s) {
            Console.Write(s);
        }

        public static string ToPrice (this int n) {
            if (n == 1)
                return "a buck ";
            else
                return " more bucks";
        }

        public static string Green (this bool b) {
            if (b == true)
                return "be";
            else
                return "gets";
        }
    }
}
```

```
using Upside;
namespace Sideways {

    class Program {

        static void Main(string[] args) {

            int i = 1;

            string s = i.ToPrice();

            s.SendIt();

            bool b = true;

            b.Green().SendIt();

            b = false;

            b.Green().SendIt();

            i = 3;

            i.ToPrice() .SendIt();

            Console.ReadKey();
        }
    }
}
```

The Green method extends a bool—it returns the string "be" if the bool is true, and "gets" if it's false.

Here's where the Margin class extends bool by adding a Green() method to it. If the bool is true, Green returns "be", otherwise it returns "gets".

The UNIVERSE 🌐

CAPTAIN AMAZING REBORN

Death was not the end!

By Bucky Barnes
UNIVERSE STAFF WRITER

OBJECTVILLE

Captain Amazing deserializes himself, makes stunning comeback

In a stunning turn of events, Captain Amazing has returned to Objectville. Last month, Captain Amazing's coffin was found empty, and only a strange note left where his body should have been. Analysis of the note revealed Captain Amazing's object DNA—all his last fields and values, captured faithfully in binary format.

Today, that data has sprung to life. The Captain is back, deserialized from his own brilliant note. When asked how he conceived of such a plan, the Captain merely shrugged and mumbled, "Chapter 9." Sources close to the Captain refused to comment on the meaning of his cryptic reply, but did admit that prior to his failed assault on Swindler, the Captain had spent a lot of time reading books, studying Dispose methods and persistence. We expect Captain Amazing…

Captain Amazing is back!

…see AMAZING on A-5

Pool Puzzle Solution

The Lamp() method sets the various strings and ints. If you call it with an int, then it sets the Bulb field in whatever object Hinge points to.

Output when you create a new Faucet object:
back in 20 minutes

```
public class Faucet {
    public Faucet() {
        Table wine = new Table();
        Hinge book = new Hinge();
        wine.Set(book);
        book.Set(wine);
        wine.Lamp(10);
        book.garden.Lamp("back in");
        book.bulb *= 2;
        wine.Lamp("minutes");
        wine.Lamp(book);
    }
}
```

Here's why Table has to be a struct. If it were a class, then wine would point to the same object as book.Garden, which would cause this to overwrite the "back in" string.

Bonus question: Circle the lines where boxing happens.

Since the Lamp() method takes an object parameter, boxing automatically happens when it's passed an int or a string.

```
public struct Table {
    public string stairs;
    public Hinge floor;
    public void Set(Hinge b) {
        floor = b;
    }
    public void Lamp(object oil) {
        if (oil is int)
            floor.bulb = (int)oil;
        else if (oil is string)
            stairs = (string)oil;
        else if (oil is Hinge) {
            Hinge vine = oil as Hinge;
            Console.WriteLine(vine.Table()
                + " " + floor.bulb + " " + stairs);
        }
    }
}
```

If you pass a string to Lamp, it sets the Stairs field to whatever is in that string.

Remember, the as keyword only works with classes, not structs.

```
public class Hinge {
    public int bulb;
    public Table garden;
    public void Set(Table a) {
        garden = a;
    }
    public string Table() {
        return garden.stairs;
    }
}
```

Both Hinge and Table have a Set() method. Hinge's Set() sets its Table field called Garden, and Table's Set() method sets its Hinge field called Floor.

15 LINQ

Get control of your data

So if you take the first word from this article, and the second word in that list, and add it to the fifth word over here...you get secret messages from the government!

It's a data-driven world...you better know how to live in it.

Gone are the days when you could program for days, even weeks, without dealing with **loads of data**. But today, *everything is about data*. In fact, you'll often have to work with data from **more than one place**...and in more than one format. Databases, XML, collections from other programs...it's all part of the job of a good C# programmer. And that's where **LINQ** comes in. LINQ not only lets you **query data** in a simple, intuitive way, but it lets you **group data**, and **merge data from different data sources**.

An easy project...

Objectville Paper Company wants to do a cross-promotion with Starbuzz Coffee. Starbuzz has a frequent-customer program where they keep track of which customers buy which drink and how often they buy it. Objectville Paper wants to figure out **which of their customers are also Starbuzz regulars** and send them a free mug and a coupon for their favorite coffee drink...and it's up to you to combine the data and generate the list of customers to send mugs and coupons to.

All of Objectville Paper's customers who are Starbuzz regulars get a free mug. Just tell us who the mugs need to go to and what their favorite drinks are, OK?

...but the data's all over the place

Starbuzz keeps all their data in classes, grouped together in a big `List`. But the Objectville data is in a database (from way back in Chapter 1). We want to find any Starbuzz customers who spent more than $90, match them to the Objectville Paper contact list, and make a final list of people: **we want each person's name, the company they work for, and their favorite Starbuzz drink**.

The Starbuzz data's in a List<T>

The Starbuzz people provided a program that connects to their website and pulls all the data into a `List<StarbuzzData>`.

Here's the class and enum from Starbuzz's code.

```
class StarbuzzData
{
    public string Name { get; set; }
    public Drink FavoriteDrink { get; set; }
    public int MoneySpent { get; set; }
    public int Visits { get; set; }
}


enum Drink {
    BoringCoffee,
    ChocoRockoLatte,
    TripleEspresso,
    ZestyLemonChai,
    DoubleCappuccino,
    HalfCafAmericano,
    ChocoMacchiato,
    BananaSplitInACup,
}
```

You need to get the list of Starbuzz data, and find the customers that match Objectville customers.

You've already got the customer data

You built the Objectville Paper Company contact list back in Chapter 1—it's got part of the data you need.

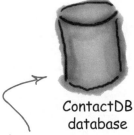

ContactDB database

All of the Objectville Paper Company customer data is in a database.

BRAIN POWER

How would you combine the data from Starbuzz and the data from Objectville Paper Company to get a complete contact list?

LINQ can pull data from multiple sources

LINQ to the rescue! You used LINQ (or **L**anguage **In**tegrated **Q**uery)
in the hive simulator to track what groups of bees were doing. You took
advantage of the power of LINQ to write simple queries to pull data out
of a collection. LINQ can work with the Starbuzz data just like it worked
with the bees, helping you use queries to pull out customer data. As long
as a collection implements the `IEnumerable<T>` interface, you can use
LINQ queries with it.

← We gave you Ready Bake Code for the LINQ query in Chapter 12. We'll see exactly how it works in a few pages.

But LINQ also lets you work with more than just collections. You can use
the same queries to pull data from a database, or even an XML document.
So once we get collections under control, we can use LINQ on the
Objectville Paper Company database.

Here was the query we used in the bee simulator to group and order bees by their state.

```
var beeGroups =
    from bee in world.Bees
    group bee by bee.CurrentState
    into beeGroup
    orderby beeGroup.Key
    select beeGroup;
```

LINQ

We need a similar query to pull data from the Starbuzz customer data, which is also in a collection.

Bee — ID = 987, currentState = MakingHoney
Bee — ID = 12, currentState = FlyingToFlower
Bee — ID = 1982, currentState = GatheringNectar

Bees — *List of Bee objects*

Bees table
ID = 987	currentState = MakingHoney
ID = 12	currentState = FlyingToFlower
ID = 1982	currentState = GatheringNec

Database

XML
```
<bee id="987" currentState="MakingHoney" />
<bee id="12" currentState="FlyingToFlower" />
<bee id="1982" currentState="GatheringNectar" />
```

The nice thing about LINQ is that the same query works on a database or XML document, of bees or customers or anything else.

LINQ works with pretty much every kind of data source you could
use in .NET. Your code needs a `using System.Linq;` line at the
top of your file, but that's it. Even better, the IDE automatically puts
a reference to LINQ in the header of the class files it creates.

.NET collections are already set up for LINQ

All of the collection types in .NET implement the IEnumerable<T> interface, which you learned about in Chapter 8. But take a minute to get a refresher: type System.Collections.Generic.IEnumerable<int> into your IDE window, right-click on the line, and select Go To Definition (or press F12). You'll see that the IEnumerable interface defines a GetEnumerator() method:

Notice how IEnumerable<T> extends an interface called IEnumerable? Use Go to Definition to explore it, too.

```
namespace System.Collections.Generic {
  interface IEnumerable<T> : IEnumerable {
    // Summary:
    //      Returns an enumerator that iterates through the collection.
    //
    // Returns:
    //      A System.Collections.Generic.IEnumerator<T> that can be
    //          used to iterate through the collection.
    IEnumerator<T> GetEnumerator();
  }
}
```

This is the only method in the interface. Each collection implements this method. You could create your own kind of object that implemented IEnumerable<T> too...and if you did, you could use LINQ with your object.

This method requires your object to define a way to move through the elements in it, one element at a time. That's all LINQ requires as a prerequisite. If you can move through a list of data, item by item, then you can implement IEnumerable<T>, and LINQ can query the collection.

Behind the Scenes

LINQ uses **extension methods** to let you query, sort, and update data. Check it out for yourself. Create an int array called linqtest, put some numbers in the array, and then type this line of code (don't worry, you'll learn what it does in a minute):

```
IEnumerable<int> result = from i in linqtest where i < 3 select i;
```

Now comment out the using System.Linq; line up in the header of the file you've created. When you try to rebuild the solution, you'll see that this line doesn't compile anymore. The methods you're calling when you use LINQ are just extension methods that are being used to extend the array.

Now you can see why extension methods were so important in Chapter 14...they let .NET (and you) add all kinds of cool behavior to existing types.

LINQ makes queries easy

Here's a simple example of LINQ syntax. It selects all the numbers in an `int` array that are under 37 and puts those numbers in ascending order. It does that using four **clauses** that tell it what object to query, what criteria to use to determine which of its members to select, how to sort the results, and how the results should be returned.

```
int[] values = new int[] {0, 12, 44, 36, 92, 54, 13, 8};

var result = from v in values
```

This assigns the letter "v" to stand in for each of the array values in the query. So v is 0, then 12, then 44, then 36...etc. It's called the range variable.

This LINQ query has four clauses: the from clause, a where clause, an orderby clause, and the select clause.

```
            where v < 37
```
This says, select each v in the array that is less than 37.

```
            orderby v
```
Then, put those values in order (lowest to highest).

```
            select v;
```
If you've used SQL before, it may seem weird to put the select at the end, but that's how things work in LINQ.

```
foreach(int i in result)

   Console.Write("{0} ", i);

Console.ReadKey();
```
Now you can iterate through the sequence that LINQ returned to print the output.

Output:
0 8 12 13 36

var

var is a keyword that tells the compiler to figure out the type of a variable <u>at compilation time</u>. .NET detects the type from the type of the local variable that you're using LINQ to query. When you build your solution, the compiler will replace var with the right type for the data you're working with.

In the example above, when this line is compiled:
```
   var result = from v in values
```
The compiler <u>replaces</u> "var" with this:
```
   IEnumerable<int>
```

And while we're on the subject of interfaces for collections, remember how we talked about how IEnumerable<T> is the interface that supports iteration? A lot of these great LINQ queries are implemented using extension methods that extend IEnumerable<T>, so you'll see that interface a lot.

Flip back to Chapter 8 to get a refresher on the `IEnumerable<T>` interface. Plus, you can read more about it in Leftover #6 in the Appendix.

LINQ is simple, but your queries don't have to be

Jimmy just sold his start-up company to a big investor, and wants to take some of his profits and buy the most expensive issues of Captain Amazing that he can find. How can LINQ help him scour his data and figure out which comics are the most expensive?

1 Jimmy downloaded a list of Captain Amazing issues from a Captain Amazing fan page. He put them in a `List<T>` of `Comic` objects that have two fields, `Name` and `Issue`.

```
class Comic {
    public string Name { get; set; }
    public int Issue { get; set; }
}
```

Jimmy used object initializers and a collection initializer to build his catalog:

```
private static IEnumerable<Comic> BuildCatalog()    ←
{
    return new List<Comic> {
        new Comic { Name = "Johnny America vs. the Pinko", Issue = 6 },
        new Comic { Name = "Rock and Roll (limited edition)", Issue = 19 },
        new Comic { Name = "Woman's Work", Issue = 36 },
        new Comic { Name = "Hippie Madness (misprinted)", Issue = 57 },
        new Comic { Name = "Revenge of the New Wave Freak (damaged)", Issue = 68 },
        new Comic { Name = "Black Monday", Issue = 74 },      ←
        new Comic { Name = "Tribal Tattoo Madness", Issue = 83 },
        new Comic { Name = "The Death of an Object", Issue = 97 },
    };
}
```

There's no special reason this method is static, other than to make it easy to call from a console application's entry point method.

We left the () parentheses off of the collection and object initializers after `<Comic>`, because you don't need 'em.

Issue #74 of Captain Amazing is called "Black Monday".

> Take a minute and flip to Leftover #6 to learn about a really useful bit of syntax that could come in handy here. This is a great opportunity to experiment!

2 Luckily, there's a thriving marketplace for Captain Amazing comics on Greg's List. Jimmy knows that issue #57, "Hippie Madness," was misprinted and that almost all of the run was destroyed by the publisher, and he found a rare copy recently sold on Greg's List for $13,525. After a few hours of searching, Jimmy was able to build a `Dictionary<>` that mapped issue numbers to values.

```
private static Dictionary<int, decimal> GetPrices()
{
    return new Dictionary<int, decimal> {
        { 6, 3600M },
        { 19, 500M },
        { 36, 650M },
        { 57, 13525M },
        { 68, 250M },
        { 74, 75M },
        { 83, 25.75M },
        { 97, 35.25M },
    };
}
```

Remember this syntax for collection initializers for dictionaries from Chapter 8?

Issue #57 is worth $13,525.

BRAIN POWER

Look closely at the LINQ query on page 690. What do you think Jimmy has to put in his query to find the most expensive issues?

Anatomy of a query

Jimmy could analyze his comic book data with one LINQ query. The `where` clause tells LINQ which items from the collection should be included in the results. But that clause doesn't have to be just a simple comparison. It can include any valid C# expression—like using the `values` dictionary to tell it to return only comics worth more than $500. And the `orderby` clause works the same way—we can tell LINQ to order the comics by their value.

```
IEnumerable<Comic> comics = BuildCatalog();

Dictionary<int, decimal> values = GetPrices();
```

> The LINQ query pulls Comic objects out of the comics list, using the data in the values dictionary to decide which comics to select.

```
var mostExpensive =
```

> The first clause in the query is the from clause. This one tells LINQ to query the comics collection, and that the name comic will be used in the query to specify how to treat each individual piece of data in the collection.

```
    from comic in comics

    where values[comic.Issue] > 500

    orderby values[comic.Issue] descending

    select comic;
```

> You can choose any name you want when you use a from clause. We chose "comic".

> The where and orderby clauses can include ANY C# statement, so we can use the values dictionary to select only those comics worth more than $500, and we can sort the results so the most expensive ones come first.

> The name comic was defined in the from clause specifically so it could be used in the where and orderby clauses.

```
    foreach (Comic comic in mostExpensive)

        Console.WriteLine("{0} is worth {1:c}",

                comic.Name, values[comic.Issue]);
```

> When you add "{1:c}" to the WriteLine output, that tells it to print the second parameter in the local currency format.

> The query returned its results into an IEnumerable<T> called mostExpensive. The select clause determines what goes into the results—since it selected comic, the query returned Comic objects.

Output:
```
Hippie Madness (misprinted) is worth $13,525.00
Johnny America vs. the Pinko is worth $3,600.00
Woman's Work is worth $650.00
```

> I don't buy this. I know SQL already—isn't writing a LINQ query just like writing SQL?

Don't worry if you've never used SQL—you don't need to know anything about it to work with LINQ. But if you're curious, check out "Head First SQL."

LINQ may *look* like SQL, but it doesn't *work* like SQL.

If you've done a lot of work with SQL, it may be tempting to dismiss all this LINQ stuff as intuitive and obvious—and you wouldn't be alone, because a lot of developers make that mistake. It's true that LINQ uses the `select`, `from`, `where`, `descending`, and `join` keywords, which are borrowed from SQL. But LINQ is very different from SQL, and if you try to think about LINQ the way you think about SQL you'll end up with code that **doesn't do what you expect**.

One big difference between the two is that SQL operates on *tables*, which are very different from *enumerable objects*. One really important difference is that SQL tables don't have an order, but enumerable objects do. When you execute a SQL `select` against a table, you can be sure that the table is not going to be updated. SQL has all sorts of built-in data security that you can trust.

If you want to get to the nuts and bolts: SQL queries are set operations, which means they don't examine the rows in the table in any predictable order. A collection, on the other hand, can store *anything*—values, structs, objects, etc.—and collections have a specific order. (A table's rows aren't in any particular order until you make a SQL query that orders them; items inside a list, on the other hand, are in order.) And LINQ lets you perform any operation that's supported by whatever happens to be in the collection—it can even call methods on the objects in the collection. And LINQ loops through the collection, which means that it does its operations in a specific order. That may not seem all that important, but if you're used to dealing with SQL, it means your LINQ queries will surprise you if you expect them to act like SQL.

There are a lot of other differences between LINQ and SQL too, but you don't need to delve into them just yet in order to start working with LINQ right now! Just approach it with an open mind, and don't expect it to work the way SQL works.

LINQ is <u>versatile</u>

You can do a lot more than just pull a few items out of a collection. You can modify the items before you return them. And once you've generated a set of result sequences, LINQ gives you a bunch of methods that work with them. Top to bottom, LINQ gives you the tools you need to manage your data.

> All collections are enumerable—they implement IEnumerable<T>—but not everything that's enumerable is technically a collection unless it implements the ICollection<T> interface, which means implementing Add(), Clear(), Contains(), CopyTo(), and Remove()... and, of course, ICollection<T> extends IEnumerable<T>. LINQ deals with <u>sequences</u> of values or objects, not collections, and all you need for a sequence is an object that implements IEnumerable<T>.

⭐ **Modify every item returned from the query**

This code will add a string onto the end of each string in an array. It doesn't change the array itself—it **creates a new sequence** of modified strings.

```
string[] sandwiches = { "ham and cheese", "salami with mayo",
                        "turkey and swiss", "chicken cutlet" };
var sandwichesOnRye =
    from sandwich in sandwiches
    select sandwich + " on rye";

foreach (var sandwich in sandwichesOnRye)
    Console.WriteLine(sandwich);
```

This adds the string " on rye" to every item in the results from the query.

This change is made to the items in the results of your query...but not to the items in the original collection or database.

Notice that all the items returned have " on rye" added to the end.

Output:

```
ham and cheese on rye
salami with mayo on rye
turkey and swiss on rye
chicken cutlet on rye
```

⭐ **Perform calculations on collections**

Remember, we said LINQ provides extension methods for your collections (and database access objects, and anything else that implements IEnumerable<T>). And some of those are pretty handy on their own, without actually requiring a query:

```
Random random = new Random();
List<int> listOfNumbers = new List<int>();
int length = random.Next(50, 150);
for (int i = 0; i < length; i++)
    listOfNumbers.Add(random.Next(100));

Console.WriteLine("There are {0} numbers",
                  listOfNumbers.Count());
Console.WriteLine("The smallest is {0}",
                  listOfNumbers.Min());
Console.WriteLine("The biggest is {0}",
                  listOfNumbers.Max());
Console.WriteLine("The sum is {0}",
                  listOfNumbers.Sum());
Console.WriteLine("The average is {0:F2}",
                  listOfNumbers.Average());
```

None of these methods are part of the .NET collections classes...they're all defined by LINQ.

These are all extension methods for IEnumerable<T> in the System.Linq namespace using a static class called Enumerable. But **don't take our word for it!** Click on any of them and use "Go to Definition" to see for yourself.

A sequence is an ordered set of objects or values, which is what LINQ returns in an IEnumerable<T>.

⭐ Store all or part of your results in a new <u>sequence</u>

Sometimes you'll want to keep your results from a LINQ query around. You can use the ToList() command to do just that:

```
var under50sorted =
    from number in listOfNumbers
    where number < 50
    orderby number descending
    select number;
```

This time, we're sorting a list of numbers in descending order, from highest to lowest.

```
List<int> newList = under50sorted.ToList();
```

ToList() converts a LINQ var into a List<T> object, so you can keep results of a query around. There's also ToArray() and ToDictionary() methods, which do just what you'd expect.

You can even take just a subset of the results, using the Take() method:

```
var firstFive = under50sorted.Take(6);
```

```
List<int> shortList = firstFive.ToList();
foreach (int n in shortList)
    Console.WriteLine(n);
```

Take() pulls out the supplied number of items, from the first set of the results from a LINQ query. You can put these into another var, and then convert that into a list.

⭐ Check out Microsoft's official "101 LINQ Samples" page

There's way more that LINQ can do. Luckily, Microsoft gives you a great little reference to help you along.

```
http://msdn2.microsoft.com/en-us/vcsharp/aa336746.aspx
```

---

there are no Dumb Questions

Q: That's a lot of new keywords—from, where, orderby, select...it's like a whole different language. Why does it look so different from the rest of C#?

A: Because it serves a different purpose. Most of the C# syntax was built to do one small operation or calculation at a time. You can start a loop, or set a variable, or do a mathematical operation, or call a method... those are all single operations.

LINQ queries look different because a single LINQ query usually does a whole bunch of things at once. Let's take a closer look at a straightforward query:

```
var under10 =
    from number in numberArray
    where number < 10
    select number;
```

It looks really simple—not a lot of stuff there, right? But this is actually a pretty complex piece of code. Think about what's got to happen for the program to actually select all the numbers from numberArray that are less than 10. First, you need to loop through the entire array. Then, each number is compared to 10. Then those results need to be gathered together so your code can use them.

And that's why LINQ looks a little odd: because C# has to cram a whole lot of behavior into a very small space.

LINQ lets you write queries that do very complex things using very little code.

BULLET POINTS

- **from** is how you specify the IEnumerable<T> that you're querying. It's always followed by the name of a variable, followed by **in** and the name of the input (from value in values).

- **where** generally follows the from clause. That's where you use normal C# conditions to tell LINQ which items to pull (where value < 10).

- **orderby** lets you order the results. It's followed by the criteria that you're using to sort them, and optionally **descending** to tell it to reverse the sort (orderby value descending).

- **select** is how you specify what goes into the results (select value).

- **Take** lets you pull the first items out of the results of a LINQ query (results.Take(10)). LINQ gives you other methods for each sequence: Min(), Max(), Sum(), and Average().

- You can select anything—you're not limited to selecting the name that you created in the from clause. Here's an example: if your LINQ query pulls a set of prices out of an array of int values and names them value in the from clause, you can return a sequence of price strings like this: select String.Format("{0:c}", value.

This is just like the {0:x} you used in Chapter 9 when you built the hex dumper. There's also {0:d} and {0:D} for short and long dates, and {0:P} or {0:Pn} to print a percent (with n decimal places).

there are no
Dumb Questions

Q: How does the from clause work?

A: It's a lot like the first line of a foreach loop. One thing that makes thinking about LINQ queries a little tricky is that you're not just doing one operation.

A LINQ query does the same thing over and over again for each item in a collection. The from clause does two things: it tells LINQ which collection to use for the query, and it assigns a name to use for each member of the collection that's being queried.

The way the from clause creates a new name for each item in the collection is really similar to how a foreach loop does it. Here's the first line of a foreach loop:

```
foreach (int i in values)
```

That foreach loop temporarily creates a variable called i, which it assigns sequentially to each item in the values collection. Now look at a from clause in a LINQ query on the same collection:

```
from i in values
```

That clause does pretty much the same thing. It creates a temporary variable called i and assigns it sequentially to each item in the values collection. The foreach loop runs the same block of code for each item in the collection, while the LINQ query applies the same criteria in the where clause to each item in the collection to determine whether or not to include it in the results. But one thing to keep in mind here is that LINQ queries are just extension methods. They call methods that do all the real work. You could call those same methods without LINQ.

Q: How does LINQ decide what goes into the results?

A: That's what the select clause is for. Every LINQ query returns a sequence, and every item in that sequence is of the same type. It tells LINQ exactly what that sequence should contain. When you're querying an array or list of a single type—like an array of ints or a List<string>—it's obvious what goes into the select clause. But what if you're selecting from a list of Comic objects? You could do what Jimmy did and select the whole class. But you could also change the last line of the query to select comic.Name to tell it to return a sequence of strings. Or you could do select comic.Issue and have it return a sequence of ints.

LINQ Magnets

Rearrange the magnets so they produce the output at the bottom of the page.

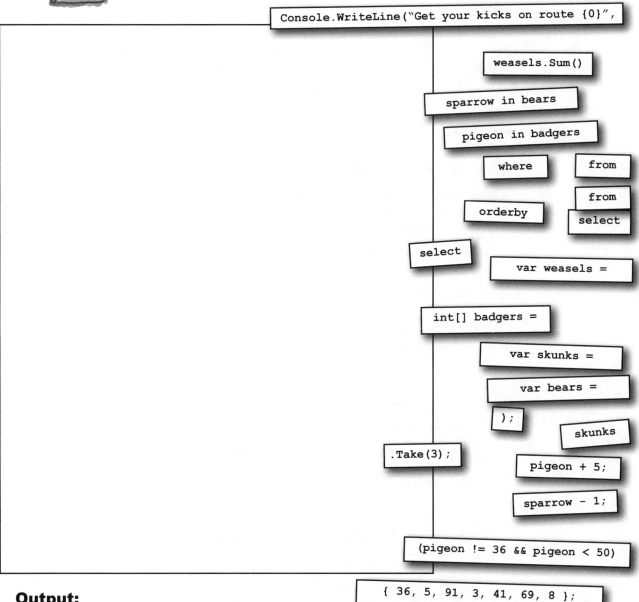

pigeon descending

Console.WriteLine("Get your kicks on route {0}",

weasels.Sum()

sparrow in bears

pigeon in badgers

where   from

                from
orderby   select

select

var weasels =

int[] badgers =

var skunks =

var bears =

);

skunks

.Take(3);

pigeon + 5;

sparrow - 1;

(pigeon != 36 && pigeon < 50)

{ 36, 5, 91, 3, 41, 69, 8 };

Output:

Get your kicks on route 66

LINQ Magnets Solution

Rearrange the magnets so they produce
the output at the bottom of the page.

LINQ starts with some sort
of sequence, collection, or
array—in this case, an array
of integers.

```
int[] badgers =          { 36, 5, 91, 3, 41, 69, 8 };
```

"from pigeon in badgers" makes for a good puzzle, but
an unreadable LINQ query. "from badger in badgers" is
more readable.

```
var skunks =
    from          pigeon in badgers
    where         (pigeon != 36 && pigeon < 50)
    orderby       pigeon descending
    select        pigeon + 5;
```

After this statement,
skunks contains four
numbers: 46, 13, 10, and 8.

This LINQ statement pulls all
the numbers that are below
50 and not equal to 36 out
of the array, adds 5 to each
of them, sorts them from
biggest to smallest, puts them
in a new object, and points
the skunks reference at it.

```
var bears =
    skunks    .Take(3);
```

Here's where we take the first three
numbers in skunks and put them into a
new sequence called bears.

```
var weasels =
    from      sparrow in bears
    select    sparrow - 1;
```

After this statement,
weasels contains three
numbers: 45, 12, and 9.

This statement just subtracts 1 from
each number in bears and puts them
all into weasels.

```
Console.WriteLine("Get your kicks on route {0}",
    weasels.Sum()    );
```

The numbers in weasels add up to 66.

45 + 12 + 9 = 66

Output:
Get your kicks on route 66

LINQ can combine your results into groups

You already know that you can use LINQ to build
your results into groups, because that's what we did
with the beehive simulator. Let's take a closer look at
that query and see how it works.

1 The query starts out just like the other queries you've seen—by pulling individual bee objects out of the `world.Bees` collection, a `List<Bee>` object.

```
var beeGroups =

    from bee in world.Bees

    group bee by bee.CurrentState

    into beeGroup

    orderby beeGroup.Key

    select beeGroup;
```

2 The next line in the query has a new keyword: **group**. This tells the query to return **groups** of bees. What that means is that rather than returning one single sequence, the query will return a **sequence of sequences**. `group bee by bee.CurrentState` tells LINQ to return one group for each unique `CurrentState` property that it finds in the bees that it selects. Finally, we need to give LINQ a name for the group. That's what the next line is for: **into beeGroup** says that the name "beeGroup" refers to the new groups.

3 Now that we've got groups, we can manipulate them. Since we're returning a sequence of groups, we can use the `orderby` keyword to put the groups in the order of the `CurrentState` enum values (`Idle`, `FlyingToFlower`, etc.). **orderby beeGroup.Key** tells the query to put the sequence of groups in order, sorting them by the group key. Since we grouped the bees by their `CurrentState`, that's what being used as a key.

4 Now we just have to use the `select` keyword to indicate what's being returned by the query. Since we're returning groups, we select the group name: **select beeGroup;**

Since the bees were grouped by their state, we call that state the "key". A group's key is the criteria it was grouped by.

Note that this query returns groups of bees, not individual bees.

you are here ▶ **699**

Combine Jimmy's values into groups

Jimmy buys a lot of cheap comic books, some midrange comic books, and a few expensive ones, and he wants to know what his options are before he decides what comics to buy. He's taken those prices he got from Greg's List and put them into a `Dictionary<int, int>` using his `GetPrices()` method. Let's now use LINQ to group them into three groups: one for cheap comics that cost under $100, one for midrange comics that cost between $100 and $1,000, and one for expensive comics that cost over $1,000. We'll create a `PriceRange` enum that we'll use as the key for the groups, and a method called `EvaluatePrice()` that'll evaluate a price and return a `PriceRange`.

1 **Every group needs a key—we'll use an enum for that**

The group's key is the thing that all of its members have in common. The key can be anything: a string, a number, even an object reference. We'll be looking at the prices that Jimmy got from Greg's List. Each group that the query returns will be a sequence of issue numbers, and the group's key will be a `PriceRange` enum. The `EvaluatePrice()` method takes a price as a parameter and returns a `PriceRange`:

```
enum PriceRange { Cheap, Midrange, Expensive }

static PriceRange EvaluatePrice(decimal price) {
    if (price < 100M) return PriceRange.Cheap;
    else if (price < 1000M) return PriceRange.Midrange;
    else return PriceRange.Expensive;
}
```

2 **Now we can group the comics by their price categories**

The LINQ query returns a **sequence of sequences**. Each of the sequences inside the results has a `Key` property, which matches the `PriceRange` that was returned by `EvaluatePrice()`. Look closely at the `group by` clause—we're pulling pairs out of the dictionary, and using the name `pair` for each of them: `pair.Key` is the issue number, and `pair.Value` is the price from Greg's List. Adding `group pair.Key` tells LINQ to create groups of issue numbers, and then bundles all of those groups up based on the price category that's returned by `EvaluatePrice()`:

```
Dictionary<int, decimal> values = GetPrices();

var priceGroups =
    from pair in values
    group pair.Key by EvaluatePrice(pair.Value)
        into priceGroup
        orderby priceGroup.Key descending
        select priceGroup;

foreach (var group in priceGroups) {
    Console.Write("I found {0} {1} comics: issues ", group.Count(), group.Key);
    foreach (var price in group)
        Console.Write(price.ToString() + " ");
    Console.WriteLine();
}
```

> The query figures out which group a particular comic belongs to by sending its price to EvaluatePrice(). That returns a PriceRange enum, which it uses as the group's key.

> Each of the groups is a sequence, so we added an inner foreach loop to pull each of the prices out of the group.

Output:
```
I found 2 Expensive comics: issues 6 57
I found 3 Midrange comics: issues 19 36 68
I found 3 Cheap comics: issues 74 83 97
```

Pŏŏl Puzzle

Your **job** is to take snippets from the pool and place them into the blank lines in the program. You can use the same snippet more than once, and you won't need to use all the snippets. Your **goal** is to make the code produce this *output*:

↓

Horses enjoy eating carrots, but they love eating apples.

```
class Line {
    public string[] Words;
    public int Value;
    public Line(string[] Words, int Value) {
        this.Words = Words; this.Value = Value;
    }
}
```

Hint: LINQ sorts strings in alphabetical order.

```
Line[] lines = {
  new Line( new string[] { "eating", "carrots,",
        "but", "enjoy", "Horses" } , 1),
  new Line( new string[] { "zebras?", "hay",
        "Cows", "bridge.", "bolted" } , 2),
  new Line( new string[] { "fork", "dogs!",
        "Engine", "and" }, 3 ) ,
  new Line( new string[] { "love", "they",
        "apples.", "eating" }, 2 ) ,
  new Line( new string[] { "whistled.", "Bump" }, 1 ) };
```

```
var _____ =
    from _____ in _____
    _____ line by line._____
    into wordGroups
    orderby _____._____
    select _____;

____ _____ = words._____(2);

foreach (var group in twoGroups)
{
    int i = 0;
    foreach (_____ inner in _____) {
        i++;
        if (i == _____.Key) {
            var poem =
                _____ word in _____._____
                _____ word descending
                _____ word + ____;
            foreach (var word in _____)
                Console.Write(word);
        }
    }
}
```

Note: Each snippet from the pool can be used more than once!

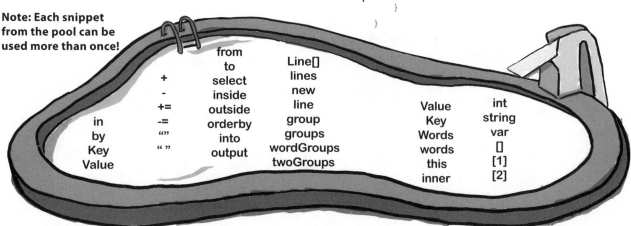

	+	from	Line[]	
	-	to	lines	
	+=	select	new	Value
	-=	inside	line	Key
in	""	outside	group	Words
by	" "	orderby	groups	words
Key		into	wordGroups	this
Value		output	twoGroups	inner

int
string
var
[]
[1]
[2]

Pool Puzzle Solution

```
class Line {
    public string[] Words;
    public int Value;
    public Line(string[] Words, int Value) {
        this.Words = Words; this.Value = Value;
    }
}

Line[] lines = {
    new Line( new string[] { "eating", "carrots,", "but", "enjoy", "Horses" } , 1),
    new Line( new string[] { "zebras?", "hay", "Cows", "bridge.", "bolted" } , 2),
    new Line( new string[] { "fork", "dogs!", "Engine", "and" }, 3 ) ,
    new Line( new string[] { "love", "they", "apples.", "eating" }, 2 ) ,
    new Line( new string[] { "whistled.", "Bump" }, 1 )
};
```

```
var words =
    from line in lines
    group line by line.Value
    into wordGroups
    orderby wordGroups.Key
    select wordGroups;
```

This first LINQ query divides the Line objects in the lines[] array into groups, grouped by their Value, in ascending order of the Value key.

```
var twoGroups = words.Take(2);
```

The first two groups are the lines with Values 1 and 2.

```
foreach (var group in twoGroups)
{
    int i = 0;
    foreach (var inner in group) {
        i++;
        if (i == group.Key) {
            var poem =
                from word in inner.Words
                orderby word descending
                select word + " ";
            foreach (var word in poem)
                Console.Write(word);
        }
    }
}
```

This loop does a LINQ query on the first Line object in the first group and the second Line object in the second group.

Did you figure out that the two phrases "Horses enjoy eating carrots, but" and "they love eating apples" are in descending alphabetical order?

```
Output:     Horses enjoy eating carrots, but they love eating apples.
```

Use join to combine two collections into one query

Jimmy's got a whole collection of comics he's purchased, and he wants to compare them with the prices he found on Greg's List to see if the prices he's been paying are better or worse. He's been tracking his purchases using a Purchase class with two automatic properties, Issue and Price. And he's got a List<Purchase> called purchases that's got all the comics he's bought. But now he needs to match up the purchases he's made with the prices he found on Greg's List. How's he going to do it?

LINQ to the rescue! Its join keyword lets you **combine data from two collections** into a single query. It does it by comparing items in the first collection with their matching items in the second collection. (LINQ is smart enough to do this efficiently—it doesn't actually compare every pair of items unless it has to.) The final result combines every pair that matches.

> Jimmy's got his data in a collection of Purchase objects called purchases.

1 Start off your query with the usual from clause. But instead of following it up with the criteria it'll use to determine what goes into the results, you add:

> **join** *name* **in** *collection*

The join clause tells LINQ to loop through both collections to match up pairs of one member from each collection. It assigns *name* to the member it'll pull out of the joined collection in each iteration. You'll use that name in the where clause.

```
class Purchase {
  public int Issue
             { get; set; }
  public decimal Price
             { get; set; }
}
```

> Jimmy's joining his comics to purchases, a list of comics he's bought.

List<Comic> → **from** comic **in** comics

join purchase **in** purchases → List<Purchases>

on comic.Issue
equals purchase.Issue

2 Next you'll add the **on** clause, which tells LINQ how to match the two collections together. You'll follow it with the name of the member of the first collection you're matching, followed by **equals** and the name of the member of the second collection to match it to.

3 You'll continue the LINQ query with where and orderby clauses as usual. You could finish it with a normal select clause, but you usually want to return results that pull some data from one collection and other data from the other. That's where you use **select new** to create a custom set of results using an **anonymous type**.

> The select new is followed by curly brackets that contain the data to return in the results.

results

LINQ Sequence

select new { comic.Name, comic.Issue, purchase.Price }

Issue = 6	name = "Johnny America"	Price = 3600
Issue = 19	name = "Rock and Roll"	Price = 375
Issue = 57	name = "Hippie Madness"	Price = 13215

Flip to Leftover #8 in the Appendix to learn more about anonymous types!

Jimmy saved a bunch of dough

It looks like Jimmy drives a hard bargain. He created a list of
`Purchase` classes that contained his purchases, and compared them
with the prices he found on Greg's List.

① First Jimmy created his collection to join.

Jimmy already had his first collection—he just used his `BuildCatalog()` method from before. So
all he had to do was write a `FindPurchases()` method to build his list of `Purchase` classes.

```
static IEnumerable<Purchase> FindPurchases() {
    List<Purchase> purchases = new List<Purchase>() {
        new Purchase() { Issue = 68, Price = 225M },
        new Purchase() { Issue = 19, Price = 375M },
        new Purchase() { Issue = 6, Price = 3600M },
        new Purchase() { Issue = 57, Price = 13215M },
        new Purchase() { Issue = 36, Price = 660M },
    };
    return purchases;
}
```

Jimmy paid $13,215 for issue #57.

② Now he can do the join!

You've seen all the parts of this query already…now here they are, put together in one piece.

```
IEnumerable<Comic> comics = BuildCatalog();
Dictionary<int, decimal> values = GetPrices();
IEnumerable<Purchase> purchases = FindPurchases();

var results =
    from comic in comics
    join purchase in purchases
    on comic.Issue equals purchase.Issue
    orderby comic.Issue ascending
    select new { comic.Name, comic.Issue, purchase.Price };
decimal gregsListValue = 0;
decimal totalSpent = 0;
foreach (var result in results) {
    gregsListValue += values[result.Issue];
    totalSpent += result.Price;
    Console.WriteLine("Issue #{0} ({1}) bought for {2:c}",
            result.Issue, result.Name, result.Price);
}
Console.WriteLine("I spent {0:c} on comics worth {1:c}",
            totalSpent, gregsListValue);
```

When Jimmy used a join clause, LINQ compared every item in the comics collection with each item in purchases to see which ones have comic.Issue equal to purchase.Issue.

The select clause creates a result set with Name and Issue from the comic member, and Price from the purchase member.

Jimmy's real happy that he knows LINQ, because it let him see just how hard a bargain he can drive!

Output:

```
Issue #6 (Johnny America vs. the Pinko) bought for $3,600.00
Issue #19 (Rock and Roll (limited edition)) bought for $375.00
Issue #36 (Woman's Work) bought for $660.00
Issue #57 (Hippie Madness (misprinted)) bought for $13,215.00
Issue #68 (Revenge of the New Wave Freak (damaged)) bought for $22
I spent $18,075.00 on comics worth $18,525.00
```

OK, so now I know Jimmy played with his comic books using LINQ queries to query his collections...but what about the Starbuzz promotion problem? I still don't see how LINQ works with databases.

Even though LINQ to SQL is very different under the hood, when you write your code it looks really similar to other LINQ queries.

LINQ uses the <u>same</u> syntax with databases as it does with collections.

You've already seen in Chapter 1 how easy .NET makes it to work with a database. The IDE gives you a really convenient way to connect with databases, add tables, and even link data in those tables to your forms.

Now, you can take that same database you already connected to and query it with LINQ. Not only that, LINQ lets you combine your data from your database with data from your objects seamlessly.

In fact, you can use the same exact query syntax...all you need is to get access to your database so you can run a LINQ query against it.

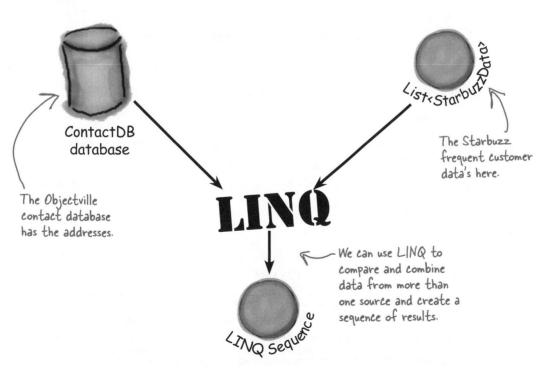

ContactDB database

The Objectville contact database has the addresses.

List<StarbuzzData>

The Starbuzz frequent customer data's here.

LINQ

We can use LINQ to compare and combine data from more than one source and create a sequence of results.

LINQ sequence

Connect LINQ to a SQL database

LINQ operates on objects that implement the IEnumerable<T> interface, right? So it should make sense that you access your SQL database using an object that implements IEnumerable. And C# makes it easy to add that object to your project.

① Add the Objectville contact database to a new console application project

Back in Chapter 1, you created a SQL Server Compact database of contacts for the Objectville Paper Company and saved it in a file called ContactDB.sdf. Start a new Windows Application project, right-click on your project in the Solution Explorer, select "Add Existing Item", and add the database. Make sure you select "Data Files" from the file type filter drop-down, navigate to the file with the SQL database, and add it to your project. (The IDE will pop up the Data Source Configuration wizard, but you can cancel out of it.)

② Use the SqlMetal.exe program to generate LINQ to SQL classes

There's one more step you need to do to connect the dots between your SQL database and your code, and you'll do it using a program called **SqlMetal.exe**. It's a command-line tool that's installed along with Visual Studio 2010 (it doesn't matter which edition you install, it comes with all of them). You can find it in a folder called "Microsoft SDKs", which lives inside your "Program Files" folder (or, if you're running a 64-bit version of Windows, your "Program Files (x86)" folder). Bring up a command prompt and run a command to add the Microsoft SDKs folder to your path. If you're using a 64-bit version of Windows, type this:

It might also be in a folder called "NETFX 4.0 Tools" under the Bin\ folder. If it is, add "NETFX 4.0 Tools" to the end of the PATH= command.

```
PATH=%PATH%;%ProgramFiles(x86)%\Microsoft SDKs\Windows\v7.0A\Bin\
```

Or if you're using a 32-bit version, type this:

```
PATH=%PATH%;%ProgramFiles%\Microsoft SDKs\Windows\v7.0A\Bin\
```

Next, change directory to your project folder (**cd folder-name**) and type this command:

```
SqlMetal.exe ContactDB.sdf /dbml:ContactDB.dbml
```

Here's what it should look like when your command is running:

```
Microsoft (R) Database Mapping Generator 2008 version 1.00.30729
for Microsoft (R) .NET Framework version 3.5
Copyright (C) Microsoft Corporation. All rights reserved.
```

After it's done, your folder should contain three new files: ContactDB.dbml, ContactDB.designer.cs, and ContactDB.dbml.layout.

Use "Add Existing Item" to add ContactDB.dbml to your project (again, select "Data Files" from the file type filter drop-down). When you add that file, the IDE automatically adds the others, too.

> **You can learn more about SqlMetal.exe here:**
> **http://msdn.microsoft.com/en-us/library/bb386987.aspx**
> **And if for some strange reason the Visual Studio installer didn't install it for you, that page has a link to the Microsoft SDK download page.**

③ Open up the LINQ to SQL classes in the Object Relational Designer

When you ran SqlMetal.exe to create ContactDB.dbml and the other files and added them to your project, you created **LINQ to SQL classes**. Remember, LINQ queries are built to operate on objects that implement the IEnumerable<T> interface. But a SQL Server Compact database isn't an object at all! That's where the LINQ to SQL classes come in. They contain classes that know how to query the tables in your database, but also implement IEnumerable<T> with an enumerator that returns the data in that table.

The IDE has a great tool called the Object Relational Designer that shows you exactly what classes you generated with SqlMetal.exe. Once ContactDB.dbml is added to your project, double-click on it to bring it up the Object Relational Designer. Here's what you should see:

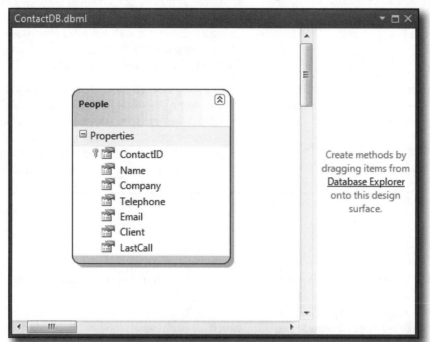

The Object Relational Designer is showing you the People class, which is a data class that you generated with SqlMetal.exe. It connects to the People table in your database and returns the data using the IEnumerable<T> interface so it can be queried using LINQ. How neat is that?

> Quick note: In the <u>non-Express</u> versions of Visual Studio, you can skip SqlMetal.exe and drag your SQL Server Compact Edition data source straight into the Object Relational Designer.

④ You're all set to write LINQ queries that pull data out of the database

Add this code to the Main() method. Notice how we used the **select new** keyword to create custom results that only contain the Name and Company.

The ContactDB class is called a data context class. Use its People property in a LINQ query to get data out of the People table.

```
string connectionString = "Data Source=|DataDirectory|\\ContactDB.sdf";
ContactDB context = new ContactDB(connectionString);

var peopleData =
    from person in context.People
    select new { person.Name, person.Company };

foreach (var person in peopleData)
    Console.WriteLine("{0} works at {1}", person.Name, person.Company);
```

Get some practice using select new. It'll pull just the values from the Name and Company columns from the database.

BULLET POINTS

- The **group** clause tells LINQ to group the results together—when you use it, LINQ creates a sequence of group sequences.

- Every group contains members that have one member in common, called the group's **key**. Use the **by** keyword to specify the key for the group. Each group sequence has a **Key** member that contains the group's key.

- Use a **join** clause to tell LINQ to combine two collections into a single query. When you do, LINQ compares every member of the first collection with every member of the second collection, including the matching pairs in the results.

- **join** queries use an **on** … **equals** clause to tell LINQ how to match the pairs of items.

- When you're doing a **join** query, you usually want a set of results that includes some members from the first collection and other members from the second collection. The **select** clause lets you build custom results from both of them.

- LINQ can query a SQL database using the **LINQ to SQL classes**. Those classes provide objects for your program that work with LINQ (which means you can access the methods on those objects directly if you want—try it out yourself!).

- The IDE's Object Relational Designer lets you choose the tables that you want to access via LINQ. When you specify the tables you want to access, it adds a `DataContext` class to your project. When it's instantiated, add its members to your LINQ queries to access the SQL tables.

---

there are no Dumb Questions

Q: Can you rewind a minute and explain what `var` is again?

A: Yes, definitely. The `var` keyword solves a tricky problem that LINQ brings with it. Normally, when you call a method or execute a statement, it's absolutely clear exactly what types you're working with. If you've got a method that returns a `string`, for instance, then you can only store its results in a `string` variable or field.

But LINQ isn't quite so simple. When you build a LINQ statement, it might return an anonymous type that *isn't defined anywhere in your program*. Yes, you know that it's going to be a sequence of some sort. But what kind of sequence will it be? You don't know—because the objects that are contained in the sequence depend entirely on what you put in your LINQ query. Take this query, for example, from Jimmy's program:

```
var mostExpensive =
   from comic in comics
   where values[comic.Issue] > 500
   orderby values[comic.Issue] descending
   select comic;
```

What if you changed the last line to this:

```
select new
   { Name = comic.Name,
     IssueNumber = "#" + comic.Issue };
```

That returns a perfectly valid type: an anonymous type with two members, a string called `Name` and a string called `IssueNumber`. But we don't have a class definition for that type anywhere in our program! Sure, you don't actually need to run the program to see exactly how that type is defined. But the `mostExpensive` variable still needs to be declared with *some* type.

And that's why C# gives us the `var` keyword, which tells the compiler, "OK, we know that this is a valid type, but we can't exactly tell you what it is right now. So why don't you just figure that out yourself and not bother us with it? Thanks so much."

there are no Dumb Questions

Q: I don't quite get how join works.

A: `join` works with any two sequences. Let's say you've got a collection of football players called `players`—its items are objects that have a `Name` property, a `Position` property and a `Number` property. So we could pull out the players whose jerseys have a number bigger than 10 with this query:

```
var results =
  from player in players
  where player.Number > 10
  select player;
```

Let's say we wanted to figure out each player's shirt size, and we've got a `jerseys` collection whose items have a `Number` property and a `Size` property. A `join` would work really well for that:

```
var results =
  from player in players
  where player.Number > 10
  join shirt in jerseys
    on player.Number
    equals shirt.Number
  select shirt;
```

Q: Hold on, that query will just give me a bunch of shirts. What if I want to connect each player to his shirt size, and I don't care about his number at all?

A: That's what **anonymous types** are for—you can construct an anonymous type that only has the data you want in it. And it lets you pick and choose from the various collections that you're joining together, too.

So you can select the player's name and the shirt's size, and nothing else:

```
var results =
  from player in players
  where player.Number > 10
  join shirt in jerseys
    on player.Number
    equals shirt.Number
  select new {
    player.Name,
    shirt.Size
  };
```

The IDE is smart enough to figure out exactly what results you'll be creating with your query. If you create a loop to enumerate through the results, as soon as you type the variable name the IDE will pop up an IntelliSense list.

```
foreach (var r in results)
  r.
```

Notice how the list has `Name` and `Size` in it. If you added more items to the `select` clause, they'd show up in the list too. That's because the query would create a different anonymous type with different members.

Q: Do I always have to add that `.dbml` file that was generated by `SqlMetal.exe`? I still don't quite get what's going on there.

A: Yes, you definitely need that file if you want to use LINQ with your SQL Server Compact database.

Remember, LINQ requires an object that implements the `IEnumerable<T>` interface. A SQL database doesn't normally implement that interface...or any interface, really, because it's not an object. So if you want LINQ to work with SQL—or any other source of data that you can query—then you need an object that interacts with it and implements `IEnumerable<T>`.

But don't take our word for it. Go to the code you just wrote, right-click on "People" and choose "Go to Definition" (or press F12). That takes you into a `ContactDB.designer.cs` get accessor that returns a `Table<People>`. Click on "Table" and go to definition again. Class `Table<TEntity>` extends `IQueryable<TEntity>`. Click on "IQueryable" and go to definition one more time, and you'll see that it implements `IEnumerable<T>`.

So the `.dbml` file (and the .cs class file it brings along with it) provides objects that implement `IEnumerable`. And the IDE is smart enough to know exactly what to do with that `.dbml` file: when you generate it, add it to your project, and open it up in the Object Relational Designer, you can see the members of the `People` data class that map directly to the `People` table in your SQL database. That data class takes care of connecting to SQL for you, and it automatically reads your database's tables and provides the data neatly wrapped up in an `IEnumerable<T>` so that LINQ can access it.

You can use "select new" to construct custom LINQ query results that include only the items that you want in your result sequence.

Use a join query to connect Starbuzz and Objectville

Now you have all the tools that you need to combine the data from Starbuzz and Objectville Paper Company into one final result set.

Do this

① **Add the SQL data to your project**

If you haven't already done it, create a new console application project and add the ContactDB SQL database to it. Then use SqlMetal.exe to create the Object Relational Designer with the LINQ to SQL classes to the project, add it to the project, and write a simple test query just to make sure it's all working.

② **Build the Starbuzz objects**

Here's the list that contains the Starbuzz customer data. Add it to your project:

```
class StarbuzzData {
    public string Name { get; set; }
    public Drink FavoriteDrink { get; set; }
    public int MoneySpent { get; set; }
    public int Visits { get; set; }
}
enum Drink {
    BoringCoffee, ChocoRockoLatte, TripleEspresso,
    ZestyLemonChai, DoubleCappuccino, HalfCafAmericano,
    ChocoMacchiato, BananaSplitInACup,
}
```

The Starbuzz data comes as a collection of StarbuzzData objects. It's got a lot of data—you won't need it all for the promotion, so you'll have to select only the data you need in the LINQ query.

Starbuzz has plenty of great drinks, and each customer has his or her favorite.

You'll also need a method to generate some sample data:

```
static IEnumerable<StarbuzzData> GetStarbuzzData() {
    return new List<StarbuzzData> {
        new StarbuzzData {
            Name = "Janet Venutian", FavoriteDrink = Drink.ChocoMacchiato,
            MoneySpent = 255, Visits = 50 },
        new StarbuzzData {
            Name = "Liz Nelson", FavoriteDrink = Drink.DoubleCappuccino,
            MoneySpent = 150, Visits = 35 },
        new StarbuzzData {
            Name = "Matt Franks", FavoriteDrink = Drink.ZestyLemonChai,
            MoneySpent = 75, Visits = 15 },
        new StarbuzzData {
            Name = "Joe Ng", FavoriteDrink = Drink.BananaSplitInACup,
            MoneySpent = 60, Visits = 10 },
        new StarbuzzData {
            Name = "Sarah Kalter", FavoriteDrink = Drink.BoringCoffee,
            MoneySpent = 110, Visits = 15 }
    };
}
```

GetStarbuzzData() uses a collection initializer and object initializers to set up the Starbuzz objects.

Again, you can leave the ()'s off of the collection and object Initializers.

We built this method so that it has some names that also appear in the Objectville contact list. If you used different names, make sure you've got matching data here.

3 **Now join the SQL database to the Starbuzz collection**
Here's the code for the query. Put it in your `Main()` entry point method:

```
IEnumerable<StarbuzzData> starbuzzList = GetStarbuzzData();

string connectionString =
    "Data Source=|DataDirectory|\\ContactDB.sdf";
ContactDB context = new ContactDB(connectionString);

var results =
    from starbuzzCustomer in starbuzzList
    where starbuzzCustomer.MoneySpent > 90
    join person in context.People
    on starbuzzCustomer.Name equals person.Name
    select new { person.Name, person.Company,
                    starbuzzCustomer.FavoriteDrink };

foreach (var row in results){
    Console.WriteLine("{0} at {1} likes {2}",
            row.Name, row.Company, row.FavoriteDrink);

Console.ReadKey();
```

We'll need to do a join to combine the Starbuzz data with the customer data in the People table.

The People member in the DataContext is a collection that gives you access to the People table in the database.

Here's where the select clause pulls the name and company from the database and the favorite drink from the Starbuzz data into one single result sequence.

Check your results—make sure it works the way you expect it to.

Nice work...with this new promotion, I'll bet we'll get tons of repeat business. I'll definitely be calling you again.

Edit queries with LINQPad

There's a great learning tool for exploring and using LINQ. It's called LINQPad, and it's available for free from Joe Albahari (one of our superstar "Head First C#" technical reviewers who kept a lot of bugs out of this book). You can download it here:

http://www.linqpad.net/

C# Lab

Invaders

This lab gives you a spec that describes a program for you to build, using the knowledge you've gained throughout this book.

This project is bigger than the ones you've seen so far. So read the whole thing before you get started, and give yourself a little time. And don't worry if you get stuck—there's nothing new in here, so you can move on in the book and come back to the lab later.

We've filled in a few design details for you, and we've made sure you've got all the pieces you need...and nothing else.

It's up to you to finish the job. You can download an executable for this lab from the website...but we won't give you the code for the answer.

The grandfather of video games

In this lab you'll pay homage to one of the most popular, revered, and replicated icons in video game history, a game that needs no further introduction. **It's time to build Invaders.**

As the player destroys the invaders, the score goes up. It's displayed in the upper left-hand corner.

The invaders attack in waves of 30. The first wave moves slowly and fires a few shots at a time. The next wave moves faster, and fires more shots more frequently. If all 30 invaders in a wave are destroyed, the next wave attacks.

The player starts out with three ships. The first ship is in play, and the other two are kept in reserve. His spare ships are shown in the upper right-hand corner.

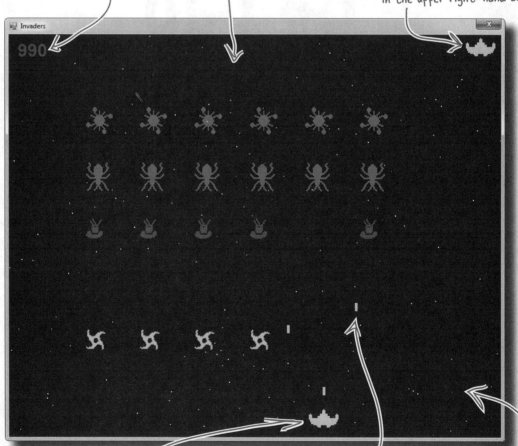

The player moves the ship left and right, and fires shots at the invaders. If a shot hits an invader, the invader is destroyed and the player's score goes up.

The invaders return fire. If one of the shots hits the ship, the player loses a life. Once all lives are gone, or if the invaders reach the bottom of the screen, the game ends and a big "GAME OVER" is displayed in the middle of the screen.

The multicolored stars in the background twinkle on and off, but don't affect gameplay at all.

Your mission: defend the planet against wave after wave of invaders

The invaders attack in waves, and each wave is a tight formation of 30 individual invaders. As the player destroys invaders, his score goes up. The bottom invaders are shaped like stars and worth 10 points. The spaceships are worth 20, the saucers are worth 30, the bugs are worth 40, and the satellites are worth 50. The player starts with three lives. If he loses all three lives or the invaders reach the bottom of the screen, the game's over.

There are five different types of invaders, but they all behave the same way. They start at the top of the screen and move left until they reach the edge. Then they drop down and start moving right. When they reach the right-hand boundary, they drop down and move left again. If the invaders reach the bottom of the screen, the game's over.

 10 20 30 40 50

The first wave of invaders can fire two shots at once—the invaders will hold their fire if there are more than two shots on the screen. The next wave fires three, the next fires four, etc.

The game should keep track of which keys are currently being held down. So pressing right and spacebar would cause the ship to move to the right and fire (if two shots aren't already on the screen).

The spacebar shoots, but there can only be two player shots on the screen at once. As soon as a shot hits something or disappears, another shot can be fired.

If a shot hits an invader, both disappear. Otherwise, the shot disappears when it gets to the top of the screen.

Fire!

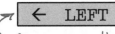 SPACE

← LEFT

RIGHT →

The left arrow moves the ship toward the left-hand edge of the screen.

The right arrow key moves the ship to the right.

715

The architecture of Invaders

Invaders needs to keep track of a wave of 30 invaders (including their location, type, and score value), the player's ship, shots that the player and invaders fire at each other, and stars in the background. As in the Quest lab, you'll need a Game object to keep up with all this and coordinate between the form and the game objects.

Here's an overview of what you'll need to create:

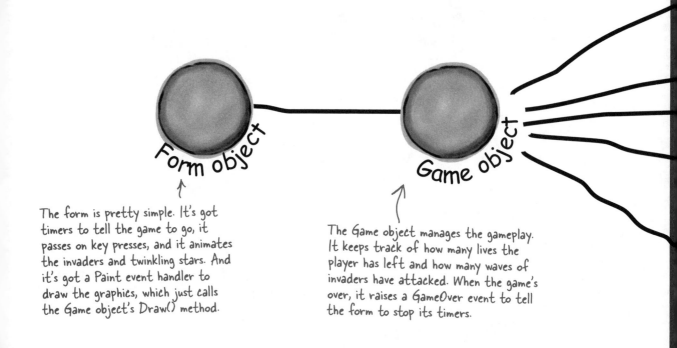

Form object

↑
The form is pretty simple. It's got timers to tell the game to go, it passes on key presses, and it animates the invaders and twinkling stars. And it's got a Paint event handler to draw the graphics, which just calls the Game object's Draw() method.

Game object

↑
The Game object manages the gameplay. It keeps track of how many lives the player has left and how many waves of invaders have attacked. When the game's over, it raises a GameOver event to tell the form to stop its timers.

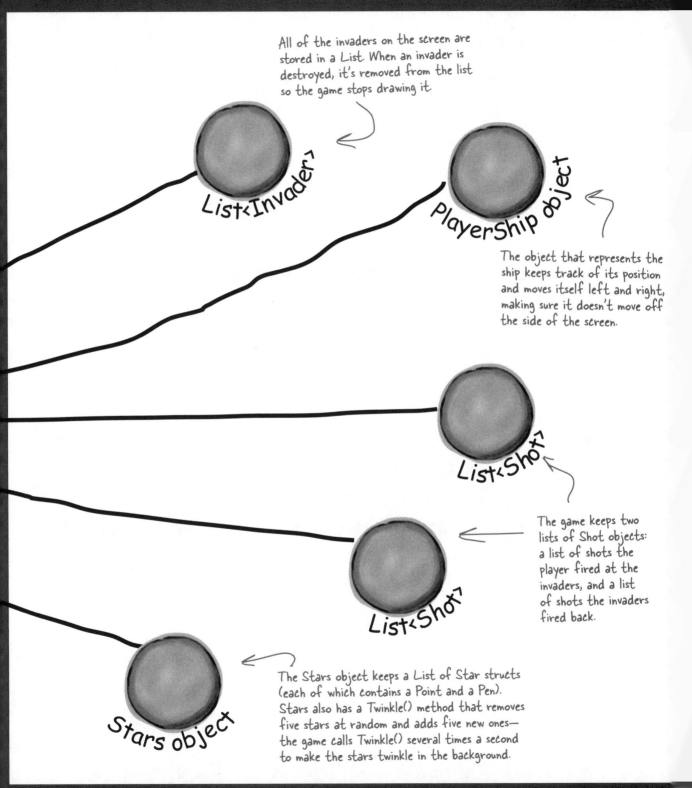

All of the invaders on the screen are stored in a List. When an invader is destroyed, it's removed from the list so the game stops drawing it.

List<Invader>

PlayerShip object

The object that represents the ship keeps track of its position and moves itself left and right, making sure it doesn't move off the side of the screen.

List<Shot>

The game keeps two lists of Shot objects: a list of shots the player fired at the invaders, and a list of shots the invaders fired back.

List<Shot>

Stars object

The Stars object keeps a List of Star structs (each of which contains a Point and a Pen). Stars also has a Twinkle() method that removes five stars at random and adds five new ones—the game calls Twinkle() several times a second to make the stars twinkle in the background.

Design the Invaders form

The Invaders form has only two controls: a timer to trigger animation (making the stars twinkle and the invaders animate by changing each invader picture to a different frame), and a timer to handle gameplay (the invaders marching left and right, the player moving, and the player and invaders shooting at each other). Other than that, the only intelligence in the form is an event handler to handle the game's GameOver event, and KeyUp and KeyDown event handlers to manage the keyboard input.

The form fires a KeyDown event any time a key is pressed, and it fires a KeyUp event whenever a key is released.

When the form initializes its Game object, it passes its ClientRectangle to it so it knows the boundaries of the form. So you can change the size of the battlefield just by changing the size of the form.

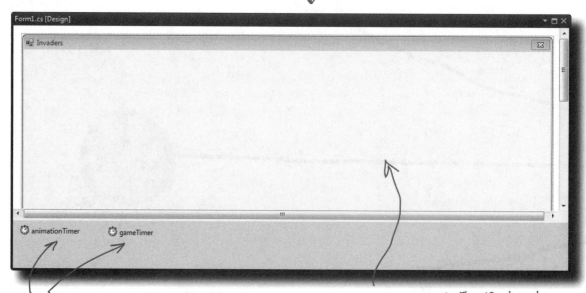

You should add two timers: animationTimer and gameTimer.

Set the form's FormBorderStyle property to FixedSingle and its DoubleBuffered property to true, turn off its MinimizeBox and MaximizeBox properties, set its title, and then <u>stretch</u> it out to the width you want the game area to be.

animationTimer

The animation timer handles the eye candy

The stars in the game's background and the invader animation
don't affect gameplay, and they continue when the game is
paused or stopped. So we need a separate timer for those.

Add code for the animation timer's tick event

Your code should have a counter that cycles from 0 to 3 and then back down
to 0. That counter is used to update each of the four-cell invader animations
(creating a smooth animation). Your handler should also call the `Game`
object's `Twinkle()` method, which will cause the stars to twinkle. Finally, it
needs to call the form's `Refresh()` method to repaint the screen.

Try a timer interval of 33ms, which will give you about 30 frames per second.
Make sure you set the game timer to a shorter interval, though. The ship
should move and gameplay should occur more quickly than the stars twinkle.

Animation occurs even when gameplay doesn't. That means that the stars twinkle and the invaders animate even if the game is over, paused, or hasn't been started.

Adjust the timers for smooth animation

With a 33ms interval for animation, set the game timer to 10ms. That way, the
main gameplay will occur more quickly than the animation (which is really just
background eye candy). At the same time, the `Go()` method in `Game` (fired
by the game timer, which we'll talk about in a little bit) can take a lot of CPU
cycles. If the CPU is busy handling gameplay, the animation timer will just wait
until the CPU gets to it, and then fire (and animate the stars and invaders).

Alternately, you can just set both timers to an interval of 5ms, and the game
will run and animate about as fast as your system can handle (although on fast
machines, animation could get annoyingly quick).

If the animation timer is set to 33ms, but the Game object's Go() method takes longer than that to run, then animation will occur once Go() completes.

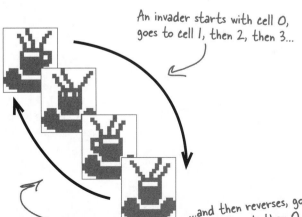

An invader starts with cell 0, goes to cell 1, then 2, then 3...

...and then reverses, going back to 2, then 1, then 0.

We tried things out on a slow machine, and found that setting the animation interval to 100ms and the gameplay timer interval to 50ms gave us a frame rate of about 10 frames per second, which was definitely playable. Try starting there and reducing each interval until you're happy.

Respond to keyboard input

Before we can code the game timer, we need to write event
handlers for the KeyDown and KeyUp events. KeyDown is
triggered when a key is pressed, and KeyUp when a key is
released. For most keys, we can simply take action by firing a
shot or quitting the game.

So if the player's holding down the left arrow and spacebar at the same time, the list will contain Keys.Left and Keys.Space.

For some keys, like the right or left arrow, we'll want to store
those in a list that our game timer can then use to move the
player's ship. So we'll also need a list of pressed keys in the form
object:

We need a list of keys so we can track which keys have been pressed. Our game timer will need that list for movement in just a bit.

```
List<Keys> keysPressed = new List<Keys>();

private void Form1_KeyDown(object sender, KeyEventArgs e) {
    if (e.KeyCode == Keys.Q)
        Application.Exit();
    if (gameOver)
        if (e.KeyCode == Keys.S) {
            // code to reset the game and restart the timers
            return;
        }
    if (e.KeyCode == Keys.Space)
        game.FireShot();
    if (keysPressed.Contains(e.KeyCode))
        keysPressed.Remove(e.KeyCode);
    keysPressed.Add(e.KeyCode);
}

private void Form1_KeyUp(object sender, KeyEventArgs e) {
    if (keysPressed.Contains(e.KeyCode))
        keysPressed.Remove(e.KeyCode);
}
```

The 'Q' key quits the game.

If the game has ended, reset the game and start over.

But we only want this to work if the game's over. Pressing S shouldn't restart a game that's already in progress.

The Keys enum defines all the keys you might want to check key codes against.

You'll need to fill in this code.

The spacebar fires a shot.

By removing the key and then re-adding it, the key becomes the last (most current) item in the list.

The key that's pressed gets added to our key list, which we'll use in a second.

We want the most current key pressed to be at the very top of the list, so that if the player mashes a few keys at the same time, the game responds to the one that was hit most recently. Then, when he lets up one key, the game responds to the next one in the list.

When a key is released, we remove it from our list of pressed keys.

**Flip back to the KeyGame project
you built in Chapter 4. You used a
KeyDown event handler there, too!**

The game timer handles movement and gameplay

The main job of the form's game timer is to call Go() in the Game class. But it also has to respond to any keys pressed, so it has to check the keysPressed list to find any keys caught by the KeyDown and KeyUp events:

> Players "mash" a bunch of keys at once. If we want the game to be robust, it needs to be able to handle that. That's why we're using the keysPressed list.

> This timer makes the game advance by one frame. So the first thing it does is call the Game object's Go() method to let gameplay continue.

```
private void gameTimer_Tick(object sender, EventArgs e)
{
    game.Go();
    foreach (Keys key in keysPressed)
    {
        if (key == Keys.Left)
        {
            game.MovePlayer(Direction.Left);
            return;
        }
        else if (key == Keys.Right)
        {
            game.MovePlayer(Direction.Right);
            return;
        }
    }
}
```

> keysPressed is your List<Keys> object managed by the KeyDown and KeyUp event handlers. It contains every key the player currently has pressed.

> The keysPressed list has the keys in the order that they're pressed. This foreach loop goes through them until it finds a Left or Right key, then moves the player and returns.

> The KeyUp and KeyDown events use the Keys enum to specify a key. We'll use Keys.Left and Keys.Right to move the ship.

> Shots move up and down, the player moves left and right, and the invaders move left, right, and down. You'll need this enum to keep all those directions straight.

```
enum Direction {
    Left,
    Right,
    Up,
    Down,
}
```

The KeyDown event handler just handles the space, S, and Q keystrokes without adding them to the keysPressed list. What would happen if you moved the code for firing the shot when the space key is pressed to this event handler?

One more form detail: the GameOver event

Add a private bool field called gameOver to the form that's true only when the game is over. Then add an event handler for the Game object's GameOver event that stops the game timer (but not the animation timer, so the stars still twinkle and the invaders still animate), sets gameOver to true, and calls the form's Invalidate() method.

> Here's an example of adding another event to a form without using the IDE. This is all manual coding.

When you write the form's Paint event handler, have it check gameOver. If it's true, have it write GAME OVER in big yellow letters in the middle of the screen. Then have it write "Press S to start a new game or Q to quit" in the lower right-hand corner. You can start the game out in this state, so the user has to hit S to start a new game.

> The game over event and its delegate live in the Game class, which you'll see in just a minute.

The form's game timer tells the game to Go()

In addition to handling movement left and right, the main job of the game timer is to call the Game object's Go() method. That's where all of the gameplay is managed. The Game object keeps track of the state of the game, and its Go() method advances the game by one frame. That involves:

1 **Checking to see if the player died**, using its Alive property. When the player dies, the game shows a little animation of the ship collapsing (using DrawImage() to squish the ship down to nothing). The animation is done by the PlayerShip class, so Go() just needs to check to see if it's dead. If it is, it returns—that way, it keeps the invaders from moving or shooting while the player gets a small break (and watches his ship get crushed).

2 **Moving each of the shots.** Shots fired by the invaders move down, and shots fired by the player move up. Game keeps two List<Shot> objects, one for the invaders' shots and one for the player's. Any shot that's moved off the screen needs to be removed from the list.

3 **Moving each of the invaders.** Game calls each Invader object's Move() method, and tells the invaders which way to move. Game also keeps up with where the invaders are in case they need to move down a row or switch directions. Then, Game checks to see if it's time for the invaders to return fire, and if so, it adds new Shot objects to the List<>.

4 **Checking for hits**. If a player's shot hit any invaders, Game removes the invaders from the appropriate List<>. Then Game checks to see if any of the invader shots have collided with the player's ship, and if so, it kills the player by setting its Alive property to false. If the player's out of lives, then Game raises the GameOver event to tell the form that the game's over. The form's GameOver event handler stops its game timer, so Go() isn't called again.

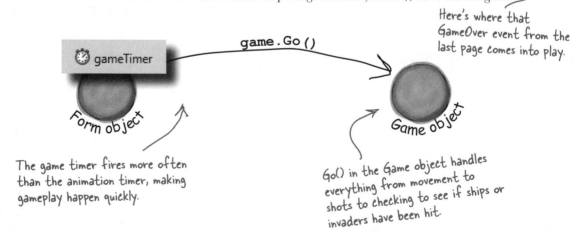

Here's where that GameOver event from the last page comes into play.

game.Go ()

🕐 gameTimer

Form object

The game timer fires more often than the animation timer, making gameplay happen quickly.

Game object

Go() in the Game object handles everything from movement to shots to checking to see if ships or invaders have been hit.

Taking control of graphics

In earlier labs, the form used controls for the graphics. But now that you know how to use `Graphics` and double-buffering, the `Game` object should handle a lot of the drawing.

So the form should have a `Paint` event handler (make sure you set the form's `DoubleBuffered` property to `true`!). You'll delegate the rest of the drawing to the `Game` object by calling its `Draw()` method every time the form's `Paint` event fires.

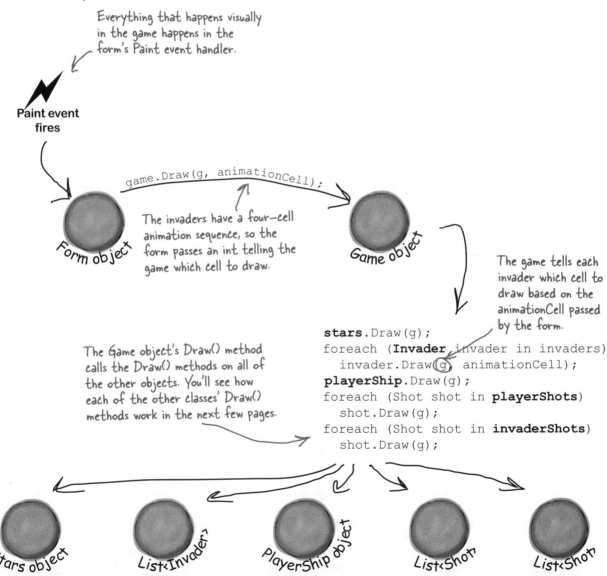

Everything that happens visually in the game happens in the form's Paint event handler.

Paint event fires

`game.Draw(g, animationCell);`

The invaders have a four-cell animation sequence, so the form passes an int telling the game which cell to draw.

Form object

Game object

The game tells each invader which cell to draw based on the animationCell passed by the form.

```
stars.Draw(g);
foreach (Invader invader in invaders)
    invader.Draw(g, animationCell);
playerShip.Draw(g);
foreach (Shot shot in playerShots)
    shot.Draw(g);
foreach (Shot shot in invaderShots)
    shot.Draw(g);
```

The Game object's Draw() method calls the Draw() methods on all of the other objects. You'll see how each of the other classes' Draw() methods work in the next few pages.

Stars object

List<Invader>

PlayerShip object

List<Shot>

List<Shot>

Building the Game class

The Game class is the controller for the Invaders game. Here's a
start on what this class should look like, although there's lots of
work still for you to do.

The score, livesLeft, and wave fields keep track of some basic information about the state of the game.

```
class Game {
    private int score = 0;
    private int livesLeft = 2;
    private int wave = 0;
    private int framesSkipped = 0;

    private Rectangle boundaries;
    private Random random;

    private Direction invaderDirection;
    private List<Invader> invaders;

    private PlayerShip playerShip;
    private List<Shot> playerShots;
    private List<Shot> invaderShots;

    private Stars stars;

    public event EventHandler GameOver;

    // etc...
}
```

You'll use the frame field to slow down the invaders early on in the game—the first wave should skip 6 frames before they move to the left, the next wave should skip 5, the next should skip 4, etc.

This List<> of Invader objects keeps track of all of the invaders in the current wave. When an invader is destroyed, it's removed from the list. The game checks periodically to make sure the list isn't empty—if it is, it sends in the next wave of invaders.

This Stars object keeps track of the multicolored stars in the background.

The Game object raises its GameOver event when the player dies and doesn't have any more lives left. You'll build the event handler method in the form, and hook it into the Game object's GameOver event.

Game
GameOver: event
Draw(g: Graphics, animationCell: int) Twinkle() MovePlayer(direction: Direction) FireShot() Go()

Most of these methods combine methods on other objects to make a specific action occur.

Remember, these are the <u>public methods</u>. You may need a lot more private methods to structure your code in a way that makes sense to <u>you</u>.

The Game class methods

The Game class has five public methods that get triggered
by different events happening in the form.

1 **The Draw() method draws the game on a Graphics object**
The Draw() method takes two parameters: a Graphics object and an integer that contains
the animation cell (a number from 0 to 3). First, it should draw a black rectangle that fills up
the whole form (using the display rectangle stored in boundaries, received from the form).
Then the method should draw the stars, the invaders, the player's ship, and then the shots.
Finally, it should draw the score in the upper left-hand corner, the player's ships in the upper
right-hand corner, and a big "GAME OVER" in yellow letters if gameOver is true.

2 **The Twinkle() method twinkles the stars**
The form's animation timer event handler needs to be able to twinkle the stars, so the Game
object needs a one-line method to call stars.Twinkle(). *← We'll write code for the Stars object in a few more pages.*

3 **The MovePlayer() method moves the player**
The form's keyboard timer event handler needs to move the player's ship, so the Game object
also needs a two-line method that takes a Direction enum as a parameter, checks whether
or not the player's dead, and calls playerShip.Move() to affect that movement.

4 **The FireShot() method makes the player fire a shot at the invaders**
The FireShot() method checks to see if there are fewer than two player shots on screen. If
so, the method should add a new shot to the playerShots list at the right location.

5 **The Go() method makes the game go**
The form's animation timer calls the Game object's Go() method anywhere between 10
and 30 times a second (depending on the computer's CPU speed). The Go() method does
everything the game needs to do to advance itself by a frame:

★ The game checks if the player's dead using its Alive property. If he's still alive, the
game isn't over yet—if it were, the form would have stopped the animation timer with
its Stop() method. So the Go() method won't do anything else until the player is
alive again—it'll just return.

★ Every shot needs to be updated. The game needs to loop through both List<Shot>
objects, calling each shot's Move() method. If any shot's Move() returns false, that
means the shot went off the edge of the screen—so it gets deleted from the list.

★ The game then moves each invader, and allows them to return fire.

★ Finally, it checks for collisions: first for any shot that overlaps an invader (and removing
both from their List<T> objects), and then to see if the player's been shot. We'll add
a Rectangle property called Area to the Invader and PlayerShip classes—so
we can use the Contains() method to see if the ship's area overlaps with a shot.

Filling out the Game class

The problem with class diagrams is that they usually leave out any non-public properties and methods. So even after you've got the methods from page 725 done, you've still got a lot of work to do. Here are some things to think about:

The constructor sets everything up

The Game object needs to create all of the other objects—the Invader objects, the PlayerShip object, the List objects to hold the shots, and the Stars object. The form passes in an initialized Random object and its own ClientRectangle struct (so the Game can **figure out the boundaries of the battlefield**, which it uses to determine when shots are out of range and when the invaders reach the edge and need to drop and reverse direction). Then, your code should create everything else in the game world.

We'll talk about most of these individual objects over the next several pages of this lab.

Build a NextWave() method

A simple method to create the next wave of invaders will come in handy. It should assign a new List of Invader objects to the invaders field, add the 30 invaders in 6 columns so that they're in their starting positions, increase the wave field by 1, and set the invaderDirection field to start them moving toward the right-hand side of the screen. You'll also change the framesSkipped field.

Here's an example of a private method that will really help out your Game class organization.

A few other ideas for private methods

Here are a few of the private method ideas you might play with, and see if these would also help the design of your Game class:

- ✓ A method to see if the player's been hit (CheckForPlayerCollisions())
- ✓ A method to see if any invaders have been hit (CheckForInvaderCollisions())
- ✓ A method to move all the invaders (MoveInvaders())
- ✓ A method allowing invaders to return fire (ReturnFire())

BRAIN POWER

It's possible to show protected and private properties and methods in a class diagram, but you'll rarely see that put into practice. Why do you think that is?

LINQ makes collision detection much easier

This seems really complex when you first read it, but each LINQ query is just a couple of lines of code. Here's a hint: don't overcomplicate it!

You've got collections of invaders and shots, and you need to search through those collections to find certain invaders and shots. Any time you hear collections and searching in the same sentence, you should think LINQ. Here's what you need to do:

① **Figure out if the invaders' formation has reached the edge of the battlefield**
The invaders need to change direction if any one invader is within 100 pixels of the edge of the battlefield. When the invaders are marching to the right, once they reach the right-hand side of the form the game needs to tell them to drop down and start marching to the left. And when the invaders are marching to the left, the game needs to check if they've reached the left edge. To make this happen, add a private `MoveInvaders()` method that gets called by `Go()`. The first thing it should do is check and update the private `framesSkipped` field, and `return` if this frame should be skipped (depending on the level). Then it should check which direction the invaders are moving. If the invaders are moving to the right, `MoveInvaders()` should use LINQ to search the `invaderCollection` list for any invader whose location's X value is within 100 pixels of the right-hand boundary. If it finds any, then it should tell the invaders to march downward and then set `invaderDirection` equal to `Direction.Left`; if not, it can tell each invader to march to the right. On the other hand, if the invaders are moving to the left, then it should do the opposite, using another LINQ query to see if the invaders are within 100 pixels of the left-hand boundary, marching them down and changing direction if they are.

② **Determine which invaders can return fire**
Add a private method called `ReturnFire()` that gets called by `Go()`. First, it should `return` if the invaders' shot list already has `wave + 1` shots. It should also `return` if `random.Next(10) < 10 - wave`. (That makes the invaders fire at random, and not all the time.) If it gets past both tests, it can use LINQ to group the invaders by their `Location.X` and sort them `descending`. Once it's got those groups, it can choose a group at random, and use its `First()` method to find the invader at the bottom of the column. All right, now you've got the shooter—you can add a shot to the invader's shot list just below the middle of the invader (use the invader's `Area` to set the shot's location).

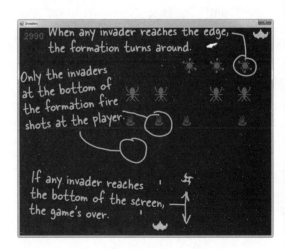

③ **Check for invader and player collisions**
You'll want to create a method to check for collisions. There are three collisions to check for, and the `Rectangle` struct's `Contains()` method will come in really handy—just pass it any `Point`, and it'll return `true` if that point is inside the rectangle.

★ Use LINQ to find any dead invaders by looping through the shots in the player's shot list and selecting any invader where `invader.Area` contains the shot's location. Remove the invader and the shot.

★ Add a query to figure out if any invaders reached the bottom of the screen—if so, end the game.

★ You don't need LINQ to look for shots that collided with the player, just a loop and the player's `Area` property. (Remember, **you can't modify a collection inside a foreach loop**. If you do, you'll get an `InvalidOperationException` with a message that the collection was modified.)

Crafting the Invader class

The Invader class keeps track of a single invader. So when the Game object creates a new wave of invaders, it adds 30 instances of Invader to a List<Invader> object. Every time its Go() method is called, it calls each invader's Move() method to tell it to move. And every time its Draw() method is called, it calls each invader object's Draw() method. So you'll need to build out the Move() and Draw() methods. You'll want to add a private method called InvaderImage(), too—it'll come in really handy when you're drawing the invader. Make sure you call it inside the Draw() method to keep the image field up to date:

Invader
Location: Point
InvaderType: ShipType
Area: Rectangle
Score: int
Draw(g: Graphics, animationCell: int)
Move(direction: Direction)

```
class Invader {
    private const int HorizontalInterval = 10;
    private const int VerticalInterval = 40;

    private Bitmap image;

    public Point Location { get; private set; }

    public ShipType InvaderType { get; private set; }

    public Rectangle Area { get {
        return new Rectangle(location, image.Size); }
    }

    public int Score { get; private set; }

    public Invader(ShipType invaderType, Point location, int score) {
        this.InvaderType = invaderType;
        this.Location = location;
        this.Score = score;
        image = InvaderImage(0);
    }

    // Additional methods will go here
}
```

The HorizontalInterval constant determines how many pixels an invader moves every time it marches left or right. VerticalInterval is the number of pixels it drops down when the formation reaches the edge of the battlefield.

Check out what we did with the Area property. Since we know the invader's location and we know its size (from its image field), we can add a get accessor that calculates a Rectangle for the area it covers...

...which means you can use the Rectangle's **Contains()** method inside a LINQ query to **detect any shots that collided** with an invader.

An Invader object uses the ShipType enum to figure out what kind of enemy ship it is.

```
enum ShipType {
    Bug,
    Saucer,
    Satellite,
    Spaceship,
    Star,
}
```

Build the Invaders' methods

The three core methods for `Invader` are `Move()`, `Draw()`, and `InvaderImage()`. Let's look at each in turn.

There are five types of invaders, and each of them has four different animation cell pictures.

Move the invader ships

First, you need a method to move the invader ships. The `Game` object should send in a direction, using the `Direction` enum, and then the ship should move. Remember, the `Game` object handles figuring out if an invader needs to move down or change direction, so your `Invader` class doesn't have to worry about that.

```
public void Move(Direction direction) {
    // This method needs to move the ship in the
    //    specified direction
}
```

Draw the ship—and the right animation cell

Each `Invader` knows how to draw itself. Given a `Graphics` object to draw to, and the animation cell to use, the invader can display itself onto the game board using the `Graphics` object the `Game` gives it.

```
public void Draw(Graphics g, int animationCell) {
    // This method needs to draw the image of
    //    the ship, using the correct animation cell
}
```

Get the right invader image

You're going to need to grab the right image based on the animation cell a lot, so you may want to pull that code into its own method. Build an `InvaderImage()` method that returns a specific `Bitmap` given an animation cell.

```
private Bitmap InvaderImage(int animationCell) {
    // This is mostly a convenience method, and
    //    returns the right bitmap for the specified cell
}
```

Each invader knows its type. So if you give its InvaderImage() method a number for its animation cell, it can return a Bitmap that's got the right graphic in it.

Remember, you can download these graphics from http://www.headfirstlabs.com/hfcsharp/.

The player's ship can move and die

The `PlayerShip` class keeps track of the player's ship. It's similar to the `Invaders` class, but even simpler.

The Location and Area properties are exactly like the ones in the Invader class.

When the ship's hit with a shot, the game sets the ship's Alive property to false. The game then keeps the invaders from moving until the ship resets its Alive property back to true.

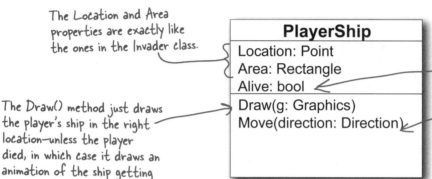

PlayerShip

Location: Point
Area: Rectangle
Alive: bool

Draw(g: Graphics)
Move(direction: Direction)

The Draw() method just draws the player's ship in the right location—unless the player died, in which case it draws an animation of the ship getting crushed by the shot.

The Move() method takes one parameter, a Direction enum, and moves the player in that direction.

PlayerShip needs to take in a Rectangle with the game's boundaries in its constructor, and make sure the ship doesn't get moved out of the game's boundaries in Move().

Animate the player ship when it's hit

The `Draw()` method should take a `Graphics` object as a parameter. Then it checks its `Alive` property. If it's alive, it draws itself using its `Location` property. If it's dead, then instead of drawing the regular bitmap on the graphics, the `PlayerShip` object uses its private `deadShipHeight` field to animate the player ship slowly getting crushed by the shot. After three seconds of being dead, it should flip its `Alive` property back to `true`.

Waiting three seconds is easy—just use the Alive property's set accessor to set a private DateTime field to DateTime.Now. The first thing the ship's Go() method does is use a TimeSpan to check if three seconds have elapsed. If three seconds haven't elapsed, continue doing the crushing ship animation. As soon as three seconds have elapsed, set Alive back to true so the game knows it should continue gameplay. (You used a similar trick in the beehive simulator.)

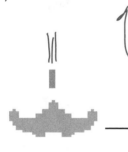

```
public void Draw(Graphics g) {
    if (!Alive) {
```
Reset the deadShipHeight field and draw the ship.
```
    } else {
```
***Check the deadShipHeight field. If it's greater than zero, decrease it by 1
and use DrawImage() to draw the ship a little flatter.***
```
    }
}
```

"Shots fired!"

Game has two lists of `Shot` objects: one for the player's shots moving
up the screen, and one for enemy shots moving down the screen.
`Shot` only needs a few things to work: a `Point` location, a method
to draw the shot, and a method to move. Here's the class diagram:

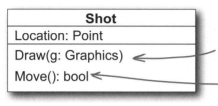

Shot
Location: Point
Draw(g: Graphics)
Move(): bool

Draw() handles drawing the little rectangle for this shot. Game will call this every time the screen needs to be updated.

Move() moves the shot up or down, and keeps up with whether the shot is within the game's boundaries.

Here's a start on the `Shot` class:

```
class Shot {
  private const int moveInterval = 20;
  private const int width = 5;
  private const int height = 15;

  public Point Location { get; private set; }

  private Direction direction;
  private Rectangle boundaries;

  public Shot(Point location, Direction direction,
              Rectangle boundaries) {
    this.Location = location;
    this.direction = direction;
    this.boundaries = boundaries;
  }

  // Your code goes here
}
```

You can adjust these to make the game easier or harder...smaller shots are easier to dodge, faster shots are harder to avoid.

The shot updates its own location in the Move() method, so location can be a read-only automatic property.

Direction is the enum with Up and Down defined.

The game passes the form's display rectangle into the constructor's boundaries parameter so the shot can tell when it's off of the screen.

Your job is to make sure `Draw()` takes in a `Graphics` object
and draws the shot as a yellow rectangle. Then, `Move()` should
move the shot up or down, and return `true` if the shot is still
within the game boundaries.

Twinkle, twinkle...it's up to you

The last class you'll need is the `Stars` class. There are 300 stars, and this class keeps up with all of them, causing 5 to display and 5 to disappear every time `Twinkle()` is called.

First, though, you'll need a `struct` for each star:

```
private struct Star {
   public Point point;
   public Pen pen;

   public Star(Point point, Pen pen) {
      this.point = point;
      this.pen = pen;
   }
}
```

Each star has a point (its location) and a pen (for its color).

All Star does is hold this data...no behavior.

> Here's another hint: start out the project with just a form, a Game class, and Stars class. See if you can get it to draw a black sky with twinkling stars. That'll give you a solid foundation to add the other classes and methods.

The `Stars` class should keep a `List<Star>` for storing 300 of these `Star` structs. You'll need to build a constructor for `Stars` that populates that list. The constructor will get a `Rectangle` with the display boundaries, and a `Random` instance for use in creating the random `Points` to place each star in a random location.

Here's the class diagram for `Stars`, with the other methods you'll need:

You can define the Star struct inside Stars.cs, as only Stars needs to use that struct.

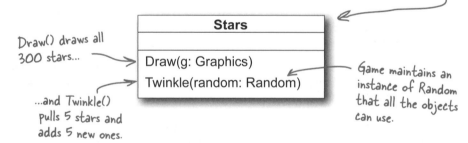

Stars
Draw(g: Graphics)
Twinkle(random: Random)

Draw() draws all 300 stars...

...and Twinkle() pulls 5 stars and adds 5 new ones.

Game maintains an instance of Random that all the objects can use.

`Draw()` should draw all the stars in the list, and `Twinkle()` should remove five random stars and add five new stars in their place.

You might also want to create a `RandomPen()` method so you can get a random color for every new star you create. It should return one of the five possible star colors, by generating a number between 0 and 4, and selecting the matching `Pen` object.

And yet there's more to do...

Think the game's looking pretty good? You can take it to the
next level with a few more additions:

Add animated explosions

Make each invader explode after it's hit, then briefly display a number to
tell the player how many points the invader was worth.

Add a mothership

Once in a while, a mothership worth 250 points can travel across the top
of the battlefield. If the player hits it, he gets a bonus.

Add shields

Add floating shields the player can hide behind. You can add simple
shields that the enemies and player can't shoot through. Then, if you
really want your game to shine, add breakable shields that the player and
invaders can blast holes through after a certain number of hits.

Try making the shields last for fewer hits at higher levels of the game.

Add divebombers

Create a special type of enemy that divebombs the player. A divebombing
enemy should break formation, take off toward the player, fly down
around the bottom of the screen, and then resume its position.

Add more weapons

Start an arms race! Smart bombs, lasers, guided missiles...there are all
sorts of weapons that both the player and the invaders can use to attack
each other. See if you can add three new weapons to the game.

Add more graphics

You can go to **www.headfirstlabs.com/books/hfcsharp/** to find more
graphics files for simple shields, a mothership, and more. We provided
blocky, pixelated graphics to give it that stylized '80s look. Can you come
up with your own graphics to give the game a new style?

A good class design should let you change out graphics with minimal code changes.

**This is your chance to show off! Did you come up with a cool new
version of the game? Join the Head First C# forum and claim your
bragging rights: www.headfirstlabs.com/books/hfcsharp/**

The top ~~10~~ 11 things we wanted to include in this book

I'm still hungry for more!

The fun's just beginning!

We've shown you a lot of great tools to build some really **powerful software** with C#. But there's no way that we could include **every single tool, technology, or technique** in this book—there just aren't enough pages. We had to make some *really tough choices* about what to include and what to leave out. Here are some of the topics that didn't make the cut. But even though we couldn't get to them, we still think that they're **important and useful**, and we wanted to give you a small head start with them.

We wish we could give this material the same kind of thorough treatment we were able to provide throughout the book, but we just didn't have enough pages to do it! But we still want to give you a good starting point and a place to go for more information.

#1. The Basics

Before we get started, here's a Guy class that we'll be using throughout this appendix. Take a look at how it's commented. Notice how the class, its methods, and its properties are all commented with triple-slash (///) comments? Those are called **XML comments**, and the IDE will help you add them. Just type "///" right before a class, method, property, or field declaration (and a few other places, too), and the IDE will fill in the skeleton of the XML comment for it. Then later, when you go to use the property, method, etc., the IDE will display information from the XML comments in its IntelliSense window.

```
/// <summary>
/// A guy with a name, age and a wallet full of bucks
/// </summary>
class Guy
{
```

The XML comment for a class consists of a <summary> block. Notice how it starts with <summary> and ends with </summary>.

```
    /*
     * Notice how Name and Age are properties with backing fields that are
     * marked readonly. That means those backing fields can only be set when
     * the object is initialized (in their declarations or in the constructor).
     */
```

Marking a field readonly is a useful tool for encapsulation, because it means that field can never be changed once the object is instantiated.

```
    /// <summary>
    /// Read-only backing field for the Name property
    /// </summary>
    private readonly string name;

    /// <summary>
    /// The name of the guy
    /// </summary>
    public string Name { get { return name; } }

    /// <summary>
    /// Read-only backing field for the Name property
    /// </summary>
    private readonly int age;

    /// <summary>
    /// The guy's age
    /// </summary>
    public int Age { get { return age; } }

    /*
     * Cash is not readonly because it might change during the life of the Guy.
     */

    /// <summary>
    /// The number of bucks the guy has
    /// </summary>
    public int Cash { get; private set; }
```

When the IDE adds the skeleton for a constructor or another method, it adds <param> tags for each of the parameters.

```csharp
/// <summary>
/// The constructor sets the name, age and cash
/// </summary>
/// <param name="name">The name of the guy</param>
/// <param name="age">The guy's age</param>
/// <param name="cash">The amount of cash the guy starts with</param>
public Guy(string name, int age, int cash) {
    this.name = name;
    this.age = age;
    Cash = cash;
}

public override string ToString() {
    return String.Format("{0} is {1} years old and has {2} bucks", Name, Age, Cash);
}
```

Here's where we're overriding ToString(). This is covered in Chapter 8.

```csharp
/// <summary>
/// Give cash from my wallet
/// </summary>
/// <param name="amount">The amount of cash to give</param>
/// <returns>The amount of cash I gave, or 0 if I don't have enough cash</returns>
public int GiveCash(int amount) {
    if (amount <= Cash && amount > 0)
    {
        Cash -= amount;
        return amount;
    }
    else
    {
        return 0;
    }
}

/// <summary>
/// Receive some cash into my wallet
/// </summary>
/// <param name="amount">Amount to receive</param>
/// <returns>The amount of cash received, or 0 if no cash was received</returns>
public int ReceiveCash(int amount) {
    if (amount > 0)
    {
        if (amount > 0)
        {
            Cash += amount;
            return amount;
        }
        Console.WriteLine("{0} says: {1} isn't an amount I'll take", Name, amount);
    }
    return 0;
}
}
```

...more basics...

It's easy to get overwhelmed when learning any computer language, and C# is no exception. That's why we concentrated on the parts of the language that, in our experience, are most common for novice and intermediate developers. But there's some basic C# and .NET syntax that's really useful, but are a lot easier to approach at your own speed once you're used to things. Here's a console application that demonstrates some of it.

```csharp
static void Main(string[] args)
{
    // We'll use these Guy and Random instances throughout this example.
    Guy bob = new Guy("Bob", 43, 100);
    Guy joe = new Guy("Joe", 41, 100);
    Random random = new Random();
```

> A really good way to get a handle on this is to debug through it and use watches to see what's happening. As you go through the book, try experimenting with some of these concepts.

> A lot of people say that jump statements are bad practice. There are typically other ways that you can achieve the same results. But it's useful to know how they work in case you run across them.

```
/*
 * Here are two useful keywords that you can use with loops. The "continue" keyword
 * tells the loop to jump to the next iteration of a loop, and the "break" keyword
 * tells the loop to end immediately.
 *
 * The break, continue, throw, and return statements are called "jump statements"
 * because they cause your program to jump to another place in the code when they're
 * executed. (You learned about break with switch/case statements in Chapter 8, and
 * the throw statement in Chapter 10.) There's one more jump statement, goto, which
 * jumps to a label. (You'll recognize these labels as having very similar syntax
 * to what you use in a case statement.)
 *
 * You could easily write this next loop without continue and break. That's a good
 * example of how C# lets you do the same thing many different ways. That's why you
 * don't need break, continue, or any of these other keywords or operators to write
 * any of the programs in this book.
 *
 * The break statement is also used with "case", which you can see in chapter 8.
 */
    while (true) {
        int amountToGive = random.Next(20);
```

> The break statement causes the loop to end, and the program to move to the Console. WriteLine() statement.

```
        // The continue keyword jumps to the next iteration of a loop
        // Use the continue keyword to only give Joe amounts over 10 bucks
        if (amountToGive < 10)
            continue;
```

> The continue statement causes the program to jump over the rest of the iteration and back to the top of the loop.

```
        // The break keyword terminates a loop early
        if (joe.ReceiveCash(bob.GiveCash(amountToGive)) == 0)
            break;

        Console.WriteLine("Bob gave Joe {0} bucks, Joe has {1} bucks, Bob has {2} bucks",
            amountToGive, joe.Cash, bob.Cash);
    }
    Console.WriteLine("Bob's left with {0} bucks", bob.Cash);
```

```
// The ?: conditional operator is an if/then/else collapsed into a single expression
// [boolean test] ? [statement to execute if true] : [statement to execute if false]
Console.WriteLine("Bob {0} more cash than Joe",
    bob.Cash > joe.Cash ? "has" : "does not have");
```

```
// The ?? null coalescing operator checks if a value is null, and either returns
// that value if it's not null, or the value you specify if it is
// [value to test] ?? [value to return if it's null]
bob = null;
Console.WriteLine("Result of ?? is '{0}'", bob ?? joe);
```
Since bob is null, the ?? operator returns joe instead.

```
// Here's a loop that uses goto statements and labels. It's rare to see them, but
// they can be useful with nested loops. (The break statement only breaks out of
// the innermost loop)
for (int i = 0; i < 10; i++)
{
    for (int j = 0; j < 3; j++)
    {
        if (i > 3)
            goto afterLoop;
        Console.WriteLine("i = {0}, j = {1}", i, j);
    }
}
afterLoop:
```
The goto statement causes execution to jump directly to a label.

A label is a string of letters, numbers, or underscores, followed by a colon.

```
// When you use the = operator to make an assignment, it returns a value that you
// can turn around and use in an assignment or an if statement
int a;
int b = (a = 3 * 5);
Console.WriteLine("a = {0}; b = {1};", a, b);
```
This statement first sets a to 3 * 5, and then sets b to the result.

```
// When you put the ++ operator before a variable, it increments the variable
// first, and then executes the rest of the statement.
a = ++b * 10;
Console.WriteLine("a = {0}; b = {1};", a, b);
```
++b means that b is incremented first, and a is set to b * 10.

```
// Putting it after the variable executes the statement first and then increments
a = b++ * 10;
Console.WriteLine("a = {0}; b = {1};", a, b);
```
b++ means that first a is set to b * 10, and then b is incremented.

```
/*
 * When you use && and || to do logical tests, they "short-circuit" -- which means
 * that as soon as the test fails, they stop executing. When (A || B) is being
 * evaluated, if A is true then (A || B) will always be true no matter what B is.
 * And when (A && B) is being evaluated, then if A is false then (A && B) will always
 * be false no matter what B is. In both of those cases, B will never get executed
 * because the operator doesn't need its value in order to come up with a return value.
 */
```

```
int x = 0;
int y = 10;
int z = 20;
```
We'll use these values in the code on the next page!

When you use /* and */ to add comments, you don't have to add a * at the beginning of each line, but it makes them easier to read.

Using the logical "or" and "and" operators' **short-circuiting** properties is another way you can effectively write an if/else statement. This is the same as saying "only execute (y / x == 4 if (y < z) is true.

```
// y / x will throw a DivideByZeroException because x is 0. But since (y < z) is true,
// the || operator knows it will be true without ever having to execute the other
// statement, so it short-circuits and never executes (y / x == 4)
if ((y < z) || (y / x == 4))
    Console.WriteLine("this line printed because || short-circuited");
```

```
// Since (y > z) is false, the && operator knows it will return false without
// executing the other statement, so it short-circuits and doesn't throw the exception
if ((y > z) && (y / x == 4))
    Console.WriteLine("this line will never print because && short-circuited");
```

```
/*
 * A lot of us think of 1's and 0's when we think of programming, and manipulating
 * those 1's and 0's is what logic operators are all about.
 */
```

```
// Use Convert.ToString() and Convert.ToInt32() to convert a number to or from a
// string of 1's and 0's in its binary form. The second argument specifies that you're
// converting to base 2.
string binaryValue = Convert.ToString(217, 2);
int intValue = Convert.ToInt32(binaryValue, 2);
Console.WriteLine("Binary {0} is integer {1}", binaryValue, intValue);
```

```
// The &, |, ^, and ~ operators are logical AND, OR, XOR, and bitwise complement
int val1 = Convert.ToInt32("100000001", 2);
int val2 = Convert.ToInt32("001010100", 2);
int or = val1 | val2;
int and = val1 & val2;
int xor = val1 ^ val2;
int not = ~val1;
```

The logical operators &, |, and ^ are built-in on all the integral numeric types, all enums, and bool. The only difference between & and && (and | and ||) on bool is that these don't short-circuit.

~ is logical negation on integral numeric types and enums, which, in a way, is an analog to ! for bool.

```
// Print the values -- and use the String.PadLeft() method to add leading 0's
Console.WriteLine("val1: {0}", Convert.ToString(val1, 2));
Console.WriteLine("val2: {0}", Convert.ToString(val2, 2).PadLeft(9, '0'));
Console.WriteLine("  or: {0}", Convert.ToString(or, 2).PadLeft(9, '0'));
Console.WriteLine(" and: {0}", Convert.ToString(and, 2).PadLeft(9, '0'));
Console.WriteLine(" xor: {0}", Convert.ToString(xor, 2).PadLeft(9, '0'));
Console.WriteLine(" not: {0}", Convert.ToString(not, 2).PadLeft(9, '0'));
// Notice what the ~ operator returned:   11111111111111111111111011111110
// It's the 32-bit complement of val1: 00000000000000000000000100000001
// The logical operators are operating on int, which is a 32-bit integer.
```

Convert.ToString() returns a String object, and we're calling the PadLeft() method on that object to pad the result out with zeroes.

This will make a lot more sense when you run the program and look at the output. Remember, you don't need to type in all of this code—you can download it all from the Head First Labs website! http://www.headfirstlabs.com/books/hfcsharp

```
// The << and >> operators shift bits left and right. And you can combine any
// logical operator with =, so >>= or &= is just like += or *=.
int bits = Convert.ToInt32("11", 2);
for (int i = 0; i < 5; i++)
{
    bits <<= 2;
    Console.WriteLine(Convert.ToString(bits, 2).PadLeft(12, '0'));
}
for (int i = 0; i < 5; i++)
{
    bits >>= 2;
    Console.WriteLine(Convert.ToString(bits, 2).PadLeft(12, '0'));
}
```

This doesn't have anything to do with logic, it's just something useful that you see reasonably often.

```
// You can instantiate a new object and call a method on it without
// using a variable to refer to it.
Console.WriteLine(new Guy("Harry", 47, 376).ToString());
```

```
// We've used the + operator for string concatenation throughout the book, and that
// works just fine. However, a lot of people avoid using + in loops that will have
// to execute many times over time, because each time + executes it creates an extra
// object on the heap that will need to be garbage collected later. That's why .NET
// has a class called StringBuilder, which is great for efficiently creating and
// concatenating strings together. Its Append() method adds a string onto the end,
// AppendFormat() appends a formatted string (using {0} and {1} just like
// String.Format() and Console.WriteLine() do), and AppendLine() adds a string
// with a line break at the end. To get the final concatenated string, call
// its ToString() method.
StringBuilder stringBuilder = new StringBuilder("Hi ");
stringBuilder.Append("there, ");
stringBuilder.AppendFormat("{0} year old guy named {1}. ", joe.Age, joe.Name);
stringBuilder.AppendLine("Nice weather we're having.");
Console.WriteLine(stringBuilder.ToString());

Console.ReadKey();
```

One thing to note here: in this particular example, StringBuilder performs worse than +, because + will pre-compute the length of the string and figure out exactly how much memory to allocate.

You typically use StringBuilder when you don't know in advance the number of concatenations you want to perform.

```
/*
 * This is a good start, but it's by no means complete. Luckily, Microsoft gives you
 * a reference that has a complete list of all of the C# operators, keywords, and
 * other features of the language. Take a look through it -- and if you're just getting
 * started with C#, don't worry if it seems a little difficult to understand. MSDN
 * is a great source of information, but it's meant to be a reference, not a learning
 * or teaching guide.
 *
 * C# Programmer Reference: http://msdn.microsoft.com/en-us/library/618ayhy6.aspx
 * C# Operators: http://msdn.microsoft.com/en-us/library/6a71f45d.aspx
 * C# Keywords: http://msdn.microsoft.com/en-us/library/x53a06bb.aspx
 */
```

```
}
```

#2. Namespaces and assemblies

We made the decision to focus this book on the really practical stuff you need to know in order to build and run applications. Throughout every chapter, you create your projects in Visual Studio and run them in the debugger. We showed you where your compiled code ended up in an executable, and how to publish that executable so that other people can install it on their machines. That's enough to get you through every exercise in this book, but it's worth taking a step back and looking a little closer at what it is that you're building.

When you compile your C# program, you're creating an assembly. An assembly is a file that contains the compiled code. There are two kinds of assemblies. Executables (occasionally called "process assemblies") have the EXE file extension. All of the programs you write in this book are compiled as executables. Those are the assemblies that you can execute (you know, EXE files you can double-click and run). There are also library assemblies, which have the DLL file extension. They contain classes that you can use in your programs, and, as you'll see shortly, namespaces play a big role in how you use them.

You can get a handle on the basics of assemblies by first creating a class library, and then building a program that uses it. Start by creating a new Class Library project in Visual Studio called `Headfirst.Csharp.Leftover2`. When the library is first created, it contains the file `Class.cs`. **Delete** that file and **add a new class** called `Guy.cs`. Open up the new `Guy.cs` file:

```
namespace Headfirst.Csharp.Leftover2
{
    class Guy
    {
    }
}
```

Notice how Visual Studio made the namespace match your class library name? That's a very standard pattern.

Go ahead and **fill in the Guy class** with the code from Leftover #1—we'll use it in a minute. Next, **add two more classes** called `HiThereWriter` and `LineWriter`. Here's the code for `HiThereWriter`:

```
namespace Headfirst.Csharp.Leftover2
{
    public static class HiThereWriter
    {
      public static void HiThere(string name)
        {
            MessageBox.Show("Hi there! My name is " + name);
        }
    }
}
```

And here's the code for `LineWriter` (it's also in the `Headfirst.Csharp.Leftover2` namespace):

```
    internal static class LineWriter {
        public static void WriteALine(string message)
        {
            Console.WriteLine(message);
        }
    }
```

> We named the class library **Headfirst.Csharp.Leftover2** because that's a pretty standard way of naming assemblies. Read more about assembly naming here:
> http://msdn.microsoft.com/en-us/library/ms229048.aspx

Now try to compile your program. You'll get an error:

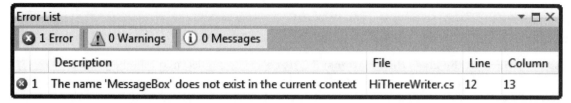

OK, no problem—we know how to fix this. Add a line to the top of your class:

```
using System.Windows.Forms;
```

Wait, it still doesn't compile! And something's weird here. When you typed in that line, did you notice that when you got as far as "using System.Win" the IntelliSense window stopped giving you suggestions? That's because your project **hasn't referenced the System.Windows.Forms assembly**.

Let's fix this by referencing the correct assembly. Go to the Solution Explorer and expand the "References" folder in your project. Right-click on it and choose "Add Reference…"; a window should pop up:

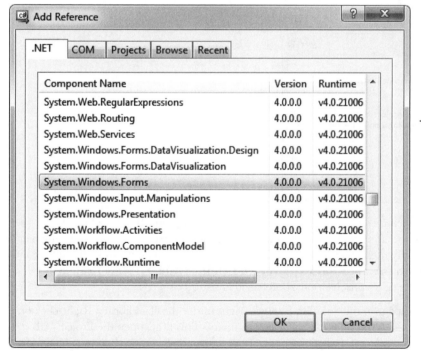

This window is showing you the assemblies your program can access. Some of them are stored in the Global Assembly Cache (GAC), but not every assembly in the GAC shows up in this window. The GAC is a central, machine-wide set of assemblies that all of the .NET programs on the computer can access. You can see all of the assemblies in it by typing `%systemroot%\assembly` into the Start menu (or Start/Run for older versions of Windows).

Take a minute and do this now. Notice how there are many different versions of some assemblies? Your programs can reference a specific assembly version, so they won't break even if a newer, incompatible version gets installed on the computer.

On the .NET tab, start typing "System.Windows.Forms"—it should jump down to that assembly. Make sure it's highlighted and click OK. Now System.Windows.Forms should show up under the References folder in the Solution Explorer—and your program compiles!

> The "Add References" window figures out which assemblies to display by checking a registry key, not the GAC. For more info: http://support.microsoft.com/kb/306149

...so what did I just do?

Take a close look at the declarations for LineWriter and HiThereWriter:

```
public class HiThereWriter

internal static class LineWriter
```

There are **access modifiers on the class declarations**: HiThereWriter is declared with the **public** access modifier, and LineWriter is declared with the **internal** one. In a minute, you'll write a console application that references this class library. A program can only *directly* access another class library's public classes—although they can be accessed indirectly, like when one method calls another or returns an instance of an internal object that implements a public interface.

Now go back to your Guy class and look at its declaration:

```
class Guy
```

Since there's no access modifier, it defaults to internal. We'll want to declare a Guy from another class, so **change the declaration** to be public:

```
public class Guy
```

Next, try running your program in the debugger. You'll see this error:

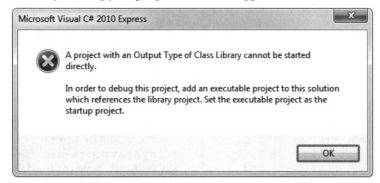

That makes sense when you think about it, because a class library doesn't have an entry point. It's just a bunch of classes that other programs can use. So let's add an executable program that uses those classes—that way the debugger has something to run. Visual Studio has a really useful feature that we'll take advantage of next: it can load multiple projects into a single solution. **Right-click on the Solution Explorer and choose Add >> New Project...** to bring up the usual Add Project window. Add a new console application called MyProgram.

Once your new program's added, it should appear in the Solution Explorer right under the class library. Right-click on References underneath MyProgram, and choose "Add reference..." from the menu. This time, open the Projects tab. You should see your class library project listed—select it and click OK. It should now appear in the References window.

Go to the top of your new project's Program.cs file and start adding this using line:

```
using Headfirst.Csharp.Leftover2;
```

Notice how the IntelliSense picks up "Csharp" and "Leftover2" as you're typing?

Now we can write a new program. Start by typing **Guy**. Watch what pops up:

```
static void Main(string[] args)
{
```

```
    Guy
    Guy        class Headfirst.Csharp.Leftover2.Guy
               A guy with a name, age and a wallet full of bucks
```

The IntelliSense window lists the entire namespace for Guy, so you can see that you're actually using the class that you defined in the other assembly. Finish the program:

```
static void Main(string[] args)
{
    Guy guy = new Guy("Joe", 43, 125);
    HiThereWriter.HiThere(guy.Name);
}
```

Now run your program. Oh, wait—you get the same error message as before, because you can't run a class library! No problem. Right-click on your new MyProgram project in the Solution Explorer and **choose "Set as Startup Project"**. Your solution can have many different projects, and this is how you tell it which one to start when you run it in the debugger. Now run your program again—this time it runs!

Why you added public to the class declarations in Chapter 13

In chapter 13, you changed the Renderer, World, Hive, Flower, and Bee class declarations to add the public access modifier. Why did you do that?

Try removing public from the Renderer declaration. You'll get an error message when you try to build your program that says this:

Inconsistent accessibility: property type 'Beehive_Simulator.Renderer' is less accessible than property 'Beehive_Simulator.HiveForm.Renderer'

Here's what's happening. Take a look at the HiveForm's class declaration:

```
public partial class HiveForm : Form
```

You've seen this declaration so many times that you probably don't even notice it anymore. But take a careful look—when the IDE adds a form to your project, it automatically adds the public access modifier. But your Renderer class is declared without an access modifier, so it defaults to internal. Your build broke when you tried to add a public property of type Renderer to the public HiveForm class. But since Renderer wasn't public, that caused the inconsistent accessibility error.

And that should make sense when you think about it. After all, a program is an assembly, too, and another assembly can access its classes. What would happen if another assembly tried to reference the HiveForm class? It would see the public property of type Renderer—but since the Renderer class is internal, it wouldn't be able to access it. That's why there's a rule: if you have a public class in your assembly, then any public property, method, or any other member can only use public types.

leftovers

Throughout the book we tell you that you compile your code. When you do, it's compiled to **Common Intermediate Language** (IL), the low-level language used by .NET. It's a human-readable assembly language, and all .NET languages (including C# and Visual Basic) are compiled into it. The IL code is compiled into native machine language when you run your program using the CLR's **just-in-time compiler**, so named because it compiles the IL into native code just in time to execute it (rather than pre-compiling it before it's run).

That means your EXEs and DLLs contain IL, and not native assembly code, which is important because it means many languages can compile to IL that the CLR can run—including Visual Basic .NET, F#, J#, managed C++/CLI, JScript .NET, Windows PowerShell, IronPython, Iron Ruby, and more. This is really useful: since VB.NET code compiles to IL, you can build an assembly in C# and use it in a VB.NET program (or vice versa).

If you have a Macintosh or Linux box, try installing Mono. It's an open source implementation of IL that runs EXE files that you've built on the PC (typically by typing "mono MyProgram.exe"—but this only works on *some* .NET assemblies). We're not going to talk any more about that, though, because this book is focused on Microsoft technology. But we do have to admit that it *is* pretty cool to see the Go Fish game or beehive simulator running natively on Mac or Linux!

We're just scratching the surface of assemblies. There's a lot more (including versioning and signing them for security). You can read more about assemblies here: http://msdn.microsoft.com/en-us/library/k3677y81.aspx

#3. Use BackgroundWorker to make your UI responsive

Throughout the book, we've shown you two ways that you can make your programs do more than one thing at a time. In Chapter 2, you learned about how to use the `Application.DoEvents()` method to let your form respond to button clicks while still in a loop. But that's ***not a good solution*** (for a bunch of reasons we didn't get into), so we showed you a much better solution in Chapter 4: using a timer to trigger an event at a regular interval. But even when you know how to use timers, there will be times when your program will still be busy and will become nonresponsive. Luckily, .NET gives you a really useful component that makes it very easy to let your program do work in the background. It's called **BackgroundWorker**, and we'll show you an example to demonstrate how it works.

Start by building this form. You'll need to drag a `CheckBox` onto it (name it `useBackgroundWorkerCheckbox`), two buttons (named `goButton` and `cancelButton`) and a `ProgressBar` (named `progressBar1`). Then drag a `BackgroundWorker` onto the form. It'll show up in the gray box on the bottom of the designer. Keep its name `backgroundWorker1`, and set its `WorkerReportsProgress` and `WorkerSupportsCancellation` properties to `true`.

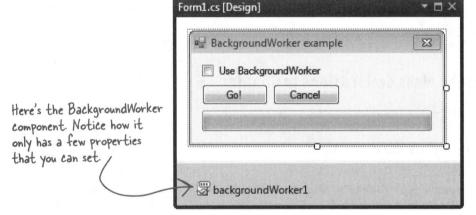

Here's the BackgroundWorker component. Notice how it only has a few properties that you can set.

Select the `BackgroundWorker` and go to the Events page in the Properties window (by clicking on the lightning-bolt icon). It's got three events: `DoWork`, `ProgressChanged`, and `RunWorkerCompleted`. Double-click on each of them to add an event handler for each event.

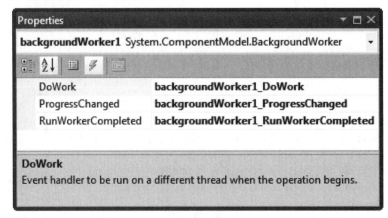

The code for the form is on the next two pages.

Here's the code for the form.

```
/// <summary>
/// Waste CPU cycles causing the program to slow down by doing calculations for 100ms
/// </summary>
private void WasteCPUCycles() {
    DateTime startTime = DateTime.Now;
    double value = Math.E;
    while (DateTime.Now < startTime.AddMilliseconds(100)) {
        value /= Math.PI;
        value *= Math.Sqrt(2);
    }
}
```

> The WasteCPUCycles() does a whole bunch of mathematical calculations to tie up the CPU for 100 milliseconds, and then it returns.

```
/// <summary>
/// Clicking the Go button starts wasting CPU cycles for 10 seconds
/// </summary>
private void goButton_Click(object sender, EventArgs e) {
    goButton.Enabled = false;
    if (!useBackgroundWorkerCheckbox.Checked) {
        // If we're not using the background worker, just start wasting CPU cycles
        for (int i = 1; i <= 100; i++) {
            WasteCPUCycles();
            progressBar1.Value = i;
        }
        goButton.Enabled = true;
    } else {
        cancelButton.Enabled = true;
```

the form's
g the
ckground
ker, it
bles
Cancel
ton.

> When the user clicks on the Go! button, the event handler checks to see if the "Use BackgroundWorker" checkbox is checked. If it isn't, the form wastes CPU cycles for 10 seconds. If it is, the form calls the BackgroundWorker's RunWorkerAsync() method to tell it to start doing its work in the background.

```
        // If we are using the background worker, use its RunWorkerAsync()
        // to tell it to start its work
        backgroundWorker1.RunWorkerAsync(new Guy("Bob", 37, 146));
    }
}
```

> When you tell a BackgroundWorker to start work, you can give it an argument. In this case, we're passing it a Guy object (see leftover #1 for its definition).

```
/// <summary>
/// The BackgroundWorker object runs its DoWork event handler in the background
/// </summary>
private void backgroundWorker1_DoWork(object sender, DoWorkEventArgs e) {
    // The e.Argument property returns the argument that was passed to RunWorkerAsync()
    Console.WriteLine("Background worker argument: " + (e.Argument ?? "null"));

    // Start wasting CPU cycles
    for (int i = 1; i <= 100; i++) {
        WasteCPUCycles();
        // Use the BackgroundWorker.ReportProgress method to report the % complete
        backgroundWorker1.ReportProgress(i);

        // If the BackgroundWorker.CancellationPending property is true, cancel
        if (backgroundWorker1.CancellationPending) {
            Console.WriteLine("Cancelled");
            break;
        }
    }
}
```

> Here's a good example of how to use the ?? null coalescing operator we talked about in leftover #1. If e.Argument is null, this returns "null", otherwise it returns e.Argument.

> The CancellationPending method checks if the BackgroundWorker's CancelAsync() method was called.

> When the BackgroundWorker's RunWorkerAsync() method is called, it starts running its DoWork event handler method in the background. Notice how it's still calling the same WasteCPUCycles() method to waste CPU cycles. It's also calling the ReportProgress() method to report a percent complete (a number from 0 to 100).

> The BackgroundWorker only fires its ProgressChanged and RunWorkerCompleted events if its WorkerReportsProgress and WorkerSupportsCancellation properties are true.

```
/// <summary>
/// BackgroundWorker fires its ProgressChanged event when the worker thread reports progress
/// </summary>
private void backgroundWorker1_ProgressChanged(object sender, ProgressChangedEventArgs e) {
    progressBar1.Value = e.ProgressPercentage;
}
```

When the DoWork event handler calls the ProgressChanged() method it causes the BackgroundWorker to raise its ProgressChanged event. and set e.ProgressPercentage to the percent passed to it.

```
/// <summary>
/// BackgroundWorker fires its RunWorkerCompleted event when its work is done (or cancelled)
/// </summary>
private void backgroundWorker1_RunWorkerCompleted(object sender, RunWorkerCompletedEventArgs e)
{
    goButton.Enabled = true;
    cancelButton.Enabled = false;
}
```

When the work is complete, the RunWorkerCompleted event handler re-enables the Go! button and disables the Cancel button.

```
/// <summary>
/// When the user clicks Cancel, call BackgroundWorker.CancelAsync() to send it a cancel messa
/// </summary>
private void cancelButton_Click(object sender, EventArgs e) {
    backgroundWorker1.CancelAsync();
}
```

If the user clicks Cancel, it calls the BackgroundWorker's CancelAsync() method to give it the message to cance

Once you've got your form working, run the program. It's easy to see how BackgroundWorker makes your program much more responsive:

★ Make sure the "Use BackgroundWorker" checkbox isn't checked, then click the Go! button. You'll see the progress bar start to fill up. Try to drag the form around—you can't. The form's all locked up. If you're lucky, it might jump a bit as it eventually responds to your mouse drag.

★ When it's done, check the "Use BackgroundWorker" checkbox and click the Go! button again. This time, the form is perfectly responsive. You can move it around and even close it, and there's no delay. When it finishes, it uses the RunWorkerCompleted method to re-enable the buttons.

★ While the program is running (using BackgroundWorker), click the Cancel button. It will update its CancellationPending property, which will tell the program to cancel and exit the loop.

Are you wondering why you need to use the ReportProgress() method rather than setting the ProgressBar's Value property directly? Try it out. Add the following line to the DoWork event handler:

```
progressBar1.Value = 10;
```

Then run your program again. As soon as it hits that line, it throws an InvalidOperationException with this message: "Cross-thread operation not valid: Control 'progressBar1' accessed from a thread other than the thread it was created on." The reason it throws that exception is that BackgroundWorker starts a separate thread and executes the DoWork method on it. So there are two threads: the GUI thread that's running the form and the background thread. One of the .NET threading rules is that only the GUI thread can update form controls; otherwise, that exception is thrown.

This is just one of the many threading pitfalls that can trap a new developer—that's why we didn't talk about threading anywhere in this book. If you're looking to get started with threads, we highly recommend Joe Albahari's excellent e-book about threading in C# and .NET: http://www.albahari.com/threading

#4. The Type class and GetType()

One of the most powerful aspects of the C# programming language is its rich type system. But until you've got some experience building programs, it's difficult to appreciate it—in fact, it can be a little baffling at first. But we want to give you at least a taste of how types work in C# and .NET. Here's a console application that gives you an introduction to some of the tools you have at your disposal to work with types.

```
class Program {
    class NestedClass {
        public class DoubleNestedClass {
            // Nested class contents ...
        }
    }

    static void Main(string[] args) {
        Type guyType = typeof(Guy);
        Console.WriteLine("{0} extends {1}",
            guyType.FullName,
            guyType.BaseType.FullName);
        // output: TypeExamples.Guy extends System.Object

        Type nestedClassType = typeof(NestedClass.DoubleNestedClass);
        Console.WriteLine(nestedClassType.FullName);
        // output: TypeExamples.Program+NestedClass+DoubleNestedClass

        List<Guy> guyList = new List<Guy>();
        Console.WriteLine(guyList.GetType().Name);
        // output: List`1

        Dictionary<string, Guy> guyDictionary = new Dictionary<string, Guy>();
        Console.WriteLine(guyDictionary.GetType().Name);
        // output: Dictionary`2

        Type t = typeof(Program);
        Console.WriteLine(t.FullName);
        // output: TypeExamples.Program

        Type intType = typeof(int);
        Type int32Type = typeof(Int32);
        Console.WriteLine("{0} - {1}", intType.FullName, int32Type.FullName);
        // System.Int32 - System.Int32

        Console.WriteLine("{0} {1}", float.MinValue, float.MaxValue);
        // output:-3.402823E+38 3.402823E+38

        Console.WriteLine("{0} {1}", int.MinValue, int.MaxValue);
        // output:-2147483648 2147483647

        Console.WriteLine("{0} {1}", DateTime.MinValue, DateTime.MaxValue);
        // output: 1/1/0001 12:00:00 AM 12/31/9999 11:59:59 PM

        Console.WriteLine(12345.GetType().FullName);
        // output: System.Int32

        Console.ReadKey();
    }
}
```

We only mentioned it briefly, but here's a reminder that you can nest classes inside of each other. Program contains NestedClass, which contains DoubleNestedClass.

Here's the entry point...

You can use the typeof keyword to turn a type (like Guy, int, or DateTime) into a Type object. Then you can find out its full name and base type (and if it didn't inherit from anything, its base type is System.Object).

When you get the type of a generic, its name is the type name followed by a backward quote and the number of its generic parameters.

...is is the ...stem.Type ...ss. The ...tType() ...thod returns Type object.

The FullName property we used in the first part of this program is a member of System.Type.

float is an alias for System.Single and int is an alias for System.Int32. They're both structs (which you learned all about in Chapter 14).

Numeric value types and DateTime have MinValue and MaxValue properties that return the lowest and highest valid value.

Literals have types, too! And you can use GetType() to get those types.

There's so much more to learn about types! Read more about them here: http://msdn.microsoft.com/en-us/library/ms173104.aspx

#5. Equality, IEquatable, and Equals()

Throughout the book, when you've wanted to compare values in two variables, you'd use the == operator. But you already know that all things being equal, some values are more "equal" than others. The == operator works just fine for value types (like ints, doubles, DateTimes, or other structs), but when you use it on reference types you just end up comparing whether two reference variables are pointing to the same object (or if they're both null). That's fine for what it is, but it turns out that C# and .NET provide a rich set of tools for dealing with value equality in objects.

To start out, every object has a method Equals(), which by default returns true only if you pass it a reference to itself. And there's a static method, Object.ReferenceEquals(), which takes two parameters and returns true if they both point to the same object (or if they're both null). Here's an example, which you can try yourself in a console application:

```
Guy joe1 = new Guy("Joe", 37, 100);
Guy joe2 = joe1;
Console.WriteLine(Object.ReferenceEquals(joe1, joe2));   // True
Console.WriteLine(joe1.Equals(joe2));                    // True
Console.WriteLine(Object.ReferenceEquals(null, null));   // True

joe2 = new Guy("Joe", 37, 100);
Console.WriteLine(Object.ReferenceEquals(joe1, joe2));   // False
Console.WriteLine(joe1.Equals(joe2));                    // False
```

Again, we're using the same Guy class from leftover #1.

But that's just the beginning. There's an interface built into .NET called IEquatable<T> that you can use to add code to your objects so they can tell if they're equal to other objects. An object that implements IEquatable<T> knows how to compare its value to the value of an object of type T. It has one method, Equals(), and you implement it by writing code to compare the current object's value to that of another object. There's an MSDN page that has more information about it (http://msdn.microsoft.com/en-us/library/ms131190.aspx). Here's an important excerpt:

If you don't do this, the compiler will give you a warning.

"If you implement Equals, you should also override the base class implementations of Object.Equals(Object) and GetHashCode so that their behavior is consistent with that of the IEquatable<T>.Equals method. If you do override Object.Equals(Object), your overridden implementation is also called in calls to the static Equals(System.Object, System.Object) method on your class. This ensures that all invocations of the Equals method return consistent results, which the example illustrates."

Here's a class called EquatableGuy, which extends Guy and implements IEquatable<Guy>:

```
/// <summary>
/// A guy that knows how to compare itself with other guys
/// </summary>
class EquatableGuy : Guy, IEquatable<Guy> {

    public EquatableGuy(string name, int age, int cash)
        : base(name, age, cash) { }

    /// <summary>
    /// Compare this object against another EquatableGuy
    /// </summary>
    /// <param name="other">The EquatableGuy object to compare with</param>
    /// <returns>True if the objects have the same values, false otherwise</returns>
    public bool Equals(Guy other) {
        if (ReferenceEquals(null, other)) return false;
        if (ReferenceEquals(this, other)) return true;
        return Equals(other.Name, Name) && other.Age == age && other.Cash == Cash;
}
```

The Equals() method compares the actual values in the other Guy object's fields, checking his Name, Age, and Cash to see if they're the same and only returning true if they are.

```
/// <summary>
/// Override the Equals method and have it call Equals(Guy)
/// </summary>
/// <param name="obj">The object to compare to</param>
/// <returns>True if the value of the other object is equal to this one</returns>
public override bool Equals(object obj) {
    if (!(obj is Guy)) return false;
    return Equals((Guy)obj);
}
```

We're also overriding the Equals() method that we inherited from Object, as well as GetHashCode (because of the contract mentioned in that MSDN article).

Since our other Equals() method already compares guys, we'll just call it.

```
/// <summary>
/// Part of the contract for overriding Equals is that you need to override
/// GetHashCode() as well. It should compare the values and return true
/// if the values are equal.
/// </summary>
/// <returns></returns>
public override int GetHashCode() {
    const int prime = 397;
    int result = age;
    result = (result * prime) ^ (Name != null ? Name.GetHashCode() : 0);
    result = (result * prime) ^ Cash;
    return result;
}
}
```

This is a pretty standard pattern for GetHashCode(). Note the use of the bitwise XOR (^) operator, a prime number, and the conditional operator (?:).

And here's what it looks like when you use Equals() to compare two EquatableGuy objects:

```
joe1 = new EquatableGuy("Joe", 37, 100);
joe2 = new EquatableGuy("Joe", 37, 100);
Console.WriteLine(Object.ReferenceEquals(joe1, joe2));  // False
Console.WriteLine(joe1.Equals(joe2));                   // True

joe1.GiveCash(50);
Console.WriteLine(joe1.Equals(joe2));                   // False
joe2.GiveCash(50);
Console.WriteLine(joe1.Equals(joe2));                   // True
```

Guy.Equals() will only return true if the actual values of the objects are the same.

And now that Equals() and GetHashCode() are implemented to check the values of the fields and properties, the method List.Contains() now works. Here's a List<Guy> that contains several Guy objects, including a new EquatableGuy object with the same values as the one referenced by joe1.

```
List<Guy> guys = new List<Guy>() {
    new Guy("Bob", 42, 125),
    new EquatableGuy(joe1.Name, joe1.Age, joe1.Cash),
    new Guy("Ed", 39, 95)
};

Console.WriteLine(guys.Contains(joe1));                 // True

Console.WriteLine(joe1 == joe2);                        // False
```

List.Contains() will go through its contents and call each object's Equals() method to compare it with the reference you pass to it.

Even though joe1 and joe2 point to objects with the same values, == and != still compare the references, not the values themselves.

Isn't there something we can do about that? Flip the page and find out!

If you try to compare two EquatableGuy references with the == or != operators, they'll just check if both references are pointing to the same object or if they're both null. But what if you want to make them actually compare the values of the objects? It turns out that you can actually **overload an operator**—redefining it to do something specific when it operates on references of a certain type. You can see an example of how it works in the EquatableGuyWithOverload class, which extends EquatableGuy and adds overloading of the == and =! operators:

```
/// <summary>
/// A guy that knows how to compare itself with other guys
/// </summary>
class EquatableGuyWithOverload : EquatableGuy
{
    public EquatableGuyWithOverload(string name, int age, int cash)
        : base(name, age, cash) { }

    public static bool operator ==(EquatableGuyWithOverload left,
                                   EquatableGuyWithOverload right)
    {
        if (Object.ReferenceEquals(left, null)) return false;
        else return left.Equals(right);
    }

    public static bool operator !=(EquatableGuyWithOverload left,
                                   EquatableGuyWithOverload right)
    {
        return !(left == right);
    }

    public override bool Equals(object obj) {
        return base.Equals(obj);
    }

    public override int GetHashCode() {
        return base.GetHashCode();
    }
}
```

If we used == to check for null instead of Object.ReferenceEquals(), we'd get a StackOverflowException. Can you figure out why?

Since we've already defined ==, we can just invert it for !=.

If we don't override Equals() and GetHashCode(), the IDE will give this warning: 'EquatableGuyWithOverload' defines operator == or operator != but does not override Object.GetHashCode().

Since EquatableGuyWithOverload acts just like EquatableGuy and Guy, we can just call the base methods.

Here's some code that uses EquatableGuyWithOverload objects:

```
joe1 = new EquatableGuyWithOverload(joe1.Name, joe1.Age, joe1.Cash);
joe2 = new EquatableGuyWithOverload(joe1.Name, joe1.Age, joe1.Cash);
Console.WriteLine(joe1 == joe2);    // False
Console.WriteLine(joe1 != joe2);    // True

Console.WriteLine((EquatableGuyWithOverload)joe1 ==
                                (EquatableGuyWithOverload)joe2);    // True
Console.WriteLine((EquatableGuyWithOverload)joe1 !=
                                (EquatableGuyWithOverload)joe2);    // False
joe2.ReceiveCash(25);
Console.WriteLine((EquatableGuyWithOverload)joe1 ==
                                (EquatableGuyWithOverload)joe2);    // False
Console.WriteLine((EquatableGuyWithOverload)joe1 !=
                                (EquatableGuyWithOverload)joe2);    // True
```

Wait, what happened? It's calling Guy's == and =! operators. Cast to EquatableGuyWithOverload call the correct == and =

#6. Using yield return to create enumerable objects

In Chapter 8 we learned about the IEnumerable interface and how it's used by the foreach loop. C# and .NET give you some useful tools for building your own collections, starting with the IEnumerable interface. Let's say you want to create your own enumerator that returns values from this Sport enum in order:

```
enum Sport
{
    Football, Baseball,
    Basketball, Hockey,
    Boxing, Rugby, Fencing,
}
```

You could manually implement IEnumerable yourself, building the Current property and MoveNext() method:

```
class SportCollection : IEnumerable<Sport> {
    public IEnumerator<Sport> GetEnumerator() {
        return new ManualSportEnumerator();
    }
    System.Collections.IEnumerator System.Collections.IEnumerable.GetEnumerator() {
        return GetEnumerator();
    }
    class ManualSportEnumerator : IEnumerator<Sport> {
        int current = -1;
        public Sport Current { get { return (Sport)current; } }
        public void Dispose() { return; } // Nothing to dispose
        object System.Collections.IEnumerator.Current { get { return Current; } }
        public bool MoveNext() {
            int maxEnumValue = Enum.GetValues(typeof(Sport)).Length - 1;
            if ((int)current >= maxEnumValue)
                return false;
            current++;
            return true;
        }
        public void Reset() { current = 0; }
    }
}
```

IEnumerable just contains one method, GetEnumerator(), but we also need to build the class for the enumerator it returns.

The enumerator implements IEnumerator<Sport>. The foreach loop uses its Current property and MoveNext() method.

The MoveNext() method increments current and uses it to return the next sport in the enum.

Here's a foreach loop that loops through ManualSportCollection. It returns the sports in order (Football, Baseball, Basketball, Hockey, Boxing, Rugby, Fencing):

```
Console.WriteLine("SportCollection contents:");
SportCollection sportCollection = new SportCollection();
foreach (Sport sport in sportCollection)
    Console.WriteLine(sport.ToString());
```

That's a lot of work to build an enumerator—it has to manage its own state, and keep track of which sport it returned. Luckily, C# gives you a really useful tool to help you easily build enumerators. It's called yield return, and you'll learn about it when you flip the page.

Just a reminder of something from Chapter 15: all collections are enumerable, but not everything that's enumerable is technically a collection unless it implements the ICollection<T> interface. We didn't show you how to build collections from the ground up, but understanding enumerators is definitely enough to get you started down that road.

enumerate this!

The `yield return` statement is a kind of all-in-one automatic enumerator creator. This `SportCollection` class does exactly the same thing as the one on the previous page, but its enumerator is only three lines long.:

```
class SportCollection : IEnumerable<Sport> {
    System.Collections.IEnumerator System.Collections.IEnumerable.GetEnumerator() {
        return GetEnumerator();
    }
    public IEnumerator<Sport> GetEnumerator() {
        int maxEnumValue = Enum.GetValues(typeof(Sport)).Length - 1;
        for (int i = 0; i < maxEnumValue; i++) {
            yield return (Sport)i;
        }
    }
}
```

> Like we said earlier, this is just the start for a SportCollection class. You'd still want to implement the ICollection<Sport> interface.

That looks a little odd, but if you actually debug through it you can see what's going on. When the compiler sees a method with a `yield return` statement that returns an `IEnumerator` or `IEnumerator<T>`, it **automatically adds the MoveNext() and Current methods**. When it executes, the the first `yield return` that it encounters causes it to return the first value to the `foreach` loop. When the foreach loop continues (by calling the MoveNext() method), it resumes execution with the statement **immediately after** the last `yield return` that it executed. Its MoveNext() method returns false if the enumerator method returns. This may be a little hard to follow on paper, but it's much easier to follow if you load it into the debugger and step through it using Step Into (F11). To make it a little easier, here's a really simple enumerator called `NameEnumerator()` that iterates through four names:

```
static IEnumerable<string> NameCollection() {
    yield return "Bob";    // The method exits after this statement ...
    yield return "Harry"; // ... and resumes here the next time through
    yield return "Joe";
    yield return "Frank";
}
```

And here's a foreach loop that iterates through it. Use Step Into (F11) to see exactly what's going on:

```
IEnumerable<string> names = NameEnumerator(); // Put a breakpoint here
foreach (string name in names)
    Console.WriteLine(name);
```

There's another thing that you typically see in a collection: an **indexer**. When you use brackets [] to retrieve an object from a list, array, or dictionary (like `myList[3]` or `myDictionary["Steve"]`), you're using an indexer. An indexer is actually just a method. It looks a lot like a property, except it's got a single named parameter.

The IDE has an especially useful code snippet. Type **indexer** followed by two tabs, and the IDE will add the skeleton of an indexer for you automatically.

Here's an indexer for the `SportCollection` class:

```
public Sport this[int index] {
    get { return (Sport)index; }
}
```

Passing that indexer 3 will return the enum value `Hockey`.

Here's an `IEnumerable<Guy>` that keeps track of a bunch of guys, with an indexer that lets you get or set guys' ages.

```csharp
class GuyCollection : IEnumerable<Guy> {
  private static readonly Dictionary<string, int> namesAndAges = new Dictionary<string, int>()
  {
        {"Joe", 41}, {"Bob", 43}, {"Ed", 39}, {"Larry", 44}, {"Fred", 45}
  };

  public IEnumerator<Guy> GetEnumerator() {
      Random random = new Random();
      int pileOfCash = 125 * namesAndAges.Count;

      int count = 0;
      foreach (string name in namesAndAges.Keys) {
          int cashForGuy = (++count < namesAndAges.Count) ? random.Next(125) : pileOfCash;
          pileOfCash -= cashForGuy;
          yield return new Guy(name, namesAndAges[name], cashForGuy);
      }
  }

  System.Collections.IEnumerator System.Collections.IEnumerable.GetEnumerator() {
      return GetEnumerator();
  }

  /// <summary>
  /// Gets or sets the age of a given guy
  /// </summary>
  /// <param name="name">Name of the guy</param>
  /// <returns>Age of the guy</returns>
  public int this[string name] {
      get {
          if (namesAndAges.ContainsKey(name))
              return namesAndAges[name];
          throw new IndexOutOfRangeException("Name " + name + " was not found");
      }
      set {
          if (namesAndAges.ContainsKey(name))
              namesAndAges[name] = value;
          else
              namesAndAges.Add(name, value);
      }
  }
}
```

The enumerator uses this private Dictionary to keep track of the guys it'll create, but it doesn't actually create the Guy objects themselves until its enumerator is used.

It creates Guy objects with random amounts of cash. We're just doing this to show that the enumerator can create objects on the fly during a foreach loop.

When an invalid index is passed to an indexer, it typically throws an IndexOutOfRangeException.

This indexer has a set accessor that either updates a guy's age or adds a new guy to the Dictionary.

And here's some code that uses the indexers to update one guy's age and add two more guys, and then loop through them:

```csharp
Console.WriteLine("Adding two guys and modifying one guy");
guyCollection["Bob"] = guyCollection["Joe"] + 3;
guyCollection["Bill"] = 57;
guyCollection["Harry"] = 31;
foreach (Guy guy in guyCollection)
    Console.WriteLine(guy.ToString());
```

#7. Refactoring

Refactoring means changing the way your code is structured without changing its behavior. Whenever you write a complex method, you should take a few minutes to step back and figure out how you can change it so that you make it easier to understand. Luckily, the IDE has some very useful refactoring tools built in. There are all sorts of refactorings you can do—here are some we use often.

Extract a method

When we were writing the control-based renderer for Chapter 13, we originally included this foreach loop:

```
foreach (Bee bee in world.Bees) {
    beeControl = GetBeeControl(bee);
    if (bee.InsideHive) {
        if (fieldForm.Controls.Contains(beeControl)) {
            fieldForm.Controls.Remove(beeControl);
            beeControl.Size = new Size(40, 40);
            hiveForm.Controls.Add(beeControl);
            beeControl.BringToFront();
        } else if (hiveForm.Controls.Contains(beeControl)) {
            hiveForm.Controls.Remove(beeControl);
            beeControl.Size = new Size(20, 20);
            fieldForm.Controls.Add(beeControl);
            beeControl.BringToFront();
        }
        beeControl.Location = bee.Location;
    }
}
```

These four lines move a BeeControl from the Field form to the Hive form.

And these four lines move a BeeControl from the Hive form to the Field form.

One of our tech reviewers, Joe Albahari, pointed out that this was a little hard to read. He suggested that we **extract those two four-line blocks into methods**. So we selected the first block, right-clicked on it, and selected "Refactor >> Extract Method…". This window popped up:

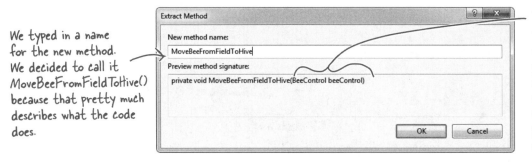

We typed in a name for the new method. We decided to call it MoveBeeFromFieldToHive() because that pretty much describes what the code does.

The IDE examined the code that we selected and figured out that it uses a BeeControl variable called beeControl, so it added it as a parameter to the method.

Then we did the same thing for the other four-line block, extracting it into a method that we named `MoveBeeFromHiveToField()`. Here's how that `foreach` loop ended up—it's a lot easier to read:

```
foreach (Bee bee in world.Bees) {
    beeControl = GetBeeControl(bee);
    if (bee.InsideHive) {
        if (fieldForm.Controls.Contains(beeControl))
            MoveBeeFromFieldToHive(beeControl);
    } else if (hiveForm.Controls.Contains(beeControl))
            MoveBeeFromHiveToField(beeControl, bee);
    beeControl.Location = bee.Location;
}
```

Rename a variable

Back in Chapter 3, we explained how choosing intuitive names for your classes, methods, fields, and variables makes your code a lot easier to understand. The IDE can really help you out when it comes to naming things in your code. Just right-click on any class, variable, field, property, namespace, constant—pretty much anything that you can name—and choose "Refactor >> Rename". You can also just use F2, which comes in handy because once you start renaming things, you find yourself doing it all the time.

We selected "beeControl" in the code from the simulator and renamed it. Here's what popped up:

This window lets you choose a new name for the item. If we renamed this, say, to "Bobbo", then the IDE would go through the code and change every single occurrence of it to "Bobbo".

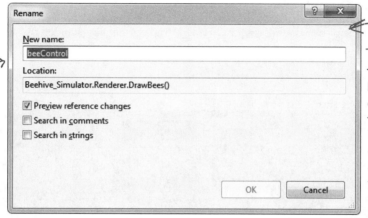

The IDE does a really thorough job of renaming. If you rename a class, it'll change every statement that instantiates it or uses it. You can click on any occurrence of the name, anywhere in the code, and the IDE will make the change everywhere in your program.

Consolidate a conditional expression

Here's a neat way to use the "Extract Method" feature. Open up any program, add a button, and add this code to its event handler:

```
private void button1_Click(object sender, EventArgs e) {
    int value = 5;
    string text = "Hi there";
    if (value == 36 || text.Contains("there"))
        MessageBox.Show("Pow!");
}
```

Plus, it'll even figure out that it should create a static method, since it doesn't use any fields.

Select everything inside the if statement: value == 36 || text.Contains("there"). Then right-click on it and select "Refactor >> Extract Method...". Here's what pops up:

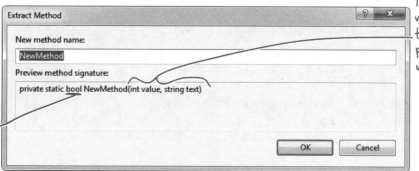

Every conditional expression evaluates to bool, so the IDE will create a method that returns a bool and replace the conditional test with a call to that method.

The expression uses two variables called value and text, so the IDE added parameters to the method using those names.

Not only will this make the code easier to read, but now you've got a new method that you can reuse elsewhere!

#8. Anonymous types, anonymous methods, and lambda expressions

C# lets you create types and methods without using explicitly named declarations. A type or method that's declared without a name is called **anonymous**. These are very powerful tools—for example, LINQ wouldn't be possible without them. But it's a lot easier to master anonymous types, anonymous methods, and lambda expressions once you have a firm grasp on the language, so they didn't make the cut for including in the book. But here's a quick introduction, so you can get started learning about them.

```
class Program {
    delegate void MyIntAndString(int i, string s);
    delegate int CombineTwoInts(int x, int y);

    static void Main(string[] args) {
        /*
         * In Chapter 15, you saw how the var keyword let the IDE determine the
         * type of an object at compile time.
         *
         * You can also create objects with anonymous types using var and new.
         *
         * You can learn more about anonymous types here:
         * http://msdn.microsoft.com/en-us/library/bb397696.aspx
         */

        // Create an anonymous type that looks a lot like a guy:
        var anonymousGuy = new { Name = "Bob", Age = 43, Cash = 137 };

        // When you type this in, the IDE's IntelliSense automatically picks up
        // the members -- Name, Age and Cash show up in the IntelliSense window.
        Console.WriteLine("{0} is {1} years old and has {2} bucks",
            anonymousGuy.Name, anonymousGuy.Age, anonymousGuy.Cash);
        // Output: Bob is 43 years old and has 137 bucks

        // An instance of an anonymous type has a sensible ToString() method.
        Console.WriteLine(anonymousGuy.ToString());
        // Output: { Name = Bob, Age = 43, Cash = 137 }

        /*
         * In Chapter 11, you learned about how you can use a delegate to reference
         * a method. In all of the examples of delegates that you've seen so far,
         * you assigned an existing method to a delegate.
         *
         * Anonymous methods are methods that you declare in a statement -- you
         * declare them using curly brackets { }, just like with anonymous types.
         *
         * You can learn more about anonymous methods here:
         * http://msdn.microsoft.com/en-us/library/0yw3tz5k.aspx
         */
```

```
// Here's an anonymous method that writes an int and a string to the console.
// Its declaration matches our MyIntAndString delegate (defined above), so
// we can assign it to a variable of type MyIntAndString.
MyIntAndString printThem = delegate(int i, string s)
                             { Console.WriteLine("{0} - {1}", i, s); };
printThem(123, "four five six");
// Output: 123 - four five six

// Here's another anonymous method with the same signature (int, string).
// This one checks if the string contains the int.
MyIntAndString contains = delegate(int i, string s)
                             { Console.WriteLine(s.Contains(i.ToString())); };
contains(123, "four five six");
// Output: False

contains(123, "four 123 five six");
// Output: True

// You can dynamically invoke a method using Delegate.DynamicInvoke(),
// passing the parameters to the method as an array of objects.
Delegate d = contains;
d.DynamicInvoke(new object[] { 123, "four 123 five six" });
// Output: True
```

```
/*
 * A lambda expression is a special kind of anonymous method that uses
 * the => operator. It's called the lambda operator, but when you're
 * talking about lambda expressions you usually say "goes to" when
 * you read it. Here's a simple lambda expression:
 *
 *     (a, b) => { return a + b; }
 *
 * You could read that as "a and b goes to a plus b" -- it's an anonymous
 * method for adding two values. You can think of lambda expressions as
 * anonymous methods that take parameters and can return values.
 *
 * You can learn more about lambda expressions here:
 * http://msdn.microsoft.com/en-us/library/bb397687.aspx
 */
```

```
// Here's that lambda expression for adding two numbers. Its signature
// matches our CombineTwoInts delegate, so we can assign it to a delegate
// variable of type CombineTwoInts. Notice how CombineTwoInts's return
// type is int -- that means the lambda expression needs to return an int.
CombineTwoInts adder = (a, b) => { return a + b; };
Console.WriteLine(adder(3, 5));
// Output: 8

// Here's another lambda expression -- this one multiplies two numbers.
CombineTwoInts multiplier = (int a, int b) => { return a * b; };
Console.WriteLine(multiplier(3, 5));
// Output: 15

// You can do some seriously powerful stuff when you combine lambda
// expressions with LINQ. Here's a really simple example:
var greaterThan3 = new List<int> { 1, 2, 3, 4, 5, 6 }.Where(x => x > 3);
foreach (int i in greaterThan3) Console.Write("{0} ", i);
// Output: 4 5 6

Console.ReadKey();
    }
}
```

#9. Serializing data using DataContractSerializer

When we put together the parts of Chapter 9 that cover serialization, our goal was to give you a good feel for the main concepts behind how serialization works, and the `BinaryFormatter` class is perfect for that. But that's not the only way to serialize objects...which should make sense, because there are many different ways that the data in an object can be represented. Let's take a look at another, really useful way to serialize data: using the **Data Contract Serializer**.

Data Contract Serializer uses a class called **DataContractSerializer**. It's part of **Windows Communication Foundation (WCF)**, Microsoft's unified programming model for building service-oriented applications. Here's an example of how we can use it to serialize and deserialize our Guy object to and from XML.

```
/* Before you can serialize an object using the Data Contract Serializer, you need
 * to set up a data contract. The easiest way to do this is by marking the class with
 * the [Serializable] attribute. By default, the DataContractSerializer will write all
 * public read/write properties and fields. But what's really useful about the Data
 * Contract Serializer is that you can be a lot more specific about exactly what does
 * and doesn't get serialized. You can associate data with this particular class by
 * giving the contact a name and a namespace using named parameters.
 */
[DataContract(Name = "Guy", Namespace = "http://www.headfirstlabs.com")]
class SerializableGuy {
    // When you set up a specific data contract for a type -- like our
    // Guy class -- you mark each field or property that you want to
    // serialize with the [DataMember] attribute.
    [DataMember]
    public string Name { get; private set; }

    [DataMember]
    public int Age { get; private set; }

    [DataMember]
    public int Cash { get; private set; }
```

> You can serialize any [Serializable] class with the Data Contract Serializer. But if you set up a data contract using the [DataContract] and [DataMember] attributes, you have a lot more control over what gets serialized.

```
    // You can decide what members you want to serialize. We added two private int fields
    // called secretNumberOne and secretNumberTwo to our SerliazableGuy and initialized
    // them both to random numbers. secretNumberOne is marked with the [DataMember]
    // attribute, so it will be serialized as part of the data contract. But we didn't
    // mark secretNumberTwo, so it won't be. They're both returned as part of ToString().
    [DataMember]
    private int secretNumberOne = new Random().Next();

    // Since the secretNumberTwo field isn't marked with the [DataMember]
    // attribute, it's not part of the contract and won't be serialized.
    private int secretNumberTwo = new Random().Next();

    public SerializableGuy(string name, int age, int cash) {
        Name = name;
        Age = age;
        Cash = cash;
    }
```

> The [DataContract] and [DataMember] attributes are in the System.Runtime.Serialization namespace, so the Guy class needs a "using System.RuntimeSerialization" directive at the top.

```
    public override string ToString() {
        return String.Format("{0} is {1} years old and has {2} bucks [{3},{4}]",
            Name, Age, Cash, secretNumberOne, secretNumberTwo);
    }
}
}
```

```
using System;
using System.Text;
using System.Runtime.Serialization;
using System.IO;
using System.Xml;

class Program
{
    static void Main(string[] args)
    {
        /* Data contract serialization typically reads and writes XML data. You use a
         * DataContractSerializer object for data contract serialization. Its
         * WriteObject() method can write to a stream, or it can write to an object that
         * extends XmlDictionaryWriter, an abstract class that controls XML output and
         * can be extended to change the way the XML output is written. Objects are
         * deserialized using the ReadObject() method, which can read XML data from
         * a stream or an XmlDictionaryReader.
         */
        DataContractSerializer serializer = new DataContractSerializer(typeof(SerializableGuy));

        // We'll create a new SerializableGuy object and serialize it using a FileStream.
        SerializableGuy guyToWrite = new SerializableGuy("Joe", 37, 150);
        using (FileStream writer = new FileStream("serialized_guy.xml", FileMode.Create)) {
            serializer.WriteObject(writer, guyToWrite);
        }

        // We can open the file we just wrote and deserialize it into a new guy using ReadObject().
        // We'll use the XmlDictionaryReader.CreateTextReader() method to create an object that
        // reads XML data from a stream.
        SerializableGuy guyToRead = null;
        using (FileStream inputStream = new FileStream("serialized_guy.xml", FileMode.Open))
        using (XmlDictionaryReader reader =
            XmlDictionaryReader.CreateTextReader(inputStream, new XmlDictionaryReaderQuotas())) {
            guyToRead = serializer.ReadObject(reader, true) as SerializableGuy;
        }
        Console.WriteLine(guyToRead);
        // Output: Joe is 37 years old and has 150 bucks [1461194451,0]

        string xmlGuy = @"
<Guy xmlns=""http://www.headfirstlabs.com"" xmlns:i=""http://www.w3.org/2001/XMLSchema-instance"">
    <Age>43</Age>
    <Cash>225</Cash>
    <Name>Bob</Name>
    <secretNumberOne>54321</secretNumberOne>
</Guy>";
        byte[] buffer = UnicodeEncoding.UTF8.GetBytes(xmlGuy);

        using (XmlDictionaryReader reader =
            XmlDictionaryReader.CreateTextReader(buffer, new XmlDictionaryReaderQuotas()))
        {
            guyToRead = serializer.ReadObject(reader, true) as SerializableGuy;
        }
        Console.WriteLine(guyToRead);
        // Output: Bob is 43 years old and has 225 bucks [54321,0]
    }
}
```

by putting a breakpoint here and adding reader and reader. Read() to the Watch window. What happens when you refresh reader.Read() a few times?

Notice how the secretNumberOne field was deserialized as part of the contract, but the secretNumberTwo field wasn't.

Open up the serialized_guy.xml file and you'll see data that looks just like this. It's a lot easier to read than what BinaryFormatter writes. But it's possible to make DataContractSerializer write binary data, too.

We took our string with XML data, converted it into a UTF-8 encoded byte array, and deserialized it into a new SerializableGuy object.

You can read more about Data Contracts and Data Contract Serialization here:
http://msdn.microsoft.com/en-us/library/ms733127.aspx
And you can read more about Windows Communication Foundation here:
http://msdn.microsoft.com/en-us/library/dd456779.aspx

#10. LINQ to XML

XML—or **Ex**tensible **M**arkup **L**anguage—is a format for files and data streams that represents complex data as text. The .NET Framework gives you some really powerful tools for creating, loading, and saving XML files. And once you've got your hands on XML data, you can use LINQ to query it. Add "using System.Xml.Linq;" to the top of a file and enter this method—it generates an XML document to store Starbuzz customer loyalty data.

```
private static XDocument GetStarbuzzData() {
    XDocument doc = new XDocument(
        new XDeclaration("1.0", "utf-8", "yes"),
        new XComment("Starbuzz Customer Loyalty Data"),
        new XElement("starbuzzData",
            new XAttribute("storeName", "Park Slope"),
            new XAttribute("location", "Brooklyn, NY"),
            new XElement("person",
                new XElement("personalInfo",
                    new XElement("name", "Janet Venutian"),
                    new XElement("zip", 11215)),
                new XElement("favoriteDrink", "Choco Macchiato"),
                new XElement("moneySpent", 255),
                new XElement("visits", 50)),
            new XElement("person",
                new XElement("personalInfo",
                    new XElement("name", "Liz Nelson"),
                    new XElement("zip", 11238)),
                new XElement("favoriteDrink", "Double Cappuccino"),
                new XElement("moneySpent", 150),
                new XElement("visits", 35)),
            new XElement("person",
                new XElement("personalInfo",
                    new XElement("name", "Matt Franks"),
                    new XElement("zip", 11217)),
                new XElement("favoriteDrink", "Zesty Lemon Chai"),
                new XElement("moneySpent", 75),
                new XElement("visits", 15)),
            new XElement("person",
                new XElement("personalInfo",
                    new XElement("name", "Joe Ng"),
                    new XElement("zip", 11217)),
                new XElement("favoriteDrink", "Banana Split in a Cup"),
                new XElement("moneySpent", 60),
                new XElement("visits", 10)),
            new XElement("person",
                new XElement("personalInfo",
                    new XElement("name", "Sarah Kalter"),
                    new XElement("zip", 11215)),
                new XElement("favoriteDrink", "Boring Coffee"),
                new XElement("moneySpent", 110),
                new XElement("visits", 15))));
    return doc;
}
```

You can use an XDocument to create an XML file, and that includes XML files you can read and write using DataContractSerializer.

An XMLDocument object represents an XML document. It's part of the System.Xml.Linq namespace.

Use XElement objects to create elements under the XML tree.

> **Microsoft has a lot of great documentation about LINQ and LINQ to XML online. You can read more about LINQ to XML and classes in the System.Xml.Linq namespace here:** http://msdn.microsoft.com/en-us/library/bb387098.aspx

Save and load XML files

You can write an XDocument object to the console or save it to a file, and you can load an XML file into it:

```
XDocument doc = GetStarbuzzData();
Console.WriteLine(doc.ToString());
doc.Save("starbuzzData.xml");
XDocument anotherDoc = XDocument.Load("starbuzzData.xml");
```

The XDocument object's Load() and Save() methods read and write XML files. And its ToString() method renders everything inside it as one big XML document.

Query your data

Here's a simple LINQ query that queries the Starbuzz data using its XDocument:

```
var data = from item in doc.Descendants("person")
    select new { drink = item.Element("favoriteDrink").Value,
        moneySpent = item.Element("moneySpent").Value,
        zipCode = item.Element("personalInfo").Element("zip").Value };
foreach (var p in data)
    Console.WriteLine(p.ToString());
```

The Descendants() method returns a reference to an object that you can plug right into LINQ.

You already know that LINQ lets you call methods and use them as part of the query, and that works really well with the Element() method.

And you can do more complex queries too:

```
var zipcodeGroups = from item in doc.Descendants("person")
    group item.Element("favoriteDrink").Value
    by item.Element("personalInfo").Element("zip").Value
        into zipcodeGroup
        select zipcodeGroup;
foreach (var group in zipcodeGroups)
    Console.WriteLine("{0} favorite drinks in {1}",
                    group.Distinct().Count(), group.Key);
```

Element() returns an XElement object, and you can use its properties to check specific values in your XML document.

Read data from an RSS feed

You can do some pretty powerful things with LINQ to XML. Here's a simple query to **read articles from our blog**:

```
XDocument ourBlog = XDocument.Load("http://www.stellman-greene.com/feed");
Console.WriteLine(ourBlog.Element("rss").Element("channel").Element("title").Value);
var posts = from post in ourBlog.Descendants("item")
    select new { Title = post.Element("title").Value,
        Date = post.Element("pubDate").Value};
foreach (var post in posts)
    Console.WriteLine(post.ToString());
```

The XDocument.Load() method has several overloaded constructors. This one pulls XML data from a URL.

Create a new console application, make sure you've got "using System.Xml.Linq;" at the top, type this query into its event handler, and check out what it prints to the console.

We used the URL of our blog, Building Better Software. http://www.stellman-greene.com/

#11. Windows Presentation Foundation

Windows Presentation Foundation, or WPF, is Microsoft's latest-generation platform for building visual applications. It's pretty amazing—it has XML-declared layout, scalable controls, a totally new system for controls, 2-D and 3-D graphics and animation, text flow and document formatting—and there's even a cross-platform web browser plug-in that uses it.

Unfortunately, while WPF is a really cool and highly capable technology, it's not a particularly good tool for teaching C#. And that was our goal—getting C# concepts into your brain as quickly and easily as possible.

Take a second and create a new WPF application. Just create a new project using the IDE, but don't create a new Windows Forms Application project. Instead, **choose WPF Application**. You'll immediately notice a difference in the IDE:

The biggest difference you'll see is that the form designer looks nothing like the one you're used to. We'll take a closer look at it in a minute.

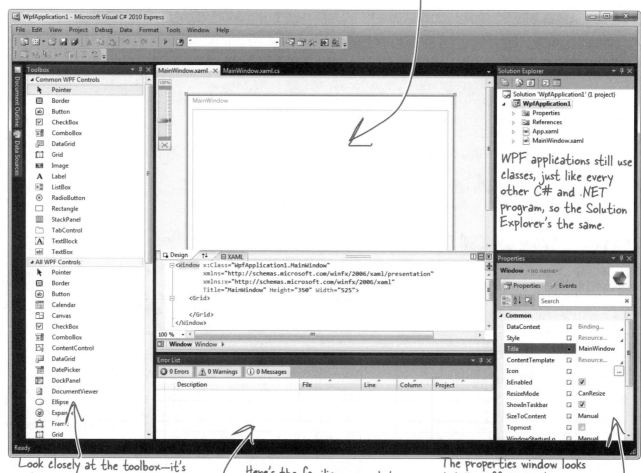

WPF applications still use classes, just like every other C# and .NET program, so the Solution Explorer's the same.

Look closely at the toolbox—it's got a whole new set of controls.

Here's the familiar error list and output window that you've been using.

The properties window looks totally different. You use it to change attributes in a XAML file, and not properties on objects.

Drag a button out of the toolbox and onto the form. If this were a Windows Forms application, the IDE would add code to `Form1.Designer.cs` to add a control to the `Form1` object. But WPF is different—it uses an XML-based language called XAML to define how the user interface is laid out, how it interacts with objects, and more.

XAML stands for "Extensible Application Markup Language," and it's the XML-based language that WPF applications use to determine where all of the controls and other UI elements go.

Drag this slider up and down to zoom in and out. When you zoom in really close, your user interface still looks good—it doesn't get pixelated.

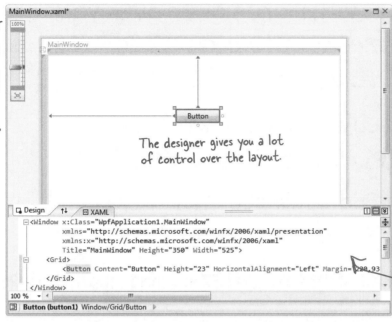

The designer gives you a lot of control over the layout.

The IDE has a really powerful XML editor that's optimized for working with XAML.

Go to the XML editor and add a second button by typing the **bold** line below into the XAML editor. You'll notice how the IDE's IntelliSense does a good job of helping you enter all the XML tags.

```
<Grid>
    <Button Height="23" Margin="98,43,105,0" Name="button1"
                VerticalAlignment="Top" Click="button1_Click">Button</Button>
    <Button Height="23" Margin="5,5,100,20" Name="button2"
                VerticalAlignment="Top" Click="button2_Click">Another button</Button>
</Grid>
```

When you get to the "**Click="button2_Click"**" part of the line, don't type in the name of the event handler. Instead, use the IntelliSense window that pops up to tell the IDE to add a new event handler. As soon as you finish the line, you'll see a new button appear in the designer. Switch over to the `Window1.xaml.cs` tab, and you'll find a new `button2_Click` method there.

That's all the WPF and XAML that we can include here. But now that you've got the tools to start learning about WPF, we definitely recommend that you take a look at ***Programming WPF*** by Chris Sells and Ian Griffiths. It's available from the O'Reilly website: **http://www.oreilly.com/**.

Here's a project to get your feet wet in WPF: try building the Contact application from Chapter 1 in WPF. Most of the steps are exactly the same! Just make sure you use an Image instead of a PictureBox, and use the Events page in the Properties window to add a MouseDown event handler to it because it doesn't have a Click event. Also, don't use the "mbox" code snippet—just use MessageBox.Show().

Did you know that C# and the .NET Framework can...

★ Give you much more power over your data with advanced LINQ queries? Serialize objects to an XML file?

★ Access websites and other network resources using built-in classes?

★ Let you add advanced encryption and security to your programs?

★ Create complex multithreaded applications?

★ Let you deploy your classes so that other people can use them?

★ Use regular expressions to do advanced text searching?

I had no idea! Where can I learn more?

There's a great book that explains it all!

It's called *C# 4.0 in a Nutshell* by Joseph Albahari and Ben Albahari, and it's a thorough guide to everything that C# has to offer. You'll learn about advanced C# language features, you'll see all of the essential .NET Framework classes and tools, and you'll **learn more** about what's really going on under the hood of C#.

Check it out at **http://www.oreilly.com/**.

Covers
CLR 4.0

C# 4.0
IN A NUTSHELL
The Definitive Reference

O'REILLY®

Joseph Albahari
& Ben Albahari

Joseph Albahari
helped us out a
whole lot by giving
the first edition of
this book a really
thorough tech review.
Thanks so much for
all your help, Joe!

Index

Symbols

() (parentheses), 184

* (asterisk), 46

@ (at sign), 411–412, 423

// (double-slash comments), 66

" " (empty string), 62, 74

! (exclamation point), 475

? (question mark), 673

' (single quotes), 127

/// (triple-slash comments), 736–737

, (comma), 329, 344

?: conditional operator, 739

: operator, 234, 274, 330

?? null coalescing operator, 739

! operator, 62, 260

!= operator, 68

& operator, 740

&& operator, 68, 77, 739–740

* operator, 62, 138

*= operator, 62, 101, 138

+ operator, 62, 131, 353

++ operator, 62, 739

+= operator
   = operator and, 534
   event handling, 513, 515, 517, 535
   functionality, 62

- operator, 132, 138

-- operator, 62

-= operator, 138

/ operator, 62

= operator
   += operator and, 534
   == operator and, 67
   casting support, 132
   return values and, 739

== operator
   = operator and, 67
   conditional testing, 68, 70
   examples, 77, 750–752

^ operator, 740

| operator, 740

|| operator, 68, 739

; (semicolon) (see semicolon (;))

< operator, 68, 70

<< operator, 741

<> (angle brackets), 335, 363

> operator, 68, 70

>> operator, 741

\\ (double backslash), 423

\n (line break) (see line break (\n))

\r (return character), 373, 423

\t (tab), 127, 411, 423

{} (curly brackets), 51, 56, 65–66, 73

~ (tilde), 654

~ operator, 740

A

abstract classes
  building a house application, 308–322
  defined, 296–297
  examples, 298
  generic collections, 335
  Stream class, 409

abstract methods, 296, 299

abstraction, 306

access modifiers
  changing visibility, 292–293
  on class declarations, 744
  defined, 291

adapters, 31

Add >> Class feature, 331

Add New Item window, 18

address book application, 4–5, 9–16, 20–34

adventure game application, 385–406

Albahari, Ben, 766–767

Albahari, Joe, 711, 748, 766

allocated resources, 427

angle brackets <>, 335, 363

animated beehive simulator
  adding forms, 570
  adding timers, 574–576
  architecture, 544, 557
  behavior considerations, 568–569
  building, 545–560, 562–567
  callback technique, 578
  collections, 581–582
  controls and, 592–593, 596, 599–607
  delegates and, 578–579
  LINQ support, 582–583
  List<T> class, 581–582
  opening/saving, 585–587
  overhauling, 635–639
  overview, 543, 554
  performance considerations, 615–617
  Renderer class and, 594–595, 607, 609–611
  testing, 577–579, 584, 614
  as turn-based system, 561
  working with groups, 580

anonymous methods, 758–759

anonymous types, 703, 709, 758–759

application development
  adding loops, 65, 69
  adding statements, 66
  adding to auto-generated code, 2, 11, 15
  auto-generated code and, 2, 11, 15, 73
  debugging code, 16, 469
  deployment and, 35
  designing for intuitive use, 32–33
  developing user interface, 12–13
  embedding databases, 18
  modifying generated code, 11
  overview, 6–7, 44–45
  source code files, 44
  testing programs, 34
  tools supporting, 46–47
  turn-based systems, 386
  using classes, 89–91
  using variables, 60–61

Application.DoEvents() method, 746

args parameter, 457

ArgumentException, 492, 495, 565

ArgumentOutOfRangeException, 501

arguments
  command-line, 456–457
  defined, 133, 669
  event, 512
  named, 672
  type, 340

Array.Reverse() method, 448

arrays
  creating deck of cards, 333–334
  defined, 150
  determining length, 151
  exception handling, 470
  foreach loops, 339
  lists and, 336, 338, 343
  of object references, 151
  reference variables and, 151
  static method for, 448

as keyword
  coffeemaker example, 286
  functionality, 283
  value types and, 668, 677

G

generic collections
    built-in, 377
    defined, 335, 340, 343

generic event handlers, 522

geocaching, 198

get accessors
    debugger and, 476
    defined, 203
    read-only property and, 206, 209
    this keyword and, 292

Global Assembly Cache (GAC), 743

Go Fish! game, 366–376

Golden Crustacean application, 533, 537–540

goto statements, 739

GPS navigation system application, 86–92, 198

graph, defined, 441

Graphical User Interface (GUI), 95

Graphics class
    DrawCircle() method, 621
    DrawCurve() method, 623
    DrawImage() method, 618, 622, 627
    DrawImageUnscaled() method, 638
    DrawLine() method, 620–621
    DrawLines() method, 623
    DrawPolygon() method, 623
    DrawString() method, 621
    FillCircle() method, 621
    FillPolygon() method, 623
    FromImage() method, 618, 632
    functionality, 620
    Paint events and, 628
    printing support, 640–645
    resizing bitmaps, 618

Graphics Device Interface (GDI+), 620–622

graphics files, 14, 616–617

Griffiths, Ian, 765

group keyword, 699

GroupBox control, 177, 217

GUI (Graphical User Interface), 95

GZipStream class, 409

H

handles, defined, 660

heap
    adding objects to, 102
    defined, 102, 667
    referencing objects, 142
    stack versus, 667–669, 676

Hebrew characters, 446–447, 458

heisenbugs, defined, 476

hex dumps, 453–455, 571

hexadecimal format
    Character Map and, 446–447
    converting to decimal, 446, 450, 473
    Debug toolbar and, 473

hex dumps, 453–455, 571

hiding methods, 246–247, 249

hit points, 386, 399, 404

house building application, 308–322

I

IComparable<T> interface, 347

IComparer<T> interface
    complex comparisons, 350
    creating instances, 349
    examples, 359
    sorting lists, 346–348, 351

icons, bundling with applications, 14

IDE
    Add Existing Item option, 263
    auto-generated code, 2, 11
    Basic Settings mode, 473
    behind the scenes, 14
    benefits using, 3
    building programs, 34–35, 45
    changing generated code, 48–50
    defined, 2, 44
    event icons, 509
    Expert mode, 473
    functionality, 8–11, 42–43
    Go To Definition feature, 427

extension methods and, 680
files and, 452
not recommended for use, 73
naming conventions
camelCase, 211
for event handlers, 513
for events, 514
PascalCase, 211
navigation system application, 86–92, 198
nested loops, 77
nested using statements, 496
.NET database objects, 6, 28–29
.NET Framework
generic collections, 377
overview, 44
System namespace, 73
using statement, 50
.NET visual objects, 6, 12–13
NetworkStream class, 409
new keyword/statement
collection initializers and, 344
creating array objects, 150
creating classes, 207
creating objects, 92–93
debugging programs and, 482
hiding methods and, 247
implicit conversion and, 522
overriding methods and, 249
passing parameters to, 207
non-visual controls, 161, 420
null keyword, 155, 465
nullable types, 673–674
Nullable<T> struct, 673
NullReferenceException, 116, 465, 467, 535
NumericUpDown control
baseball simulator example, 519
event planning example, 183, 221–222
GPS navigation system example, 90
Value property, 519
ValueChanged event, 513

O

Object class, 353, 445
object data type, 127
object declaration (see declaration)
object initializers
beehive simulator example, 602
collection initializers and, 344
functionality, 117
initializing properly, 206
object oriented programming (OOP), 306, 459
object references
arrays of, 151
callback techniques, 535
Controls collection and, 591
defined, 156
examples, 287
garbage collection and, 142, 147, 156
interface references and, 279, 294
as labels, 141, 156
multiple, 144, 149
reference variables and, 140–141
Object Relational Designer, 707–708
objects
accessing with IntelliSense, 287
adding to heap, 102
allocating, 427
base class for, 353
as black boxes, 199–200
built-in, 419
callback technique, 534–535
chaining, 515
comparing, 347
controls as, 591
converting to strings, 353–354
creating, 92–94
dead, 655
defined, 92
deserializing, 438–439, 442, 585
downcasting, 286
enqueuing/dequeuing, 378
enumerable, 693
Equals() method, 750–752
event handling, 511
exceptions as, 469

P

protected fields, 253

public access modifier, 291, 294, 512

publish folder, 36

Publish Wizard, 35

pushing onto stacks, 379

Q

queries
  combining values into groups, 700
  defined, 19
  editing, 711
  joining data results, 703–704
  LINQ support, 690–695, 763
The Quest lab exercise, 385–406

question mark (?), 673

queues
  Clear() method, 378
  copying to stacks, 380
  Count property, 378
  creating, 378
  defined, 377
  Dequeue() method, 378
  exercises, 381–382
  FIFO support, 377–378
  lists and, 377, 380
  Peek() method, 378
  stacks and, 377, 379–380

R

racetrack simulator application, 169–178

raising events
  baseball simulator example, 514
  defined, 509–510
  this keyword and, 515

Random class, 331, 559

random numbers, 194, 559, 563

range variables, 690

reading data
  BinaryReader class, 450
  bytes from streams, 456–457
  excuse manager program, 429–433
  File class, 422
  FileStream class, 410
  serialized files, 451–452
  Stream class, 408–409
  StreamReader class, 415
  switch statement, 436–437

read-only properties
  adding, 205–206
  beehive simulator example, 546, 551
  event arguments and, 520
  functionality, 549
  get accessors and, 209

Ready Bake Code, 583, 688

real numbers, 126

record IDs, 21

Rectangle struct
  beehive simulator example, 638
  functionality, 676
  The Quest lab exercise, 392, 403

recursion, defined, 669

ref keyword, 671

refactoring, 756–757

reference types
  == operator and, 750
  value types and, 664–666

reference variables
  arrays and, 151
  code example, 526
  declaring, 150
  defined, 140–141
  delegate types and, 527
  objects and, 154

Renderer class
  beehive simulator example, 594–595, 607, 609–611, 637
  building, 609–611
  functionality, 594
  ResizeImage() method, 618

reserved words (C#), 156, 164

resizing
    backing fields, 219
    images, 618, 632
    lists dynamically, 339

Resource Designer, 608

resource files (.resx), 46

resources
    allocated, 427
    defined, 14
    finalizers and, 654
    managed, 654
    storing as Bitmap objects, 619
    unmanaged, 654

rethrowing exceptions, 490

return character (\r), 373, 423

return statement, 51, 88–89, 753–755

return types, 88–89, 208

return values (methods)
    = operator and, 739
    on class diagrams, 394
    constructors and, 207, 209
    defined, 51, 88
    delegates and, 527
    multiple, 670

robust programs, 478, 674

RSS feeds, 763

S

Save As... dialog box, 421

SaveFileDialog control, 425

SaveFileDialog object, 421

sbyte data type, 126

sealed (access) modifier, 291, 678–679

seeds, 194, 559

select clause
    anonymous types, 703, 709
    beehive simulator example, 699
    functionality, 695–696
    LINQ support, 690

Select Resource dialog box, 13

Sells, Chris, 765

semicolon (;)
    interface requirements, 273
    statements and, 47, 66, 73
    void return type and, 88

sequences
    CurrentState property, 699
    defined, 695
    examples, 700
    keys and, 708

[Serializable] attribute, 443–444

serialization
    beehive simulator example, 585
    classes, 443
    DataContractSerializer class, 760–761
    exception handling, 478
    finalizers and, 659
    objects, 438–442
    reading/writing files manually, 451–452

SerializationException, 477–478, 484

Server Explorer window, 18

set accessors
    callback methods and, 534
    defined, 203
    this keyword and, 292
    value parameter, 203, 209

setup programs, 36

short data type, 126

single quotes ('), 127

Size struct, 642, 676

snippets (IDE), 47

Solution Explorer window
    adding SQL databases to projects, 18
    changing filenames, 11
    displaying files, 14
    functionality, 46
    opening designer code, 48
    project files, 8
    switching between files, 10
    viewing databases, 18

solution files (.sln), 44

T

W

Learning for the Way Your Brain Works

Learning isn't something that just happens to you. It's something you do. But all too often, it seems like your brain isn't cooperating. Your time is too valuable to spend struggling with new concepts. Head First books combine strong visuals, puzzles, humor, and the latest research in cognitive science to engage your entire mind in the learning process.

Get even more for your money.

Join the O'Reilly Community, and register the O'Reilly books you own.It's free, and you'll get:

- 40% upgrade offer on O'Reilly books
- Membership discounts on books and events
- Free lifetime updates to electronic formats of books
- Multiple ebook formats, DRM FREE
- Participation in the O'Reilly community
- Newsletters
- Account management
- 100% Satisfaction Guarantee

Signing up is easy:

1. **Go to: oreilly.com/go/register**
2. **Create an O'Reilly login.**
3. **Provide your address.**
4. **Register your books.**

Note: English-language books only

To order books online:

oreilly.com/order_new

For questions about products or an order:

orders@oreilly.com

To sign up to get topic-specific email announcements and/or news about upcoming books, conferences, special offers, and new technologies:

elists@oreilly.com

For technical questions about book content:

booktech@oreilly.com

To submit new book proposals to our editors:

proposals@oreilly.com

Many O'Reilly books are available in PDF and several ebook formats. For more information:

oreilly.com/ebooks

Spreading the knowledge of innovators   www.oreilly.com

Buy this book and get access to the online edition for 45 days—for free!

Head First C#, **Second Edition**
By Andrew Stellman & Jennifer Greene
May 2010, $49.99
ISBN 9781449380342

With Safari Books Online, you can:

Access the contents of thousands of technology and business books

- Quickly search over 7000 books and certification guides
- Download whole books or chapters in PDF format, at no extra cost, to print or read on the go
- Copy and paste code
- Save up to 35% on O'Reilly print books
- **New!** Access mobile-friendly books directly from cell phones and mobile devices

Stay up-to-date on emerging topics before the books are published

- Get on-demand access to evolving manuscripts.
- Interact directly with authors of upcoming books

Explore thousands of hours of video on technology and design topics

- Learn from expert video tutorials
- Watch and replay recorded conference sessions

To try out Safari and the online edition of this book FREE for 45 days,
go to **www.oreilly.com/go/safarienabled** and enter the coupon code LZZFTZG.
To see the complete Safari Library, visit safari.oreilly.com.

O'REILLY®

Spreading the knowledge of innovators

safari.oreilly.com